I Also Walked On This Earth

By Reverend Eugene Stefaniuk

I Also Walked On This Earth
Copyright © 2016 by Eugene Stefaniuk

No part of this publication may be reproduced, distributed, or transmitted in any form or by any means, including photocopying, recording, or other electronic or mechanical methods, without the prior written permission of the author, except in the case of brief quotations embodied in critical reviews and certain other non-commercial uses permitted by copyright law.

tellwell

Tellwell Talent
www.tellwell.ca

ISBN
978-1-77302-505-6 (Paperback)
978-1-77302-506-3 (eBook)

TABLE OF CONTENTS

Forward vii
Genesis - The Beginning 1
Early years 9
Train fascination 28
Lake and Sporty the dog 39
Sports and school 45
Storms and community activities 50
Our first car 58
Leaving home - a teacher 64
A family tragedy 75
New life - RCAF 78
A water car? 89
My own car 91
Parents leave the farm 99
Job hunting 111
Childhood actions begin to fulfill 120
A traveling summer job and engagement 123
Ordination and parish work 135
Dauphin, Manitoba Parish 154
Fraud - a scam? 165
Parish work continues 169
A real holiday 174
A miracle? 177
This and that - tidbits 180
My illness 185
A new manse and family health 188
Moving to Prince George, British Columbia . . . 195
Life in Prince George 201
California - here we come ! ? 214
Marriage - falling apart 219
More problems 230
Hyas, here I come! 234
Hyas, Saskatchewan - population 175 238

Mary passes away.	249
Parents moving out of Winnipeg	254
Work must go on day after day.	262
Others already making plans for me.	265
People want Father Stefaniuk	268
To close to death.	271
Don't burn God's Church.	275
Calm before the storm.	278
Life must go on	283
Who was it?	286
Hyas Parish grows	290
More health problems.	293
A new friend - George Alexandro	297
A strange dream and a missing car	301
And now the "kolomayka" starts	307
God's new life - for me ?	319
Twenty-five years of Priesthood	333
Betrothal - Marriage	336
House purchase and trip to Australia	344
New life in Salmon Arm and Vernon	349
Marusia's and mother's health.	353
On the move again - to Vernon	362
Work and long trips	365
News from Phoenix comes to us.	372
What - another move? Again?	377
Visitor from Ukraine.	381
What a disastrous trip	385
A new life in a new place - Yorkton	395
A broken chain link - mother's passing	399
Peace River country again.	402
A Historical Move - Phoenix, Arizona.	409
Work in a new country.	417
Family from Canada arrives.	420
Back to Canada?	429
Life goes on in Phoenix	436
Looking for better church property	442

Marusia's health problem	444
Returning to Canada	453
My illness and home to Canada - Calgary	462
That Buick car trouble	471
A bad painful time	478
Oh those Buick car problems	484
Yellowknife NWT - Raven Mad Daze	490
Busy at home after the trip	500
Marusia - another health problem	505
More trips	510
Our first computer - a new experience	516
Moving - Again?	519
Lac La Biche - here we come	523
A new world? - 2000 Millennium year	532
Completion of an earlier project	536
Are there false records?	545
So where is father?	548
Strange but true!	555
Marusia's health begins to fail	560
Marusia passes away and funeral	587
Father ends up in the hospital	611
Father's house is sold	616
Father moves to Wakaw seniors place	621
Father not well	623
John and Kay's trouble trip	628
Another chain link broken - Father passes away	630
Life Must go on	635
A scam and not a scam?	646
Time runs along and waits for no one	648
More health problems	654
Surgery time	659
Family reunion and gout problems	669
What a night at the Toronto Airport	676
Eugene caught in a scam trap	681
Day to day life goes on	686
Unexpected event at a church service	692

Joyce	698
Day to day activities carried on	700
Betrothal (engagement) Joyce and me	705
House hunting in Osoyoos	711
Pre-marriage problem	714
Garage sales and moving	723
Settling in Osoyoos, British Columbia	728
Leaving for Ontario	736
Homeward bound	742
Life goes on in Osoyoos	745
Busy daily life	752
Another family reunion and car problem	763
Another car?	769
Cats	772
Bits and pieces	776
And still working day to day	779
Health problems again	787
I publish a book	790
Windsor, Ontario and home	797
Osoyoos life goes on	800
Life moves along	804
Speed limit and Helen Malchuk funeral	809
Osoyoos "KOLOMAYKA" starting	816
Closing words	827
Do you believe in miracles?	829
How I have escaped death five times	838

FORWARD

This is my third book I have published. My first one "Whose will is it" was published in 2013, based on spirituality. Sales have not gone well. Had I written a book on pornography, I would need police to control people traffic who would be rushing to get such a book, but because it's spirituality, and as you probably very well know, people are running away more and more each day from religion and God. My second book is presently at the publishers and being published is "Our forefathers pre-Christian and present beliefs." This book in your hands is based on my life of some eighty-three years on the face of this earth. Having lived to that age and if I wanted to write everything without missing a minute of my life, it would take eighty-three years to write and it would take years to read the works. So in this work I have the highlights of what my memory tells me and what I have in my diaries from 1962 to 2012 (fifty years)

The language. Oh yes, very simple that even a grade four student will be able to read and understand, and my sight and plan was to write so a young child could and would understand. When I started school I did not know one word or letter of the English language. My parents came from Europe in the later 1920's and I learned the Ukrainian language from them which I speak even today as well as the English.

But why are my publications in the language of grade four? Having entered seminary and mother knowing I would be ordained, she time and again and again gave me the same talk. "Eugene, when you will be a priest, always talk in such a way so people will understand you. Many priests come to our church and they give sermons, but when the service is over, I don't understand what they were talking about. So when you will talk, speak so people would understand what you are saying."

I took mother's advice to heart. I can recall and remember how in one congregation where I served, that following the service I was invited by this one family to come to their place for lunch. On this yard lived two families. The parents lived in one house and their son and daughter-in-law with their family in another house on the same yard. During conversation at the lunch, the owner of the house had made some remark about something. His five year old grand-daughter breaks in and says: "Dido, the priest said not to say and do that." Dido means grandfather in Ukrainian. I can still see that little girl (who today is a grandmother herself) telling her grandfather what I had said in church. Had I used language of grade twelve or university level, that child and probably the people where I was having lunch would not have understood what I was teaching and talking about. For this I am to this day thankful and grateful to my late mother for instilling in me to use a language that people can and will understand. I myself remember when I was a teenager and in church or some other gatherings, priests or higher educated people spoke using big fancy words that I did not understand or know what they were talking about. This also reminds me that the words spoken by Christ and His Apostles were not high vocabulary words, but simple that people could understand. That is why I wanted to have it be the way as I wrote it.

That is what I learned - to speak an understandable language for even Apostle Paul in his writing to the Corinthians says: *"Yet in the church I had rather speak five words with my understanding, that by my voice I might teach others also, than ten thousand words in an unknown tongue."* (I Corinthians 14:19) That is why I want the younger people to read this work and understand the times I lived in, in the "Dirty thirties" and we survived. People had more morals at that time and love among each other. Today in larger towns and cities people live together but ask them who their next door neighbor is and they don't know. People have become to live to themselves and not needing anyone else. In my days if we had two horses, one neighbor had a plow and another neighbor had a seed drill, our two horses were hitched to the neighbor's plow and his field was plowed, then our field and then the third neighbors field. The same with the seed drill. Today in the farming communities everyone has their own tractor, plow, seed drill, combine and they don't need anyone else. What a different world in half a century it turned out to be.

As you read along page by page, I hope maybe you will remember of a same incident or activity during your lifetime that I had lived. Those days are gone and will probably never return, but if they should ever return to what they were a hundred years ago, how many people would survive not knowing how to produce food. How many people would die from the hands of others who would come to a strangers' house looking for food. Whether such a time will come, no one knows, but only One, the One above us all.

Happy reading. Take care, stay well and God bless.
Eugene

GENESIS - THE BEGINNING

The world moves along. People come and people go. Some leave behind them great works and become famous. Others leave no trace of themselves and are lost to this world. Still others look for glory and are at times remembered, while others will receive glory in the other world when they depart to the earth from which they were created. As the years kept piling up on my back, I decided to put a few words and thoughts together on paper to leave for the kin and for those that will come after me, so they would know of the life I had lived. Life at the time I lived was what we call, "those good old days," or "those dirty thirties."

I, Reverend Eugene Stefaniuk, was born at Cudworth, Saskatchewan, on October 6th - 1932. My father the late Fred Stefaniuk, who lived to be 101 years of age, was born in the district of Horodenka, village of Torhowitsa in Western Ukraine on April 15 - 1901. My mother the late Mary Stefaniuk (nee Tesarowski) was also born in Western Ukraine in the village of Mooshkativka, in the district of Borschiw on April 13 - 1906 and lived 87 years of her earthly life. I know one thing that the name Tesarowski is recorded in history books in Ukraine. Some 400 years ago there was a Bishop by that name in the Ukrainian Orthodox Church in Ukraine and he took part in the ordination of the Saint Peter Mohyla (1596-1647). When I was a seminary student at St. Andrews College in Winnipeg, Manitoba in the late 1950's, I asked the late Metropolitan Ilarion, the Primate of the

Ukrainian Orthodox Church of Canada at that time, if there was any way to find some information about Bishop Tesarowski. He said it was nearly 500 years ago and records were lost during the two World Wars. So was the late bishop Tesarowski related to my mother in any long way around? I guess only God knows and I will know if he was or not related to our family, when I leave this earth.

My late father came to Canada on July 2nd 1927 and my mother on June 29th 1928. Father arrived at Meacham, Saskatchewan and my mother at Ethelbert, Manitoba. After a year or two of working at the people who had sponsored them to Canada, they moved to Saskatoon, where they met. Their life together started at Cudworth, Saskatchewan in the early 1930's.

Times were hard and tough when I arrived into this world at the Cudworth General Hospital on October 6 - 1932. The depression years had already sneaked into Canada when I came along. They were called: "The Dirty Thirties." I do not remember anything from birth to about the age of five or six years. From what my late parents told me, the times were hard. When I wasn't even a year old, father, mother and I traveled with a covered wagon from Cudworth, Saskatchewan to Grandview, Manitoba. It took three weeks to cover some three hundred miles. As we traveled along and as the sun would be setting, my parents would turn into some farmyard and ask the owners if we could stay overnight on their yard. The parents said people always welcomed us into their homes. One day near Kamsack, Saskatchewan we stopped overnight and it was at a Doukhobor family. We were treated well the parents said. When I grew up the parents told me that the Doukhobor family wanted to buy me from my parents. Parents did not oblige and next day we carried on in our journey. We were going to Grandview, Manitoba because mother had a cousin there Tillie Korzeniowski. Parents had heard that life was somewhat better in Manitoba, so they headed out east to start a new and better life

While residing at Meharry, a few miles west of Grandview, we lived at Andrew Balak's place. Here in Grandview my brother John came into the world on January 20 - 1934. Now the parents had two toddlers to look after when the family was short of livelihood necessities. My father like other fathers tried to make a living. What did he do? He had a pair of bronco horses, so he would take some food with him into the bush and would cut cordwood all day long. Towards evening he would return home with the cordwood. Next morning he would take the wood to Grandview to sell to make a few cents to buy necessities for the family. No one would buy the wood, because they said they had enough wood or had no money to pay for it. As a last resort Father would go to the store and ask the owner to take the wood and give him at least a few essentials so that the family could survive.

After having lived in Grandview, the parents saw that they could not make a living in Manitoba either, so they decided to return back to Saskatchewan. They sold the horses, and the wagon was put on the train. They boarded the train with me and my brother and we all returned back to the Cudworth area. We settled and lived in vacant houses in the Cudworth surroundings. Father would find out who the vacant house belonged to and then asked for permission to live in it. My parents would clean the house and we would move in. We lived many times in such houses. Sometimes the house had been vacant for a number of years. At times after we had been living in such a house, the owners son or daughter were getting married and the owner said he was giving his children the farm with the house where we lived, so we had to vacate that house and find another place to live. This style of living was like gypsy living, "here today, there tomorrow" and just about each year or second year found us moving to a new place. As you will find out later it was move after move after move that we made. There was no money to buy a house or a farm like there is today. We lived where we could find a vacant house.

We had lived on Peter Guydych's farm. It was a woody place a few miles from Cudworth. Many times father would leave at sunrise to Cudworth to see if he could find a job where he could make a few dollars to buy life sustaining goods for the family. Some days he would not get a job and would return in the evening with what he had left in the morning - empty hands and pockets. Sometimes someone would hire him to do something and that would take a day or a few days after which he was paid a few dollars. He would receive anywhere from fifteen to twenty-five cents an hour for his labor and it was ten to twelve hours of work a day. Because food was necessary, he asked a storekeeper to give him goods on credit. He would return late in the evening with a sack on his back carrying the goods home. He got flour, sugar, matches, yeast and other necessary items. He had walked to town and back for we had no horses now. The horses had been sold in Grandview.

My first memory goes back to when I was about four or five years old. It is something that I have a good memory at what happened at one of those places we lived. One day father had returned home after finding some work for a day or so. This time he had bought my brother and me two small toys. John and I were each given a toy policeman on a motorcycle. These toys lasted maybe a hour or two. John was younger than me. Where we had been living, someone had dug a cellar for a new house to be built on that place. John and I played in that cellar daily and now we played there with our toys. Somehow turning around here and there, our toys got covered with dirt and we never saw them again. That was the only toy I had received in my childhood. This was in 1936 and this year my sister Alice was born at Cudworth on March 14 and now there were three more pre-school and hungry mouths in the family.

The years kept rolling and slipping along. It was time to start attending school. By this time we lived at Andrew Kindrachuk's place south of Cudworth, about half a mile. There was a vacant house there so with permission from Mr. Kindrachuk we moved into this place. Cudworth was not far to the north from where we lived, but for some unknown reason I did not go to school to Cudworth where it was closer. I had to attend school south of where we lived about two miles. I started school at Carpathian School which is still standing today along side highway #2 south of Cudworth on the west side of the road. A farmer was using the school as a granary or storage shed. As this is written in July 2016 my first school was still standing and my first teacher, Mr. John Luciuk, had passed away a few years ago at Wakaw, Saskatchewan.

Times were hard on many people or I could say most people. I remember my lunches to school. There were no school lunches provided by the school as there are in some schools today. I had to bring lunch from home. What was my lunch? One day it was - mother moistened a piece or two of bread in water, put sugar on it, wrapped it in some old newspaper or some other paper that she had and I was off to school. The following day she may have smeared a piece of bread with pork fat, put some salt and pepper on it, wrapped it and I was on the way to school. There was no such thing as an apple, orange or peanut butter sandwiches. There was no money to have bought such luxuries. Yes, other students may have had some of such foods, but I did not, because there were no funds to buy such items. There was no such thing as a school bus or to be driven with a car to go in comfort to school. It was walking miles in the morning and return in the afternoon.

I had to walk the first mile and a half to school all alone. The next half mile I was on a main road where other students were going to school, so it was better to walk with company. Some morning mother would put me on a horse and would lead the horse for the mile and a half until I got to the main road. Then I walked the rest of the way to school, while she led the horse back home.

One day coming home from school and about a mile from home, I ran into trouble. Coming along the farmers road, I spotted a skunk that was some ways from me near some bushes beside the road I was going home on. That was the most scariest thing for me at that time - to see or meet a skunk. I was not afraid if a wolf happened to come along, but a skunk, no way. Stay away from that animal. We had smelled the skunk many times when the wind blew from some direction and if that smell was so terrible, imagine what the skunk would do if you met it. So what do I do now? I can't walk past that skunk, because if she sees me, she will destroy me. I stopped in my tracks. Oh yes it was a few hundred yards where I could see that skunk moving near a brush pile. I started tiptoeing backwards in the direction I was coming from.

After I had moved away some distance walking backwards, and seeing that the skunk was not coming after me, I turned around and as fast as my feet could move I was flying back towards the school. Having gone a while, I stopped and looked back. I could not see the skunk anymore, good, but I will not go there. I must get home, but how - which way? I walked back to school and took the road straight north of the school. I knew that road, because we had traveled on it before by horse and wagon after we bought a pair of horses. As I had headed back towards the school, tears as large as marbles, were falling like raindrops from spring rains. What a scary experience for a six year old. This second road was farther to get home. I knew mother would be looking to see if I'm coming home and waiting for me in the yard. I don't know what she was thinking after I never showed up at home when I should have been home already.

After making the extra distance, I finally got home. I remember that mother had been worried and asked where I had been that I was so late coming from school. I told her the story about the skunk, but she only laughed it off. It was funny for her, but a most fearful thing for me. She said the skunk was probably more afraid of me than I of her and probably had run away. I said that when I had gone back towards the school, I looked and saw that the skunk had not moved and said that she was still there.

Next day was off to school again. But - how can I go past that pile of brush where the skunk was. Mother said she would go with me to that place. I was put on the horse, while mother lead the horse. Now we are nearing that brush where the skunk was yesterday. As we came closer, I could hear my heart beating faster. What is going to happen if that skunk is still there? Will she eat mother and me? From the top of the horse I could see the brush pile and sure enough I could see the white stripe on the skunk. I told mother to stop because the skunk was still there. "Where? Where is the skunk? I can't see any skunk" she said. Mother being brave enough left me on the horse and herself walked towards the pile of brush. I was beginning to cry, because the skunk would eat her. To my embarrassment mother stops near the white spot and picks up an oldnewspaper that the wind had blown against the brush. Each time the wind blew, the paper moved and it looked like the skunk with the white stripe was moving beside the brush pile.

Another incident which happened at this my first school was, when I started school I did not know one word or letter of English. A day or two after the first day of school my parents were going with the wagon south of Cudworth towards Prud'homme for some reasons which I don't remember. They said I would have a ride, because they would be going right past the school. When we came to school, I was late for classes had already started. I knew where my desk was, so I walked in and headed straight for my desk. The teacher Mr. John Luciuk, asked me to say "Good Morning" when I came in. I did not understand what he was saying. He took me by the hand and led me to the porch (cloakroom). He told me in English to come in and say, "Good Morning" when I walk in. This was being done in English and what good did it do me, when I did not understand what he was saying. As soon as he turned around to go in, I rushed passed him and to my desk. I have to study at my desk not in the porch. He tried that over and over, but nothing helped and tears like marbles were rolling down my cheeks by this time. Finally he told one of the older Ukrainian students to take me out and tell me in Ukrainian what I have to say in English when I come in. I don't remember if I ever learned anything that day or what I had to say when I came in late. By this time I had enough of schooling. Everybody is watching me and laughing. I'm not going back to school again. I have all the education I need for now.

When I came home that day after school, I told the parents what had happened, but could not explain to them what everything was about. That evening we all went to see someone for the parents wanted to know what had happened. They found out and laughed. That's it no more school for this boy. He goes to learn, but people laugh of him, schooling is done. My parents being older and wiser convinced me that I will not be late for school again and nothing will happen. Somehow they left me at ease and with hesitation I did journey back to school the following days and years.

Another thing that happened one day where we lived in Kindrachuks' house is something that got carved into my memory to this very day. It was Sunday afternoon. It was very early spring with snow still in many places in the shades or where there had been big piles of snow. The roads were nothing but mud up to the knees whichever way you went. We had gone with the wagon to church at Cudworth. Coming home from church, John and I had noticed a large nest in the bush maybe 100 yards east of the house. We asked the parents if there are any baby birds in the nest and they said, "no."

I was not convinced. When we got into the yard, the parents were unhitching the horses and doing chores, so what did John and I do? Oh yes, we have to investigate that nest and see the baby birds in it. If it's a crow's nest we have to kill the baby crows, because they will grow up and then will catch and kill our baby chicks. John was younger and smaller so he would follow me to do what I was doing. He came along with me to check the nest. We did not tell the parents where we were going or what we were planning to do. We came not to far from the tree, but in the bush there was still big piles of snow. John being lighter walked on top of the snow, me being older and a little bit heavier, I sank into the snow. Finally that was as far as I could go. I sank into the wet soft cool snow up to my armpits. I could not get out of the snow in which I had broken in. I told

John to help me get out, but he wanted to see the baby birds in the nest first so he went. He tried crawling up the tree, but the branches kept breaking and he couldn't get up. In the meantime, I'm stuck and can't move out of the snow. John finally came and tried to help me out, but he could do nothing and said that he was cold and was going to the house. He started for the house and I was left in the snow crying and trying to wiggle out in some way out of this mess. I told John to tell the parents to come and get me out of the snow. After wiggling, kicking and twisting in the cool snow, I was beginning to make headway. Slowly, slowly I kept pounding and kicking at the snow as it softened from the warmth of my body heat and slowly I managed to crawl out, wet, cold and hungry. To this day I never again went to check any bird's nest or look for little baby crows.

EARLY YEARS

My parents were always church goers as far back as I can remember. Us children were never left at home or with any baby sitters while the parents went to church or other places. The whole family went to church, for as a saying says: "The family that prays together stays together." This next incident that happened a number of times, also took place on Kindrachuk's farm. This happened many times over, when we were still small. We had been to church a number of times and had seen the priest serving, dressed in brilliant robes. People carried banners around the church, the priest made sweet smelling smoke (censing). People sang in church. Many times as soon as the parents were out of the house, I would put two chairs in the middle of the room. I would tell John to sit on one and Alice on the other. I would put on a long coat or sheet on my back and pretend to be the priest while John and Alice were the parishioners-faithful. I would sing to John and Alice and shake my hand as with a censor. Sometimes I would tie a dish towel to a broom and carry it around the house and tell John and Alice to follow me. To John and Alice this made no sense at all at that time. Could anyone have said at that time that some thirty years later I would be standing in front of the altar serving God? Was that a calling from God already at that early hour what I was to do in my adult life? Many times I would be caught by mother doing this when unexpectedly she would walk into the house from the barn or the garden. Then she would want to give me a spanking, but she couldn't do that because first she had to catch me. Sometimes she did catch me if I was too far away from the door, but if she caught me than the yard stick or her hand would smack my back. She would say: "And what do you think you are doing?" I usually got the yard stick, because John and Alice were innocent bystanders (parishioners?)

Because I was the first born in the family, naturally I was the first one to start school. As previously mentioned when I began school I did not know one word in English. Later when John started school, I by this time knew some English words and I would teach him what I knew. When we knew even more English, oftentimes the two of us would converse in English in the house. Mother hearing us speak English would say: "How are you talking in the house? Talk so I can understand. You can talk English in school, but at home talk so father and I would understand." If we did not pay attention to her words, she would smack her hand or a dish towel over our necks and backs. Today both parents are gone and I am thankful and grateful that they instilled in me their language, customs and traditions. For that may God reward them blessed a life in His heavenly Kingdom.

As mentioned above when I started school I had to walk over two miles, summer or winter. In the spring of 1938 we moved to William Sopotyk's place and lived with them. They had a large house and they had half of the house and half where we lived. Now it was much better. Here I had to go to school only across the road. I could come home every day for lunch. But one thing that will always stick in my mind is the day we moved to Sopotyk's place. All our belongings that we had were packed in a wagon. We arrived at Sopotyk's shortly after lunch. Just as we entered the yard we could see an absolutely huge, dark, black cloud rolling across the sky from west to east. It was a dust storm, "those dirty thirties."

My mother and Mrs. Sopotyk were lucky to get into the house with us children. Father and Mr. Sopotyk had unhitched the horses and barely had time to scramble into the barn with them. They could not make it to the house, because it got so dark that you could not see anything outside as if it were in the middle of the night. Wind and dust flew into your face. You could not walk in the wind, because the wind would knock a person over and dust flew into one's eyes, nose and ears. The belongings that were on the wagon, some became victims to the wind. The wind had pushed the wagon against the barn and there it stood till the storm died down about two or three hours later. Mrs. Sopotyk had lit the lamp in the house for it was dark and no one could see anything. We children were afraid and some of us hid under the table and others under the bed and you could only see their eyes shining in the dark from the dim coal oil lamp. Some were screaming and crying because of the howling sound of the wind and the darkness. The noise from the storm sounded like a freight train passing right through the room. There was three children in our family and there must have been three or four in Sopotyk's family. During those "Great Depression" years hundreds of dust storms raced across the prairies blowing away everything with them and taking away the top rich soil. Even the windows on the west side of the house were blown out and I remember that mother and Mrs. Sopotyk held quilts and pillows against the broken windows to keep the wind and the dust out.

The storm lasted about two or three hours, but it seemed like it was there for days on end. The fear of such storms was instilled in everyone. Some of our belongings that were on the wagon were broken and destroyed because there had been no time to bring them in. Some things that the storm blew away were never found. Anyone who has never experienced such a dust storm when daylight turns into complete darkness does not know what fear is. You would think the world was coming to an end. One cannot even begin to explain to today's people what those dust storms were. There just seem to be no words to describe such horrific catastrophe as it was called.

It was also around this time in my time or maybe a year or two sooner that I remember having my tonsils taken out. It was such a time in history that every child had to get their tonsils removed, why, I don't know. I was brought to the Cudworth Hospital where I was born a few years earlier. I was more scared being left there than a rabbit was afraid of a fox. Afraid and crying with no parents around and complete strangers all dressed in white. What does a four or five year old child do, when all around everything is strange, unknown and unfamiliar. I don't remember being put under for surgery. What I can remember is that someone gave me something to smell and that was it. Then I thought I heard music playing. It seemed to me that a radio was chasing me and I was running away as fast as I could. Next thing what I remember was when I awoke after the surgery. This was the time I liked to be in the hospital because the people dressed in white were feeding me with marshmallows. The marshmallows were soft and easy to eat and brought no pain to the throat after surgery.

At this same hospital a few years later my youngest sister Oksana was born. My both sisters and I were born in the same hospital at Cudworth, only brother John is a Manitoban for he was born at Grandview while we resided there for a year or two. I was born October 6 - 1932; John January 20 - 1935; Alice was born on March 14 - 1937 and Oksana was born on August 11 - 1940.

I believe that it was in the spring of 1939 when we moved again, this time about two or three miles east of Cudworth. There had been a vacant house and we moved into it. We lived only half a mile north from Mr. Mike Stefaniuk, which was no relation to us. There were children from that Stefaniuk family that attended this same school. The school, St. Cunageneda, was only about three or four hundred yards east of where we lived. Today it is there no more, but only a marker stands there to tell that there stood a school. We moved here in the spring as the snow was just starting to melt. I went to school the very next day. I had now been in school for one year. Miss Frey (or Frie) gave me a grade two reader to read. I could not read what she asked me to read, so I was put in with grade one.

It was also in this school that I had some misfortunes. This was the school where I got the only two straps while attending different schools all my school life. As mentioned in the above paragraph, we lived less than a quarter of a mile from school, so each day I would come home for lunch. This school had no well, so there was no water in the school and children had to bring water to school for themselves in jars or whatever. One day I had just returned from home from lunch and was playing with other children outside. The school bell rang and everyone rushed to get into their desks. After everyone was in their desk, the teacher Miss Frey (or Frie) asked me to come to the cloakroom with her. I thought she was going to teach me something or ask me to do something. She came and brought the strap with her. Then in the cloakroom she told me that I had drank the water that one boy that brought to school. That boy was a bully in school. How much English I understood, I told her that I did not drink any water because I was at home. I was at home and if I wanted water, I drank it at home, so why would I drink some one else's water? There were no if's and but's for the teacher and for that I got two straps, all for nothing, because the bully made up a lie against me and I could not defend myself still not knowing the language that well.

Another thing that this bully did was on a cold winters day. This day I did not go home for lunch because it was cold and some stormy weather was churning outside. I brought my lunch with me to school this day. The lunch was in a paper bag. The teacher dismissed the class for lunch, and she went for lunch to the teacherage next to the school. As soon as the teacher was out the door, this bully walks past my desk, grabs my lunch, pulls up a chair beside the blackboard and puts my lunch on top of the map cabinet. Maps used to be in a drawer type cabinet which you would pull down any map you needed to show something to the class. There sat my lunch. An older student, Mary Stefaniuk, (the daughter of Mike Stefaniuk mentioned above) began to argue with the bully to give me my lunch back. No way. He bullied her also and with the poker that was used to stoke the fire in the wood stove, he would poke her with it. At other times when I knew he would come to grab my lunch I would guard it, but he would still come around and grab my sandwich from hands and either eat it himself or throw it into the garbage pail or into the stove. He would keep an eye on the teacherage and as soon as he saw the teacher was leaving the teacherage coming to school, he would quickly give me the lunch back at which time there was now no time to eat. I sat hungry throughout the whole day until I came home from school. I would not eat my lunch when classes started because I was afraid so that I would not get a strap again. In that school I lived in fear all the time because of the "big bully."

One other funny thing that happened at this place where we lived was in the spring time. The snow had just about melted when one day when John, Alice and I were playing outside and we happened to find a beautiful pin with a red ruby stones on it. I was going to pin it on myself, but John began to cry that he wanted it, so I pinned that on him to keep him quiet. And who got a spanking for that pin? Yes I did, for pinning it on John. Mother tried taking the pin out of his shirt, but the pin would not come out until the shirt was partly damaged. Why? Because later we learned that this pin was a fish hook and the fish hook has a barb the other way and you would have to tear a small hole in the clothing to get it out.

Another silly thing that happened at this place was with John and me. A hundred yards south-west of the house was a slough. The snow was just about all melted, but here and there in the bush were still small piles of snow. One afternoon father and mother took Alice and went to Cudworth some 2-3 miles west of where we lived. They told John and me to play outside and be good and they would be back soon. John and I were home alone. So what do two young rascals do for action? First we played around the yard and then decided to go to the slough and play with the water. From first we threw little pebbles into the water that we found, then would throw some sticks and see who can throw farther. There were no bathrooms and bathtubs in homes at that time in the places where we lived. Baths were seldom taken, maybe once a month or so in a tub in the house. John and I thought it would be a good time to go into the water. We rolled up our pant legs and went into the water, but we soon found out that was not very much fun. We undressed and fully naked ran into the slough. The water was ice cold, since as mentioned snow was still standing in shady places. But two young rascals splashing around in the water that was bellybutton deep, was no time to feel cold. Having a good time in the water we never even noticed when the parents arrived home. They saw us in the water and yelled to us, what we were doing and to get out of the water. We did get out and were dressed in shorter time than we were undressing to go into the water. Mother said we were half blue and half white from the cold water. Mother pick up some kind of a stick and warmed our butts for what we had done. We never went bathing into that slough again without the permission of the parents.

After spending a year living in this place, the following spring we moved again, just as the snow was beginning to melt. This time father had found a place one mile east of Wakaw which is eleven miles north of Cudworth and we moved there with father renting a quarter section of land from the late John Kwasnicia. Mr. Kwasnicia had a store in Wakaw and lived in Wakaw, but he also had a vacant house on the farm. By this time we already had four horses, one or two cows and other livestock. Here for the first time father started farming by renting the farm, quarter section of beautiful level land. In the north-west corner of the farm was a small Orthodox church and cemetery which is there to this very day. (the church is no more there.) We attended this church whenever services were held. There is another side to this story where we lived. Nearly half a century later I was married to Mary Kwasnica who was a niece to John Kwasnica, but at that time when we lived there, I never knew Mary (Marusia). The story of this will be told later as we come to that era in time.

Moving to this area early in the spring, John also started school here. The name of the school was Crooked Lake and was just over one mile south east from our place. It was one mile to Wakaw, but why we went to the farm school instead of to Wakaw, I don't know. When I came the first day to the new school, what does the teacher do? Does he put me in grade two or grade one that I had already spent two years. He gives me a grade three reader to read, but with new and harder words it was difficult to read. Seeing this the teacher keeps me in grade two. I had to repeat the same grade again and by this time I nearly knew the grade one and two readers by memory, but the teacher thought I was not ready for grade three. For this reason it is a very bad decision for families to move in March if there are children going to school. We lived at the east end of the quarter section and about two or three hundred yards east of where we lived, was another family the Fereniuks. Children from that family also went to the same school, so we had company to and from school in this school district. During free times we played with the Fereniuk children in their yard or in ours. The school was south-east of where we lived and to get to school we walked past Fereniuk's place and east to get to the main road. There was a lake from east to west and we had to go around to get to the road that went past the school.

As mentioned above we already had four horses by this time. Now there was something to work the land with. Father was still asking and looking to get some work around the community, while mother did most of the work around the yard and also in the house. Father had gotten some kind of work someplace and was not home a day or two. One morning probably during July, when we woke up we found the horses had broken out of the pasture and were missing. Now where do you start looking for the horses? Mother left John, Alice and Oksana at Fereniuks and took me with herself to help find and catch the horses. We tried to follow their tracks but soon lost them. We stopped in at different farmers places to ask if they did not see four stray horses. Later we found some horse tracks by the railway. The first thing that came to mind was that if the horses got on the railway, they may be dead now, being killed by the train.

We followed those tracks and lost them also. Were those the tracks of our horses? The day was hot. It was summer and I was thirsty and tired. After walking and searching for miles and miles, we returned home with no horses seen anywhere. This same evening father came home from where he had been working and mother told him that the horses were gone. He was upset and angry, but what could we have done when they broke down the fence during the night and got out. Next day father himself went looking for the horses, but had no luck finding them. Later towards evening Peter Hryciuk from Cudworth came with the car to our place and told us that our horses are at Cudworth where we used to live. Wakaw to Cudworth is eleven miles. One of the horses we had was smart and many times we had problems with her. We thought that this was probably the work of that mare Lucy, who got out and took the other horses with her. Father got into the car with Mr. Hryciuk and went to Cudworth to bring the horses back. He brought back all four horses, only I don't remember if it was that same night or the following day.

Because of the hardships that followed us wherever we went, I being the oldest was expected to do more to help out with chores around the yard and house. When I was about eight years old father put me on the discer to disc the summer fallow when school had been out for the summer. Father had other work to do around the yard at home. The field was exactly half a mile from east to west. He tied me down to the discer seat so that I would not slide off and down under the discs and get run over. I went from the east end of the field, where the yard was, all the way to the west end where I had to make a turn and come back again.

As I was making the turn, the steering pole fell of the horses neck yoke and I stopped. I could not get off the seat because I was tied down and the knots were under the seat where I could not reach them to loosen myself from the rope and seat. So what does an eight year old do at the end of the field half a mile from home and no one around? I sat in the hot sun but I was lucky that the horses did not decide to leave the hot sun and take off. It would have been a catastrophe and I could have been made into hamburger under the discs. I sat in the seat and cried, for what else could I do? Maybe someone will come along and will help me. In the meantime whatever father was doing in the yard and he would glance from time to time to see if I'm still discing. One time he said he looked and thought that the horses were standing and not moving. He looked the second time, and sure enough there was no movement. He said that his first thought of seeing the horses standing, was that I must have fell off. He could not see me if I was sitting because of the color of the horses and my clothing, so he could not distinguish if I was on the seat or not. He knew something was wrong, but did not know what. I was lucky that the horses were quiet horses and they would have rather stood and rest than move and pull the discs. Father seeing that the horses were standing, he came running towards me. I had already made half a turn, so I was sitting in a way that I could turn my head and see the yard at home half a mile away. When father arrived he saw right away what was wrong. He put the steering pole back in place and then shortened the pulling straps of the harness by one or two rings and than I disced the rest of the field, for the rest of the day without incident.

Summer came and went. There was time for work for an eight year old, but than there were times for play. Now harvest was around the corner. Father had seeded half of the field in the spring and there was a bumper crop that year. When harvest came in late August or early September, school had already started. Our crop was now cut, stooked and ready to be threshed. I had seen a threshing machine before from a distance, but I would not go too close to one, because it was too frightening, making a huge noise and it looked dangerous.

One day after school we learned that the threshing crew will be threshing at our place the following day. I was told that I would have to stay home from school, because I will need to help at the machine by shoveling grain in the bin. The machine and crew arrived and the following day our crop was threshed. My job was in the granary. I shoveled and shoveled that wheat and ate the dust that was in the bin. This was my first experience with a threshing machine and crew. Everybody had something to do. Racks on the field were being filled by sheave pitchers. An engineer was keeping an eye on the machine to see that everything was working properly. Someone else would do something else and everybody was busy. As the threshing machine hummed along, more wheat kept pouring into the granary. I shoveled until there was no more room to shovel the wheat. An empty wagon was brought by the granary and the wheat was directed into the wagon.

When I was shoveling in the granary it got hotter and hotter and harder to breath in the dust. Father brought me a wet rag and tied it around my face. Oh what a relief that was when it became so much easier to breath. Finally all the sheaves were threshed and it was supper time. As the threshing was going on, inside the house there was just as much commotion as from the threshing machine outside. Mother was preparing lunch and coffee to take to the workers by the machine, and then also prepared dinner and supper for the crew. Another thrill came to me in the evening. About ten to twelve men sat around a large table having supper after they first had looked after their horses outside, to be watered and fed. All day mother had prepared this meal for the hungry crew. Someone had noticed that I was standing in a corner in the house, (because children were always taught to respect the elders and not say anything or do anything, but stand quietly and watch) and the person says that I should sit down to eat with the men because I was helping with the threshing. A place was soon made for me and what a thrill to sit at the same table with the threshing crew. Was I grown up and a man now? An eight year old man?

Life at Wakaw lasted only one year. It was a good place there. The land was nice and level, no rocks, close to town, etc. But, father had found another place to rent land and so when spring came at about the end of March or early April we were on the move again. This time we moved from Wakaw to Reynaud which was about fifteen miles east of Wakaw towards Basin Lake. There father was going to rent a quarter section of land from Mr. Shchitka. About a mile south of where we lived father rented another quarter section of land. This second quarter had been neglected and no one had worked that land for a few years. It was overgrown with weeds and small shrubs had started to grow here and there. Usually on Saturday and during summer holidays it was my job to work this second quarter of land. Now with half a section of land, more crop will be produced and more funds will come for the family.

Chances looked good. After we had worked that second quarter section of land all summer long and looking forward to seeding it the following year, a bombshell fell. People had seen how well the land was worked up, clean and ready to seed, so someone went and purchased that quarter section from the owners of the land and we were again left with the one quarter were we lived on Shchitka's farm. I don't know if father even got one red cent for having worked the neglected land to bring it to productivity. The dark, misfortune evil was always looking where we were, to make things harder and harder for the family.

Moving from Wakaw to Reynaud we traveled as nomads. We borrowed one wagon from a neighbor and piled all our belongings unto it. Mother will drive this wagon. The other wagon which father was driving had the wagon box divided into two parts. In one part went the sow with the piglets and in the other half the poultry. Alice and Oksana were with mother in the wagon. John and I had the job of walking behind and chasing the cows. One oldest cow was tied to the wagon while the others were loose, so John and I had to see that they followed the cavalcade. The trek began at Wakaw sometimes before noon. At about the half way point just east of a small lake, about 7 miles east of Wakaw we stopped for lunch. John and I were still keeping an eye on the cattle and eating with the rest of the family dry bread and drinking water which had been taken from the well at the last place we lived. One piece of bread in one hand and a stick in the other to keep the cattle together. The horses and cows were given hay because it being the time of the year, there was still no green grass. I do not recall the rest of the trip to Shchitka's but we must have gotten their sometimes in the late afternoon. Things had to be unloaded and placed in the house in their places. The animals had to be put into their place, so that we may start our life in the new place. The house sat on a hill and to the east we could see Basin Lake. It was a large lake. People from the area told us that at one time the place was a meadow where farmers from the area around came and cut hay for winter for the cattle. People told us that one night there was a very large rumbling noise and everybody was afraid of what may have been happening. In the morning when people got up, a large lake met their eyes and is there to this day. It is called Basin Lake because of its round shape looks like a basin.

Having moved to a new area, we now have to find a new school. Again we would start in March or April and that was a bad time to change schools. This school that we would attend was about a mile west of where we lived. It was called Cranberry School. To get to that school by road, it would have been about five or six miles, but to make it closer we would walk across the fields and then through some bush, down a steep hill and there at the bottom was the school. Here we made new friends again. The teacher was Mr. MacFadden. He had a son Garfield who was the same grade as John. We became very good friends with Garfield also with Eddie and Mickey Balon, and other children. Last I heard was that Garfield was a pilot living at Peace River, Alberta.

    It was also at this place where father had to spend a few days in the hospital at Cudworth. The year had been good. It was a bumper crop and good harvest. Now came winter and at winter comes the Nativity of Christ (Christmas). The parents had invited some closer friends over for the festive celebrations. Father served refreshments. At that time it was different than today. Father would have a drink to one friend and then give that friend a drink. Than he would have another drink to another friend and than that friend would have a drink. By the time each friend had a drink, father had already had half a dozen drinks or so. At that time that was the tradition. Doing greetings this way gave father maybe more than he could handle. He must have felt bad and somehow slipped outside in the dark for some fresh air. He only had a white shirt on in the -30 degree weather in the month of January. While outside, he lost his balance or what, to which one knows, and he fell into the snow. Someone noticed that father was missing and started to look where he was. Someone checked the rooms in the house and someone went outside to have a look. Near the steps of the house father was found lying in the snow. He was brought into the house. Next day he felt really ill aching all over. Mother drove him to the train station at Reynaud where he caught the train to Wakaw. At Wakaw he took the train to Cudworth, because he knew the doctor in Cudworth. He stayed in the hospital a few days. A young new doctor was substituting for the regular doctor who was away. The young doctor gave father medication to make him sweat. Later father said that the nurses changed his bedding three times a day from the sweating. He returned home from the hospital and till his passing away at the age of 101 he never had any side effects. Till the day he passed away, we had never again seen that our father had too much to drink.

    We lived for a year or two on Shchitka's land. It was by this time that father said the only thing to do was to have your own property - farm. We had to have our own land where all the income would be ours and we would not have to give any share for the owner of the land. We could get farther ahead by owning land than by renting. At the same time we would not have to look for another place to live, for it would be our home for as long as we lived. This thought stayed with father and he started to look and ask around about property for sale, mostly interested to purchase land.

He saw in a paper or learned from someone that there was a shoemaker shop for sale at Porcupine Plain, Saskatchewan in the Hudson Bay area. Father knew some shoe making, because he had done that in Ukraine before he came to Canada, so he thought that he could do the same here. One day father got on the train at Reynaud to go east to check the place out. He had $16.00 in his pocket. He paid for the return train fare and I don't know how much he lad left. When he got to Porcupine Plain he found the shoemaker shop place in a very dilapidated state. The owner asked father if he had any children and father said there were four. The man looked at father and says: "Don't bring your children out here into the bush, take them among the people into the city and give them an education." So now what? Father thought it over and started back for home.

An incident happened to father at Melfort as he later told us himself. When he was going to Porcupine Plain he had to change trains at Melfort. Coming back it was the same. He got on a train that other people were getting on. After going out of Melfort the conductor came to pick up the tickets. He looked at father's ticket and saw that father was on the wrong train heading to Prince Albert wrong train to where he had to go. The train was stopped in the middle of the field and than had to back up into Melfort to drop father off. When they returned to Melfort the train to Saskatoon had already left, so father had to spend the night in Melfort. Where? In a hotel? No. There was no money to pay for the hotel, so he stayed at the station the whole night until next day when he caught the right train. One thing that the railway people learned from father's mistake was that next day at the station as you were boarding the train, the conductor checked your ticket to make sure you were getting on the right train and they shouted out where the train was going. In small centres this was not necessary, but where a number of trains arrived and departed each day at nearly the same time this was needed because many people who traveled at that time did not know English.

Having had no luck with the shoe repair business at Porcupine Plain, father was now heading back home to Reynaud. Coming home he met some people on the train who told him that a man is selling a farm near

Tarnopol. Having taken some information about where, what and who, next day father went to see the man who was living on the land that was for sale. He met Mr. Gach, an elderly and retired gentleman bachelor who lived on a small plot of land in the south west corner of the farm. When father and mother were giving us their life biographies in 1988 at Salmon Arm, B.C., father said he bought the farm from Mr. Gach, but John says that the farm belonged to a one Mr. Waschuk in Winnipeg. So I don't know who is correct. The owner of the land wanted $500.00 down and the rest in annual payments. The land had not been worked on for a number of years and lay vacant. Rocks, wild weeds, quack grass and brush in some places four and five feet high had already grown over the land.

Father came home and told mother about the land and they decided to buy the property. There was an old clay log house on the land, a barn and a granary. The house with three rooms was only about 150 feet from a lake. With a lake on the property, cattle at least will have a supply of water. The lake was about forty or fifty acres in size and stretched from our farm and across to the neighbors farm. That lake is still there as this is written. There were rocks and more rocks and still MORE ROCKS on the land. Small ones, middle sized and large ones. The north side boundary of our farm had a fence, but there was no need for one. The rocks from our side and the neighbor from his side had picked and thrown enough rocks that it formed a rock fence about three to four feet high. Father seeing the rock piles around the field and along the north fence was sure that they had all been cleared. What a surprise when we started working the land.

So father is buying the farm. He needs $500.00 for down payment, but where do you get such money from? The parents knew of a family who were very good friends They decided to go and see if this one family would borrow father $500.00. This family had been farming for many years and were in good financial standing. They did borrow father the money and father purchased the land. Now we will move once more and will not have to move again - OR WILL WE?

Before we moved, us children kept going to school at Cranberry. When we were in school, at the same time the parents with Oksana (to young for school yet) would go to the new place to clean it up and prepare for the move. We have to move as soon as possible, because spring was starting and work on the field will have to be done if we want to plant anything this year. The parents made a number of trips back and forth to the new place and each time they went they would take some articles to leave so there would be less to move on moving day. The place was only about four miles north from Schitka's place.

Again everything was ready and time to move to our own home place. Good-byes were said to the people (neighbors) who had come to help us load the wagon with the heavy things. Now we were off to the new place to our home to call our own. Soft tears came to the eyes as we were leaving, since we had grown up more by now and parting was different than when you are a small child. We had to leave that place where we had come to love and enjoy, but we also looked forward to better things to come.

One must remember that by this time we were already "rich". A bumper crop at Wakaw and another on Shchitkas farm made us wealthy. Imagine: We owned a wagon, four horses, a hay rack, a buggy, a few head of cattle, some pigs, chickens, etc. The trip was not far, four miles north. Excitement was high and the blood flowed rapidly through the young veins as we looked forward to our own home place. Now we will not move until we finish schooling or maybe even never, but stay on our farm. At least now we will have our own farm and what we will grow or produce will be ours. As mentioned, parents had already made a few trips to prepare the place and had moved a number of things. They clayed the house inside and out. They whitewashed the walls inside, put a new door on, fixed up the windows and chimney to make the house look habitable. As we were making this trip sister Alice already remembered that we had moved once or twice and during the ride to the new place she asked: "When will we move again after we stay in the new place?" The parents smiled and said: "We will not be moving no more, because this new place will be our home for always." Later as we will see, Alice and her husband John Hnatiuk rented this land when no one was living there anymore. Why? As we go along time and events will tell the rest of the story.

So when we move to a new area, there is a new school to attend. Again as in all previous times moving was in the early, early spring so that spring seeding can be done on the land. This also was bad moving for children when they have to start classes in a new school not at the beginning of a school year but towards the end. The school was one and a half miles away called Old Tarnopol School. In that surrounding area there was an older Ukrainian Orthodox Church. There was a store, a blacksmith and a community hall. The area Tarnopol was named after the city in Ukraine when people from that area came to Canada and settled here. The hope was that a railway one day would go through this place and it would grow. But when the railway came along, it went a mile south of this place and a new place, New Tarnopol was started. Today neither place exists, just the name of the area - Tarnopol.

As for school, the first day here also brings a memory. John and I immediately made friends the first day in this school which was called Tarnopol School. I can't recall where Alice started school, at Cranberry or Tarnopol. Oksana, yes she started school at Tarnopol. The new friends first day we made, told John and me that the strap which the teacher had, they threw it into the stove and burned it. When the school bell ran everyone hurried to their place. The Lord's Prayer was said and O' Canada was sung. The teacher first wanted to know who we were and we told her our names. The teacher looked mean. She saw that the strap was missing and she wanted to know where the strap was. No one was admitting anything. Then came the news. The teacher (Dorothy Cipiwnyk, maiden name, was still living at Penticton, B.C. in the late 1990's), announced that the strap has disappeared. She asked for admittance who knew anything about it. Having received no answer she gave instructions what to do. "You all have fifteen minutes to go behind the barn, except the two new students, John and me, and each one bring a small twig at least twelve inches long." She dismissed the class for fifteen minutes and asked John and me to stay in school and enquired from us what our names were, our grade, where we came from, when our birthdays were, etc.

A short while later all the children were back in the classroom each one holding a twig or branch in their hand. The students by this time had already figured out what this was all about. The teacher told them to line up along the wall where the blackboard was. Then she asked the children once again where the strap was and no one said anything except one or two younger children said they don't know anything. The teacher then took each child's little branch and gave each one a few strikes over their outstretched hands. The school was filled with ouches, sobbing and crying. There was one older student who thought he would outsmart the teacher, so he brought a thick stick about an inch thick. He knew the teacher would not hit him hard with that because it could hurt his hands. When the teacher saw what he did, she left him to be the last one for punishment. At the end she called him beside her desk and told him to lay down on the chair. Now he knew what her idea was, but it was too late. He did as the teacher told him and she wacked him a number of times over his seat shaking off the dust from his trousers. The teacher did get a new strap later, but she hardly ever used it unless it was for some serious offense. The children were obedient to the teacher. When the time had come that she was moving away to another school, there were more tears and sobs than had been from all the strapping which all the children had previously received that one day. Faces were saddened and the children did not want the teacher to leave.

School had to be attended. Grades seemed to be easier now that we were settled in one place and from year to year in the same school. Teachers at that time were tough and they fought tough kids in school. Yes there was some bullying going on, but it was always handled and things turned out well in the end. When I taught school I also had a bully, and that was taken care off as later we will talk about this when the time comes. In those "good old days" you made spelling mistakes, you got strapped for it. You used foul language, you got strapped. You did things you should not do and the strap spoke out - slap, slap, slap. The strap made people out of us. When you walked into a classroom, there was order, quiet and obedience. At that time there were no children wandering around the classroom. There were no caps on the heads and turned around backwards. Our hands were on the desk and our feet on the floor. Nowadays you see feet on the desks and the hands God knows where. There was less mischief and vandalism, name calling, street prowling or juvenile delinquency as compared to today. You could walk down the sidewalk and there was room for everyone on it. Today an older person coming down the sidewalk with a cane towards a group of teenagers and the older person has to get off the sidewalk to make room for the gang. Where is the respect today, which was so prevalent in the "good old days?" When you came home from school and the parents found out you got strapped in school, then father's belt came off and he would finish the work where the teacher left off. Those days and teachers made people out of us where we learned respect and obedience.

But look at today's world. When we went to a store as small tots in those days, our hands were in our pockets or behind our backs. We looked at toys or anything else in the store, but God forbid if we touched anything that was not ours. Compare that to today. You go into a store and kids at the age of three, four and older go to the toy department. On the floor are all kinds of toys scattered around. Kids come and try out the toys, play with them, spoil them and probably even break them. Someone has to pay for the damage - and that is you and me. Toys all over the floor on the isle that you can't even walk through. Look at those people's homes, is it any different? No. Children have no respect for their parents. They call their parents by their first name, they disobey them, they don't listen to what they are told. Discipline actions these days is nil while the discipline in our times made people out of us. Youth today grow up with no respect and obedience to anyone. Today the teachers in the school are powerless. If the teachers in school had power, I know that the world would change back to normality as it should be. Today youth grow up as though the world owes them a living. We are thankful and grateful to our parents and the teachers who taught us, for they made respectful people out of us.

So, now we had our own farm. Spring was here and spring work had to be done. As mentioned above, father bought the farm for $1500.00 with $500.00 down and the remaining $1000.00 to be paid in four installments of $250.00 each year. Now the crop had to be put in. But how do you work the land when you have no machinery. We had accumulated some smaller implements and other implements we borrowed from the neighbors. As time went on father would go to auction sales and buy used machinery. Some seed grain was borrowed from the neighbor which had to be given back in the fall after harvest. This year the summer was dry. Rains never came when they were needed. At the end we harvested one hundred and twelve bushels of wheat as father told us. From this, thirty bushels had to be given back to the neighbor which had been borrowed from in the spring. Eighty bushels of wheat was left for seed for the following year and what about feed for the livestock. The cattle will need straw for the winter and where is that to come from when there was a drought and not much straw. Than there was a payment of $250.00 to be made for the land. What about the $500.00 to return that was borrowed to make a down payment on the farm? How does one make a living and get ahead? And at the end there are six mouths to feed. Times were tough and we made the best with what we had.

The family was always worried not to have any debt, but how can you eliminate that word when all around you debt just seemed to climb higher and higher above one's head. Today there is so much money that people just want more and how true it is: "the more they have, the more they want."

Today's problem with people is people want to work less, but at the same time to give them more money. I have one thing to say. I would ask the person: "Do you want this?" and they would probably say "yes." I would then say: "Do you need it?" Maybe some might say yes, but I know they don't need it and if they got along living without it till now, they can get along without out it and they don't need it. Why do people have to: "keep up with the Jones's?" Where in the Bible or in a country charter or constitution does it say that if someone has a million dollar house, that I have to have one too? Where does it say if someone is driving a Lincoln car, that I have to drive one too?

TRAIN FASCINATION

With all these hardships looking into the eyes of the family, father decided that something had to be done. He went to Prince Albert to look for a job for the winter months. Mother and us children stayed and worked on the farm what had to be done. Father found a job in a factory that produced railway ties. He was making forty cents an hour carrying and helping to tar the railway ties. It was a ten hour day with heavy work making four dollars a day.

Because father was away and I was the oldest in the family, so more chores fell to me. Each and every morning mother would milk the cows. She would not let anyone else milk the cows unless she was away during milking time. Sometimes in the summer mother was away from home for two to four days being a head cook at a wedding. People heard and word got around that Mrs. Stefaniuk cooked at such and such a wedding and they were very pleased with her work. When for weddings mother would be away we would have to milk the cows, but this was usually in the summer when weddings were taking place. For those two to four days she would get paid $25.00. Today don't some cooks get more than that an hour? That was great help to get a few cents for the family. Every morning before we went to school, chickens, hogs and cattle had to be fed and watered. Manure had to be cleaned out of the barn so that it could be hauled out unto the field. Then came breakfast and off to school.

Returning from school, chores again awaited us summer or winter. In the summer bring the cows home for milking. Hogs had to be fed and checked to see that there was water for them. After chores came supper and after supper school home work and then bedtime. We had no power, so a coal oil lamp was placed in the middle of the table for light. Later we even acquired a high test gasoline lantern with mantels. Every night at 8:00 PM CBC news came on the radio with Earl Cameron. We already had purchased a radio that was operated on a battery power pack. Parents would not let us listen to the radio whenever we wanted, because they said that when the battery wears out, there will be no money to buy another battery. We listened to the news for fifteen minutes each evening. As soon as the news was over the radio was turned off to preserve the battery. At this time I could already read and write in English. As the news hour approached I would take a piece of paper, a pencil and would write brief messages of what was said in the news. At the end of the news I would convey to the parents in Ukrainian what was happening around the world.

I vividly remember one news item that held the families attention, suspenseful and its as vivid today as the time it happened sometimes in the late 1940's or early 1950. Earl Cameron reported that there was a ship sinking in the Atlantic ocean. It was said that the Captain of the ship had gotten every one off the ship safely and he stayed on board the sinking vessel. Today I can't remember how it ended whether the Captain went down with the ship or if he was rescued with the rest of the people. That news item had caught the attention of all the people around us and even we children in school talked about it during class period.

With father being away in the winter time some fifty miles from home, we did not know what was happening with him. Did he have enough to eat? Did he have a good place to sleep? We had no power and no telephone. It was very expensive to get power and telephone. There were bills to pay and things that were needed, so we could not afford to have any luxuries. Mother could not read nor write in Ukrainian or English. We could have written to father in English, but that would not help him very much, because he could not read or write in English. One week-end father gave us a surprise and came home for the week-end. Father said that mother should learn to read and write in Ukrainian and then at least there would be correspondence between father and home. One evening mother says: "Children, where is that Ukrainian reader father bought you a year ago?" We found it. Mother sat down and started to look at the pictures and the letters underneath and putting them together. By putting the letters together she made words and slowly, slowly she began to read and write a word at a time. In a few days she could read and write at a slow pace, but as time went on she learned more and more so that she could write a letter to father in Prince Albert. Father would write back and when I brought home the mail and a letter from father had come, we crowded around mother like baby chicks around the mother hen and with eagerness listened to the letter father had written. Sometimes father would send a money order and would tell mother to pay off some of the debts to certain people where money was owed. Mother would have to go to town to cash the money order at the post office and pay some bills that had been incurred.

When springtime arrived father also arrived home because there was spring work to do on the field. He brought home some money he had made and paid off a few more debts that were hanging over the family's head. Father wanted to pay back the $500.00 that he had borrowed to buy the land, but he did not have enough. He took what he had and said that the rest would come as soon as he could get some more money. It took some time, but father paid everything off. Money was needed for clothing, for school supplies, for purchasing machinery and other items needed for survival. Food on the table was not a problem. We had eggs and chickens, meat, milk, cream and butter. We had vegetables from the garden. Mother made dill pickles and sauerkraut in forty gallon wooden barrels. The first year food for cattle, hay and straw, had to be found at friends or neighbors place because it had been a drought and had no grain or straw. Money was desperately needed at all times to try and catch up with debts. People to whom we owed money had hearts that were bigger than they were themselves and they patiently waited to get their money back. In the end as we will see later, everyone was repaid in full with thanks for their goodness and kindness. They could see that the family was struggling, so they never rushed to the lawyers office to take us to court. I believe that had father not paid off the debts, he would have hated himself for the rest of his life and would have probably felt guilty that he could not support his family. May God grant eternal rest to those who has passed away and had helped us in any way by borrowing us money and patiently waited to have it returned.

I ALSO WALKED ON THIS EARTH

One interesting thing living in this place for us children, was that there was a railway running east-west about three hundred yards north of our yard and house. The railway had cut off an acre of our farm in a kiddy corner in the NW part of the farm. Trains had always been an exciting thing in my life. I knew that when you drove horses, you had reigns to steer them and there was a steering wheel in a car, truck or tractor, but what steered such a big machine on two thin steel rails? We could hear the train whistle for miles away. During the summer holidays when the train whistle was heard, we children all raced towards the railway trying to beat each other. We would come to the fence and knew there we were safe that the train would not harm us. As the train passed by we would wave to the engineer and he in turn would give us a little toot-toot of the train whistle. We always kept thinking if we would ever ride on a train and if that day would ever come. On week days the train came from Melfort to Saskatoon at 9:00 AM in the morning and returned back at 4:30 PM. On Saturdays it would run about 5:00 PM and return at 10:00 PM. Sunday there was no train.

This habit of rushing to the railway to see the train go by and wave to the engineer became rewarding to us children. To this day we don't know who the engineer was, but he must have passed away as this is now written and may God grant him life in eternity for his goodness and kindness he showed to us. He must have seen us a few times standing by the fence and waving to him. He seemed to know that we would be there and he would have his head out the window and would wave to us. One time we did get a good fright and wondered what had happened. As the train passed us by, he turned on the valve and steam from the locomotive hissed and came towards us as the train passed by. Oh yes, we were afraid. I don't know who was the first one to run away from the fence. The engineer had seen us four ragged youngsters stand and wave to him each day.

One day we were standing and watching as the train neared us, the engineer throw something at us. We jumped with fear and ran from the fence. As the last coach passed we turned around and began to wonder why he would throw something at us when we never did anything wrong. Maybe he was just cautious and wanted to make sure that we don't come on the railway and get killed by the train. Anyway, as the train passed we thought we should go and find what he threw at us. There was tall grass and two or three foot shrubs. We all crawled through the fence and started to look for a rock or whatever that was thrown towards us. Low and behold we found a paper bag that was tied with a piece of string. We picked it up and all four raced towards the house to show mother what the engineer threw at us. Mother untied the little package and out came chocolate bars, suckers, gum and candy. These kind items we saw only once a year at Christmas time and here a good engineer threw us some of these goodies in July. This seemed like a dream come true from heaven. What a thrill that was for us.

This thing went on for about three or four years and then it stopped. We kept coming to the fence of the railway, but we could not tell if it was the same engineer or another. The train went by quickly and always the engineer had the special cap on. When no more goodies came for us father and mother told us that maybe the man had retired, maybe he is on another train someplace else or maybe he is sick or died or maybe he saw that we were somewhat older and did not need those kind goodies anymore. Whatever it was, but today by this time he must be in the other world, and may God reward him with life in heaven like he was rewarding us small children with goodies beside the railway.

Another episode of the railway happened a few years later. This took place in the fall and I must have been about fifteen years old by now. It was harvest time. Father was cutting the grain with the binder while John and I were stooking. It was Saturday and the train went to Saskatoon about 5:00 PM past our place. John and I were stooking at the east end of our farm on an up slope and from there we could see the yard, the whole field, the railway and neighbors farms. John and I could hear the train whistle and we knew that it was about 5:00 PM, so we were trying to get the stooking finished because we never did work on Sunday. We were a bit more than a quarter of a mile from the railway. Being in this higher place on the field we will be able to see the train very well. In a little while we could hear that the train was nearing our crossing. But something looked unusual today. We had lived a few years by the railway and were accustomed to the speed of the trains going east and west. Not this time. Something was wrong. We stopped stooking for a moment and were looking at the train. It was traveling at a very fast rate of speed, something we had never seen before. Was something wrong? Was the train late and trying to make up time? Was there a sick person on board and the train was rushing to get to

Wakaw to the hospital? John and I looked at each other and said: "Boy is he ever going."

As the train went around the bend behind the bush we could not see it anymore and went back to stooking. In the meantime father had made the last round cutting before 6:00 PM, unhitched the horses and gave them something to eat. Mother was milking cows. John and I were now down the hill and coming closer towards the yard with our stooking. Then we see father coming towards us and stooking as he comes so we would finish before 6:00 PM. As we neared to father and could hear each other talk, father speaks out loudly to us saying: "The train came off the tracks around the corner." WHAT? How does he know?

Joy ran through our veins. If that train came off the tracks, than we'll have a chance to see it from close. We finished stooking in no time flat and hurried with father as fast as we could to were the train was standing. As we came around the bend we could hear the locomotive hissing steam and the coaches standing on the tracks. We looked at each other and say: "But the cars are all on the tracks. Looks like nothing tipped over or anything wrong." We could see people milling about the train and in the ditches. The train was still about two and a half miles from Tarnopol and about five miles west of Yellow Creek which had been the train's last stop. Than we saw that the railway ties had been damaged by the train.

Don't remember if it was the trainman or conductor saw us coming towards the train. He came towards us and looked angry. He looked at John and me and says: "What do you want here? What are you doing here?" We said that we came with our father because we hear a noise here and we came to see what it was and maybe give some help." "Have you been playing on the railroad?" he says to us. "No. We were stooking and father was cutting the crop with the binder, and we heard noises so we came to see what it was." John and I understood English so we could talk to him and tell him what we were doing. Father did not understand the conversation, so he kept asking us what the man was saying.

So what had happened? As John and I were stooking we had noticed that the train was really flying this day. Never had we seen a train go by so fast as it did this one time. Probably with such great speed around the curve the water tank was swaying too much with the water swishing inside the tank and threw the water tender off the tracks. There were no injuries, the water tender was off the rails but everything else was on the track. There were a lot of broken railroad ties and the water tender was sitting in the gravel and the broken ties standing upright with one side outside the rails and the other inside. We looked at the train for a few minutes and then through the bush headed for home about four hundred yards. We had supper and after supper John and I again rushed back to where the derailment took place to see the excitement and what was happening.

After a while the section foreman and his crew that looked after that part of the railway arrived from Reynaud. By now it was beginning to get dark. John and I had climbed up the large high bank on the north side of the track to watch. Like owls we perched ourselves on the edge at the top of the bank and stared to see what was going on. Over and over again the men would set steel blocks under the derailed tender. Then the locomotive would slowly try to go forward so that the tender could get as high as the rails and hopefully slide back unto the rails. Each time as they tried this method, the tender would just about be on the rails but then would slip off again. Then they start all over again with the same thing. Over and over and over again they tried and just could not seem to succeed. It was already dark by this time, but there were lights set up that were shining where the men were working. John and I were tired from stooking that day and it was cooling off in the night, so we decided to go home and come back in the morning to see what is happening.

Next morning we got up and dressed quickly, had breakfast and told our parents that we are going back to the derailed train to see what is happening. As we hurried through the bush on the shortcut, we could hear no noises. No people talking and no hissing of the locomotive. It all seemed so quiet. As we came nearer to the railroad and could already see through the trees, disappointment met us. There is no train. We came out of the bush and walked up to the railway. All that was left was a pile of broken railroad ties and a roughened up area where the accident had taken place. Later we learned that it was about 6:00 AM that Sunday morning that the tender had finally been replaced back on the rails and the train made its journey on to Saskatoon.

This same railway later served as my link with the high school in New Tarnopol. It was a shorter route for me to walk on the railway to school than all the way around by road. By railroad it was only two and a half miles and by road it was more like four to five miles. Than if it was raining, it was always dry and no mud on the railroad as one did have on the road. I usually left home about 8:15 AM to be in school for 9:00 AM and had to walk the two and a half miles.

It was about this same time that the railroad section crew from Reynaud would come up to check the railway. They would go another half mile east, past our place and then turn around because that was the end of their territory. The train came through at 9:00 AM each day, so they went up and down the track to inspect if everything was all right. After they turned their motor car (jigger) around they would come back towards Tarnopol and they would stop along the way wherever they had to do something. Nearly every day of the week as I was going to Tarnopol, they would be coming towards me. I got off the track about ten, fifteen feet and waited as they go by and waved to them. After they passed me, I got back on the track and keep walking to school. After I had walked a few hundred feet, I hear them coming from behind me. As they neared me, I would again get off the track and they just went past me. I guess they found out later who I was and where I was going. So one day as I stepped off the track when they were returning back to Tarnopol and Reynuad, I could hear the little jigger slowing down.

My heart took a skip and a beat and I knew I was in trouble for being or walking on the railroad. As the jigger neared me, it stopped and the foreman calls out: "Come on, get on, we'll give you a ride." Yes I felt glad that I was going to get a ride. But what if they maybe picked me up and will take me to the police. When we reached the railway station at Tarnopol, they stopped so that I could get off. The station was located in such a position that no one could see me get off the jigger. If anyone heard the jigger stop, they paid no attention, because it often stopped beside the station to check if there was wood for the stove or maybe to sweep up and clean up the station inside. There was no station agent there, so it was up to the maintenance crew to look after the cleanness of the station. As soon as I got off, I would thank them for the ride, they started up and went on their way. From the station to the school it was now only about three hundred yards. This went on for four years until I finished school.

Life seemed to go normally on the farm if there is such a thing as normal life on the farm. But still it was normal for what a farmer had to do day after day. We had no tractor and larger machinery, but four horses and machinery fit for horses. The horses were our tractor for a number of years. At times for days on end those horses, beasts of burden, pulled the plow, discs, harrows, seed drill, mower, rack, binder, wagon, buggy, etc. The only time the horses rested was on a Sunday and a Holy Day. But when a church service was held on a Sunday once a month or even less, then a pair of horses was hitched to the wagon or a buggy(democrat) to go to church. It was only during the late fall, early spring and winter that the horses could rest more often. Sometimes in the summer the horses were so tired that if you even tried to bribe them with oats to catch them, they would not come, but would stay put. If you came nearer to them they would try to move away, so that they would not be the ones to be caught and hitched up. Horses usually rest and sleep standing up, but when you see horses lying on the ground, resting, that was a sign they are tired.

For the family as for horses it was not a pushover life either. Rocks had to be picked and there were millions of them. Each year you pick and pick and pick and they just seemed to be growing along with the crops each year. To this day there are huge piles of rocks on the field and along neighboring fence. Year after year we picked and it seemed that the more you picked the more there were. I hated picking rocks, because it was done year after year after year. I did not mind picking roots where new land was broken, because you picked the roots once and there was no more of them. And there were trees to be grubbed for opening up more land. Grubbing was done by hand. First with the grub hoe, we'd move the soil away from the roots. When the roots were exposed then they were cut with an axe and the tree would be felled. If that did not work we would bring a team of horses and tie a long chain to the tree and have the horses pull the tree out. John and I usually did the grubbing while father would cut the roots. When the tree was felled, branches were cut off and piled and later they would be burned. The cleared trees of the branches were piled and later hauled home, so that it would be cut into firewood. Sometimes mother would come out to help us in clearing the land, and she was not afraid of work as was neither member of the family. Work had to be done and it was done not waiting for someone else to come and do it.

Then in the summer time also hay had to be made so there would be feed for cattle for the winter. There were no balers at that time. Every stem of hay was pitched by hand. First it was cut with a mower that we had bought at some auction sale. Two horses pulled the mower and father always cut the hay. After a few hot dry sunny days the hay was ready to be racked and hauled home. I usually racked the hay. Two horses pulled the rack and you racked the hay into rows and piles. Then another team of horses with the rack on the wagon would pick up the hay. Father and mother usually threw the hay unto the rack and John would drive the horses and trample down the hay, so it would be well stacked and solid and not slide off as it would be transported to the home place. At home it was thrown off the rack and one person on the ground would trample it to hold it in place.

One year father says that he will take us children to Prince Albert to the exhibition. We had heard so much about those fairs and exhibitions, but had never seen or attended one. That itself was something else to see for our eyes. We have only two eyes, but to see all that was going on at the fair-exhibition, we needed eyes on every side of the head to see everything. Rides, people, noise, food, prizes, all at once, and it seemed like there were a million people around us. We had never seen so many people. What a sight to behold. Father had hired someone who had a car to take us to Prince Albert to the fair-exhibition.

We still had to watch our finances. Father paid the admission to the grounds, but we could not afford to go on any rides except on one a merry-go-round. Riding a horse at a merry-go-round was sure different than riding a live one on the farm. What a thrill. We could not take chances in any games because money was short and was needed for other things at home. Mother and Oksana did not go with us on this trip. Oksana was still small and mother stayed home to do the evening chores should we come home late. Father thought it would be a good idea to have a picture taken of us four while in Prince Albert. We went looking for a photographer in the city to have a studio picture taken. A photograph studio was found and we had the pictures taken. After the pictures were taken the photographer asked for our address and money for the pictures so he would have them ready to send out to us in the mail. When he told father the price of the pictures, father just about blew a fuse. I can't remember what the price was, but it was exuberant for that time of what father thought it should have been. Somehow after arguing, with John and me being the translators between father and the photographer, the man lowered the price and father paid him. The pictures later arrived by mail to Tarnopol at the post office. I still have on hand one copy of that photograph. I don't know how many pictures we had received and where the rest of them went I don't know. I can only assume that some of the other family members had taken a copy and somehow in some way either their children damaged them or they were just thrown out. Today when people look at themselves in a picture that was taken of them when they were ten or fifteen years old, they didn't like the hairdo they had at that time, so many times a picture like that just goes into file number thirteen - garbage.

LAKE AND SPORTY THE DOG

I must also mention a word or two about the lake we had on our farm. As was already mentioned, the lake covered a part of our farm and a part of the neighbors. Had there been no lake here, there would have been a road built right along the west side of our farm, but because there was the lake, there was a road from the north and from the south, but they ended when you reached the lake. Father thought it would be good and fun to have a boat where we could spend time on the lake in the summer. One day father got some boards and started construction of the boat. We watched with anticipation of the progress of the boat building and hoped that it would go sooner. In the summer many Sundays, or on other days, when there was not too much work we would get into the boat and paddle around and have fun. One thing is that the lake was not very deep. We could walk across the lake and the water at the deepest place would only reach below our shoulders. We had a dog named Sporty. He would go with us in the boat. When we got into deeper water we would through him overboard and he would swim back to shore. We would paddle back to the shore and then he comes back himself into the boat with us. We would again repeat the same action and he enjoyed it, because he would come back into the boat without asking him in. He would wag his tail and we would pat him and start the same game over again.

Many times we would row the boat across to the south side of the lake with Sporty in it. The lake was only about four hundred yards across. Sometimes Sporty would go into the water and wait for us to get into the boat. We would call for him to come into the boat, but he would look at us as if to say; "well paddle and I will swim and see who gets across first." Many times he swam across the lake beside the boat. To us Sporty was more human than some people are. We used to have a lot of fun in the water during the summer months. We would play in it even though there was no sand, gravel or rocks. It was the real black loam mud. When you stepped into the mud you would sink in it about three to six inches. At times when it was milking time we would take Sporty into the boat, paddle across, then drop him off and say: "Sporty, go get the cows home." He knew what was said and understood us. He would wag his tail, take a look at us and he was gone. We would turn around and paddle back while he would bring the cows home around the lake. Sometimes we would take him on the dock that father had built and pointed to the other side of the lake and say: "Sporty go get the cows." He wagged his tail, jumped into the water and would swim to the other side of the lake. Ten or fifteen minutes later the cows and Sporty were by the barn.

One other thing about Sporty. One day father butchered a hog. After it had been cleaned, he cut the head off and put it in the snow to stay cool. This was in early winter time. The rest of the hog was cut up into pieces and taken to the granary to cool off over night or to freeze. By the time all was cleaned up, it was late afternoon and the days being so much shorter in the winter, we all went about to do chores. Now it was dark and supper had been prepared with fresh pork. That evening the parents were still cutting up some meat in the house and preparing to get it for cooking (preserving) in quart jars for the summer months.

Outside it was cold maybe 25-30 below F. When it got that cold Sporty was always in the house with us. He had his place by the door where he always slept. This night when we were going to bed father opened the door to let Sporty in from outside. Sporty was not by the door. Father called him and waited a moment but no Sporty came. Father told us that Sporty is not around, so we wondered where he was and nobody thought too much of what could have happened. Some of us thought that maybe he had found a cozy place and was spending the night there. When morning came father was up and went to start a fire in the little hut we had built in the bank of the lake for heating water for the hogs. As father walked down, there was Sporty laying beside the head of the hog which we all had forgotten about the day before. Some snow under sporty had even melted and formed a little ice crust under him. Sporty had spent the whole night guarding the hog's head. He knew that if we did not tell him that he could have it, it meant it was not his and he must watch it. That is the kind of dog Sporty was.

We also had another dog besides Sporty. He was a huge, huge German shepherd dog, a really big dog. He was not afraid of anything or anyone, but he dare not go near Sporty, even though sporty was smaller, for Sporty was in command as he was older. I don't recall what we called him or where we got him, but my brother John said we called him Teddy. He also was an ideal watch dog, but not in the sense that Sporty was. One day we were grubbing and cutting down trees to open up more land on the south side of the lake. Because we did not want to walk home for lunch around the lake, we took lunch with us. Both dogs came with us to where we were working. Father put the lunch beside a tree in the shade. As we were leaving the lunch, Teddy was already scampering towards our lunch. Sporty seeing Teddy coming there, attacked him and Teddy jolted away. Even though he was probably about two times as big as Sporty, he still kept an eye out for him for his own safety.

One evening the neighbors came to our place for a visit and their three dogs came with them. Father was giving us boys a haircut outside. It was summer about 7:30 PM, the days were long and warm. When the neighbors came around the corner of the house, a dog's third world war broke out in our yard. I don't know what or where Sporty was, but when the German Shepherd saw the three dogs who were smaller than him, did they ever start a war. The fight was horrific. They barked and growled and snarled and tumbled one over the other. They came close enough around us that they tangled around neighbors legs and that dog war, tripped her over. There was nothing that anyone could have done, until the neighbors dogs took off in every direction yelping and each one to get away as fast as possible. One dogs took off for his home direction. One took off for the bush not far from the house, the third headed out towards the field and then only our shepherd dog Teddy was left. I don't know if all the dogs were in the fight or there may have been one that was standing idly by his master, but he saw what was happening and took off in flight. When all had calmed down, the neighbor says: "I guess your dog won the war, but wait if he should ever come into our yard, my dogs will cut loose your dog's pants." The neighbors stayed for a little while, mother made some lunch and then they left for home.

It was this same year, shortly after the dogs' war took place, that very early one morning father got up to go and bring home the cows for milking. He looked for the cows, but could not find them. He had the German shepherd Teddy with him. He went along the fence line thinking maybe the cows broke down the fence and got out into the field of crop. He walked but could not find the cows. He thought he would go and see if the neighbor had by any chance seen if any cattle were around. Father approached the yard and the three dogs that had been in the fight with our dog began barking. The neighbor had probably been up also, for the screen door opened a bit when father was getting closer to the house and the three dogs shot out like a canon ball towards father and the German shepherd. Again the dog war continued from the last episode where this time the three dogs are to cut off our shepherd's dog pants. All of a sudden the war was on. Later father was telling us what all had happened. He said that when the war started and the dust rose up, one of dogs took off and ran under the granary. The other ran off behind some building and the third took off in still another direction. When the dust began to settle only the German shepherd remained. Father came to the neighbors' house and asked if they had not seen any cattle roaming around. Father said that he did not want to ask the neighbor whose dogs cut whose pants off, but just thought to himself of those words that were spoken at our place some days earlier. One day Teddy wasn't around. We called for him and looked all over but he did not come. One day when father was hauling a load of hay with the rack, he was sitting up high and when he was crossing the railway, he noticed like some animal about seventy feet away. He stopped the horses and went to check out what it was. It was Teddy. Teddy was killed by the train. He used to run at cars and bite on the tires. This day he must have been by the railway, a train came along and he went chasing the train and was killed.

Just to end the story about Sporty. It was a few years later that after the family was all separated the parents were left alone with Oksana on the farm. They made an auction sale and moved out from the farm. I was in the RCAF in Winnipeg. John was in Saskatoon training to be a mechanic and Alice was married and living near St. Benedict which was some fifteen miles south of our farm. The parents and Oksana were the only ones on the farm now. After the auction sale, there was no one left on the farm, so Alice took Sporty to her place. The first night Alice put Sporty into the barn and closed the door. Next morning she let him out and he stayed around the yard. Night came and Sporty was by the house, but next morning when they got up Sporty was not around. They called for and went to look in the barn thinking maybe he slept in the same place he did the day before. Not finding him they thought he would show up sooner or later. About four or five days after the auction sale John, Alice's husband, went to the farm in Tarnopol to see if all the things that were sold had been taken away by the buyers at the auction. As he drove into the yard, there beside the door lay Sporty. Now he had been taken in a truck when Alice brought him home to St. Benedict. How did he find the way of those fifteen miles to get back where he had grown up. John took him back home to St. Benedict.

A day or two later he was missing again. Alice thought that he must have gone back to Tarnopol, so she gets into the truck and goes to see if he is there. Sure enough there he was in front of the door. He knew that this was his home and he had to guard it against any intruders. Alice brought him back to St. Benedict. For another few days he was around, but then they missed him again. Alice went back to Tarnopol, but there was no Sporty there. A few days later she made another trip to Tarnopol, but Sporty was not there this time either. They thought maybe a car may have killed him when he was heading back to Tarnopol, or maybe he may have been in a fight with a bunch of coyotes or just died some place of starvation. John and Alice had a dug out on their farm for storing water. One day John or Alice were walking by the dug out and noticed something in the water. On coming closer to have a look, it was discovered it was Sporty. Did he commit suicide seeing no one cared for him? He had swam hundreds of times in the lake, (larger than a dug out) where we lived, so why did he die in the dugout? And we think that animals are dumb?

The lake we had was a good thing. We never had to pump or pull water from a well for cattle. In the summer they had freedom to drink all they wanted, but in the winter it was different when the lake was frozen over. I always used to get up early and would go to the lake to cut open the hole in the ice for the cattle to drink water. I would cut the hole out and before any cattle would drink, I would wash my face in the clear cold crisp air. Oh that felt good and fresh and woke every muscle in my face. Till today I always wash my face in cold water whether it was morning or any other time of the day. Hands, I always prefer to wash in warm water with soap. Cold water woke me up and kept me awake the whole day long.

SPORTS AND SCHOOL

In school we children always took part in sports and school activities. I did not stay behind others if there was sports or things to do. In the spring and fall we had baseball and soccer, in the winter time hockey. We did not have money to buy sports equipment as some other children did. In the summer time we had no baseball gloves. For catching the ball we used the mitts that we used on the farm for picking rocks or roots, for pitching hay or manure and other work around the farm. For playing hockey we used the old horse collars for leg padding that father would throw away or some boys used old felt socks. These would be wrapped around the legs and tied up with twine to keep them in place. I played in goal for our high school in New Tarnopol. Sometimes we won games and sometimes we lost them, but we played for the sport and fun of it and no one became a millionaire like we have today.

    I recall one time when our high school team went to play hockey against the Wakaw high school. We caught the train and in less than an hour we were in Wakaw. There were only about nine or ten of us boys that went this one day so that there wasn't even enough boys to have a line change so that some could rest while others played. The Wakaw team playing at home had enough players that they could change. I had no goalie gloves, but had the mitts that I used at home to do chores. I was lucky enough that I had goalie pads and a goalie stick from the school. There was no such thing then as a mask or helmet. We did the best we could with what we had. As we were playing on the outdoor rink in the minus twenty-five degree weather, one of the Wakaw forwards got a breakaway and came towards me. He fired a shot that came straight for my head. I docked but to late and the puck struck me in the forehead. At that time boys wore big thick round caps with a front like a sun visor. The puck hit me in the cap and all I felt was like if someone threw a marshmallow at me. Had it not been for that cap, I probably would not be writing this today to tell others. We lost the game eight to nothing on that cold crisp day, but we had fun.

Another incident happened one day in school. It was recess and the boys were playing soccer. It was a fine spring day. Two captains would be chosen. The captains than chose players for their side. Then away went the game. Two teams rushing and scrambling around the school yard chasing the soccer ball. I always like to play goal. I did that during hockey and soccer. This chum of mine, from the other team, got a breakaway and was rushing with the ball towards me to score. I was defending the goal and we collided. In the process he fell on top of me. I felt a sharp pain go through my ankle. I started to get up and I could barely stand on my foot. The pain was just excruciating. I was helped to the school hobbling along.

After classes were over, I had to walk home two and one half miles. I could hardly walk. I found a stick and with the help of that stick I slowly hobbled along to get home. It took me longer to get home that day than other days. When I got home I did not want my parents to see me struggling to get around, but it did not take long for them to realize that something was wrong. They asked me what was wrong and I told them. Father said that he was going to go to see the teachers and the trustees and ask them, how come I go to school all right and come home with injuries. I convinced the parents that it was no one's fault, but that it was an accident. They thought it over and did not say much more.

Next morning the pain was still there and I could not walk. Father decided that I needed to see a doctor. Mother took us to town to catch the train to Saskatoon which left at 9:00 AM on week days. As we were on the train father met someone he knew and the people told him that he should take me to a chiropractor. Arriving in Saskatoon we looked in the telephone book and found a chiropractor. I think we took a taxi there because I could not walk. The doctor told me to lay down on the table. He stood at the end of my feet and felt things around. Then all of a sudden he jerked my foot and I saw all the stars flying around me. What pain. Oh it hurt. The doctor told the nurse to wrap up my ankle and to get up. I got up and stepped on my ankle and it hurt, but it was a much less pain than it had been for the past eighteen or twenty hours. Father paid the doctor, but I don't remember how much and we left. We still had about two hours to kill before the train headed back. We looked around and may have bought something, but at this time I do not recall. We got on the train and arrived home. Today I don't even remember which ankle it was.

This had happened when I was already in high school a lad of about eighteen years old. Boys my age would be going around together to dances, weddings, parties, etc., but I was too shy for such things and especially where there were girls. I was very shy and timid with girls until 1959 and that is another story which will be told later. I would never go near girls and if any girl or girls would come towards me, I would be sure to get away from them like a rabbit from the fox. I would just have nothing to do with girls.

I never brought home any homework from school unless there had been some special assignments given. I did all my work in school so that I did not have to carry books in the knapsack on my back. Now isn't this something? Students in school were laughing and making fun of me for carrying a knapsack on my back. Do you know what? Today in the twenty-first century you can see students and others carrying knapsacks on their backs. I bet if one stood on a street corner and watched, nearly twenty percent of the people walking are with a Knapsack on their back. I carried lunch and books in my knapsack, but today God knows what some people carry in their knapsack.

When there was a dance in the community hall on some week-end, we always knew about it, but that week-end I made sure I brought home a lot of books. Why? I did not want to go to the hall where there were girls. I would pretend and tell the parents that I have a test on Monday morning and I have to study. This was a good reason and way to stay home and away from girls. Parents always wanted us to study, pass our grades and become school teachers. Days in advance the parents would tell us that on Saturday we are all going to the dance at Old Tarnopol Hall. My excuse was to stay home and to study (for the test that there wasn't to be.)

EUGENE STEFANIUK

I stayed home while the rest of the family went to the dance a mile and a half away from home. The teacher from school was there and he saw that other boys and girls from the school were there but I wasn't. The parents asked some of the students if they have a test on Monday, and they said no. They talked to the teacher and he told them the same thing. This time I did not get away. I got caught in my own trap which I had set myself.

When they came home they really gave it to me verbally. First for lying to them and then that I did not go where everybody else was, people from the whole community. When another dance or social came along, I would try to wiggle out not to go, to find some reason, but it did not help. Everybody was going to the social including me. I could not get away this time. But, what will I be doing there at the dance? I'm not going to dance. This time the parents said; "Homework or no homework, you are also going." No way to get away now. They said that I was sixteen years old and it was time that I started to go out with other boys to dances. I had no choice. Either run away from home or stay home, listen and obey the parents.

We all got dressed and in a wagon (or democrat buggy) we went to the social at the Old Tarnopol Hall. It could have been fall time for it was cool outside. In my mind all this time, I was thinking how I could avoid being there. Father paid the admission for the whole family. At that time adults were twenty-five cents and school children ten cents for admission. It cost seventy cents for four of us, since Alice and Oksana would still get in free. Even seventy cents for the family at that time was hard to get sometimes. In the hall there was an old wooden barrel stove that was used for heating the hall. On one side as you entered the hall was a place to hang your clothes and on the other side a confectionary room where Mr. Fisych sold refreshments during the socials. Refreshments like soft drinks, chocolate, gum, peanuts, etc.

When we got to the hall, I found that the best place for me would be to stand near the stove. There it was nice and warm and somewhat hidden from the crowd. If anyone came towards me, especially girls, I would have an easy chance to escape to the outside. When the music started and the dance was on, I kept my eyes peeled as to who was doing what. I dare not go to the middle of the hall where people would see me and maybe some girl would come and ask me to dance with her. During those days there were many times when the orchestra would tell the people that they will play the next dance and it will be "ladies choice." Oh that did it. As soon as that was announced, I was gone. I would go outside, walk around by the hall and when I could hear that the music stopped, then I would come back in.

One time when the music and dancing stopped, I saw two girls get up and start to come towards the back where I was near the stove and hall entrance. Before they made it halfway to the hall, I was already outside. I wandered around outside, but those girls never came out. Maybe they weren't coming after me or to talk to me. Maybe they came to stand by the stove to warm up. Maybe they came to talk to someone who was at the back of the hall. When the orchestra started playing again, slowly I made my entrance back to the hall. Cautiously I opened the door and looking inside I saw no one near the entrance. Carefully I walked into the hall and back by the stove. I looked around to see where the two girls were and they were way at the front of the hall sitting on the bench along the wall and drinking soda pop. Oh, so that's why they were coming to the back of the hall. They weren't coming for me, they came to get pop. That is how I felt all the time, shy, shy and still shy. As mentioned above, this shyness stayed with me until 1959 when I was discharged from the RCAF and was working in the summer operating a Ferris wheel. This story will unfold as we roll along.

STORMS AND COMMUNITY ACTIVITIES

At this time I should also mention some of the storms that went through Saskatchewan and our area where we lived in those "good old days." The storms in the "good old days" were something else, when there were no roads or vehicles like we have today. One particular storm I can recall that can never be forgotten. This happened sometimes in March in the late 1940's. Mother had gone with the train to Cudworth to visit friends and help some people write Easter Eggs. First it started snowing one day afternoon. Then came the wind and the storm followed in full force. The winds picked up and it looked like they were becoming stronger each hour. Drifts began to pile up. The chores were done in the storm and then everybody was in the house for the night. The animals were all in barns in those days where it was nice and comfortable for them, not as today in minus forty below zero and howling storms the animals spend the time shivering outside from the cold. Getting up next morning we knew there would be no school, for how can one go to school if you can't see ten feet in front of you in the storm.

Father dressed to go and feed the animals. He returned very soon and in an excited way tells John and me to hurry up to come help him look for the barn, because its all blown in with snow in the snow drift and you can't even see where it is. To look for a barn? We hurried and all three of us were walking close to each other so that we can see where the other is, not to stray away in the storm and be lost in your own yard. The barn were the horses stayed was a tall barn and that one was okay. The barn where the cows were was low with a flat roof and was made of railway ties which keep the animals nice and cozy inside - the wood is a good insulator.

We came to the barn where the horses were and found some shovels and forks in the lean-to. Then more less where the cow barn was we walked through the storm on top of the snow and father had a fork and was piercing the snow to see where the roof of the barn was. At this time father was saying all the time that the cows have probably suffocated in the barn with no air coming in or going out. We soon had the barn located and started to check where the door was. We poked with the fork the wall of the barn to a hear a different sound. We found the door and started to shovel to get the door opened. Frantically we shoveled just enough to try and get in to open the door. Our hearts were throbbing. What if we really lost all the cattle to suffocation? How will it be for our family to survive? Where will we get our milk? As father opened the door, a steam vapor like smoke came out. We walked into the barn. Our eyes swept the stalls. Cattle stirred in their places. Thank You God, the cattle are alive. The barn was warm and cozy as the inside of a house. Had the cattle suffocated at this time, it would have been a disaster, another dark moment for the family.

The barn where the cows were kept for the winter was made of railroad ties. If the railroad crossed people's land, those people could ask the railroad for old railroad ties that are taken out each year. Father asked the foreman for the used railroad ties because we wanted to build a barn for the cattle. There was not enough railroad ties taken out from a small piece of land on our farm that the railway crossed, so father asked if we could have more ties from those places where people don't need them. The foreman brought us all the ties we needed and from those ties we built the barn and the floor in the barn. The roof was a flat roof with a slant and was covered with sticks and dirt. The barn was beside the bushes and was only about eight feet tall. For this reason it was very easy for the storm to cover the building completely in a large snowdrift when such fierce winds blew. Drifts in some places in the "good old days" were, yes as high as fifteen feet high. Yes we can walk on the snow banks along the railroad and touch the phone lines and the top of the poles which where higher than fifteen feet.

There were many other such storms that raced through the prairies. Today with paved highways, good roads, snow plows, good motor vehicles, electricity and telephones, people don't even think of storms as they travel from place to place. In the "good old days" transportation was by horse and buggy in the summer and horse and sleigh in the winter. When storms came up, children in the farming communities stayed home and did not attend school, because it was not a necessity to go to school in a storm and lose one's life getting lost or freezing in the storm. Today probably less precipitation falls than it did in those times. Lands have been cleaned of bush and so the storms are not as severe for there is no place to pile up the snow into snowdrifts.

When the above storm had subsided, we were to go to school, but how? There is no one going on our road for three quarters of a mile before we come to the main road. The road we had was only going to our place, for it was a dead end road because of the lake. When the storms were over we had to make our own tracks to get to the main road. Father would hitch the horses to a stone boat to try and make a trail. Having the horses pull a sleigh to break a trail was harder than with a stone boat. A stone boat was a piece of equipment made on the farm with two runners and than a floor on top of the runners. This was used on the farm to pick rocks and then haul the rocks(stones) to the piles or the fence bordering a neighboring farm. It was also used in the winter for hauling the manure to the fields. When this stone boat was pulled by the horses it ran right over the top of the snow without any sinking because it had wide runners and was light.

In places where it was impossible to go on the road for the snow drifts were too deep, fences were cut and traveling was done through the field. Sometimes the snow was so deep that the horses could not even walk through it, so they jumped to keep going. Sometimes a horse would stumble over in the snowdrift and would fall down and then thrash itself in the snow trying to get up. Times were hard and tough but today's times are easier for people. How many people today would know how to cope if they had to go through such times as we did? There were no school buses or snow plows. Snow plows were only used on highways. After the trails were opened up, we could walk to school or would be taken by the parents. In the spring and fall we walked to school. In the winter when it wasn't too cold we also walked. There was no such thing as a school bus coming to your door each morning to pick you up. The horses were hitched to a sleigh or a caboose and that was our winter transportation. The caboose had a window to the front and often inside was a little wood burning stove heater, so it was comfortable even when it was thirty or forty below zero outside. A door was made on the side and one on the back. Should the caboose tip over on the side the door was on, people would be able to get out the back door. A caboose was built unto a set of runners, like four walls, roof and floor built on the runners.

Another storm that came up was on a week-end. Children went to school in the morning, but by the time school was out a storm had already been howling outside, so the parents came from home to pick up the children, so no one would get lost and freeze to death. This storm howled for three days and nights before it disappeared. It had blown so much snow that even the trains were canceled because of the drifted railroads. On our railroad crossing, snow had drifted up into huge snowdrifts. When the railroad snow plow had gone through we could stand on top the of the snow bank and look at the train like in a ravine. The snow was so deep in places that one could walk along railroad telephone wires and they were about waist high to us. The banks of snow after the railroad snow plow had gone by, it took father, John and me about two or three hours to shovel the snow so that it could be made possible to cross the railroad. The banks on the railroad were so high that they looked like two walls on each side of the track. We had to shovel down the eight foot banks to make it passable to get across the railroad. I remember hearing on the radio and reading in the paper that in those days there was so much snow that even the snow plows on the railroad at times got stuck. The steam locomotives could not push the plow through at times in longer stretches of snowbanks. Today we can only see photos of those by-gone days of such snow banks and trains trying to plow through them.

It was also about this time that I took a plunge into business. Looking through the Winnipeg Free Press Weekly which we received each week, I found a company, The Gold Medal People, who were looking for people to sell their products like greeting cards, wrapping paper, ribbons and other articles. There was no cost on my part. I ordered their products, sold them to neighbors and others and than sent so much money back and the rest was my commission. In January 1951, I received a surprise in the mail when the company sent me a Grand Diploma for being an honest salesman. I still have that diploma.

Our farm was only a mile and a half from the church, school, hall, store and blacksmith shop. Such places were centres of community activities. There was no TV at that time. Not everyone even had a radio until later. People gathered in such community centres and presented plays, concerts, held bingos, meetings, dances, pie socials, etc. I recall that many times we were left home alone while the parents went to the community hall to practice their parts in a play or concert. Younger children were left at home with older children of the family and there was no such thing as "baby sitter". The children went with parents when there was a church service or when there was a social activity at the hall. The parents at home in the evenings, spent time to rehearse and learn their parts for plays or concerts.

Finally came the day of performance for the concert or play. Everyone came, the whole community and no one stayed home. The halls were always filled to overflowing. Most people came with horses, for not everyone had a car yet and it was a few years later that cars began to appear. People walked to the hall. Some came by horse and buggy or wagon in the summer and a sleigh or caboose in the winter. Admission was twenty-five cents for adults and ten cents for school children. As far back as I can recall there were times for some events that admission was only ten cents for adults and a nickel for school children. The money collected sometimes amounted to ten, twelve or fifteen dollars for the evening. This was used to pay for the priest for services, for hall expenses, orchestra, taxes, to buy coal oil or gas for lamps, or to buy gifts for children for Christmas concerts. There were always costs to run a community hall.

It was sometimes in the late 1940's or the early 1950's that mother received a letter from Ukraine. I remember that day when I brought the letter home when I was in high school. It was an air mail envelope and had a black cross marked on it. When I brought it home and gave it to mother, she began to cry even before she opened it. I knew something was wrong, but at that time I did not understand much as to what the black cross on the envelope meant. When mother read it she found out that one of her parents, I don't recall which one, had passed away. Up to that day we children still had a grandparent even though we did not know any of them.

When there was a service in the church, the church was filled to capacity every time. There was no TV, sports, marathons in those days in the mornings. People went to church and afternoon different activities would take place. A picnic with ball games, or a sports day or some special guest speakers, etc. No one stayed away from church yet everyone was happy even though they were poor. If there was a service, there was always lunch in the hall after the service. During the lunch period the priest would enlighten the people about other congregations or about church and religious events happening around the world. The services were not held every Sunday, for the priest served five, six, seven, eight or more congregations so he would visit a congregation once a month to give an opportunity for people in other districts to have a service. The priest had no car and his transportation was by train.

The priest would always come on a Saturday when the train would arrive from his home town. The priest residence was at Wakaw, Saskatchewan. The train would arrive at Tarnopol at 10:00 PM on Saturday night. Father would be at the station waiting for the train to arrive. When he went to pick up the priest, he would wait in the store and post office before the train arrived. The store and post office was run by Sam Dziadyk. When the train arrived, mail arrived at the same time. Father waited for the mail to be sorted and than with the priest they would come home. It took about three quarters of an hour to get home with the caboose. When father and the priest arrived, it was about 11:00 PM. Mother had lunch waiting for them, for the priest could not eat after 12:00 midnight. By the time father got home with the priest us children would already be fast asleep. When bedtime came father and mother made their bed on the floor in the living room and gave their bedroom for the priest. There was no basement under the floor and the floor was not very warm. In our house there were four rooms. The parents had a bedroom. There was the kitchen and there was a living room. The fourth room was the bedroom for the children and there was a curtain separating John and me from Alice and Oksana. We started out with three rooms in the house, but later we built another room which were bedrooms for John and me and for Alice and Oksana.

Next morning father did a few chores and left very early in the morning for the church a mile and a half from home. He had to shovel the snow from the sidewalk by the church and start a fire in the wood stove so that it would be warm when the people came for the service worship. It was still dark in the winter when father left walking to church. The rest of the family got up a few minutes later, did the chores, had breakfast and got dressed to go to church. When all was ready the horses were hitched up to the sleigh if it was not too cold outside or to the caboose if it was cold. After the service there was lunch in the hall. Following the lunch the priest would come back home with us to our place. The priest would not be leaving for home until Monday morning when the train would come through. And father would take the priest to town to catch the train. This kind of schedule went on for years until the priest finally bought himself a car even though some roads were not very much improved for travel by automobile. In the winter time the priest still came by train to have services, but traveled with his car in the summer.

On Sunday after we arrived home from church, the priest would spend time talking with the parents about different things and he would give us children some lectures of catechism. If Monday morning was a very cold morning, father would take the priest in the caboose to town, while mother with the other team of horses would take us to school with the sleigh. Why would we have to be taken to school if there was no storm? Walking for a mile and a half to school, one could freeze their feet or fingers and if it was against the wind, it could be that even hands could be frozen. By riding in the sleigh, we could turn our backs against the wind or get off the sleigh and walk behind to warm up. About ninety percent of the time when there was a service our family would host the priest in our house. Yes, there were people that had more modern and better houses than we did and lived beside good roads and lived closer to the church than we did, but for some reason they would not have the priest over at their place. Why? I don't know, but maybe they were afraid of the priest?

Later when a priest already had his own car he did not need to stay overnight at people's homes during the summer season. When he would have a service in Yellow Creek or Tarnopol, he always stepped in to our place after the service. Father, John and I would fill the trunk of his car with wood as much as we could put in. In the meantime mother would get him a jar or two of cream, two or three dozen eggs, butter cheese, etc., to take home with him. Because we had a bake oven outdoors, mother baked bread and she would always give the priest a few loaves of bread. When mother baked bread she could put fifteen or twenty loaves of bread to bake at one time in the outdoor oven.

OUR FIRST CAR

I mentioned above that the priest now had his own car. I should also mention how we got our first car. One Sunday afternoon I was going to Tarnopol to a sports day. When I was still about a mile from town, I heard a car coming behind me. I got off the road and stopped, looking who was coming. It was a friend that I knew very well. This friend was all by himself in the car going to Tarnopol. He knew me and seemed to slow down, but then just kept on going. When I came home that evening, I told father about this and father was somewhat upset, because we all knew that family and had visited them many times and they visited us also. Father said: "So I go and help them from time to time when they need help during harvest and other times and his son would not even give my son a ride? No, we'll get a car so that my children could ride and would not have to walk." It seems that because when some people were poorer than other people, better off people seemed to ignore and bypass the poorer ones.

That day finally arrived to fulfill father's words about our own car. Father also wanted to have a car, because he wanted the horses to have a rest on Sunday, trips to town, to visit people, go to church or whatever. Some weeks later father took a train trip to Meacham, Saskatchewan. From his previous times, (father arrived in Canada at Meacham in 1927) he knew that there was a business man who sold cars. Father made a deal and bought a 1940 black two door Chevrolet car. The dealer showed father a few things how to start and drive the car, but father had no licence to drive, so how could he bring the car home without a drivers licence and having no car registration? When father went to get a car, we did not know when he would return. One morning when we awoke, there in our yard stood a bright shining black car. We had to rob our eyes and look two or three times to see if it was true, or whether we were still asleep and only dreaming.

Father had purchased the car and because he had no drivers licence how do you bring the car home? It was about thirty to thirty-five miles south from where we lived where he purchased the car. What happened was that the dealer and father came with our car and father was shown how to drive. Another car followed behind them. When they got to our place the other car and the salesman returned home and our car was left at our place. The car that father had purchased was a well built sturdy car. For the years that we owned it, it plowed through snow, mud, fields, water, etc., to get us from place to place. This car was later traded off in Winnipeg when the parents moved from the farm to the city of Winnipeg.

Now there was another problem. No one in our household had a drivers licence. Father would have to pass written and driving tests, but he can't read or write in English. John was always more mechanically inclined than father and me, and maybe that is why as this is written, John has spent over sixty years as a mechanic. Even still in school, John was already ahead of me about cars and mechanism when he talked with friends about cars and seemed to know more about them than father and me combined. Even though none of us had a drivers licence we still had to learn to drive. Father had driven the car part way home when he bought it, still there was so much to learn about the operation of an automobile.

Just north a few hundred feet from the house, we had a summer fallow field of about thirty acres that year. This would be a good place to learn to drive. No buildings in your way and lots of space to turn one way or another or go straight or back-up. It was an open field and we learned different things about the car. John and I did not have any problems to drive, and it was easier for us to find out from chums in school or to read the information booklet that came with the car of how, what, where, etc. The steering was much, much easier than the clumsy old 10-20 McCormick Deering tractor we bought later and thus it made learning more simple, easy, unhindered and pleasant. Anyway we gave that car and the summer fallow a good going over and that even kept the weeds down on the summer fallow. Mother never wanted to learn to drive, even though John many times had put her behind the steering wheel, but she was always afraid. Alice and Oksana learned to drive later when Alice got married and Oksana learned to drive in Winnipeg.

The car was a standard transmission and had the gear shifter on the steering wheel column. It was very easy to shift from gear to gear. Father always had a problem starting out from standing position. Instead of shifting the transmission into first gear and starting out, he would shift into third and then try to go but the engine would stall. This happened time and time over and over again. John tried to show and tell father what or how, but father would have none of that. How can a younger person teach an older person. Father would even get angry at times when he was told how or what. When the whole family was going someplace, mother and the girls sat on the back, while John and I sat on the front with father. Sometimes we took turns driving. Mother would than say: "How come when one of the boys start to drive, the car starts out nice and even and when you drive it always jerks and sometimes stalls?" Father did not like that and would not say anything. This was even happening after we got our driver's licences.

Time went by. We learned to drive better and better on the summer fallow near the house. So now came the time to go and get a drivers licence. Where does one get a drivers licence? We inquired from different people and they said that you have to go to the RCMP detachment. The closest detachment was at Wakaw. When we were ready to get a licence we drove to Wakaw and not one of us had a licence. Then as now, one had to have a written test first, before you had a driving test. For John and me it was no problem, because we could read and write, but father did not know English, so how can he write a test? The constable at the detachment had an answer. He phoned someone and in a few minutes a man showed up at the detachment. I don't remember who that person was. The man was asking father the questions in Ukrainian and father answered him the best he could. John and I sat and listened. Some of the answers that father gave were wrong, and so father did not pass the written test. John and I passed our tests. Than the constable took each one of us for a driving test. So now John and I got our drivers licences, but father did not. As John later recalled to me, father and him one day went to Yellow Creek and another man went with them to Melfort. There father again went for a written test and this time he passed, so when he arrived back home, he had a drivers licence as did John and I.

Father still had problems with the driving. One day in early spring we went to church on a Saturday to have the Easter Paska blessed. Tomorrow was Christ's Resurrection(Easter). The whole family piled into the car and put the Easter basket with all the food in the trunk of the car. Away we went. Everything was fine; the priest arrived and had the service and blessed the Paska. After exchanging some talk with the friends on the church yard, people got into their cars and headed for their homes. Coming home, there was a hill to go up. As we got half way up the hill, the car started to jerk. John told father to shift to a lower gear, but we know that, "Father knows best." He did not shift the gears and the car eventually stalled. Then the car started to roll backwards down the hill. Father stepped on the brakes, but than he could not start the car, because the starter was on the floor and was started with a foot. One foot was on the brake, one on the clutch and there was nothing to push the starter to start.

When he would take one foot of the brake or clutch the car would start to roll back. Mother would start to holler: "What are you doing? Watch out because you'll kill all of us here." Everybody was excited. What's going to happen to us? Will we end up in the ditch? Will the car tip over? Will we be killed? Slowly, slowly, inches at a time father got the car down to the bottom of the hill. When the car would not roll farther anymore, than he would start the car and start going up the hill. Again he had the car shifted in third gear. As he would start, the car began to jerk and then a few feet going up the hill, the engine would stall again. Back again we roll with mother again screaming at the back. Mother got angry and says: "What's the matter with this car? Give it so one of the boys can drive it." Father was not happy with that. How could someone younger than him drive the car when there is something wrong with it. Reluctantly he let John try and drive the car. John got behind the wheel, started the car, put the car in first gear and before we knew it we were all at home. Father was not happy with that. That car was really a sturdy, well built car to take the abuse that it had from our family in all kinds of weather and roads.

Yes we did build a garage type of building to house the car. When roads were improved and better to drive on, we even drove the car in the winter time when there was not much snow. But there was a problem, how do you start a car when it's -30 or more in the winter time? We knew that to start a car in such cold weather was difficult, so how do you warm up the car? Yes father thought up a way to warm the engine in cold weather. I don't remember if we had a large tub, or had a large piece of flat tin. Father put that under the car and started a fire under the engine. How that car never blew up to this day it is still puzzling. There was the gasoline tank, plus gasoline lines and oil and gasoline and nothing caught fire. I guess God or the Guardian Angel must have watched that fire each time father was going to warm up the car.

During the Second World War, Canada went through a time when there were shortages of many products. Each person was given ration coupons and you could only purchase so much of the goods. Sugar and other commodities were in short supply. So that we would have enough sugar to make preserves of jams and fruit for the winter father decided to order a hive of bees and in this way we would have enough sugar to make preserves. The bees came and father was the beekeeper. From one hive he later expanded to two hives.

It was about this time that if we wanted to get ahead on the farm, we would need more than one quarter section of land. It was hard for a family to survive on one quarter. In 1951 at the end of July as we were making hay and father says to me: "If you are going back to school this fall, than go and become a teacher. Or if you want to stay on the farm, than I'm going to go and buy another quarter section of land." At this time I had finished grade eleven in school. It was a hard decision to make. Father was not that well. He had been in the first World War and was seriously wounded. Now was he was having some side effects from that injury? My brother John was also not to well and was always saying that he wants to go and become a mechanic. My sisters were much younger and could only help with some smaller and lighter chores. So who is going to help on the farm if both John and I leave? Even though I said that I would continue to go to school, father still went ahead and bought another quarter section of land, kiddy corner to our farm. Now we had two quarters of land. This second quarter is still in the family owned by sister Alice as this is written in 2016.

When the parents were still living, they said that when they die, they will give the farm to Alice and her husband John to work it. The home quarter was sold to the neighbor. Before the parents passed away, they gave Alice the quarter section that had been bought later and told her to give John, Oksana and me $5,000.00 each and the farm will be hers. When John and Alice retired from farming, they tried to sell that quarter but there were no buyers for land and the prices went crashing down. Alice rented out that quarter and still doing that today, because no one wants to buy land. She just gets enough rent money only to pay the yearly taxes on that quarter.

In 1952 spring looked beautiful and came early. Crops were seeded and were up about four inches and looked very promising. Than it happened. During the night of June 6th it snowed so much that everything was white. The snow was wet and heavy. Many tree limbs broke from the weight of the snow. Crops and gardens were flattened. Some vegetables froze in the garden. Another doomed year lay ahead for the family. But after the warm sun came out, the snow melted, everything rebounded and that was the best crop we ever had on that farm. Because the crop had turned out well, father had enough funds to purchase a used 10-20 McCormick Deering tractor in the spring of 1953 and also to pay off some debts. He also purchased a brand new one way discer on rubber wheels from a dealer at Yellow Creek, Sask. I did not get a chance to work with that tractor very much, for father worked with it when we children were in school.

LEAVING HOME - A TEACHER

The parents were always trying to tell us children to get the best education we can, so that we would not have to work as hard as they did. They had learned from someplace that St. Andrew's College in Winnipeg was having summer classes for students to learn the Ukrainian language, dancing, customs, culture, traditions, religion, etc. They asked me if I would want to go to these summer classes. At first I was hesitant to go so far from home, but than accepted the proposition for it sounded good and so I went. How did I go there?

Father and mother decided they would drive me with the car to Winnipeg, because along the way we could stop to see mother's cousin, Mrs. Tillie Korzeniowski near Grandview, Manitoba. We had never been there before, and now that I knew enough English, there would be no problem driving me to Winnipeg. School was finally over and the day came to leave for Manitoba. We started out for Winnipeg. Who was left at home, no one but John, Alice and Oksana. John was already a fully grown adult, Alice was grown up and Oksana was at this time about twelve or thirteen years old. We drove to Korzeniowski's and stayed overnight there. Korzeniowski's had a daughter Jennie who was married and living in Winnipeg. They said we should stop there, see her and maybe even stay overnight at her place.

Next morning we left and drove all the way to Winnipeg. We got to Winnipeg and when father saw all the traffic he said that he was not going to go any farther into the city, but would leave the car on the outskirts and take a taxi to Jennies' place. Father stopped at a service station and filled the car up with gas. We asked the owner of the service station if we could leave the car there for a day or two at the service station. The owner said it was okay and they would keep an eye on it. We called a cab and it took us straight to Jennies place. We spent a nice time visiting and Jennie did not live far from St. Andrew's College where I would be attending.

After everything was set, father and mother were ready to return back home. All was ready, BUT ONE PROBLEM. Where is the car? We had not taken any address, phone number, name or street. When we were leaving to Jennie's place with the taxi, I remember that I had seen the name Ferry Street or Ferry Road near the service station. Nick and Jennie did not know where to take father and mother, but when I said I remember Ferry Road, they said they knew where it was. The five of us got into a car and Nick drove to Ferry Road. Sure enough as we neared the place there was the service station and the car sitting where we had left it. Father and mother put their belongings into their car, good-byes were said and they left for home, while Nick, Jennie and I returned back to their place. As I stayed at St. Andrew's College, Saturdays there were no classes, so that day I would go to see Nick and Jennie, or would just go downtown to see the city.

At St. Andrew's College we learned different things, language, religion, Ukrainian dancing, culture, etc. While there I would read the daily Winnipeg Free Press which was coming to the college every day. One day I was looking at the ads to see if there are any kinds of jobs in Winnipeg, so that maybe I could get a job, make some money and help the parents out on the farm. As I was checking the ads, there was one ad that caught my eye. "Wanted teacher to teach in school." I took the address and wrote a letter. It was to the Department of Education in Winnipeg. Maybe I could get this job to teach and surely father and mother would be very happy and proud of me.

One afternoon as we were in class, I got an unexpected phone call. Who would be calling me, when no one knows me in Winnipeg. I had forgotten about the letter I had written about teaching. I went to the phone. It was the Department of Education calling, wanting to know if I was still interested in the teaching position I applied for. They said they had four applications for that position in the Flower School near Oakburn, Manitoba and they are willing to give me the job if I am still interested. I said I am and they asked me to come to the Legislature to see them possibly the following day. I went and they took down information they needed. They told me that I have the job and would have to report to Mr. W. J. Smith at Oakburn to sign the contract.

Everything was done and sealed. Now when I come home, what will the parents say and think? Will they be happy that now Eugene is a teacher? Will they be happy that I will be so far away from home for at least a year? All kinds of questions filled my mind now. Did I do the right thing? But than I recalled what father always used to say: "Look at your cousins in Manitoba, they are teachers, so why can't you be?" Yes I did the right thing. Father will be happy, that now his son is a school teacher.

The summer school came to an end. It was time to head back home to Saskatchewan. To get home, I would take the train. I had written letters home telling the parents when I would be arriving home, but I never mentioned anything about the teaching position. This would be a surprise to the family and I would leave that to the end when all are together to hear the news. Now I would be able to make a few dollars and help the parents with the costs to run the farm. There was still debt to be paid on the second quarter section of land that father purchased. When I arrived home and told the family the news, they were happy for a minute or two, and then mother says: "But you will be so far away from us, from home. That will be three hundred miles away."

I stayed at home for a few days and than it was time to leave for Oakburn. Decisions had to be made before I left. Would it be okay for me to be alone and so far from home where I don't know anyone? Finally we all decided that my youngest sister Oksana should also go with me and she can go to school there and I would have company and would not be alone. At home the parents would now have two mouths less to feed and she was still small and could not help very much on the farm. So Oksana and I will be venturing out into an unknown place where we have not been before.

Father would have taken us to Oakburn, but he could not, because harvest was started and to lose two or three days during harvest could be a great loss. So Oksana and I would have to take a train or bus to get to Oakburn. Father took us with the car to Humboldt, Saskatchewan, from where we caught a bus to Oakburn. We had a few suitcases and boxes in which we took our clothing and things we would need while staying at the Flower School. Good-byes were said, mother shed a tear and says: "My children are always going away to some place that you don't know anyone. What will you be doing so far away from home?" The bus arrived and we boarded and were on our way to start a new life in a new place. When we arrived in Yorkton, Saskatchewan we had to change buses. We had to take another bus that went through Russell, Manitoba. The Department of Education had also said that I must contact Mr. W. J. Smith at Oakburn and he would give me instructions about the school for he was the official trustee of Flower School Number 1843.

Oksana and I arrived at Oakburn on August 24th, 1953 at about 4:00 PM. The school was slated to start tomorrow, August 25th. The bus dropped us off with our belonging and now what do we do? Can't carry all the luggage with us to go looking for Mr. Smith. After we find Mr. Smith, how do we get ourselves and our things out to the school? Anyway we had to make a decision. Oksana would stay at the bus depot with our suitcases, while I go to find Mr. Smith. I asked people where to find Mr. Smith and people told me where to go, and I walked a few blocks and found his office. We got acquainted and I told him that my belongs and my sister are at the bus depot. The kindness of Mr. and Mrs. Smith is recalled and remembered to this day. We never knew each other, but they were like parents to Oksana and me. Mr. Smith left his office, took his car and we went to pick up Oksana and the luggage. We packed the things into the trunk and than went back to the office. We were told that the school is fourteen miles NE of Oakburn. Mrs. Smith was in the house and was preparing supper. They invited Oksana and me to have supper with them and after supper they drove us out to the school. Beside the school there was a teacherage where Oksana and I will spend the next year.

There in that teacherage Oksana and I spent a scary frightful first night. All night long there was a sound like something or someone was running on the roof of the house or trying to get into the house. Outside there was a wind blowing. It sounded like someone or something was trying to break into the house. I was afraid to go and check what was happening.

There was power in that house to turn on the lights, but I was afraid to get up and check. Finally when daylight came, that puzzle was answered. I knew that it was not a ghost or anyone else, because it was now daylight, and that noise was still coming. The teacherage had a porch and the porch did not have windows, but had a plastic like covering with strong thread in it. When the wind blew, the loose plastic moved and made a sound as if someone or something was on the roof or trying to get into the house.

At Flower School I taught for one year. I had twenty-four students ranging from grade one to ten and teaching all subjects to all grades. It was not as it is today, that a teacher has one subject or maybe two and that is all he or she teaches that one grade. My salary was $1400.00 for the year, $140.00 per month. Today the teacher makes more in a day, than I made in a month. Of this income, we used a part of the money to buy groceries, and the rest of the money I sent home to help the family with the debt that was hanging over their head. Money in those days was hard to come by, so every cent that came along the family spent only for the most essential needy things.

The people in this new place were all very friendly and kind. I was Ukrainian as were all the students, every one in school, for it was a Ukrainian settlement in that area of Manitoba. There was one student in school who knew everything, but didn't understand anything and that was the "bully." When people learned that a new teacher was already at the teacherage, people brought us different vegetables and food. Many people always invited us to come to their place for meals and visits when we were free. Oksana at this time was taking grade five and she was helping with housework as well as doing her studies.

So began my first paying job in my life. The work was good and I enjoyed working with the students, with the exception of one student who was more of a trouble maker than a student but just a regular "bully". Even after I dismissed the children to go home, he would cause problems for children along the way home. He would push the children into the ditch. He would throw dust at them and snow in the winter time. He would knock them down and kick snow into their face. He always found a way how to intimidate and instill fear in the children. There were no school buses then, so children walked to and from school whether it was half a mile or three miles. There were times that the parents brought children to school if the weather was inclement or if they would be late for classes. When I saw that there was a problem with this student I decided on a plan. I would let the children of this one family which he bullied the most, leave the school five minutes sooner. This gave those two children a head start to get away from this bully. Or there were times that the children would all go, but I would hold the bully after school, because I wanted to talk to him. This also gave the children the chance to escape his bullying tactics on the road.

Farm schools in those "good old days" were also famous for one other thing - to hold annual Christmas concerts before the school was dispersed for the winter Christmas break. It was up to the teacher to prepare the Christmas concert. I wrote out different parts and passed them out to the children to learn. Children learned quickly and knew their parts well before the concert date. Every part had to be written out by hand. There were no such things as computers or even typewriters to do these things. Maybe in large city centres there may have been more elaborate ways of doing these things, but in poorer country schools the hand and pen did all the work. I did this after school hours and in the evenings in the teacherage. That year the concert was going to take place on December 19, which also for Ukrainians was St. Nicholas Day. On December 17th and 18th, the men from the district gathered in the school in the evenings and built a stage where the students would perform and act out their parts.

Before the concert was held children would practice their parts in the front part of the school and than on the stage after it was built. The teachers' desk was moved to one side and where the desk was before now that place had a stage. One afternoon as the practice was going on and I was watching the action of the children in their performances, when suddenly there came a sound of "ouch" and than crying. The bully that was in school had taken the stove poker and hit one girl across the legs with it. The child screamed and cried from pain. Everything stopped and I had to check the situation to see what had happened. I learned that the bully hit the girl with the poker for no reason at all. I saw that trouble might come from the parents of the hurt child if I did nothing. I called the bully to the porch (cloakroom) where I wanted to talk and bawl him out. I asked him why he hit the girl and all the answers I got for each question was: "Because." Why because, and again the answer was the same. I have had enough of this bully in the last few months since August. I grabbed his clothes, took him by the collar and threw him and his clothes outside and told him: "Don't come back here anymore this year." It was winter. He picked up his clothes and took off for home.

I knew that I may have caused trouble for myself and the school trustee Mr. Smith. I did not know if Mr. Smith would be on my side, and I hoped that I would not be reprimanded too severely for what I had done. Whenever I had an opportunity to be in Oakburn, I always stopped in to see Mr. Smith and chatted with him about the school and he was pleased with how things were going. I knew that the parents of the bully would cause me trouble. I did not care anymore, because in two days school would be over and than whatever will be, will be. When visiting many of the families of the school children, they would always tell me the same story, that previous teachers all had problems in school with that bully but I saw that at least I had support from the parents on this matter.

Since Oksana and I moved to Manitoba, we had been corresponding with the parents all this time. I wrote letters to them and always sent them money to help them pay bills that they had on the farm. I wrote a letter and said that there would be a concert in the school on December 19th, than the school will be dismissed and Oksana and I will be taking the bus to go home the following day and asked the parents to meet us at Humboldt at the bus depot. But on December 18th, Oksana and I got a surprise. Late, late that afternoon, father, John and Alice arrived by car to see the concert and to take Oksana and me back home for two weeks of school break. John and Alice knew English well, so they kept asking people for directions to the school, found the school and they surprised Oksana and me.

Next day was the last day of classes and the concert in the evening. We practiced for the concert a few more times and I dismissed the children an hour or so earlier so that they may go home and get ready for the concert in the evening. After classes were over some men from the district came and moved all the desks to one side piling them up and bringing in benches so the people would have something to sit on when they come to the concert in the evening. After supper people started coming to the concert and before we knew it, all the benches were filled and people were standing along the walls and wherever there was room. The concert went well, the children knew their parts and at the end Santa Claus arrived and brought gifts and goodies for the children.

Next morning father, John, Alice, Oksana and I started for home to Tarnopol. It was winter time but the roads were better than they had been in the Tarnopol area as I remember them, so there was no trouble getting home before too late in the night. Oksana and I stayed at home until January 9th 1954, because classes did not start until January 11th. Oksana and I spent our old fashioned Ukrainian Christmas at home with the family.

Again Oksana and I returned back by bus to Oakburn. We had made arrangements with a family, Peter Spak, to pick us up at the bus depot when we return in two weeks. Whenever the Spak family was going to Oakburn, they would pass a note with their two boys telling me that they are going to town tomorrow and if we need anything to write them a note what to get for us. They would get us what we needed and pick up our mail. The following morning they would bring their boys to school and would drop off our mail and the things they bought for us. I would pay them what was owed. This went on for the whole year when Oksana and I lived there. When Oksana and I arrived back from Saskatchewan on January 9th, we also brought back the bicycle we had on the farm.

Before father had bought the car which they now had, he had bought a bicycle with balloon tires. That bicycle was a mode of transportation for us before we got the car. Many times each week we would send a can of cream to Saskatoon to the creamery. The train picked up the cream at 9:00 AM and next day the cream can was returned by train at 4:00 PM. When the cream can would be returning back from the creamery, father and mother would say: "Ewhen, you take the bicycle today and bring back the cream can." The bicycle had a strong built large basket over the front wheel. I would pick up the cream can from the station and bring it home. At times when I had to go against the wind, it was hard peddling, so I was not be able to ride, but would push the bicycle. Whenever it was going up hill, I never rode, but had to walk, because there was no ten speed at that time on the bicycle and it was just too hard and impossible to pedal up the hill and especially if you had weight over the front wheel.

So this was the bicycle that we brought back with us to Oakburn. The parents had a car at home, so they had transportation. Oksana and I had none, and if we wanted to go and visit someone, it was by walking. Now when spring comes, we will have a bicycle to get around. When the road was dry and we were free, Oksana would sit on the handle bars and I would pedal and this was our transportation to get around visiting the families of the children. Many, many times we were invited for supper after school hours or on week-ends to different families. There was Mrs. Spak who had a special recipe for making beef soup. To this day I have never eaten such good beef soup, like the one we always had at Spaks. They butchered their own steer and they made soup and other meals from that beef. Whenever they butchered, they would always bring Oksana and me some beef for consumption. I always had good relations with the families which I can recall; Spaks, Manuliaks, Kustiaks, Barans, Glods, Rybaks, and others.

It is now January 9 - 1954. Oksana and I are back from Saskatchewan. When we arrived at the teacherage, it was cold inside like in a deep freeze. At that time there was already power, but there was no automatic furnace. When we went away there was no fire in neither the heater nor cook stove, so the house cooled off to the cold winter temperature outside. There were no waterworks in the house so nothing froze or was damaged over that period.

School started on January 11th on a very different note than it had ended. As soon as the Lord's Prayer was said and O Canada sung, I welcomed the children back and slowly started school work. Oh yes the bully came back today as did all the children. As soon as classes started, everyone was startled by a knock on the school door. No one comes here unless of some urgent need. Who could be coming and for what purpose? I went to answer the door. I opened the door and there before me stood the School Inspector. My heart sank into my heels. Now I'm in trouble and I know why he came, probably the bully's parents reported me to the him that I threw their son out of school. I said "Good Morning" and asked the Inspector to come in. I already knew him, because he had been here in the fall to check with the progress of the school. When the Inspector walked in, he said, "Good morning" to the children and the children all stood up and said "Good morning" to him also. I had told the children when I first arrived in the fall that when the School Inspector comes to visit the school, so they would always stand up and say Good morning or Good afternoon, whichever time of day it was. I knew that today I would have plenty of explaining to do as to the event that happened before the Christmas break.

The children had seen the Inspector previously and after he walked in, the children dug their heads into their books and carried on. I do not remember the Inspector's name, but he came to the front of the class and told me to carry on with my work as if he is not there. In the meantime as I was going over a subject with one grade, he would ask another grade to put their scribblers on their desk. I was doing what I had to do, but my heart was racing and skipping beats faster than a jack rabbit fleeing from a coyote. One ear and one eye was on my class, while the other one was on the inspector, watching what he was doing. He came to each student in that grade, was picking up their scribblers and looking over page by page flipping them over as his eyes skimmed over the children's work. I had been correcting the children's work, so he had everything before him, all information he was interested in.

When he finished checking with one grade, he would go to the next and do the same. Then came recess. I dismissed the class for recess and they went outside to play, while some huddled beside the stove to stay warm. When the bell rang and the children came back, he continued checking their scribblers as he had done before and during the recess break. I carried on with my work. Now came lunch hour. I dismissed the children for lunch and Oksana went to the teacherage to prepare some lunch and I asked the Inspector to come and have lunch with us. He said that he was in a hurry to get to another school and thanked for the invitation. Than he turns his back to the children and softly says to me: "I have checked the children's work and I see you are up to date with class work. I am pleased with that and their exercise books are very satisfactory to me. Carry on with your work as you have till now." Than he asked me if I am having any problems with any children. In short I told him the story about the bully and what had happened. He told me something that has stuck to me to this very day. He said: "You do what you are doing, and don't be afraid of that student. You let Mr. Smith know if you are still having trouble with that student and I will see to it so that student not attend this school anymore." I just about broke out in tears when I heard this, that I was having support from the Inspector for what I had done and was doing.

I must say a word about how things were after the Inspector had left. When he left and to the end of June, I thought that a bunch of Angels had flown into my Flower School. The bully that had been causing all the problems for me and previous to that for other teachers, himself changed so much that I to this day don't know if it was him or someone else in his place. He became the best student in the school. Prior to that during school hours he would raise his hand. I would ask what he wanted and he asked to leave the room. As soon as he was out of the classroom going to the rest room outside, when all of a sudden, bing, something hit the window which was on the east side of the school high above the floor. He had picked up a small rock and threw it at the window or at the wall if he missed the window. Later privately I would ask him why he threw rocks at the window at the school, he would say it was not him. Well than who when all the children were in school and only he was outside.

After a number of years later when I had left that school area I was living in Winnipeg with my parents and working in the city. One evening I received a telephone call. Mother answered the phone and said someone asked for me and she passed me the phone. I said "hello" and than a voice on the other side says: "Can you guess who this is, calling you?" I tried to guess, but no way could I know. I had never heard that voice on the telephone. Anyway he said who he was. Than it hit me. Oh yes, it's that bully that had been causing me all the headaches and problems in Flower School. Thoughts ran thick and fast through my mind. He found where I am, and did he come to take revenge against me? Does he want to cause some problems for me now? Than he starts to apologize to me and saying that he is sorry that he caused me all the problems for his misbehavior in the school. I heard his voice change as though it was somewhat emotional. I said that I forgive him and hope that he learned well from his mistakes. I wished him the best in what he was doing and that ended our conversation after a few minutes on the phone. Now after all the problems I had faced with this bully, he finally saw and admitted his wrongs and asked for forgiveness.

A FAMILY TRAGEDY

Now it was just about spring. Snow was slowly being eaten up by the warm sun and calm south winds. There was only a small snow bank in the shade here and there. Another month or two Oksana and I will be heading back to Saskatchewan to be with the family. At home father and John had been doing spring work on the fields. John also used to go to the neighbor to help with the spring work when there was nothing to do at home. The neighbor had a nice new case tractor and John like to work with it on the field. When evening came, John came home. During the day father had also been working on the field with his McCormick Deering 10-20 tractor that had steel lugs on the rear wheels. Father had been discing and harrowing the summer fallow to prepare for spring seeding. After supper John asked father if he could go and finish what father did not finish earlier in the daytime. Father said he could and he did. Mother was milking cows after supper. Father was doing something else in the yard, preparing seed for seeding next day or doing some chores.

John went out with the tractor, one way and harrows and was working the field. Next day father will be able to seed the field. Will he? After a while father looked from what he was doing and noticed that the tractor of the noise was the same and it was going around in a circle, and John was not on the tractor. A shock ran through father's body. What happened? Where is John that the tractor is turning on one spot on the field? Father yelled to Alice to come with him to the field. They jumped into the car and raced to where the tractor was. They came and the tractor was turning in the same spot because the front wheels had became locked. So where is John? Father jumped out of the car and jumped on the tractor to stop it. Father stopped the tractor and shut it off. Father and Alice started looking for John and than they spotted a piece of cloth. Sure enough it was John all covered with dirt that you could hardly make out that it was him.

John had been discing with the one way and three harrows behind. The one way discer had a power take off, that if you pulled on the rope the discer lifted up out of the ground. John must have slipped or lost his balance and down he went on the power take off rope and the one way lifted up. When there was no one to steer the tractor, the wheels locked and the tractor started turning on that one spot. The front wheels of the tractor had just been missing John's head and the rear lugged wheels were going over his chest along with the discer and the harrows. How many times the tractor ran over him, only God knows. Someone may say how come he was not crushed to death under all that. The ground had been worked over and was very, very soft, so that the body was pushed into the soft earth and did not kill him.

Father and Alice dug John out of the earth and father felt him to see if he was still breathing. Then father tore out the back seat of the car and with Alice together they pulled John unto the floor where the back seat was. They rushed with John to the yard with father honking the horn and yelling to mother to leave the cows for Alice and to come with him to the hospital. Mother who was milking the cows did not know what was going on. When she saw what the commotion was, she dropped everything and got into the back of the car where John was lying. Alice looked after the remaining of the milking. After they left the yard, father says to mother: "If he is still breathing, I'll go all I can, but if he stops breathing, let me know and I can slow down, for no use speeding than." They took the old #44 trail highway north of Old Tarnopol, towards Tway and then on to Wakaw. On one curve as they were speeding father just about lost control of the car on loose gravel and the first tragedy could have turned even to a worst second one. Father managed to control the car and they arrived at the hospital all in one piece and John still breathing.

John was taken into emergency to Wakaw and they tried to take his shirt off, but the tractor lugs had pushed the shirt into his skin and body, so the major part of the shirt was cut off and the little pieces left in the skin to be taken out later. Father and mother returned home that night with all kinds of thoughts on their mind. Now what? Will we need to prepare for a funeral? Will John be an invalid? I guess all kinds of thoughts race through a persons mind at times such as this. Next day after John had come back out of unconsciousness he was taken to Prince Albert, Saskatchewan for x-rays. The x-rays showed that all he had was a cracked chest bone. He was brought back to Wakaw and spent a few more days in the hospital before the parents brought him back home. God's hand must have been with John as he lay in that soft earth and the tractor with machinery trampling over him. He was saved from sure death. Oksana and I found out about this accident while we were still in Oakburn and had received a letter from home telling us what had transpired on the farm.

John escaped death at that time. I myself have escaped death five times. You will read this at the end of this biography. I have written at the end a few incidents that happened in my lifetime that no one has an answer why or what. Also the five escapes of death closes this bio of my life in 2016. If God willing and I still am around after 2016, I don't know how much longer I would want to stay on this earth with all the ruthless happenings each and everyday around us. Shootings here and shootings there. Terrorist attacks here and terrorist attacks there. Murders here and murders there. Assaults here and assaults there. No love among people like there was a hundred years ago. Today the world has become, "dog eat dog." As long as I have and I don't care about the next door neighbor. So who wants to live in such a society in such a world not knowing when you may be attacked for no reason. No thanks, such a world is not in my lens to look through.

NEW LIFE - RCAF

Wednesday, June 30th was the last day of school at Flower School. This same day father and mother unexpectedly arrived from home to pick Oksana and me and to take us back home. They also brought news that there will be no teacher in the Old Tarnopol School for the coming school term. Father said that when we get home I should apply to teach there. He said that I would probably get the position, because father had talked to some people and they were of the opinion that I should be the teacher in the school where at one time I attended. On July 1st I bid farewell to the Flower School, the area and to Oakburn and we headed for home. I did not know that fate would bring me back to these areas years later and in a different profession as we will see in the forthcoming pages.

Coming home on the first of July which is a Canadian holiday, Canada Day, we ran into an accident that involved one vehicle about ten miles north of Humboldt, Saskatchewan. On the north side of highway #20, a car was sitting in the ditch, in a slough, in the water. The driver side was higher and the driver was standing outside by the car on the road. The woman, a passenger, was sitting in the car with her feet in the water. What we learned was when we stopped to check what happened was the husband had a few too many and drove into the ditch and ended up in the water. The woman through the open driver's side door of the car was shouting to her husband: "Wait when we get home, I'll give you whiskey."

We wanted to help, but could not do anything and by this time there were already a few more cars that had stopped to see what happened. The people needed a tractor to get pulled out of the mud and water.

When we arrived home, I made an application to teach in the Old Tarnopol School, which was just a mile and a half from home. Teaching at this school, I would have no expenses and all income would be directed towards paying off the debts on the land and running the farm. But there was the question: What will father, John and I do during the two summer months? What will I do when there is no school for another two months? Three men on the farm and not enough work for two men, not alone for three. I decided that I would go to Saskatoon and get a job for the summer. We knew that the airport in Saskatoon was being developed, was expanding and there was much construction work going on during the summer months.

It did not take long. The next day found me on the train at 9:00 AM heading for Saskatoon to get a summer job. Arriving in Saskatoon, I went to the employment office to look for a job. I said I was looking for work at the airport for the summer, and was told I would have to go to the airport and apply in person for a job. I caught a bus and headed for the airport. When I arrived at the gate the guards measured me up and down and asked me what I wanted. They asked me a few questions and what I was doing until now. I told them that I had taught school and will be teaching again come fall. I told the guard I was looking for people in charge of getting a job for the summer months. They told me that I would have to go downtown and apply in person at the recruiting unit.

The guard looked at me again and went inside the guard house while I stood outside in the hot sun waiting for an answer. After he had made a telephone call, he told me to go to the Recruiting Unit downtown and gave me the address. I thanked the guard and turned back towards the city to catch a bus. Because the airport was also a military base, I knew that there were strict regulations as to who can come onto such a base and for what reason, purpose or business. Everything looked up and I thought the bus was flying while going back all the way downtown. At least now I'll have a job for the summer and a few more dollars into the family coffers will come in handy. Many times father a return soldier, would speak how tough it was to get into a military base if you had no business to be there. I took in all that thought that I would have to go through a tough period of questioning of why I want to get unto the base.

When I came to the Recruiting Unit, the receptionist asked if she can help me. I told her my story that I had been at the airport to get a summer job for two months and was told to come here. Before I knew what was happening, I was given some forms to fill out. Good. Eugene will get a job and maybe start work tomorrow morning. I filled out the form with no problem and in no time at all. I handed the form in and was told to have a seat. Spirits were running high. Everything looked better than I had anticipated. Luck is on my side. I could have rubbed my hands in glee and joyfully cried out how happy I was inside. A while later I was called again and was asked to complete a "time allotted test." Me being a teacher, what's that for me to answer some time limited questions. As long as I get the job, I'll write the tests they want.

I completed the test and handed the paper in. The receptionist was surprised that I was finished and she said that I still had a few minutes. On the top of the test paper and on the back there was some fine print, but who needs that and who reads the fine print on papers. I'm writing a test and no time to read fine print. In my mind was running the thought of what kind of a job I will get. After waiting for a few minutes, I was called in to see a man in the another room. As I walked in, a man in military uniform stood up and greeted me with his name, which I don't recall now. The man said I would have to take an oath. No problem, no bother. I'll take the oath to get the job, maybe even tomorrow morning. All this time I had on my mind that because I will be working on a military base I may have to be careful what I tell people as to what I may have seen or heard, so oath was an oath. I knew that secrecy sometimes is very important from the military side of things, so I was not afraid of any oath. What's a small oath to take, to get a summer job. As soon as we went through the oath, the man in uniform says: "Congratulations, you are in the Air Force." I didn't quite get what he had said, so I asked: "So when can I start work?"

Now the officer told me to sit down. Yes I needed to sit now. He told me that I can go back home now and return back to Saskatoon on August 6th, a month from now, and would be leaving for St. Jean late that evening. St. Jean? Where in the world is that? I asked. The man said that I will be in a sleeper car and all my meals will be paid. But, hold it, wait a minute.

What he was telling me was not making any sense to me. I will be going in a sleeper and the meals will be paid. What is all this about? Again I ask, where is St. Jean? I had not heard of St. Jean anywhere in Saskatchewan. The officer looks at me and says: "St. Jean is about thirty miles from Montreal and that is where your training will begin." For a while I thought I was in a deep sleep and was having a dream or that I was under some spell. The officer handed me two railroad tickets, one to go home and one to return to Saskatoon on August 6th. "Now you can go, and we'll wait for you to come back on August 6th, said the officer. Now I can go, go where? I wanted to go to work at the airport for two months. What has happened here?

After coming to my senses what had transpired I was whisked into the military service in just a few minutes being at the Recruiting Unit. As I walked out the door, the first thought came into my mind: "And what will mother say now? Will she disown me? Will she tell me not to come home ever again?" Over and over all kinds of thoughts raced through my mind. Should I go home, or should I run away someplace and hide so no one will find me? What shall I tell the family at home who are all waiting for me, their son and brother, to come home and report he got a job at the airport. As all this kept flashing through my head, one little thought came flying from nowhere. "Hey, you are old enough to do as you want. How long will your parents have to keep telling you what to do?" There was still enough time to catch the train back home. I had a ticket to go home, so I did not need to pay my fare. I took the train home and all the way home I kept peering out the window with all kinds of thoughts racing around in my head. I didn't even realize when the train came to Tarnopol, until the conductor came and shouted, "Tarnopol, next stop." Maybe I should just keep on going on the train and don't stop until I get to the end of the earth

Instead of getting and working in a summer job, I ended up in the RCAF when I signed the papers writing the tests. I should have read the fine print in the application and the test that I wrote. Maybe I would have still been teaching at home starting in the fall.

As I walked home from Tarnopol along that railway track, many memories and thoughts flew by about the times that I had a ride to high school nearly every morning on the jigger car. Or how about the time when the train derailed near our place? What about the time how accurate I was, when I could pick up a little stone on the rail road and throw so perfect that I could hit the fence post or some tree fifty feet away. How about the cold, cold and snowy mornings when I tramped the railroad to school each winter day?

When I got closer to home, my heart began to beat faster and heavier. I will have to leave my family and go away maybe forever, maybe never to see them again. What have I done to them? What shall I tell them if I am asked if I got a job? Should I tell them now or not say a word until maybe some time later? If I don't tell them now, than I will not be telling the truth. To this day I don't remember how I broke the news to the family. I just had too much in my head at that time, so I can not recall today what happened then, but however, I broke the news to them somehow. It was for the next three years that my time would be spent in the RCAF, July 1954 to July 1957.

Then came the day when I was to leave my family and head out to St. Jean on August 6th. It was a hot and dry Saturday day. The train left Tarnopol for Saskatoon on Saturdays about 5:00 PM. This day the family was making hay for the cattle for winter. I was raking the hay while father and mother were pitching the hay unto the rack where John was tamping down the hay. As I was raking the hay all kinds of thoughts went through my mind. Maybe this is the last day that the family will see me. Maybe I will be sent to war and die there never to return home again. Maybe the next time I come home I may be an invalid, where I was injured in a war. All of such thoughts climbed all through my head, but nothing can change anything now, unless I should become ill or pass away before I have to board the train to Saskatoon.

The hay was in the stacks at home all ready for winter. It was time for me to get ready to leave for the railroad station. I got ready and the family all piled into the car to take me to Tarnopol. When the train blew the whistle that it was one mile from the station, we all started to cry. Parting was sad. Farewells were said a dozen times before the train arrived. Mother cried the most and was always repeating: "My son, why are you going away so far from us? Will I ever see you again? You'll be killed in the war or in an airplane and we will never see you again. Why do you have to leave us and go away?" Over and over mother repeated similar words and that made the heartache greater.

The train approached the station, slowed down and stopped. Everyone had eyes filled with tears as I boarded the train. "All aboard," shouted the conductor and slowly the train started to pull away from the station. I could see through the window as the train slowly moved away that all were crying and waving farewell to me. Again thoughts came: "Will I ever see them again? Will I ever see the people that I knew, lived with and loved? Will I ever see my old school pals?" Many of such thoughts circled in my head as the train picked up speed from the station. I looked a few more times behind me to see the grain elevator and Tarnopol disappear behind the hill and bushes. How many tears were shed that day because of me, and I felt guilty that I brought this on upon the family. The parting was sad and emotional, but than a thought came to me: "You are a soldier now and you have to be brave, strong and courageous. You are not the first one that ever left home and you had left home just a year ago to teach. People have done that before and it will continue to be that way as long as this world will last." My tears stopped and I kept looking out the window of the train as the wheat fields, meadows and prairies swiftly flew past.

When I arrived in Saskatoon I reported to where I had to get my instructions as to what farther was to be done. I was taken to a railroad car that was standing beside the station. There I was assigned a room in a sleeper and where I would stay until we came to St. Jean. A while later a few other men were brought into the same car and they had the same instructions given as I had. We introduced ourselves and found out that we were all heading to the same place for training in the RCAF. It was sometimes late during the night when I was asleep when our sleeper was hooked up to the train and we were off. When I awoke in the morning and looked out the window, I could see prairies flying past us as the train sped along the rails singing clickety-clack, clickety-clack. As the train sped on east, more and more men were boarding the train along the way when it stopped at stations, and we were finding out that we were all going to the same place. By the time we arrived in St. Jean the car was filled with men all going to the RCAF training station. As all this was taking place, thoughts of the family were fading away more and more, so that by the time I arrived in St. Jean, so many things had happened that the family was now someplace on the back burner.

At St. Jean we were met by RCAF personnel and a military bus. We boarded the bus and headed out to the training base. It was night time and all we could see was many buildings with lights as we rode along the streets. At the base we were assigned living quarters (barracks) during our training session. The very next day training began. I was given a regimental number of which I remember to this day. This number has stuck in my head till this very day. We were also given medical and physical check-ups. We were measured for uniforms and were given out supplies. A large suitcase was supplied to keep our belongings and personal things in. This large suitcase was usually under the bed and it was locked if you had purchased a lock to lock it.

Our training started immediately. Drill was the program day after day as well as tests and exams almost every second day. The tests were given to see what the person was best qualified for - a trade. There is the service, but in the service there are trades or as one may say vocations. One person may be best qualified to work in the hospital, another in the kitchen, a third in the mail room, a fourth as mechanic and so forth. After the tests and exams were written each person individually was called up before an officer who would recommend or suggest what trade you would be suited to go in. During this period the interviewing officer would also ask which trade a person would like. According to the tests we wrote, they knew our IQ and we were encouraged to go into the trade that we would be best suited for.

The officer that was interviewing me asked if I would like to go into air crew, to become a pilot, navigator or some other trade to fly in the airplanes. He said they would like me to consider the air crew because my IQ at that time was somewhat above average. At this time we were still all on ground crew until we had our basic training completed. I ask the officer if I could think about it for a day or two and than would give him my answer. He booked me to come at a certain hour a few days later. After some consideration of the request from the officer in charge, I made my decision to stay on ground crew. If you went into air crew, you immediately were an officer rank.

When I returned a few days later to see the trades officer I told him that I made my decision to stay on the ground crew and I would be interested in the trade of Mobile Equipment section. I chose this, because I knew that one day I will be out of the air force and than what will I do? I can return back to the farm and any mechanical knowledge that I can pick up would sure come in handy. The mechanical training would help me to maintain machinery, car, tractor, etc. Another thing that was telling me not to go air crew were the words mother was crying when I was leaving home: "Son, you are going to the RCAF and you will be flying, the plane will crash, you will be killed and I will not see you again." Those words of mother stuck with me and for that I was hesitant to go into air crew. In the ME (Mobile Equipment) trade that I had chosen it was an important duty like other trades.

After my basic training of eight weeks were complete at St. Jean, I was to go to Aylmer, Ontario for my trade training for a period of two months. This was not fulfilled, because at that time there was no vacancy in that trade for two more weeks. Instead of staying at St. Jean and not doing anything, I was sent to Trenton, Ontario on contact training. What a beautiful place that was in Ontario. There I was working in the Mobile Equipment section doing what I was asked and told to do. I changed tires, oil, washed and cleaned vehicles. I washed and swept floors. Since I had not received any training for my trade, I could not drive vehicles until I finished the trade course even though I knew how to drive and had a Saskatchewan Drivers Licence. After a two week stint at Trenton, I was sent to Aylmer to start my trade training. Here the instructors taught us how to drive, operate and in instances to find the problem with stalled or broken vehicles. One thing that we were taught here was: "There are three ways to drive. The wrong way, the right way and the Air Force way."

I had left home on August 6th for St. Jean, Quebec. Here I spent eight weeks training and this was all mostly drill and military etiquette. It was about the end of October when I started my training in the Mobile Equipment Unit in Aylmer. After this course in Aylmer I would be sent to any military base of the RCAF to work and be a regular service personnel in the RCAF. We had already been told that there were two ways of being sent to a full time base. One was you were posted which would probably last one year, while the other a transfer, which would be of indefinite duration. Where I would be going was anyone's guess. One was usually sent to a place where there was an opening for that particular trade. Someone may have retired, or promoted, or moved to another station and that vacancy would have to be filled.

During all the time that I spent at St. Jean, Trenton and Alymer, I kept in touch with the family by mail. I could not phone them, because they had no power and no phone on the farm. Mother was the one that was always writing the letters to me in Ukrainian as well as she could. She probably wrote better Ukrainian than I wrote back to them. She told me of the news about the family and the surrounding district. She mentioned each time that father was not very well. I also received news that John had left home and had gone to Saskatoon to train as a mechanic. Father with mother, Alice and Oksana were left on the farm.

I graduated from my trade training on December 17th - 1954 along with other graduates. We each received a certificate saying that we completed such training. As training was coming to an end, now came the day when each would be notified where he was being posted. Everyone was excited to find out who would be going where. The names of us graduates were already written on the blackboard when we came in for the last day of class. In the military things were done in alphabetical order, and it may still be the same today. As my surname was Stefaniuk, it was the last one on the list. As we assembled for the last time in our classroom, my heart was in the throat, than in the heels, back into the throat and again into the heels. Where will I be going? Will I be going to Saskatoon? Will I be shipped out to Gander Newfoundland? Will I get a posting to Cambridge North West Territories? Will I stay on in Aylmer or someplace in Ontario? Will I be sent to British Columbia? Will I be sent overseas? The instructor in charge brought out his paper and started to write beside each name who is going where. Following my name the instructor started to write: **S a s k a t o o n**. I will be going to Saskatoon and will be about Sixty miles from home. I did not get a job in Saskatoon when I went to get a two month job, but now I will still be working in Saskatoon. God sure works in wondrous ways.

Two days after the completion of my course found me in a sleeper car on the CNR railroad heading west to Saskatoon. I arrived in Saskatoon on December 20 - 1954 and reported to work immediately. Because I was newly arrived in Saskatoon, the corporal in charge asked if I wanted to work over the Christmas holiday and on January 1st. I said I would be willing to work those days, if later I could get January 6th to 8th off. "Why?"

he asked. I answered him and said I want to be home with the family for the Ukrainian Christmas season. I was told I could have that time off and so I agreed to work during the festive season.

Parents knew that I would be coming home for our Christmas. I had written a letter and told them that I would be home on the 4th of January. Of this I knew, because I was told that I can have that time off for working during Christmas and New Years as the corporal had informed me. I had written home asking father to come and pick me up at the station at 4:00 PM on January 4th. This was already January 1955. I do not know if there was anyone else from Tarnopol that had served in the RCAF before me. I know that there were several men that served in the military, but they were in the Army, I was in the RCAF.

When the train arrived at the station, father was there to meet me. The train slowed down and came to slow screeching, braking halt. When the trains arrived at the station people usually came out to see who was leaving or arriving. As I disembarked from the train, I could see father's face was gleaming with pride. Other people present were looking at me. Is this Stefaniuk's son Eugene? He is a soldier in uniform? We got into the car and went to Sam Dziadyk's store and Post Office. We waited until the mail was sorted. While in the store I could see people watching me like a hawk watches a baby chick, or a coyote watching a rabbit. Some people more brave, stepped up to me and asked me about my career, where I was, what I was doing, etc. Father in the meantime was as proud as a peacock walking around, that his son is now finally someone and did not waste his life. Father had served in the First World War and knew what military life was, so that made him more pleased to see me following in his footsteps.

Father and I arrived home. Now there was even more joy. Mother and sisters were glad to see me again and mother kept hugging me over and over again. It is only a little more than five months since I left home, but the way the family accepted and treated me, you would think that I had been away for decades. When I was away I did not forget the family either. In the RCAF, I was receiving free clothing, food, lodging and a small pay. The pay was about $76.00 a month. Because I only needed to buy tooth paste, shaving cream, shoe polish, etc., I would keep anywhere from $15-20.00 a month and the rest of the money I would send home to help the family pay their bills. A day later after I had been home, brother John also arrived by train from Saskatoon. At that time there was no such thing as paved highways or each son having a car. Travel by this time was still mostly by horse and wagon or horse and buggy. John and I stayed home together for a few days, but I don't recall if we both went back the same day or different days.

I stayed in Saskatoon until March 1956 when I was transferred to Winnipeg. While in Saskatoon, John and I got together quite often when I was not on duty. We would walk downtown and look at the places or sometimes we would go to a movie. And each opportunity that I had more than a day, like three or four days, I tried to get home as often as possible. By this time the parents and family had already been accustomed to me being not to far way and coming home each time I had the chance. Coming home I always found time to give a helping hand on the farm of whatever time of the year it was.

A WATER CAR?

While in Winnipeg I met a man by the name of Ken Sullivan. He was in the same trade as I was and we even resided in the same barracks and the same room. There were usually four people in a room. Because of this we had many things in common to talk about. He was a quiet man like I was, so it was easy for us to form a friendship. He like me, did not spend money foolishly like some others spent a lot of time in the bars or going downtown.

One time as we were talking, we somehow stumbled unto the subject of high gasoline prices. We talked about it and said that it would be so much cheaper or cost nothing if a car could run on water. Today as this is written there are cars that run on hydrogen and produce water. We sat and planned and planned, how a car engine could be built so that it would operate on water for fuel. We drew pictures, had equations and whatever we could think of. We finally came to the conclusion that such a theory could work, but not in cold climate temperatures. If you left water in the gas tank when it is very cold in sub zero temperatures, the water in the tank or cylinders would freeze and that would cause damage to the engine and car.

We knew that in school we were taught that water is composed of hydrogen and oxygen. We knew at that time what an atomic bomb could do, and we learned from school experiments the power that hydrogen had. All we would need is to separate the hydrogen from oxygen. If we fill the gasoline tank with water, than through electrolysis separate hydrogen from oxygen and we would have that conquered. Hydrogen is lighter than oxygen and it would rise to the top in the tank. Have a pump to pump the hydrogen to the carburetor. From a spark in the cylinder and we would have great power in driving the engine for a long way. We even had said that we would call that kind of a car: "The Water Car."

It was well understood by us that when oxygen came from outside and mixed with the fired hydrogen, we get water. Now we can put little pumps in the bottom of the cylinders and pump the water back into the tank. Then split the water again and get hydrogen and it would come back and the same process would be repeated over and over again. Fill your tank once with water and forget everything. We had it mastered. But than we had a problem. When the car would stop there would always be some water left in the cylinder. What would happen if you did not use the car each day and the water sat in the cylinder for a week or more? Of course rust and or corrosion would set on the cylinder and pistons of the engine. We knew that there was nothing at that time that did not rust. Yes, today there are many alloys that do not rust or corrode and could be used for this purpose. We had to scrap our plan. Another reason that we never got any farther was that in 1957, I was discharged from the RCAF and Ken Sullivan was sent over to the Suez Canal with our forces to keep the peace. After we said our good-byes that year we have never had any contact with each other. Today I don't know if Ken is still around or not, since it is nearly sixty years ago.

MY OWN CAR

It was also during this time in Winnipeg that I purchased my first car. I wanted to get out to see the family and the only way was by train, bus or have a car. I purchased a 1946 used Chief Pontiac car. I wish I had that car today. It was in very good shape. It had a sun visor over the windshield. It had a heater that warmed the car inside in the front and rear. This car gave me very good service, UNTIL one time when I was returning from Saskatchewan to Winnipeg. Coming back I took the road through Rossburn and Oakburn heading east. I was bringing Oksana back with me from Saskatchewan to Winnipeg to live with the parents who had already been in Winnipeg for a few months. How the parents happened to be in Winnipeg will be explained shortly.

I am one step ahead since I'm talking about the car I had. But some may want to know why Oksana and I are coming from where and why. This is just a few words before the actual happening why this took place. The parents had an auction sale on the farm and moved off the land. Oksana went to live with a family who were good friends with the parents. After the parents were settled in Winnipeg, I went to Saskatchewan to pick up and bring Oksana to Winnipeg.

When Oksana and I were returning back to Winnipeg, it was already dark when we hit the Elphinstone area. Having come as far as Elphinstone, I began to notice that something was not normal with the car. From

Elphinstone we had a high hill to climb. I had the gas pedal all the way down to the floor and the car just had no power. The farther up the hill it went, the slower it went until finally, it would not go any higher. I had to back down the hill in the dark, so that I could get another try at the hill. I tried about three or four times to get to the top. Then I took one more chance, one more try. This time barely, barely we climbed up to the top. Now that I'm here I will be ok on the straight road and no more hills to Winnipeg.

Having finally climbed and reached the top of the hill, the car seemed to go better but still not as it had and should. We could not gain any speed to go faster than maybe thirty-five to forty miles per hour. As we kept driving, it seemed that near Minnedosa the car was again losing power. I had to stop and see what could be wrong. I pulled over unto some side road off the highway. I opened the hood, and there I saw more than I ever want to see again. There staring at me from under the hood was the engine absolutely red hot as fire. I told for Oksana to get out of the car and run away from the car, while I shut off the engine. Should an explosion occur, so we would not get hurt. We stood for a while in the cold winter air and waited to see what happens. A while later I started to walk slowly towards the car to see how things were. The engine was now cooled off enough that it was not red, but standing near the edge of the car, you could still feel the warm heat coming from the engine. How Oksana and I got to Winnipeg with the crippled car was a mystery. To this day I don't know how the car did not explode when it was red flaming hot with gasoline lines around so close to the engine.

Oksana and I stood waiting for the engine to cool off more and at the same time wondering, how we would get to Winnipeg, in the dark night when we were still over a hundred miles from home. The question on my mind was: Why did the engine turn all red color? It was red like the top of the stove when you turn on the element. In the winter time the engine cools down sooner than it does in the summer. We waited and after I thought it had cooled down enough we got into the car to keep going on our trip. I tried to start the engine and it was firing, but would not start. After coaxing it for a while it finally started. We started to drive, but the thought was always there as to why the engine had become red like a tomato. Even though the engine was red hot, the heat gauge never showed that the engine had heated up. WHY? After driving for half an hour, I pulled over on an approach and went to see if the engine was red or not. I opened the hood and it was not red, but you could see that it was starting to change color. I shut the engine off and we sat and waited so it would cool off again. We must have stopped about three or four more times before we got to Winnipeg. We'd wait for the engine to cool off and than we would proceed for another hour or so. We stopped again and again and in such manner we finally did reach home in a somewhat crippled way, tired and worried.

I dropped Oksana off where the parents were living on Maryland Avenue and myself went to the RCAF base to my quarters. Next morning I was back on duty. After work I took the car to the garage where I had bought it. I told them of the problem and left it with them to see what the matter was. I took a bus back to the barracks. Next day the garage phoned me and said they found the problem. The engine blocked was cracked. They replaced the block, but that car was never again the same after that. So the engine block was cracked. Where did it crack and the main question was WHY? As time went on, I later traded that car off for another, but can't remember what kind it was.

While I was in Winnipeg, the time was getting near that I would be called up before the Commanding Officer of the station to resign for another period in the service. When I first joined the RCAF, I was later told that I was on the last group of people who had signed up for a three year service. The people that came after me were now signing up for a minimum of five years. My term in the RCAF would be up in June 1957. At that time I could sign up for another two years to make five years of service. One day I got a message that the Commanding Officer wanted to see me. There were two reasons why a Commanding Officer would want to see you. Either your term in the service is up and he will ask you to re-enlist again or you had done something wrong and you would get a good lesson from him. I knew my term was running out, so I was not worried that it would be something different.

The RCAF station in Winnipeg was in two sections. One part was on the west end and the other one the east end of the base. A bus usually carried people from one side to the other. The only time when I enjoyed working in the Mobile Equipment Unit was when I was on night shift.

One day I asked if I could drive the bus for the evening shift. This started at 4:00 PM and went on to midnight. There was always someone that was going from one side of the station to the other. The bus transported the people because the hospital was on the east side of the base, while most of the other places were on the west side and the refueling of the planes was also on the NE area.

One time in the department where I was working a notice was posted on the notice board. I looked and read it. "Needed one airman to work in the refueling Unit." I had heard about that unit. I went to the corporal and told him that I would be willing to go to the refueling Unit. He checked things over and in a few days I found myself in the refueling section. This unit was the refueling of the planes. Pilots were trained and planes flew. After they landed, the plane had to be refueled to be ready for the next training flight. In this unit we always had to make sure that the fuel trucks were full of fuel.

When the planes landed, we would get a phone call that such and such a plane or planes needed to be refueled with such and such fuel. There were two or three different kinds of fuel that was used for different planes. Myself or who would be designated to go and refuel the plane, gets into the truck and drives up to the plane. There always was a person with the plane to help in the refueling. The tanks on the planes are in the wings. You need one person to hold the nozzle to fill the plane while the other one operates the pumps on the fuel truck. The truck and the plane always had to be grounded, other wise an explosion could occur. When we had to do something in the refueling unit we all took our turns. We refueled the planes and filled up the trucks. We also washed and cleaned the trucks and the place where we worked. I completed my service in the RCAF in this unit and was released from the RCAF in June 1957. I remember one incident that happened to me when I came to refuel the plane(s). I came to the plane and one airman was already on the wing of the plane waiting for me. I grounded the fuel tender and plane and opened the two doors of the truck where the hoses were. As I reached to pull the hose, one door came down on my head and put me on my hands and knees. Yes there were stars flying around me in broad daylight for a few moments. The airman on the plane asked if I was alright. I said I was and we continued to fill the plane with fuel. By the time I had refueled the plane(s) the pain on the head had disappeared and only a lump was left after this episode.

The time came when I got a message from the Commanding Officer to appear before him at a certain time. I knew what the reason was, because I knew I had done nothing wrong, so the only reason was to re-enlist for another two years minimum to make for five years. I arrived at the appointed time and you made sure you were on time, otherwise you would also hear about being late.I came in, saluted the Commanding Officer and told him who I was. He asked me to sit down. He took my file from the table and looked at it. Than he looked up at me and asked me if I would like to re-enlist again for another two years. I was prepared and said that I would be leaving the service. He looked at me again and says: "I would be very pleased if you stayed on in the service. I would also like to ask you if you would consider going into air crew." I told him that I had thought things over and would leave when my time came up. Once again I saw the Commanding Officer on the day when I was released, because he was the one that was giving me my release certificate. Another reason for not re-enlisting was that mother always said not to go into air crew, because the plane will crash and I will be killed. The last day when I was leaving, there were some things you had to turn in before you left. The Commanding Officer H.C. Vinnicombe at the end thanked me for the three years of service, handed me my release certificate and I walked out of the RCAF.

Another thing as mentioned previously was that the station in Winnipeg was of two areas with about a mile apart. The hospital was on the east side and the mess hall on the west end. There was no kitchen in the hospital, so food for the patients had to be transported three times a day to the hospital from the mess hall, morning, noon and night. The order was that you go to the hospital, pick up a person, take him or her to the mess hall and there pick up the food and bring them back to the hospital.

Since I left home, I always had a feeling that there was something missing in my life. Always seemed like there was something lacking and an empty space. A missing link in my life was with me. When Oksana and I had been living at Oakburn for a year, we never attended any church services. There was a Ukrainian Orthodox Church in the area at Seech, about five or six miles NW of the school. One time there was a Ukrainian

Catholic priest who had come one Sunday to have a service in the school. People from the surrounding area knew and they came to the service. Oksana and I attended that service in the school, but it seemed not to what we had been accustomed back home even though the Ukrainian Catholic service is the same as the Orthodox.

When I was in the RCAF I had to attend church services from time to time on the base. While there I attended both, the Roman Catholic and the Protestant services taking turns, once there, once there. Yes they were services, but to me they were strange and cold and not to what I had been accustomed too. I longed for my own church and service. But where can I get my own church when there was none in the military service. I never received satisfaction for my soul from other services. The services seemed as though they were lacking something and that they were empty. When I was stationed in Saskatoon I could have attended service there, but at that time it seemed too far away and also there was no one that I knew in Saskatoon except brother John.

It wasn't until I got to Winnipeg that I started going to my church. When I was not on duty, I would go to the service at the Holy Trinity Ukrainian Orthodox Cathedral on Main Street in north Winnipeg. It was about six miles or so from the base. I could have taken a bus to go there, but I always walked there and back. I left early in the morning to catch the service on time and I always wore my uniform. When I walked I had the opportunity to see and get acquainted with the city of Winnipeg. At this time I had a car, but I still walked there and back. I was young, the body was strong and good physical condition and there was no problem to walk any distance. Unless the weather was not favorable, than I would take the car or city bus to get to church.

When I attended the service in the Cathedral, the services were held in the basement, because the upper part had not yet been completed. I sat on a chair like others, for there were no pews yet. One time someone approached me and asked if I could hold the candle during the service. I obliged that I could. When the priest reads the Gospel two or three people on each side stand holding candles. At that time a young looking priest the late Father Michael Yurkiwsky was the parish priest. Something in the back of my head would whisper to me: "You can do that, why don't you?" When I attended the service, the whole week went well for me, successfully and very quickly. When I was not in church, that week for me seemed that it would never end and always something seemed lacking and not right. Isn't it mysterious how God works in wondrous ways. Yes God is a Mystery, for no one has ever seen His Face, and no one will, for God Himself said His Face will not be seen. In the second book of Moses we read: *"And I will take away Mine Hand, and thou shall see My back parts: but My Face shall not be seen."* (Exodus 33:23)

While I was still in Saskatoon, it was at that time that my older sister Alice found someone she wanted to spend the rest of her life with. So on October 15 - 1955 Alice married John Hnatiuk. She had met him through his work. John and his late brother George had a bull dozer and they were cutting and piling brush for the farmers in the Tarnopol area. Father had hired John and his brother George to bull doze some bush on the farm he had bought from Fisych. That quarter was only about half cleared and the rest was still bush. While John was clearing this bush, he met with Alice and after that it is all history. They were married and started their home in St. Benedict where John, his brother George and their mother lived on the farm. John and Alice lived there most of their life. In 2002 they decided to retire from the farm and purchased a house in Wakaw, Saskatchewan. They lived in that house for one year and found it too large for them, so they sold it and moved back to the farm. They lived on the farm for another year while a new house was constructed in 2004 after which they again moved to Wakaw to their new house. On October 22nd of 2005 in Wakaw, Saskatchewan in the Legion Hall, they celebrated their 50th Wedding Anniversary with their family, relatives and friends. John and Alice have five lovely and beautiful daughters who are married and have their own children and they are the ones who prepared all the food and organized the whole anniversary celebration for their parents.

Even though John and I were older than Alice, she took the first step to the church Altar in the Sacrament of Matrimony. They were married in the historical St. Michael's Ukrainian Orthodox Church in Lepine some two or three miles east of Wakaw. That church is over one hundred years old. The reception was held in the church hall near the church. As mentioned above they have five daughters Pat, Kathy, Carolyn, Darcey and Corrine. I recall attending John and Alice's wedding and I had come home from the RCAF in uniform. The weather that day was beautiful and warm. That whole evening long, people came up to me and many whom I did not know asked me who I was and from where. When I told them who I was many were surprised that I was Stefaniuk's son for they knew my parents but not me. Many school chums, other friends and acquaintances came up to me to talk and ask things about me. Many people congratulated me on the occupation which I had reached in my life in the RCAF.

PARENTS LEAVE THE FARM

When I was transferred to Winnipeg, I never stopped assisting parents with monetary help on the farm. Every month as mentioned I would send them money to help make payments on the second farm father had bought, plus tractor and other machinery. Even though what I sent was not much of some fifty to sixty dollars a month, that at least helped to pay for the gasoline or repairs to machinery on the farm. The harder the parents tried to work and prosper on the farm, the bigger the expenses seemed to crawl in. There was no one on the farm now except father, mother and Oksana. There was no one to help them on the land. They finally realized that they will not be able to make headway on the farm, so they decided to sell everything through an auction sale, so they could pay off the debts. They were thinking of moving to find some other form of work to earn a living. Father was one of those people who never wanted to owe money or things to anyone. The way things for them were going, I also encouraged them to sell everything and move to Winnipeg where at that time there was an abundance of jobs. Alice was married and lived fifteen miles south of their place, John was in Saskatoon and I in Winnipeg.

The auction sale took place on November 10 - 1956. I asked for a few days off from the RCAF, to go home and help the parents with the auction sale. That day they sold everything they had: livestock, machinery, household goods, garden vegetables, books, etc....... I still have the original poster of the auction sale. They cleared some $2000.00 dollars from the auction sale. Father paid off some bills and there was still $1800.00 of debt left. Father paid up some debt and to others he promised he would pay off as soon as he can from work that he would get. He kept his promise and slowly as the years slipped by he paid off every penny he owed to anybody. Father was always too honest and he did not want his name to be mud.

Next day, which was Sunday after the sale, I was leaving back for Winnipeg, because come Monday 8:00 AM I have to be back on duty. Father before this time had already been in contact with one of the Derzak boys about a job in the oil fields near Estevan, Saskatchewan and he was assured that there will be a job for him if he comes. Father was already fifty-five years old. But now what about mother? Where is she going to be, do and live? I told mother to come with me to Winnipeg and I will help her get a job there. That is what she did. Early next morning bidding farewell to our home place we left with heavy hearts. At one time there was hope and future, but now it is all gone. But what do you do when you try and try and things just don't work out? You have to turn to something else. We traveled with two vehicles. Father drove his car and I drove mine. Mother was coming with me and father was following us behind. I had already planned out which way I would go so that later it would be easier for father to get to Bienfait in the Estevan area. We drove until we got to highways #16 and #35 at Elfros, Saskatchewan west of Yorkton.

There we stopped and said our good-byes. Our hearts were heavy. A lump formed in my throat and it was hard to say good-bye. Would we ever see each other again? If so when, where and how? I told father to stay on that highway #35 south and he will get to Weyburn. From there he was to go east on highway #39. When he gets to Estevan he can ask people how to get to Bienfait. I also wrote out a paper for him, so he could show it to someone and they would direct him to Bienfait and to where the oilfields were.

There in the middle of the prairies the family again separated. Father went his way, mother and I to Winnipeg, John is in Saskatoon, Alice married and living at St. Benedict, and Oksana went to stay with John and Helen Chytyk in Tarnopol. From there she went to school. It was later that year as already mentioned above that saw Oksana and I were coming to Winnipeg we had trouble with the car engine on the highway. No one knew what would happen in Winnipeg with mother if she will have a place to stay or what, so Oksana could not come to Winnipeg at that time. She could not go with father into the oil fields. Alice was busy on the farm herself and Oksana could not go to stay with brother John. By staying at Chytyks Oksana was only about ten miles from Alice and Alice could visit her from time to time. The family was now scattered like little chicks when a hawk comes down upon them. How will father do alone in a completely new environment and surroundings. The separating of the family did not help the lump in the throat.

Mother and I arrived in Winnipeg in the evening. Where does one start to look for a place to stay at night? The only place was to drop mother off at some hotel or motel which I did, and myself I headed for the barracks at the station. Next day on Monday I was on duty during the day until 4:00 PM. I had told the hotel people so that they would keep mother in the lobby the following day until I came and picked her up. Next day I did not go for supper, but straight from work, I headed out to the hotel where mother had been waiting for me. She was anxious and somewhat uneasy, because she did not know anyone and than her English language was not good. She said it was a long wait for her all day, which I believed her. We had supper together and than went to look for a place where she could stay, to rent a room or apartment.

We drove and looked at places, but they were not the best kind. Mother said she would like to stay where there were Ukrainian people in that apartment or rooming house and than she would be able to converse with them. We looked and looked and finally we found a place on 187 Maryland Avenue where we saw a notice in window of a suite to rent. I may be wrong, it could be other than 187, but it was Maryland. We rang the door bell and a lady answered the door. I asked her in English about the suite for rent, how large and the cost. The lady told me and than I translated for mother what she said. The lady looked surprised and than says to us in Ukrainian: "You talk Ukrainian?" When mother heard the Ukrainian language, she immediately said that she is not going any place else and she will stay there. The owners had immigrated to Canada and they knew Ukrainian because they came from Ukraine. Now communication would be good for mother in this place. It was in this same place that later father joined mother, than Oksana and I followed and we lived there for a number of years. We also brought from Poland mother's sister and niece and we all lived in that place on the third floor.

Mother had a place to stay. Now she wanted to find a job so she could do something and make money to pay for the room where she will be staying. I cannot recall how much the rent was each month, but it was reasonable, because the parents lived there for a number of years.

But what could mother do? What kind of a job? She can't converse in the English language, so she would have to find something that she needs no knowledge of the language. She had no education so her English was just about nil. She asked me to find her a job even if its to wash dishes. After mother was settled in and I brought her luggage in, I returned back to the barracks. Mother asked me to come back the following day and help her find a job. That took place. I did not want to get mother into the city centre, because she could not read and talk in English and could get lost or have problems. Next day I picked mother up and we drove west on Portage Avenue. We kept looking for signs where help was needed.

Finally we saw in one little café a sign saying they needed help. Mother said that she would not be a waitress, because she can't speak English. We stopped at this small café and went in to ask about the position for help. The owner said that he wanted someone to wash dishes, wash floors and to help the cook in the kitchen. I told him that mother would be willing to do that, but her English is poor. The owner looks at me and says: "Did you see the for help sign in the window? Does it say that you have to speak English?" I said, "No." Than he says: "I want someone to help in the kitchen, not to give lectures." Mother was hired and she could come to work next morning. This was mother's first job in Winnipeg at the "Chatterbox café." After she had worked at this café for a while, she heard from other people that there was a job at the Leland Hotel and the wages were much better there. She left the Chatterbox café and got a job at the Leland Hotel in downtown Winnipeg.

There was another experience with mother. Every day she would walk back and forth to work. It was one mile one way. I told her to take a bus and it will be quicker and easier on her feet, since she was on her feet all day long. The bus stop was right in front of the café and also on the other side of the café going downtown which was perfect. From Portage Avenue it was only two blocks to the rooming house where she stayed. Mother said that she will not take the bus, because she will not know where to get off and will get lost and will not know where she is. Another reason she did not want to take the bus, because it cost ten cents each way. She said that in one week she could save a dollar by walking there and back.

I worked one week a midnight shift and I told mother that I would be at the café to pick her up after she is finished work. When I got to the café she was already waiting for me. We crossed the street and I told her that we are going to her place with the bus. We got on and I told her that if she wants the bus to stop, to pull the cord above her. As we rode along, I told her to look for certain landmarks or buildings so she would know where to get off. As we got near Maryland, I told her to pull the cord. The next bus stop came and we got off. Mother was very surprised that she got home that quickly. I also showed and told her that she can go to work the same way, but she would have to catch the bus on the opposite side. We both walked home. It did not take long and mother was riding the bus to and from work. She learned quickly. Mother had worked in the Leland Hotel for a while until someone told her to apply for a job at the Misericordia Hospital. Mother made an application and she was hired. Here she worked until she retired and the hospital was only about three blocks from where she lived.

Mother was now settled in Winnipeg, had a place to stay and a place to work. Father in the meantime was also working in the oil fields near Estevan, Saskatchewan. The pay there was very good, but he did not stay there very long. He had served in the First Word War and had been severely injured. His stomach had been ripped open by a hand grenade and the intestines were badly damaged. He still had pieces of shrapnel in his chest and in his cheek when he passed away. When he worked in the oil fields he had to climb up the oil derricks and carry a heavy steel cable up with him to be flung across to another derrick or some sort of equipment. This all was taking part some twenty to thirty feet up in the air, standing on a ladder. This was just too heavy a job for father. At this time he was over fifty years old already. He had to give up that job even though the wages were good. Father left the oil fields and came to Winnipeg to find a job there. Somehow I lost this piece here. I do not remember how father had found where mother was now living, but it seems that mother had written a letter to father with her address, so when he arrived in Winnipeg, he found the place where mother was staying. When he arrived in Winnipeg I again took time looking in the papers to help father get a job. Without education and a language barrier this was not an easy way to get a job even if there were jobs available.

Finally I found something for him that was warm in the winter and cool in the summer. I found him a job to work as a "newsie" on the Canadian National Railways. This gave him a chance to travel on the train from Winnipeg to Thunder Bay, Ontario, Churchill, Manitoba, Edmonton, Alberta and places in between. The job on the train involved selling newspapers, soft drinks, chocolate, gum, etc. Because he could not read English he had problems in this work, even though he enjoyed it. He was constantly cheated by the boss. Instead of giving father the right amount of items to sell, he always gave him less, but charged him for more. Instead of giving him sixty bottles of pop, they would give him forty, but charge him for sixty. Father would sign the papers for the goods received and he was off on the trip. He would sell everything he had and when he returned back home after four or five days, he would be paid two or three dollars. It did not take long for father to find out how things were functioning. When he saw that he was being cheated, he came back one day from the trip and said that he was quitting. One thing he got from that job was to see the country for free and different places which he never saw before.

Since he left that job, once again I started to look for a job for him. Yes, jobs were available, but they required the English language which he was lacking. I found a place where a caretaker was required. It was the Regent's Park United Church in St. Vital. He said that he would take that job right now. I told him that job may be okay, but that he should remember that he will not have any Sunday off, but must be at the church to open the doors and look after everything. He said that he could do such a job. We drove to see the people at the church. He was hired right there and then. He said that he'll take that job for now and later maybe something better will be found. After he started working there, I did find more jobs that he could have taken, but he liked the place where he was now working.

This care taking job father held at the church for nearly two decades until he retired. It was not very easy for him either, but money was the shortage problem and any dollar that could come to the house was always very welcome. After he started working there the church was torn down and a new church was built with a large auditorium, kitchen, classrooms, storage area, furnace room in the basement, a caretakers room, etc. The place was steam heated. In order to operate a steam furnace, a person needs to have special papers for steam fitters. Father had none. The executive of the church saw that father was doing a good job did not want to lose him. One day they took him into the furnace room and explained and showed him everything how the furnace worked. The furnace was run by burning oil. Each spring after the furnace was shut off, the furnace had to be taken apart, the flues and everything else cleaned and than put back together again. Once or twice the steam heating inspector would come around to check and investigate the furnace to see its operation. When the inspector came around to check it, he always made a report to the church board reporting that they had the best cleaned and looked after furnace that he inspects each year. Because of that, father stayed there for years, and no one ever demanded for him to go and take a steam fitters course to run to operate the steam furnace.

Many times in that span of time father would tell the executive that he was quitting his job. The executive would get together and each time decided to give him a raise and father stayed on year after year at the same work. Father was given a small room in the building where he could have a rest whenever he wanted. He had a little hot plate and many times cooked his own meals there. He also had a small bed in which he slept many nights not going home and also during the day if he was tired, he would lay down to rest. There was a Safeway food store next door to the church, so father could always buy for himself whatever he wanted in food. Only he had the key to his little room. Many times when some function was going on in the church into the late hours of the night, father would not come home, but slept in his little room since next morning he would have to be up early to set up the hall or something else to have the place ready for eight or nine o' clock in the morning. The minister and staff liked him very much and he worked well with them. Every Sunday they always asked father to help count the church collection plate. Because of the burden of work that he had at that church, he said that many times all he had for a meal was tea and bread.

Reading the article above we see how people became rich in the "good old days." Times were hard and when a man was honest, he did everything he could so his name was not dragged through the mud. With God's help the family paid up every cent they ever owed anyone so that they could have and live with a clear conscience. The parents had been living on Maryland Street and paying off the debt as well as the rent and support of themselves. Not long after the debts were all paid off, they started talking about buying and owning their own house. They did buy a house just a few blocks from the Manitoba Legislature on Young Street and just a few blocks from Maryland where they lived. For a laugh we always used to say that maybe father was thinking of running for the premier of Manitoba and that is why they bought a house so near to the Legislature, so it would not be far to go to work.

After having lived on Young Street, Oksana who was married, moved in with the parents occupying the upper suite and she lived there until the parents sold the house and bought another house on Bannerman Avenue north Winnipeg. Why they sold the house on Young Street was as they later said: because of the "hooligan hippie type" of people who were always bothering them and had no respect for someone else's property. They made a lot of noise and if told to be quieter, they came and caused damage and vandalism to their property. The parents said they had no alternative, but to sell and move to another area. In May 1982 they also sold their house on Bannerman and moved out of Winnipeg back to Cudworth, Saskatchewan for some peace and quiet in their older age.

What had happened was that the hooligans also caused destruction to their house on Bannerman. The noise was also like it was on Young Street. They said that it was unsafe for them on Bannerman Avenue to go out whether day or night. Someone was always robbed, assaulted or attacked in that area. In August 1981 mother needed to have her prescription refilled. They both went to the pharmacy and were gone for half an hour. They left at 12:00 noon and were back very soon. When they returned, their house had been broken into, vandalized and damaged. Someone who had broken in tipped over furniture and flipped the mattresses looking for money. They opened the cupboards and the refrigerator and than threw eggs inside the refrigerator and into the cupboards. Those hippie hooligans probably were staking out and watching when the parents are out, and than they broke in and did vandalism damage. They saw both parents leave the house, so they crashed the rear door and ransacked the house inside.

When the parents came back from the drug store, they got a shock of their lives. Father seeing what happened, rushed into the house, grabbed a knife, hoping that maybe a hooligan was still hiding inside and he would at least have something to defend himself. Than he ran outside to see if anyone was around, but to no avail. When this happened, I was living at Hyas, Saskatchewan that time. They phoned to tell me what had happened and I told them to get in touch with the police and the insurance people and not to touch anything. I was some three hundred miles away from them. Later they told me that the insurance people came within an hour, but the police did not come for five hours to make the investigation.

Father said that where they lived there was a little corner store in the area. They told the owner of that store of what had happened to them. The owner said that he was not surprised. He told father that he had break-ins into his store frequently and it was not new to him of a break-in. The store owners residence was above the store. He told father that one time he heard someone had broken into his store, so he called the police at that moment. He said that the police asked him if the thieves were still in the store and he said they were, because he can hear them. The police told him: "Do you think we're going to go in there when someone is around so we could get shot or killed?" I don't blame the police one bit for that. The criminal today has the rights over the victims and no punishment for the criminal. That is probably why it took so long that the police did not come to investigate for five hours after they received the call from the parents. The parents said that Winnipeg had become a place of crime and hooliganism and it was not a city fit for older people, but for criminals, and that is why they made a decision to move out of Winnipeg.

Both parents had enjoyed not too bad of health until 1981, which turned out to be an unsuccessful year for them. Living on Bannerman father one winter day decided to go to town. Instead of driving, he will take the bus. When he was on the way to the bus stop, he noticed the bus was already coming. He wanted to hurry to be at the bus stop, so he started to run. As he ran he slipped on the curb, fell down and with his head and shoulder hit the curb. The bus driver saw what happened, stopped to help him. Father had separated his shoulder and hit the side of his head against the curb. He was taken to the hospital and spent three days in the hospital in Winnipeg. He was also stricken with appendicitis or some other problem with severe pains in his stomach. Later the pain disappeared and he never knew what had caused the pain. It may have been that when he fell down, muscles were stretched and caused pain.

When father was still working at Regents Park United Church being the caretaker, something happened to him that his skin on his hands and feet would blister and than peel off. Where the skin peeled off, there was raw flesh exposed to the area and it was painful. He went from doctor to doctor seeking help, but no cure came about. This problem sent him to the hospital. One day being in the hospital, he said that eight doctors came to see his problem. They looked at his at hands and feet and after studying the situation they came to the conclusion to amputate his legs, because they can't find any cure or problem what was causing the peeling of his skin. Father told the doctors that he would not permit them to amputate his legs. He asked his personal physician to send him to Rochester, Minnesota to the hospital there. When he got to Rochester, they discovered that he was allergic to chemicals such as cement, cleansers, detergents, chemicals, soaps, etc. In Rochester they gave him some medication and told him to wear rubber gloves. After this his hands and feet began to heal, he would not touch any chemicals. At that time he was seventy plus years old. He lived to be 101 and passed away on December 3 - 2002 with both hands and feet in tack and no amputation.

Mother also did not fare too well in 1981. It was March 12th when late one evening Oksana called and said mother was in the hospital and the doctors told her they did not know what the problem was. They told Oksana to phone the family members to come, if we wanted to see mother still alive. She had been taken to the hospital by ambulance in a semi-conscious state. The doctors held out no hope for her and said that she could go anytime. As soon as we got the message, John in Edmonton and I made arrangements that we would meet in Yorkton at a prescribed place and time about 6:00 or 7:00 AM. John would leave Edmonton before midnight to be in Yorkton at the prescribed time. After we met in Yorkton, I left my car in Yorkton on the church parking lot and went with John. John had been driving all night, so he asked me to drive and give him a break. Alice and her husband John from St. Benedict also had left for Winnipeg the evening before.

When we got to the hospital, we saw that mother was ill. She had her arms tied to the bed, so she would not scratch her face or take out the intravenous. She was talking funny. She told us that some people dressed in white came to the house and took her and father and brought them to this building where we are gathered. We told her that she is in the hospital, but that did not seem to come to her. She told us she was taken to some room and there on the wall she saw a long saw, like we had on the farm, and the people used this saw to cut off people's heads. When people heard that mother was ill, many warm and sincere prayers were offered. Slowly, slowly mother recuperated from her illness and lived until 1993 when she passed away at the age of eighty-six at Wakaw, Saskatchewan. Later the doctors came to the conclusion that she had a brain hemorrhage, a stroke and heart attack all at the same time and that was why it was hard for them to designate and decipher what was wrong with her because of the sympt

I have already mentioned above that Alice was married in October 1955 and was living at St. Benedict, Saskatchewan some fifteen miles south of Tarnopol. As for the marriage of the rest of us, it was a few years later that, John, Oksana and I got married. John had taken special training in Saskatoon to be a mechanic. After completing his course he worked in Saskatoon for a while. There in Saskatoon he met Doreen Kluz who was in a wheelchair and he married her at Wadena, Saskatchewan on July 16 - 1960. They lived for awhile in Saskatoon and than moved to Winnipeg where John got a job. John and Doreen had two boys, Gregory and Philip. Things did not work out, their marriage broke up and they were divorced. The older son Gregory went to be with John and Philip stayed with his mother in Winnipeg. John moved to Edmonton and worked there and Gregory attended school. Later John worked in such places as Inuvik, Hay River, Tuktoyaktak and other places in the North West Territories. He worked for Wajax company in Edmonton. In Edmonton he met Kay Vesochyn and they got married in May 1980. At the time of this writing (2016) they are still living in Edmonton and are retired.

As for Oksana her life did not fare much better. After the parents had the auction sale and moved out of Tarnopol, Oksana was still attending school so she stayed with John and Helen Chytyk at Tarnopol and went to school from their place. Oksana could not have gone with the parents after the auction sale, because the parents themselves did not know what would happen to them in the days to come. After the parents were settled in Winnipeg, it was at the end of 1956 that I went to Saskatchewan and brought Oksana to Winnipeg. Here she lived with the parents and has been in Winnipeg since that day. Oksana finished her schooling and than went to work in hospitals, drug store, restaurants, motor hotels, etc. Her life carried no roses either. She married Lawrence Foley in December 1960 and she had three girls, Brenda, Gail and Cathy and one son Lawrence. Misfortune struck Oksana's family on April 3 - 1975 when her husband passed away from a sudden and massive heart attack at home at the young age of forty-two. Oksana was left with the three girls and son Lawrence who was only one month old at the time of his father's passing. The year 1960 brought much pain to our family. I was married in June 1960, John in July 1960 and Oksana in December 1960. All three marriages suffered. In my life, I married Mary Olinec and she passed away in March 1982. John was divorced from his wife Doreen and Oksana lost her husband in 1975 at an early age.

JOB HUNTING

Let us go back to the year 1957 when I was discharged from the RCAF. June came as it did in past years. The parents and Oksana had been living on Maryland Avenue, so naturally after I got discharged from the service, they told me to come and live there also. It's not a matter of living with the parents, but I would like to do something to help contribute to the welfare of the family. I have to find a job. But, what kind of a job can I find and get ahead anywhere? Well, go to the unemployment office and see what there is and leave my name there. Because I was in the military and was released, I thought I had a better chance of getting a job than someone who just walks off the street looking for employment. In my case it did not work, because my name was Stefaniuk. I went day after day to the unemployment office but the answer was always the same: "Nothing today, try again tomorrow." This went on from one day to the next. I also bought the Winnipeg Free Press Daily and looked for jobs there. One day when I came to the unemployment office, I was asked if I would consider working as a waiter in a hotel. I was ready and willing to do anything, as long as I get some money coming in to help pay for the room and board with the parents.

I was sent with a paper to the Cabinet Hotel in Winnipeg. The hotel owner gave me a licence badge to work in a hotel in the bar room and waiting on customers. I was now on work for two full days, before I quite as a beer waiter in a hotel. After staying for two days in the hotel, smelling cigarette smoke and fumes in the parlor, I became ill. I became nauseated and pain in my stomach. I wasn't feeling well at all and thought it would be easier to die than survive the way I was feeling. Another thing that brought on this problem was that it was the roughest part of the city. As I would bring beer to the tables, I was paid by the customer. I would give change to the customer, turn and go to another table. The customer where I had given the change yells to me: "Waiter, you gave me the wrong change." Well at first I thought, maybe I did. It was a new job, and I wasn't feeling well already and I was not familiar with the scams that the customers pulled on the waiters. When I turned away from the table and unto the next one, the customer quickly pulled of the table the dollar bill or some change when my eyes where not watching. Than he calls and says that I did not give him the correct change. So what do I do? Maybe I did short change the man. So I shovel out the difference and give it to him. This happened a few times, but than I caught on to the tricks of the customers and made sure I counted out the exact change each time I put the money on the table.

As mentioned, after two days, I had to give up this work. I lost my appetite, was nauseated, and pain in my stomach. The two days I worked there I had to go to the bathroom and get a drink of cold water each time to help carry me through the day. Later after quitting that job, I was at home and was still ill. I tried to eat or drink different things, but nothing seemed to help. My eyes could have eaten a horse with hooves, but when the food came to the mouth, there was no taste nor appetite. I would maybe swallow a spoonful of something and that was my meal. I had started to lose weight and was now only a hundred pounds, and mother said that I go and see Dr. Buchok, who was her doctor. The family would sit to a meal, and I would look at the food and say I'm not hungry. Mother would tell me to eat, and I would say I have no appetite and not hungry. Looking at me mother would say: "Well look at you. If I put you outside on the back lane tonight, two cats would not have enough of you for their meal by morning."

Even though I was not feeling well, I still knew in my heart that I should help the family with costs. After more coxing from mother, I got enough courage and went to see Dr. Buchok. I had some tests done and later the clinic called that Dr. Buchok wanted to see me. I went to see him and the result was that I had a nervous stomach. Dr. Buchok gave me a prescription. I started taking the pills and soon began to feel and got better.

Very well I can remember how I went to the unemployment office each day seeking employment and the answer was always the same: "Nothing today." When I went to the unemployment office, I went very early, so that if there was any job, I would be first in line. When I got there, I would find a lineup from the door before the office was opened. I stood in line as did the others. It was summer and the days were nice and warm and for a young man nothing to stand for a few minutes. The door would open and the line would move inside. Everyone was going in order that they arrived at the building. I saw odd people getting papers and leaving, having gotten a job. I don't know what kind of jobs they were getting. When I came up to the wicket I even mentioned to them that I had served in the RCAF and was just released and was looking for employment. The answer was as before: "Nothing today."

It was still early in the morning. Slowly, taking my time I walked the slow walk. Along the way I stopped and bought the Winnipeg Free Press to check the ads for employment. As soon as I bought the paper, I stepped a few feet away, opened the paper to check the want ads. There I found an ad that said: "Wanted, shipper, packer and receiver." Well I can go and try that job and see what its all about. Maybe no one has yet beat me to that address. Now as fast as my feet could carry me, I thought I was flying, hurrying to the address to inquire about the job. The address was on Market Street which was north, just across the street from the old Winnipeg City Hall.

I walked quickly and hoping that someone had not beaten me to the address by this time. I knew that it would not be worst than what I had heard a while before: "Nothing today." I found the address and the large sign above the door saying: SNYDER and McCULLOUGH. It was right on the corner of the street. I walked in. A lovely lady was sitting at the desk in front of a typewriter. We exchanged hellos, and I said I came to inquire about the job mentioned in the paper. The lady with whom I later worked went to see the manager, Mr. McCullough in the next room. She came out a minute later and asked me to step inside and see the manager. After introducing myself and being asked a few questions by Mr. McCullough, he said that I can start working tomorrow morning at 8:00 AM and asked me if I would be satisfied with forty dollars a week for pay. I said I would be very pleased with that pay. I could have kissed the man for his good heart. Wow, now I have a job and that will be $160.00 per month. Forty dollars a week is better than nothing. Tomorrow I start work at 8:00 AM. Someone will have to tell me and show me what to do, but that is for tomorrow, today I fly home in midair, I have a job. I taught school it was $140.00 a month and now I will be getting $160.00 a month and increase of $20.00 a month in some four years. Yes I know today there are many people working who get that in an hour and they are still not pleased and satisfied.

It was a good place to work. In the summer and winter the work was indoors. Out of the hot sun in the summer and out of the cold in the winter. My work was to keep records of all things that came in and went out as well as pack and ship out orders. When shipments came in, I had to unpack and keep track of all. It was a small firm. Mr. McCullough was the manager. Mr. Sandison was a salesman, Mrs. Mildred Empson the secretary and I was the shipper, packer and receiver. Mr. Sandison was away most of the time. He traveled from Thunder Bay, Ontario to Lloydminster, Saskatchewan. He sold and took orders for the products that the firm carried. Mr. Mccullough did all the selling in Winnipeg and looked after the operation of the company.

This company had Richards glass. They were pill bottles and containers that were sold to drug stores for filling prescription medications. There was also the Noxzema line of beauty cream. The firm also carried the Moore-Clinger veterinary line of products. A few other smaller lines of products were carried by this firm. Sometimes orders came in the mail, but mostly were coming in from Mr. Sandison who was out selling the above products. When the orders came in, my job was to fill the orders, pack and ship out. When goods were received I had to check the supplies, I had to unpack and restock the shelves.

The place were I worked also had an alarm system installed. Why? Because there were drugs for veterinary use that was stocked in the place. The alarm system was hooked up to the police station. Every time someone came in first or left last, they had to send a signal to the police. About a week after I had worked in this place, Mr. McCullough gave me a key to the front door. He showed me how to operate the alarm system and said: "Now if you ever want to come in earlier to do something or stay later you have the key and know how to operate the alarm." He said I can come and go whenever I feel I need to do something in the place. I was happy. In only one week, Mr. McCullough had put enough faith and trust in me, that he gave me a key and alarm system code.

I had started working here sometimes probably in late July or early August. I had been released from the RCAF in June. I had been looking for work everyday before I found this job. After I started working here the people found out I was Ukrainian. Later came winter and the Christmas season. Then came the New Year and after that what sometimes is called "Ukrainian Christmas." On January 6th as we were getting ready to leave for home and to lock up, Mr. McCullough stopped me before I went out and says: "Is it your Christmas tomorrow?" I said, that it was. He put his hand into his pocket, took out a ten dollar bill handed it over to me and says: "Here take this small gift and I don't want to see you here tomorrow." I just about cried from joy. I'm hardly known and here such great expression of confidence towards me. It showed me than and there that there are still some good people in this world, only they all don't live together.

The staff where I worked were very friendly and kind to each other and because of that it was a healthy place to work. Sometimes when someone had to take some time off for some reason, no one ever questioned anyone why or where they were going or how soon they would be back. Everyone just substituted for the other person. I worked at the back of the building and in the basement where some goods were stored. I had a large table which I used for packing and unpacking. When I had the goods packed, I let the secretary know and she phoned the railroad or trucking company that there was a parcel to be picked up.

One day after I had been working for a few months, I got my pay cheque. I glanced at it and saw that it was more than it had been before. Must be some error. I looked at it again and told the secretary that there was an error. She looked at me from behind the counter, smiled and said that she was only following the boss's order. She said that Mr. McCullough had told her that he was very pleased and satisfied with my work and for that he gave me a raise.

So now I had a job and was helping out the family with expenses that were around us. In the meantime, come Sunday it was always church day. As I have already mentioned previously, that when I was still in the RCAF, I had found that something was missing. When I ended up in Winnipeg, that empty void began to fill when I could go to my own church every Sunday, when I was free and not on duty. Sometimes some people are funny and queer, if one can call them that. When I was in the RCAF and used to come to church, I came in uniform. After many weeks of attending church at the cathedral, I was never approached by anyone to come forward and ask: "Who are you? Where did you come from? What are you doing here in Winnipeg?" Everyone just seemed to mind their own business and everything else was of no concern to them. They were seeing this man in uniform coming to church week after week, you would think someone would became interested and wanted to know who this fellow was. One time they gave me to hold a candle during the service one Sunday and than another Sunday. When they saw that I wasn't swinging the candle and attacking anyone, they thought it was safe enough to step forward and find out who I was.

Finally after many weeks, one single man, Paul Misiak, got enough courage and approached me. He introduced himself and asked who I was. Now I knew someone in the church. He asked me to go with him to his place and we had dinner at his place that Sunday afternoon. After this our friendship was more like brothers than just friends. He was single and so was I. He had no girlfriend and neither did I. When I was off duty, I would jump into the car and go visit him. We sat many times at his place and talked for hours. Other times we would drive out to some café to have ice cream and chat. Many times we would just sit in the parked car on a street and watched the life of the city move about as we talked about many different subjects. After I became friends with him, he began to introduce me to other people in the church. He also sang in the church choir. One year when it was Easter Sunday, when the parents were still on the farm, and I was in Winnipeg, I went to church for the Easter service. One family Andrew and Nellie Pawlik stepped forward and invited me to come to their place for the blessed Easter morning breakfast. In 2015 Mrs. Pawlik passed away.

When I was out of the service, I was in church every single time, never missing a service on Sunday. The whole week would just go so well for me, but if I happened not to be in church, the whole week long seemed to bring some form of bad luck as we say. Than one time after the church service it happened. The late Father Michael Yurkiwsky came up to me and asked me to teach Sunday school. I was hesitant to talk on something that I was not acquainted with. He kept convincing me that I would have no problem and that he would prepare the lesson for each Sunday and I would just have to teach it to the children. I finally accepted and was given the task to teach the oldest class. Younger children were taught in some small closed rooms in the church basement, at the same time the services were being held. My class was held at St. Andrew's College at 259 Church Avenue, about two or three blocks north of the cathedral. When it wasn't cold, it was alright, but when it was cold, it was just **soooo** cold to walk the few blocks to the cathedral.

One day after the service father had taken a day off from his work and we went to see William Shewchuk who lived south-east of Winnipeg on the farm. This Sunday I did not teach Sunday school. Once a month, Father Yurkiwsky taught Sunday school himself on that afternoon in the church basement where all the children from the cathedral would gather. As father and I were returning from Shewchuk's place I was in a hurry, because I wanted to be in the cathedral when Father Yurkiwsky was teaching the sixty or so students of Sunday School. We took a different road coming back. Coming out to a crossroad, I saw there had been a new wide road constructed. It was a new road but there were no signs placed along that road. As we were entering the crossroad, I looked in both directions and could not see anything for a mile or so each way, I just slowed down and kept on going.

Suddenly from nowhere a police cruiser is approaching towards us with flashing lights. The cruiser stops and the constable steps out and puts his hand out to stop me. I pull over and father and I started to talk, that maybe some prisoner escaped from the jail or the prison and he wants to know if we didn't see anyone. I stopped and rolled down my window. The officer comes near and says: "Do you know that you must stop when you enter a trunk highway?" I looked at him and say: "But officer, I have never traveled here before, I did not know this is a highway, and besides there is no stop sign." He asked me for my drivers licence and car registration and took them to his car with him.

Father in the meantime is already in flames and tells me: "You go and get his police badge number and we'll fix him." I kept telling father not to say anything, because we could get into more trouble. I told father that I remember not stopping, for I did not know it was a highway and there was no stop sign. Anyway it ended up, that I got my first ever ticket for not stopping entering a trunk highway. The officer came back to our car and handed me a ticket saying: "You can get rid of this anytime this week after Thursday at the Law Courts Building in Winnipeg." Then father and I continued on our way to the cathedral where Father Yurkiwsky was holding Sunday School classes.

Next day I was back at work. When Thursday came, I asked Mr. McCullough if I could have a few hours off because of what had happened the past Sunday. I told him that I would probably have to pay a fine. He said that I could go and asked me if I needed any money and I said no. How could I take money from him, when its not his fault that I did not stop. On the way to the court house, I stopped at the bank and took out $25.00 hoping that this would be enough to pay for the fine, if I am not sent to jail.

I reported to the clerk at the desk in the Law Courts Building on Broadway Avenue, not far from the Manitoba Legislature Buildings. The clerk took my ticket and said to have a seat and they will call me. After a while my name was called and I was told to go to a certain wicket. I approached the wicket and there sitting on the other side was an old grey-haired judge. His glasses were on the tip of his nose. He read something to me and than says: "Are you guilty or not?" So what do I tell him? I say: "I guess I'm not guilty, but I have to be guilty here." When I said that I thought his glasses would fall of his nose to the floor had he not grabbed them. He looks at me sharply and says: "What?" I than try to explain to him what happened and how I got that ticket. I told him there is no stop sign and I had never traveled in that area before and did not know that it was a trunk highway. Later I found out that highway was highway number #59 going south from Winnipeg to the USA border.

The judge again has another look at me like he could eat me alive without salt, and in a gloomy looking mood and again asks: "Guilty or not guilty?" Afraid of getting into hotter water with this judge, than I am now, I had no alternative at that time, so I just thought: "Whatever will be, will be." I say to him: "Not guilty, but this time I'm guilty." He pounds his gavel on the counter, so hard I thought it would break off and than says: "Five dollars fine, plus two dollars and fifty cents, court costs or seven days in jail." Without even thinking, I say: "I'll pay." He hands me a piece of paper and says: "Go see the clerk over there", pointing with his gavel. I paid the $7.50 and that was my first fine ever I had to pay. Later I paid another fine at Yorkton, Saskatchewan in 1959 which again was not my fault. The fine I paid in Yorkton, I later received back from the man I was working for. This will be explained later when we get to that period of time. The fine that I paid in Winnipeg was a good lesson for me. From that day to this whenever there is a stop sign and it says stop, that's what it means, to S T O P. It does not mean: "Spin Tires On Pavement." I have been driving since 1951 and only paid two traffic fines in that time and have probably covered between two and three million miles since. When I returned back to work and told them at work of the episode and it cost me only $7.50, they laughed and said that I had gotten away Scott free. The place were I was working later was all torn down because Winnipeg City Hall took the land for the New City Hall. There was one more ticket that I got and this was on the 16th of April 2010 in Osoyoos, British Columbia for going to fast past a school. It was a $138.00 but the kind constable wrote across it: "warning."

CHILDHOOD ACTIONS BEGIN TO FULFILL

While still working at Snyder and McCullough, as stated above, I always attended church services on Sundays. One day after the service Father Yurkiwsky called me to the side away from everybody else and says: " Ewheny, why don't you go to St. Andrew's College to study and become a priest?" I never gave much thought to it and probably gave him some answer just to get away from the topic.

It was a few months later, a theology student who was later ordained and now deceased, the late Father Mykola Stetzenko, came up to me with the same question. I don't know if maybe Father Yurkiwsky had told Mykola Stetzenko to approach me with the topic, for he says: "Ewhen, come to St. Andrew's College to study for a priest." I gave him a few excuses like: "I can't sing." He says, "They will teach you to sing." Than I say: "I can't speak well and give sermons." Again he answers: "They will teach you." Whatever excuse I gave him, he had an answer for that. In the end I told him that I can't read or write in Ukrainian and again he says: "They also teach that at the college." So I was left with no excuses, but still said that I would not go. Then Mykola Stetzenko says: "Where do your parents live?" I told him that they live in Winnipeg and he said that he would like to meet them. We get into my car and I drive home to Maryland Avenue this one late Sunday afternoon.

I introduced Stetzenko to my parents and after a few exchanged words of who, where and what, he says to my parents: "Panstvo Stefaniuky! We would like to see your son Ewhen become a priest, to come to St. Andrew's College." Mother said that I am old enough and can make my own decisions and no one don't have to tell me anymore what to do. Father was different because he first would sit still and say nothing but think and than says: "Let him go to university for two years and than he can go out and teach in school. He could teach six hours a day and not have to worry about any hard work."

At that time it was easy to get into the priesthood because there was always a shortage of priests same as today. I began questioning Stetzenko: "Suppose I go to study for a year or so and than I wouldn't like it, than what will I do?" He answers me saying: "You'll enjoy this type of school and work so much that you won't want to quit." Yes he was correct. For every question I put before him, he had an answer. He along with Father Yurkiwsky kept convincing me that year to get into theology. It was spring of 1958, that I finally gathered enough courage to say yes and to enroll at St. Andrew's College to start theology classes in the fall of that year.

When fall 1958 came around, I found myself sitting in a desk with other students at the old St. Andrews College on 259 Church Avenue in north Winnipeg. When October 6th came, on my birth date, I began my four year course of studies. Tuition fee at that time was $100.00 per year. Because I lived in Winnipeg with my parents board and room were not charged. I did though have to take a bus each morning and afternoon to get to classes which was about four or five miles away. I don't recall whatever happened to my car I had that I had to take the bus to the college. Other students from outside Winnipeg lived right at the college.

After completing one year of study at the seminary, I noticed that the students which stayed at the college gained more knowledge. Why? Because many times there were some extra curricular studies going on in the evening which I was missing out on. Sometimes special guests would speak or be invited in the evening for discussions which I was missing out. There were prayers held morning and night which I was not present for. They sang prayers and learned which I did not because I was not there. I would have had to make another trip by bus in the evenings to participate in extra programs. And yes it was as I was told, that once I start, I will not want to stop my studies. The more time I spent in learning and listening the more I was enjoying the studies and for looking forward to the profession being a servant of God. It took four years and then it was out unto your own to put into practice what I learned at the college. The late Metropolitan Ilarion used to say: "My sons, I can teach you theory, but the parishioners will give the practical work on your parish." How true those words are even today.

A TRAVELING SUMMER JOB AND ENGAGEMENT

I decided that for my second year of theology I will stay at the college to take part in all activities that take place. By doing so, I would need extra finances besides the tuition fees. When classes concluded in the spring of 1959 with one year of studies behind me, I started job hunting for summer work. Getting a job only for the summer months was not that easy to find. But God was on my side. Looking through the paper one day, I found an ad that someone was looking for summer help. I took the address, got on the bus, and hurried over to get there before someone else beats me. As the bus rolled along the Winnipeg streets, many thoughts were flooding my mind. What kind of a job is it? What is the pay? What kind hours? How long is this summer job? I got off the bus and started to walk towards the address. What kind of a job is this? This is all residential homes here. What kind of work for the summer could be here in a private home? As I walked I was becoming hesitant about the job, as I got nearer the address. Should I go on or return? Maybe this is some kind of a trick or some crooked job?

I came to the address and walked up to the side door of a private house. As I was coming up, I noticed a man in the back yard painting some long pieces of four by four lumber in different colors and designs. What in the world is that for, was my first thought. We introduced ourselves and I told him that I was answering the ad for the job. The man kept painting as we talked along. He began to tell of his business and said that he owns the "Great West Shows", a carnival where he goes to summer fairs. He needs someone to drive a three ton truck for him and to operate a Ferris Wheel. When he said to operate a Ferris Wheel, all my hope fell into my shoes. I never operated a Ferris Wheel before and don't know anything about it. Another thing I need, but didn't have, was a chauffeurs licence to drive a three ton truck. The man assured me that if I have a driver's licence I will have no problem getting a chauffeurs licence. After talking for a while the man hired me for the summer, because we would be finished at the end of September and that would be in time to start my second year classes. The man was right. Going back home I stopped at where drivers licences were issued and just filling out a form I got a chauffeurs licence even before I got home.

The job was now mine for the summer. He said he would teach me how to operate the Ferris Wheel and I would have no problem. He would pay me $40.00 per week. If t rains and we don't operate that day or even for a whole week, I still get paid. Hey, that's a good job. I would be in charge of my own meals and a place to sleep. We would be starting the first day of operation in Kildonan Park on Henderson Highway north-east in Winnipeg. After that we will head out to Saskatchewan to summer fairs and from there we will go to Ontario. Well that sounds to good to be true. I knew that through this work I would get to meet many and all kinds of people for all kinds of people go to fairs. Now I knew what the man had been painting when I first met him. He was painting the long poles which were a part of the Merry-go-round. The man owned three rides, a Ferris Wheel, a Merry-go-round and another smaller airplane ride for the children. I operated the Ferris Wheel, another man operated the kiddies small ride and the owner ran the merry-go round. The man that operated the children's ride had only one eye and he also drove the small vehicle which pulled the children's ride on a trailer. The owners wife sold tickets for the rides.

Now came the day when we started to play at the fairs. After I arrived where everything was stored, we drove to the Kildonan playground. I had to learn the ins and outs of the truck operation first. The Ferris Wheel was on the truck. After the truck was driven where the Ferris Wheel would operate, came the time to get the Ferris Wheel of the truck. "Who is going to lift that thing off that truck?", I thought to myself. But the owner had everything figured out. All we had to do, was move the Ferris Wheel two feet or so to the back of the truck. Than push on it and it just lifts and slides off the truck. Nothing to it. The seats for the Ferris Wheel were above the cab of the truck in a built shelf. Once everything was ready and operational, the boss showed me what and how to run the Ferris Wheel. Always the Ferris Wheel had to be loaded evenly, balanced, otherwise if the wheel is out of balance, problems could arise. As the operation went into motion, I got the handle of what and how and away I went for the rest of the summer.

After we finished playing at the park, everything was put back in the way it was before setting up, only this time in reverse order. When all was in place the vehicles were driven back to the storage area and left there for a few days before we start the trip to Saskatchewan.

So now came the day to leave Winnipeg. The first stop in Saskatchewan was at Sturgis on July 1st 1959. Who would have said that some twenty years later I would be living near Sturgis and serving the church beside the highway. Sometimes I wonder if there were any people from the church I served later going for a Ferris Wheel ride when I was there on July 1st 1959. Only God knows the answer to that question. I told members of the congregation about this later, but no one could remember or recall that far back if they remembered me. Unless someone may have been there with a camera and taken a picture, today we would know. But what a small world this has become and holds unexpected futures for each and everyone of us.

Then from Sturgis the work took us farther west into Saskatchewan. We stopped at places like Watrous, Unity, Stoughton, Creelman and many other places in between which took us to the end of July and the first days of August. We arrived back in Winnipeg and had a few days rest before venturing out east into Ontario. On August 10th we left for the east and did not return back to Winnipeg until October 6th, the day of my birthday. As mentioned earlier I was paid $40.00 per week for my labors. By the time we returned back to Winnipeg in October my wage had been substantially increased.

For meals many times we would grab a hamburger from a booth at the fair with a coke and that was our lunch. In the evenings, sometimes after everything was finished and ready to roll to the next town, we might go to a café and have a meal, but this was seldom done. Sometimes we would buy something at the booth on the grounds and would consume it after the work was finished. As for sleeping, the man with the one eye would put his sleeping bag on the ground under the three ton truck and would sleep there. I copied his system. This was also a kind of security, because if anyone approached the vehicles we would hear and they would be frightened off. The owner and his wife slept in their large station wagon. If the weather was not very warm or rainy, I would take out two or three seats of the Ferris Wheel out of the shelf and crawl myself into the shelf and sleep there like in a house. The man with the one eye in such times would sleep in his vehicle which he drove during the day.

As I traveled around the country with this show, thoughts came and went from me that if I'm going to finish my schooling to become a priest, I will need to find a girl whom I can marry, and who would be my helpmate in my future life. If I would not marry, I would not be ordained, for in the Orthodox church the man must first be married before he would be ordained. I would have to find a Ukrainian girl, same faith as mine. How could I look for such a girl at this job? Do I ask each girl that comes for a ride if she is Ukrainian and Orthodox? Than I still had that shyness with me. No it still had not left me, even though I already had taught school for a year and spent three years in the military. How do I approach a girl and start talking with her? What do I say? What kind questions could I ask? One day as we were stationed in Long Lac and Geraldton, Ontario, the boss came to take over the operation of the Ferris Wheel from me, so that I could have a break for a bite to eat. It was evening and the sun was setting. The lights from the show lit up the area around the grounds and the rides. As I returned back with my snack and stood at the side watching things, there I see that the boss is talking to the people as they board or dislodge from the seats of the Ferris Wheel.

As he was taking the tickets from the people going on the Ferris Wheel, I see the boss pat one lady on the back or hug her to make her feel happy. The boss would shout to the ladies to come and take their boyfriend for a ride. He would encourage the ladies, talk and smile to them. After watching this for about ten fifteen minutes, I realized that the women were not angry at him or insulted, but seemed to enjoy that sort talk. As I watched all this I noticed that this encouraged the ladies or girls to get another ticket and come back for another ride. The more rides people had, the more money came in for the owners. After watching him operate in this manner, I thought I should try the same kind of system. I saw the ladies and girls never bit, spit, or got angry with him. If they did not do that to the boss, they probably would not do any harm to me either.

So I started a new page in my life that evening. As people walked by or lined up to go for a ride, I would shout out: "Okay sweetie pie, come on for a ride of your life." Or I would say: "Come here beautiful, why are you waiting. You can be next. Get your ticket and I'll give you a ride." Another time I would say: "Okay, now where is your boyfriend? Get him to take you for a ride. I won't send you to the moon, only into the sky." One other time I would say: "Now, now ladies look at the beautiful sky up there and you can't see it as well from here, as you can up in the air. Get your boyfriend and come for a ride." All kinds of things I shouted out and I saw some that were coming back for second rides.

As we settled for the night that day and I was laying in my sleeping bag under the truck, thoughts of the past few hours came back to me. Before falling asleep I thought to myself: "See Eugene, how you talked to people and no one got angry and hit you, but all seemed to have fun and enjoyed it." With all these past scenes flashing past me under the truck, slowly I drifted away and fell asleep. This style and type of work changed my life and slowly that shyness that had been with me from my earliest days was slowly beginning to sink into the deep dark pit and I was beginning to see a new world coming out before me. Now I seemed to be like all other normal people. By the time we got into southern Ontario around Paris, Orangeville, Kincardine, Hanover and other places, my shyness was lost somewhere in the deep forests of Northern Ontario along the Trans Canada Highway. I felt like a big hero. I would be able to talk to any girl or lady if she wanted to talk to me.

Before I get back to Manitoba and on the trip to Ontario, let me mention one more thing. My memory just reminded me of a girl that I knew in Winnipeg which I met through church services and CYMK. CYMK means: Canadian Ukrainian Youth Association. This girl in

Winnipeg was also of the shy nature like I was. I had met this girl in the winter when I was attending St. Andrews College. At this time I do not recall her name, but she was Ukrainian, Orthodox, so was this maybe my girl for my future? I had been looking for friendship and companionship before I would consider any serious talk about marriage. Maybe she was only looking for a good time to go out and have fun. She had come to Winnipeg from someplace in Saskatchewan and was working in the city, but I do not recall what she was doing. We had gone a few times to movies or just went for a ride and than sat in the car by her place and talked. Her parents, also lived in Winnipeg, so she was at home. I told her that I was taking theology and someday would become a priest in the church. She had nothing against me to be a priest or against priests in general.

After we had been going around for a while I brought her home to meet my parents. Mother was very happy because this girl talked very well in Ukrainian and she was a pretty girl. One time my parents and I took her out for a ride to Seven Sisters Falls, NE of Winnipeg. After we had been going out together for a while, I brought up the subject of marriage. I asked her if she would marry me and she said that she still wanted to stay single for a number of years. After that we never went out again. Maybe that was just a good excuse to brush me off. We had known each other for about half a year and during that time we never embraced or kissed each other. Was it my shyness that brushed her off from me? Maybe she saw that I was not very romantic, so she wanted to stay single. After this we only saw each other at church services.

Now we move deeper into Ontario and to what transpired after we left Long Lac and Geraldton. My shyness was beginning to get left behind. More and more I began to think that now I will be able to find someone who will spend the rest of her life with me. I had three more years of theology left. If I want to be a priest, I have to be married. Yes at fairs and rodeos many people come and go, but you don't get to know them who they are. We were here today and gone to another place tomorrow. There is no time to get acquainted with anyone when you are busy at work. Than how do you know what nationality and faith they are as they come for a ride on the Ferris Wheel? At fairs I did not carry a sign with me saying that this man is looking for such and such a girl. Even if you see someone you like during the fair, you can't talk to them, because you are busy keeping an eye on the Ferris Wheel to see that nothing happens. If you want to meet someone they will not wait for hours until you finish your work. That was my situation, that at the fairs I would not find a mate.

But it was not so. I did meet a beautiful angel while working the Ferris Wheel. Just to have looked at the girl, you thought you were looking at an angel sent from God. She was, oh so pretty and I remember her name, Christine, even a Christian name. This happened in a little town in Kincardine, Ontario on the shores of Lake Huron, south-west of Toronto. We just happened to stay in Kincardine for two days before we had to move on to the next town. This Christine was a very pretty and beautiful girl. When you looked into her eyes, you thought an angel was looking at you. We met and talked when I was free from work. We had met when I was operating the Ferris Wheel. I must have called her some pretty name or something like that which she liked. When she got off the ride, I don't remember what I said to her, but after that she roamed around the fair grounds and would always return back to be not far from the Ferris Wheel.

I believe that she had fallen for me as I had for her. I learned that she was English and an Anglican. I had told her what I was doing and if I could have stayed a few more days and seen her a few more times, maybe things could have been different and progressed with our acquaintance of each other. She said that she attended church every Sunday and her family were religious. If we could have continued with a relationship, I know she would have learned Ukrainian and she would have loved our faith, for her eyes told the whole story. We exchanged addresses and promised to write to each other. I wrote her a few letters from Ontario and asked her not to write to me until I get home to Winnipeg, because I have no address on my travels at work on the road.

When I got back to Winnipeg, I wrote her a letter and told her that I was home and she could write to me to the address I enclosed. I never heard from her and all my hopes were quelled. Maybe if the distance between Winnipeg and Kincardine would have been shorter, maybe there could have been a romance started. I guess she was not to be mine, and that was the end of Christine, God's angel in Kincardine. God works in wonders and it will never be the way we want but the way He wants. My late mother used to say: "We make plans and God changes them." How true that is in our lives.

When I got back from Ontario, I went back to college. I was a few days late this year for the studies had already started three or four days ago when I was still on the road heading home. This year I was staying at the college. About two weeks after I got back from Ontario a friend of mine Bill Kyrdiak, met me after church service and says: "Ewheny, I have a girl for you." "Who? Where?" I asked. I did not know if to believe him, but he said that he would make arrangements for me to meet her. And so he did. He made arrangement and I met this girl, Mary Olinec, who was the only child in the family. Seeing a person for the first time, one can't tell too much, but she looked like a nice quiet person. I remember one thing, she smoked as did her father. It was after we had met and began seeing each other that I asked her to quit smoking. She did. We began to phone each other and meet whenever possible. At this time I was already twenty-seven years old and she was twenty-two. We began to know each other better and better acquainted with her parents. She was Ukrainian and Orthodox but went to a different Orthodox congregation in Winnipeg. There are four or five Ukrainian Orthodox congregations in Winnipeg

I told her that I was at St. Andrews College studying to become a priest. I don't know if she cared for me at that time, because later, much later after we were married, I learned she had an eye for another boy she knew, but I never asked her about it. Her late mother Lena Olinec, always kept telling her about me: "Mariyko, if you marry him, you will not have to go to work again." Later I myself told her that if we marry, she will have to change her way of life, because a priests wife must live somewhat different than other wives and to spend more time for church and God. When she said she could live with those changes, we began to get serious talking about marriage. She had been working for the "Nutty Candy Company" in Winnipeg.

We met about the middle of October 1959. Approximately one month later on November 15th we were engaged after one month courtship. Now I knew I had someone by my side for the rest of my life. I continued my school and we set our wedding day for June 4th 1960. Before we got married, I believe that we had gone out to a few movies and I think to one dance. Eight months after we met we were married in the Holy Trinity Ukrainian Orthodox Cathedral on Main Street in Winnipeg by the late Father Michael Yurkiwsky. Looking on the Internet on July 15th 2016 I found a sad and disturbing item. The cathedral on Main Street in

Winnipeg where I was ordained a Deacon had a fire. It says the fire is suspicious and looks like arson. The damage has been placed at one million dollars. Talking with my sister in Winnipeg on Skype, she said there is talk that a ten year old boy probably set fire to the cathedral, but nothing has been confirmed yet.

Marriage. What a joyful time. But we had to live someplace. I wanted to rent out an apartment or house, but Mary's parents would hear nothing of it. They had a three bedroom house and they said there was enough room for all of us to live there. She was the only child in the family. I wanted to be out on our own for I knew that sometimes in-laws do not always get along too well. I had no choice, but had to go with what her parents were saying. There were three of them and I was one. I soon found out after living together that her parents always did things their way, and their daughter and my wife always sided with her parents instead of her husband. Many times when I would say something, her parents would disagree with me and she would take the side of her parents. They in turn would always take her side if she said anything. I could already see that there may be a problem in the future life together. I also knew that we will be with her parents for two years and than we would be going on our own, once I was ordained and sent to serve a parish. As time will show later, things did not work out any better when we were alone, because she was always lonely for her parents and their house.

That same year when we got married on June 4th. I had to serve with Metropolitan Ilarion at a service the day after our marriage for he was having a service in the cathedral on Sunday and the next day and after that being Monday I went to work. I had already gotten a summer job with Orange Crush and was making sixty cents an hour. I was the helper for the truck driver who was also the salesman. We delivered pop to stores around Winnipeg and on each day we had a different territory or route to serve. It was hard work. Many times we had to carry three full cases of drinks into basements through which one could hardly squeeze through and coming back up, we would carry three empty cases of glass bottles. At that time it was still all glass bottles, no plastic or cans. In some places there was enough room that we could use a two wheeled cart and haul down four, or five cases at a time. As mentioned it was heavy work and the pay was not very large. Sometimes when the sales were larger and we needed longer hours to cover the territory there was overtime and the pay than came to time and a half which gave me a large salary of ninety cents an hour with overtime. At this same time Mary was still working at the "Nutty Candy Company" as a stenographer. She had taken a typist-stenographer course and knew that type of work. We could have easily lived in an apartment, but I had to abide by the three against one to keep peace in the family. I had no choice.

In the fall of 1960, I went back to school. This was now the beginning of my third year in college. We were still living with Mary's parents. Living with in-laws is not always the best. Yes it is very good in some cases, I was not that lucky. I soon found out her parents John and Lena Olinec, were not very religious people. At times I had disagreements with them about church and religion and Mary always took the side of her parents. Her father worked for the CNR and was cleaning railroad coaches. Her mother worked in the laundry department for the large Marlborough Hotel in downtown Winnipeg. When father-in-law retired, he was only a few days short of working for the CNR to have received a pension. Living for two full years with the in-laws, I never ever heard how much they made at their work. When I worked for Orange Crush and got paid, I brought the cheque home and everybody saw it and touched it with their hands. When I cashed the cheque, I turned over fifty to seventy-five percent to Mary's parents to help pay for cost of food, etc. They never talked about money, how much they made or how much they had, yet Mary knew everything but never told me anything. How much their bank account was I didn't know. Maybe that was none of my business, but usually family matters are known by all family members. No one ever told me anything.

Mary's father was a drinker. On Saturdays he did not work, so afternoon he would go downtown and spend the evening in a hotel or in a friends house. He had friends and they were kept busy buying rounds of beer for each other in the hotel. Many times he came home drunk, but I was already asleep when he would come home late Saturday night. Next morning I would learn that he was drunk, because mother-in-law would be making fun of him that he had been drunk the night before. The morning following the drinking spree of the night before, there was no interest for them in going to church. There were times that Saturday night the phone would ring at 10:00 PM and his friends would ask that I come and pick up father-in-law at such and such a place. This would happen a number of times during the year. I recall how one time I was called to come and pick him up at his friends' place and when I got there he did not want to come home. He wanted to stay longer and drink more. I had a whale of a time to get him to come home, to get him into the car. In such a case, will church be interesting next morning? Absolutely not. Another thing was that when Mary and I would go to church Sunday morning and return home, he would have cut the lawn Sunday morning or did other work around the yard or garden. Why did he not do that work Saturday morning, but on Sunday?

Mary nor her parents ever owned a car or knew how to drive. Living in the city, they used the city transit to get around. When we got married, people had given us gifts and enough donations at our wedding day that after a few weeks we went and bought ourselves a brand new 1960 Pontiac from a friend I knew who was a salesman. It was a straight cash deal, so we got a very good bargain. After we had the car, many times during the week, on Saturday or Sunday afternoon I would always take them someplace to visit relatives or friends or to go shopping. Mary's father had a brother that lived in Charleswood, the south west end of Winnipeg, and every time once a week we would go there during the day or evening to visit. Other times I would drive them to Vita, Gardenton or Tolstoy area where they had friends and some far distant relative. Mary's mother also had some relatives in Fort Frances, Ontario and in the two years I lived with them we went Fort Frances to visit the relatives a number of times. Because they never had a car, they never visited people out of town, unless they hired someone to take them there. Now with a car in the yard, I would drive them many places. In this way I learned to know some of their relatives and friends.

So I finished my third year of studies and I was looking and hoping that the fourth year would come sooner so I could finish my course and move to a parish. Maybe than things would be different. This third year I got a summer job working for Pepsi Cola in the bottling plant. My job with a few others was to take empty bottles out of the cases and put them on the machine to be washed and sterilized. Here I was now getting a bigger salary of $1.00 an hour. I made some money to help pay for the school for my last year and at the same time was always giving some money to the in-laws to help with expenses. There were a few times they did not want to take money from me, but that was very, very seldom.

ORDINATION AND PARISH WORK

In the fall of 1961, I was starting my last year of studies. I knew that I would have to make a request to the church to ordain me a priest. That was the usual norm, that you write a letter requesting to be ordained. At this same time in 1961, the Holy Trinity Ukrainian Orthodox Cathedral in Winnipeg had begun to construct the upper part of the church. To this time the services and functions were held in the completed basement. It was beginning to look like the first service would probably be held on "Ukrainian Christmas Day", January 7th 1962. I made a request to the church to ordain me on that day. And so it was, that when that day arrived the first service took place in the upper part of the cathedral and I was ordained into the rank of a Deacon. I was the first one ordained at the first service in the upper part of the cathedral by the late Metropolitan Ilarion, my college professor and the primate of the church in Canada. After being ordained a Deacon the church delegated me to the St. Mary the Protectress Ukrainian Orthodox Church on Burrows Avenue in Winnipeg for practical training under my College professor, Father S. Gerus who was the pastor of that church at the time. Now I have about four months of classes left at the college.

In Winnipeg at this time also lived a priest, Father I. Skakalski who was the secretary for the church primate, the late Metropolitan Ilarion. Father Skakalski was a monk and never married. It was many, many times that Father Skakalski asked me to drive him on Sunday morning to a country church where he would hold a service. He had no car. It was the same with the late Metropolitan Ilarion. When he was invited to hold a pontifical service outside Winnipeg, I would get a phone call from his secretary saying: "Ewhen, the Metropolitan is asking if you could take him to Yorkton, for this coming Sunday for service." I drove them when they asked whether just near or farther away. If it was a trip of a few hours out of Winnipeg, we would leave Saturday morning or afternoon. If it was an hour or less from Winnipeg, we would leave early Sunday morning. So in one way or another I became part-time chauffeur for the Metropolitan and Father Skakalski.

I remember taking Metropolitan Ilarion to Yorkton, Saskatchewan, Dauphin and Petlura in Manitoba and to other places. When I drove Father Skakalski after I was already a Deacon, I would assist him with the services. Traveling an hour or more each way to a service, we had ample time to talk about church life and the church services. Father Skakalski had come to Canada from Ukraine after the Second World War. When he lived in Ukraine, he lived and served in the monasteries. He knew the ins and outs of each service by memory. He knew when, how, where, what about church services. Because of him, I was more privileged to learn and know the services. Father Skakalski told me when he was twelve years old, he ran away from home to a monastery and so from that age on he lived and learned the monastery way and life and I was very privileged that I had that opportunity to learn about the church. It was the same with Metropolitan Ilarion. I heard first hand from him of rules, laws, history and regulations about church law. He was a man of great learning. When he was in Ukraine he was a minister in the Ukrainian Government. It took him twenty years to translate the Bible into Ukrainian and that was during the Second World War.

Now came April 1962. I completed my theological courses at St. Andrew's College after four years. This same year the church sold the college building to the Church of the Nazarene. The church was now in the final stages of moving St. Andrew's College to the Campus of the University of Manitoba and thus becoming affiliated with the University. Starting in the fall the seminary students had no place to continue their studies, so the church purchased an older house next to the Consistory building to house the students and hold classes. Here classes were held until the spring of 1964 while the new college building was constructed on the University campus. I was one of the class of the last students who attended classes in the old college on 259 Church Avenue.

After completing my studies and already being a Deacon, the next step was to ask the church to ordain me a priest. I made a request to the church and at their monthly meeting they took the request into consideration and said that I could be ordained at Fort Frances, Ontario where Metropolitan Ilarion would be holding services on St. George's day, May 6th which was a Sunday. Taking part in my ordination were the late Father S.W. Sawchuk who was the chairman of the Presidium of the Consistory and also the late Father Hryhorij Udod who was the parish priest at Fort Frances at that time. Present at my ordination also were my parents, Mary and Mary's parents. We drove from Winnipeg to Fort Frances on the Saturday before Sunday.

Ordination is a different feeling. I've seen other men get ordained in Winnipeg in the churches, but when it comes to you, it's a feeling out of this world and one that just can not be explained, how or what. The Holy Spirit comes down upon you and you feel God's presence around you. You feel a trembling in your body. You feel the shivering. You feel a sensation that cannot be described. The church in Fort Frances was full, because this was also the congregation's Feast Day or Patron Saints Day as some say. After the ordination you just feel that you are a different person. Something around you makes you feel different than you did before ordination. Now that I am ordained, next Sunday I will probably be out to serve as other priests.

When we got back to Winnipeg, I was informed by Father Sawchuk, that come Sunday I go to Sioux Lookout, Ontario to have a service with the late Father T. Kowalishen. I went with Father Kowalishen to Sioux Lookout for the service on May 13th and we stayed at the home of the Stogran family. In 2002 when the Canadian Armed Forces were serving in Afghanistan, there was a person by the name of Stogran who was in charge of the troops there. Later when I went a number of times to serve at Sioux Lookout by myself, I remember there was one or two boys in that family. Could it be that this person in the Armed Forces is the same one that I stayed at their place at Sioux Lookout?

One day Father Kowalishen, one of my professors at St. Andrew's College was having a funeral at Transcona, Manitoba, at that time a suburb of Winnipeg. He asked me to come and assist him and this will give me a chance to learn the funeral service. Two days later Father Kowalishen was having a memorial service at Gonor, Manitoba, just north of Winnipeg and again asked me to come with him. The funeral service was hard the first time when I was closer to family members of the deceased than I had ever been before. People crying and weeping. A corpse lying in the casket. What if that corpse decides to get up? Who is to run first? I had never attended funerals before and here for the first time to stand beside a corpse, all kinds of ideas ran through my head. I had always been afraid of a dead body and now here I have to stand beside one. It was good that Father Kowalishen had asked me to come, because had I to serve a funeral myself, I don't know what would have happened. When the funeral was over, it somewhat gave me more courage, seeing that nothing unusual occurred. Maybe next time when I have a funeral alone, everything will be the same again.

I had spent four years at the college, and now comes the real test after the ordination. A service at Sioux Lookout, a funeral at Transcona and a memorial service at Gonor all in one week was good practical training. When this week was over, I was than allowed to serve alone and the Consistory would let me know when and where I am to go for services. At the college we did not practice, baptism, marriages or funerals, but than when the real thing comes in your life, than what? The college gave you theory and as for practical experience you will gain that once you are sent out to the parish. You have books and the books tell you what, how and when to do things.

So on May 20th I was given the green light to hold services without anyone else assisting me. I believe that Father Kowalishen saw I was ready and able to carry out services by myself and he told the Consistory that I can be on my own now My first service alone was at Sandhill, Manitoba, north east of Winnipeg, near Beausejour. The following Sunday I was sent to Poplarfield some seventy-five miles north of Winnipeg. After that I served many other little congregations around Winnipeg, and at Pleasant Home, north-west of Winnipeg, I performed my first baptism.

And life rolled along from day to day. Mary and I still lived at her parents' place. I knew that sooneror later I will be getting a letter notifying me where I will be going to serve a parish. I waited anxiously for that day when we would move out of Winnipeg. We would have to be on the parish on September 1st. We are now about middle of June. Two more months in Winnipeg. Clergy were moved on September first of each year, if there were requests made for transferred, so that their children could start school in their new place of residence.

On July 31st a letter arrived from the Consistory telling me that I will be going to my first parish. Where? Sheho, Saskatchewan. That would be some sixty miles west of Yorkton. That would be a good place to go. It was not that far from Winnipeg with good train and bus service as well as being on a main highway. Yorkton was only an hour away, while Saskatoon was two hours west. Regina to the south was about two hours and Dauphin, Manitoba some two hours to the east. Sheho was like the hub. Sheho was only some hundred and twenty-five miles from where I was born. Things looked fine and I was beginning to think more and more each day when finally we will be out on our own. Slowly now and than we were starting to pack and to get ready for the move.

In the meantime, John was living in Saskatoon. I thought that now being two hours out of Saskatoon, we would have more time to get together and catch up on the lost time not seeing each other for many months at a time. Alice also was only two hours away and now we would be able to visit more often. As I was preparing and pondering how and what else to do, so nothing would be forgotten, when all of a sudden news came. The very next day on August 1st John moved from Saskatoon to Winnipeg with his family. Where we would have been two hours away, now we will be some six or seven hours apart again. Even though we will be farther apart later, at least now in Winnipeg for one month we will be just a stone's throw away from each other. In Winnipeg lived Marys' parents, my parents and Oksana and now John will be here also. Living in Sheho and whenever there will be a reason to come to Winnipeg, at least there will be family, and also a place to stay and visit.

Mary and I were packing now more and more as the day of September drew nearer and nearer. I looked forward to the move, but I could see and feel a sense that Mary was not pleased. How will she leave her parents and be away six hours from them? Mary's mother always had much to say. Her father was more quiet, like my father who would sit and think. Mary's mother would say: "So why are they sending you out to some farm? Let someone else go there. Can't you stay here in Winnipeg?" Another time in a sly remark she said: "Let the one that wrote you that letter, go there on the farm, or let the bishop go himself." This was no encouragement to Mary. She backed her mother and would say the same as her mother.

Than just about a week before we are to leave for Sheho, another shocker came. I got a phone call from Father Skakalski, that Metropolitan Ilarion wanted to see me. He said to come immediately. Now what did I do? When you got a phone call that Metropolitan Ilarion wants to see you, you knew something was serious. You knew you must have done something wrong and now you will get cut down by the Metropolitan. There was no way that you miss an appointment with the Metropolitan. When the secretary calls that you have to appear, you don't make excuses. You go for "whatever will be, will be."

I got into the car and went. The news, was it better or worse? Metropolitan Ilarion informs me, that he had to change my move to Sheho and that I will be going to Lac La Biche. Lac La Biche? Where in the world is that? How far from Winnipeg? Than he asks me to stop in at the Consistory to see Father Sawchuk and he will inform me more about the change. I took the Metropolitan's blessing and walked out, not knowing what to expect from Father Sawchuk.

At the Consistory Father Sawchuk said that because of sudden things that came up, I would have to go to Lac La Biche. I asked him where that was and he said in Alberta. I asked how big a parish and how things are there. He said: "Well I'll tell you what ...., when you get there you will see for yourself." He told me the reason for the change. There were two priests living at Sheho, father and son, Father Tet and his son Boris Yakowkewich. Father Boris served the Theodore parish and father Tet serve the parish of Sheho. At times they changed and served in each others parish. Father Tet's daughter, Father Boris's sister, Dobrodeyka Nowitski had passed away and because of that they wanted to stay on in Sheho and Theodore, because they knew all the people and it will be easier for them to carry this burden of their family loss. So the Metropolitan fulfilled their wishes, and I had to go to Lac La Biche in Alberta.

I left the Consistory somewhat saddened, but what can I do? I came home and told the news to the family. If there had been any uneasiness before of going to Sheho, how much more will it be going someplace to Alberta of which I never heard of before. When I told what happened, just about all hell broke loose. Mary's mother began to scream: "You're not going no place. Who makes all those rules? Let me speak to them." On and on it went. I was one and there was three of them. To get out of the house, to get away from all this, I said I was going to see my parents. Maybe by the time I come back, things will have settled and cooled down somewhat. I told my parents that we will be moving to Lac La Biche, and mother only said: "So we'll probably not see you again for being so far away." I told her that today people have cars, there are buses, trains and planes and people can go from place to place in a short time. The atmosphere was completely different than at Mary's place and her parents.

When I returned from my parents', I wanted to see where Lac La Biche was. I took out the map of Alberta and looked up the index where my new home will be. If Mary wants to stay by my side, she will come, but by the actions of her mother, it was doubtful if she would want to go to some unknown place. Now the map is open. Alberta. I looked and sure enough, there is such a place. On the 1960's road map of Alberta, Lac La Biche was at the end of the world. There at Lac La Biche ended the road. There was no road farther north. It was some hundred and fifty miles north east of Edmonton. Whatever comes and "whatever will be, will be." I am moving there because my church is sending me to go there. I will now be farther from my parents, Oksana, from John and from Alice too. Instead of being closer, I will be farther and venturing out into an unknown and unheard of territory. No family, no friends or relatives, just all total strangers.

The day was coming to leave Winnipeg for Lac La Biche. Things were packed and we were only taking things we could put into the car and only bare necessities. We did not know what we will find in the house (manse) where we will be living. Are there any dishes there? Is there a bed? Are there a table and chairs? Are there any utensils? Question after question about going into the unknown. But if there are none of those things and we wanted to take them with us, where would we put them when the car is full? Finally the day to depart arrived. We left Winnipeg at 9:30 AM on September 3rd - 1962. That first day we drove to St. Benedict,

Saskatchewan and stayed over night at John and Alice's place. It took thirteen hours to get there. We must remember there were no such roads then as we have today. The roads were there, but with gravel and barely any pavement. Today this same distance on the paved roads one can travel in nine or ten hours. We also spent the next day at St. Benedict, for who knows when we will see each other again.

We left St. Benedict on September 5th and were heading to Edmonton. Before we got to Edmonton, we stopped at Wakaw, Saskatchewan to visit with the late Father Mykola Stetzenko who was the parish priest there and the person who had encouraged me to attend St. Andrew's College. When we get to Edmonton, we have to stop and see Bishop Andrew. He will now be my bishop. I had known bishop Andrew from Winnipeg when he was still the parish priest at the St. Mary the Protectress church on Burrows Avenue. Bishop Andrew was ordained a bishop in 1959 at Edmonton. In Edmonton we stayed at a relative of Mary's mother. Next day we visited Bishop Andrew and than also with the late Father Kowalishen who had been previously transferred from Winnipeg to Edmonton. After that we left Edmonton for Lac La Biche and arrived at 4:00 PM, on a cool, cloudy, dreary, rainy and wet day. There was no pavement to Lac La Biche or in town. When we got to Lac La Biche, the car did not look like a car, but like one large huge chunk of mud. We arrived in Lac La Biche on September 6th.

When we were leaving Winnipeg, we knew whom we had to contact when we got to Lac La Biche. We soon found Mr. & Mrs. Eli Tkachuk who were owners of a store in Lac La Biche. They took us into their place and we had supper with them. After supper we went to the manse to unload our things into the house. People already knew when we were arriving. I don't know how they found out the precise day that we would arrive. Maybe Bishop Andrew had called and told them that we were on the way. Mr. & Mrs. Tkachuk came with us to the manse and gave us a key to the house and church. Inside the manse there was a surprise awaiting us. The manse was nice and clean. There were plates, utensils for cooking, silverware, beds, bedding and furniture. Mary wanted to check the refrigerator to see if it's working. When she opened the door, there staring at us into our eyes was a full refrigerator of food, bread, meat, milk, cheese, and vegetables for meals.

I ALSO WALKED ON THIS EARTH

We hadn't quite yet unpacked and settled in when we got an invitation to attend the graduation at the high school to take place on September 8th. My first service in the Lac La Biche Parish was held at Athabasca on Sunday September 9th. After this we got into the groove of fulfilling parish duties, services, marriages, funerals, meetings, baptism, etc. The first duty was to attend the graduation. When I had spent a few days in Lac La Biche getting acquainted with the people and the area, I very soon organized religious classes to be held in public schools at Lac La Biche, Grassland and Wandering River. What happened in Lac La Biche in the next five years will unfurl as pages are turned. I have a daily diary of the more important happenings in my life starting from 1962. For this reason what is written here from 1962 is 99% accurate. Not every minute is recorded, but all major things that I did or that occurred are recorded each day in my diary from which this is taken and put here on paper.

This same year an unusual thing happened during a service at Noral, Alberta some twenty-five miles south-west of Lac La Biche. It was December 19th, a Holy Day celebrating St. Nicholas the Wonder-worker. I had finished the sermon and was continuing the service. The priest in the Orthodox Church serves at the Altar with his back to the people. He is the pastor and is leading his flock who follow him all going in the same direction to meet Christ. When I was serving, I heard some noise and commotion behind me, but I never turned around to see what was happening. There were people in church and they can take care of what was transpiring. What happened was that Mary had passed out and they took her outside for fresh air. I did not know what happened, but right after that the unusual happened again. As I was serving, I also passed out and fell backwards away from the altar. I remember that I was at the altar and the next thing I recall is that some women were saying: "Give him some snow in his hands." Mary and I passed out. Why? No one else passed out that day. To this day I don't know why or what had happened.

The following year nothing unusual happened with the exception of maybe that I had to baptize eight people at one time on one day at one place. This happened on June 30th 1963 outside in the yard of the family that was being baptized. Baptized was the mother, her five children and the mothers two brothers. There were about eighty to a hundred people present. There was no church large enough to accommodate all the people, and for that reason the baptism was outside. The family had not been baptized, because the mother and her husband had been married by a judge. Now what happened was, the daughter wanted to get married in an Orthodox Church in Edmonton and she needed a baptismal certificate. Because she was not baptized, the priest would not marry the couple in Edmonton. The family came to me for help, what to do. After having learned what was said to me, I told them that they could all be baptized at one time. The time was set for baptism on June 30th. There were eight people to be baptized. Each had two God-parents and they could not be husband and wife for the same child. Plus all friends and relatives made this a special day and celebration. Baptism took place under the open skies. Alice and her husband John had come to Lac La Biche to visit us and they also witnessed this special event.

This same year in 1963, I was given extra duties by Bishop Andrew. There was no priest at Glendon-Bonnyville parish area since the late Father Peter Zubrytsky had been transferred to Two Hills, Alberta. Glendon, Bonnyville, St. Paul, are approximately seventy-five miles south east of Lac La Biche. The only road to that area was a dirt road and no gravel on it and went through the area of Rich Lake, Iron River, La Corey and Sandy Rapids. If it rained the road was virtually impassable, but yet rain, snow or shine I was given to serve that territory until a priest would be sent there. There were the congregations of Glendon, Bonnyville, St. Paul, Elk Point, Nova Bukovina, Therein, Big Meadow, Sandy Rapids and maybe another one or two that I may have forgotten. The farthest from Lac La Biche was to Elk Point with some ninety five miles south east. Later in about 1966 a new road, highway #36 south of Lac La Biche was built and that connected to highway #28 near Vilna. This new road was wide and had gravel, so it was much easier to go to the above mentioned congregations, even though it was farther than through the old dirt road. Today that old dirt road has become highway #55 and is paved all the way to Cold Lake. So I now had eight congregations in Lac La Biche Parish, plus the seven or eight congregations in the Glendon-Bonnyville Parish to look after.

The late Paul Balaban who lived twelve miles south of Lac La Biche was the cantor who always went with me to the congregations when I had a service. The only place he did not go with me was when the service was at Athabasca in town and Richmond Park about twenty miles north of

Athabasca. In those two congregations there was a combined Orthodox-Catholic choir under the direction of the late Mr. Chrusch. In the spring of 1964, Mr. Balaban and I left home at 7:00 AM on Saturday morning for Easter services and did not return home till some thirty-four hours later on Easter Sunday at 5:00 PM, before evening. We traveled all day Saturday, all night and Sunday before we got home. It was non-stop with our families at home while we visited every congregation to have different services and bless the Easter Paska in each congregation. At this same time two young teen-age girls from Lac La Biche asked if they could go with us. We picked up the two girls in Lac La Biche early Saturday morning. We asked them why they wanted to go with us, since we would not be back in Lac La Biche till some twenty-two hours later. They said they had school projects and did not know what to write about so they wanted to visit the churches, see the people and the different services we were serving. After we had completed most of the trip north and west we arrived at Noral for the service and Paska blessing about 4:00 AM. In Noral the girls came in, looked at the church and went out. When the service was over, Mr. Balaban and I came out to go to Lac La Biche our next stop, we found the two girls sleeping in the back seat of the car. When we arrived at Lac La Biche for the service at 5:00 AM, the girls did not go with us any farther.

In 1964 I received a letter from the Consistory (church headquarters) that the church will be moving me to a new congregation St. Andrews, in Edmonton, which is located on Wayne Gretsky Drive. This did not materialize. For one, when the parish in Lac La Biche heard that I would be moved, they got everything in motion, got the gears into high with letters and telephone calls to Winnipeg, they asked that I not be moved from Lac La Biche. Another reason was that I did not know if I was ready to make such a big jump after only two years being a priest. I had only arrived to Lac La Biche in the fall of 1962 and here two years later after being ordained, the church wanted to move me to Edmonton. Did I have enough experience to move to a large one city congregation? Was I really fit for that kind of promotion? When all had settled down, I was left to continue to serve the Lac La Biche Parish.

Since Mary and I had been married in June 1960, we had not gone anywhere for even one day of holidays. This year, four years after marriage we took holidays and went to British Columbia and the USA for a trip.

Neither one of us had ever been to or seen the Rocky Mountains, so we decided to go west and south. When I first saw the mountains, I fell in love with them at that moment, than wished and hoped that some day I may live in those mountains. This dream was fulfilled seventeen years later, in 1977 as we will see.

The year 1965 had a few different things happen. One thing was that Mr. Humeny of Boyle, Alberta passed away. On February 12th we had prayers in the evening in church. The funeral director from Athabasca did not take the body back to Athabasca that evening, but the body was transferred to the little hall the congregation has at the back of the church. Men had agreed to change shifts and watch the body. The funeral director was coming back next day to Boyle and he had to bring back the rough box, because he did not have room in the funeral coach for the coffin and rough box together. After prayers I returned back to Lac La Biche. During the night a howling snow storm came up. The roads were drifted by the swirling snow driven by the north wind. Next morning in the storm I drove back to Boyle to have the funeral service.

I arrived in the howling storm in time to get ready and start the service. When 10:00 AM came to start the service, no funeral director. So what do we do? I tell the people to come to the little hall and we will bring the body to church. I got six men to take the casket and one to take the cart and we all moved to the church. Everything was set up and the service started. Half way through and no funeral director, so in my mind the cells are working overtime and telling me that the funeral director must be stuck in a snow drift someplace, because he is never late. The service is coming to the end and still no funeral director. As the service was winding down, I thought that all we can do is take the casket and put it on someone's truck and drive to the cemetery and bury the body without the rough box. Just as I was about to ask someone to volunteer their truck to haul the body, when the door opens to the church and the funeral director walks in. He was surprised to see what had transpired and that the service was all over. Just as I had thought. He had gotten stuck on the highway in the snow, and had to get a farmer to pull him out with a tractor. All that took time.

Another strange thing that happened this year was the clergy of the Western Diocese were having their conference in Edmonton. When the conference was over, I went to one of the Edmonton hospitals to visit a patient who was a member of my parish from the Sarrail congregation and had been hospitalized in Edmonton. I visited with the patient and was ready to leave for home, when low and behold as I was turning away to leave I passed out and crashed to the floor. When I came to, I was lying on the floor and nurses and orderlies were around me. The nurses were trying to open my shirt collar so I could get air into my lungs. They brought a wheelchair and hauled me away to the emergency where I spent about two or three hours. The doctors examined me and said they could find nothing wrong and sent me on my way.

By this time there was now a priest in the Glendon-Bonnyville area, so I did not have to serve that parish any longer since September of 1964. Bishop Andrew seeing that I was young, energetic and able to move and do things that were loaded unto me, gave me another duty. He asked me to look after the Peace River country. The priest that was there became ill and had surgery in Edmonton. His age was also against him. Later he passed away in Edmonton. So another milestone began for me which brings back many fond memories of that northern Alberta territory. My first service in that area was at Spirit River, north of Grande Prairie. There was a congregation of people in Spirit River, but they had no church building where to pray. Whenever priests used to come to that area to serve, they always stayed at George and Mary Zyha's place. I became friendly with this family, and it seemed that I was now a member of that family.

Because there was no church building in Spirit River, the services were held in the theatre. On Saturday night there were movies shown which lasted late into the night. Very early in the morning Zyhas and I would get up and go to the theatre to clean and set up for the service for 10:00 AM. We had to dust, sweep, and set up a table for the altar and everything else needed for the service. This kind of schedule went on for many a service, before the congregation got their own church building. They bought an older Roman Catholic church some six miles east of Spirit River at Rycroft and had it moved to Spirit River. They paid five hundred dollars for the church, the same amount for the land and the same amount to have the church moved the six miles. The church was remodeled inside and is used for services to this day whenever services are held in that area.

This year also brought some bad news for us. Mary's father had taken ill and was admitted to the hospital where he had surgery. Five days after he was admitted to the hospital, Mary left for Winnipeg. This was the first time that Mary and I had been apart for a longer period of time since our marriage. She did not return back home until August 20th. She had left for Winnipeg on July 17th. Prior to this we had been apart maybe for a day or two, if I had taken a train to Sioux Lookout for services, but now she was gone for over one month. I must also mention that when we moved into Lac La Biche, it was not long after that, that Mary's father had come to visit us. He had a CNR pass, so it cost him nothing to travel by train.

Also this year after visiting the Peace River country a number of times for services, I made a decision that I would like to move to that area. I saw a great need for missionary and potential work in that part of the country and I was ready to tackle that. There was a future for the church in that area. What it's like there now, I cannot tell. At the Lac La Biche Parish things were more less organized and things were running along smoothly, but in the Peace River country there was a tremendous amount of work to be done and in order to do it, one would have to reside in that area. On September 21st I let the church headquarters in Winnipeg know, that I was ready to move to the Peace River country. This did not materialize. Bishop Andrew and others insisted that I stay on at Lac La Biche. I did stay in Lac La Biche until the summer of 1967 when the church moved me to Winnipeg to be a missionary. In the Peace River area there were congregations at Spirit River, Reno, Berwyn, Deadwood, and Hotchkiss. There are many Ukrainian people who moved into that area when the west and north were opening up. There they took up their homesteads, raised their families and continued to live in that country. The church could have grown and flourished in that part of the country.

In 1966 many things happened. Mary's father was not feeling better since his surgery. His health was failing. On May 4th Mary again went to Winnipeg to be with her parents. She stayed with her father at home while her mother went to work. Mary called from Winnipeg saying that her father was getting worst. On June 6th I left for Winnipeg to visit her father. Our wedding anniversary was on June 4th and Mary's birthday on June 7th. I thought at least I would be with her on her birthday. I returned from Winnipeg on June 10th while Mary stayed on in Winnipeg. I had just come home when on the 12th of June I got a call from Mary that her father had passed away. Early the next morning I once again left for

Winnipeg. The funeral was on June 16th after which we both returned to Lac La Biche on the 17th after a long, long drive from Winnipeg, from early morning until late at night.

When I arrived in Winnipeg for the funeral, I talked over with Mary that maybe we should ask Mary's mother to come and live with us. When we told her this, her mother got upset and told us not to chase her out of her house. We told her that we don't want any money from her to pay for us, because wherever we will be, there will always be a house for us and a room for her. We told her that she would not have to go to work anymore either. But no, she would have nothing to do with this and did not even want to listen to what we would tell her. We told her that she could sell her house, put her money in the bank and she would not need to spend any money for utilities, taxes, or whatever. For a while I thought that if she came to stay with us, maybe Mary would be different because than her mother would be with her at all times.

While I was serving the Lac La Biche Parish, I also took part in serving in two summer camps for children. I spent two weeks teaching religion at Camp Bar-V-Nok, south west of Edmonton on the shores of Pigeon Lake. Another camp was started a year later near Bonnyville, Kyviski-Haj. The camp near Bonnyville was closer to Lac La Biche than Camp-Bar-Vinok. People from Lac La Biche had gone to help build the camp near Bonnyville. Camp Bar-V-Nok was a good camp. Each night after the campers were all tucked and in bed, the councillors would come and asked me to come to the activity room and talk with them. They asked me thousands of religious questions about God and the church and sometimes it was late into the night before we all retired to our cabins for a rest. The councillors were always eager and wanted to know about their faith.

In 1967 another important event took place in my life. I was enjoying my work in the parish very much and I could see progress being made as the years slipped by, but my married life was beginning to deteriorate. It seemed that Mary's heart was set on Winnipeg, her mother and her mother's house instead of her husband. It happened that Mary's mother was going to have a memorial service for her husband and Mary's father. Mary wanted to go and I would have loved to be there, but parish work during May and June had me bottled and tied up, that it would be impossible for me to leave. Mary left for Winnipeg on May 24th, for the service that was to take place around the middle of June.

I know God knew all along what was happening to our marriage, and He intervened to help the situation. I could have stayed in Lac La Biche to this very day and served the parish and may have built up a larger parish. But than it happened. This year in 1967 I was transferred back to Winnipeg. Next year in 1968 the church in Canada would be celebrating its fiftieth golden anniversary. The church asked me to come back to Winnipeg to be a missionary and travel across Canada to help organize the celebration countrywide. The main anniversary was to take place at Saskatoon, Saskatchewan in July of 1968. Now with the move to Winnipeg, maybe things will be better. Mary will be with her mother all the time. When we moved to Winnipeg, the church was going to rent out a house for Mary and me to live in. Mary's mother would hear nothing of that sort. We must and have to move in and live with her in her house.

So started a new life, a life of living for nearly a year out of the suitcase as my home had became where I hung my hat for the night. I'd leave Winnipeg and be gone sometimes as much as six weeks on the road before I returned back to Winnipeg. I traveled with the Consistory station wagon automobile. My travels took me from the borders of Alberta and British Columbia and all the way east to Thunder Bay in Ontario. I did not have enough time to go farther east as the day of the celebration in Saskatoon neared and after the celebration, my work as missionary was over. During my travels I was on the road each and every day traveling from one parish to the next covering the provinces from the north to the south, east and west. I spoke in each parish in the evening, showed a slide presentation and answered people's questions. Each day before bedtime I wrote a report, where I was, what I did, what I saw, questions that people asked, how many people at the meeting, how many miles traveled, expenses of the day, where I stayed over night and all other details. Some nights when I went to bed, I was so tired that I could feel my whole body shivering-quivering. From first I did not know why this was and what, but when I was rested up this did not come about. In Alberta at times during the day when I traveled I had to pull over to the side of the road on an approach and catch a nap. I was that tired.

One time when I was leaving Winnipeg on a trip, I wanted Mary to come with me on the trip which was not as long as other trips but only a few days. She did not go with me. Her mother said that Mary is not going anywhere and will be home with her. Mary listened to what her mother said not what her husband asked her to do, to get out and meet the people. This was another sign that this marriage was not working out. What her mother said was holy and saintly, but what her husband said it was not worth listening to. Many times I just had to keep quite and not say a thing, just to "keep peace in the family." One thing that credit has to be given where credit is due and that is Mary's mother never charged the church anything for rent, not one red penny that we lived in her house. This was a financial saving for the church. When I traveled in Western Canada, the only cost the church had was for gasoline and oil changes for the car. Everywhere I went people always took me in to come into their place to spend the night with them. When I was in Lethbridge, I stayed in a hotel and nothing was charged because the owner of the hotel was a church member.

I believe it was shortly thereafter that I was admitted and became a member of the Order of St. Andrew. In the early 1960's a few men had a vision to help St. Andrew's College - financially. The college was having financial difficulties to support itself, pay the professors and maintain itself. Those few men said that if they could get one thousand men into an organization and each man donate $50.00 per year to the college, that would ease and help the financial burden on the newly constructed college which had a mortgage. The organization has five degrees and the fifth is the highest. In 2002 at the Order of Saint Andrew Canadian general meeting gathering in Calgary, Alberta, I was awarded the fifth degree in the organization.

Than came the year 1968, the fiftieth anniversary of the church. There were meetings and more meetings and still more meetings, discussions and plans and more meetings in order to get everything ready for the anniversary. The diocese across Canada held their celebrations. The parishes and congregations also held special occasions to honor the event of the church. The main celebration took place in Saskatoon where the genesis of the church occurred. The Sunday celebration was the highlight of the anniversary. That morning I celebrated the Divine Liturgy at 7:30

AM. At 10:00 AM another Liturgy was held at the same place, but this was a pontifical Liturgy celebrated by the Primate of the church, the late Metropolitan Ilarion with other bishops and clergy assisting. Afternoon a concert was held and the main attraction was the one hundred plus voice youth choir from Toronto and area. Thousands of people attended this celebration in Saskatoon. Many people whom I met in my travels as missionary recognized me when attending the celebration and personally came to thank me for informing them about such a great event. Till the end of June my time was mostly spent on the road notifying people of this event. After the celebration in Saskatoon, I spent my time in Winnipeg at the Consistory church headquarters, winding up post work after the celebration. On Sundays I would be sent to some smaller congregations to the outlying area of Winnipeg to hold services.

As the year was scampered along, it had rolled and rolled and now it was August 1st the day when the clergy who were to be moved around to other parishes were to be on their new parish. At the Consistory this time the late Father Frank Kernitsky was the chairman of the Presidium. Father I. Trufyn was the secretary in the Consistory and I was the missionary. One day Father Kernitsky called for the late Father Trufyn and me into his office. Before we went in we kind of wondered what was so important that both had to come in and see him. Did we do something wrong, or is there going to be more work? When we came in, Father Kernitsky says: "You both know that there is no priest at Dauphin at the present time. I have to send someone to Dauphin on the parish there. Tomorrow I am going on holidays, and when I return I will have made up my mind which one of you will be moving to Dauphin." Yes, we looked at each other and what was there to say? We have to wait for what decision Father Kernitsky will make.

In the meantime the late Father Maksym Olesiuk who had been the priest in Dauphin was transferred to Kamsack, Saskatchewan and Dauphin was left vacant without a priest. Father Kernitsky also told me to look after the Dauphin parish for any services that may be needed there while he was away. Father Trufyn and I seemed to be walking on needles. Which one of us will be going to Dauphin? Which one will be moving from Winnipeg? When Father Kernitsky came back from his holidays, he called me into his office and says: "I have made my decision which was not easy, as to who is going to Dauphin. I have decided to send you to Dauphin on a TEMPORARY basis, probably for a few months until I get someone to go there permanently." This temporary transfer lasted nine years and could have lasted many more had it not been for illness that struck me. On August 27th we moved to Dauphin and a new chapter in my life was begun which I will try to put down on paper for people to know.

DAUPHIN, MANITOBA PARISH

When I arrived in Dauphin, the first thing I did was organize a fiftieth anniversary committee to celebrate the anniversary of the church in the Dauphin Parish. This was done and together with the committee a program was planned and the celebration took place on October 20th with many, many people attending. Our own parish hall was too small to accommodate all the people, so we had to rent the town hall which was so much larger and in the end even that was too small. Two days later after this celebration, another celebration took place. The parish made us a welcome tea, welcoming us to Dauphin and to the parish. After this I dug right into parish work and as we travel along time will show what happened.

Having arrived in Dauphin, the congregation had a hundred and eighty-six family members. There was an old residence for the priest next to the church. The church was incomplete and the hall that the parish had was old, outdated and too small for the needs of the parish. I had three or four other smaller congregations outside of Dauphin that I had to serve. There was Ashville, Valley River and Kosiw. Very soon I saw that something did not look right to me. The congregation in Dauphin was having only one service a month and the rest of the services were given to the other smaller congregations. Somehow it made no sense to me to leave a hundred and eighty-six families on a Sunday and go out to the country where maybe fifteen or twenty people attended. Yes I know the story that Christ told about a man losing one sheep and he left ninety-nine and went to search for the one that was lost. At the succeeding weeks at a monthly meeting of the congregation I mentioned that we should have a service every Sunday in Dauphin and for the farm congregations, I could go and serve them during the week when there are Holy Days. When I brought up this suggestion, there were some people who would have eaten me alive without salt, for thinking and saying that. The church does care about each congregation and member, so the smaller congregation members can always come to Dauphin to church with today's good roads and vehicles.

The reason was that a number of people said it would be too costly to have a service in Dauphin every Sunday. Some said that the other smaller congregations outside Dauphin also needed services. I explained the benefits of a service every Sunday and after a goodly heated discussion a motion was made and barely passed to go on a trial basis for two or three months and see what happens, how it would work. After this had been done and about two or three months later at another monthly meeting I made the suggestion that maybe we should go back to having one service a month. When I said this, all I heard was a very loud: "No, no, no." To this very day the congregation has services every Sunday. No, the smaller congregations outside Dauphin are not neglected but have services from time to time in the summer. In the winter heating the small congregations is really impossible where the walls of those congregations have no insulation, no basements and some had no power.

This same year in November the treasurer of the congregation gave me a cheque for the services for October telling me the following: "Don't cash this cheque, until I let you know, because we have no money in the bank to cover it." I guess that was my fate for wherever I went, there was always a shortage of funds to pay me my honorarium. In the Lac La Biche parish, the same thing had happened. In one congregation they took in the collection plate and were to pay me $40.00 for the service, but I got only $20.00, because the treasurer said they did not have enough money in the bank. Yet in Lac La Biche out of the $40.00 per service I was receiving I had to pay for car expense, all utilities in the manse as well as look after Mary and myself for food and clothing. A similar situation happened in Prince George, British Columbia, but this will be told later.

When the year 1969 came, it was the same as the year before, work, work and more work. In April of this year Father Shwetz passed away at Oakburn, Manitoba. He had been the priest in that parish for a few years. It was Easter time. He went to each congregation he had to serve, brought out the Holy Shroud and on Easter Sunday when he served the last congregation and blessed their Easter Paska, he came home. He passed away as soon as he arrived home. What a blessed way to have passed away after serving each congregation, come home and pass away on such a great day. When a priest passes away, it is the duty of other priests to come together to the funeral chapel, wash the priests body, anoint the body with oil and dress the priest in full vestments as he dresses to serve the Divine Liturgy. The late Father Hryhorij Fil' who was the parish priest in Brandon and I had to go to Shoal Lake, Manitoba to the funeral home and prepare the body for the funeral and burial.

As has already been noted above, the church in Dauphin was not yet completed. The time had come to think about an Ikonostas for the church. This was brought to the church meeting one time and the members passed a motion to have an Ikonostas installed. But who is going to build the Ikonostas, where and when. We began to check for prices and at the same time a fund was started to collect donations towards this project. As this was starting to unfold, I learned again that God works in wondrous ways. One day in the mail I get a catalogue from a church goods store, Light and Life Publishing Company in Minneapolis, Minnesota, that they have a man who carves Ikonostasis for churches. When I got this catalogue and saw the item about the Ikonostas, so naturally I wanted to get as much information as possible about the topic at hand. I immediately wrote to the company for more information.

On June 7th Mr. K. Papadakis from Minneapolis arrived by bus in Dauphin. He came to see the church, discuss what kind of Ikonostas, the price, etc. He measured the place where the Ikonostas would stand and that evening a special meeting of the congregation was called in regards to the Ikonostas. An agreement was reached with Mr. Papadakis. He would hand carve the Ikonostas and install it for the sum of $14,500.00. For this same work in the USA, he would charge $25,000.00. He said he was giving the congregation a bargain, since this was the first work that he would be doing in Canada. The price did not include the icons.

One thing that he wanted was for the congregation to agree to a certain height for the Ikonostas. I was in favor with him on this topic, for I had seen enough Ikonostasis by now and knew something about them, maybe more than ordinary people. The executive was not in favor of his proposal, for it would have cost a thousand dollars more. The congregation was to give him $5000.00 deposit so that he would have enough money to get materials and expenses. Another $5000.00 would be paid when half of the work was done and the remainder when the work was completed and the Ikonostas installed.

The contract was drawn up that evening by a lawyer, Mr. Ed Demkiw. A deposit was given and next day Mr. Papadakis returned back to Minneapolis to start work on the Ikonostas. The agreement stated that the Ikonostas was to be completed and installed in the church in June 1970. This never happened till six months later after I had spent many sleepless nights and days with headaches. Mr. Papadakis was in Dauphin on June 7th and he said that in a years time he would have the Ikonostas installed. In December of 1969 the congregation received a letter from Mr. Papadakis' lawyer that the installation and completion of the Ikonostas would be delayed, because Mr. Papadakis was involved in a automobile accident and was recuperating in a hospital. When this letter arrived in Dauphin, all hell broke loose. The congregation became jittery and some people started talking that an unknown man came to Dauphin, took $5000.00 and that will be the last of anything we will ever see of that money. Some said that the congregation had been swindled by some unknown person from the USA.

I kept assuring the congregation that nothing is lost, because we have a signed contract and everything will turn out all right. If the man was injured, how could he work if he was lying in the hospital on a bed? It was a serious neck injury and the doctors said that he was very lucky because one bone still held his neck in place. Some people began to whisper that the man who took the money was not an honest man. Some time later we got another letter from the lawyer that Mr. Papadakis was out of the hospital with a neck collar and a head brace and will be starting to do work on the Ikonostas as soon as the doctor gives him the green light. I kept telling people, that when a lawyer writes letters, take it seriously that things are not lost. Some time later another letter arrived from the lawyer that Mr.

Papadakis was working on the Ikonostas and that the congregation should give him the next installment of payment because half of the work was concluded.

When the people heard this letter which I read at the meeting, some began to say, that not another red penny will be given until the work is done and they see the Ikonostas with their own eyes. I kept telling the people that we have a contract and we should abide for if we don't the congregation may be sued for breaking the contract. To satisfy the congregation, I made a proposition. I said that it will not cost the congregation a penny, and let them elect or designate three people and I will drive to Minneapolis take these three people at my own cost to see what has been done on the Ikonostas. Somehow I convinced the people and the congregation gave me a cheque for $5000.00 to give Mr. Papadakis if we see that half the work is done. Very early on the morning of March 4th - 1970 with three other people the late, Wasyl Grodzick, Harry Klapouschak and Maxim Stanko we left for Minneapolis. We did not phone or let Mr. Papadakis know that we were coming. The congregation said that we should arrive unexpectedly, unannounced and so we did.

When we arrived in Minneapolis, we found Mr. Papadakis' residence and surprised him. When we came in to see him, he was working on the Ikonostas in his basement and was wearing a neck collar and a body brace. Immediately I saw that there had been a lot of work done because there were carved pieces of wood all over standing against the walls of the basement. The congregation and the men who came with me thought that the Ikonostas would be one whole large piece. The problem was that the Ikonostas was constructed in pieces, so that it can be moved and than assembled in the church. I had a Polaroid camera with me and took pictures and also a number of slides. When these were developed, people saw them and still there were some who were not convinced after seeing proof of the photos and slides. At the same time I was convincing people that everything will be all right and if no Ikonostas will be built and installed, I would personally take the responsibility and with my own money and in some way will refund the money to the congregation. This was a big proposition to make, but I knew that the Ikonostas would be built and I was not worried about this. The people who had gone with me to Minneapolis also began assuring the congregation about the work done, but some people still were not convinced. It was now summer and people were more on the move and outside, so less talk and gossip was going around about the Ikonostas.

It was sometimes in October that I received a phone call from Mr. Papadakis that he was hoping to have the Ikonostas finished in one month or so and would be bringing it to Dauphin. People were now waiting with anticipation to see if really the Ikonostas project will come to fruition. There were still some skeptical people who would say: "I won't believe it until I see the Ikonostas with my own eyes." At this same time I kept telling the congregation that they will have to have the remainder of the money when the Ikonostas is brought and installed. During the summer, talk was falling on people's ears from some disgruntled members and because of that the congregation began to see a dropping off of funds considerably during the summer months.

On December 9th - 1970, I got a phone call from Mr. Papadakis that we meet him at the Canadian-American border at such an hour and date, because he will be bringing the Ikonostas. He said he learned from his lawyer, that we would have to be present to sign papers at the border that the Ikonostas was being delivered to a church. This would than eliminate for the congregation to pay a duty fee at the border for the Ikonostas is for a church not for resale or profit. So finally on December 11 - 1970 the Ikonostas arrived in Dauphin in a U-Haul trailer. When Mr. Papadakis arrived with the U-Haul trailer behind his car, some people were still skeptical. How could you put a sixteen or twenty foot long Ikonostas in such a small trailer. There were some people who whispered: "So where is the Ikonostas?" They thought the Ikonostas would come in one piece and all you had to do was to carry it in and place it on the floor. Some people had gathered at the church to meet us after we arrived from the border.

Anyway the time came to unload the trailer. There were pieces and pieces that were carried into the church, so the wood would warm up since it had been in the trailer and cold frosty air for more than a whole day. After all the pieces were in and warm, Mr. Papadakis began to arrange and put the pieces together. As soon as the pieces were beginning to make sense to some people another problem occurred. Some people began to grumble in Ukrainian that the Ikonostas is too low. The Deacon Doors are too low and when a person walks through them they will have to bend down their head or they would hit the top of the doorway with their head. One church member who was a carpenter by trade tells Mr. Papadakis: "You made a mistake, how will someone walk through those side (Deacon) doors?" Mr. Papadakis pulled out the contract and said that he built things according to the contract. He took a tape measure and it showed the same as the contract. He had built everything according to contract specifications. He was right. I reminded the congregation when the contract was being drawn up, Mr. Papadakis was telling the congregation to have the Ikonostas higher, but the congregation did not want it.

To remedy the problem, I suggested that they go to the lumber yard and get some lumber, lay it on the floor and than put the Ikonostas on top and that would raise it enough for a person to pass through the Deacon Doors without hitting their head. That is what was done. While this was being done, Mr. Papadakis had nothing to do, but wait until the congregation put the six inch risers underneath the Ikonostas. This was done and it is there to this very day. Mr. Papadakis and I had told the congregation during the drawing up of the contract to built the Ikonostas higher, but the people would not hear of it. When the Ikonostas was finally finished, than all those who were saying that the money was lost and there would be no Ikonostas just began to hide somewhere and you could only see them once in a while here and there. Why? They had nothing to say now that the Ikonostas was built and installed as was promised. Mr. Papadakis after he finished his work left back for home. To show his honesty, he also donated to the congregation a carved Gospel stand in the value of $1000.00. Those who talked the most that money had been lost, now had nothing less or nothing more to say

Now that the Ikonostas was installed we would need icons to be placed in their respective places. This also was another story. It seemed that I knew nothing, while everyone else knew everything. At times I had told many people of my saying: "Some people know everything, but don't understand anything." I knew of a lady, Marie Northrup, who did paintings. I took a small icon of Christ praying in the Garden of Gethsemane about 2"x4" and asked her to paint that picture to a size of twenty by thirty inches. When she finished I came to pick it up. She charged me $50.00 for that painting. I brought the icon to the church meeting to show the congregation what kind of work she did. The people saw the beautiful icon and asked how much it cost. I told them $50.00. "Oh no, that's too much. We should be able to get those icons for less, for about half the price." The congregation would have nothing to do with this painter. I told the congregation that they don't have to buy this icon, since I paid for it and it will be mine. That icon has been in my home since 1970 and some people who have seen it were offering me $400.00 for it, but I would not sell it. It turned out later that the congregation ordered the icons for the Ikonostas from Winnipeg and the cost was $75.00 per icon.

I recall one day of February 1969. There was a snow storm roaring outside when a knock came on the front door of the manse. Who in the world is out in such a storm? I opened the door and there on the stairway landing were standing the late Mr. & Mrs. Mike Demchuk, church parishioners. I asked them to come in, but Mr. Demchuk began to recite a poem by Taras Shevchenko, Ukraine's greatest poet. The storm is roaring with stormy force winds and he is reciting a poem in the doorway, so I finally took him by the arm and pulled him into the house. He and his wife had no telephone, so he wanted to ask me something so they walked the two blocks to see me. God works in wondrous ways. As we were talking about something, the telephone rang. I answered the phone and it was a salesman from the Schullmerich Carillon Bell Company in Calgary, Alberta. He said they have some specials on electronic bells and he wanted to know if we would be interested in ordering a set. I told him that we would not be interested at the present time, because the congregation was in the process of collecting funds for icons for the iconostas. He gave me his name and phone number and said that he would send out some information about the bells.

I returned from answering the phone and Mr. Demchuk asked me who it was. He understood English very little. I told him what the call was about. Mr. Demchuk stood and stared at me for half a minute and than he says: "How much will the bells cost?" I told him that I did not know and I had told the salesman that we are not buying any bell at the present time because the congregation has no money. Mr. Demchuk keeps staring at me while I tell him this and than he says: "We will buy the bells for the church." Now just hold everything, just a minute." I just about fell when he said that because I knew that bells like those were a very expensive article. I told the Demchuks that it could cost a lot of money but I would have to ask the salesman how much they cost. He told me to ask the man how much they cost and they would buy the bells. So what do you do? God works in such wondrous ways. After a while I drove the Demchuks back home even though it was only two blocks, but because of the storm, I did not want them to go out in such weather. God works in wondrous ways. Why did the Demchuks come to see me in the wintery day storm? Why did the phone not ring half an hour earlier or half an hour later when the Demchuks were not at my place?

When I returned after driving them home, I called the salesman in Calgary to inquire as to the cost of the bells. The salesman said that he will send the bill to me and the bells would be installed early in the spring when its warmer for people to work outside. When the bill for the bells came, I went with it to the Demchuks. I showed them the bill and it was $4975.00. After Mr. Demchuk saw and heard the price, he says to me: "You take me to the bank and I will get the money for you." Now let's take it slowly piece by piece, one thing at a time. Could this really be true or am I in a hazy dream? After Mr. Demchuk was so positive that they will buy the bells, I came home and called the chairman of the congregation, the late Fred Chaykowski, and told him to come over to Demchuks and I will meet him there. I did not tell Mr. Chaykowski why I wanted him to come to Demchuks place. I walked back to Demchuks and shortly Fred Chaykowski arrived. When he came in I gave him the bill for the bells. He looked at it surprised and than says: "What is this?" Than I went into the story and told him what was what. Mr. Chaykowski was as surprised as I was of this whole ordeal. Machinery was put in motion. Demchuks gave the money to the congregation and the congregation sent the money to the company in Calgary. On June 30 - 1969 the bells were installed and bring joy and pleasure to the congregation to this day. The Demchuks are now deceased, but their memory will live as long as the bells will ring in the church. On the control box of the bells is an engraved inscription telling who purchased the chime bells and when the bells were installed.

Now 1970 was upon us. A milestone in my life again for the next five years was that the General Church Sobor was held in Winnipeg this year. At that Sobor I was elected as one of the eighteen members of the Consistory church board. This was the ruling body of the church and I was elected for a five year term. It is composed of nine clergy and nine lay members from across Canada plus the bishops. One can be re-elected to the same position at the following Sobor if that was the wish and will of the people. I was elected on August 1st and was a member until the following Sobor. My name was again put on the ballot, but I declined to accept the position for a second term.

If anyone has ever been to the Black Hills of South Dakota in the USA, they will know what I am talking about. There is one attraction there that is held each summer at Spearfish, S.D. It is the Passion Play, the Crucifiction of Christ. This Passion Play takes place three times a week, Sunday, Tuesday and Thursday. I don't recall how I learned about this Passion play. I believe that I must have seen it already four or five times in my life. It is a live performance performed outside to an audience of six thousand people. If you have never seen this before, you should make an attempt to see it once in your lifetime. Mary and I had seen this performance twice before and we told people in Dauphin about it. One time the late Harry and Anna Klapouschak said they would like to see this performance. They said they would pay all the costs, so Mary and I would go with them for they do not know how to get there.

On August 25th, very early in the morning (5:00 AM), we left for Spearfish with Klapouschak's car. We arrived in Spearfish in the late afternoon and rented a place to stay overnight. In the evening we took in the performance and the following day we toured the Black Hills. Among other things to see there, are the faces of some of the presidents of the USA carved in the mountain. There is also a mine where you can go and see the formations underground. Later Mary and my parents also went to see the same performance. Again after Marusia and I were married, again I saw the performance in the summer of 1988. Don't miss this in your lifetime to see this extra ordinary performance. As this is written in 2016 I must let the public know that a few years ago the Passion Play is no longer. People that played in the show retired and the company decided to close and cancel the event. It's too bad because a live outdoor attendance enjoyed by millions for all the years it took place does not run and operate no more.

A marriage of interest this year was on November 4th. A young lady Janice Gorchynski had been my Sunday School teacher. After graduating high school, she moved to Winnipeg to work and there met a young man Mykola Derewianka who had come from Belgium to St. Andrew's College.

They were married and later in May 1972 the ordination of Mykola into the priesthood took place in Dauphin. After the ordination they were given a parish at Ethelbert some thirty five miles north of Dauphin. We became close associates working for God and the church. When their first child, Pavlo, was born I was the God father for Pavlo. We had been close until 1988 when I had to leave the priesthood due to my illness. Father Mykola passed away in 2013.

This year in Dauphin there was another milestone for the congregation. As previously mentioned, the congregation had an old hall, the Ukrainian People's Home. It had become overcrowded and aged. The congregation in Dauphin had grown tremendously in the last few years and the hall was just too small to hold functions. It could accommodate a hundred and twenty five people while the congregation had over two hundred families by now. Talk about building a new hall had taken place as far back as the 1960's, but nothing had been accomplished. The manse where the priest lived was also outdated and the congregation needed a new manse for the priest. So at one or two meetings during the year the subject was always brought up about a new hall.

FRAUD - A SCAM?

Let me tell you a story that could have cost me my life. Mary had gone to Winnipeg to see her mother. I was home alone. One day towards evening I was getting ready to be picked up by the funeral director for prays in the chapel and funeral tomorrow, when there came a knock on the door. Now starts a story that may have been the end of my life. How? Well let me explain. I opened the door and a huge man was standing by the door and he asks me: "Are you Reverend Stefaniuk?" I told him I was. He told me his name (whether it was true, I don't remember) and said that he is from Saskatoon. I asked him to come inside and then his story begins. He said he worked for the highway department in Saskatchewan, but he got a job at Dauphin, Manitoba on the highways and is moving to Dauphin. He said his wife is coming tomorrow from Saskatoon with their furniture in a U-Haul truck, but he left a day earlier to check the house. He said he bought a house earlier in the NW section of Dauphin in the four hundred block.

He asked me if I know Father Maxim Olesiuk in Saskatoon. I told him I did because he lived here in this house were we are standing right now. Then he told me the story of the Saskatoon parish where he was a member and asked a few questions about the Dauphin parish. What he spoke about Saskatoon, I knew exactly those things so he was correct. He goes on and tells me that he was driving with his car and had a car breakdown near

Gilbert Plains, Manitoba so he called Martin Motors in Dauphin, they came with the tow truck and brought his car into Dauphin. He tells me he spent his money on the tow truck and has no money to call his wife and tell her what happened to him on the way to Dauphin. He asks me if I can borrow him a few dollars so he could phone his wife in Saskatoon. I took out my wallet and had about three or four $20.00 bills and one $10.00 bill. I gave him the ten dollars and he said that is enough to make a phone call to Saskatoon.

Then he goes on and asks a few questions about the Dauphin parish. I told him what he wanted to know and was glad that he was that interested in knowing some information about the parish. I told him I was waiting for the funeral director because he should be coming any minute to take me to the funeral home for the prayers for I have a funeral tomorrow. I told him that there is a bingo going on in the old hall and so he would go there and introduce himself to the men that were running the bingo and wait for me there. I told him to tell them that he saw me. I asked him where he was going to stay over for the night and he said he did not know where, because he had no money with him until tomorrow when his wife comes with their furniture. I told him that we have three empty beds and bedrooms and he can stay here and he thanked me and said he would come. He left and I saw him walk towards the Ukrainian People's Home where a bingo was going on. The funeral director came, picked me up and we went for prayers. After the prayers I was driven back home and started to put things together for tomorrow's funeral.

Having done that, I walked over one block to the hall to see the bingo and the man that came to tell me that he will be living in Dauphin and will want to be member of the congregation. I came to the hall and looked around, but that man was not there. I asked some of the bingo working people if such and such a man was there, but not one worker had seen or heard of him. Well that sounds somewhat irregular, for he said he was going to do as I suggested. Because he was not there, I walked over to the "Jug Store"(corner store) to get some things for tomorrow for breakfast since the man from Saskatoon will want breakfast and he has no money. The late Fred Chaykowski worked at the "Jug Store" I told him that we will have a new member in the congregation, but I told the man to go to the hall and wait for me, but no one saw the man that I had sent to the hall. Fred hearing the story says: "Reverend, you go home, close and lock the doors and go to sleep." When Fred said that, I kind of felt a chill go down my back, but I did as he said. The little store was one block from the church both on Main Street.

I came home and checked the basement windows to make sure non were broken, that no one had gotten into the house. Having the feeling that things were secured, I went upstairs to bed. Yes I fell asleep, but some time later I was awakened by the knocking on the door on the house. Did that man really come back to spend the night because he has no money for a motel? I did get out quietly from bed and putting on no lights in the house I tip toed from window to window to look down and see if I can see who was knocking on the door. Seeing nobody nowhere around the yard, I went back to bed.

Come morning I had the funeral and came home after the funeral was over. Now that I am free I will go and see if I can find the man and the house he bought and maybe help him unload the truck when his wife gets here from Saskatoon. I drove to the NW side of Dauphin looking for the four hundred block where he bought the house. Now something hit me here good and well. Just a minute now. There is no such house and number as he had told me. Maybe it is not NW, maybe NE. I drive to the NE area, but there is no such number. I checked with SE and SW streets also, but there was no matching number as he had told me. Well maybe he made a mistake. Oh, I know what I'll do. I'll go to Martin Motors, maybe he is there where they are fixing has car. I came to the garage and went straight to Peter Hrytsay who was a member of the congregation, and he worked in the body shop and ask him if they had the tow truck bring in a car from near Gilbert Plains the following day. I told Peter the story of the man that had come to see me. Peter went and got the book from the tow truck to check what kind of car and what else. We looked in the book, and what do we see? Low and behold, the tow truck was not even used anywhere yesterday. So now I guess I have a real problem on my hands. I leave the garage and the next stop will be the RCMP detachment to let the police know about the "scam defrauding person." The constable hearing the story tells me that was the last time I will see that $10.00 bill. So if that man did return at night to come inside to stay over the night, would I have lost the rest of the money I had, or would I have lost my life during the night and then he could have had a chance of getting away before anyone would have found me. He could have been long gone before someone would have discovered anything that something was wrong.

PARISH WORK CONTINUES

The highlight in 1971 was the blessing of the completed church. The Ikonostas was now in place and the ordered icons were in their proper positions. The interior of the church was repainted with a new coat of paint and all was in readiness for the blessing. Everyone was ready and prepared for the occasion. Because the hall was too small to accommodate all the people for the banquet, the congregation rented out the curling rink where there was a larger hall available. People saw that something had to be done since the congregation did not have proper facilities to hold its functions. Any bigger event that the congregation wanted to put on, a hall had to be rented. This year a new hall committee became more active and more meetings began to take place. More about the new hall will come later.

In 1972 I got more duties and obligations. The late Father Wasyl Aponiuk who was the parish priest at Ethelbert, Manitoba had retired due to his age, so there was no priest there. This happened a month or two before Easter. Since I was the chairman of this missionary district and closest to Ethelbert, the Consistory wrote me a letter to take the responsibility to give service to the Ethelbert Parish, so that people would have their Easter Paska blessed and other needed services. This continued most of the summer until a new priest arrived at Ethelbert on August 1st. The priest that was assigned to Ethelbert was Father Mykola Derewianka. In the meantime Father Aponiuk had retired to Dauphin and was renting an apartment next to the church.

As time slipped by, more and more meetings were held about a new hall. Some other people were saying that the congregation should build a new manse for the priest. A new hall and a new manse was just not feasible to build at the same time. Yes, of course I would have liked to have a new manse, but let first things come first. One time at a meeting, I had mentioned to the people to build a hall first, because the hall will later build the manse, but the manse will not build a hall. I told the congregation that a manse will not support the church, but the hall will. As the hall meetings continued, it looked like the hall may be built this year. In April 1972 a hall meeting was held in the church basement. Discussions continued and as in other previous meeting, I had always suggested to put a basement under the hall. There were only about two or three people who favored my opinion. Finally a day or two before the construction of the hall was to begin, a meting took place and I once again suggested to put at least a partial basement under the hall.

When I mentioned this at this meeting, one member stands up and says: "What is this about a basement? We have been talking about building an auditorium for the last few years and someone always comes to the meetings and speaks nonsense about some basements." That was it. I finally had enough. I picked up my papers and walked out of the meeting. If I speak nonsense, than I'm not needed at meetings - right? That same evening I sat down and wrote a letter to the Consistory asking to move me to another parish immediately. I had the letter all addressed and stamped to mail the following day. Next day on the way to the post office, I stopped to see Fred Chaykowski, congregation chairman, and give him a copy of the letter. Fred read the letter and says: "And what is this?" I told him that if I talk nonsense at meetings, than I'm not needed in Dauphin. We both sat for a few hours and hashed things over. He begged me to reconsider because neither the congregation nor the Consistory will accept my resignation. He said that he will see to it that things will be fixed up.

I did not mail that letter that day. I waited. When the next hall meeting came up, Fred asked that I also attend and he'd fix things up at the meeting. I went to the meeting with hesitation. What happened was that Fred asked me what I would like to see or say. I asked for one thing. I asked that it be recorded in the minutes that Rev. Stefaniuk was always suggesting to have a basement under the auditorium, but the people were against it. Today some forty odd years later when I meet with members from Dauphin, they tell me they feel like kicking themselves in their behinds for not listening to me about at least a partial basement under the auditorium. Many have told me personally that it is an error that they never put no basement under the hall. I did not need a basement, but what I was doing and proposing was for the good and the benefit of the congregation and the people. In 1982 when I was the parish priest at Hyas, Saskatchewan, the Dauphin congregation was planning to have a tenth anniversary celebration of their auditorium. The congregation was inviting me to come and partake in the celebrations. I told them that I did not know if I would attend. They said that if I don't attend than they will not have a celebration. My heart softened up and I did attend during which time I was given a plaque which mentions my participation in the new auditorium.

Early in the spring a surprise happened. Mary had gone to Winnipeg and wasn't home. It was ten years since I was ordained a priest. The congregation learned of this in some way and made me a surprise anniversary celebration. My parents and Mary came from Winnipeg, but they never came close by the manse, so that I would not know anything. It was all planned so well that I had no inkling of what was happening. One church family member, Peter and Rose Hrytsay, came over to the manse in the afternoon and said they were going to Clear Lake, Manitoba in the Riding Mountain National Park and they wanted me to go with them for ride. I was hesitant, but after some coaxing I went, but where? They turned around and started to go towards the direction of the old parish hall. We were going in the wrong direction, but he was driving so I did not say anything. When we came near the old hall, we see a lot of cars parked around. He slowed down and kind of looking around says: "I wonder what's going on in the hall today?" Than he turns to me and says: "You didn't hear of anything that was to be in the hall here today?" I said, "No, no one told me anything." Than he stopped the car and says: "Maybe we should just check and see who rented the hall and for what." Yes I was ready to have a look and see what all the cars where doing by the hall. Was there some bridal shower? Was there some meeting? Was it some birthday or anniversary party? When we walked in, the hall was packed to the rafters. My parents and Mary were sitting at the head table. Than I knew that something was cooked up for me. The congregation presented me a surprise tenth anniversary of priesthood tea get together..

As mentioned above already, the work on the new auditorium began in April 1972 and was progressing on time. I organized another event to take place on September 10th. In a little more than a month the auditorium will be opened for the first function in the new hall - a wedding. I had organized that we have a cornerstone blessed and installed in the corner of the auditorium. The Sneath-Strilchuk Funeral Home in Dauphin donated the marble cornerstone with the inscription on it. We had some special papers put in behind the cornerstone. A large crowd of people had assembled for this occasion. Present where the mayor of Dauphin, the contractor, workers, church members and others.

On October 28th of this year the first large event took place in the newly constructed auditorium, a wedding of 1000 people attending. That same night it was decided that never again that many people will be put into that hall. It was over crowded, and I mean OVERCROWDED. It is against fire regulations, and it was just lucky that it was not very cold outside that many people could convene outside and so the wedding went through. The people learned that it was just not feasible to hold such large events in that hall. After this wedding on October 28th, I had another marriage on November 3rd. Who was this second marriage? It was the sister of the groom of the first wedding in the auditorium. She was Sharlena Manchur who was a Hollywood actress. She starred in movies and she came to Canada with her fiancé to her brothers wedding. Seeing her brother married, a few days later they came to me to perform their marriage. Another wedding this year was held on October 6th, my birthday.

On November 25th of this same year the official opening of the new auditorium took place. I was asked by the executive to be a participant and sit on the stage with dignitaries. I did not participate. Why? Let me tell you another reason in a few words. When talk had started about the official opening, I suggested that we have the *blessing* of the auditorium and then the official opening.. I thought that at least the smallest thing I can do is read a prayer of blessing and maybe sprinkle the auditorium with holy water. The people were just dead set against this idea and no way would they permit any blessing. Than I figured out what two and two are. No blessing, no participation by me on the stage at the official opening ceremonies. When the day of the official opening came, I did not participate even though there had been a chair placed for me on the stage. I sat down among the people in the main part of the auditorium and took slides. I had warned the MC of the program that if he will call me to come and say anything, I will no go up. When the people saw what happened, they realized that what I said I meant and was not fooling or intimidating anyone.

Now 1973 had come. This year on August 19th is Holy Transfiguration, the Feast Day of the congregation in Grassland in the Lac La Biche Parish where I had served. I received an invitation to attend the blessing of their church. Mary, myself and Mr. and Mrs. Joe Beigun of Dauphin went to Grassland. After the blessing the following day we took a one day trip to Fort McMurray to see the oil tar sands that were starting the development. We could not stay any longer, because I had already received a message that a man passed away in Dauphin and I was needed to return for the funeral.

About ten days after we returned from Alberta, Dauphin was hit with a severe thunder and hail storm. Hailstones the size of **goose eggs** fell from the absolutely darken and black sky. It was so black that the street lights came on about 4:00 PM. Lights also had to be turned on in houses, because it was just so dark. The hail pounded everything in its path. Mary and I held pillows against the windows facing to the west, so that the windows would not get blown out. I had never ever seen hail the size that showered Dauphin that day. Some people as well as I had picked some hail stones as the storm was letting up and put them in the freezer. Pictures were taken of the hail size.

A REAL HOLIDAY

This was also the year that Mary and I went on a real holiday. Yes we had gone before for a few days here and there not to be too far away from home. This time it was different. This time our trip took us across the Pacific Ocean all the way to Hawaii. We drove by car to Vancouver and left our car at Mary's relative and took the Canadian Pacific flight out of Vancouver to Hawaii. It was a trip to another world. I have over five hundred slides of that trip. Let me say just a word or two about that trip.

We left home on October 21st and drove to my sister Alice and husband John Hnatiuk at St. Benedict, Saskatchewan. There we stayed over night and left next morning and drove all the way to Golden British Columbia. From Golden we drove through Kelowna and stopped overnight at Princeton. The fourth day we were in Vancouver at Tony Zaharias, who was a distant relative of Marys. When we left Vancouver for Hawaii in the morning, it was cool, wet and rainy. We had our heavier clothing on. A surprise awaited us when we got to Honolulu. It was eighty six degrees above zero. People looked at us as if we had arrived from outer space or from the North Pole when everyone was dressed lightly for Hawaii. We did not go to Hawaii with any group, but just on our own and because of that we were more lost not knowing where to go or what to see.

In twelve days that we were in Hawaii, we visited four islands, Oahu, Maui, Kauai and Hawaii. Many people asked me which island I liked the best. I could not give them an answer, because each island was different from the other for what it was. There was always something unique about each island. When we were on the big island of Hawaii, on November 3rd and 4th, a volcano erupted at that time. We had the opportunity to see the eruption and were only about a quarter of a mile from where the lava was pushed out of the ground. We could not come closer because guards were posted and would not let people get near the volcano. The lava flowed down towards lower levels and it looked like a red river slowly moving along the ground. There is so much about Hawaii that one can write a separate book about the trip and the sight seeing.

When we got back to Vancouver, we could not get out of the city, because a huge snow storm had closed all the roads out of the city. The Trans-Canada Highway was closed so we had to wait until the roads were opened. We finally left one day after the storm and as we drove we encountered snow plows opening up the roads. The roads were still heavy, but in some places the snow was beginning to melt. We had plans and wanted to get to Edmonton for Saturday, because there was a special celebration taking place on Sunday, the fiftieth anniversary of St. John's Ukrainian Orthodox Cathedral. We got to Kamloops after traveling the whole day from Vancouver which normally would be a three or four hour trip. We stayed over night in Kamloops and early next morning we headed out north to get to Edmonton before dark. We did not make it. We got about eighty five miles north of Kamloops and that was the end of our trip before noon. A vehicle had passed us and as it went ahead it lost control and headed into a ditch about eight feet deep landing on its roof. We wondered why and what happened. As we drove another mile or two more, we found out the problem - B l a c k i c e. We slowed down and we got about half way up an incline hill and nearly ended up in the ravine deep down below. It had rained during the night and the roads became skating rinks for the cars.

The car started spinning tires and we could not go any farther. We stopped at the side of the road and the car started sliding towards the curb, towards the deep ravine. It was just luck that as the car slid of the pavement and touched the dirt and gravel shoulder it stopped sliding, otherwise who knows where we would have landed. It wasn't until noon that some large semi-trucks put on chains and started to break up the ice on the pavement. Then we started to move after the trucks. Being still some three or four hundred miles from Edmonton, we knew that we would not make Edmonton that day. In the summer time when days are longer, yes, but in November the days are short and driving is not the best at night and in the winter. Then the snow storm that we followed from Vancouver was still ahead of us and the roads were rough and heavy. We finally made it home to Manitoba after the storm, but always a day behind following the storm. Near Roblin we found a large gasoline tanker in the ditch because of icy conditions. When we got home, we could not get into the driveway because there was snow and the plows had cleared the streets piling up banks of snow along the curb. I had to shovel that bank and the drive way for over an hour, so that I could drive into the garage.

A MIRACLE?

Then came the year of 1974. This was a year of unhappy events which was to end sadly some eight years later. There were other things that happened and they could be called miracles. Spring had begun with rain. It rained and rained and rained day and night. The rain began to remind us of the time of Noah and the ark. Water had formed in the fields and farmer could not get out to put the crops in. The ditches were filled and running with water towards creeks, streams, rivers and lakes. Rivers rose and overflowed their banks bringing more problems and misery. Water was all over. Flooding was starting to take place in lower areas in the town. Some churches began to hold special services praying for the rain to stop, but nothing helped. One Sunday during the service the altar server passed me a slip of paper. The late Anna Klapouschak had written a note to me saying: "Father, if you are free tomorrow, have a service in church so that the rain would stop. Announce so that people would come to pray tomorrow."

This special request service we held on May 24th. It was late, because usually by this time the farmers were finishing with their spring work. This year no farmer has even been on the field yet. Some farmers hired airplanes to do air seeding, because machinery could not get out into the fields. When we started our service at 9:30 in the morning it was still raining like it had for weeks. After the service and the veneration of the cross, people began to leave the church for home. I was taking of the vestments, when I heard someone came in and seemed very excited. Someone who was the first out of the church, rushed back into the church saying: "God heard us. You could see the clouds breaking up and blue sky beginning to show." Sure enough, an hour later the sun was out as the clouds moved to the east. Many people later told me that it was a miracle because God heard our prayer and gave the good weather. Farmers still seeded their crops and planted their gardens that year, even though it was late, late.

A few weeks later we had another opportunity in the congregation to make history. The choir conductor, the late Helen Lazaruk-Henderson, had been directing the church choir for over two decades. It was decided to make LP records of the choir so members could have a souvenir of the choir. This was done even though a number of people complained and said it was only a waste of money. They said money will be spent to produce the LP's and but no one will buy them. Today some more than forty years later, even if one wanted to buy one of those LP's, you couldn't because they are all sold out and not one left. The congregation made money from the sale of those LP's. It had also been a year before this that I had asked Helen Henderson to teach children to sing parts of the Divine Liturgy. A children's choir was formed and the children's voices are also recorded on the LP. The children came up from Sunday school and sang their parts in the service in the choir loft.

Why I wanted to have a children's choir is that when I went blessing homes with holy water after Epiphany, I saw that there were children in the congregation, but many of them and their parents I never saw in church. Some of the parents brought their children to Sunday school, dropped them off and went someplace else, only later to return and pick up their children after the church service. I believed that if the children sang a part of the service each Sunday, the parents would also like to be in church to hear their and see their children singing. It worked. As soon as the children began to sing their parts in the Liturgy, the church began to fill up with more parishioners. The time had come to the point there was no more room in the pews for people to sit. It happened that during the service younger men carried benches from the basement to put along the walls so that people may have a place to sit. Now some thirty years later I have hear from people from Dauphin saying that half of the pews could be carried out of the church, with so few people left in the congregation.

I can't tell how it is now since some have told me that some people have started to return back to church. I also had a good group of boys who were serving by the Altar with me - Altar servers.

THIS AND THAT - TIDBITS

It was also in the 1970's that the late primate of the church of Canada passed away. The late Metropolitan Ilarion had been my professor for four years and I always held high respect for him. When he passed away I went to the funeral to Winnipeg and I was one of the pallbearers at the funeral. As each priest continues his duties in the church, he is rewarded with different titles. I had received the latest title of wearing a gold cross and title of Very Reverend. These awards are usually bestowed upon the candidate at a service when the bishop is serving with the candidate that was awarded the award.

A very strange dream happened to me this year. It was the night of June 30th to July 1st a long week-end. As we were sleeping in the upstairs bedroom, I had a dream at 5:00 AM. I dreamt that some young girl dressed in a white wedding gown was running towards me across a meadow and was shouting: "Help, help." I could not see her face, for it looked blank like a bright light. When I heard the shouts for help, I jumped out of bed and glanced out the window. Nothing. I went to the three other directions to see who is calling and there was nothing there either. Seeing nobody around and no more voices, I went back to bed. The day rolled along. In the late afternoon at 5:00 PM sister Alice called. As soon as I answered, I knew by the tone of her voice that something was wrong. She says: "Eugene, we have some bad news. Linda Kochan died in a car in the lake this morning about 5:00 AM." Linda was John Hnatiuk's niece, his sister's daughter. My dream at 5:00 AM told me someone was in trouble, but who and where? It was at that time that the car with Linda Kochan had gone of the highway between Wakaw and Cudworth where Linda perished in the water inside the car. From that day on I began to wonder if dreams told you anything. Yes, the church does say that we are not to believe in dreams, but do we not read in the Bible how many times Joseph had dreams and also of many other dreams found in the Bible? There are over forty places in the Bible mentioning dreams.

Again this year Mary and I had an opportunity to take off some time from work - a working holiday. I had received an invitation from the Vernon British Columbia congregation to come to the Feast Day of their congregation on September 1st. We were going to spend a few extra days in the Okanagan, but an unfortunate drowning accident took the life of a young husband and wife from Dauphin in the Kalamalka Lake near Vernon. The couple had been vacationing in the Okanagan. They were on a boat and something happened that both perished. They had two small children which they had left at home in Dauphin with their parents. It was a very sad funeral to have two coffins in the church side by side, husband and wife.

On July 12 - 1970, Her Majesty Queen Elizabeth the Second was on a tour in Canada and was in Dauphin on this day. The clergy of Dauphin were asked to be at the grandstand this day where an ecumenical church service would be held with Queen Elizabeth, Duke of Edinburgh and their daughter in attendance. The service was to start at 10:00 AM. On Sundays our service also started about the same time and yet many people wanted to be present at the grandstand. I told the congregation that we would have a service in our church at 8:00 AM and than everyone would have ample time to get to the grandstand and be part of the service there. The service was served by the Anglican and Roman Catholic clergy. All the rest of the clergy sat at the side on the grandstand stage. After the service was over each clergyman stepped forward and introduced himself who he was and what denomination. The late Effie Perepeliuk took a picture with a cheap camera, had the film developed and gave me a copy of the picture when I was shaking hands with Her Royal Highness and her family. I enlarged it and have a copy to this very day. There was a large crowd in attendance for this ecumenical service. People from all denominations came to witness the service and to see the Royal Family. The large grandstand in Dauphin was full of people. Many of my parishioners later thanked me that we had the service in our own church early in the morning and still had ample time to get to the grandstand and be participants in the event that followed to see the Royal Family.

This was the year that for the last few months Mary was not feeling very well. She began to loose weight and while the doctors were saying they could find nothing wrong, we could see that there was something wrong. This was the problem that some eight years later took her life, that dreaded disease - cancer. On October 10th she left for Winnipeg to visit her mother and while there she went to see a doctor on October 18th. In Winnipeg the doctors immediately diagnosed the problem, admitted her to the hospital and surgery was performed.

On October 28th she had surgery at 2:00 PM in the Misericordia Hospital. I could not be in Winnipeg that afternoon, because I had a memorial service and a panakhyda (requiem) service on the 29th. The memorial service had been booked weeks in advance and on the 30th I had a funeral in the morning. Because I was not in the hospital when she had her surgery, she later held this against me. Many times later she told me that when she awoke from surgery, I wasn't there, but her mother was. How could I have left the memorial service when people had it booked weeks in advance, prepared meals and all. Than that evening a prayer and a funeral the following morning. I had asked the people to postpone the funeral for one day, but they could not. Than if I would have went, what would have I done for her when she came out of surgery? Her mother was now retired, nothing to do, so yes, she could spend hours and hours with her. On October 30th right after the funeral I left for Winnipeg leaving the rest of my scheduled meetings and all for another time.

She stayed in the hospital until November 6th. She did not come home, but went to stay with her mother. That was good, because she was close to the doctors, the hospital and her mother could give her better care than I could at that time. She stayed in Winnipeg until December 7th. When I had gone to see her on October 30th, I also went to see the surgeon to find out what was wrong. The doctor confirmed that it was cancer in her lower bowel and he was sure that they got everything out and there should be no more problems. The doctor had also asked me not to tell her that it was cancer because it would be better that she not know what the problem was. It was hard to hold a secret, but I had to do as the doctor had asked me. It wasn't until her second surgery that the doctor finally told her what was what, but about this I will come back later. When the illnesses started in our families, it seemed like it did not know when to stop.

The new 1975 began with more illnesses. On January 10th we received a call from Winnipeg that Mary's mother was found unconscious in the house and was taken to the hospital by ambulance. We both left for Winnipeg immediately. Fifteen minutes after we got the phone call we were on the road heading to Winnipeg. It was winter, cold and snow was beginning to fall. We got as far as Portage La Prairie and I had to turn back home. A bad, bad snow storm was already in progress before we even got to Portage La Prairie. The visibility was reduced considerably at times that it was hard to see in front of you. I had to be home the next day, because again I had a service on the 11th and a few other things to do. We stopped at Portage La Prairie at a service station that Matt Kereliuk managed and who hailed from Dauphin and were our friends. I told Mary that I have to turn back and head home. I left Mary at the service station with the hope that someone will stop at the service station that is going to Winnipeg and she can hitch a ride with them. Returning home, I did not know if I would make it home or not. The storm became worse around St. Rose, some thirty miles east of Dauphin. It was so bad that I could not see where to go, so I crept along and at times even stopped at the side of the road by hearing the sound of the wheels if they were on the pavement or on the shoulder of the road. From time to time the wind would let up for a minute or two and I would drive up until another blast of snow and a gust of wind would blind everything and nothing would be visible. It was night time. It took me just over two hours to drive the last twenty miles to Dauphin.

Mary's mother stayed in the hospital from January 10th until March 3rd, just about two months, before the doctors diagnosed and got her diabetes under control. The doctors had to get her sugar down before sending her home. That same day her mother came home, Mary also had surgery again in Winnipeg. Mary did not come home until the middle of March after being in Winnipeg since January 10th. In the meantime when I had a few free days I had made a number of trips to Winnipeg to see her and her mother

This figure three was both joyful and sad. As mentioned above Mary had her surgery on March 3rd. This same day Oksana gave birth to her only son, Lawrence. Than the figure three brought grief to the family. On April 3rd, one month after Lawrence was born, Oksana's husband Lawrence passed away suddenly at home. He died from a massive heart attack. He had seen his little son for only one month and Lawrence grew up not knowing his father, only what he sees on pictures. When Lawrence passed away I knew something was wrong someplace. I just had a feeling that I can not even begin to explain. It was as if something was gnawing at me and I could not tell what. Mary and I had just sat down to supper and this feeling was just not giving me any peace. It was a little while later that mother called from Winnipeg and broke us the news that Lawrence had passed away. On April 8th was the funeral. He left surviving a young thirty year old wife with four children, three daughters and one son, Brenda, Gail, Cathy and Lawrence. Than as if the figure three was not enough add twenty to the three and you have more pain when on the 23rd of April, mother was rushed by ambulance to the hospital. While doing something outside she got a stroke and heart attack. With prayers of many faithful people, God heard the prayers and restored her life but never again to be as previously. Some eighteen years later that number twenty-three again played a role in mothers life, for on June 23rd, 1993 she passed away

As was already mentioned, the year 1974 was a bad year, with heavy rains in the spring and then an early snowfall storm. Why do these things happen? Because of people's sins. People forget God and made gods themselves and want God to listen and obey them. People think they can live without God. Well in 1975 God again showed His hand against sinful people. This year the rains came again, but not in the spring. They came when crops had been swathed and ready for harvesting. So much water appeared that the waters were running off the fields and were taking the swaths of grain with them into the ditches, streams and creeks. The town of Dauphin again experienced flooding as it did the previous year. This was happening in the month of September. I drove around Dauphin, St. Rose and area and took many slides of the damage that was done.

MY ILLNESS

Then as if this was not enough, I also became a victim of illness this year. Beginning on October 5th, 1975 coming home from a wedding in St. Benedict, Saskatchewan I began to get a pain in my left leg. Mary, my parents and I had been to Bill Noble and Gracie Kochan's wedding. Gracie Kochan was the daughter of the late Tina Kochan and the sister to late Linda who had died in the car accident in the lake. The leg pain was not going away. Next day I purchased some liniment and smeared the calf of the leg where the pain was, hoping that it would ease the pain. When nothing helped after a day, I went and bought a different kind and stronger liniment. Again I smeared the left leg for a few days, but the pain would not go away. Because of this pain it was difficult to sleep at night and I was not getting enough rest. I did not know what the problem was, so I was trying different liniments trying to cure the pain, but no help was coming.

On October 10th the pain was so bad that I was up at 5:30 AM. Mary was asleep and not waking or telling her anything, I dressed and went to the emergency. I thought that before Mary gets up, I would be back from the hospital, but that did not work. I thought maybe I would get a needle to ease the pain and would be back home in an hour. The good doctor Sigurdson knew better. He checked my leg and said that I had phlebitis (blood clot). He admitted me to the hospital and went to tell the nurses to get a bed and room ready. There was no way that I was going to be admitted, because tonight I have a marriage rehearsal and a marriage tomorrow and than a service on Sunday in church with special missionary activities on Monday. The doctor went and told the orderly to bring a wheel chair and take me to the nurses station and they will tell where my room is. The doctor returned and I said that I would like to take the car home and than I will walk back to the hospital. No way. It would not be so. The doctor said that I must be off my leg and can't use it for mobility. It was at this time that I spent seventeen days in the hospital recuperating from this illness. While staying in the hospital, I asked Mary to bring me a few scribblers and pencil and it was at this time that I started to put down on paper what you are reading today some forty years later.

The doctor told me to get into the wheel chair and stay off my feet. For the first ten days I was not allowed to even step off the bed. One nurse that worked in the hospital was my parishioner, Mrs. Storozuk. When she came into the room I began to tell her what had happened. I told her that I rubbed and smeared my leg for a few days with liniment before I came to the hospital. When I told her this, she suddenly left and went out of the room. Some time later when she returned she told me why she had left so suddenly. She told me that it was not a wise thing to do to rub a blood clot. She said that a piece of the blood clot could have broken or separated, could have gone to the heart or lungs and that would have been the end of me. But how does one know what the pain is from? I tried to help myself and not to bother anyone. I guess God still needed me and had some other plans for me on this earth. After this episode of spending seventeen days in the hospital, changed many things in my life.

After I got home from the hospital, I was put on medication - blood thinners. Every week for six months I had to see the doctor in the afternoon after I had blood samples taken in the hospital in the morning. This was to check the clotting of the blood. Because of the medication that I was on for some six months, it gave me side effects that are still with me to this day and will be to the last days of my life on earth. From that day I was somewhat stricken with memory loss. I was told later by people that my blood thinners did cause memory loss. I can read a book or something and if you asked me the next day what I read, it was already forgotten. I do not know to this day, how I survived with the memory loss. If someone would ask what I read, I would say: "I forgot." I remember many things that happened before illness, but it's after and till this day that memory loss is with me. And finally 1975 came to an end after a tumultuous year of ins and outs, good and bad.

But as the old year ended and the new 1976 came upon us, it was starting as the old one left. On February 25th I had minor surgery done to my face. I was having some growths between my nose and my cheek. The growth was like a wart and would grow and than it would bleed. The doctor decided that I should have that removed. After this was over, I thought things would be well, but it was not to be. A few weeks after this surgery, the growth began to reappear. I went to see the doctor and he said that more surgery was needed and back I go to get it done. This time the doctor said that he would cut deeper. After this second surgery the growths have not reappeared.

My parents had heard from Mary and me about the Passion Play in the Black Hills of South Dakota. They asked about it and mother said that she would like to go and see it. On June 8th, my parents, Mary and I left for the Black Hills. This I believe was already my third or fourth time that I saw this performance. You should make an attempt to go and see for yourself. It may change your life. I learned in 2016 that those performances have been cancelled because the people (actors) retired due to age and health.

After the parents were retired in Winnipeg, they had more time to go visiting. Because mother had been a cook for weddings and other occasions when we stilled lived on the farm at Tarnopol, she was hired for the summer months to be the cook for the children's church summer camp, Veselka, north of Winnipeg near Gimli, Manitoba.

A NEW MANSE AND FAMILY HEALTH

It was at one annual meeting in 1974 or 1975 a motion was passed that the congregation build a new residence for the priest. It was decided to build the manse in 1977, so that it would be the congregation's fiftieth anniversary project. This would be the main event of the celebration. Usually anniversaries last one or possibly two days, they get over and are forgotten and gone. I made a proposal to the congregation to celebrate the anniversary whole year long. How can that be? Very easy and simple. People seemed surprised because anniversaries are celebrated on one or two days and it's over. My idea was that each month of the year be dedicated to someone or something. One month we would honor all the presidents of the congregation, both living and deceased. The next month we would honor the choir members. The third month we would recognize those that assist the priest by the Altar, the elder brothers and Altar boys. One month would be to celebrate and have official opening of the new residence. Another month the Ukrainian Women's Association who have financially and otherwise supported the congregation from its beginnings would be honored. When the members heard this, they were in agreement that this would be something worthwhile. A plan was made how we would celebrate the anniversary each month for the fiftieth anniversary of the congregation.

It is ok to build a manse, but with what when there are no funds. The members decided they would make donations to raise funds for a new manse. Monetary funds began to flow in and it grew. As months passed by, I was again beginning to have sleepless nights. What was happening was, that some people behind my back began to gossip that the congregation is building a house for Stefaniuk. Why for Stefaniuk? No such thing was ever talked at any meeting. It was a manse for the priest. Why not say a manse for the parish priest, but saying that the congregation is building a house for Stefaniuk. At monthly meetings I talked, explained and asked members to tell those who say such things that the house is not for Stefaniuk, but for the congregation and the priest to live in it. I was telling the people that when time comes to move from Dauphin, I will not take the house with me, because it's not mine and it will stay here in Dauphin. But the talk of a house for Stefaniuk continued.

When May 2nd came this year the congregation was celebrating its Feast Day which falls each year on May 6th, St. George Holy Day. By this time I had already heard enough about the house being built for Stefaniuk. That day after the service there was a meal in the hall. After the meal I made a promise to the congregation. I told the people present that as soon as the new manse is constructed and ready to move in, I will leave and move out of Dauphin the day before and I will not live in the new manse. The congregation was stunned and if you would have been in the hall that moment you would have heard a feather fall through the air. At first everyone thought that I was joking and took nothing to heart. By this time I had heard enough of such talk and had to take some action. After the Feast Day when people met me anywhere, they said that I was joking about moving away when the manse will be ready. I kept telling them: "Wait when the manse is ready and built and than we will see if I'm joking." Other people were telling me, that I was trying to scare people. Why would I do that? When the time came, the people found out the truth. I never lived one night or day in that new manse.

While all things were happening around us, father and mother did their things. They were now retired and resting more in their golden years. Father had joined some organization, I believe it was men who had served in the first World War in the Ukrainian Army. Father served in three armies during his time. First he served in the Austrian Army when Ukraine was under Austria. He was captured by the Poles and then served in the Polish Army and lastly he served in the Ukrainian Army when Ukraine liberated itself from under the Russian yoke in 1918-1921. Father went to their meetings and functions. Father also had a brother in Ukraine who had lost his leg in the war and was an amputee.

My health problems still were not over. Mary was still not feeling well. We went to Winnipeg on August 31st. She stayed behind in Winnipeg to see the doctor while I returned home. When I returned from Winnipeg I was not in the best of health. Probably tension and stress were following me around. Mary is not well and neither is her mother plus all the work and the mind could only hold for so long. On September 7th I went to the clinic to get tests and examination done. The tests all showed negative, nothing wrong. But why than was I not feeling well? Something was wrong, but what? Mary went to see the doctor on September 18th in Winnipeg and was admitted to the hospital. Three days later she had surgery - hysterectomy. Her troubles weren't over by far. She stayed in the hospital until October 4th when she was released and went to stay with her mother to recuperate.

This same year took me to a small community in Saskatchewan at Hyas for a special Thanksgiving service and program. I was invited to the special thanksgiving program and was the guest speaker at that occasion. Who would have thought that some years later I would be the parish priest in that same area of Saskatchewan and would live in Hyas for eight years.

Finally on October 18th Mary returned home from Winnipeg. For nearly two full months she had been away. All the while I still lived with prayer, hope and faith that everything will turn out to be fine, even though the doctor had told me that she had that dreaded disease. Hope was that maybe she will pull out of this and be a survivor. But as we will see later that did not happen because at the young age of forty four she passed away. As time passed by, I somewhat began to feel better and thought that now maybe things will be better for us all. That happiness did not last long, for five days after she came home, she had to rush back to Winnipeg, because there were complications after the surgery. She did not return home again until November 25th.

After she returned from Winnipeg and as if those worries were not enough another thing happened. I was at a church meeting in the new auditorium. Mary was home alone. As she later told me, some one had come and knocked on the side door of the house. When she went to answer the door, there was no one. When I arrived from the meeting, I got a big shock. At the side of the house lay a Union Jack flag and looked like two rifles were wrapped in it. I was shocked, scared, afraid and froze in my tracks. What is happening and going on here? For a minute I stood outside and thought what to do. Do I rush into the house? Do I not go in? A number of thoughts ran through my mind. Maybe someone is in the house. Maybe someone came and murdered Mary and waiting for me inside. Maybe there is a kidnapper in the house. The only thing I could do at that time was to be careful, - VERY CAREFUL.

I stood and thought what action I should take. I know what. I'll open the door slowly and call into the house to see if Mary is all right. If I hear no answer I let my feet carry me to the back lane and to the nearest telephone. I will speak through the open door. If I hear an unusual sound or voices, I'm gone from there. Slowly and quietly I opened the door and called out for Mary, if she is home and if there is company. She answered that she is alone. Than I called her to come to the door to be sure she comes herself. She came and when I saw she was all right I asked her what the flag and the rifles are doing by the house. She came to the door, looked and said she knew nothing about it. She said someone had knocked on the door, but when she answered there was no one. She did not see the flag and the rifles because the door opened in the direction of the guns and she did not see them for they blinded in that area.

When I saw that things were normal inside the house, I called the RCMP without touching or moving anything. I knew that the police would want to investigate the matter, so best not to touch anything. The police arrived quickly in no time at all, but in that short period of time many thoughts flew through my head. Maybe someone wanted to murder or kidnap us, but it did work out, they got scared and took off. Or did someone commit a murder someplace and than dropped the rifles off beside the house to put the blame on us. Did someone want to scare or frighten us for some reason. All kinds of thoughts raced through my mind in such dramatic moments.

When the constable arrived he picked up the flag and riffles, put them in the trunk of the cruiser, than came to the house to get some information, ask some questions. As it turned out, we later found out that someone had broken into the Dauphin Museum and stole the articles from there.

Why he or they would drop them off at our residence was and still is a sixty four dollar question. We were a about half a mile from the museum and whoever it was before they came to our place they passed dozens and dozens of houses. Why did they not leave it at some house but at our place? Than the question still remains, why did someone knock on the door and not answer when Mary had come to the door. I do not know if any of the guilty were ever discovered, caught and brought to justice. Nerves and tension were not getting any help from such a situation. I believe that the tension was just too much because at 3:00 AM I had to get out of bed and rush to the bath room where I was sick and threw up.

As the year was coming to an end, there was hope to look forward for maybe the coming year will bring happiness instead of the grief we were going through. On December 18th the congregation was holding their annual bazaar. I bought a few tickets for a raffle from Mrs. Effie Perpeluk. As I paid her for the tickets, the left palm of my hand became itchy and I had to scratch. As I did that Mrs. Perepeluk says: "Your left hand is itchy, so you're going to win something." I laughed that off and said: "I never win anything." Then she says: "If your left hand is itchy, you will win or get something. If it's the right hand, than you will be shaking hands with someone." As the bazaar progressed, towards the end there was a draw for some prizes. My name was drawn and I won a Ukrainian ceramic clock. That clock is still in our possession and running to this day.

Always when the New Year is bearing down to start its cycle, people look forward that maybe the New Year will be better then old one was. The year 1976 was gone and the eyes were now looking into the far distance to see what may lie ahead. What would this New Year bring? Will it again be grief and sorrow? Will it be more heartaches? Will the sun shine on us in the New Year? But when 1976 came to the end it was just as ruthless as the previous year had been in the families life. The New Year took over and was continuing where the old year had left off. Just three weeks into the New Year Mary left for Winnipeg to see the doctor, because she was just not feeling well. She went to get a checkup. To this time neither the doctor nor I had told her or her mother that Mary had cancer. On February 3rd the doctor brought the news to her and said that he would have to send her to the cancer clinic in Winnipeg to have some tests done. For years she had dreaded this disease for she saw what it had done to her father and many times she would say: "You know I could cancer inside me just like any other people."

As Mary was in Winnipeg, I was alone at home. The work of preparation for the fiftieth anniversary had to keep going ahead. The building of the manse was to begin in 1977. When people saw that the manse was really in the stages of planning, donations began to pour in again. Plans had been drawn and the contractor was hired. Than there was also the matter of what to do with the old manse, for the new manse is to be built in the same place. The congregation said they would have to pay some contractor to demolish the old manse and clear the lot. The congregation was now worried that they would have to fork out a number of dollars to get the old manse removed, but I had another plan - idea.

At one meeting I suggested to put an ad in the paper that there is a house for sale and it must be moved off the lot and bids will be received and opened at a certain day and time. People looked at me as if I had fallen off the moon for saying such a thing. "Who will give you anything for that old house?" They began to question me. I replied: "Neither you nor I know that, but if we don't put an ad in the paper, we will never know." Somehow my words were more convincing than those of the pessimists. I had talked to the treasurer and a few others of the executive and told them what I had in mind, so they supported me to try and see if it would work. Someone said that the ad would cost a few cents and not big money, so that we should maybe go this way and might sell the old manse. The motion was passed and an ad was put in the paper. The bids that came in were not opened until the designated day, time and place.

When the hour to open the bids came, the executive gathered in the church basement for a meeting. As the bids were opened and revealed, some of those who were against such a plan, got a good shock when they realized that there were some people who were interested in the old manse. After all the bids were opened I told the executive to call the people with lower bids to tell them if they want to up their bid, they may do so as it is as an auction sale. The lowest bid that came in was $200.00 and the highest was $3000.00. As the evening rolled along the end result was that the manse was sold for $5000.00. The buyers would have to come and move the house of the lot by a certain day at their own expense. When all was over and done, people could not believe their ears nor eyes what they had seen and heard. They had made $5000.00 clear money and it did not cost a single red penny to get rid of the old manse. The manse was moved to a farm south west of Dauphin to the Kosiw-Keld area. When the manse was sold, Mary and I had to move to another place to live. The congregation rented out a house at 419 Jackson Avenue, behind the hospital. On March 30th we moved out of the old manse..

The day of fulfilling the dream of the congregation's anniversary project was drawing near. On May 4th, the old manse was removed from the lot. The lot was cleaned and readied for sod turning ceremonies to be held on the Feast day of the congregation on May 7th. On this day late Fathers Dmytro Luchak of Winnipeg and Father Mykola Derewinka of Ethelbert and myself served the Divine Liturgy and after the service on a beautiful sunny day had the sod turning and blessing of the lot to commence building of the manse. Hundreds of people looked on, some surprised to see the progress, others still not sure what was happening. The building of the new manse began a few days after the sod turning took place.

MOVING TO PRINCE GEORGE, BRITISH COLUMBIA

Next came two things which again brought changes in my life. I was in Winnipeg on May 11th, attending a Canada wide clergy conference. At the same time in Dauphin the beginning of the construction of the new manse was starting. In Winnipeg the conference at St. Andrew's College was in progress. At that conference I still know till this day that I received a message from God. Father Luchak was speaking to the conference and was telling how the church is living with a shortage of priests. He said that just a day before the conference he received a letter from a small group of people from Prince George, British Columbia who were "crying in the wilderness." They were asking the Consistory to send them a priest, otherwise their little congregation will fall victim to "sheep in wolfs clothing." It was at that time as Father Luchak was reading that letter, that something in me kept saying: "Go, go, go." I had heard of Prince George before, but never even came to my mind of ever being interested where it was, what is was, etc. Now something stirred my soul in me telling me to go north and help those people. As we already have seen, I had once asked the church to send me to northern Alberta, the Peace River country to serve, and nothing came out of it. Now something was whispering to me to go to this northern British Columbia community.

At the first opportunity during lunch break, I had a chance to talk to Father Luchak. I told him that I was interested in Prince George and would like to go there to serve. I said I would like more information about the congregation. I had now been in Dauphin just about a full nine years when I was sent to Dauphin on a **temporary** basis away back in 1968. After my bout with a blood clot, the doctor had advised me to stay more off my feet. If I do get the chance to move and what I had promised in Dauphin, that I would not live one day in the new manse will be fulfilled. Father Luchak gave me a copy of the letter from Prince George later that day and the more times I began to read it, the more times something was telling me; "Go, go, go."

On June 3rd another blow hit our family. Mother was taken to the hospital after receiving her second heart attack and a mild stroke. More worries clouded my mind. Why do all these things happen to us? Prayers were offered, God heard the prayers of many and partially restored mother's health from which she pulled through and did not stay in the hospital very long this time.

Even though with mother's illness, Prince George was not leaving me and my thoughts. While the body was in Dauphin, my thoughts were flying over a thousand of miles to Prince George. Finally Mary and I decided that we would drive out to Prince George to see for ourselves the people, congregation, city, etc. On the 19th of June, after the service, we left for Prince George. We arrived at Prince George at Mr. and Mrs. William Tarnowetski's place. We got acquainted with them and later they drove us to show the church. And what a sight. Tall grass growing around. Windows broken. Dust which was coming through the broken windows was inside the church on everything from a dusty and gravel road past the church. Fence on the south side property broken and partially lying on the ground. The paint on the church in khaki color peeled, blistered and peeling off. Things looked more like a haunted building. But what can one expect when there are only ten families in the congregation. Still over $30,000.00 are owed for the church which had been purchased from the Mennonite people. No manse for the priest to live in, because the priest used to come from Vancouver once in a while. Move here and where do we begin anything. Leave Dauphin with all facilities and everything organized and come here into nothing?

Things began to turn and twist in my head. More questions popped up than answers could be found after I saw the church. How much will I get for support if I move here? Will the congregation be able to give me support with their debt, no manse, etc.? A thought flashed through my mind: "Why did I come here?" In the other ear I heard a whisper say: "Remember the pioneers. They came here and they did not even have this. They started with absolutely nothing. They survived, you will also."

The next evening the congregation in Prince George had a meeting, because people heard we were in town and they wanted to see and meet us. When the people arrived at the church the following evening, it seemed like we had known them all our lives. The friendliness was great. We all jellied together like jello in a bowl. At the meeting people were interested and wanted to know the situation of the church in Canada. I told them what I knew. They asked us to move to Prince George to be their priest. I told them that what I had already seen, that if the church sends me here, I would be willing to work and help them. They also wanted to know what honorarium I would want. I told them they would not have to worry about that, because I would not demand from them that which the congregation did not have. Everything went well and we were sure as sure could be that this is going to be our move. After spending another day in the city of seventy thousand people I felt even more that I wanted to stay here already and be a part of this congregation and community. We left for home the following day. Before we reached Dauphin, we stopped overnight at St. Benedict at Alice and John's place. From there I called the Consistory and told them that I was ready to move to Prince George on the day when the clergy are moved to new parishes.

When we got back home to Dauphin, we told the people where we were, what was happening and the conclusions we had reached. The people could not believe what they were hearing. Some were telling me I was joking and were having a good laugh. They soon found out the reality. Mostly I wanted to go and help the small congregation and also because it would give me less work to be off my feet as the doctor had told me to do. When the congregation realized it was not a joke, they made us a farewell tea on July 20th after I held my last service in Dauphin. We received gifts from the congregation and good wishes, many tears were shed by many people and many went home with heavy hearts. Now they knew that

Stefaniuk was not joking and that he always did what he said which was to help the church. The promise which I had made that I would move out as soon as the new manse was ready was now being fulfilled. I think that many of the people later learned their lesson that it was not a house for Stefaniuk, but a parish manse.

The day came to leave Dauphin. We had packed our belongings and I went to get the U-Haul trailer. The people hooked up the trailer to the car and I came home with it. Everything was packed into the trailer on the 27th of July and at 5:00 AM, and we left Dauphin for Prince George. The car was loaded with more delicate items and the trailer with everything else. Things were going well until about six or seven miles east of Roblin, Manitoba. We had just gone across a railroad overpass and coming down an incline towards a small river. As we traveled down the incline, the car started to speed with the trailer pushing on it from behind. I tried slowing down the car by braking, but no way, it just would not yield to braking. I thought that death would meet us before we reached the bottom of the incline on either side of the ditch. The car went from one side of the road to the other and when it got off the pavement you could hear the gravel pounding under the car. The trailer and car were roaming from side to side and as I tried braking to slow down, nothing helped. Death was staring us in the eyes. At the bottom of the hill a bridge and river. If we don't hit the ditch than surely we'll crash into the river.

God and/or the Guardian Angel must have been on our side at that moment and helped in avoiding a crash that could have occurred. We had been coming down the hill at about fifty to fifty five miles an hour. I had never before driven a car with a trailer behind. What was I doing wrong that I could not control the car and trailer? Why was the car not holding back the trailer? It was not the brakes on the car, because they were working when we left Dauphin, for I had stopped at stop signs and slowed down at speed limits on level roads. Yet down the hill, we just about met death.

After that scary incident I was afraid what would happen when we come west of Roblin and will have to descend a steep hill to the lake below and climb up the hill on the other side of the lake once we cross the lake. When I was just about to start the descent of the hill, I put the car in low gear. Than using the brakes, we made it safely and without an incident. Than why did I have a problem a few miles back? As we crossed into Saskatchewan, past Yorkton and coming past Sheho another low long incline was before us. As we were coming down I could feel the trailer again starting to push on the car and the car was starting to move out of control. Because we had been going much slower now about forty miles per hour, I suddenly stepped on the gas, the car with more speed straightened with the trailer and everything turned out well. Am I driving too slow or too fast that I am having such problems? If such small inclines are giving me such fears now, what will the mountains do? So I started to gear down before each downward incline and the rest of the trip to Edmonton went well.

We finally arrived in Edmonton and stopped overnight to see John. We had supper at John's and I told John of what had happened along the way to Edmonton. John being a mechanic said that there is something wrong and he wanted to find the problem right now. I also knew something was wrong, but what? After supper John and I went to check and see if the problem could be found. John looked at everything and all things looked okay. Than he says to me: "You drive slowly along the curb and I will walk beside and look to see if I can see anything." I drove slowly and than would step on the brakes. John was watching what was happening. After a few tries, he said to stop. He went, got a wrench and unscrewed the top off the master cylinder on the trailer. He took the cap off, checked, and the master cylinder was drier than the Sahara Dessert. Not one drop of brake fluid. We drove to the closest service station and bought two pints of brake fluid. We put one pint in and then I again drove around the block while John was walking along the curb and watching. John bled the brakes and then he said that to him it seems like things are working now.

I was still not satisfied. I still have at least four hundred miles before us and mountains to boot. What will happen when I hit the steep down hill inclines? Would we make it to Prince George or will we end up in some ravine a few hundred feet below? I thought that before we get to Prince George, I will try on some smaller hills to see if it will be any different. Next day July 28th we left Edmonton for Prince George. I was driving, but felt uneasy, because I was not sure what was awaiting us on the big hills. Here and there as we drove I tried to brake going down small hills when there was no one behind us. It seemed like it was better and the car was stopping easier. Later on the first steep hill I tried to stop. The car and trailer both stopped on the downward slant as I wanted. Half way down the incline I braked again and the car and trailer stopped. Now the brakes on the trailer were working. From then on there was no more problem all the way to Prince George. The U-Haul trailer should have been checked over before it was let go for the road. That was negligence on the part of the U-Haul company for renting out a faulty piece of equipment to people. What would have happened if we would have ended up with an accident and even killed? The dealers who have the U-Haul equipment should be checking everything before they let it get out on the road.

That was not the only thing that was lacking with that trailer. Coming through the mountains here and there we ran into rain showers like many times in the mountains it happens. We arrived in Prince George at 9:00 PM and stopped at Tarnowetski' s place. The congregation had been informed by the Consistory that we were coming to Prince George, so they had made arrangements that when we arrive to find an apartment for us to live in. Next day Tarnowetski's took us around to look for an apartment. We did not want anything fancy, just so there would be a roof over the head and a bed to sleep on. Another thing the congregation had no money to pay for luxury apartments. We drove all morning from one place to the next looking at dirty, filthy and expensive apartments. Finally we found a two bedroom apartment near the main street and less than a mile from the church. When we came to unload the trailer, it was then that I found another fault with the trailer. There was a leak in the floor and the water from the showers along the highway got inside and damaged some Encyclopedia books on the floor of the trailer.

LIFE IN PRINCE GEORGE

Mary and I had still not fully unpacked our things and settled in on August 4th, when there was a knock on the door. We thought some church members had come to see us or check and see how things are. We opened the door and there standing in the hallway are my parents, laughing. What a surprise. I never found out where they got our address that they found us. A relative of ours was getting married at Williams Lake some one hundred and fifty miles south of Prince George this coming Saturday, so father and mother drove to Prince George so that we can go together to the wedding. They also came because they wanted to see Prince George, the church and the people.

I have to mention one thing about the wedding. The day before the wedding father wanted to go to a liquor store and buy a bottle of liquor to take to the wedding. I took him to a liquor store, he got what he wanted and we came home and brought the bottle into the apartment. Next day as we were dressing and getting ready to go to Williams Lake, father took the bottle of liquor to put in the car trunk so he would not forget it. He did not think to ask for the keys to the car and I did not know what he was doing. He went outside and than realized that the trunk of the car is locked. Instead of bringing the bottle back with him to the apartment, he placed it beside a fence post in the shade away from the sun. Then he came into the apartment and we were all busy dressing and talking, he forgot about the bottle and the locked car trunk.

So far everything is fine. We are all dressed and leaving the Prince George for Williams Lake. All four of us walk out, get into the car and leave. After the marriage in church the family went to Mike and Anne Derzaks motel before the reception will start in the hall. Mike and Ann Derzak owned the Lakeland motel in Williams Lake. When we got to the motel father asked me to open the trunk of the car for him. I thought he wanted to put something inside. I opened the trunk, he looked inside all over and than says: "Where did you put the bottle of liquor?" I told him that I do not know anything about any liquor. He looked confused and said that he put the liquor in the trunk and I must have did something with it. I tried telling him that I don't know anything about any liquor. He looked restless the rest of the day. After supper at the reception we stayed for a little while and than had a three hour drive back home for tomorrow I have my first service in Prince George.

When we got home it was already pitch dark. As I pulled into the parking spot to park the car when all of a sudden father says: "Oh there it is, the bottle of liquor beside the post." I remember mother telling him in the car: "You are always like that, you put something someplace, than can't find it and you blame someone else for it." Father got out of the car quickly and went to check the bottle. He was sure it had been empty by now. He lifted it up, but it was still full. I remember him saying many times later when we reminded him of that event and he would say that the people in Prince George were honest people that they didn't take that liquor.

Tomorrow is August 7th, my first service in Prince George. Oh yes, there will be mistakes and lots of sweating. It always happens that when you come for the first time to a new job or new place, you are not accustomed to the surroundings, people and are somewhat unnerved. And how poorly that first service went. No one to sing the responses. Everyone is tense, excited and afraid to make a mistake, but with God's help the service did go over. Later that evening in the apartment after we had been sitting and discussing things I remember till this day what father said: "You won't last here six months and than you will be looking someplace else for a piece of bread." How wrong he was at that time. I stayed in Prince George for three full years and much progress was made. I could have stayed on even longer had the church not taken me from there to go to Hyas, Saskatchewan. When we came to Prince George there were ten family members. Three years later when I left there were twenty family members and had I stayed there longer, even more members would have been in the congregation. At Hyas there were some two hundred families while at Prince George only twenty. The church thought a priest is needed more where there are more members.

So Mary and I have now been a few days in Prince George. The parents stayed a few days in Prince George and were leaving back for Winnipeg. By this time Mary had already decided that she will go back with my parents on August 8th, because her mother is in Winnipeg and she is going to go and see her. She also said that she wanted to go and see the doctor in Winnipeg. She left with the parents on August 8th and did not return until September 8th, one month later.

That same day when the parents left for Winnipeg, the congregation called a special meeting to discuss a few things with the arrival of the parish priest. A few things were discussed and than they brought up the topic of the priest's honorarium. Different ideas flowed back and forth among the members. At the time when I left Dauphin I was receiving $650.00 per month. In Prince George after some discussion, Steve Essar made a motion that the congregation give me an honorarium of $1000.00 a month. That's very good, but who is going to make payments which were still owed of $30,000.00 on the church, pay all utilities, pay for apartment where the priest is staying, etc. etc.?

As they were talking about the honorarium, I interjected and said: "I thank you so very much for your decision and generosity, but I will not accept such an honorarium. If you think you can give me $500.00 a month, good. If you can also pay for the apartment, good. I will look after the utilities at the apartment suite. If I will be short, I'll turn to the Consistory for they have a missionary fund for such a purpose and they can help me out. If I will have no food, I'll go to one member and will ask for potatoes. I'll ask another member ask for a loaf of bread, but I cannot take $1000.00 each month when you have all that debt sitting on your shoulders and no manse, appliances, etc. To me it would be a sin to take such money from you when you don't have it." At that I sat down. The congregation thanked me and said they would abide by my wishes of $500.00 per month honorarium.

In Dauphin I was getting $650.00 per month and now in Prince George I will get $500.00 a month. Is that a $150.00 raise? Would - or did any other priest or any worker in Canada do the same? Everyone always wants the most for himself, not thinking about others, but only, give, give, give. When I was getting $500.00 a month in Prince George, did I ask the Consistory for aid? No. When the congregation paid off the debt on the church two years later, they themselves raised my honorarium and I did not have to ask for a raise. In November 2005 when I was living in Lac La Biche, Alberta, I received a telephone call asking me if I would consider coming back to serve the congregation in Prince George. I told them that the bishop or Consistory have only to write me a letter and I start packing the same day I receive a letter.

But one can't pray very well when there is dust flying all over and around you. Windows are broken by the vandals and cars go by and the dust flies into the church. Sticks, paper, rocks, cans on the church yard, paint peeling off, etc. There was physical work that had to be done that was for sure. So on September 10th a work bee was organized where members came and everybody did what they could to clean up the church yard and the church. I asked why the windows were not replaced. I was told they had been replaced time and again, but are broken again and again. I suggested that they put plastic windows even in different colors and plastic will not be broken. This they did and on the day when I was leaving Prince George three years later, and not one window had been broken during my stay in Prince George..

The beginning of a new life in Prince George was not easy, but I did not mind that. It was much less work than had been in Dauphin and that was better for my feet. The same money matter as had happened in the Lac La Biche parish, and in the Dauphin Parish, now even the same found me in Prince George. The treasurer had given me a cheque one time and says: "Reverend don't cash this cheque for a few days because we are short of funds in the bank." No funds, than we have to do something to make funds. We started to hold bingos in the church basement, rummage sales, sale of varenyky, caroling and other fund raising activities. We checked and found out on what days there were no bingos in the city and we started to have bingos on that free day. Bingos were bringing in thirty to fifty dollars a week which was a great help. Than an organization heard that we were having bingos on a certain day, they began to hold bingos on the same day in a larger hall, with better prizes to take the people away so that we would not make any money. Our bingos fell off so much that we had to give up on that project. But God was on our side. Even when others were trying to hinder and eliminate the Ukrainian Orthodox church in Prince George, it was to no avail, because things began to expand in other ways and the congregation was moving forward. Yes there are such people and organizations that do not want to see the truth and they try different schemes to destroy the church, but Jesus said: *"The gates of hell will not prevail against it."* (Matthew 16:18)

As time crawled along, Mary's health did not improve. On October 4th we were in Vancouver at the cancer clinic. The news from the clinic was not good or encouraging. Her cancer seemed to be spreading slowly. The doctors were telling her that she should have surgery and chemo-therapy. Numerous times she asked me if she should take chemotherapy. I told her straight forward that I cannot tell her what to do in this case. I said it was between her and the doctor. I was not a doctor and I did know about medicine. If I say that she takes chemo-therapy, and it does not work, she will blame me. If I tell her not to take it and she will get worst, she will blame me again. I said she must listen to what the doctor says. All this time she kept in touch with her mother by phone. Her mother usually called when I was already in church on Sunday mornings. On Sunday when it was 9:00 AM, I was already in church, when in Winnipeg at that time it was already 11:00 AM. Mary never came to church until just before the service was to start, so her mother called when I was not in the house. Calling from Winnipeg, her mother always said: "Don't take any chemo-therapy or any kind of treatments." I knew that her mother told her this, because sometimes she would tell me that her mother had called. Even if I would have told her to take-chemo-therapy, she would not have listened to me as she didn't listen to the doctor but only to her mother.

After living in Prince George we got a phone call from Dauphin that a very good friend of ours and worker in the church William Perepeluk passed away. The family called and asked me to come to the funeral. About a month before this the congregation had sent me an invitation asking to come and participate in the official opening and blessing of the new manse. I was not going to go to this function, but now that the funeral will be held on October 21st and the official opening of the manse the following day, we went and attended both functions.

As stated already, things in Prince George were poor. Services were now held every Sunday. Before we came to Prince George, services were held once a month or less often. When services began every Sunday, people began to attend more often and regularly. Families saw that we needed things for the church and some began to purchase things that were needed. One lady, Olga Wynnychuk, who was a seamstress and lived at Bear Lake, some fifty miles north of Prince George said that she would sew anything that the church needs, like banners, robes and other items. When I had left Prince George, she had sewn three pairs of vestments, two banners and other things. Material was purchased by a family and she would sew the article.

Mary's health was not improving and that was at the top of our list of things to do. Once again she had to see the doctor in Vancouver. She left for Vancouver on November 22nd by bus to see the doctor at the cancer clinic. It is five hundred miles from Prince George to Vancouver. There were other patients in Prince George that had to travel to Vancouver to see a doctor or get treatment at the cancer clinic. Later Vancouver and Prince George made arrangements that a doctor from Vancouver would come to Prince George to see the patients. It was better for one person to come north than for dozens of people to go south. This made it cheaper and the patients were at home. When the doctor from Vancouver would come, Mary would have an appointment in Prince George to see him. She was told time and again to start chemo-therapy, but because her mother said no, she would not consent to it. It was not till some time later I learned from our family doctor who said that; "If Mary does not want to take chemo-therapy and take the doctors advice, than she should not go and see the cancer doctor anymore."

The year 1977 did not end on a sad not. After all it was the year that the congregation got a resident priest. After many meetings, discussions and planning, it was December 12th that the construction of a manse was started. It was a prefab house and when it was ready, it was moved unto the lot on December 17th. Previous to this we had a sod-turning and the blessing of the site were the manse would be built. The church had engineers survey the church property and subdivide it so that a manse could be built next door. On December 13th, it was cool, foggy and rainy in Prince George. It was on this day that the basement was dug for the manse. Things were beginning to look brighter on one side, but a financial dark cloud on the other side still hung over the congregation. The debt on the church was still unpaid and now the congregation brought another debt of $40,000.00 on the manse. On one side of the face you could smile of the advancements made in such a short time, while on the other side you could cry that the financial load was increased.

Now came the new year 1978. New hope that things will be better. On January 4th I had to appear in court. No I did not do anything wrong. I got a call the from the court clerk to come and be an interpreter at the court. I received a phone call from Manpower and Immigration to come to their office because they have a lady who can't speak English, only Ukrainian. I arrived at the office and found that the problem was not a small one. A Ukrainian lady had immigrated to Canada from Poland and got married. She arrived here and had a small child with her. The marriage had gone sour and she said that her husband had thrown her out of the house. The manpower hearing this story called a lawyer. I was told to take this lady and child and go over to see the lawyer and to be the interpreter at the same time. This lady and her husband later were to appear in court and I again was called up to the courts to interpret for the judge. There were two or three more appearances in court and each time I had to interpret during the court case. One day in the evening I get a phone call from this ladies husband who said that he doesn't want to see me in that court again and to be an interpreter or I will have trouble. I felt that there was a feeling of guilt on his part and that was why he called to intimidate me. I knew that the lady needed help, but because of his threats I did not want to have anything to do with that case.

One day the court clerk called again to tell that the case will be set for such a date and that I come as interpreter. I told the court clerk that the husband of the lady had called me one evening and gave me a threatening talk not to interpret anymore. I told them to get someone else and I gave them names of two or three people. Whatever happened with that case and that man, I don't know for I never heard from anyone anything more.

At the end of January came a happy day. On the 30th of January everything was completed in the manse. The final inspection had been done and was passed that we could move in. We moved in, but there was a problem. This is January and there is no power in the house. How do we keep warm? We had to plug in a two hundred foot extension cord into the church to get power into the house. You could not put too many lights or appliances on, otherwise the breaker would jump out and I would have to go the church even in the middle of the night to trip the break back on.

So why was there no power in the manse? Why was it not hooked up? The power people in B.C., were on strike at that time and they would not hook up the power. We could not live this way where you have to dress up in the winter each time to go and push a breaker in or else neither the furnace nor any appliance would operate. I went to see the hydro people about this matter and complained. They told me that the only thing I could do was to call the Labor Department in Vancouver and tell them what the situation is and they may give them an injunction so that the power would be hooked up. I told them I had a wife in the house who has cancer and we need power in the house. The strike was still on, when orders came from Vancouver that the power to our manse must be hooked up. Two days later the phone was also hooked up, even though the telephone people were reluctant to do so because they said that the power poles were also used for telephone, and those poles were declared "hot" because of the strike.

As mentioned previously, my honorarium was minimal and there were no other services like marriages, funerals, baptisms were funds could come in. In November 1977 when we were still in the apartment, Mary say: "If we had a colored TV, I would stay home more often and watch TV." She had been going to the shopping malls, found friends and they would meet each day in certain places for coffee or whatever. Hard as it was for finances, we decided that we would get a colored TV to please her, because she was not well. In December 1977 we purchased a color TV at Woodward's, but had to take it on monthly payments. That did not solve the problem. Mary was still going out two or three times **a day** visiting friends that she would find in the malls. She would see someone on the street or the mall, start a conversation and the next thing she was at their place drinking coffee.

Work in the parish continued. In 1978 we prepared a Taras Shevchenko concert in March. Mrs. Wynnychuk and I had been teaching Ukrainian language classes with students and with them we prepared the concert. The people from the local TV station got wind of our program that we held in the church basement and called me one day if we could come to the TV studio and they would tape the program to air on TV. We did this on March 23rd. I remember that day very well. While taping the program inside, outside other things were happening. It had begun to rain and rained so hard that when we were going home many streets were flooded and there was water everywhere.

In 1978 a little financial light came on, but that came with extra duties. I was asked by Bishop Boris from Edmonton to look after the Peace River area in Alberta. This is the same place that I had previously served from Lac La Biche a number of years earlier. From Prince George to Spirit River the closest congregation was three hundred miles one way and the farthest to Hotchkiss it was four hundred and twenty miles. How many people would be willing to travel that far to hold services? When I would have services in Peace River area, the congregation in Prince George said that whatever I get for those services, I may keep for myself.

Spring had now arrived. New ideas came with spring. I made a suggestion to the congregation to paint the church on the exterior. The answer was: "We haven't got money." I made another suggestion that each member contribute a few dollars to buy the paint and we would not need to take any money out of the account. If we donate our labor as a "work bee" than we do not have to pay for that either. The members agreed to this. About the middle of May we started scrapping off the old paint. After that the church was painted a white color with light blue trimmings. It had been painted previously in a khaki color. Later everyone agreed that the church now looked very pretty as compared to what it was before.

The church was painted. The manse was built and now it should be blessed. At a meeting it was passed that we invite Bishop Boris from Edmonton and Father Michael Fyk of Kelowna to come to this occasion. This event took place with many people in attendance and the first time that a Ukrainian Orthodox Bishop was in Prince George. Father Fyk had been the first priest to hold services in Prince George away back in August 1971.

Another thing that happened this year was that one day I received a phone call from 100 Mile House, British Columbia from a couple who wanted to get married and if I could come and see them. The bride was Greek and the groom a different nationality. They could not get a Greek priest to perform the marriage on the day they wanted to be married. So one day I drove to see the young couple. When I got there, I discovered that the groom was not baptized and the father of the bride owned a restaurant in 100 Mile House. The father also wanted the restaurant to be blessed. There was no Orthodox Church in 100 Mile House. On September 25th after the service in Prince George, I drove to 100 Mile House. I baptized the groom in the home of the bride. Than all went to the restaurant. I blessed the restaurant and after that we had the marriage ceremony. Following the marriage, the reception took place in the restaurant.

This year was also the Special Sobor(Synod) held in Winnipeg. On the 9th of July after the service, Mary and I left for Winnipeg and we also took our holidays for this time, so we were not expecting to get back to Prince George until July 24th or 25th. After the Sobor in Winnipeg we stopped at St. Benedict for a family wedding. John and Alice's daughter Cathy was getting married. I participated in the marriage ceremony in church at Lepine about three miles east of Wakaw, Saskatchewan.

Financially things were still tight with us. I knew I had to do something to get a few extra cents. I began to look for something. It had to be something that I could be free on week-ends to conduct services. At manpower there was nothing at that time. I looked in the daily paper and found ads, but they were not suitable for me because sometimes I would have to work week-ends and I need week-ends. One day I found an ad that said you work when you are free. I called the number and the man gave me an address to come immediately. I went as fast as I could so as not to be late. It was the Filter Queen Vacuum Cleaners. They were looking for people to go from door to door to sell vacuum cleaners. At first I hesitated to take this on, but than I knew that my week-ends and other days I needed would be free. I agreed to take on that work and try it. There were also a few other men in a room and we were given training for an hour how to go about selling the vacuum cleaners

It did not take long to find out that this was not the easiest job. In order to make a sale you had to tell how good the product was. You go from house to house trying to sell. Every house has a vacuum cleaner, so how many more do they need? I was too honest and in the three months that I was selling, I sold one vacuum cleaner and that was not even in Prince George. There was no limit to which territory or area you went. You could go and sell wherever you wanted.

The one that I had sold was out of Prince George some hundred and fifty miles at Valemount, British Columbia. The sale I made was that God sent me there. I had stopped at a few homes, but no prospects. Just as I was about to leave back for home, I stopped at one more house. Never say, never. I guess God was with me that day also.

I knocked on the door and a lady answered. I told her who I was and why I came to see her. As I was telling her this, she stared at me as if dumbfounded. For about a good half minute or more she never said anything, just stared at me. She looked at me and studied me over up and down and then says: "Are you God?" Now I was dumfounded. Why would she ask such a question? I did not know what she was thinking when she said that. As she was still looking me over, I said: "No, I am not God , just trying to sell a vacuum cleaner." She says: "Than God must have sent you, because I was vacuuming the house about ten minutes ago and the machine stopped and I am not sure what I should do." We talked for another minute and than I said I could demonstrate the machine I have in the car. She and her husband said that they would be willing to see the demonstration. I went to the car and brought the machine in. I showed them, how and what about the vacuum cleaner and they bought it. Their old machine was standing in the middle of the room watching my demonstration.

For each vacuum cleaner you sold you would get one hundred dollars salary. I sold the one vacuum cleaner, but to this day I never saw even a red penny not alone a hundred dollars. Later I found out that the dealer was not an honest person. Others told me later they also had trouble with the man collecting their due wages. Some had even gone to the Department of Labor to get their pay from the man. Had the man been honest and just, he should have paid his workers. I left that place and never even went near there again.

As already was mentioned, Mary received sad news from the doctors when she visited them on November 2nd. She had gone to the cancer clinic in Prince George for her checkup. After the doctors examined her, they said that unless she starts Chemo-therapy treatment immediately, she has only one year to live. Such news will make anyone sad and depressed even more when it is a family member. She was already going through anguish and I was not feeling any better with such news. She would not listen to the doctors, but only to her mother. The doctors told her that she had one year to live, but she still lived for three years until March 1982.

A week after Mary received that news from the doctors we were on the way to Edmonton, because there was a clergy conference. When we got to Edmonton, she caught the first bus out of Edmonton for Winnipeg, because she wanted to see her mother. She stayed in Winnipeg until December 18th. In the meantime I was alone at home and had as many worries as there are stars. I had gotten to such a point in my life that it also became at stake. I had to go and see Dr. Staniland but he could not diagnose the problem, so he sent me to a specialist on December 19th. I was having a feeling that there was something in my throat and was choking me, like shortage of breath. After the doctor checked me over, he said he needs some x-rays done. The x-rays were taken on December 21st. Later when the results came in, they showed there was nothing wrong. What was happening was that the tension, stress and nerves were causing me that condition. The year 1978 ended on this unhappy note.

Now will a new year 1979 bring better news? Always when a new year comes, hopes and dreams give a boost to a person. The happy thing this year was that on January 17th, the congregation paid off their mortgage on the church, the full sum of $17,000.00. At least now the congregation had less debt, only on the manse. It is interesting to note that the $35,000.00 loan which was taken out for the church for a period of ten years was paid off in just five years. All this was possible because of the dedicated faithful families of the congregation who sacrificed their time, energy and money to see the debt paid off. When there was anything to be done, everybody pitched in and helped. The congregation held two large events each year. A Fall Ball in November and the Malanka, Ukrainian New Years Eve, in January. Each of these events brought in a very good profit for the congregation. These kind of events brought in enough funds that the debt was eliminated sooner.

In April Mary and I took a one week trip to Winnipeg to visit our parents since April 13th was mother's birthday and April 15th was fathers birthday. We wanted to be there for this occasion. At the same time I had to visit the church headquarters, the Consistory, to get some things from the church goods store. I should mention one other thing. Since Mary and I had been married, both our parents lived in Winnipeg. Anytime we ever visited Winnipeg, we always had to stay at Mary's parents' place overnight. Oh yes my parents also asked many times that we stay over at their place, but it was never to be. To keep peace in the family, I went her way and stayed with her parents. I tried telling her and her mother that one time we could stay here and the next time there, but Mary and her mother would hear nothing of it. It was always one way, and one way only.

CALIFORNIA - HERE WE COME ! ?

Again this year we had a financial setback when we purchased a used 1971 Volkswagen camper. When Joan Matvieshen, Mary's friend from Dauphin, had visited us in Prince George the year before, the two of them had begun to plan for holidays for 1979. Mary had always talked about California and wanting to go there. I said that I would like to go there too, but it was just not possible, because it would be too expensive. Mary was always suggesting that we get a camper and we would not need to sleep in motels or eat in restaurants, but we could use the camper for that and the expenses would be small. Many times when we traveled and met campers on the highway she would say: "It would sure be nice to have a camper like that one and than we could go wherever we wanted." She talked about campers and said that we should buy one and than we could go to California with it.

 Finally I gave in and said that if we ever find anything that is in good shape and cheap, we can try and buy it. I knew what the doctor had told her some time back, that she had one year left to live. I was now seriously thinking that I should fulfill her wish and make that trip to California. On May 15th we did purchase a camper which was all finished inside for sleeping and cooking. When we bought this Volkswagen camper she wrote to Joan to come to Prince George and we will go to California, but she did not tell me anything that she had written to Joan and asking her to come to Prince George and we can go to California..

Joan wrote back when she was taking her holidays and that she would come to Prince George. When we got the letter, I was not sure what to say and do. It took a few days to worry over how three people could go on such a long trip with a small Volkswagen camper. Earlier, when we lived in Dauphin, we had met a from Porterville, California and I thought that if we get to his place, he would direct us or go with us to show us California. We had met George Alexandro, when he came to the Ukrainian Festival in Dauphin a number of years back. I wrote a letter to Mr. Alexandro in California and told him that we would be coming and will stop in and see him. He replied back very quickly and said that if we come he will pay us for the trip. Well now, that was a very good gesture from his side. Before we start on our holidays, let us stop here before we leave and learn what else happened before then.

Where we lived in Prince George, we also had a small garden by the manse. The garden was planted and all was fine until one day on August 1st. The ladies were making varenky in the church basement. Mary and I were there helping them. About 9:00 AM I had to go to the house to get something that was needed in the church basement. As I came near the garden and the house, I looked and a cold shiver ran down my back. In broad daylight between 8-9:00 AM, someone walked into the garden and tore out the vegetables scattering them around the garden. Never did find out who the culprit was and never bothered calling the police, because they wouldn't have been able to do anything. All it did for me, was give me a good scare and some worries.

Then came a historical date for the congregation. On August 11 - 1971 was when the first service was served in Prince George. Since that day, the small congregation pushed ahead and flourished, slowly fulfilling its duties to God and man. They purchased a church but went into debt. They got their very own parish priest. They built a manse for the priest and furnished it. Than just eight years later from when the first service was held, on August 12 - 1979 Father Michael Fyk was again invited to attend a service in Prince George. This day the congregation burned the mortgage on their church. The burning of the mortgage papers took place in the church basement. What a happy and joyous occasion. Now they have their own church and owe no one anything. Tears were seen in some of the eyes as the flames ate up the mortgage papers. Now they can say that the church is "OURS." My parents and Mr. and Mrs. Hawaleshka from Winnipeg also were in attendance at this mortgage burning ceremony. I never told father anything, but very well remembered his words which father had previously said that I would not last six months in Prince George and that in six months I would have to go looking for work.

Another first for the congregation this year was an open air service. This service was held on the shores of a beautiful Davie Lake some fifty miles north of Prince George. After the service followed a barbeque, sing-song, swimming and fishing. Everyone enjoyed themselves and made a pledge to hold such an event every year weather permitting. A date was later set to hold another service in 1980, but because of bad weather that came on the day of the service, it was canceled and the service was held in the church in Prince George. I was moved out of Prince George in the fall of 1980 and I don't believe that any more open air services were ever held there.

Now let us go back to the California trip. Joan Matvieshen had phoned us on Saturday September 1st that she will be arriving in Prince George on Tuesday morning September 4th and so we would pick her up at the bus depot. Mary said that as soon as Joan arrives we should leave for the trip to California. Another important thing about this planned trip. George Alexandro knew that we were coming and he had mailed us a letter telling us he is awaiting our arrival. Enclosed with that letter was an American one hundred dollar bill to help us pay for expenses along the way to California. As mentioned earlier he wrote he would pay for our trip to his place and back. More about him will be told later.

Everything looked fine and even by now I was getting excited to go on such a trip. But before Joan arrived in Prince George, Mary became ill. She got a severe back-ache so that on September 3rd she did not even get out of bed because of the pain. By evening she began to feel somewhat better with reduced pain even though she was still complaining that she had a sore back. She had to hold on to me or to the wall when she walked because of pain. On September 4th when Joan was arriving she felt somewhat better but had a hard time walking due to pain. We both went to the bus depot to pick up Joan. Seeing the condition Mary was in and knowing that she had cancer, I made a quick decision before Joan arrived that we would not be going to California in Mary's condition.

What would happen if we left and were over a thousand miles from home and she became worse on the trip? We would be in a foreign country and what happens about doctors, hospitals, medication, etc.? Before Joan arrived we already had talked and knew that we would not be going to California if anywhere. All three of us were somewhat disappointed that we would not see California, but health must come before holidays. There was no other thing we could do. Yes we could fly, but who had the funds for such a trip? That same morning we were to leave, I sat down and wrote a letter to Mr. Alexandro that Mary's illness became worse and we can't come. I also returned him the one hundred dollars that he sent us. With Mary's condition, we stayed home, sat in the house and talked.

The next morning September 5th Mary thought she was feeling somewhat better. Around noon she says: "If we couldn't go to California, let's go to Prince Rupert." It is about five hundred miles to Prince Rupert and it is nearly noon. I did not want to disappoint Mary because of her condition, so I said: "Yeah at least if we go it will be in British Columbia and should you get sick worse, our health system will take care of us here in B.C." We got things thrown together in no time at all and just before noon we were already on our trip. It was a picturesque trip with mountains, rivers, forests, etc. We pulled into Prince Rupert about 9:00 PM that evening, just as the sun was starting to go to bed.

Arriving in Prince Rupert, the first thing we had to do was get a motel for the night. We found a motel and I went inside to check and see what is what. Mary and Joan stayed in the camper. I did not know what was transpiring in the camper when I was in the motel, until 1980 when I got a letter from Joan. She wrote me and said what happened. She said that while I was in the motel getting two rooms, she and Mary had quite a talk. She said Mary turned to her and said: "Why did you have to come with us when we are married and you are single?" What else happened I don't know, but I knew something had transpired while I was in the motel, but I did not question anyone and no one said anything more. I was not surprised from the letter that Joan had written to explain those events.

We stayed overnight in Prince Rupert and the next day we went sight seeing and took a chairlift to the top of a mountain from where we could see Prince Rupert and the Pacific Ocean with all the islands around. We had dinner and after that we left back for Prince George. We stopped along the way here and there and took pictures and viewed the scenery. We stopped at Kitimat to see the town and than drove on to Terrace where we spent the night. Next day taking our time we drove leisurely and arrived home when it was already dark.

Next morning I was up as usually in the summer time at 6:00 AM. I had a lot of typing to do so I was in the office typing. Mary and Joan did not get up until later. They made breakfast for themselves and were eating in the kitchen. I could hear that they were not talking normally, but they were whispering. I got up and was going to the basement to get something and went through the kitchen. They must have heard me get up and as I neared the kitchen and I heard one of them whisper: "He's coming." To this day I don't know what they were whispering about..

That evening when all were already in bed, Mary said that Joan will be leaving for home in the morning. Next morning I drove them to the bus, dropped them and the luggage off and went to park the car. After I parked the car and was going to the bus depot, I met a man whom I knew and we talked for a moment or two. Than I started towards the bus depot. When I was coming to the entrance of the bus depot, Mary was already coming out and we met near at the door. She said that Joan was already on the bus.

MARRIAGE - FALLING APART

On November 3rd, my oldest niece, Pat Hnatiuk was getting married in Saskatchewan, John and Alice's oldest daughter. Mary and I left for the wedding driving the first day to Edmonton on November 1st. Next day brother John took his car and his son Gregory and the four of us were going with one car to St. Benedict. My car was left in Edmonton. Mary had already decided at Prince George, that she would not be returning with me back home, but she will keep going to Winnipeg with my parents. And she did. After the wedding on November 5th, my parents were returning to Winnipeg and Mary went with them, while John, Gregory and I returned to Edmonton. Mary said that she would stay with her mother for a month before returning home.

When Mary got to Winnipeg she wrote me a registered letter, that's right REGISTERED. To this day I don't know and will never know why. What happened was that after two months she and her mother had already hatched up some kind of scheme. By now we had been married for nineteen years. In that time we wrote many letters to each other when she was away from home, but never a registered letter to one or the other. But this time a registered letter? Why? I was upset to get a registered letter from my wife, and that was on my mind, why? In her letter she stated that her mother was not feeling very well and since winter was coming she would stay a bit longer in Winnipeg. Her mother was a diabetic and was going blind.

I wrote a letter back to Mary (not registered) and told her that if her mother needs help with winter coming that maybe she could stay longer even if all winter long. I told her that I would take care of myself so she would not worry about me. When her next letter came, I was even more confused and upset. She wrote and said: "By the sound of your letter, you don't want me to come home." What is going on here? Those words at that time sliced me like a sharp knife slices warm butter. I did not know what was happening there in Winnipeg that she was writing such things. To this day I still say it was all her mother's doing. We had never written such words to each other in the nineteen years of marriage. All I could do was sit, think, worry and wait to find out what is going on.

Around the middle of December I got another letter from her stating that she would be coming home the following week (December 17-22) only she did not say what day. I did not know when she would be coming, so I went to the bus depot each day, December 19, 20 and 21st at 4:00 PM when the bus came in. But she never arrived. I thought maybe she changed her mind and was going to spend the winter in Winnipeg, or maybe her mother was worse so she decided to stay on. I thought if she is not coming, than a letter will probably come and explain.

On December 21st three buses were coming from Edmonton to Prince George, but I did not know that. It was the Christmas season and more buses were put on the road. I went to the bus depot and when the bus arrived, she was not on it. As I was ready to leave for home when another bus approached. I quickly returned back to the bus depot. The second bus unloaded and she was not on it either. The third bus came in much, much later after I had already left for home. I did not know there were three buses arriving from Edmonton that day. Two buses came and she was not there, so I went home. I came home and put some supper to warm up. Myself I sat down at a piano that we had and was playing (learning) and singing to myself. My back was to the kitchen and the house entrance. Playing the piano I did not see or hear anything. Suddenly ice cold hands touched my cheeks from behind. Did I get a shock. Because of this we will see what happened to my health.

Mary had arrived on the third bus when I was already at home. She said she tried phoning me to pick her up, but no one was answering the phone. No one could. Why? Till yesterday there had been one phone with the same number in the manse as in the church. The day when Mary arrived from Winnipeg, the telephone people installed a new number for the manse. When she phoned, the phone was ringing in the church basement, but there was no one there to answer it. Mary did not know about this so she called the old number which she knew but there was no one in the church basement and she did not know that there was now a new phone number for the house.

When she could not get in touch with me she took a taxi home. She had the keys to the house. I was playing little keyboard and singing with my back to the door, I did not hear or see when she came home. She had a key, unlocked the door, walked in and from the back touched me with her cold winter hands. Than she began to yell at me, why I'm not home to answer the phone, because she called from the bus depot, but I was not answering. I told her that I had just come from the bus depot, but she was not there when two buses arrived. I asked her how she got to Prince George when two buses came and she was not on them. She said that there were three buses and she was on the last bus. I told her that I saw two buses, everyone got off, she was not there, so I came home. I also told her that the phone number for the manse is not the same any more as it was.

Next day was Saturday. Nothing unusual happened all day long. In the evening we were sitting and watching TV. I sat on the chair and she was laying on the chesterfield and had herself covered with a blanket. I do not remember if the fireplace was burning or not. All of a sudden as we were watching TV, she jumps up from the chesterfield and went to the bedroom, to bed without saying a word what was happening. This day she had also called her mother in Winnipeg and gave her the new phone number that we now had in the house. I had also called my parents that day when the new phone number was given us.

On Sunday December 23rd I was having a regular church service. As I was getting ready to go to church at 8:50 AM, the phone rang. I was in the office and answered the phone. Mary in the meantime picked up the phone in the kitchen where she was having her breakfast. It was Mary's mother calling from Winnipeg. When I answered the phone, the first thing her mother said was: "How come you are not in church? Don't you have a service today?" In Winnipeg it was already 10:50 AM. She forgot or did not realize the difference in time. I answered her and told her that I am all ready to leave for church, when she asks me : "What time is it there?" She thought it was like in Winnipeg nbear noon already. I told her it was 8:50 AM and I still had an hour before the service is to start. Mary at this time was on the other phone in the kitchen listening what we were talking.

Before anything more she asked how Mary was feeling. I was going to answer, but Mary answered first and said that she had a cold that morning. As they were still talking, I said good-bye because I have to go and I hung up the phone in the office. Mary kept talking with her mother. When I was leaving for the church, Mary was still on the phone and finishing her breakfast. I could sense by their talk that something was not right only I did not know what. I could not get it out of my head the words her mother had asked, why I wasn't in church. It was only later I learned her mother always called Mary on Sunday morning when I was already in church. I went to church, got everything ready and by 10:00 AM people were in church and the service started. Mary was not in church.

Because Mary was not in church, I took it that she had a cold and for that she did not come, but probably went back to bed. I made nothing of it even though I thought maybe she will show up later. Halfway through the service and she still was not in church and so I was not worrying, because probably her mother told her not to go to church but back to bed if she has a cold. That's all right. If a person is ill, a person can stay in bed and at home. When the service ended, Mrs. Malayko asked me for some papers that I had prepared for her, but had forgotten to bring them to church. I told her that the papers are on the kitchen table and before I disrobe from my vestments, I told her she can go to the house and take them from the kitchen table and Mary will help her.

Before I disrobed following the service, Mrs. Malayko returned back from the manse with the papers. She told me that she rang the doorbell, but no one answered, so she walked in because the door was unlocked and took the papers. That seemed strange. No one answered the door? Mary is in the house and she should have answered the door, unless she is so sound asleep that she did not hear the door bell? After everyone was gone from the church I locked the church and went to the house for I was the last one to leave the church. I walked into the manse and sure enough the door was not locked. I walked into the kitchen, and into the office. Mary was not around. She must be sleeping because of her cold. I took my coat off and figured she is sleeping, so I'll go and start to prepare something for dinner.

I did not want to bother waking her up if she is not feeling well and tired from the trip, her illness and a cold. I quietly went into the basement to the freezer to get a few things to prepare for dinner. When I was in the basement, I thought I heard the door open and someone yelled: "Keys, keys." I thought maybe some one had forgotten something in church and wanted keys to get in. I just yelled from the basement: "Coming." Before I got some things from the deep freeze, I heard the door slam and like someone walked out. I hurried up the stairs and went into the kitchen to see who had come for the keys. As I glanced through the kitchen window, I saw Mary walking away on the sidewalk and going towards the church. I looked again and wanted to see where she was going and noticed that she was going towards a parked truck between the manse and church. The first thing that hit me was that I should get the licence number of the truck that she is getting into. I could not see the truck too plainly from the kitchen window, so I thought I'll see better from the bedroom window. Quickly I hurried to the bedroom and another lightning shock hit me. Boxes, papers, bags and everything strewn on the floor and bed. Dresser shelves opened and emptied. I still managed to get the licence number of the truck before she got in and it pulled away.

While I was in church for over two hours, she had plenty of time to get her things packed, call someone with a truck, whom she probably knew, and vacated the house. When I saw what was happening, I immediately called the police, told them what was happening and told them I would like to know whose truck it is with such and such licence number. They said they could not reveal that information to me. When they told me that, I told them that I want to register a complaint that a truck with that licence number picked up and took my wife from the house.

After that I sat down wandering what happened. I did not fix any dinner already. I was not hungry and now my appetite was even gone. I felt more ill than hungry. It was later in the evening when my parents called me from Winnipeg and mother asked how things are. I told her that everything was okay. I did not want my parents to worry about my life. Than mother asked where Mary was. I said that I didn't know. How could they know where Mary was? In Winnipeg they already knew what was happening in Prince George. Mother said that Mary's mother had phoned her and said that Mary was on the way to Winnipeg. She had just come from Winnipeg two days ago, picked up her things when I wasn't around and headed back to Winnipeg.

When I learned that Mary was on the way to Winnipeg, I sat down and wrote a letter to Mary addressing it to the address of her mother in Winnipeg. In the letter I asked her what happened and what was wrong. I told her that if she wants her mother more than her husband, so be it. I wished her happiness, good wishes and told her that I would like to hear from her what she has to say and the door to the house will always be open for her to come back home. I waited, but no reply came. I was worrying myself into illness. I was getting nightmares from the time when she frightened me when she came up unannounced from behind and touched me with her cold hands. I know that I was frightened and screamed at times during the night waking myself and to find no one in the house. All it was, was a bad dream and nightmare. All kinds of thoughts kept flooding my head. Why, why, why and why? Still I was not sure if it was true. Was it maybe only a dream? A trick? Did she leave for good? If she left, what will the people say? Will I be able to go through all this? Question after question filled my head.

I could not sleep at night, so I called a doctor and made an appointment. I know that already for some days I was seeing things as though I was seeing them through thick smoke or fog. The receptionist asked what my problem was, because the doctor was busy and booked for the day. I told her I could not sleep. She asked which drug store I dealt with. I told her and she said to go to that drug store and they will have a prescription filled for me later in the day. Later that day I went to the drug store and picked up sleeping pills that the doctor had ordered for me. I started to use the pills, but that did not give any relief. Nightmares and sleepless nights followed on. On this occasion ended the old year 1979. Will the new year bring better results? If we live, we will find out.

The new year 1980 did not start out any better, maybe worse. I wanted to know what to do, so on January 9th I went to see a legal aid lawyer to ask for advise. I was told that my wages of $500.00 a month were too high to get legal aid. I would need to get a private lawyer. When I learned that legal aid would not help me, I let everything be and let the chips fall where they may.

In the meantime, things were not getting any better. Everywhere I looked it seemed like there was thick smoke or fog at everything I saw. I knew there was no smoke, because I could not smell smoke. Was it a fog? No it could not be, for I would have heard about it on the radio and than there is no fog inside buildings, and the sun was shining. On January 3rd we were having a carol practice with the children in the church basement. Mrs. Wynnychuk was teaching language to the younger children and I had the older class. Because Ukrainian Orthodox Christmas falls on January 7th, we were preparing the children so that they could go caroling on January 7th. This would be the first time in the congregation history that children would go caroling to church members homes. Mrs. Wynnychuk and I would have to go with the children. I would drive my car and Mrs. Wynnychuk her car with the children when we went caroling because we could not all get into one vehicle.

After the practice, the children went home. Mrs. Wynnychuk's bus was not leaving for Bear Lake for another hour. She made tea in the church basement and we sat and talked about the Ukrainian school and what we would be doing in this new year with classes.

I was telling Mrs. Wynnychuk what happened with Mary. I had told her that I was planning to leave the church and head south into the USA and get lost someplace. When I told her this she tore into me like a lion into a hare. She said that the congregation had waited for years to get a priest and now I would do this to the church. The congregation went into expense to build a manse and all other work and now I would be doing this to the congregation? She just tore into me, up and down and across. I felt hurt. I thought we were like a family and here she rips into me tearing me apart into shreds and scolds me left and right. She said that if I did this, God would not forgive me for this. Sharply she told me to go and see a doctor next morning. If the doctor is busy to tell the receptionist that it is important. I felt even more hurt now. I did not even feel like driving her to the bus depot that evening, but I did.

EUGENE STEFANIUK

Next morning, I thought things over again and made up my mind that I would go and see the doctor. Maybe that was good advise to see a doctor and tell him what happened. I guess it was my lucky day. When I called for an appointment, the receptionist said that they could take me in, in about twenty minutes. I rushed to get there to see the doctor. When I got to the doctors office, I told the doctor what had transpired in the last few days, Mary left me and I cannot sleep. I asked doctor Staniland why everything is so grey, cloudy like smoke or fog. After listening to me, he must have realized that there was a problem. He gave me a prescription to take nine pills a day for ten days. He said that after taking the pills for a week or so, I may still not see too much relief, but to stay on the pills and about the tenth day things will start to improve. After about the tenth day, the fog began to clear out off my eyes as the doctor had said. The doctor told me he wants to see me each week. For ten weeks every week I went to see doctor Staniland. At one of those times when I was seeing him, he told me one thing about Mary. He said that he had seen many patients in his life and work, but Mary was a very hard patient to deal with. I never asked why.

Things were beginning to look up. The fog from my eyes was slowly clearing away and I was beginning to sleep and look better. One time the doctor told me that I was very fortunate and lucky that I had come to see him when I did, because another few more days and it may have been too late. He told me that I was on the verge of a nervous breakdown. He said he caught everything before it happened and got out of hand.

On January 22nd - 1980 about 10:00 AM when the mail came, I got a letter from a lawyer from Winnipeg, stating that my wife had come to see him and that she is not living with me anymore. He also stated that I would have to give her support and maintenance. I knew that now I needed a lawyer also. Mary went to see a lawyer in Winnipeg and this was all her mother's doing. When I got the letter, I called the church chairman and member of the congregation if he knew of any divorce lawyer in Prince George. He got in touch with his own lawyer and a while later called me back and told me to see a lawyer Mr. H. Johnson.

I called the lawyer's office, talked with him and told him my problem, that I received a letter from a lawyer in Winnipeg. He told me to come and see him. When I went to see him, I also brought the letter from the Winnipeg lawyer. He looked at the letter and said that the law in Canada states the person which is receiving a wage is supposed to support the one that has no income or wage. I told him that I never chased Mary out of the house, because I was in church when she took her things and left. He told me that the law was the law and I would have to abide by it. He asked if I could give Mary $25.00 a month. I thought about it for a second and said that if I have to I will. I will find a way to do it. A few weeks later Mr. Johnson called and said that he wanted to see me, because he got a letter from the Winnipeg lawyer. When I came to see Mr. Johnson, he said that Mr. Walsh from Winnipeg wrote and says that I get $500.00 a month and Mary wants $250.00 a month for support. I told Mr. Johnson that I would not be able to give that much. He asked me to go home and get all the figures together of what I get and the expenses I have each month and to bring them to him. He would look at them and said that then he would write to Winnipeg.

I did as the lawyer asked me to do. I went home and than back to him and brought him the figures. When all my monthly bills were paid, I had only $120.00 left. This did not include the food that I had to buy each month to live on. Mr. Johnson said that I would have to give more than $25.00 a month and asked if I would be able to give $75.00 each month. I was hesitant because if I have to give $75.00 a month that would leave me about $50.00 for food and unforeseen expenses each month. I told Mr. Johnson if that is what I have to give, I'll have to give. I will scrap and scratch to survive and will send her $75.00 each month. He wrote a letter to Winnipeg and said that our final offer was $75.00 per month. He also sent to Winnipeg a list of all my monthly income and expenses and what was left after for my sustenance each month. Later the lawyer called me in again and said that there was an agreement from Winnipeg and that I would have to pay for the past four months that have gone by starting in January 1980. My first payment of $300.00 was tough, for my income was small and very little was left over after expenses.

Even though unofficially we were more less apart, I still lived with hope that maybe, MAYBE Mary would change her mind and return but than I knew that as long as her mother was living, she would never change and do things on her own, but only what her mother would say. Mary had no relatives, she had been the only child. As time went on things did not work out that way. Her mother meant more to her than her husban

On February 16th I had some unexpected company come to see me. Brother John had a few weeks of holidays from his work. He also had found a friend by this time and with his friend Kay (Katrusia) they came to see me. They brought a whole carload of food with them, maybe they thought that Prince George is so far north and there may be no food here. They visited for a few days and than returned back home to Edmonton. It was a nice break from the loneliness I was living in, but when they pulled away from the house to head back home, I returned to the house, broke down and cried bitterly wondering: "Lord! Did I not serve you at any time? Did I not fulfill my duties to You? Did I ever miss a service? Why do I have to be so alone and blue in this world? Why do other people have joy and happiness and all I have is heartache?" Such thoughts swept through my mind, but no help came.

Not very long after John and Kay left Edmonton for home he called me to say that they will be getting married on May 31st. Father and mother from Winnipeg had come to see me in Prince George. They stayed for a few days and they even went with me to the Peace River country where I had a service. We returned back from the Peace River area on May 27th. We spent another day at home resting and relaxing. On May 29th we left early in the morning for Edmonton, because John and Kay will be getting married tomorrow at St. Michael's Ukrainian Orthodox Church in Edmonton. Father Steve Semotiuk and I are to perform the marriage. When everybody was in church, it was discovered that the cantor(dyak) is not in church. Whether he forgot or what happened, we don't know, but than I could not serve, so I had to be the cantor instead. Next morning June 1st I had to be back home in Prince George. I caught a plane from Edmonton and was in Prince George by 9:00 AM and still in plenty of time to have the service.

On June 29th, I left for Winnipeg, because this year the church was having its General Sobor from July 1 to 6. This time when I was at the Sobor, I stayed at my parents' place. The Sobor went with resolutions being passed on different topics. Delegate to the Sobor from Prince George was Mrs. Wynnychuk and Mike Wynnychuk was the guest. This was the first time that the Wynnychuks had been to a sobor. Following the sobor I returned back to Prince George.

About a month after the Sobor when I got home, I got a call from the Consistory that the church will move me from Prince George to another parish. They were telling me that I have only twenty family members in Prince George while other parishes have over a hundred families and have no priest. Another reason they would be moving me would be as the story will now reveal in the next paragraphs.

MORE PROBLEMS

As mentioned previously, Mrs. Wynnychuk was the church secretary. She was also the president of the Ukrainian Women's Association in Prince George local. She was the chairman of the School Committee (Ukrainian and Sunday School). She also taught Sunday and Ukrainian school and sang in the church choir. Mike Wynnychuk was the chairman of the congregation. Because I was the parish priest, many members naturally turn to their parish priest for help or advice asking how to do this or that. The congregation was young and needed a lot of organizational work. At times I drove to Bear Lake to Wynnychuks to explain and help them with church matters.

Because Mrs. Wynnychuk was involved in so many activities in the congregation, naturally I had more dealing with her to help and explain how or what to do, write, etc. They lived fifty miles north of Prince George. Many times she would phone and ask for some advice or I would call her and tell her what had to be done. Sometimes things came up suddenly and had to be done quickly, so I had to make a trip to their place or they came to town to see me. Sometimes I would take someone with me to go for a ride and other times I went myself. At times we also held church singing practices at Wynnychuks home so that they would not have to travel to town each and every time. Church work was progressing slowly and one could see the advancement and growth in the church. Because the congregation was small, naturally you could not see progress as you would in a congregation of a hundred members.

When Mary was still with me, Mike and Olga Wyynychuk had decided to build a large Ukrainian Easter egg. Mike built it and than it was Olga's job to paint it. Every day for a week or more Mary and I drove each day to help paint the egg. When all was finished the egg was displayed in the park during Folkfest and it was also used in the parades that were held in Prince George.

One year Mr. Wynnychuk built two membership boards (plaques) to hang on the wall in the church basement. One was for church membership and the other for Ukrainian Women's Association. When they were built Mr. Wynnychuk brought the boards to a meeting and the names of all members were to be put on the plaques. The ladies had just been organized a year or so, so it was easy to get all the names on the plaque. It was a different story with church members. Some had died, some moved away, others joined later etc. The church had been in existence for only nine years, but all names could not be remembered or had not been in the record books. When these plaques were brought to the meeting, someone had to be appointed or elected to check all the records and get the names for the plaques. When it was time to elect someone to do this, the people at the meeting would say: "Let Reverend and Olga do it." Whether it was to do something with the library, minute books, records, etc., it would be: "Let Reverend and Olga do it." I agreed I would try to do what I could to bring all the names of the members for the board.

The records of the congregation showed quite a bit of discrepancies as to when some people joined and became members of the congregation. In some places one could not figure out one thing from the other. One evening in the winter time I drove out to Bear Lake and Mrs. Wynnychuk and I sat till 11:00 PM checking the church records. Mr. Wynnychuk was not home, because he was a cook in some camp in the bush. Their son Fred was home doing his home work and watching TV. We spent hours checking and rechecking and things just did not seem to come together either with names, the years or months. I drove home that evening with a small accomplishment, besides getting acquainted with the minutes. We decided that we would have to meet again to make some headway before the next monthly meeting comes up.

EUGENE STEFANIUK

Another thing that was coming up was a Ukrainian concert in honor of Lesia Ukrainka, Ukraine's greatest woman poetess. Sometimes there are things that can be done through the phone, but other times you just have to get together in person to do what has to be done. Songs, recitations, program, speaker, MC, which child to do what, etc. At times parts had to be written out by hand. There were no computers as there are today where you can send and do things by email. Because the Wynnychuks lived fifty miles north of Prince George, many times I had to drive out so that we could get things organized and ready for whatever the event was coming up.

Mrs. Wynnychuk was also a seamstress as has already been mentioned. The congregation needed some new vestments for the priest. Material for the vestments was ordered from Winnipeg and some family member would pay for it. Mrs. Wynnychuk would sew the vestments and never charged anything. When the material had arrived I had to make not one trip to Bear Lake to help out with how and what about the vestments. Vestment material is very expensive and Mrs. Wynnychuk was afraid to cut it or do anything with it until she was sure it was right. If an error was made, than a few hundred dollars was lost, because once the material was cut wrong, it cannot be fixed up. I would bring an older pair of vestments from the church for measurement. One time she phoned and was ready to cut the material but she called so I would come over, because she could not figure out which was face of that material. I know of a congregation in Alberta that has two banners sewn and one of the banners has the face of the material sewn upside down. It was many times that the two of us had to make decisions about things and when it was finished the congregation would say it was good and was done professionally.

In the springtime the Ukrainian Women's Association was going to have their spring bazaar and they needed Ukrainian Easter Eggs to sell at the bazaar. Mrs. Wynnychuk wrote Easter Eggs. One day in the morning she called and asked how busy I was. She wanted to know if I have time to come out and give a hand writing Easter Eggs. I said that I didn't think I could do that, but she said that she will write the designs and then Mike and I would just fill in certain places. I went. She wrote about two dozen eggs that day. The women needed six to seven dozen for their bazaar. Next morning I again went to help out. When she made the designs, she told

Mike or me which to cover up with the wax. While Mike and I were doing that, she started with another egg or continued making a design over the color of those that had been already written.

One day in early August mother called from Winnipeg to see how I was and I told her about the episode in Bear Lake. I believe that next day father must have gone to the Consistory or to see the bishop and told them this story. Why? Because after all the priests had already been in their new parishes since August 1st and now I was asked to move to a new parish. I had not asked for a change in parishes and I knew I was staying on in Prince George. On August 14th, I get notification by phone from the Consistory that I will be moving to a new parish. I did not tell the congregation anything about this until I had something black and white from the bishop or the Consistory.

HYAS, HERE I COME!

On September 4th the congregation and the Ukrainian Women's Association were making a farewell tea for Steve and Iris Ciona. They had done so much work in the congregation and now they were moving out to Hinton, Alberta. At the end of the speeches and gift presentations, I made a surprise announcement that I had been notified from the church headquarters that I will be moving from Prince George shortly. I still had no letter, but said that I was awaiting for the letter from the Consistory. I had been informed by phone that I would be moving to Hyas, Saskatchewan some sixty miles north of Yorkton. This news was a shock to all that were at the farewell tea.

Yes there were ten family members when I first came to Prince George in 1977. Now three years later I will be leaving the congregation with twenty family members. I was told that in Hyas there were two hundred family members who were waiting for a priest. The Consistory told me that a priest is needed more at Hyas than at Prince George and that is why I have to move. After I had broken this news of moving to the congregation, the very next day I began to get phone calls asking me not to leave Prince George. My mind was already set and made up and now no one was going to change it.

On September 10th I got a letter from the Consistory that I am to move to Hyas, Saskatchewan and to be there on October 1st. I had only twenty

I ALSO WALKED ON THIS EARTH

days to pack and move. I had already checked out about the Hyas parish and learned that there were eleven congregations to serve with some two hundred and fifty families. I told the congregation in Prince George about the situation in Hyas and that I was leaving. There had been no priest in Hyas for three months now. Even the Holy Bible says that when they persecute you in one place, get up and go to another. *"But when they persecute you in this city, flee ye into another...."*(Matthew 10:23) Good time to follow the Biblical command.

Now came the questions. How will I move? How would I go? I made the decision to sell the nice car I had and purchase an older car or a station wagon, rent a U-Haul trailer and move. I sold the 1979 Ford Fairmont car for $1500.00. And bought an old Acadian station wagon and rented out a U-Haul trailer. I had packed things sooner and now just to move. I loaded the station wagon until I could put nothing else in it. Than I loaded the U-Haul trailer. When I could not put anything more in the trailer, I had to leave a few items in the church basement and hopefully someday I will pass through Prince George again and then will pick them up. On September 24th I left Prince George. Instead of going south and to Edmonton, I headed up north into the Peace River country. Why? Because before I had any information of moving, I had made arrangements with the congregations in the Peace River country that I was going to have services there on the planned dates. I had services at Spirit River, Berwyn and Reno, before I started going down south towards Edmonton and unto Saskatchewan.

When I was at Spirit River, I stayed at Zyhas place. This was always a stop over point and we were like family. When I was at their place they told me that at the far west end of the town is a man that wants to make a monetary donation to the church. I went to see the single man. He said that he had a problem with his health and one day looking at the icon of the Virgin Mary he prayed very humbly and sincerely so the Virgin Mary ask Her Son to heal him. He said as he was praying, he could feel healing power come into him and he was healed that moment, so he wanted to give some money for the church. I thought maybe he wanted to give $50.00 or $100.00 dollars, so I asked him how much he wants to give. When he said he wants to donate $100,000.00 dollars I could not believe what I was hearing. I told him that because I am traveling on the road with a load and moving, I undoubtedly do not want to take such a sum of money with me because who knows what could happen, but as soon as I get to Hyas, I will call the consistory of the church and someone will come get his donation. After having arrived at Hyas, the very next day I called the late Father Udod in the consistory and gave him the news so that someone from Edmonton go and get that money. It was later a year or two when I was passing through Spirit River again that I saw Zyhas. I asked them if the man donated the money to the church as he promised, and they said he did, but not for our church.

I arrived at Hyas, Saskatchewan on September 30th at noon. I was to report there on October 1st, so I was in time to be at my new parish. I immediately went next door by the church and reported to Mr. and Mrs. Paul and Victoria Kurkowsky who I was and they gave me a key to the manse. They lived right next door to the manse. Because it was noon time, they invited me to have dinner with them. Shortly after dinner Mr. Kurkowsky and I started to unload the trailer and station wagon when from nowhere my parents appear. They knew I was moving and had to be on such and such a day at Hyas, so they came to see where I would be living. Father and mother helped to unload and in no time at all everything was unloaded. Now I had to take the U-Haul trailer to Yorkton, some sixty miles south. My parents went with me to Yorkton for a ride. After leaving the trailer, we headed back to Hyas. Arriving at Hyas, I began to unpack some things. Mother wanted to help, but I said that I would do it myself, because when I will need something, I will know where it is if I unpack it myself. We unpacked the boxes of bedding so that we could make up the beds and have a place to sleep on. Next morning my parents left back for Winnipeg. It was three hundred miles to Winnipeg from Hyas. When I lived in Hyas, many times I left early, early in the morning for Winnipeg, got what I needed and the same day in the evening I was back home.

Before I go into Saskatchewan, let me say another word about Mary. It was about the middle of June when I was still in Prince George that the lawyer had called me and said he needed to see me. When I came he showed me a copy of a letter he had received from the lawyer in Winnipeg. Mary had asked for a legal separation and on June 13th, she signed the papers and a copy was sent to the lawyer in Prince George, so I would sign them also. I hesitated to sign because of some of the clauses that were in it. One of the things in the paper was that we have no right to visit each other or to step unto each others premises. I could not agree to this, because I knew that no one knows what tomorrow holds or may bring. I told the lawyer that I do not agree to sign such a document. He told me to think it over and let him know in a few days. When the time came for me to move, I went to the lawyer and told him what was happening and that I still do not agree with the papers. The lawyer advised me that if I did not sign than sooner or later we would have to appear in court and I would have no way out. On September 20th or thereabouts, reluctantly I put my signature on that document.

Before I left Prince George for Hyas, the congregation made me a farewell tea after my last service on September 21st. They were going to get me a farewell going away gift, but I had warned the people that I would not accept and take any gift, but would leave it in the church basement or in the manse. At the farewell tea, one lady, late Sophie Ludvigsen, stood up and says: "Reverend we don't buy you any gift, because we are loaning you for a year or two and after that we want you to be returned back to us."

HYAS, SASKATCHEWAN - POPULATION 175

It was quite a difference to move from one place to another. Prince George had a population of over seventy-five thousand and Hyas (a larger city?) with a population of one hundred and seventy-five. I don't know if that included the dogs and the cats. There was only one grocery store, one hardware store, a small hotel, post office, three or four churches and a municipal office. It was a quiet peaceful little village in comparison to the hustle and bustle of a large urban centre. Maybe that is what I needed after the stay in Prince George. But I did not know what awaited me in this new place.

After I arrived at Hyas it was only seventeen days later that Alice and her husband John Hnatiuk were celebrating their twenty fifth wedding anniversary. At this time John and Kay from Edmonton had been visiting family at Thompson, Manitoba. Coming back from Thompson they stopped overnight to see me. Father and mother also had come from Winnipeg and stayed overnight and than we all left with our cars to the anniversary the following day.

When I arrived in Hyas, I wanted to trade off the Acadian station wagon for another smaller car. I looked and checked around and I found and bought a 1979 Pontiac Phoenix car at Sturgis, Saskatchewan. Who would have thought that thirteen years later I would be serving a parish in PHOENIX, Arizona. That car worked well, but it had one problem - a flaw. On December 18th as I was backing out of the garage, I spotted oil leaking underneath the car. I stopped and checked and it was transmission fluid that was leaking. The car had to be towed back to Sturgis where I bought it. It cost me $300.00 to repair the transmission and the garage paid the same amount since they had given me three months warranty. Later I learned from some people in that area that this was already the third or fourth time that the transmission had to be repaired on this car. When I heard that, I was hesitant to drive it for who knows when in the middle of the road I may be left stranded again in cold winter weather. I started to look for something better. I looked and checked around and ordered a 1981 Ford Fairmont car similar to the one I had in Prince George. The new car was to have arrived in February at the Ford dealer in Canora, Saskatchewan, but it never arrived until April. The railway company that brought the car from the east shuffled the railroad car in Winnipeg to some siding and forgot all about it. There it sat in Winnipeg until my dealer began to inquire what happened to that car I had ordered.

So I returned back to Saskatchewan. I know from my early years, of the winters in Saskatchewan. I was expecting the same kind storms as they were in the 1940's and 50's. I was dreading even to think of winter and the minus forty below weather. But what can one do when such weather comes? We just have to accept what is offered. This first winter though gave me a surprise. The winter was not like it was in the olden days, but it turned out with little snow and milder temperatures. Some winters on the prairies in the 1980's were still very snowy and frosty, but none could be compared to what people endured in the 1930's to 1950's.

Then came spring 1981. Many ups and downs in my life. Sad and happy events were greeting me this year. Everything seemed to go normal if there is such as thing, until March 12th when I arrived home from lectures that evening which I was having with parishioners. When I returned home a phone call greeted me. Oksana was calling from Winnipeg that mother had been stricken with a hemorrhage and was taken to the hospital by ambulance. The doctors were not sure what had happened and they told Oksana to call in the family, because chances for her recovery were very slim. This same night Alice and her husband left for Winnipeg. John and Kay also left from Edmonton and I was to meet them in Yorkton at a designated area. I left my car in Yorkton and we went together in John's car.

When we arrived in Winnipeg in the afternoon, we went directly to the hospital to see mother. She had her arms tied down to the bed because she had intravenous in one arm and was pulling out the needle from her arm. She talked about things that made no sense and was saying that she was having a headache. It wasn't until the following day that the doctors could pin point what was wrong. Mother spent exactly one month in the hospital and was released. After being home for about two or three weeks she got a heart attack and was once more rushed to the hospital. This time she spent one day in the hospital. Prayers by faithful people were heard by God and He restored mother to partial health, but she was never again one hundred percent normal herself. Some days she talked well and other days she talked things that made no sense. She also would repeat the same thing she had said before when we visited her.

Things seemed to normalize until April 16th a day after fathers birthday. At 4:30 PM the sky turned black that lights had to be turned on in the house. A wind storm came up, blew the dust off the ground into the air and blew it into any crack there was in any building. Even though I had all the windows and doors closed, when the storm was over I had to dust the whole house, because wherever you turned or touched anything, there was dust on and under it and you could write with your fingers in the dust.

As things were going along, one day I get a phone call from the church Consistory asking me if I would be willing to go to Prince George. I told the Chairman of the Presidium that they only have to tell me when to go and I'm leaving. They said that I would also have to look after the Peace River area as I did previously. I was so glad that I felt as though I was walking on air. I would be going back into the mountains, because it seemed that the mountains were calling: "Come, back, come back." The mountains and me, it seemed we were made for each other. I had told many people that I would always like to be closer to the mountains or the mountains closer to me.

A few days later father called from Winnipeg to see how things were with me. Naturally, I was glad to tell father the news that I will be going back to Prince George. That was my mistake for breaking that news to him, for next day he probably went to see the bishop or the consistory and told them not to send me to Prince George. It was later sometimes in July I also learned that father had gone to see the bishop and asked him not to move me back to Prince George. Somehow from somewhere the parishioners got wind of the news that I would be moving back to Prince George, they got in touch with the consistory asking that I not be moved but to stay in Hyas. This same scene was again repeated two or three times as history will reveal as we go on.

Then an unusual thing happened on July 14th. I was in the house and thought that I heard something fall someplace in the house. I looked all around and could find nothing. A second or two after, another noise was heard in the house. It seemed like someone else was in the house and was snoring in their sleep. I tried to find the noise, but each time I was getting closer to it, the noise seemed to move to another place. I could feel shivers were beginning to crawl up on my spine and I was not sure what to do. Should I call the neighbor? By the time he gets here from next door, the noise may be gone and than people will say that something is wrong with the priest. As I pondered what to do, the noise seemed to fade away into the distance and I heard it no more. To this day I do not know what the mysterious noise was. Later there was another interesting noise that happened in the middle of the night, but that will be explained in due time as we get to that time in history.

When I lived in Lac La Biche from 1962 to 1967, I used to travel nearly two hundred miles to the children's summer camp, Bar-V-Nok, south of Edmonton near Pigeon Lake. Living in Hyas, I was now the closest priest to a summer camp, Trident Camp at Crystal Lake, some seven miles west of Hyas. This year I spent two weeks at the camp, but held my services in the churches that I had scheduled during the year. At the close of camp my parents from Winnipeg arrived to be at the concert that the children prepared. They were going to stay longer, but mother realized that she was running low on some pills, so they had to get back home to Winnipeg.

When they got back home, next day on August 10th at noon they went to the drug store to get the prescription refilled. They were gone for half an hour as they told me. When they returned, their house had been broken into, ransacked and vandalized. The rear door had been smashed in and things were topsy-turvy in the house. Cupboards had been opened and eggs flung into the cupboards. Eggs were thrown against the walls inside the house. The insurance company cleaned up the mess and it did not cost the parents anything, but this was a shock and not good for mothers condition. Father than began to seriously think of moving out of Winnipeg.

While the parents were having their trouble in Winnipeg, the people in the Hyas area in 1981 were moving up in style. On August 11th we had private telephone lines hooked up. Prior to this Hyas had been on a party line system. There were four of us on the same party line. Now everybody is getting a private line and all this happening in 1981. Real advancement in the telephone technology. Sometimes it was good for me to be on the party line. Kurkowskys next door and I could hear each others rings. When I was not home and they knew that I was away, they would answer the phone for me in their house. Later when I was home they would convey me the message what someone had called me about. In other ways it was not good, because people could listen on and you could not have any personal conversation on the phone. It was in the fall of 1980 that I moved into Hyas and I had started to feel a pain in my left leg. I was worried that maybe I was getting another blood clot like I had in Dauphin. I went to see the doctor a number of times and was put on different medications, but nothing seemed to help. I was sure that a blood clot was coming back for the pain was the same as when I had the blood clot in Dauphin. When I would lay down to rest the pain would go away. When I had a service and had to be on my feet two to three hours the pain would start to come back again. Many times during the service I just bit my lip from pain and hoped to finish the service. As long as I moved around or walked there was no pain. The moment I stood still at the Altar, the pain would return.

Than it happened. On August 19th after the service at Norquay and the pain was just getting unbearable. I finished the service and came home. It was afternoon. When the pain was not letting up this time, I decided to go to Canora to see Dr. Alex Danylchuk. When I got to Canora, the clinic was already closed, so now what? The only thing to do is go to out-patients in the hospital. That is what I did. The doctor checked my leg over and said there was no blood clot. He thought it was maybe some arthritic pain and gave me some pills and a prescription. Later as the pain was not easing up, I made a few more trips to Canora, thirty miles each way, to see Dr. Danylchuk. The doctor sent me to the hospital to have x-rays taken of my back. When the results came back, he found that I had a problem just as he had suspected and thought that problem was bothering me.

He showed me the x-rays of my back and a picture how a normal back should look like. I could see there was a difference in my back. He said that my back was causing me the pain in the leg. He gave me some material to read about my problem called Ankylosing Spondylitis. He prescribed me two different kinds of pills. I started taking the pills and after two or three days I found out that they were causing me pain and upsetting my stomach. I went back to the doctor and he told me to take only one kind of pill and to throw the others away. He also suggested that I drink lots of milk and that should help the stomach as well as help build up the calcium in the backbone. He said if the calcium would build up in the backbone, than the pain should disappear. The problem was that the last two bones seemed to be coming apart from each other and that was causing pain. He said that if the calcium build up would not help, than I would have to spend time in the hospital stretching my back. If that would not help, than the last resort was surgery. That's all I needed to know to make me feel even more ill.

Later I found out from some parishioners who had also been on the medication I was on and they informed me that those medications caused stomach ulcers. Now that's all I needed. As soon as I finished the last pill, I did not go back for refills. I began to drink a lot of milk. Never drank that much milk in my life as I drank that one year. The pain did seem to get less. When I was in Prince George, I was much less on my feet and I did have some pain, but tolerated it, since it was not so harsh as it was in Prince George. But in Hyas, there was so much more work and special activities with services which required me to be on my feet constantly. The doctor in Dauphin had told me to get off my feet more, because that had some doing with the blood clot.

By this time I had already been in Hyas for a year and should be entitled to some holidays. I never cared and wanted holidays, but the law says you have to take them. I don't know how news can travel that quickly, but somehow people in the Peace River country knew that my holidays were coming, so they began calling me to come to their area and give them a service, because since I left a year ago they only had two services. I guess my problem all life was that I can't say, "No." I let the people in Peace River know that I would be leaving Hyas on September 6th and could have a service at Reno on September 11th and at Spirit River on September 13th. In the meantime, even before I left on the 6th, I had to spend one more day at home, because I had a funeral on the 7th of September. Also just before I left I got a phone call from the Peace River area, that a man passed away at Reno and they will wait for me to come and have the funeral on September 10th. So I did the funeral in Stenen, plus the funeral and services in the Peace River country.

After the services in the Peace River country, I traveled down to Prince George, because I had to pick a few items that I had no room for when I was moving from Prince George. I had left the Solovox piano and some smaller items. Now being closer to Prince George than to Hyas, might as well stop and pick those items up.

When I arrived at Prince George, I first stopped at Tarnowetski's place. We talked for a while and they said that the members of the congregation would like to see me. I said that I would not be able to visit because next morning I was heading south to the Okanagan Valley to see my "koomy", Peter and Doris Chaykowski, because they are waiting for me. Mrs. Tarnowetski called all the members and made arrangements that all meet in the church basement for coffee that evening and there we can all see each other. That was a good idea and that is what happened. People were glad to see me again and I was glad to see old acquaintances and parishioners. I told them how much work I have in the new parish and we exchanged news events and thoughts. I stayed over at Tarnowetski's and next morning I headed for Vernon, B.C.

I spent two days in Vernon visiting Chaykowski's and other friends that I knew from Dauphin who had moved to the Okanagan. Peter and I spent some time in the hot pool which I thought would help my pain in the leg. After spending those few days in Vernon, I headed for Edmonton and spent a day or so at John and Kay's place and visited other priests that I knew. I arrived home safely in one piece after putting on nearly three thousand miles in less than two weeks. One thing that I could say about the trip is that it was LONELY. Drive miles and miles and miles and no one to talk to. Oh yes, there is the radio, but once when you get into the mountains that thing doesn't work there either and than the radio talks its own subjects and my thoughts are different. The radio also does not talk back to answer me. The radio never pays attention to me, but does its own thing.

On October 14th, St. Mary the Protectress Holy Day, I was going to Danbury some twelve miles north of Hyas to a service. Mr. Mike Tymryk always went with me when I went to all services. This time he told me to go on another road, because there is construction going on and we may get stuck for it had rained a day or two before that. We took the other road and when we were about four miles from Danbury as we were turning unto the old road, we got stuck in the fresh clay that was being used to build up the old road at the crossroads. We could not get out, so we had to get a farmer with a tractor to come and bail us out of the gumbo mud.

This fall my parents, sister Oksana and her son Lawrence, all from Winnipeg, came to visit me. At this time Oksana brought some sad news. She said that she had met up with Mary and her mother in a shopping mall and Mary did not look good at all as she had lost a lot of weight. It hurt to hear such news. Yes I was six hours away from Winnipeg and I could have run out many a time to visit and see her. But as Mary had wanted in the signed papers we were not allowed to go near each others house or to see each other. This was still her mothers doings. If I stepped on the yard, I would probably have the police sent after me. I had not wanted any kind of agreement and was hesitant to sign the papers before I left Prince George. I was still wishing that she would have gotten well and maybe things would have turned out better all around. But it is not what we plan, but what kind plans God sets for us. I can still even today as this is written more than thirty years, after her passing, do not believe it was her work that she wanted such an agreement. That agreement was all her mothers work. Mary just went along, because what her mother said it was holy. Her mother provoked her to such an agreement. If not her mother, than it had to be someone else, because I knew Mary for over twenty years and she would not agree to such an agreement. But as the saying says: "What is done is done and cannot be undone."

It is fall time and it became a very beautiful fall. Now the days and nights were getting cooler as we headed closer to winter. On December 3rd in the afternoon I was going to Hudson Bay, Saskatchewan to have a singing practice and religious classes with the adults and the youth during their programs. It was a sunny afternoon. About two miles east of Sturgis,

Saskatchewan a man was picking rocks on the field. Usually by this time there is a foot or more of snow on the ground with lots of coldness and the ground frozen like a rock. This year it was nearly a third of the winter season gone, but still no snow and mild for that time of the year. It was just a super fall. Winter finally did come with snow arriving on December 20th and with it also came hail, sleet and wind. The roads became very slick and icy. Winter had arrived with a fury and sent many motorists into the ditch and the rest had to learn to drive more carefully.

At times I felt so depressed that I could not think, watch TV, read or anything. When conditions became that bad, I would get into the car and go drive around the country for miles and miles, hours and hours, just to chase that depression away. I would come home two or three hours later after having made about a hundred miles along the country roads. At this time I was also using pills to get me through the depression, but now even those were not of much help. There were times that I wished I could have broke down and cried and maybe that would have released some of the pressure, but I just could not cry. I had no tears left, for all my tears had been shed in Prince George into the Fraser and Nechako Rivers.

It was also this year that I had the premonition that something was happening someplace, only I did not know what and where. It was away back in June 1980 that I started to keep track of all my dreams. I have a little book and all my dreams are typed in it as to November 2005. On December 31 - 2001 I typed all my dreams and printed ten copies of them. Many of the dreams have been fulfilled. Others probably needed some interpretation to know if they to were fulfilled.

In regards to dreams the church teaches that we are not to be involved with dreams. I look at it from a different angle. I do not believe in dreams, but I know that they do mean something. Do we not find dreams in the Bible? Did Jacob not see rams in his dream? Did Joseph not have dreams? The kings butler and baker also had dreams. Dreams are mentioned more than thirty times in the Bible. Are dreams mentioned in the New Testament? They sure are. Did the Angel not appear to Joseph in his dreams? Were the three Wise Men not warned in dreams not to return back to Herod? Did Pilate's wife not suffer in dreams about Jesus? We see there are many places in the Holy Scriptures that talk about people having dreams. People had dreams and will continue to dream as long as the world will exist. It is not up to us to interpret dreams and waste our time. I had a strange dream, if that can be called a dream, in March 1985 when I was living in Hyas and that will be mentioned when we come to that period in this bio.

But I do want to mention two dreams. One dream November 21 - 1985, was that I was in the city of Regina, Saskatchewan and was walking on Albert Street north but why I don't know. I came to a tall office building about four stories high on my right side. Next to this building was a very small office. Something kept telling me to go inside, but why I don't know. I went into that office and there was a very beautiful blonde lady, but her face was not visible, just like a shallow light. The lady got up from her chair came towards me, threw her arms around me and hugged me saying: "I have been waiting for you to come and I thought you would never come." I had never seen the lady before but yet her voice was soft and gentle like an Angel. I can tell you that some three years later I was married to such a lady who at one time worked in a mental institution in different departments

Another dream two or three weeks later (1985) once again I dreamt that I was traveling west of Yorkton, Sask., going east. There was a long, long grade down hill going east into a somewhat valley type prairie, (there is no such place west of Yorkton). As I was going down towards a little village, I thought I got a flat tire on the car. The road being very narrow I pulled off the road unto some summer fallow, because there was traffic behind me, and I did not want to stop the traffic. I stopped to check the tires. The tires was okay, so I got back on the road and because it was noon hour and I still had over an hour before I get home to Hyas, I stopped at a café to have lunch. At this café a blonde haired beautiful lady waitress came to serve me. She came and stood by my table looking at me and says: "So where have you been all this time?" I was surprised because I had never seen this lady and the way she said that to me. Some three years later I was married to such a lady who at one time had worked in a restaurant I believe in Moose Jaw, Saskatchewan. Now there are dozens of dreams from January 1980 to end of December 2001 when I stopped keeping track of my dreams.

To start the new year 1982 off, it started being very terribly cold. Windy, frosty and terrible cold. Nothing as cold as when the north wind blows and you can feel that its pulling your breath out of the body.

On January 5th, my parents came from Winnipeg to spend Ukrainian Orthodox Christmas with me. Coming to see me they also brought me a yellow budgie bird which my nieces (Oksana's daughters) had bought and passed it with the parents to give for me. Next day also John and Kay from Edmonton arrived also. The five of us spent Christmas Eve and had the Holy Christmas Eve Supper meal together.

The weather was extremely cold that January of 1982. I did not wait for it to warm up. I was still making my rounds blessing homes with holy water. Paul Kurkowsky always went with me to help in the singing. One evening as we were returning home in that terribly cold weather and less than a mile from home as we entered off the highway to the road that leads to town, the rear end of the car spun around on the cold icy road and we ended up in the ditch. We got out after Maudest Yurkiw came with the big gasoline tanker truck and pulled us out in that forty below weather and the cold, cold north wind. That cold spell was finally broken on February 19th when the temperature raced up all the way to a +41 Fahrenheit (+5 Celsius).

MARY PASSES AWAY

I learned of the sad news that came to me from my parents that Mary had passed away on March 20th. My parents found out about her passing two days after her passing and immediately called me to let me know. They learned the news from their friends and from Metropolitan Andrew, who was the primate of the church at that time. Father and mother had been working for a few years for the Metropolitan. Mother used to wash his clothing, prepare meals for him to last one, two or three days. Father would drive him to see the doctor or other business and to purchase his groceries. He also did some work around the yard of the house. After the parents had called me to tell the news of Mary's passing, some time later Father Hryhorij Udod also called me to tell of the news. I left for the funeral to Winnipeg not knowing what to expect once I got there.

Mary's mother took charge and care of the funeral. In the obituary it was said that she is survived by her mother and other relatives. My name was not mentioned that her husband was still living. I told the funeral director that I was her husband, but he said that his orders were to put only in the obituary what there is and nothing else added. He said that Mary's mother told him that was the only way it was supposed to be. Mary did not give that order, it was her mother.

Another thing that I discovered was that one lady after the funeral stepped up to me and says: "Father you know, Mary wanted to see you before she died, but her mother told the doctors and nurses in the hospital not to let you come in to see her should you come to visit her." Mary wanted to see me and I wanted to see her, but I knew that all along her mother was the doer of all what had happened. Maybe at the end Mary saw that her mother was wrong and wanted to say something, but her mother would not allow for it. Her mother would not allow me to come and see Mary on her death bed. What kind of a person would do that?

One other hurt that I have and will always remember. Mary spent one month in the hospital prior to her passing away. Our church had twelve clergy serving and retired in Winnipeg at that time. I don't know, but did at least one had come in to see her as she was lying on her death bed? I do not know. If one of them had visited her, could he not have let me know? They all knew my parents in Winnipeg, and they could have told them that Mary was in the hospital?

I did go to Winnipeg, not to see her, but attend her funeral on March 26th. When I got to Winnipeg my parents and I went to the funeral home. When we got there, I learned that the funeral was pre-arranged and was fully paid for in November 1981 for a total of $1992.00. When we looked at the floral arrangement on the casket, it said that the flowers were only from her mother. My parents and I went over to the flower shop and I got six red roses which I put into the casket with her. The parents from themselves, they bought a wreath.

To this time I had not cried for over two years. I just could not have gotten into a mood that would make me shed a tear. Now the pain was great. The heart was sad and broken. It is hard to part with people that are living and leaving for some other place to live, but when you part with someone you have not seen for over two years and had been restrained because of someone else' s doings, the pain is so much greater.

It was after the funeral and the dinner that was in the church hall, that someone came to me and said that Mary's mother wanted to see me. NOW? When I came to see her, she said that Mary wanted to see me, but they did not know where I was living and did not know where and how to get in touch with me. This is absolutely not true. They knew very well where I was, but had I known this sooner, the outcome may have been different. They knew where I was. How?

1. Oksana, my sister, had met Mary and her mother in a mall and while they were talking Oksana knew where I was, if not they could have asked Oksana: "Where is brother Eugene now?"

2. My parents were still living in Winnipeg and they knew very well where their son was living. All they had to do was call up and ask, but Mary's mother did not want that. Mary's mother talked from time to time with my parents, and she could have asked where I was if she didn't know. My mother called me many times and said that she was talking with Mary's mother.

3. The headquarters of the church are in Winnipeg. All they had to do was pick up the telephone and call the Consistory and ask for my address or phone number if they wanted to know where I was.

4. I had been sending payment by cheque to Mary every month from 1979. On each cheque my name, address and phone number were on it. Each time I mailed Mary a cheque, my return address was on the envelope. My address had come into their home over twenty times since Mary left to go and be with her mother. So how could she say tell me at the funeral, that they did not know where I was. And when someone does not tell the truth what are such people called?

I knew there was nothing more that I could do for Mary, but pray for her soul. Yes she listened to her mother and made an error, but that is easily forgiven. Now all I can do is ask God to be merciful to her soul and forgive her the wrongs she did, which her mother had instigated into her. As I was talking with Mary's mother at the funeral luncheon I took out my wallet and gave Mary's mother $200.00 cash and said that is towards the purchase of a headstone for Mary. There was nothing else I could do for Mary anyway. It was some time later that I heard through the grapevine, that Mary had left me, because she did not want me to see her suffer. It was some people from Winnipeg who were coming from Winnipeg west and they stopped at Hyas and told me this. These people did not know me and I did not know them, but they knew the story about Mary and my life and told me this news. Whether that was true, I don't know.

I must mention one thing more here that touches the funeral and that is my trip back home After the funeral lunch in the church basement I left for home which was getting late afternoon. Beside Portage Avenue where Mary is buried I stopped once again at the cemetery to bid her farewell. Leaving the cemetery I started the trek home. One thing that happened on the road I was going is lost. After I left Neepawa it started to snow pretty heavily and I caught up to a truck and was following him with much visibility reduced in the twirling snow. I know that was so, but what happened after that I don't recall. It was someplace before I hit the Saskatchewan border that I remember the snow was not falling, the road was clear and I was traveling in the night for the sun had already set. Yes I recall going through Yorkton and then stopping at Canora, Sask., to see Father and Dobradeyka Derewianka. I had tea with them and talked for a while and then left to drive home foe the last thirty miles. I do not remember a part of the trip between Neepawa and the Saskatchewan border, and it is blanked out. I have had a similar experience in 2015 near the Kelowna airport where I was traveling and then lost sight and sound but then I remember the car facing the highway about three hundred feet from where I was to begin with.

Now with all hope vanished, the world seemed even lonelier. What else can I look forward too? The house is always empty, sad and lonely. No one to turn to for help. Many days you want to ask or say something, but there is no one to talk to. No one to welcome me home from a trip. Neighbors and friends are fine, but it is not family. You do not live with your friends and neighbors. They have their own homes, families and problems. You can confide in your friends and neighbors only so much. And in my situation it was even so much harder. No children for comfort. Parents, brother and sisters are three hundred miles away and more and they have their own families and don't have time to bother with me each time and day. All these thoughts creeping around in the head made it so much harder to live through pain, grief, loneliness and sorrow.

Not quite a month after Mary's passing, I was asleep when at 4:30 AM on April 12th, I got a frightening experience. I was awakened, by what I thought was a noise in the bedroom as if something was fluttering about in the house. It was dark and I could not see anything. I was not sure what I should do, should I get up, or just wait and see what will happen next. For a while I thought maybe the house I'm living in is haunted. Maybe someone broke in and I didn't hear at first. As I slowly turned my head towards the window, I caught a glimpse of a bird. Oh, so that's you, that budgie bird. I got up and put the lights on. And now, tell me how did you get out of your cage? Who let you out? Who opened the door of the cage for you? I tried to catch that budgie, but no luck. Oh, I know what I'll do. I'll put out this light and turn on the light in the bathroom. It's a small bathroom, no windows and you'll fly in there and I'll get you in one way or another. It worked. In another minute the budgie was in my hand and than back in the cage.

On April 23rd, just a few days short of forty days after Mary's passing, I had a memorial service in Hyas. My parents came from Winnipeg as did Alice and her husband John. The church was full of parishioners from every congregation and I had eleven congregations to serve. Father Derewianka of Canora did the service. After the service the ladies served lunch in the church basement. After everything was over people began to disperse and my family members had gone to the manse. A few minutes later mother wanted to talk with someone she saw outside by the manse. She opened the doorway saying something, when all of a sudden the little budgie bird flew past her outside never to see it again. We tried calling its name, hoping that it would hear and return, but never saw it. The day was very beautiful and warm. Later some people told me that what happened with the budgie was, that as soon as the service for Mary was over, the budgie disappeared. It was Mary's soul and it flew out of the house and out to heaven. So let it be it so by your beliefs.

PARENTS MOVING OUT OF WINNIPEG

For quite some time the parents were trying to sell their house in Winnipeg since they had the incident of a break in and vandalism. Finally on May 4th - 1982 they phoned me and said they sold their house and will be moving back to Saskatchewan. Now they would have to find another place to live, but where? Father always wanted to go back to Saskatchewan and now that the house in Winnipeg sold, his only thought was to move out of Winnipeg. When their house was sold they came to my place and I went with them to help look for a house. Mother did not mind where it would be, but father had his mind set on Cudworth.

But no one knew our father as our family knew him. I went with them to look for a house in Cudworth and than to Wakaw. There were not any houses that looked appropriate for the money they had to spend. We stopped at Alice's and suggested that they wait for a few weeks and maybe by that time something will come up. No, father said it has to be right now, because the buyers in Winnipeg want to move in already to take possession. Alice and John suggested to the parents to bring all their stuff from Winnipeg to their place on the farm where they had many empty granaries and they could store the stuff there until they find a house. It was spring and the granaries were empty and would not be needed till September and by that time surely there will be houses for them to choose from. But no, father said it has to be right now if not sooner. When father found the house which they bought, he later was saying that there were no other houses except that one and they had to buy it. But that was our father, it had to be right now and not after tomorrow. Alice and John were telling them that they could stay at their place until they find something. I also suggested that if they get tired of being at John and Alice's they could come and stay with me for a week or so, than go to John's in Edmonton for a week, but no, for father it had to be right now - today. We looked in Wakaw and there were two or three houses and one was not fit for a cat or dog to live in. There were also two houses in Cudworth. One was a more modern Mexican style house but the price was twice the money they had and the other one is the one they bought. We drove up and down every street in Wakaw and Cudworth and there was nothing selling in those communities.

The man wanted $25,000.00 for the house. The house in Winnipeg sold for $19,000.00, so they were $6000.00 short. This house was an older type house with two bedrooms. After the deal was made, the owner said that he wanted the remaining $6000.00 within a week, or the sale is off. Father started to worry. Now what? We drove back to Hyas and I called brother John in Edmonton and told him the story of what was what. I said that I will give (not borrow) for my parents $3000.00 and asked John if he could do the same. He agreed and I told him to send the money out the following day. He said a cheque will be in the mail the next day. It was. Later father gave me back what I had given him for he said that he does not want our money. John did not get his money back until after the parents had passed away.

Another item was the refrigerator that the parents had in Winnipeg was to be left with the house in Winnipeg. Now they would need a refrigerator here in Cudworth. Father kept calling from Winnipeg that they will get a refrigerator in Winnipeg. In the meantime, brother John, Alice and I decided on the phone that we would buy them the refrigerator, but not to let them know. In the meantime when father would talk about the refrigerator, I would stall and ask him, why they have to haul a fridge from Winnipeg, when there is a store in Cudworth that sells refrigerators. When they move, we'll measure the size of the space for the refrigerator and than they can buy it in Cudworth. That finally settled father down agreeing to such a proposition. They bought a house just two blocks from the hospital where I was born more than eighty years ago. The parents did not move into Cudworth until June 1982

As these paragraphs start one after another, someone may think that my brain is like a computer to remember things in such details. Come to my place and I will show you all the five year diaries that I have filled from which now I can dip into the information as to what happened when, how, etc. I kept track of all more important things and they are written for each day as it happened. I kept track of life as it rolled along, but never had time to sit down and put everything as you are reading it now until August 1993. Even since that time to now many things have transpired and changed and they will come in these paragraphs as the months and years roll along.

This story of my life may not be important to some people, like someone else's story may not be important or interesting to me. If someone wants to boast with how much liquor they drank, how many times they were drunk and had good times, that to me would not be worth anything. That kind of life is useless to a family, community, church, country and God. Of interest to me would be: what did you do with your life for the good of mankind, your church, your country and God? That is what counts and will count when we are gone from this world. It is not important to God to know how many bottles of beer a person drank in their lifetime, or how many times they were drunk or how many good time parties they had. God will only take into consideration what we did for the hungry, the naked, the ill in the hospital or at home, how much did someone benefit on our behalf. Read in the Bible about the rich man and Lazarus in Luke 16:19-31. Read and see the reward that the rich man received for not knowing the poor Lazarus who lay hungry and naked at the rich man's gate.

The years had been tough living alone. There was always hope, but when Mary passed away, that was so much harder on me with nothing to look forward too. Days came and days went and each day brought something new and different. On June 1st I made a trip to Winnipeg to help the parents move. On the 2nd of June my car was loaded as much as I could put things into it. Father's car was the same, loaded up to the top. Oksana's friend with his truck loaded all the rest and the heavier things. When all was loaded, away we headed to Cudworth in a three vehicle cavalcade.

When John, Alice and I bought the refrigerator for the parents, Alice asked the man to deliver and install it in the house on the day when the parents would arrive from Winnipeg. That was done. As we were about to leave Winnipeg, father again brought up, the topic of the refrigerator, that we should buy one there and take it to Cudworth. I asked him if he knew what size it is to be, and he said, no. I said if you buy in Winnipeg and than it's too big, what are you going to do with it than? Who will exchange it for you if you did not buy it from them? I told him that the first thing we'll do when we get to Cudworth we will unload everything, than we'll go and get a refrigerator. That was the end of the refrigerator conversation. Father drove first, than followed by Oksana and her friend with the truck. I was last and was keeping an eye out to see that nothing was getting loose or out of place on the truck. If something was not right, I would have to signal the truck driver so he would stop and tighten things up. What father was saying to mother in the car, I don't know, maybe he was grumbling all the way that there was no refrigerator.

When we arrived at Cudworth, there was a surprise waiting for them. The house had a brand new refrigerator in its place and plugged in. At first they did not notice it as we were unloading things into the house. As we were nearing the end of unloading, I say: "Maybe we should go right away and look at the refrigerators." Just as we were about to walk out, mother noticed the refrigerator and says: "Ah, look, there is a refrigerator here." Later they found out about it and father wanted to refund us the money, but we three decided that it was our gift and you don't take money for giving a gift.

Things were already not starting out very good for mother in the new place. Living only for one month in Cudworth, she became ill and landed in the hospital at Wakaw eleven miles north of Cudworth. She would not go to the doctor in Cudworth, because she could not converse with him in English, so father had to take her to Wakaw where there is a Ukrainian doctor, doctor Fred Cenaiko and who has been a doctor for over fifty years in that town (he is now deceased). By this time she had been a victim of brain hemorrhage, stroke and heart attack. Now she was diagnosed with a new illness, a diabetic. It is strange that in Winnipeg they never knew she was a diabetic? She comes to a little country hospital and immediately is found to be a diabetic. Now she did not become a diabetic in one week or

257

month since moving from Winnipeg. Maybe life would have been better and longer for her if she would have listened to the doctor more. She was told by the doctor not to use sweets, but she used them often. At times we would tell her don't use sugar or don't eat this because its sweet. She would only reply: "Oh yea, but I only take a little bit." We knew we could not win, so we just let things take their course.

This first half of the year was not looking very good. Mary passed away in March. Parents moved from Winnipeg to Cudworth, Saskatchewan. Mother was diagnosed a diabetic and than on July 12th John and Alice had their beautiful crop destroyed one hundred percent by a severe hail storm that threshed their crop before it even had fully developed. This was a serious setback for someone who works so hard on the farm and than have the hail come and destroy everything in minutes. So this was the first half of the year, but what does the second half hold in store?

When the parents purchased their house in Cudworth, there was no garage. Father was insisting that he has to have a garage because the car cannot stay outdoors in the summer sun nor winter cold. I was telling him to look around in Cudworth and see how many people do not have garages and yet the vehicles are outside year round. No, father had to have a garage. Father found a carpenter in Cudworth and asked him to build the garage attached to the house. He also called me and asked if I would be able to come and help him in building. I went and spent two days helping and than had to return home because priestly duties were waiting to be carried out. It was about a week or more that I made another trip to Cudworth. Father and the carpenter could not get the overhead garage door hooked up properly and were having difficulty. So what do I understand and know about installing overhead garage doors? I knew about it as much as mother used to say: "He knows about that as much as a bear knows about the stars." Anyway I made the trip to Cudworth to see if this "greenhorn" can learn anything about overhead garage doors.

In three hours I was in Cudworth. I took the instructions for hooking up the door, read it over and looked at the diagrams and in two short hours the door was hung and working. It's still probably working till today. The door was opened by hand until a year or two later that brother John and I purchased an automatic door opener for father for a Christmas present. John bought the opener in Edmonton and the parents didn't know anything about it. One day John and I agreed to come to Cudworth to hook up the door opener. John and I were hooking it up and father would keep asking what that box was for. John would just answer: "It's to keep watch if any thieves are coming to steal anything." When we attached the braces unto the ceiling father still did not know what it was. Than finally somehow it came clear to him what we were doing and he says: "Ah, why do you need that? The door works good without that and now with that I won't know how to operate it." He had figured out what it was all about. That was our Christmas present for them. If you asked father a few years later if the door opener was good, all he would say: "That was a wise person who invented the garage door opener."

Like everybody else in the free world, I again went for holidays. I hated to take holidays, but I had to go because of the law. To me it was just a waste of time and money. Often when someone asked me when and where I was going for holidays, I would say: "How many holidays did Jesus take when He was on earth and how many holidays does God have each year?" No one ever gave me an answer for that question to this very day. I was born on this earth to work, not to holiday. Grudgingly I would go and left Hyas on September 27th after the church service and drove to Lloydminster where I stopped for the night. Next day I drove to Edmonton and in the evening went with John to look at new cars. The new cars for 1983 were now arriving at the dealers. I had by this time put on quite a number of miles on my car and time was coming to trade it off for a newer vehicle.

I made a deal purchasing a 1983 Ford LTD. I was short of $5000.00 to pay for the car. I told the dealer that next morning I would call my bank at Stenen, Saskatchewan and get a loan to pay for the car. That evening as we were sitting at John and Kay's place, I told Kay about the deal for the new car. I told her that I will call the bank at home and get a loan. Kay asked me how much I needed and I said $5000.00. She said that she would borrow me the money and I would not have to get it at the bank. I said I know the bank manager at home and there will be no problem to get a loan. Than she says: "Brother-in-law, I will borrow you the money, because what are family members for?"

Next morning John went to work. When the banks opened, I took Kay to her bank. She took the money out of her account and gave it for me. We went to the dealer and I paid him and had the plates transferred. Kay was the first one to have a ride in the new car. I told her that it's also her car because she gave money for it, so she should have a ride in her car. I spent another day in Edmonton and than headed out to Spirit River to visit the Zyha family. I arrived at Spirit River on October 2nd. Zyhas knew that I was coming their way, so they made arrangements that I have a service there at that time. That is what happened. After the service I drove to Dawson Creek and down towards Prince George and all the way to Quesnel where I spent the night. The following day I drove to Jasper and spent the night there and from there on to Edmonton on October 6th.

As was stated earlier, the year 1982 was not such a good year. Before the year ended I was beginning to get headaches and nose bleeds. Many times I even got chest pains and would rush myself to emergency to the Canora Hospital thinking maybe I was getting a heart attack. Each time the results were negative. I knew something was wrong and the doctors were baffled with my problem. To add to this problem, warts began appearing on my body and the doctor asked me to come in and have them removed. This was done on October 18th. On November 23rd I was sent to Regina to see a specialist to find out why I was getting headaches and nose bleeds. The results were the same : "We don't know."

Now the new year has arrived. Just four days into the new year and things began to happen. Mary and my engagement was in the fall of 1959 and my parents had given us a 400 day clock. You wind it up once a year, but I used to wind it twice a year to be sure that it did not stop. This particular clock was fully wound and then it just stopped at the hour of 8:45 PM in the evening of January 4th. Next morning on January 5th I received a phone call from a church parishioner from Swan Plain, Saskatchewan, that her husband passed away at 8:45 that morning. A twelve hour difference. Is this some coincidence? Was this some omen for what the new year may have in store? Is this still maybe a continuation of the old year?

It looked like wherever the old year left off, the new year took over for on January 11th, I again found myself in Regina in a doctors office. Dr. Danylchuk from Canora sent me (this time to another specialist) to check out my headaches and nose bleeds. Those health problems looked like they followed me wherever I turned. It was so bad that on January 29th I had to take my first tranquilizer(Valium) pill. The headaches were not leaving me, but seemed to be getting worse as each day came and went. I was going into a depressing state.

As mentioned above, it was October 1982 that I had purchased a new car in Edmonton. Kay had borrowed me money to pay for the car. I checked with the bank and found I had enough money that I could repay Kay the money she loaned me. On February 7th I left home at 7:00 AM and headed west to Cudworth. At 10:00 AM I picked up my parents and we headed to Edmonton. I had some extra money to give Kay as interest, but she would not take an extra penny. I felt bad, because she could have earned some interest with that money, so when no one was around, I left the extra money in a candy dish that they kept in the TV room.

The car I had purchased in 1982 in Edmonton, I did not keep that car very long. Seemed there was something wrong with the rear shocks or the springs. It seemed that the front of the car was always much higher than the rear and looked like the car was going to take off into the air. I had bought the car in October 1982 but by June 15th not even a year old, I had put on over eighty thousand **miles** on it. I started to look for another vehicle and bought a 1983 Celebrity from the General Motors people, Ortynski Brothers at Canora. This car was something different because it was a front wheel drive.

WORK MUST GO ON DAY AFTER DAY

Since I was ordained, I have always been busy, very busy at times. You hear some people say: "I'm bored, nothing to do." Well I can say the opposite: "I'm bored, I have too much to do." There have been marriages, funerals, baptisms, meetings in the congregations, parish organizations, Sunday and Holy Day services, Evening Vespers, Morning Matins, choir practices, religious and Ukrainian classes for adults, anniversaries, graduations, banquets and other events that I had to attend from time to time, here and there. And how about people coming to get a signature who were applying for a passport; me visiting the hospitals and nursing homes, being called out in the middle of the night to the hospital because someone is nearing death, or someone needing a birth certificate, or some even came to have a letter from Ukraine translated into English. These are just a few examples of what I experienced on parish life. And how many other things that I did not mention, but have them in my diary.

To do all that type of work it took hours and miles of driving when you have to look after one congregation that is over a hundred miles from your residence. When I was in Lac La Biche area, it was nothing for me to put on the car eighty five thousand **MILES** a year. When I served the Hyas Parish I could put on anywhere from seventy five to eighty-five thousand MILES a year and it was like a blink with an eye. Multiply this in Hyas for the eight years which I was there and you get the figure. When I was in

Prince George, I also served the peace River area. From Prince George to Hotchkiss, Alberta it was four hundred MILES one way to hold a service. Multiply that by a few times a year to make that trip and you see there is no time to get bored that maybe I had nothing to do. From the time I started driving in 1951 or 1952, I know that I would not be lying if I said that I have three or four million miles behind me. How about when I lived for nearly three years in Phoenix and traveled through USA and to Canada for a number of occasions. The miles added up each time. All those miles were made for the benefit of the parishioners, the church and mankind.

I had left Lac La Biche in July 1967 when the church moved me to Winnipeg. Since than I have served the parishes of Dauphin in Manitoba and Prince George, British Columbia, at Hyas, Saskatchewan and lastly Phoenix Arizona about which will be mentioned when that period comes. I dedicated my life for the church and the people. Maybe that is why the people in Lac La Biche did not forget me, when I was in Hyas. I got a call from Lac La Biche on June 25th - 1983, asking me to come back to Lac La Biche to serve there. I told them that if the Primate or the Consistory write me a letter to go, I will start to pack. I told them that when I had left Lac La Biche, it was not my doing, but the church needed me to help organize the church's fiftieth anniversary. I was ready and willing to go back to Lac La Biche knowing that when I was there, there wasn't ONE INCH of paved street or road at that time in that area. Nothing materialized from that phone call, because when the people in Hyas heard that I may be moved, they made their calls to Winnipeg and I stayed on in Hyas. Every parish wanted Reverend Stefaniuk, Lac La Biche, Dauphin, Peace River, Prince George, Phoenix and others.

My health was still not what it should or could be. My records show that at one time in two days I had three appointments to see three different doctors. When a person is feeling well, they don't need to go see a doctor. I was in dire straits never knowing what one day from the other held in store for me. The headaches at times were so bad, that each time it felt like a bang, bang in the head. Maybe the next time the bang comes the head will explode and than I will not have any more pain.

After having served for nearly two decades, I saw something different that I had not seen before. I had a funeral at Whitebeech, Sask. When I came out of the church to meet and lead the casket in, I saw something that I was shocked. To this time there were always pallbearers who were men. Here standing and lifting the casket where six young ladies. What? After the funeral and the lunch, people flocked to me saying: "How come women were carrying the casket? How could that be?" At that moment the guardian Angel told me the answer and I told the people. I mentioned to them that in the Bible when Jesus was Crucified, Joseph of Aramethia looked after Christ's funeral. But the Bible also says there were women there also. I am sure they helped in the process of the funeral and burial. (Matthew 27:55-56 : 27:61) (Mark 15:40) (Luke 23:55) Was it not women who early on Sunday morning hurried to anoint the Body of Jesus? If women could help in the funeral of Jesus, why can't they be pallbearers and help in the funeral nowadays? Today there are even women who are undertakers. When my parents passed away we had the granddaughters of our parents for pallbearers in both their funerals.

OTHERS ALREADY MAKING PLANS FOR ME

It was now over a year ago when Mary passed away. Because I was a widower, the church looked to me as a candidate to be a bishop. A number of priests also told me the same. I was not interested. For one, because for my health issue and the other that I wanted to be on a parish with people where there is always activities going on in a parish. I wanted to be that "little papa" serving people on the parish level. Being a bishop, I would sit and on Sundays get out for a service if a congregation had invited the bishop to come for a pontifical service. No I would rather stay on a parish. Another thing was also disturbing to me that when Mary died, I went to her funeral. The day before the funeral I went to the Consistory to get some candles and other things that were needed for the congregations back in the Hyas parish. When I came to the Consistory, the first thing I met was: "You know, you are now alone, you should be the bishop now." No one knew me when Mary left and I nearly had a nervous breakdown. No one knew me that I am living alone. No one asked me if they could help me go over my loss, but the first thing was that I'm alone and now to be a bishop. Mary was still lying in the funeral home and here already people have things planned out for me. No respect for people who are in grief and sorrow. I said than and there that I was not interested in such a position.

Than the Primate of the church called me on August 18th asking me to accept the candidacy to be a bishop. And where was the Primate when Mary left and I nearly had a nervous break down? No one asked me how things were and how I was feeling. Each time a request came about the bishopric position I turned down the proposition. I needed health first. What kind of a bishop would I be if two days, two weeks or two months later I would be laid up in a hospital or have a nervous break down? On a parish I could do more good than as a bishop sitting in a house and waiting which congregation will call next to book me for a pontifical service. My goal was to serve the people on the parish. Staying in the office was not my piece of toast or cup of tea. I wanted to be with the people where I could serve them in their times of need. A bishop is more of an administrator instead of "people server". There are people in all other kinds of professions who are sometimes slated for higher promotions, but many turn the promotion down, so why could I not turn down to be a bishop, when I feel that I would not be and do well in that position? My health had to come first, it was priority for me. No health then also no service as priest or bishop.

I knew all the time that I would not be comfortable to do bishops work. I was sincere and told from my heart there was no desire for me for such a position. If I took on that position and than things did not work out as people expected, than what? If someone today asked me to be a lawyer, a nurse or doctor, would I take that job? Surely not, because I know I cannot fulfill such work. If I know that I cannot do something, I don't take it on, let someone else do it who has the ability and knowledge for such work. As time passes by, we will learn that this same proposition was asked of me many more times, but each time I turned it down.

As mentioned above this was a good year for growing crops and gardens. Harvest came earlier than normal this year. On August 30th sister Alice called and said they were combining and asked if I could come out and help them haul grain from the combines to the granaries. I was only three hours away from their place. I checked my schedule and there was nothing too important to do, and I said I could be out there in three hours.

For two solid full days I hauled thousands of bushels of grain while John and Alice with two combines worked on the fields.

This year another event happened in my life, an event that seldom ever happens to a priest in his lifetime. North of Sturgis, Saskatchewan stood an old unused church that had no services in it for a number of years. Beside the church there was one grave of a man who had been buried some twenty five years ago. The family of this deceased man asked me if they could have the body of their father moved to a cemetery where their mother was buried. At one time the congregation thought a cemetery would be beside this church, but another cemetery was started about a mile farther west. To have a cemetery by this old church never materialized. When the man was buried, there were no roads like today and there was a creek that flooded and at times was hard to get across. When the road was built now people could travel on the west side of the creek were the cemetery was located.

I knew that to exhume a body, I had to get permission or orders from the bishop to do so. I wrote a letter to the bishop, explaining the situation that the family wants to have both their parents buried together in one cemetery. The bishop wrote back and told me what to do. In the meantime the funeral director, Mr. Leson from Canora, Saskatchewan got permission from the Vital Statistics in Regina to exhume the body and move it to another place. On September 1st the remains were exhumed and buried beside his wife. How many times in a priest's lifetime does one have such an experience?

PEOPLE WANT FATHER STEFANIUK

This year another mysterious illness struck me. On October 28th at 11:15 AM I lost the full strength in my right arm. I could not hold nor lift anything. It felt like it was numb and no feeling nor strength in it at all. I became afraid, thinking that maybe it was a stroke. I was planning to go and see a doctor, but how could I go when I need my right arm to shift gears in the car? In fear I sat and waited, thinking and wondering what to do. Shortly afternoon the strength began to slowly return. As the strength began to return, my back was beginning to ache. I never did go to see any doctor and as things began to get better, I just sat and thought: "Whatever will be, will be." God can take care of everything. I have never again since that time had such an experience.

Another tough time for the orthodox clergy in the winter time of the year was, visiting and blessing homes for the parishioners. After January 19th the priest visits each parishioners home with holy water, blessing the family that lives there. This goes on until February 15th or until all the homes are visited. Someone may say: "Why does this have to be done each year? Isn't it enough to bless the house once?" Yes you bless the house once, but what about the family? There is a difference between a house and a home. A house is a building and a home is a family. The priest blesses the family. And yes there are such families that the priest should bless some of the homes every day, the way some families live in those houses. Are they faithful to God? Do they obey God's laws? Do they follow the church laws? There are many families in the world that know very little about God. In many homes there is much alcohol abuse. Abuse of children and/or spouses, drugs, etc. Many use profanity and swearing in their house in front of their children. How many watch vulgar and obscene movies? In such homes maybe even every day is not enough to bless that home. Maybe such a home should be blessed three times a day.

It is now nearly a year when I had a phone call from Lac La Biche asking me to come to serve the parish there. On May 19th of this year I again got a call from Lac La Biche asking and begging me to come to serve the parish. As before it was the same. I told them to get in touch with the primate or the Consistory, tell them what you want and when I hear from Winnipeg, I will start packing and be on the way to serve there as I did from 1962 to 1967. I was willing to go, since I knew the parish was smaller than in Hyas and that I would be able to have more rest. Maybe my headaches and nose bleeds will cease in a new area, in a different atmosphere, etc. In Hyas I had eleven congregations while in Lac La Biche there were eight. The farthest congregation from Hyas was Hudson Bay, Saskatchewan a hundred and nine miles one way. In Lac La Biche the farthest congregation was at Richmond Park some sixty-five miles away. What happened in Winnipeg is that I was not moved.

The following day on the 20th I got another call, this one from Vernon, B.C., asking me to move there. Everybody always wanted Stefaniuk to be their parish priest. I told the Vernon people the same I told for the Lac La Biche, call the Consistory or the bishop. When I get the go ahead, I start packing and I am on my way. I was positive that now I would be moved out of Hyas, since two parishes are after me and getting in touch with Winnipeg. I was sure Winnipeg would oblige to at least one of the requests. Nothing ever came out of those requests and I remained in Hyas. That was still not the end of those requests. On May 28th I got a call from Prince George asking me to move back there. The people in Prince George had a notion that I would go to Saskatchewan for two years and than would be returned back to Prince George. Nothing ever materialized of those requests by the parishes.

It is now four years since I left Prince Gorge and the peoples hopes were once again dashed that I did not return after the second, third and even fourth year. The deadline for applications for clergy transfers was May 31st. It may be different now, but at that time the deadline was May 31st. It was now June 13th. Is June 13th lucky or unlucky?

TO CLOSE TO DEATH

It was June 13th and I was cutting the lawn by the manse and the church. It always took me about three hours to do everything also cutting along the roadways-streets on three sides of the church and manse. I had been cutting the lawn since I moved from Prince George starting in the spring of 1981. I told the parish not to touch the lawn mower as I will cut the lawn, since I need exercise and they let me do it. On June 13th I had finished the lawn and was now cutting along the street on the south west corner. I never wore gloves, but this time as if something told me to put gloves on. I also used to wear old shoes and this day something whispered and told me to put on rubber boots. I know that it seemed stupid, and I wondered what people would say when they see me cutting the lawn wearing boots in June when it was so hot and dry outside. I guess God or the guardian Angel knew better.

Anyway I did wear the boots and gloves as the message seemed to be relayed to me. I was cutting around the hydro poles like each and every other time since 1981 and this time on June 13th something happened. I was cutting around the guy wires running from the power pole to the ground, when all of a sudden a big flash of lightning flashed before me. The lawn mower flew into the air and out of my hands about eight to ten inches above the ground stalling the engine on the mower. I stopped and did not know what happened. I've been cutting here the same way for the last few years and nothing, and what's wrong now? Everything jumped in my hands and I had no control in the lawn mower which now lay at the side and dead. What happened? That was the question. What would have happened if I would have had no gloves and not wore the rubber boots that day while cutting the lawn? Yes I could have been a pile of ashes beside the lawn mower and the hydro poles. The Guardian Angel was with me that day for sure. I could have been electrocuted at that moment. When all this had happened and I came out of the shock, dazed and somewhat stunned, I began to get frightened and wandering what had happened. I stood and looked at the guy wire. Ah ha, low and behold I saw the guy wire was attached to the live power wire. I ran quickly into the manse and called Sask Power telling them what happened. The power people were stationed at Norquay about six or seven miles east of Hyas. Then I rushed back outside to see that no one comes around near the place.

It took the power people less than ten minutes to be at Hyas by the church. I showed them the problem and the cut, melted part of the lawn mower that the flash of lightning had made. In a few minutes everything was repaired and the power crew went back to Norquay, while I started the mower and went on cutting the grass. After this ordeal, how can I say there is no God? Had I not had gloves and rubber boots on that day, I would not be writing this today. The power people told me that there was anywhere from six thousand to thirty thousand volts of electricity in that guy wire. If that amount of power would have gone through me that day you would not be reading this now. God was with me and the Guardian Angel knew what would happen and told me in advance, put on the gloves and rubber boots. Thank you God for saving me from what could have happened that day and been a tragic accident. What happened was that two hydro poles were about eight feet apart. There was a live wire connecting both poles and then the poles had guy wires going into the ground. Somehow the wind must have been more stronger or blowing in a certain direction it moved the live wire and it touched the guy wire. I guess they kind of melded or joined together and now power was going into the ground. How long this had been going on I do not recall, but I would guess from the last time I cut the lawn till this happened was about two weeks ago.

The following day after the above ordeal, I get a letter from the Primate of the church asking me to consider to be a candidate for a bishop. I wrote back the same answer as I had written before or said it on the telephone or in person. I said that my health conditions do not allow me to even consider anything of that sort. I told them that I prefer to be on the parish and serve the people this way. I also wrote and said that if I accepted and than I did not fulfilled the expected duty, would that not be heartaches and headaches for the church and also for me? This way just leave me alone and let me be what I am, doing what I am doing for the people and the church.

Things seemed to normalize if there is such a thing, until June 22nd when a heavy rain and hail storm hit the Hyas area. Damage was done to crops and gardens. My garden was not damaged as bad as for some other people. Why? In the Orthodox Church on February 15th the priest always blesses thunderstorm candles (hromovee sveechky). When a storm approaches, light the candle and say a prayer that the storm may by pass. I lit a candle and said a prayer. My garden hardly had any damage while other people's gardens around me had everything destroyed and plowed under into the ground by the hail. As this was written in 2016, I still have those candles on hand and they have worked each time even while living in Lac La Biche. Candles are always blessed on February 15th, on the Holy Day of the Meeting of the Lord in the Temple on the fortieth day after His birth.

On June 30th I had been invited to go to Canora for a memorial service. After the service was over everyone went to the Rainbow Hall for a memorial lunch. I had parked my car about a block from the hall, because all the parking spaces had been taken up. After lunch everyone was going home. I went to the car and when I came to the door to unlock the car another shock hit me like a hot flash down my spine. The front window on the drivers side was smashed into a million pieces and shattered glass all over the street and inside the car. I don't know what happened, but I did find a rock the size of a golf ball inside on the floor of the car. Did someone try to steal my car? Had someone done this on purpose against me, knowing my car? Did another car drive by and there was a rock on the road, its tire hit the rock and the rock flew right into my window? Did someone try to steal something from the car? Nothing was missing. What happened to this day I don't know. I did go to the RCMP in Canora and told them what happened and gave them that rock, and never heard anything from anyone to this day. All I know is that I went straight to Formo Motors in Preeceville and ordered a new window which cost me $200.00 to have replaced.

DON'T BURN GOD'S CHURCH

This year another incident happened that I must mention. It happened at Hudson Bay, Sask., area. Just about ten miles east of Hudson Bay is a village of Erwood. There was an old church that had not been used for a number of years. Most of the people from Erwood had moved to Hudson Bay and were members of the church in town while the one at Erwood was neglected. There are some people in this world who think that when there are no services held in the church, than you can do what you wish with that church. It is not so in the Orthodox Church. There are rules what has to be done with such a building. The church cam be burned, but the ashes must be buried in the cemetery.

Anyway what happened was that one time I drove by there and stopped just to see what the church looked like inside. Yes, the door was unlocked. Articles from the church had been taken away previously. Birds flew in through broken windows and made dropping on the Altar and other places in the church. As if that was not enough, some hunters that came through that area made the church their motel. They slept and ate in there and who knows what language was even used. When I saw this I told the people that it's a bigger sin to have the church in the condition it is now, than burning the church down. One time John Rurak from Hudson Bay had asked me what to do with that church. I told him to burn it down after everything had been removed from it. He brought this up at the church meeting one Sunday after the service.

After I told the people at the meeting what I saw in the church, they decided that it would be better to burn it down. The following day John Rurak and a few other men were going to go and burn that church down because the wind was blowing in the favorable direction west to east, towards an open field. Next morning as John Rurak was putting on his coat to leave and go burn the church, he got a telephone call. The mayor of Hudson Bay was calling him to ask if the town could have that old church from Erwood. They were starting a heritage museum in Hudson Bay and they were looking for older buildings to be moved to the proposed museum site. He told John Rurak that it would not cost anyone a penny to move the old church. Mr. Rurak gave his consent and the church was moved that winter to the museum park. In the summer time, summer students looking for work repainted the church and it was restored to its originality.

The Heritage Park is on the west side of Hudson Bay and has many more buildings now and is nicely developed. Our church was the first building that was moved unto the park grounds. It was restored to its original state and than on July 22 - 1984 the late Father Mykola Derewianka and I held a service in that church and blessed it. A large amount of people turned out to see the ceremony. God did not want His church to be burned, so He gave people another use for that old church and today tourists traveling through, stop at the Heritage Park and can see that church. God knew there were many humble prayers said in that church and He did not want to see His church go up in smoke and flames. But if an old abandoned or closed church must be destroyed the church says it may be burned but the ashes must be dug into the cemetery grounds.

As already mention that when a priest wanted to be transferred or a congregation wanted another priest, they had to have their request in at the church headquarters before the end of May each year. Here it is already July 31st and the priests know by this time who is going where so that on August 1st they must be on their new parish. On July 31st I received a phone call from the Consistory asking if I would be willing to go to Lac La Biche or London, Ontario to serve the parish. I was excited and said that I will start packing today and that I would rather go to Lac

La Biche. Why Lac La Biche? Because here in the west is where all the family members lived and there was no one in the east. When I received that news, I told the Hyas people that I will be moving. That was my error that I did that. The Hyas Parish committee got together that I did not even know, had a meeting and got on the phone to Winnipeg and talked things over with the Consistory. I was informed by Winnipeg that I would not be moved but stay on in Hyas. The committee in Hyas said they did not want another priest, but they wanted Stefaniuk, the one they had now. They must of had a strong influence on Winnipeg, for I was left where I was and remained in Hyas.

Starting each year on September 1st I would start taking vitamin pills. I did this for years and when winter came I had no colds or flu. I took the pills during the months that have the letter "R" in them. Well as one may guess, I forgot to start pills in September in 1994, and that winter I had a cold, after cold, after cold all winter long. From February 22nd to 27th, I suffered terribly with a bout of the flu. Every morning when I awoke, I was always wishing and hoping that it would already be evening, so that I could stay in bed and not attend any meeting, have services, etc. But that was not to be, for on February 24th I had three different services: Divine Liturgy at Arran, afternoon service at Norquay and Evening Vespers at Sturgis, and was I ever sick with the flu, but yet never missed one service. When I finally arrived home that day, I was already in the house, but it seemed my feet were still between the house and garage. I was t-i-r-e-d.

Time rolled along and I was always busy, always something to do. There was enough work in the parish for two priests, but I carried on and on with non-stop. Than on March 23rd I had surprise visitors,- not one, two or three, but five Jehovah Witness ladies. They came with the hope that the more of them there is the more frightened I would be and they would convert me to their faith and get thousands of dollars for it. There was no deal and I had gotten into a debate with them, and still I won - five against one, but after they left, they never came back again.

CALM BEFORE THE STORM

One day I had to make a trip to Hudson Bay. The day was beautiful, sunny and mild. The road was clear and dry like in the summer. This was the calm warning before the storm. Coming back I left Hudson Bay about 5:30 PM and had to stop at Endeavor to have a lenten Passion service at 7:00 PM. This service is served five times during the lenten period. When I left Hudson Bay, it was nice and sunny, but as I was driving south I could see on the far horizon, miles away somewhat of a dark, dark cloud hanging in the sky over the Porcupine Forest. When I was some twenty miles from Endeavor, I was now in cloudy weather and snow was beginning to fall. The farther south I came, the more and heavier the snow was falling. As I neared Usherville, the wind had already picked up and was swirling snow all around and the storm had begun. I could sense that it was going to be a bad one. When I got to Endeavor, the storm was in a lion state, roaring with the wind and cutting down the visibility. I drove to the chairman of the congregation, Joe and Isabelle Greba and he said that maybe we should cancel the service, because nobody will come. I looked at him and said: "Joe, I'm still having the service, because God will be there and I will be serving God and if anyone else wants to come they can join in." He looked at me smiled and says: "I guess you are right Reverend." So we went to the church and got ready for the service. Including me there were six of us in the church for the service. I finished the service, but had no sermon, so that I could get out for home sooner, before the roads get plugged up with snow. When we opened the door of the church to get to our cars, the storm was raging in full fury. It was now about 8:00 PM in the evening.

It was not bad to travel from Endeavor to Sturgis, because there was more bush here and there on the west side of the road from where the wind was blowing and so the road was somewhat sheltered from the storm. Passing Sturgis and heading south east on highway #9, the visibility was getting worse each mile of the way. At times the wind gusts were so severe that I had to stop, because I could not see anything where I was. As the gusts subsided and I could barely make out the road, I slowly would proceed forward. All I could go was about five to ten miles per hour if that. Suddenly I could see red lights flashing before me. And what is this? As I neared to this flashing light at a snails pace, I could make out that it was an ambulance coming towards Sturgis. I don't know who had how much of the road, but slowly we slide past each other, not knowing where the edge of the road was. It was dark, night time. When I first detected the flashing red lights, fear hit me, for I thought it was maybe police at an accident scene.

Slowly the car crawled along, a foot at a time. About a quarter of a mile ahead I could barely make out the lights at the highway junction. There I turn to the east onto highway #49 and only about four or five miles from home. I was traveling very slowly and then I could feel the car coming to a stop. It seemed like I was stuck in the snow, but where was I? Was I on the highway or am I in the ditch? I could feel that I am stuck in the snow. If I was in the ditch, which side of the road was I in? I must be on the right side because the car is lower on the right side. I'll have to get out and check this out. I opened the door and it seemed like someone was standing near the car and was throwing shovels of snow at me and inside into the car. I closed the door, sat for a minute thinking, what to do and hoping that no one comes from behind me and runs into me.

I thought I might as well try moving backward or forward. I realized that the right side of the car was somewhat lower than the left side, so I must have gotten of the road and am at the edge of the ditch. I tried slowly to move forward and backward and as I slowly advanced a few inches at a time to the front, I tried to turn to the left to get back on the road but the car got stuck again. Now if I'm at the edge of the ditch on the right side, than that's were I am. Slowly, slowly inches at a time I was moving backward and then forward. Again I felt the car on solid ground, so I knew I must be back on the pavement. As I crawled along, I would wait once in a while so the gust of wind would die down that I could see the yellow lines on the road if they are visible. After minutes and minutes of snail pace movement I came to the highway junction. Maybe now with the wind in the back it will be easier to go. I should be home in a few minutes for it's only four or five miles to go.

When I turned east, the wind seemed to be coming from the south east now not the west like it had been earlier. I was going very, very slowly and could clearly see the outline of the road. But I thought I was going too fast, so I stepped on the brakes to slow down, but the car keeps moving along. I pressed the brake pedal with all strength I had, but the car is still moving. How could this be? I looked at the speedometer and it was zero, but yet why was the car in motion going forward. All it was, was an illusion with the snow rushing along the road towards me and it seemed like the car was moving forward. I stopped a number of times before I got to Hyas. The visibility at times was nil - zero. It was a cat and mouse travel. After minutes and minutes and minutes, I finally came to the Hyas turnoff from the highway. As I neared the turnoff, I could make out in the blowing snow that there were two cars standing with their lights flashing.

When I had advanced close enough to the two cars a man came out of one of the cars. The man came to me and asked if there is a hotel in Hyas. I told him there is and that he can follow me and I will lead him to the hotel. He told me that they were from The Pas, Manitoba going to Yorkton to a hockey tournament, but they thought they should not go any farther in this weather. The bad weather caught them on the road, so they were not going to go any farther. For the last four miles from the junction of highways #9 and #49, it took me exactly ONE HOUR to travel in that storm.

When I got home, did I get into the garage? Off course not. The trouble was that the manse and garage are in such a position that when a storm comes, you can't get in cr out of the garage until after you shovel out the driveway. The overhead door, I could not even open, because of the snow piled right against it. It took about twenty minutes of shoveling before I could get into the garage Finally after all this ordeal I'm in the house and its 10:10 PM. What a trip. Normally it took thirty five to forty minutes to get from Endeavor to Hyas, this time however it took just over two hours in the raging blizzard. Next day I was to have a service at Danbury, twelve miles north of Hyas, but the people phoned and said to cancel the service, because the roads were blocked.

I remember that I was in a similar blizzard a few years earlier when I was a traveling missionary. This happened in April 1968. I had come with beautiful weather the day before into Lethbridge, Alberta. I had a slide presentation, an address and than took questions from the public. When I was on my travels, I usually stayed at peoples homes. In Lethbridge one of the church members had a hotel and I was put up in that hotel for the night. As I was getting into bed after I had said my prayers, I looked out the window and it was a beautiful clear, warm night. Tomorrow I have to be at Moose Jaw, Saskatchewan and that will give me plenty of time to get there from Lethbridge. I had been tired and fell asleep very quickly.

I was not worried what time I would get up next day, because I had plenty of time to get to Moose Jaw. In the morning when I awoke and while still lying in bed, it seemed like the sun was high up in the sky, for it was very light in the room. I jumped out of bed, looked out the window and, low and behold, you could barely see the buildings across the street. How am I going to get to Moose Jaw? Which road or street do I get on, to get out of the city, when you can't see anything in the snow storm? I have not been on these roads before and I won't know which road to take to get out of the city. How can I drive in such a storm? Anyway, I quickly dressed, said my prayers and was going downstairs to the car with my suitcases. The hotel owner and church member saw me coming down with the bags says: "You're not going anywhere. You can't go anywhere in such a storm." I told him that I was only taking my bags to the car out of the room and I'll be back. When I walked out of that hotel, I haven't been back since.

I brushed the snow off the station wagon, started it up and ready to go. But which way? Where is the highway? I pulled out of the parking lot and drove and got behind some large semi-trailer truck. I was following him. I hope he is going in the same direction that I need to go. Maybe I will see some road signs and than will know if I am on the right road. I followed the semi, and when he drove a little faster and I was losing sight of the truck, I'd speed up to be closer by him. If the truck became too dark, I knew I was too close to him so I slowed down. As long as I could see some of the dark shadow ahead of me, I'll keep going. I followed that truck until we got to Bow Island which is about seventy some miles east of Lethbridge. It took two full hours to drive those seventy some miles. When I got to Bow Island, the sun was out and it was a beautiful day and no wind. When I had left Lethbridge, I turned on the radio and heard the warning not to leave the city and that the police had closed all the highways and not letting anyone out of the city. Well how did I get out, I didn't see no police anywhere. They also said on the radio that a Greyhound bus was heading to Lethbridge was five hours late due to the snow storm. I did meet a Greyhound bus heading towards Lethbridge, but whether that was the bus, I don't know.

After I got out of the storm at Bow Island it was clear sailing all the way to Moose Jaw. I was somewhat late arriving in Moose Jaw because of the time spent on the road between Lethbridge and Bow Island. I traveled the speed limit and only here and there maybe went five miles over so that I could make up the time that was lost. I did arrive a bit late at Moose Jaw, just as some people were starting to come out of the church basement. When I arrived people returned back to the church hall and the program proceeded. Those two storms I will never forget and they were the worst that I ever encountered in all my sixty plus years of traveling and driving. The other bad one was when we were still on the farm and the storm had covered the barn that we could not see where it was. Many storms come and go, but those two will never be forgotten. I loved to travel in the winter when a storm was on but not in such storms. In the car it is cozy like a bug in a rug while a storm in brewing outside.

LIFE MUST GO ON

As everything slipped along, I was bombarded by priests and at conventions and letters from the Primate, when will I give my acceptance consent as a candidate for a bishop. This was nothing new to me and my answer was always the same for everybody: "My health does not let me accept such a position, and than I only want to serve people in a parish." I never liked fanfare and a bishop is most of the time encircled in that. I looked at Jesus, He never boasted and he never made any great showing of who He was. He was just as humble as humbleness came. And what did Jesus say: *"If any man desire to be first, the same shall be last of all, and the servant of all."* (Mark 9:35) How many problems are being faced each day in the world, because of people wanting to be first and are looking for glory and honor.

I have mentioned time and again that my health was giving me problems. Yes I suffered, but I would not let the people know of it. Anyone who would see me would say: "Oh you look well." My reply always was and still is: "Its not how a person looks, but how a person feels what is important." Because of my health problems, I found myself at the University Hospital in Saskatoon on May 21st, seeing a specialist. One other thing I should mention is that in the past two or three years each morning when I would wake up, both my hands were swollen up to nearly double their size, but caused no pain. Why I don't know and the doctors could not find an answer. Sometimes the swelling was so huge that I could not even put my fingers together for they were so swollen and stuck out as we say: "Like a sore thumb." When I got up and started moving around, the swelling would slowly dissipate and the hands became normal. A few times it happened that even my face was so swollen in the morning that I could not recognize myself when I looked in the mirror. I should have taken a picture of my hands and face. But at that time it never came to my mind. I was more worried what was happening to me. There never was any pain, only bad swelling and as soon as I started moving, the swelling would dissipate.

There was this one time that one family had made arrangements with me they wanted confession and communion one morning. Because of my own different illnesses which I was concerned with, I had forgotten to go and visit that family while they waited for me. They sat and waited for me without breakfast. I was embarrassed that this thing had happened. They phoned me to ask if I was coming. It was already noon time, so I said I would come the next morning. The night before I was to see those people, I had a very terrible bout of heartburn. I did not know what to do with myself and where to put myself. Maybe because of my own illness, I was neglecting other people their confession and communion or help they needed.

Because of my health condition, was now wondering myself, if I should move to another parish. Maybe new climate or environment might restore some health. On June 17th at a parish meeting held at Whitebeech, Saskatchewan, I made an announcement that I may be leaving to another parish because of my health condition. The decision that I had made never materialized, because the parish executive called Winnipeg and gave them their suggestions not to move me out of Hyas. Again I was left in the same parish when other clergy moved to their new parishes on August 1st. Maybe I should have not said anything to anyone and I may have been moved at the last minute.

On July 11th, I got a call from the Yorkton Hospital telling me that I am on a waiting list for surgery and she wanted to know if I want to come in for surgery or not. I was dumb founded. Slated for surgery? On the waiting list for surgery? I asked the lady what the surgery was to be for. She said she did not know only that my name is on the list. I told her that

I would not be coming. I don't know anything, she doesn't know anything, why go for surgery, for what? I told her to take my name of the list.

Summer had come and was in full swing. My work in the parish continued day after day with no letups. This year it was my turn to be at Trident Summer Camp with the children at Crystal Lake. The week that I was there had come and gone. July was over and August 1st came again and priests were in their new parishes while I still sat at Hyas. On August 11th I received a phone call from Prince George B.C., that they are awaiting my return as parish priest to their congregation. I told them the same as before, to contact the Primate or the Consistory because my orders come from Winnipeg. I told the Prince George people that as soon as I hear from Winnipeg, I will start packing - nothing again became of that petition by the Prince George congregation.

I carried on with my duties and everyday something was always different. On October 5th I got a surprise at Stenen. Tomorrow is my birthday, but that was far from my mind. The local Women's Association in Stenen called me and asked to come to the church basement because they will be having a day of certificate presentations to their honored women. They wanted me to be present, to say a prayer and to say a few words on that occasion. Sure, I'll come. That was not the first time or the first congregation that such events took place and I attended to help out as much as I could. I came prepared to the event. I had put down on paper what I would say. The ladies always served lunch during such an event. Everything was lined up and ready to go. I said grace and than the president of the local, Mary Kurkowsky, makes an announcement that everybody is gathered to celebrate my birthday. I came to my surprised birthday event. I was the only one surprised that evening. What wonderful people and their gesture to do such a thing. May God grant them a good, long and healthy life for thinking of me. Because Stenen was the closest to Hyas, only some four miles, I enjoyed visiting in that area more than in other places and many, many times visited with Peter and Mary Kurkowsky..

WHO WAS IT?

A very unusual thing happened in Arran on November 3rd. This morning I am having a service in the Arran church in the village of Arran. I always used to arrive at the church about forty five to sixty minutes before the service was to start. This gave me the chance to say my prayers, get everything ready for the service, put on the vestments and maybe someone will come sooner for confession and when 10:00 AM rolls in everything was ready to start the Liturgy. Before I would come to any of the churches that I served, some church member had already been there, unlocked the church and started the fire or turned up the thermostat. If there was snow in the winter he would have the sidewalk cleaned. Than he would go home to change and come to church for the service.

I arrived at Arran about 9:00 AM this morning and went about like every other time. It was still cool in church, but the furnace was running and it would be warm in a while. I put on my cassock, and said my prayers in front of the Ikonostas. Having finished that I went into the Sanctuary, found the Gospel reading for the service, got the chalice and everything else ready. Than I went and started to put on the vestments. As I was doing this, I could hear someone walking in the church. It was queer that someone was in church when I never heard anyone come in and open or shut the door. I looked through the north Deacon doors, but there was no one. I could still hear the footsteps moving around from place to place in the church, yet could not see anyone. I felt a funny feeling, but was not afraid, because I knew that I was in God's House and there it is always safe. Only God Himself or some Saint must have been in the church that morning. After the service during coffee, I told the people what had happened that morning, but they all seemed unconcerned. Maybe some were even thinking that I was sick in the head and was hearing things. I know that what I heard was true, but to this day, I do not know who or what it was.

Stenen and Hyas are only about four or fives miles apart and yet the weather between the two places can be so different at times. On December 22nd I had a service at Swan Plain some twenty miles north east of Hyas. The weather was warm and mild outside and the temperature had gone up all the way to plus four this day. After the service I headed out to Hudson Bay for a 3:00 PM Baptism. After the Baptism there was an early supper and I was in a hurry to get back to Stenen for a 6:00 PM potluck supper and an annual meeting was to follow. The road was smooth and dry until I hit the Usherville-Endeavor area. Here wet snow must have been falling for quite some time because the road was wet with slushy snow.

Driving along I caught up to an older half ton truck that was traveling at a slow pace in the middle of the road. I wanted to pass him, but the driver would not pull over to the side to give me room. He stayed in the middle of the road. I was going to pass him, because I was in a hurry to be at Stenen for people will be waiting for me. As I was passing him, my left front wheel of the front drive Tempo grabbed some loose fresh snow and before I knew it I was in the ditch. I was saying: "Whoa, whoa, where are you going?" Nothing doing, the Tempo ran until it got stuck in the snow and I had to get out and shovel. That old truck in the meantime never stopped, but just kept a going. So what do I do now when no one is around? Oh yes, every winter I had a shovel in the trunk. I shoveled and than I started going back and forth making a path until I finally got back on the road. I threw the shovel back in the trunk and started to drive, hoping to catch up to that truck. I was ready to give the driver a lesson or two about courtesy and on which side of the road he should drive. By the time I got out of the ditch he had disappeared. He may have turned off to some side road or was already in Preeceville or Sturgis, so where do you look for him? Because of this I arrived in Stenen about twenty to thirty minutes late and the members were waiting for me.

After the meeting was over, people began to come out and go home. Rain met us at the door. It was really raining, coming down and the wipers were going on fast speed. This is happening on the 22nd of December. About half way home the rain started turning into snow and by the time I got to turn off the highway into Hyas, I was already in a blinding blizzard. What a difference in four or five miles the weather can be.

Ending this year was not on a good note. On December 15th, I got a severe headache. The following day it was even worst and on the third day I got a bad nosebleed. I went to see a doctor but he could not find anything wrong even though to me it seemed that the next pounding in the head I hear will be the one that will explode and shatter my head. I took aspirin for pain, but there was no relief. On such a sickly note ended 1985 for me and the year 1986 started with the same headaches carried over from the year before. It was not until January 11th that the headaches started to leave and that was when the temperature outside reached plus four Celsius. After this warm spell it cooled off and my headaches began to return. Does weather have anything to do with headaches?

Because my headaches were not easing up, the doctor in Canora made me another appointment to Regina to see a specialist on February 12th at 4:00 PM. In the morning I had a service at Sturgis and than had to rush to Regina. Six days later I was in the Yorkton Hospital getting more tests. By this time the weather was again starting to turn colder. And on February 20th it sank to minus forty below Celsius. Was it ever c - o - l - d. With the cold winds, one could not even breath properly outside. Br-r-r-r-r, just too c o l d.

By this time I had already been in the Hyas Parish for five years. The parish grew in membership as well as morally and spiritually. Other priests knew about the growth in the parish from the parishioners. Because they learned of this, newly ordained priests began calling me to ask when and if I will be moving from Hyas, because they would like to come to this parish. This happened on March 11th. I told the newly ordained priest to talk to the Consistory and that clergy transfers are still a few months away. I told him that I will be willing to go to another parish and he can take over in Hyas, but asked him to talk to the Primate or the Consistory. Nothing became of this and I was still in Hyas.

HYAS PARISH GROWS

The most likely reason why the parish grew was when I arrived in Hyas I saw that there was a large amount of work to be done. First there were no cantors in some congregations to sing the services. People could not read in Ukrainian, so they did not attempt to be a cantor. I noticed that many people were not very much versed in the faith either. They attended church like everybody else, but they knew very little what was what. So when I saw this, I knew something had to be done. I found people who could help me and we organized classes for adults. Classes would be held once a week for three hours. Bill Nowosad would teach the Ukrainian language for one hour. Mrs. Lillian Steranko will teach singing, choir for one hour. I would end the evening with one hour of religious studies. Members from Endeavor, Sturgis, Stenen, Hyas and Norquay traveled each week for these classes. Each week the classes were held in a different congregation, so that everybody had a chance to travel four times to the classes and the fifth time they would be in their own congregation. There were eighty-five adult students attending these classes.

People flocked to these classes like people flock for Holy Water when it is blessed. We met in church basements, or an attached building to the church, and in schools wherever there was a place. Quarters were small but we had anywhere from seventy-five to eighty-five people attending and the oldest person was Anton Yurkiw at the age of eight two. One day at the classes Mr. Yurkiw asks me a question after he had heard my lecture. "Father, how come all those priests that were here before you, never told us these things?" So what should my answer be? I said, you would have to ask those priests, because I don't know why they did not tell and explain to you about the services. Some people at times had to stand because there were not enough seating for all. These classes carried on for two years, until Bill Nowosad, a school teacher, left the area. Ukrainian was not taught anymore in the public school in Norquay so he moved out of the area. Ukrainian classes could have continued, but people became surprised of themselves that they learned enough Ukrainian in two years that they could read and write. As to speaking the Ukrainian language, people spoke and understood, but it was to read and write that they did not know. There were some that could read and write in Ukrainian. The singing and religious classes continued in the years to come. Mrs. Steranko had taught singing in a choir. Later whenever there was a service in any of the congregations, those that learned singing came to each congregation and sang the services beautifully.

There was complete love and harmony among the people. People at the east end of the parish at Arran, heard of these classes and they asked me to come and teach them too. Later the congregation in Hudson Bay was given these same religious classes, so I drove out to Hudson Bay and started the same thing. It was not long when parishioners in Danbury, north of Hyas, heard of these classes, so than I had classes started there also. In Danbury we used the public school for classes in the evenings. Than four nights each week of my time was given up for classes. It was twelve miles to Danbury, a hundred and nine to Hudson Bay, about twenty five miles to Arran and than the other congregations were somewhat closer.

Before these classes had started, I want to mention one person in particular, the late Joe Greba (deceased in April 2014) who was the postmaster at Endeavor. He understood and talked Ukrainian, but could not read one Ukrainian alphabet. In two years he learned to read well enough, that some twenty years after I left the Hyas parish, I heard that Joe Greba was the cantor for the whole parish. After he started to pick up the reading and writing, he tells me one day: "Reverend, could you order me a Ukrainian newspaper, so that I could keep learning to read." He subscribed to a newspaper, Ukrainian Voice out of Winnipeg, the oldest Ukrainian paper in Canada and his reading was increased even better.

MORE HEALTH PROBLEMS

My health gave me more problems this year. On April 17th in the afternoon I attended the monthly meeting of the Ukrainian Women's Association at Sturgis. After the meeting I went home, had a bite to eat and was on the way to Stenen for the evening to attend the monthly meeting of the Ukrainian Women's Association there. Everything was fine. As I neared Stenen, I could already see the village and the church. I had to cross the railroad to get to the church about a hundred and fifty yards to go. As the car crossed the tracks, I felt like an electric current went through me. I began to feel funny and nauseated. It seemed that I was falling over to right side, and the car seemed to be tipping over to the side. I still drove in front of the church and parked. Was I getting a heart attack? A stroke? I sat quietly for a moment thinking what was happening. I started to feel better. I took the briefcase and started to walk towards the church basement entrance. As I walked I felt that I was again falling over, walking like a drunk man. I came into the church basement and I felt like I was falling over to the right. There were a few people in the basement already. I came down stairs and sat down at the nearest table by the bottom of the stairs.

The people saw that something was wrong with me and Mrs. Mary Kurkowsky came towards me and says: "Are you all right? You look white like a ghost." I was sitting on the chair, holding unto the table and saying: "Hold the table, because its falling over." It seemed like everything was turning over and around. Peter Kurkowsky asked me if I wanted to go to the hospital in Canora. I told him that I cannot drive, unless he takes me with my car. Peter Kurkowsky and Alex Kozmeniuk drove me to Canora. They waited until the doctor had checked me over. The doctor having checked me, said that he was admitting me to the hospital. I told the two men to take my car back home to Stenen and leave it at their place. I spent four days in the hospital and came back home on April 21st at 3:30 PM.

During my stay in the hospital I had to cancel two or three services. Someone had called my parents in Cudworth and told them that I was in the hospital and the very next day they came to see me. The problem was that I had an inner ear imbalance. What caused it the doctors said they did not know. There is medication to ease the nauseating feeling and the falling over sensation. The doctor said the best thing for this condition was to lay down, be very still and not move at all, not even to blink an eye and the problem will slowly get back to a normal condition.

After the hospitalization I tried to take things somewhat easier, but how could you take things easier when the greatest Holy Day (Easter) of the Christian Year was just around the corner. The busiest time of the year for the priest at this time is having extra services and I just got out of the hospital. People want to come to the special services and have their Easter Paska blessed. What about those that die, do we not bury them? You have to take them to their resting place. There was no time for taking things easy.

On May 23rd I got an unexpected call from the Primate of the church. As soon as I heard his voice, I knew why he was calling. I thought he was calling for the same reason as before, but this time I was wrong. This time he was calling and asking me if I would go to the parish at Oakburn-Rossburn, Manitoba. I told him that he is my bishop and if it is his will that I go there than I go. I also told him that I had been in the hospital a month ago. Did this move materialize? No. When the parishioners got wind that I will be moving, they got on their phones calling Winnipeg and my move ended before it started. I was again left to serve in Hyas. The very next day I received a phone call from Kamloops, B.C., asking me to move there to be the parish priest. Nothing became of this either.

Health wise I did not think I was getting any better. I visited the doctor in Canora and Norquay quite regularly hoping that maybe, maybe here or there one of them would find what the problem was. On June 13th I once again found myself in Regina seeing another specialist. All this time when these health problems were creeping unto me, anyone who saw me would say that I looked well. I kept telling people, its not how you look, but how you feel. You could be a hundred years old, but if you're well everything is fine. Yet you could be only twenty years old, but if you have some illness, nothing is happy or joyful. And I know I was not feeling well, even though people said I looked well.

Then it happened.

On Sunday July 13th - 1986 (I'm not superstitious), I was having a service at Norquay. It was their Feast Day, St. Peter and Paul. I had finished the Liturgy and we were going to bless the water outside and walk around the church. Someone peeked outside to see what was happening and said that it was starting to drizzle. So the blessing of the water will have to be inside and there will be no procession around the church. There was a full church of people. Everything went well until after I read the Gospel at the blessing of the water. I felt somewhat weak and seemed like everything was slowly starting to turn black. I still had enough memory to sit down in the front pew, so I would not fall down.

What happened after that I don't remember. The next thing I recall is that I was all wet and a few men were holding me up in the pew, so I would not fall over. Then the men took me into the sanctuary and sat me down on a chair. They took the vestments off me and I was driven to the local hospital at Norquay a few blocks from the church.

I was put on a bed in the corridor of the hospital. The doctor was away for the week end and he was the only doctor in the community. The nurses placed a phone call to Canora the larger hospital. They took my blood pressure and heart beat. They ordered for an ambulance from Canora. While waiting for the ambulance, the nurse gave me a needle. It took the ambulance about half an hour to arrive the thirty five miles. When the ambulance arrived, I was put unto the ambulance and we started out for Canora. The driver was going pretty quick as I could feel by the way the ambulance was moving. There was one attendant at the back with me and he was taking my pulse every few minutes. I had enough memory and I asked him where we were already. He said we were passing Stenen. The next thing I remember was I thought I would, throw up, I felt very nauseated. At that time the attendant took my pulse and I remember him saying to the driver: "Speed up, because his pulse is dropping and is only forty eight."

Arriving at the hospital the doctor was already waiting for us. I spent four days in the hospital and the first day was spent in intensive care. The doctors could not find anything wrong. After four days in the hospital the only thing the doctors found was that I had high blood pressure. Just prior to this my blood pressure on June 17th was 150/105. I know that this was not good as a the doctor later told me that it was on a stroke level. The doctor put me on medication, but it did not seem to help very much.

Because of all these health problems which I was having, I decided that maybe I should go someplace into a different atmosphere or place, a different parish. They say that a change is as good as a rest. Then I thought that the best thing for me to do would be to go and visit my old friend at Porterville, California, George Alexandro. Just a year earlier he had come to Hyas to visit me with his friend. I drove them around and they went to the services with me. They were very surprised of the flat lands in Saskatchewan. Here I should stop for a minute and say a word about his story as he had told it to me. He can't tell it himself because he has passed away.

A NEW FRIEND - GEORGE ALEXANDRO

When George Alexandro was still a small child living in Ukraine, he was kicked out and thrown out of school because he was accused of being anti-bolshevik. As history tells us, Ukraine was under the occupation of Russia for four hundred years and was not a free country. George Alexandro still being a youngster knew who and what the bolsheviks were(some call them communists). He saw his people suffering. He tried to stand up for the rights of people while still being a young school child. He grew up in Ukraine and when he was an adult he was arrested and sent to Siberia to be executed. As he was awaiting his execution, one night he escaped the day before he was to be shot. He said that every day Ukrainians were lined up against a wall and the orders were given that every third person in the row was to be shot. Time was coming that he would be shot the following day, but he escaped. For three days and nights he was running away and hiding without food, until he reached Germany the American side of the World War Two. He got a job in the USA Army in Germany working in the kitchen. There he learned the trade of cooking. When the war was over, he immigrated to the USA and ended up in the northern part of California. There he began to work and make money. He made enough money that he bought his own restaurant business. He got married and had three children. He knew what he had gone through in his life and he did not want his children to go through the same fate.

Something went wrong with his marriage and it was broken up the last few years of his life. Than he moved to Porterville and bought another restaurant and ran it until he retired and sold it. In 1974 he took a trip to Canada about which we have already read when he arrived in Dauphin at the Ukrainian Festival. He had heard much about Canada and he wanted to see what this Canada was that people were talking about. He had arrived in Calgary and while there he heard someone talking in Ukrainian. He became interested and stepped up to them and asked if they were Ukrainian. In his discussion the people in Calgary told him to go to Dauphin, if he wants to see Ukrainians. When they were still talking, he began to cry and than revealed why he was crying. He later told me in Dauphin, that he had been crying from joy, because after what he had seen and lived through in Siberia he did not know if there were any more Ukrainians left in the world. He was sure that Russia had executed every Ukrainian.

Because there was no regular air service to Dauphin from Calgary, he took the bus. Arriving in Dauphin and not knowing anyone, somehow he looked in the phone directory and found the Ukrainian Orthodox Church. He phoned and I answered the telephone. He said he wanted some information where he could stay. I told him to wait at the bus depot and I will pick him up right away. Because I had a clergy collar on he recognized me when I came to the bus depot, because I told him who I was so he was looking out for me. We introduced ourselves and I brought him home. After a while I phoned William Perepeluk that I have company from California who came to the Ukrainian Festival. Mr. Perepeluk said to bring him over immediately so that he could meet him. When we went there Mr. Perepeluk said that he can stay at his place. Later I took Mr. Alexandro to the Festival grounds and when he saw what all was on display and going on he cried and wept like a child. His handkerchief was all wet from his tears and I gave him my handkerchief. He said that he cried being so happy to see Ukrainians still living, because when he escaped from Siberia, he was sure there were no more Ukrainians left on the face of the earth. Mr. Alexandro is now deceased having passed away in 1991 in the summer after he had visited his homeland in Ukraine earlier that year. Later we will come back and he will be mentioned again.

Now back to my story.

In 1985 George Alexndro paid me a visit when I was I Hyas. With his friend he flew to Regina and I met them at the airport. The following year I made a trip to Porterville to see him. This trip was a great experience that maybe someday I may write another story about it. Even though I went for a visit to California and came back, my health did not improve for on October 21st I again was seeing a specialist in Regina.

The work in the parish continued. After people began to sing better, we arranged to have a Taras Shevchenko concert in the parish. Each year this type of concert was held in one or two congregations. One year the choir decided to prepare a half hour program dedicated to Taras Shevchenko and to see if we would be able to appear on the Yorkton TV station. There was a once weekly time that people with different talents would appear on this program. The TV station obliged and a combined choir of people from Endeavor, Sturgis, Stenen, Hyas and Norquay traveled to Yorkton and had the program taped and than it was broadcast over the wider area of Saskatchewan.

When I lived in Hyas, I did some experimenting with gardening. Each time I planted anything in the spring, I kept track of the name, when planted, which row, etc. In the fall when the harvest came, I marked down the results and remarks about each vegetable, how it produced, size of product, date harvested, etc. Did it grow well? Did it produce well? Did it freeze or grow to maturity? The following spring I bought the seeds that had given me the best produce from the past year. I did the same with tomatoes. When January 15th came around, I used up the last tomato that came from my garden. I know it was called "Longkeeper." I had gotten those seeds in the mail from the USA. It was a very good quality tomato and kept for a long time without spoiling. Later when I was moving from Hyas, I threw all those papers out.

By this time my nose bleeds were still coming, but at least not every day, but still a few times a week. I usually got the nose bleeds in the morning. When I got up and went to wash, that's when the nose bleeds would start. I would have to lay down on the chesterfield for five to eight minutes and they would cease for the rest of the day. Than on February 13th it was different. When I was washing, I got a nose bleed. I did as before, lay down and wait for it to stop. This day when I got up and started to move around the nose bleed would come back again. I would lay down again and wait for it to stop. When I got up, it would start bleeding again. I played around with this nose bleed all morning long and was already thinking of phoning the neighbor next door to take me to emergency to see a doctor. But slowly just before noon the nosebleeds finally stopped. Later on in the year the nose bleeds came not only in the morning, but any time of the day and even in the evening. Many times I would be sitting at the typewriter typing a sermon or what and suddenly I would get a nose bleed. At times, before I felt the nose bleed, a drop of blood would drop on the paper or clothing.

A STRANGE DREAM AND A MISSING CAR

I have already mentioned that I have all my dreams on paper since June 1980 and to the end of 2001. Some of the dreams were beautiful and quiet, others were nightmares, terrifying and scary. As we know, Mary had passed away on March 20th 1982. I had been sad and alone and only much work kept me from going insane. Because of the work, I had no time to sit and ponder what will be next. There was no one in the house to share my problems with. Then on March 20th 1987 (five years to the date of Mary's passing) something strange happened when I was sleeping. I do not know if I can call it a dream, because I did not see anyone, only heard a beautiful, lovely, mellow, deep baritone voice.

I was asleep like every other night when suddenly from nowhere this voice came to me at 3:00 AM. I heard the voice tell me: "Get up and look at Genesis 2:18 and Ecclesiastes 4:7-11." I was horrified. Who is talking to me when there is no one in the house. Where and who are you who talks to me? What do you want? I was startled, got up and sat at the edge of the bed and could not get over what was happening. Was this real? Was it a dream and if it was what kind? I looked around the house in the dark, but could not see or hear anyone. Darkness filled the house at 3:00 AM. With fear I got up and with shaky hands and legs I moved around to see if there is anyone in the house. Fear filled me, but yet at the same time with the sound so soft and mellow I was hoping I could hear it again.

Stumbling with fear to a light switch, I turned on the light and went to the kitchen to get the Bible that I had sitting on the table. What is so important in the Bible that I need read it? As I picked up the Bible, I was still shaking and wondering where the voice had come from. Who was speaking to me when there is no one in the house. I sat down by the table and with trembling hands opened the Bible to the first page. My eyes went down to chapter two and verse eighteen. Than I read: *"And the Lord God said, It is not good that man should be alone; I will make him an helpmeet for him."* (Genesis 2:18) Startled from the sound and staring at the passage, I read it again and than again. I must have read it a dozen times and each word one at a time. No, it's still the same words. What does all this mean? Why do I have to read this? Who told me to read this? What is all this about? What is the purpose of such a dream (if it was a dream). What has this to do with me?

Than I remembered the other quotation. I fumbled through the pages with shaking hands looking for the passage and still thinking about the first one I had just read. I found the second passage and read: *"Then I returned and saw vanity under the sun. There is one alone, and there is not another second; yea, he hath neither child nor brother: yet is there no end to all his labor; neither is his eye satisfied with riches; neither saith he, For whom do I labor, and bereave my soul of good? This is also vanity, yea, it is a sore travail. Two are better than one; because they have a good reward for their labor. For if they fall, the one will lift up his fellow: but woe to him that is alone when he falleth; for he hath not another to help him up. Again, if two lie together, then they have heat: but how can one be warm alone? And if one prevail against him, two shall withstand him; and a threefold cord in not quickly broken."* (Ecclesiastes 4:7-11)

I sat trembling beside the table. What is the meaning of all this? Why do I have to read this? Who told me to read this? I sat and contemplated, got up and took a drink of water. Maybe the water will wake me up to reality as to what is happening here. I put the lights out and went back to bed. Do you think I could sleep? No. The voice I had heard and the words I just read in the Bible were rushing around in my head a hundred miles an hour. I could not sleep, but the voice I heard a few moments ago seemed to be rebounding over and over again. I could not understand the meaning of why I had to read the passages and what the meaning of it was. But than, who told me to read those passages? The night finally dragged into daylight and since 3:00 AM when I first heard the voice, I have not slept. The passages stuck to me like honey sticks to bread. What am I supposed to learn from these passages? Question after question whizzed around in my head. What, How, When, Who, Where I questioned myself but no answers came. Than it hit me. This is the night that Mary had passed away, but what has this to do with her passing? It is exactly five years when she passed away. Because I could not sleep anymore, I was up with the sun this morning. When I think of that incident at that time, the message is somewhat clearer today after what else has happened and transpired since then. God or an Angel must have spoken to me at that time but it made no sense to me. When I look back now, I see God made a lot of sense which I did not understand at that time.

Things rolled along and I was fulfilling my duties to the parish as best I knew and could with the health problems I had. Than on April 6th at 8:30 PM, I got a call from Dmytro Belbas from Rossburn, Manitoba asking me to move there to be their parish priest. Again as in all other times, I told him the same I had told the people at Prince George, and Vernon, Kamloops and Lac La Biche and others. When I get a letter from the Primate or the Consistory, yes I will move and come to your parish. As with all the other previous requests, it was the same this time also. I stayed on at Hyas. What would I have to do to get moved to another parish? People calling me from Western Canada wanting me to move to their parish, but each year the answer to them all from the Consistory is the same, "nyet, no."

This was also the second year that my nephew Lawrence, Oksana's son, was staying with me over the summer holidays. This gave Oksana a break, rest and some time to relax when she would come from work. Lawrence stayed at the summer camp with the children for two weeks and the rest of the time he stayed with me. After Lawrence was not in camp, I still used to go to the camp quite often to check and see how things were coming along and if any help was needed with anything.

One day in particular in the evening after supper Lawrence and I went to the camp. It was about 9:30-9:50 PM when we were coming home. Did we both witness a miracle. Just south of the Stenen turnoff there is a small hill on the road on highway #49 going east. There was a car traveling in front of us of about a hundred and fifty yards or so. The tail lights were very visible. The car in front was over the top of the hill and two seconds later we also were on top of the hill. As we drove along, the tail lights of the car ahead had vanished when the vehicle had gone over the hill. As we came over the crest of the hill there was no more car ahead of us that had been there a second before. It was Lawrence who first noticed the event and says to me: "Uncle, where did that car in front of us go?" Yes, than it hit me. Where is that car we were following? I pulled off to the side of the road to see what happened to that car that had been in front of us.

There was no sign of any car anywhere. It could have not turned off the road, because there were no roads to turn off and no approaches. It could not have gone into the ditch, for we would have seen it when we got to the top of the hill. It did not go into the bush for there is no bush. Did a U-F-O, grab the car of the road? If it did would we not have seen it lift up before our eyes? Well, where did that car disappear? We both looked and listened and looked, but no car. To this day I don't know what happened to that vehicle. Next day we went back with Lawrence to check the place in the daytime. There were fields on either side of the road. We looked for any tracks that a vehicle could have left. Nothing. On each side of the road there is a ditch some eight to ten feet deep with a long incline. No tracks of any car going there. Nothing, absolutely nothing not even a mark anywhere. Last night we were traveling at sixty miles an hour behind a car and it vanished from in front of us. Even if someone would have floored the gas pedal to go hundred miles an hour, we still would have seen the car for a while before it pulled away. Whatever happened there on that hill to that car, to this day I do not know. It is a mystery and will be for always. I have no answer to the disappearing car. The car was traveling, moving, so if a U-F-O grabbed the car, there were people in it. We should have heard on the radio or TV that there were people missing, but no such thing was broadcast anywhere. If there would have been some news item of missing people I would have told investigators or police what Lawrence and I saw that evening - the disappearance of a vehicle. But there was absolutely nothing just a mystery. Both of us saw the car in front of us, not only one of us.

Like every other year again that dreaded time, holiday time. The parish was telling me to take holidays. Maybe they now realized that my health was not the best. They have seen me in the hospital and knew that I was going to see specialists from one city to the next, Regina and Saskatoon. So this year again I go for holidays. I made plans that I would again go and visit George Alexandro in California. When Mr. Alexandro was visiting me he became acquainted with my parishioners. Peter and Mary Kurkowsky had invited us to come over to their place for supper one evening. They got to know him and the people were calling him, Uncle George. One time as I was visiting Peter and Mary Kurkowsky, they had mentioned that it would be nice to visit uncle George. After talking about this seriously, one day we decided that there would be four of us going to see uncle George, Peter and Mary Kurkowsky and Mary's sister Eileen Gryba and myself.

We left for this trip on September 12th traveling to Edmonton where we would leave the car by John and Kay's place. Going to Edmonton with us was also Peter and Mary's daughter Genia. She would visit family and friends in Edmonton and than go back home with the bus. We stopped at John and Kay's for a brief visit before we were going to a motel, but John and Kay would not let us out of the house. We had to stay over at their place. Next morning John took us to the airport. We flew from Edmonton to Calgary and than on to Los Angeles.

When we arrived at Los Angeles, we rented a car and spent a day at Disneyland and on Sunday went to a church service. After the service Father Holutiak and his wife drove us around Los Angeles and took us to beautiful large cemetery. Who would have told me that some seven or eight years later Father Holutiak and I would be serving together at the Altar in Phoenix, Arizona. Next day we drove out to uncle George to Porterville. Mr. Alexandro was very happy to see us that his house was filled with guests from Canada. We stayed that day at his place and the following day we went to see the Giant Redwood Forest in the Sierra Nevada mountains.

After our visit in California we returned back to Edmonton where John picked us up at the airport. We spent another night with John and Kay telling them about the trip. Next day we did not drive straight home from Edmonton, but headed out west to Banff and Lake Louise to see the Canadian Rockies before we headed for home. I knew I had to be back home on September 25th, because on the 26th of September I had a memorial service booked in Hyas. When we arrived home, I dropped off Peter, Mary and Eileen and came home at about 9:30 PM that evening when it was already dark.

AND NOW THE "KOLOMAYKA" STARTS

Now starts a new chapter in my life. A kolomayka is a fast twirling Ukrainian dance. One that changed the status of my profession and of the things to come. Because of the events about to unfold, I had to make tremendous changes in my life, all because of the circumstances that were caused to me from the church I served. This new "kolomayka" is now beginning.

Early on September 26th at 7:00 AM a Saturday, I was awakened by a telephone call from Winnipeg, from the Consistory. The late Father Stephan Jarmus was calling me and from Winnipeg and the time there was one hour ahead. When I answered the phone he says: "I know you have a memorial service this morning, so I will not hold you long, but I want to ask you if you would be willing to move to Vernon, B.C." I was stunned. Saturday the Consistory is closed. The priests have already been on their new parishes for two months. Now two months after the priests transfers, I'm getting a phone call to move to Vernon. Why? I knew that I was not moving again this year, for the transfers had already taken place two months previously. I was settled to stay in Hyas this coming year. Stunned as I was to this proposition, I asked: "What is the problem and why at this time?" Father Jarmus said that there were some problems in Vernon and they have to make the change at this time. I thought for a moment and than said: "If you will sleep better at night and have less problems and headaches if I move, I'll go to Vernon." I could hear by the sound of his voice change that he was pleased with my answer.

I asked him, how soon and when I would have to be in Vernon. He said that I should be in Vernon on November 1st. This gives give a month and a few days to pack and move. I knew that I would have to step on it to be packed and moved out in a month. I knew I would have to start packing right now. At the end of our conversation I told Father Jarmus to write me a letter that I am moving. Father Jarmus assured me that a letter will be in the mail first thing come Monday morning. In less than a week I should have the letter on hand from the church headquarters.

I had the memorial service that morning, but much as I hated, yes I sinned that morning too. Half of my mind was set on the move to Vernon and half on the service. I had to get boxes and start packing. I will need a trailer to move. I knew that the parish in Hyas would not be in favor of me leaving. I have to hold back and not tell anyone anything until I get a letter from the Consistory. If I even as much as whisper to anyone that I am moving, the phones from here will be sending messages to Winnipeg not to move me. I made it set in my mind that this time, I'm not telling anyone anything, no matter how hard it may be to keep the secret.

Now all kinds of questions were loading up my mind. How do I move? Do I get a U-Haul? Do I get someone with a truck to move me? Do I get a moving company? Then other questions: why at this time of the year? What kind of problems are there in Vernon? Will I be able to do anything to fix those problems? Question after question kept flooding my mind and me trying to find and think of an answer.

I learned of the move on Saturday morning September 26th. On Monday morning I went to Canora to get some boxes for packing. I did not want the people in Hyas to learn that I was getting boxes from the store to pack. If someone saw me loading boxes, they may get suspicious why I need boxes. If they learned about this, they would not give my phone a rest, because everybody would want to know what is going on. I started packing on the week of September 28th on Monday. I packed and carried the boxes downstairs into the basement. I did not want some church member to walk into the house, see packed boxes and start questioning as to what is happening. I packed everything I had in the basement. And than only a few things from the main floor. I would leave the rest to pack after I get the letter and I am ready to leave in a few days. A week passed, it is now October 3rd and still no letter from Winnipeg. Most of the things I had packed in one week and was awaiting a letter from the Consistory. It is one week since I had received the phone call from Winnipeg that I will move from Hyas to Vernon but still no letter of confirmation.

Sunday October 4th I had a service at Hyas and than afternoon a service at Sturgis. After the service at Sturgis a parish meeting was scheduled to discuss the topic of the manse in Hyas. Some people and I wanted to have the manse located more centrally at Sturgis or Preeceville. Others were dead set against this. Sturgis and Preeceville were bigger centres and more central for the parish. Others were saying to repair the present manse and leave where it is. Others said to sell the manse and relocate the priest to a larger centre. The manse in Hyas was getting up in age and something had to be done. Even the foundation, concrete, was beginning to crumble on the south wall. You could move the palm of your hand over the south foundation in the basement and the concrete was crumbling. Why, I don't know. Because of age or some other reason? At the meeting ideas were going back and forth among the delegates. The chairman of the parish asked me if I had anything to say, or any suggestions. Oh yes I have, but said that they discuss and talk and I will say what I think at the end of the meeting. As they talked, discussed and debated, I sat back listening and thinking of what I knew and they didn't. Finally the meeting was coming to the end with no results, with the exception to let the manse be where is, as is.

Finally the chairman asked me to say a few words. I got up and said something like this: "You know, you are talking about the manse. To me it matters not anymore if the manse will be where it is, if it will be moved to Canora, Sturgis or Preeceville. It matters not if its going to be old or new. I got a phone call a week ago from Winnipeg and I am moving at the end of October to Vernon, B.C. I have to be on that parish on November 1st. I already have almost everything packed, just a few more items to pack away. You can come after the meeting to the manse and you will see everything is being packed." When I finished speaking, it was so quiet in the basement that all you could hear was people breathing. Everybody looked at each other, stunned and in disbelief. They could not believe what they were hearing. Some people could not even speak because of the shock. Then

I just added on: "I'm still awaiting for a letter from the Consistory for the confirmation and than I am gone. The letter should be in the mail any day now." The meeting concluded that everything is left as it is until we know if we will be getting another priest or not.

Time was not standing but moving along. Now that the cat was out of the bag, I could pack everything and people can come and have a look if I was joking or did reality come to Hyas and me. Each service that I had from now on, I would bid farewell to the parishioners in that congregation telling them that it was my last service in their congregation. We shook hands and bid each other farewell extending best wishes for the future. Some people cried that I was leaving and others were still in disbelief, whether it really was happening or was it only a joke. I bid my farewell at Arran after the service and than at an afternoon service with the Norquay parishioners on October 11th. It was now two weeks ago, since I had the call from Winnipeg to move to Vernon, but still no letter of confirmation about my move. In the meantime I was still packing during the week with things that I would not need at the present time until I get to the new parish. I kept things unpacked that I needed for the services. A few things were left that will be packed on the last day, the last minute.

On October 14th, St. Mary the Protectress, I had a service at Swan Plain and there I also bid farewell to the parishioners. I still had a few services left in the parish and as I visit those congregations, I will bid them farewell at that time. Coming home from Swan Plain, I stopped at the post office to pick up the mail. I took the mail out of the box, and low and behold, finally a letter from Winnipeg from the Consistory for which I have been looking forward to receive. Over two weeks ago when I learned of the planned move, that I finally got the letter I was waiting for. I drove home and once in the house, the first thing I have to do is read the letter that I am moving and have the letter to show the people. I opened the envelope than the letter and read about my transfer to Vernon. But wait a minute. Something is not right.

No. It can't be. It's an error. I have to read it again, one word at a time. I read it again with trembling hands and with disbelief. Wait a minute. Something here is not right. Did I get the right letter? I looked at the letter again and could not believe what I was reading. Impossible. It can't be true. My hands began to shake and tremble. Now the parishioners will call me a liar. I still have that letter on hand as I write this. It is from the Consistory and dated October 8th, saying: **"With the blessing of his Beatitude, Metropolitan Wasyly, we inform you with this letter that the matter of a change in your parish this year will not take place."** What? I read the letter again and again. Am I reading something wrong? But no, that's what it says, there is no change and I continue my stay in Hyas. What do I tell the parishioners now? Will I be called a lair? I have bid farewell to a few congregations, and what happens now?

I was sitting with tears starting to fill my eyes. Why? You asked me to move and I said I would help you so you don't have headaches and can sleep peacefully at night, and you do this to me? I have done two weeks of packing and everything is in boxes, so now what? I am packed and ready to leave in a few days and now this, you telling me that nothing is changed and I stay where I am? I seemed to be disoriented for a while, not sure if I was reading correctly or was there a word misspelled or something. What happened? Why the change? Was all this done just to make me look like a fool among people? No one else in the house. No family. No one to talk over about what is happening. No one to turn too for comfort. No one to share this calamity with. All alone. So where do I go from here? Again I read the letter, maybe I made a mistake in reading. I was still not sure that the letter was correct. Each time I read the letter, it was the same thing that my move is canceled and I stay on in Hyas. It just can't be. Something is wrong here. After I packed almost everything and bid farewell to some parishioners and now you say I stay where I am? There's got to be something wrong here.

Will the parishioners believe me now after all what has happened? Will they say that I lied to them. I still could not believe it. I was upset and who would not be in such a situation? I didn't even have dinner that day, because I lost all appetite after I read the letter. I went to the garage got into the car and drove out of town, but where was I going? I don't know. Going just to get away from this place so that I don't go insane. I wanted to get my head cleared after this news. I did not want to go to see anyone in the parish, because I was embarrassed to see anyone. How could I look someone in the eye now? How can I go on and say that I am not moving after what has transpired in the last two weeks? How can I face anyone now? I drove out of town and unto some country roads to get away from everything and everyone.

That same day I got a headache like I never had before and for the next four days the headaches stayed with me. My nose bleeds were worst than they were before and I was sick the whole day long. The nose bleeds that had been starting to ease off somewhat, where now more severe than previously and occurred any time of day or night. If I had not been feeling well till now, well this was the topper. At times I did not know if I was coming or going. Do I unpack what I packed or just pack up the rest, load it up and go to the end of the world? All kinds of questions hounded me. No one to share this burden with. When I met parishioners on the street, they responded differently to me and looked at me as if I was a bad boy. I felt coolness from the parishioners in the coming days. When I see that kind of betrayal, there is nothing left to do, but take off to the end of the world. At least God was still with me and was giving me enough strength and energy to carry on through those last two weeks.

After I got the letter from Winnipeg, I took it with me to every congregation. After the service I would read the letter to the people in church, showing them the letter, that I was not moving and the that the letter was written October 8th. Some people were relieved to hear that I was not moving and others still had doubts about me as a person, not only as a clergyman. Will the people believe me at this time that I will be staying after I had told them I am moving, all packed and ready to go?

Slowly I began to get back into the groove of things. I would unpack a box here and another one there to get to the things I needed each time. This was happening but at the back of my mind was the thought that I have to get a letter telling me to move to Vernon. As I was slowly getting settled back into the daily routine, when suddenly as from a clear blue sky comes another lightning bomb shell.

Every spring and fall the full Consistory Board of the Ukrainian Orthodox Church meets for their meeting in Winnipeg. Nine clergy and nine lay people plus the bishops compose the Consistory board. Such a meeting was taking place in Winnipeg on the last days of October 1987. On October 31st a Consistory board member, the late Sam Lebedowich, calls me from Winnipeg at 8:00 PM and tells me: "You are moving to Vernon, because we talked about this matter today at the Consistory meeting." W H A T? Am I dreaming? Am I hearing correctly? I tell Mr. Lebedowich: "But it can't be, because I have a letter from the Consistory telling me that my transfer is canceled and I stay where I am." I told him about the letter I received, but he said that I would be hearing from the bishop next week.

Next day on November 1st I get a phone call from Vernon (can't remember who called) asking me if I am moving to Vernon. I said that so far as I know, I have a letter stating that I'm staying where I am, but last night Sam Lebedowich called and said that I am moving to Vernon. Now I don't know where I am and where I'm going. Until I get confirmation, I'm staying where I am. On November 4th I get a phone call from Tony Burkowski from Kelowna, B.C., asking me if I'm moving to Vernon. I gave him the same answer I gave for the Vernon caller.

How can a person survive this? This juggling around with phone lines, news and everything else would make a well and healthy person sick, not alone me who already had health problems. This kind of confusion can drive one into mental illness. A person with steel nerves would have a hard time surviving such abuse and misunderstanding. How I withstood all this trauma, to this day I don't know. Only God was with me to give me the strength to go through these events.

Time is going by and I'm doing on the parish what I have to do. It is now November 14th and I still haven't heard from Winnipeg if I am moving to Vernon or not. Sam Lebedowich told me on November 1st that the bishop will speak to me about this in a week. Two weeks of November are gone by, and I have not heard anything from any bishop or anyone else, so I will be staying put where I am. I had unpacked a number of boxes getting things I needed for use at the time. On November 14th in the evening I get a phone call from Vernon from Peter and Doris Chaykowski, asking me if I am moving to Vernon, because they heard that I was moving there. Everybody seems to know everything about me, only **me** doesn't what **me** is doing or has to do. I told them that I don't know anything, because no one has told me anything. I told them that I had a letter stating that I stay where I am. It was later some three years after I was living in Vernon, that I heard another story from people. The late Alex Romanyk told me that the congregation in Kelowna had received a telephone call from the Consistory telling them I was moving to their parish and that they would meet the plane at a certain hour to pick me up. WHAT? They went to the airport and when the plane came I did not arrive, they went home and made some phone calls to learn what was happening. When they called, they were told that I was not moving, but staying in Hyas. Aslex Romanyk who told me this at that time was living in Kelowna. He later moved to Winnipeg and passed away in 2016.

    The following day, November 15th I got a phone call from Archbishop John at 8:30 PM asking me to move to Vernon. I told him that the latest letter I have is that I am staying at Hyas. I told him unless I get a letter black on white telling me otherwise to move I'll move, but I can't do anything without orders on black and white. I also told him of what had already transpired and I'm hanging in mid air not knowing which way I will fall or swing. I told him that after I had been packed and ready to go, my last letter said to stay where I am and I have unpacked some of my things. Phone calls coming from Western Canada asking when I'm moving to Vernon, and here I'm sitting not knowing what is happening. This evening had been bad and I had to take a tranquilizer(Valium) pill to keep my nerves from exploding.

    I was getting into a terrible health state at this time. Was I coming, going or staying? Was I packing or unpacking? Was I blind or could I still see? Was I dreaming or was it reality? Was I still alive or am I already dead? Anyone who has not gone through such hassles will never know the pain, hurt, deceit and misunderstandings. When people called at times, I had to think even what my name was. Many times as I was doing something, I had to stop and think what I was doing and why. When the phone ran, I answered and than I had to think who was calling, even though they would say who they were. I know that there were times I was saying things that made no sense, because people looked at me as if I had fallen off from Mars. I was so low in life and now on tranquilizers that I don't remember what I was doing. How I ever drove to the congregations and had services, I do not know till this day. Only God must have been doing everything for me. I was thinking of leaving everything, get into the car, head south to the USA or Mexico, get lost among the people and than at least I will have peace and know who I am. I was ashamed and embarrassed of being pulled, manipulated and made fun of, which to this day I don't know how I survived all that. Why can't someone make up their mind once and for all and tell me what is happening?

Tell me either this or that, but don't push a person around and change things every day. I was by this time already thinking of leaving my priestly work. If things don't change soon, I'll end up in a mental asylum. From one day to the next I sat on pins and needles, not knowing what to expect, what to do. When the phone rang, I would jump up from the tension and nervous condition. When a person is in such condition, how can you perform your duties? How can you work properly? Either I should have been in Vernon in a day or two, or I could not have been a priest any longer in my condition.

It seemed like someone was really mean and wicked against me to send me through such a horrendous state. But this still was not the end of it. I at times was not sure what was happening, but it was not well at all. The only thing that was coming to my mind was to step out of my profession, so that I can reestablish my mind and mental condition back to some normality. My body needed a rest after all the goings on in the past few weeks. My mind needed to get away from thinking too much so that it don't go blank. Nose bleeds had come back. My body at times at night in bed would tremble, quiver and shiver from exhaustion. Nerves pills I began to eat like bread. Nothing was helping. I felt like I was becoming a wrecked ship on some deserted shore on the ocean. Physically and mentally I was a wreck in bad shape and there was no help coming from anyone. Whoever met and saw me, would say: "You look well." I replied: "It's not the way a person looks, but how one feels." Only God, the doctors and I knew how I was feeling then even the doctors could not find the answers to what the problem was with my health.

I was already making plans that at the end of 1987 I would ask for leave of absence or just plainly say, take sick leave, or just leave my profession so that I don't end up in some mental institution in Saskatchewan. I was so ill and even more tired mentally than physically, but I wanted to carry on to the end of the year. It was so hard with things when everything was coming to confusion. From that time things seemed to get more muddled up each day. Nights were becoming restless. Instead of trying to carry on my duties, I was spending more time laying on the chesterfield, once in a while falling asleep, but more often laying there restless and sleepless with millions of thoughts running around in my head. Many times I prayed and prayed, but it seemed to no avail. It seemed that God had forgotten me. I thought of the Righteous Job and wandered if I was in the same boat as he had been.

As if all this worrying and illness was not enough, on November 19th, I get another phone call from Winnipeg. Father Jarmus was calling. He is the one who called on September 26th asking me if I would move to Vernon, B.C. I answered the call and after our hellos, Father Jarmus says: "So are you all packed and ready to go to Vernon?" I did not even think this time, but said straight out: "I am so ill from all that Vernon talk, that I don't even know what day it is, because I'm so confused with Vernon and Hyas." Then he says to me: "The Metropolitan will talk with you." Then the Metropolitan says: "We are talking here that you go to Vernon, because of all the priests in Canada we think you are the only one that would be able to fix up the problems in Vernon."

I could fix up problems in Vernon? And who is going to fix my problems? I answered Metropolitan saying: "The way I feel right now, I'm so sick that I don't know from day to day how long I will be able to last. On November 21st the parish is having its annual meeting and I may have to tell them that I will have to leave the parish and maybe even leave the priesthood, because of my health, for I don't want to end up in a mental asylum." Metropolitan answered me like this: "Okay, you tell the meeting that you are leaving." At these words he hung up the phone on me. For a moment I thought maybe we were disconnected by the operator, so I waited for a while and am still waiting till today to get reconnected. How can someone hang up when you can sense that there is something wrong?

If you phoned your child and heard that they are ill, or some other problem, would you hang up on them? If the Metropolitan is the shepherd, is that the way to treat your sheep, workers, your priests, by hanging up on them? I waited for a while and thought they would call back because we were disconnected. I waited and nothing came back. When that last phone call came from Winnipeg and they hung up on me, I made up my mind there and then saying: "THAT IS THE LAST NAIL IN THE COFFIN." Right there and then I thought and decided: if that is how the church thinks and looks after its clergy, than there is no room for me in this church. I made a decision to get out of the church and my profession and then no one will bother me and I won't bother anyone else. What else could I do in such a case? I did not want to go through all this hell, because I knew I had served God faithfully all my life. I did not know, but God already had made different plans for me, for my future.

The annual parish meeting took place at Hudson Bay, Sask., on November 21st after the service. At that meeting I explained and told the parish what had transpired in the last few weeks since the end of September and they understood my position. I was emotional as I spoke and tears filled my eyes. I had given so much of myself to God and the church and now here I stand on the threshold, uncertain of my future. I told the parish that I would give them one month notice before I left the parish and that hopefully at the end of December 1987 I would leave. **Now** - people felt sorry for me and they understood my feelings, hurts and illness. I told them and promised I would not just walk out from them in the middle of the night, but they would have a month notice before I left. The people were disappointed in what they were hearing and now they knew that I was not well but was seeing doctors in Canora, Norquay, Yorkton, Regina and Saskatoon. People at the meeting began to ask and beg me to stay with them until the end of January 1988, so that I could still come and bless their homes for them.

That same evening when I got home from the meeting from Hudson Bay, I got another call from Kelowna, British Columbia from Father Deacon Isidore Woronchak at 8:30 PM. He asked me if I was moving to the Okanagan to serve the area. I told him what had happened with the phone call from Winnipeg and what had transpired at the annual meeting in Hudson Bay. I told him that I will be leaving the church at the end of January 1988.

The following day was Sunday November 22nd, and I had a service at Sturgis. After the service I had a requiem memorial service and this was followed by a baptismal of an infant. After this I left for Moose Jaw, Saskatchewan, because that evening along with two other priests we were having a missionary service. Father Mykola Derewianka from Canora and Father Michael Zaleschuk from Regina were present. After the service everybody gathered in the church basement for lunch and then it was followed by the program and I was the guest speaker.

After this missionary service things changed my life, the plan that God had already set up. All I knew was that I had just a little over two months of service left. After that I would have to think and decide my future life. I had also told my parents before the annual parish meeting that I may have to leave my service. They told me that when I do, to come and stay with them. They told me to bring all my belongings to their place and live with them until I decide what will be next.

GOD'S NEW LIFE - FOR ME ?

After the missionary service in Moose Jaw on November 22nd things started to work in a different direction when I received a letter from a Mary Paziuk from Moose Jaw. She had been at the missionary service, heard my speech, thanked me for coming to Moose Jaw and giving the speech and asked if she could have a copy of my talk-address. This was not the first time people in my life had asked for copies of my sermons or talks. People from The Pas, Manitoba after the marriage of their son at Dauphin, Manitoba asked for a copy of the sermon at that marriage. They said they cried at the marriage and were remarried during the service. Another couple from Calgary after the funeral of their family member at Sturgis, Sask., wrote to me and asked for a copy of the funeral sermon I had delivered. There were other times people asked me for copies of sermons or speeches which I had and I made copies and mailed to them or gave it in person. I always thought that if what I had said made sense to the people and helped them find God or the church, than please here is a copy and use it for your own benefit and salvation of your soul. If my sermon or talk can save a soul, so help them God.

When I got the letter (which I still have on hand) from Mary (Marusia) Paziuk, I obliged, made a copy and sent it out to her. At that time I did not know who the lady was. With that copy of my speech I also wrote and told her that I was not feeling very well and that I will probably be leaving my services in a few months. It was later that I learned why she wanted the copy of that speech. She was working in Moose Jaw in the mental institution. At that time she was a seamstress working in the sewing room. During their coffee break the people would talk and tell what they did for the week end. Mary Paziuk told them she was in church because there was a missionary service with three priests serving. One particular lady, Ena Nelson, who was of a different faith wanted to know what the speech was about. Mrs. Nelson said she would like a copy to see it. Ena was a religious person. Mary Paziuk told Ena that she would try to get my address and will write to me to see if I would give her a copy of my speech. When she wrote for a copy of the speech, I sent it for her.

By this time God had all His plans set and they were in motion and only He knew about them, for God works in wondrous ways. Neither Mary Paziuk nor I knew what was happening at that time. I received the letter from Mary Paziuk on December 10th about twenty days after the missionary service in Moose Jaw. I replied and sent a copy of the speech within a week. She wrote me another letter thanking me for the speech. This second letter from her I received December 22nd, and this letter began to change my life as well as for Mary (Marusia) Paziuk. It is a story in itself that must be told and is now starting.

After I had received the letter from her on December 22nd, it was two days later that I got a phone call from her. I had not talked or hear her talk before, but when she called and said who she was I could sense some emotion in her voice. She told me who she was and thanked me for sending her the speech. I felt that something was wrong when she spoke on the phone. It sounded like she was crying. I asked her if something was wrong and she said that she got my phone number from the operator and wanted to thank me personally for the speech. Still I could here the emotional tone of speech that was there and I asked her again if something was wrong.

She began to tell me what happened. Her husband had passed away in March of 1987. When he was still living, people used to visit them. Now that she is alone no one comes around any more. She also said that she used to prepare the Ukrainian Christmas Eve Supper and used to have ten to twelve people for supper. Now that her husband is gone and Christmas is a day away, no one even phoned her to see if she could come to their place for Christmas. This she said, had upset her and that is why she was feeling that way. Now the Christmas season is here again and no one even wants to know her she said. I could feel she was she was heart broken and sad. I knew what she was going through, because I was going through the same thing. I told her not to worry, believe in God and things will always work out for the good. I told her that maybe someone will still invite her to go visit with them at Christmas. It seemed to cheer her up and I told her that if she ever wants to talk to someone she can call me and cry on my shoulder for my shoulders are tough and she can cry all she wants and sometimes crying helps a person release their problems. I was also in an emotional stress myself, but I was still willing and eager to help people in their troubles.

Than we started to talk about other things, weather, church, work and I asked her where she was from originally, because I come from Saskatchewan and was born at Cudworth. She said she came from the Wakaw area. I asked her what her maiden name was. She said it was Kwasnica. I remarked that we lived at Wakaw one time on John Kwasnica's farm, just one mile east of Wakaw and this Kwasnica had a store in Wakaw. She came back and says: "That was my uncle John's farm and my father's brother." After having learned that we were born about eleven miles apart, our conversation became different and we must have talked for another half hour or more on the phone asking each other if we knew these people and those people, etc.

A few days later my parents called to see what I was doing and if I would be able to come for Christmas Eve supper to their place at Cudworth. I told them that I would not be coming because I have a service at Sturgis at Midnight after supper and I would not have enough time to get back in time and in case a storm came up, I could be stuck somewhere on the road. The parents lived a hundred and eighty miles away, a three hour drive. When they knew that I would not be coming to their place for that supper, mother says, they will come to my place and we will have supper together at Hyas. I said that would be very nice and fine. Mother said they would come on January 4th so we would have time to prepare for the supper on January 5th and 6th. She said they wanted to be an extra day or two with me, so that is why they will come sooner. I guess God always knew what He was doing.

I believe it was about January 2nd or 3rd when I got another call from Mary Paziuk. I should mention at this time that whenever I will mention her name I will use Marusia as I called her that and this will be different from my first wife who was Mary. Marusia called and wanted to know how I was feeling, because I had told her that I was not well. She also said that she was in a somber state since it was only a few days before Orthodox Christmas and she will have to spend the time in her house alone for no one had called her to ask her for Christmas. We talked on the phone for quite a while and I could again hear emotion in her voice. Than a thought came to me, must have been God sent. I told her my parents are coming here for Christmas Eve supper so maybe if she wants to come out to Hyas so it would help her get over the loneliness and have supper with us. She immediately said that we don't know each other and my parents don't know her either. She also said that it may not be good for her to come out when I am alone and she is also alone. She said she did not want to cause any problems for me. I told her that there would be no problems, because both of my parents will be here. She thought for a moment and said that she would see if she could get some time off from work.

She said she would ask to take a few days off and if she can and she will call me back in a day or so. Next evening she called again and said that she would be able to come but so it would not cause any problems for me and she wanted to be sure that my parents will be there. We talked and I asked when she could come and she said on January 5th. I asked how she would come, with the car or bus. She said that she would come with the bus, because in the winter time she did not care to drive the car out of the city too far away from home. I told her that if she took the bus in Regina that goes to Preeceville, I would meet her at the Stenen junction, because many people do that and the bus stops there to drop off or pick up passengers.

It also happened that on January 7th (Orthodox Christmas) I had an appointment to see Dr. Nattrass in Regina at 1:00 PM. I told Marusia I would be driving to Regina on the 7th of January and can take her back there, and so she would take a one way ticket. Than from Regina she could catch the bus to Moose Jaw. Things seemed to be working out, but when she gets off at the Stenen Junction, how will I know her when she gets off the bus and maybe a few other people might be getting off. She told me what she would be wearing and I should be able to recognize her. There was another thing that I was concerned about. What if there will be someone else there waiting to pick up a passenger? What if some parishioner sees me picking up some woman from the bus, what will people say? I did not want to have a problem with people's talk because I already have enough problems without adding more.

From the time my mother had heart attacks and strokes in Winnipeg a number of years ago, she never was the same. Her reactions were slower and at times she would repeat the same story to you each time you visited her or she visited other people. At other times she would say things that did not seem to make sense. So when Marusia had decided to come to Hyas and have supper with the three of us, I knew that mother might say something to some people that would not be right. We had not seen or met each other yet, but with mother's condition one never knew what to expect. I had told father privately that there would be another person for supper and that father knew of her uncle years before, because we lived on her uncle's farm, and shopped in her uncle's store in Wakaw. Father seemed to be thrilled when I told him that she was a relative to the late John Kwasnica. He already wanted to know who, what and everything else, but I said that I don't know myself yet, because I have not seen her yet. Father and I did not tell mother anything until the night when Marusia was to arrive. While washing supper dishes on the 5th of January, I told mother that she will have company tomorrow to help her prepare the Holy Christmas Eve Supper. My parents had arrived in Hyas on January 4th, 1988.

January 5th came, the day was over, and now it was night and it was time to go to the bus to pick up Marusia at the Stenen junction. I was some what jittery, not knowing what to expect. I got to the junction and waited for the bus to arrive. As the bus was coming which I could see about a mile away, shivers were running down my spine. Was it excitement? Was it nervousness? Was it the unknown that was before me? What if someone on the bus recognizes me picking up some woman. There would be gossip I did not need, because I was already stretched miles with my nerves. I have had enough problems of mine and this time I was just trying to help another unknown desperate person during the Christmas period. The bus arrived at the corner and stopped. A lady got off the bus and no one else and I asked if she was Mrs. Paziuk. "Yes" she said. We got into the car and introduced ourselves and started the four mile trip to Hyas.

The parents knew that I had gone to pick up a passenger at the bus stop. When Marusia and I arrived they were still up, not sleeping. I introduced Marusia to my parents and than we still talked for about an hour, drinking tea, before we all went to bed. Father was really interested in Marusia and he wanted to know who, what, when, etc. We had lived on Marusia's uncles' farm and shopped in his store at Wakaw. When we finally turned in for the night, father and mother had one bedroom and Marusia the second one upstairs. I slept on the chesterfield in the living room. There was a bedroom in the basement, but it was good for summer and not winter sleeping. If you slept in the basement in the wintertime, than next morning someone would have to call for the undertakers to come and pick you up. Why? Well when you have hoar frost on your walls in the basement, what does that tell you? It tells you it is cold, COLD there. That is how cold it was in the basement and I should know, because I spent eight years - winters there. That is why I had also been pushing that the parish get another manse for the priest, but that did not fly as you know from reading about it some pages back.

The next day the four of us were getting acquainted with each other and worked at ease preparing for the evening supper. We talked and our acquaintance got better and we seemed to be like a family. I felt happy that I could help another soul to make her life a teeny weeny happier. Together the four of us had Christmas Eve Supper. After supper we all dressed and went to a midnight service at Sturgis. Father had already been working on a plan all day in his mind how it will be so that if someone in church would ask who Marusia was what he would say. When we got to the church, father said that I should go in myself first and they will come a few moments later. Father had planned out in his head that Marusia would sit beside the wall in the pew. Than he would sit beside her and than mother nearest the aisle. Father figured that if anyone would ask who Marusia was, he was going to say it was his cousin from Saskatoon. No one knew of this plan father had devised and it was only much later that he told us what he had planned in his mind.

There were not too many people in church that night because for one it was a cold night and the second that it was a midnight service. Everything

I ALSO WALKED ON THIS EARTH

went over well in church and no one had asked who Marusia was. We came home after the service and it was already 2:00 AM, and immediately went to bed because in the morning everybody is leaving. Next morning we had breakfast and father and mother were leaving for home at about 8:00 AM, because they wanted to be home when the Carollers will come. At the same time father and I had loaded his car with some of my things that I had already packed and he would take them into the basement when he got home. When father and mother were leaving for home, I was leaving at the same time for Regina to see the doctor. Marusia was coming with me as far as Regina and from there she would take a bus back to Moose Jaw.

Before Marusia and I had met and talked, I had let the parish know that I would leave the parish at the end of January 31st - 1988 as the people had asked at the annual parish meeting at Hudson Bay. Now one week is gone in January. As mentioned, my parents took some of my things when they were leaving for home. The rest of the things I will bring to their place hopefully before the end of the month. The following week I made two trips to Cudworth taking more of my things to father and mother's place. Some of the things had been packed previously from the time I was packed to move to Vernon. The parish executive told me they will make me a farewell tea. I told them I did not need any farewell, but at my last church service at Endeavor, if they come, they can squeeze my hand and say farewell and thank you. They had been good to me and we had no hard feelings. The executive insisted of having a tea or something but me being only one, and many of them, I could not convince them and I had to abide by their wishes.

As Marusia and I were going to Regina, we had some three hours of time to talk about many different things. She knew that I was leaving Hyas at the end of the month. She asked me, what I will be doing and where I will be living. I told her that I did not know what I will be doing, but as to where I will live, I'll stay with my parents until such time that I will know what is what. As we were driving, Marusia said that this summer she will be going to Australia with a tour to the Expo and asked me if I would be interested to go on that trip. I told her I would not, saying that now I will have to watch my pennies for I don't know what will happen in the future. She said it would not be expensive, but I said that absolutely I am not interested in any trips at the present time. A White Hackle Scottish

Pipe Band from Moose Jaw was invited to play at Brisbane at the Expo and a tour was being lined up for this trip. She said about a hundred people would be going. I told her that at the present time, nothing interests me, until I find out what I will be doing and what lies in the future for me. I dropped Marusia off at the bus depot and went to see the doctor that I had an appointment for 1:00 PM. I returned home that evening about 6:00 PM and had to prepare for a service next day at Endeavor.

This same day when I got home, I got a call from Marusia. She wanted to know how I made out at the doctors and how I got home. I said that everything went well. She once again asked me if I would be interested in going to Australia and whether I had thought about it on the way home. She thanked me for the time she spent with the parents and me and said that she was very grateful for the hospitality shown her. She said she was very happy meeting my parents and happy to know someone from the same area where she came from. Was this a coincidence that we had lived on her uncle's farm a few miles from where she lived and we yet never knew each other? Or was this God's plan for other things to follow? God works in wondrous ways. It is more than half a century ago since we lived on her uncle's farm. There is a saying in Ukrainian that goes: "A mountain with a mountain will not meet, but a person with a person may." My late mother quoted this saying often a time.

After Christmas I was now packing every day whatever was still not packed. I wanted to get everything packed before January 19th, because after that I will be busy blessing homes and will not have time to pack. It was after Marusia had visited Hyas that she began to call me two or three times a week to ask how I was feeling and I guess she just wanted to talk to someone. Than one day around the middle of January she called and again asked me about going to Australia. She said that she would put my name on the list of tourists. She said a trip like this would only come once in a lifetime. Again I reassured her that this was not even on my mind or plan, because I have a few days of work left and after that I will not know what will happen with me. I told her I did not have funds for such a trip at the present time.

Then she said something, that the telephone nearly fell out of my hand. She said that she would like to see me go to Australia and that she would be willing to pay for my trip. I had never had such a proposition from anyone in my life before. What am I to do? She said that there were already over a hundred people on the list. She said she wanted to do this as a favor for me because she knew what I was going through and she thought a trip like this may help me. She said she also wanted to show her appreciation of what I had done for her that she had a place to be for Christmas Eve Supper. She said it would be good to get away from the surroundings and forget what is happening. She had worked twenty six years in the mental institution in Moose Jaw and maybe she knew I needed to get out of the health problem I was having.

I told her that we are not married, and I would not think of going, because than there will surely be gossip flying around like never before. I told her that if we were related, it would be a different story, but this way I do not think I would want to go. Again I said it's different when people are married and they go on trip. Than somehow when the word marriage was mentioned we started talking about marriages. I told her my first marriage broke up and she told me her problems that she had. I told her that I would like to go and visit her some day and we could talk about different things we have in common, but right now I cannot go because I have to bless homes before the end of the month before I leave Hyas. But one thing lead to another and I said that if things don't work out for me, I may get married again just to settle down someplace if that is what God has in His plans for me. On the other end of the line I could not hear any voice, and I asked if she was still there, and she answered she was listening. I don't know how, but during the conversation I asked her if she would marry me, if I ever decide to do that. When I asked her this, I heard a loud: "Yes." I don't remember how long we talked on the phone after that. It could have been a hour or maybe more.

How many instances have you heard of people proposing and accepting over the telephone? How many times have you heard of people who had seen and met each other once and than proposed to marry? To this day I say that all that happened was God's doing, for nothing is done without Him and what is impossible for man, all is possible for God. (Luke 1:37) It had never been my wish, or even a thought occurred for even a split second to leave the service in the church or to marry again. Once I had become a priest I put myself into full service only for Him and His church. I never thought of any marriages again because my first marriage did not work out well, so I had no decision of ever getting married for the second time. Today as I sit and write this, my memory goes back to what happened on March 20th 1987 - a dream and not a dream that I had and was told to look at Genesis 2:18 and Ecclesiastes 4:7-11. Was God already at that time setting up my future life?

It was January 25th at 10:30 PM that I asked Marusia if she would marry me. Why? She was in Moose Jaw and I was in Hyas, more than two hundred miles apart. God does things in such ways that we would never think of doing. Here I will be leaving the parish in six days, not knowing what lies before me with no job, no house, and an unknown life ahead. But God had planned a new future for me. I do not know how much I slept that night, but next morning I was back on the road heading to Arran congregation to visit and bless homes of the parishioners with holy water. This was my last day of blessing homes.

I finished blessing homes at 3:00 PM that afternoon and came home to get things organized for my last service in the parish. Before me lay packed boxes of my belongings and these I had to get to my parents' place before the 31st of this month. I loaded the car with all the boxes I could get into the car and even though it was getting late afternoon, I was taking a load of my belongings to Cudworth. Maybe I will stay overnight at my parents' place or maybe I will yet return home later tonight, it's only a three hour trip one way. When I got to Wadena, Saskatchewan, I thought I should call Marusia, because I knew she would probably be calling me and there will be no answer, she will be worried. It was about 6:00 PM when I was at Wadena. From a pay phone I called and told her where I was and that I was taking a load of my belongs to my parents' place. But Marusia comes back and says: "Why are hauling your things there, when after you will have to bring them back here to Moose Jaw?" I thought for a second, and sure, she was right. Instead of me going another ninety miles west, I turned south and headed towards Fort Quapplle, Regina and Moose Jaw. But where do I go when I don't know where she lives? Oh yea, when I get to Moose Jaw, I'll call her again and she will tell me how to get to her place, her address.

When I got to Moose Jaw, I stopped at a pay phone and called her for directions to her place. She gave me the directions and I was there in a short while. I came to the house with fear and yet with joy at the same time, because I was not knowing what to expect and not quite knowing what the future is being planned. I came to the door and rang the door bell. She opened the door and told me to drive to the back of the house to unload the car. I carried the boxes into the basement and there was an empty bedroom in one corner in the basement. It was about 8:00 PM by this time. She had prepared some supper for me and we both sat at the table and had supper. As we ate we talked about our plans for the future. I said that we should be betrothed(engaged) in Moose at the first service that will be held. She looked at the church schedule and the service in Moose Jaw will be on February 7th. We decided that this would be a good day to be betrothed after the Liturgy service.

Marusia did not want anyone to know about our plans and I thought it was a good idea not to tell anyone anything. We kept everything secret until after the Liturgy service. She told me that I should move to her place and she had a spare bedroom upstairs and also an empty one in the basement. I was hesitant to this idea, but she said it would be okay and not to think of anything bad or wrong. I said that the only way I could agree would be if I stayed in the basement bedroom until at least our betrothal. It was just before 10:00 PM when I left her place for home which was a four hour drive. I knew it would be late and I got home at 1:30 AM. I had some rest and in a few hours was up again on my feet, packing, cleaning, for I had only a few days left to move out.

Next day Marusia called again to see how I got home. We talked for a long time on the phone setting plans. We talked about setting a wedding date. She said she would like us to get married on April 21st of that year, because this was also her birthday and the birthday of the present Queen Elizabeth the Second. We talked about our attendants for the marriage. It was hard to think of someone who was not working on the week day. I said that I knew a couple, good friends who lived in Sturgis and I could ask them to stand up for us. They live on a farm and should be free on a week day. Than I said there was my brother and his wife, John and Kay in Edmonton. Marusia said she has friends in Regina, John and Jean Sawchyn and she would like them to stand up for us, but they are in Arizona for the winter and she did not know if they will be back by April 21st.

Next day I took another load of things to Moose Jaw. I unloaded my things into the basement and as we were having supper, she mentioned that she would like to be present at my last service which is scheduled for

Endeavor on Sunday January 31st. I thought it would not be good, but than I thought: "How could I not let her have her wish? She is willing to help me with my health by paying for a trip to Australia and to take me for her husband." I said that would be fine, but I would have to find a place for her to stay when she comes. I said I would ask the same people that could stand up for us and I'm sure she can stay over at their place on the farm.

When I came home that evening I went to see Eddy and Sophie Kozushka at Sturgis and broke the news. When I told them what was happening, Eddy got so excited that he grabbed me, lifted me off my feet, squeezed me so hard that I thought he would squeeze all the air out of my body. They were both so happy and I think they were even happier than I was. I asked them if Marusia could stay over night at their place this coming Saturday. They said they would be very happy to meet her and have her stay there overnight. I told them I would bring her over because she does not know where they live. I also asked them if they would be our attendants for our marriage. They were very happy for me and said they would do it with pleasure. I asked them to keep this secret until after the service and the farewell tea that the parish is planning for me in Endeavor. When I came home from Kozushkas I called Marusia to tell her the news. Marusia sounded happy on the phone that this had been arranged.

On Saturday January 30th, Marusia came with her car to Hyas in the late afternoon. She helped me pack the last few things and about 6:00 PM, I drove to Eddy and Sophie Kozushkas and Marusia followed behind me in her car. There she spent the night and had a good opportunity to get acquainted with Eddy and Sophie who later stood up at our marriage.

Next morning as I'm leaving for church, I go past the hotel in town and what do I see? Father and mother's car standing by the hotel and father is outside. They had come to my place, but I wasn't home, so they went to the hotel. Father could not start his car and was waiting for someone to come and give him a boast. It had been a very cold night. I was upset. So they decided to come, and could they not phone that they are coming so that I could have left the house unlocked or stayed home until they came . I would have wanted to stay and help father, but I had to go, so I would be in church on time. When they got the car started, they came to church on time and also to the reception that the parish had prepared for this day.

The church was cracking on the outside from the frost and inside it was cracking from the overflow of people who had come to be at my last service. People as we sometimes say, "Were hanging from the rafters." I don't know if the people saw Marusia in church or not, but she stayed with Eddy and Sophie. At dinner Marusia sat with Eddy and Sophie in the corner of the hall where they were not very visible. After dinner each congregation had someone say of a few farewell words and passed a thank you card. I had told the people that under no circumstances will I accept any away going gift or money. I told them if they want to give me a card, that will be very fine. They did not give me a gift, so what they did, each congregation put a small token in the envelope, and I had told them not to do that. Had I not been in a hurry to leave that day, I would have opened the envelopes there and given all the money back, but I wanted to be out of the manse that day in case a new priest would be arriving tomorrow. Yet no one was saying if another priest was coming or not.

Many people cried this somber day in the parish. I myself had many of such somber days in the past number of years, that I had no more tears left to cry. At the end after all was over, I was asked to say a few words. I had written down things I wanted to say and was prepared for it. At the conclusion of my farewell words, a shock and surprise hit the present people. I told them there was a certain lady present in the hall which I had met less than a month ago (January 6th), and that we would be betrothed in a week. Than I asked Marusia to come forward to the front table. When she got up and started to make her way to the front, the roof in the hall lifted off its moorings a few inches. The people started to clap and clap and clap. There was a standing ovation, a long, long applause for us. Following the introduction of who Marusia was and how we met over the phone, I said the closing prayer. Than the hall of people burst towards us. People came and hugged both of us. They shook our hands, congratulated us and tears were appearing in people's eyes from the joy they had just witnessed.

From Endeavor we drove and stopped at Eddy and Sophie's place and picked up Marusia's car and drove to Hyas to take the rest of the things from the house. We loaded up both cars and put some into the parents' car to take to their place at Cudworth because they had followed us to Hyas. I knew and I could see that father was happy what transpired this day in Endeavor, but mother had different feelings. She said that I broke their heart by leaving to serve the church. But I told mother that I could not have carried on anymore because of my health and I had no other choice. After that she thought different. Just before I left the manse, I called Paul Kurkowsky from next door to come and take a look at the manse and see if everything is in whole, nothing damaged, broken or missing. I gave him the keys to the manse and we were all gone. When we arrived in Moose Jaw, I carried everything into the basement. Than we had something to eat and after the big day we turned into our beds. Marusia was asking me to sleep in the spare bedroom upstairs, but I would not agree to it and said that I will stay in the basement for another week and nothing will hurt me there. Than all my belongings were in the basement where I can use whenever I needed anything. I also said that in case she gets some company, they can stay upstairs in the spare bedroom.

Before we left Hyas, I showed Paul Kurkowsky two boxes full of books valued at least a minimum of a thousand dollars. I asked him to phone a certain priest to come and pick up those books and all my sermons of over twenty five years of service. I was told later that the priest got the books, but to this day 2016 I never received a word nor a five cent card of thanks for all the books. That is the thanks priests get from other priests and or from their church. The people in Hyas knew how to be grateful and thankful to their priest.

Before I carry on, I should stop for a minute and say what kind thanks I got from my church for over twenty five years of service which I gave of my life. When I first lived in Lac La Biche 1962 to 1967, I sometimes was away from home for a week as already previously was mentioned. Dobrodeyka Mary stayed home alone, answering the phone and took care of the house when I was in the Peace River area. Than we both worked in the church whatever needed to be done. The church was poor. We swept and washed floors. Helped preparing meals in the church basement. Cleaned the church. Washed dishes. Worked with children and adults in teaching religion and singing. On and on our help went for the church. It was the same in Prince George and in fact even more help, because it was a young congregation and needed twice the amount of work. Sometimes we worked into late hours helping the congregations. It was nothing less in Dauphin where we gave time and time again of any needed help.

TWENTY-FIVE YEARS OF PRIESTHOOD

I must not forget my twenty-six years of work in the church which came before I left (retired). On May 6th 1987 I was remembering my twenty five years of priesthood in the church. The Hyas parish wanted to make me a dinner and celebration to honor my twenty five years of service. I asked, begged and pleaded not to do anything, because all I needed was their prayers to get my health restored. I was myself, but the executive was many, half a dozen of people and I just could not convince or overturn their plans. I could not win and had to give in. On May 6th 1987 at Endeavor I had a service. When I arrived at Endeavor to get ready for the service, very shortly after that arrived more clergy which my parish had invited without me knowing. The late Father Iftemy and Dobrodeyka Trufyn from Dauphin, Manitoba and Father Myron Pozniak and Dobrodeyka from Kamsack, Sask. The three of us served the service and than there was a dinner in the hall in Endeavor. I was thanked and praised by the congregations for all the work that I had done for the church in twenty five years.

The year is 1987. The following year the Ukrainian Orthodox Church would be celebrating one thousand years of Orthodoxy in Ukraine and the church in Canada will be celebrating its seventieth anniversary. Because of the coming important year in the Ukrainian Orthodox Church, I asked the executive not to give me any gifts, but I from myself will give $100.00 toward the St. Volodymyr Fund at the Consistory to commemorate this celebration. The parishioners did not listen to me and made monetary contributions for me from the eleven congregations and the organizations that were attached to each congregation. At the end when I counted everything at home, the parishioners had given **me** a total gift of $2400.00 for **my** anniversary. I knew that the jubilee Fund needed money for the thousand year anniversary. I added my $100.00 and sent in a total of $2500.00 to the jubilee Fund in Winnipeg at the Consistory.

This money went FROM ME to Winnipeg, to the Consistory for the Jubilee Fund. The thanks and reply I received from the church headquarters was the same as the person that donated $5.00 from anywhere in Canada. No recognition from the church or headquarters for such a donation. Why could the church not have used this as an example and maybe some other priest or person would have done the same thing. I remember being told by some people (now deceased) that the church was even hesitant to put an article in the church paper about my anniversary and about the donation. When other priests celebrated their anniversaries, oh yes, there was lots of write up about it. When my anniversary was celebrated they did not even want to mention it in the paper. When you work and than you get no thanks, you don't have any encouragement to continue working in such an environment. You miss meals, have sleepless nights, failure of health, worries and no support from the senior staff of the church, than the best is leave and go. I remember when I came to each parish how many members there were and when I left that parish, how many members had increased in that parish. If anyone wants to know for sure, all they have to do is go to those congregations which I served and look at the list of membership for those years and the records will speak for themselves.

In Dauphin the congregation was growing so fast that during the services people had to bring old benches from the basement and place them along the walls, because there was no seating space left in the pews in church. In Dauphin a children's choir was organized. There had been no children's choir in our church in Canada, but later some other congregations followed with this example. Children that were very well under sixteen years of age were members of the choir. I could spend hours and hours of writing of the activities that had been organized. I organized a Ukrainian Self-Reliance Association of men in Hyas and it was prospering.

After I left it fell apart. A large CYMK group was organized in Hudson Bay. Is there one there today? All I got as a reward from my church were nose bleeds, headaches and visitations to doctors and clinics. So I had no choice, but to get out, because no one at the church headquarters could make up their mind if I go to Vernon or not.

My health was not good, when I was leaving the parish. In 1987 from June 9th to October 1st I saw the specialist doctors in Regina and Saskatoon six times. How many times I saw the doctor in Canora, Yorkton or Norquay I don't even mention, but the records in those places will show in my files. How about the time that every second day for a few weeks I had to drive to Yorkton to the hospital, get a harness put on me and have my back stretched. The headaches were terrible. Each time my heart beat, it felt like a sledge hammer was hitting my head inside. I always thought that the next pound would shatter my head into hundreds of pieces. I started taking aspirin, but even that did not help, in fact it started to cause trouble to my stomach. I did not want to get an ulcer added to the many problems that I was already having at that time, so I quite taking aspirin.

Because of all that had happened until January 31st, 1988 I left my work or as someone may want to say, "retired due to health problems." But other plans were already unfolding at that time. Marusia also had her retirement come up on February 2nd after putting in twenty six years of work in the Valleyview Centre in Moose Jaw. When she worked there, she worked in different departments. She was a switch board operator than she worked as a nurse's aid, than worked in the pharmacy department and finished her work as a seamstress in the sewing room. She retired after twenty six years and I was present at her retirement. People with whom she had worked all those years came out to bid her good health and success on her retirement. Later she received a plaque from the Saskatchewan Government showing how many years and days she had worked in that field. This was more which she received for the same amount of years than I had received from my church. I say church not congregation or parish. The parishes and congregations wherever I served were very good to me and I can't complain about them at all.

BETROTHAL - MARRIAGE

As was mentioned earlier we made arrangements to be betrothed to each other on Sunday February 7th at Moose Jaw in the church after the service. Marusia called Father Michael Zaleschuk in Regina that she wants to see him and will come to Regina one evening. No one knew anything about our betrothal only Father Michael Zaleschuk, my brother John and Kay, Sister Alice and John and my parents.

When Sunday came we both were in church for the service and both went upstairs to sing in the choir. No church member in Moose Jaw knew what was going to happen after the service. When the service was over, Marusia and I went down from the choir and stood at the back of the church. Father Michael made an announcement that a betrothal service of Mary Paziuk and Eugene Stefaniuk was going to take place. People were shocked and bewildered. They were absolutely stunned. I still feel that some of them thought it was a dream they were having. You could have heard a pin drop to the floor after the announcement. We both had also gone to confession and communion that morning before the service. Before this had happened I had written to the Primate of the church asking for his blessing to get married. He gave his blessing with the stipulation that from now on I cannot perform any priestly duties because I become as an ordinary lay person.

I ALSO WALKED ON THIS EARTH

After the betrothal service there was lunch in the church basement. People came and congratulated us and there were some which seemed they did not want to have anything to do with us. My parents, John and Kay, Alice and John stayed over at Moose Jaw for the rest of the day and night and left to their homes the following day. Marusia and I stayed another day in Moose Jaw and than we headed west. Marusia said that she lived for forty years in Moose Jaw and thought she would like to move out to some other place. She said she had never seen the mountains and would like to go west. She wanted to live somewhere in a new place. She said she had seen pictures of mountains and would like to live in such a place. We started out west to British Columbia. We passed through Calgary and headed west into the mountains and we were looking forward to Kelowna, because it looked like a retirement place for seniors of what we heard from people. We left Moose Jaw to investigate what possibilities there were to move to the Okanagan. We heard from people that the Okanagan was the place to retire. Marusia also had said she would like to be where it would be warmer than it is on the prairies in the winter time.

We left Moose Jaw on February 9th and got to Calgary that day. The next day we traveled the Trans Canada Highway going west hoping to get to Vernon or Kelowna before sunset. Approximately ten miles east of Revelstoke we ran into a problem. Hundreds of vehicles were stopped on the highway because of an avalanche. The highway was closed and the crew were working to clear the road. The line of traffic was for miles and miles. The man that was stopping the traffic said it would be about an hours wait. It was 1:00 PM in the afternoon. This was the first winter trip into the mountains and what an experience we had.

The day was beautiful and sunny when we left Calgary and the same all the way into the mountains. When we got stopped for the avalanche, there it was a different story. Standing with hundred of cars, what can one do? Nothing moves. We waited for an hour. Nothing. We waited another hour and still no movement. Some people who were impatient behind and ahead of us, turned around and went back towards Rogers Pass, or maybe even to Golden. The sun was now starting to set in the mountains. It is 4:30 PM and still no moving forward. On the horizon what we could see in the mountains were dark rolling clouds approaching from the west. A little while later and it was already dark. We had nothing to eat since noon and had no food in the car with us. We had filled up our gas tank at Calgary and the gauge is beginning to go lower and lower to the empty sign on the dash. We had to keep the car running for a while then shut it off and turn it on again so we do not get cold. There are no bathrooms in the middle of the road. Snow had been piled up high on the sides of the highway by the snowplow. I was starting to think of the worst. It was now dark. No food in the car. The fuel is running low and we are in no man's land.

Than large snow flakes started falling and it was 6:00 PM. The snow began to fall heavier and the wipers had to brush of the snow from the windshield if you wanted to see what was happening. When some cars ahead of us turned around and headed back, this gave us a chance to sneak up closer to the front of the line of cars. We were now only about a hundred and fifty yards from the front of the line and only about eight or nine cars ahead of us. What we learned from this trip was that when you go into the mountains always have food with you in the car and make sure your gas tank is full. This was in the winter time, but it could also be the same in the summer only it could be a rock or mud slide. Traveling in the mountains you must be prepared for the unforeseen, unexpected and the unknown. By this time there was a good accumulation of snow on the road for it had been snowing heavily for over an hour or more. Yes I lived in the mountains in the winter (Prince George) and traveled but never had any experience as this to sit and wait in no man's land.

Finally the all clear was given from the man who had held back the traffic. It was now past 7:00 PM. It was pitch dark with the exception of the car lights. As we were nearing Revelstoke, two snow plows came towards us clearing the opposite side of the road. Was I ever glad when I saw the lights of Revelstoke. Now I knew we would have enough fuel to get to the gas pumps and maybe a warm bowl of soup would be waiting for us someplace. Arriving in Revelstoke the first place we stopped was at a motel to get a room before all rooms are taken up. There were only three rooms left and we took one with two beds for each to sleep on. After this we went to a restaurant and had something to eat because its's already eight hours since we last ate anything. After supper we went and filled up the tank with gas, returned to the motel and hit the beds.

Next morning as we were having breakfast, before we leave Revelstoke and go farther west, we learned that during the night another avalanche came down blocking again the road west where we were heading. So now what do we do? We'll have to wait like everybody else until the road is opened. We decided to go and look around some of the shops in Revelstoke. Maybe by noon the road will be opened. While we were shopping in one store we heard a radio announcement say that the road west will be opening at 11:00 AM. Hearing that we just left everything with the basket we had, hurried out to the car and out unto the highway. We got a few miles west of Revelstoke when we came upon a line of vehicles waiting for the road to be opened up. We waited only about ten minutes and the line of cars began to move. We drove through but the car behind us was stopped, because it was only one way traffic for the whole highway had not yet been cleared. We arrived at Sicamous and already had no more windshield fluid left, so we had to get a gallon of washer fluid for the roads were very slushy from the newly fallen snow overnight. As we left Sicamous and headed south and the closer we got to Vernon, the less snow there was.

We arrived at Vernon after noon and as we entered from the north we saw a Real Estate firm. We stopped in and told them what we were looking for. A lady took us out and showed us a few houses. Than she showed us a brand new house in which no one had yet lived. When we saw that house, that was what we wanted. We saw the inside of the house and went back to the office and put down a $1000.00 deposit on the house with the understanding that the builder pour us a concrete pad at the rear of the house eight feet by twelve feet. The lady said that the owner had forty eight hours to accept or refuse our offer. After this we went to see my koomy, Peter and Doris Chaykowski. I knew them from Dauphin, but they moved to the Okanagan in the 1970's. When we first came in, Doris began to cry, because this was the first time she saw me without a clergy collar.

We told them that we put down a deposit on a new house in Vernon. Peter asked where and we told him. Right off, Peter said that we should not buy a house in that area, because it was a bad area and houses loose their value in that area of town. We visited Chaykowskis for an hour and than headed south to Kelowna to visit Emil and Mary Rubashewski who were house sitting for a couple who had gone south to the USA for the winter.

On February 12th we took Emil and Mary Rubashewski with us and went to Vernon to a church service which was a Holy Day, The Three Hierarchs. After the service we went and had lunch and than drove to show them the new house we were purchasing in Vernon. During the time when we put a deposit on the house and heard from Peter Chaykowski that it was a bad area, we began to hope that the offer would not be accepted. It was now not yet forty-eight hours since we made a deposit on the house, but anyway we stopped in to see the Realtor and she said the owner would not accept the our offer. The lady told us that the offer was turned down and the builder said he would not make the patio larger than eight feet by eight feet. He also did not accept the condition that we pay him as soon as the house in Moose Jaw will be sold. He wanted the money up front before he would agree to sell. We were delighted that the offer fell through. Now we can go and look for something else. Our cheque was returned and we drove to Kelowna to try our luck there.

In Kelowna we got in touch with Peter Mosychuk, a Realtor. He took us and Rubashewsks to show us some houses. We saw houses in Kelowna, Peachland, Westbank and Winfield. Did we ever see houses. You drive by the house and beautiful outside, but enter inside and it's just the opposite. In some houses we had to grab our nose and back out to the outside. I do not recall if there was at least one house that was clean and tidy inside of about fifteen houses that we saw. Clothes all over the house wherever you looked. Some kitchen utensils in the bedroom. Running shoes in the kitchen sink. The bathrooms and in fact the whole house was just dirty, filthy and messy with some unknown odor. How people could live like that I don't know and understand. Why doesn't the government have health inspectors visit homes unexpectedly at any time to check and see how people live. I had seen pig sties that were cleaner than some of the houses. And than we wonder why and from what all the germs and diseases come from. Also the prices were just way, way out of our range and more expensive than in Vernon.

We thought that maybe it would be easier and cheaper to buy a lot and have a house built on it. We asked Peter Mosychuk if there were any lots for sale. He looked into his book and said that he would show us a beautiful lot. On the east you could see Lake Okanagan and it was a flat level lot. We asked the price and he said it was $32,000.00 dollars. I looked at him and say: "Peter I can go to Saskatchewan and buy a whole quarter section of land for a cheaper price." Quarter sections of land at that time were selling for around $25,000.00. After that we told him to take us back to the office for we had seen enough.

On February 15th we went to church in Kelowna. It was a Holy Day, Meeting of the Lord in the Temple. The following day we ourselves went to look for houses in Kelowna, but nothing was found that we could have thought to buy. Nothing was accomplished, so we decided to drive back home the following day. We arrived back home on February 18th after having found nothing worthwhile for us. As mentioned we saw many houses, but the price was not what we could afford and the shape of some of the houses were in.

After we arrived back in Moose Jaw, Marusia put her house up for sale. We knew that if the house sold, we could always go back to the Okanagan and surely there will be something that we would be able to purchase. People came and looked at the house, but there were no buyers. When we had arrived home from the Okanagan, I wrote a letter to the Town of Salmon Arm, B.C., asking them if there were houses for sale. They passed my letter to a Realtor, Lisa Knobs, and she sent us a list of houses that were for sale. We looked at the list and it seemed like the houses were cheaper there than in Vernon and Kelowna.

Our life was moving along like everyone's else in their own way. Spring was around the corner and our wedding day on April 21st was coming up. Finally that day came. The house still had not been sold. Relatives and friends began arriving for our marriage. The marriage was in the same church we were betrothed and than we had a small reception in the church basement. The day of our marriage, we got a call from the Realtor in Moose Jaw that some people would like to see the house. Marusia said: "Not today, because its our wedding day and we have a full house of guests."

By this time plans for Marusia's trip to Australia were going ahead and being finalized. The trip was starting on July 3rd 1988. Marusia had made all the plans for the trip and she wanted me to go, but there was no room available for me. The only way I could have gotten on the trip was if someone single would have backed out. The tour people would than be able to put us together in one room. Because there was no room and the time was getting close, I told Marusia so that she would go as she had planned and I would stay home and look after the house. I told her to stick with the plans that were already made even before we had ever met. She kept insisting that there will be room made and she did not give up hope. Than it happened. Someone had to cancel out of the trip at the last moment and a space opened up for me to get on.

Before we left for Australia one other thing happened. The house in Moose Jaw had been up for sale for three months. Nothing happened, so we canceled with the Realtor and told him to take the sign down. On June 1st the sign was removed. Then God did the rest again. We were now thinking that we would not put the house up for sale again until we returned from the trip. But on Saturday June 3rd, one month before our trip there was a knock on the door. We opened the door and there were two young men standing. They asked us if we had sold the house, because they did not see the for sale sign. They were two military men from the military air force base in Moose Jaw. They said they had driven a number of times past our place and they had seen the for sale sign and liked the house on the outside. They told us later that they wanted to buy the house, but did not want to go through a Realtor, but buy it privately.

They looked at the house and agreed to buy it for the price that was quoted. Next week we went to the lawyer and had the deal drawn up and signed. So now what? Where do we go from here? Where are we going to live? We leave in a month for Australia and will not be back until the end of July. We have to be out of the house by August 1st, because the boys wanted possession on that day. So it happened that we got into the car the following morning and headed west again. Traveling west I told Marusia to pick out the place where she would like to live and we will go directly there to look at houses. She said she would like to be where it would be warmer than Saskatchewan. We arrived in Calgary on June 7th and next morning kept on going west.

We drove into Salmon Arm which is on the Trans Canada Highway. It was a picturesque setting of the town as well as the surrounding area with the beautiful Shuswap Lake. We had already seen Vernon and Kelowna and there was nothing too inspiring in those places. We decided to go farther west to Kamloops and see the area. We stopped in Kamloops and had lunch in the Aberdeen Mall. While in the mall, we saw a Real Estate firm in the building. We went and talked to the man and looked at some pictures of houses that were on display. We saw beautiful houses for sale at Logan Lake with unbelievable prices. Beautiful homes selling for $25,000.00 each. We asked the man where Logan Lake was and he said it was about twenty miles south of Kamloops. We said we would go and have a look. We did.

When we got there we were very surprised. Beautiful three year old homes were selling for $25,000.00. For what we sold the house in Moose Jaw, we could buy two of those houses in Logan Lake. We wandered why the houses were so cheap and we asked people in the café where we stopped for a break. There was a mine in the area, but it closed and people moved out and left their houses to be sold next to nothing. People were desperate to get out of there since they had no more job. The little town or village was well set up. Streets were all paved and there were services hooked up, two small stores, a restaurant and a service station. It was only twenty miles from Kamloops, but the area did not appeal to us, because it was in a forest with bush all around the town. If a forest fire should break out, there was no hope for the area. We headed back to Kamloops to see what we could find there.

Coming into Kamloops we could already feel the scorching summer heat. It if is so hot in June, what will it be like in July and August? The hills around Kamloops were already all brown and burned up from the heat. Coming back from Logan Lake, we never even stopped in Kamloops, but just kept going back to Salmon Arm. For some reason Salmon Arm had impressed us and seemed to be calling us. We arrived at Salmon Arm later in the afternoon and looked for the Realtor, where Lisa Knobs worked who had sent us some material about houses in Salmon Arm.

HOUSE PURCHASE AND TRIP TO AUSTRALIA

We found the office and went in. We asked for Lisa and she came out and told us that she was busy at the moment and could not go to show us any houses. We told her to give us a list and we could go ourselves and have a look to see if anything appeals to us. If we find anything we will come back and talk with her. She gave us a paper with a few addresses of houses in our price range and she mentioned that there was a new house and she put that address down too. We had a list of about eight or ten houses to look at.

After we left the office, Marusia said to go and have a look at the new house first. The new house we were told would be ready to move in, in two weeks. We looked at the address and checked the town map which Lisa gave us and we were off to find the address. In no time flat we were stopping in front of a new house. In front of the house was parked a red half ton truck. We rang the door bell and it was the contractor himself who was still working in the house finishing up the cupboards in the kitchen. We introduced ourselves and said why we came. He showed us around the house. Both Marusia and I fell in love with that house. Two bedrooms upstairs and one in the basement completed. For some reason we knew and had the feeling that this was our house to be. It was 5:30 PM by this time and we knew that Lisa the Realtor may have already gone home, so we did not go back to the office. We went and had some supper and than went to the Lucky Lady Motel and got a room for the night.

From the motel we called Lisa and told her we were interested in the new house and would like to purchase the new house on Seventh Avenue south east in the Little Mountain subdivision. Lisa came over to the motel and we gave her a deposit on the house. She took the signed papers and went to see the builder and said she would be back in a short while, because the builder lived just a few blocks away from the motel. It was not long at all before Lisa was back. The offer was accepted. Now we have a brand new house to move in and start our life. We gave her more money for a down payment as the builder had wanted. Next morning we headed back home to Moose Jaw to get ready for the trip to Australia and to prepare for the move to Salmon Arm.

But now another problem stood before us. In less than a month we are leaving for Australia. When we get back home from our trip there will be no time to pack and be out of the house by August 1st. The only thing left to do was to get a mover to pack our things and move everything to Salmon Arm while we are away in Australia. We checked out with the movers that were in Moose Jaw and came to the conclusion that MacCosham Movers were giving us the best deal and promised to have our things in Salmon Arm on the date we wanted. We were kind of not sure if we will get our things on the date promised, because we had heard many stories from people about movers, how their things were never delivered on the day promised and at times even damaged. We paid MacCosham in advance for packing and moving.

As we got this settled, than another thing came to mind. We made a deal for the house in Salmon Arm, but we just never thought of going to the town to apply for hook-ups of water, sewer, power and telephone. The movers had told us they would not move perishable things. So on June 23rd we loaded up the car full of perishables and headed out to Salmon Arm. In the meantime the boys who had bought the house in Moose Jaw wanted the appliances that were in the house which we sold to them separately. Now we would need new appliances for the house in Salmon Arm. We arrived in Salmon Arm on June 24th shortly after noon. We made arrangements to have utilities hooked up on August 2nd. Than we went to the house and found the contractor was still finishing things around the house. We asked him if it would be ok to leave the perishable things in the basement in some corner. He said that it was okay, because it was our house. From there we went to Salmon Arm Home Furnishings and picked out the appliances to be delivered on August 2nd. After all this was taken care of, we returned back home and started to prepare for the trip to Australia.

When we returned back to Moose Jaw we told MacCosham people that we will leave some things in one room and so they would not take anything from that room to move. There were still a few perishable items that we had to take and things we will need before we move out of the house. Time was now flying faster each day. Eventually everything was organized and we are ready to leave for the trip not knowing what and how we will find things in the house when we return from Australia.

On July 3rd we drove to Regina to John and Jean Sawchyn's place and left our car at their place. They drove us to the airport in Regina. We boarded the plane and that day we flew to Calgary, on to Vancouver and went through USA customs. We boarded another plane and landed in Seattle, San Francisco, and Los Angeles. We boarded another plane again and flew to Hawaii all this traveling in one day. When we got to Hawaii, we were so tired that when we were already in our hotel room, our feet were still somewhere on the sidewalk outside. There were a hundred and thirty four people on this tour group. As for the trip to Australia, I will omit this because I have twelve hours of the trip on video and I can show it to people if anyone is interested. Some day God willing and I find the time, maybe I will write a separate booklet about that trip. We flew from Hawaii and landed in New Zealand. From there we flew to Australia. We traveled along the east coast of Australia. Returning home we stopped in New Zealand for a few days and than on to California. We spent a week in California before we returned back home.

We arrived home on July 30th and when we came into the house, all we found were empty rooms, with the exception of the appliances that the boys bought with the house. MacCosham had done a very good job. They packed everything and even vacuumed the house. Next morning we drove to Regina to the church service. The late Father Mykola Derewianka was the parish priest there. After the service we spent the day with John and Jean Sawchyn telling them about our trip. On August 2nd we wound up the final agreement with the two airmen that bought our house and around noon we headed west to Salmon Arm where our new house was waiting for us to begin a new life.

Traveling west was a good trip and we arrived in Salmon Arm the following day just before noon. First we had something to eat and than went to see Lisa and get the keys to the house. We also went to the furniture people and let them know that we are in Salmon Arm and they can bring the appliances, which they did that afternoon. MacCosham had promised us that they would deliver our things on August 4th at 8:00 AM. We did not believe that they would be on time, because we had heard too many bad remarks about furniture movers. We were not expecting our furniture to arrive until maybe at least three or four days after we were in the house.

That evening we went to bed early being tired from the travel. We had an air mattress with us that had been left in the closed room in Moose Jaw when we had gone to Australia. We pumped up the air mattress and that was our bed the last night in Moose Jaw and the first night in Salmon Arm. The following morning we were still sleeping when we heard some loud noise outside and we thought some large machine like a bulldozer was doing some work around the place. I got up and went to check what the noise was, and what do I see? MacCosham is parking in front of the house to bring our things in. They promised us they would deliver our things at 8:00 AM. Here it is only 7:00 AM and our goods are in front of the house. Is that service or what?

MacCosham gave us better service than what we had expected. Marusia and I from then on put trust in that company and told everybody we met about the service we received from them. Later when we needed to have things moved again, MacCosham were the movers that we got. In three hours, that's right in THREE hours everything was in the house out of the big truck. We had boxes all over the house staring at us from every which way. Now came the next job, to unpack and place everything in its place. The only damage that was done to our things, was a small broom handle had broken and one small dish. We were pleased and satisfied with the service that MacCosham had given us at that time.

So now came the unpacking and in a few days everything was in its place where Marusia wanted. But there was still a lot of work ahead of us. The basement would have to be finished. The landscaping is not done. The garden to be prepared. The drive way has to be paved. A shed for storage has to be built. But even though all this was before us, we did not hurry or rush. What we did, we did, and what we did not do that was left for another day. We had no obligations now, so we took our time in doing things. We can do what we want and when we want. I remember my mother-in-law in Winnipeg used to say many times: "Let the one who invented work, let him work." We can take our time and we did. Our koom, Peter Chaykowski from Vernon came and helped build the storage shed. The rest of the things we did ourselves as time progressed.

One month after we moved into our new place, we got company. My parents went to Edmonton and together with John and Kay the four of them came to see us. It was not that they wanted to see us as much as they wanted to see the house and the place where we were living. They stayed over the week-end. When they arrived mother was upset and kept saying the whole time: " We will never come to see you again. Why did you move so far away? We traveled all day and it's so far past the mountains." Just two months later the four of them came to see us again. We were having the house blessed and they knew about it and came to be present. The blessing took place on November 12th - 1988. Present from Vernon were late Father and Mrs. Stetzenko, the late Father and Mrs. Blazuk, the late Peter and Doris Chaykoswki, From Kelowna the late Tony and Elsie Burkowski, the late my parents from Saskatchewan and John and Kay from Edmonton and our next door neighbor, Ed and Liz Waddell.

The rest of the year went by very quickly. We had the driveway paved. We put in the lawn with sod. We did the landscaping in the front and prepared the garden at the rear of the house. We also planted a few fruit trees. All that we had at the end of the year were memories of much work.

NEW LIFE IN SALMON ARM AND VERNON

Something different of an experience in British Columbia is the winter snow. Out on the prairies you take a shovel full of snow and you could hardly feel the weight of it. Not so in B.C. The snow in B.C., is damp and moist and when you take a shovel full of snow it feels like a shovel full of sand or wet cement. Than when it starts snowing, it sometimes does not know when to stop. That first year we lived in Salmon Arm we did not know what the sun looked like for two months starting in the fall. Our house was up on top of the hill, Little Mountain area. When it was snowing at our place, down town in Salmon Arm it was raining or snow mixed with rain. It was devastating not to see the sun for so long after being used to seeing sunshine all of your life. Every day we had snow, fog, rain, clouds for two months. But than summer is different, warm and more sunshine and then hot.

When it snowed, it snowed. There were times that I had to shovel the drive way three times a day, that's right, three times a day. About eight to ten inches of heavy wet snow would fall. I would shovel it in the morning and around noon had to go and shovel again. After supper had to shovel the third time. If I did not do that, than who would be able to move two feet of heavy wet snow? How would we ever get out with the car in two feet of heavy wet snow? That evening after all the snow shoveling, when it came to go to bed, my arms and back were screaming with pain.

During the time we lived in Salmon Arm we did not miss one church service, Sunday or Holy Day, unless we were away from home, but than wherever we were we would still go to church in the area we were visiting in Saskatchewan or wherever it was. When we were at home we were in church either at Vernon, Kelowna or Kamloops. We also attended choir practices, meetings, funerals, church functions, etc. We lived thirty miles north of Vernon, so it was thirty miles to church to Vernon, sixty miles to church to Kelowna and seventy miles to Kamloops. We were church members at Vernon. It did not take long to realize that living in Salmon Arm it was wearing us out as well as the vehicle. In the winter time when we left for church it was still dark and at times we returned home late in the evening if there were other functions going on after the service or if we had visited some friends.

As for my health, I began to feel better as the days came and went. My headaches disappeared that I never even knew how and when. It was the same with the nose bleeds they came less often until they stopped completely that I did not even know how and when. Headaches and nosebleeds are things that I have even forgotten about. Now thirty plus years after Hyas, I don't even know what headaches or nosebleeds are anymore. They went and have not come back. So in Hyas was it stress, high blood pressure or what?

Since we were retired, there was more time to look into a book or a paper, or even to sit and relax. Marusia, she was different. She always had to have everything done on time and things for her always had to be spick and span. Marusia had never written Ukrainian Easter Eggs. As Easter was coming in 1989, I asked her if she will be writing Easter Eggs. She said that she never did that before, because she was always at work and did not have time for such fine art. I had some old articles for writing Easter eggs, so one day I got them out and showed her how to do it. When she saw how it was done, she took off with it. At times I even thought why did I have to show it for her, because she would start to write in the morning and would not quite until going to bed at night. Now for that it was extra work for me. During that time she wrote Easter eggs, I had to be the cook, dishwasher, floor sweeper, duster and all other housework. But I felt glad and happy that she learned something that I showed her and she enjoyed doing it, because before she passed away she must have made a few hundred dozen Easter eggs. What she did with them was - ninety five per cent she gave them away as gifts or donations to bazaars, bake sales, family, friends etc. When she learned how to make the Easter eggs, she entered exhibits and won many prizes for her Easter Eggs. She won a total of eleven prizes at competitions in Dauphin and British Columbia with her Easter eggs. When she was not doing Easter eggs, she would do embroidery, sewing, Brazilian embroidery, baking or cooking. She was special in all kinds of work and she looked happy in doing all that.

This first winter went over very quickly because we had lots of time to do things even though we did it leisurely at our pace. We were retired. We got married. Looked and found a new house in another province, went to Australia, New Zealand and California. All the yard work that we could do, we did before winter came. We became involved in church activities. All those things and more kept us busy and it was our pleasure and enjoyment that now we could help the church and church organizations.

It did not take long for the congregation in Vernon to involve us in church activities. We thought, that once we retire, we can take things easy, but it is not so. When people see you are retired, they make you a go-for. Go-for this, Go-for that. At one monthly meeting at Vernon, someone made a motion that Marusia and I prepare a half hour Ukrainian Christmas program for the local radio station for January 6th, Christmas Eve. There had been such a program years before, but somehow and somewhere it fell off the rails and was not produced anymore. We did this program for January 1989 and the following years that we lived in Salmon Arm and Vernon. I got the script all ready and Marusia did the English part, while I did the Ukrainian with Ukrainian carols playing in between. We pre-recorded the program at the radio station CJIB, but the following years it was carried on CICF radio because we were told that more people listened to CICF.

After the Christmas season was over, I wanted to get into preparing a weekly Ukrainian program on the radio. I went to CICF and talked with the program director and he said that their station is strictly Country and Western. So that was out. Than I went to the other station, CJIB and talked to the manager and the manger said: "nyet" in Russian, meaning "absolutely not". That was the end of the Ukrainian weekly program.

MARUSIA'S AND MOTHER'S HEALTH

The year 1989 did not start out very well for Marusia health wise. On January 15th we left to visit our families in Saskatchewan. We got to Calgary the first day and stayed overnight in a motel. Next morning we got up and Marusia said that her left leg was sore and she thought it may be arthritis because of winter conditions and milder and more damp-humid weather in the mountains. We drove to Saskatoon and Cudworth to visit our families and stayed overnight at my parents' place. The following day her leg was still sore and I said that maybe we should go to see a doctor in Wakaw and get it checked, but she said that it will be ok.

That morning we drove to Prairie River, Sask., to visit Fred and Larraine Waskowic and returned back for the evening to Cudworth. On January 18th her leg was still sore and I again said that we should go and see a doctor, but she said it would get over. That evening we attended a Epiphany Eve Supper in the church basement at Cudworth. On the 19th of January we left for Edmonton, because tomorrow is John's birthday and we wanted to be there on January 20th. My parents went with us to Edmonton and later they returned home by bus.

On January 20th at 4:00 AM Marusia awoke and said that her leg was very sore. I said that she dress and I would take her to the emergency, but she said to wait till morning. That morning she thought she felt better and wanted to go to Superstore to get some things. While in the store she said she was not feeling well and felt like passing out. We returned to John and Kay's and were going to have dinner, but Marusia said she was not hungry, but tired and wanted to sleep. She fell asleep immediately on the chesterfield. When she awoke, she told John and me to take her to emergency. We took her to the University Hospital in Edmonton. With special machines, the doctors immediately found the problem - a blood clot in the leg. One piece of the blood clot had broke off and was in her left hip and was moving towards the heart. A specialist told her later that if she would not have come in, in twenty fours hours she would have not been alive. The same doctor also told her that she got her blood clot from using the medication Premarin that she was on for eighteen years. She was taken off Premarin in the hospital when she was admitted there.

When she ended up in the hospital John and I stayed until she was in her room and on the bed. We went back to John's place and had supper. After supper I went again to the hospital. Did I ever get a shock when I walked into her room. Marusia was not there and her bed was all made up. The first thing that hit me was, that she passed away or something serious happened. I went to the nurses station and asked about Marusia and was told that she was moved to another room. Was I ever relieved to hear those words.

The doctor said she would have to spend a week in the hospital. When he said that, we decided that I would go to Salmon Arm tomorrow because its nearly a week since we left home and I must check out and see that everything is all right. I left for home next morning and arrived home finding everything in order. Next day I got a phone call from the hospital that Marusia will be released the following day. It was to late to drive back, so I did not leave until next morning. The day when she was released from the hospital we spent that day in Edmonton and left for home the following morning. On the way home just east of Golden we ran into a cavalcade of vehicles which were standing on the highway because an avalanche had blocked the highway.

By this time we had been living for over half a year in our new house and we thought it was time to finish off the basement. On February 23rd, this "green horn carpenter", picked up a hammer and a few nails and went to work. I did all the work only calling Marusia from time to time when I needed a third hand to hold something. The ceiling was done by our koom, Peter Chaykowski from Vernon with me helping him.

Then as we thought spring was around the corner and than summer will follow another thing happened. On April 1st, and it was **no** April Fools joke, father called and said that mother is in the hospital with another stroke. How many strokes she had by this time, only God knows. We said we would leave, but father said not to come, because it was too far for us to travel and so we would be at home. We prayed for mother's health at home. We kept in touch with father and he said that mother was getting better and improving. Then another shocking phone call came. Alice called crying on the phone that mother had a massive heart attack in the hospital and the doctor said that if any family members wanted to see mother, to come quickly.

The time was 11:00 AM B.C., time. This morning Marusia had started dough to make paska and babka for Easter. We couldn't just throw the dough out and go, so we had to see it through. We started to pack while the dough was rising and baking. After the baking was finished we left at 5:30 PM for Saskatchewan. We were in Saskatoon at 7:00 AM in the morning having traveled all night. It was now April 12th, one day before mother's birthday. We drove straight to Wakaw Hospital and we were there at 8:30 AM. As soon as mother saw us, she began to be more cheerful and seemed to perk up. She was hooked up on oxygen and intravenous. We stayed for a few moments and than went to father's place to lay down and have a little rest. Everyone was sure that mother was on her last leg of life on this earth. In the evening, April 13th, on mother's birthday, the whole family gathered in the intensive care unit, father, John and Kay, Oksana, grandchildren, Marusia and I. The family had brought a cake for her. When she saw all of us, she looked so much better, and she even had some birthday cake. But than it was also father's birthday two days after mother celebrated hers in the hospital. The family got together and we went to the restaurant in Cudworth and had a meal to honor father on his birthday. Oksana had already left for home while Marusia and I still hung around for a few days and when we saw mother was improving we too headed for home.

As previously already mentioned I had been a parish priest in Prince George B.C., for three years. It is now ten years when I left Prince George. In Prince George we had Ukrainian and Sunday schools and a Ukrainian dance group Yalenka, was also organized by Peter and Diane Bihun. It is ten years since this group was formed and they held their tenth anniversary spring concert. We got an invitation to attend this anniversary, so we packed and went.

We left Salmon Arm on May 26th and attended the performance. Following the concert we motored to Edmonton to see John and Kay. From there on to Cudworth to see my parents and on to Saskatoon to see Marusia's side of the family. Mother had lost some use of her right arm and leg and her speech was partially impaired, but to how she looked in the hospital and now, she had improved so much more. She got around slowly with a walker, or holding on to the wall or some other article. She also used a cane. On May 31st we motored to Moose Jaw to attend to some unfinished business and arrived home in Salmon Arm on June 1st. Arriving home, we went straight to emergency because Marusia had a very sore throat that had to be checked out.

After all this excitement we somewhat slowed down the pace and relaxed more. Marusia had a sister-in-law at London, Ontario, Beth Kwasnica, and Beth wrote a letter that she will be coming to Vernon to a seniors hostel and so we pick her up at the airport in Kelowna on June 9th. After she was finished with her activities at the hostel we picked her up and she spent a few days with us. We drove her to Lillooet, Nakusp and Revelstoke. We were happy to have her stay with us for a few days and a chance to meet her.

This year also happened to be the bi-annual convention of the Ukrainian Self-Reliance League of Canada taking place in Regina, Sask. We left home on August 13th first going to Saskatoon and Cudworth to see the family. Marusia had five nephews and nieces in Saskatoon. When we would come to Saskatoon, we would stop at one of their places and the rest would come and we always had a good chat and visit with them all.

Than on to Regina to the convention. In Regina we stayed at John and Jean Sawchyn's place. We returned home on August 21st, because Marusia's niece Judy (Beth Kwasnica's daughter) from London, Ontario, was coming to visit us. She was coming to Banff, Alberta for her holidays and since it was only some two hundred miles from our place, she was coming to see us. Other friends came this year to visit us were: Emil and Mary Rubashewsky, Fred and Lorraine Waskowicz, Pat and Vern Walker,

George Semeniuk, Denis and Mary Prefontaine, Ed and Sophie Kozushka, Allan and Corrine Olynuk and others. Allan and Corrine Olynyk came after the wedding for their honeymoon to Salmon Arm. Allan and Corrine came in October. Many people had never even heard of Salmon Arm before and now they came to visit us and also saw the beautiful setting of the town on the Trans Canada Highway. Every time someone came to see us, we would take them up to the top of the mountain Fly Hills from where you could see the beautiful valley below, took them to Margaret Falls and other places.

Come September we made another trip to Saskatchewan to my niece's marriage and visit Marusia's family in Saskatoon. My niece Corrine Hnatiuk was marrying Allan Olynyk on October 7th. The rest of the year slipped by with work around the yard and shoveling snow in the winter time. Marusia and I taped another Ukrainian Christmas program for January 6th. Having made the tape earlier, this gave us a chance to slip to Saskatchewan for our Christmas to be with the parents and help mother prepare the supper for mother was still not fully recovered from her illness. She had been in the hospital back and forth a number of times since her major illness. We wanted to be with the parents, since maybe this will be the last time that we would be with mother at Christmas. She was in her eighty fourth year and her health is not getting better. Father also was not a spring chicken, for he was in his eighty ninth year. We left for Cudworth on January 4th and returned one week later on the 11th. The trip to Cudworth was seven hundred and twenty miles one way and driving in the mountains in the winter, one does not know what to expect.

Because John's birthday fell on January 20th, we made another trip to Edmonton. The last time when we were at John's birthday, Marusia spent time in the hospital and she wanted to be at John's birthday to make up for the past year. Father and mother surprised everybody when they appeared on the doorstep at John and Kay's place. Father was eighty nine years old and drove himself from Cudworth to Edmonton in the winter time. Father could never find his way to get to John's place. Once they hit the city, they would stop a taxi and ask the taxi to go ahead and father will follow him to the address. Father would then pay the taxi fare whatever it was. When we returned back home from Edmonton, I had to go to emergency because it seemed like everything was turning topsy-turvy and I was nauseated.

What happened was that I had another attack of inner ear imbalance as I had in Saskatchewan in 1986.

After all the activities, things seemed to normalize. Everyday there were things that had to be done, but we did not rush with it. Can we call church services, meetings, choir practices, funerals as normal everyday activities? We drove to each function in Vernon every time. It was thirty miles one way to Vernon and that brought a lot of wear and tear on the vehicle and us because there were times we had to make three trips a week to Vernon. In the summer time I built a fence around the back part of the lot and a six foot retaining wall at the back of the house where the garden was. On top of the retaining wall, I put a meshed fence.

My father had come to Canada in 1928 and mother in 1929 but neither had ever been back to Ukraine for a visit. One reason they never went back was due to a shortage of funds and another that when the communists enslaved Ukraine they would not let anyone in or out of the country. Than things began to change in the later 1980's. The communists saw that their socialist policies do not work, they saw the coming downfall of the country, and so they decided to ease up and let people visit back and forth. It was sixty two years since father came to Canada and he always longed to go back to see the place where he was born. Mother was never interested to go back and she always said she was happy that she got out and had come to Canada.

John also picked up enough interest and said he would like to see the place where the parents were born. Kay was born in Ukraine and she also said she would be interested to go back and see her birthplace. Father and John got talking and more interested each day and they decided they would go to Ukraine for a visit, father, John and Kay. John went to the travel agent and made all the arrangements. They would leave on May 18th. But what about mother? She cannot be left alone at home. She could not go to Oksana's because Oksana was working and not home. Alice was on the farm and always was too busy. She could not stay with us, because it was too far for her to travel by herself, because if something happened on the way, than what? It was decided that mother would spend two weeks in the nursing home at Wakaw in the respite. We could not go to be with her in Cudworth, because the day father, John and Kay left for Ukraine,

Marusia had to be in Kamloops to get the stitches out of her trigger finger on which she had surgery..

Because we could not see father, John and Kay leave for Ukraine, and father was ninety percent sure that the communists would kill him in one way or another, we decided that we would be there to welcome them back home from the trip. We drove to Cudworth and than with Alice and her husband John and other members of the family we met the returnees at the Saskatoon airport at 10:00 PM on June 2nd. We spent another day in Cudworth to hear what father, John and Kay had to say about their visit to Ukraine. In the meantime mother had been complaining about the nursing home and just did not want to stay there. She said that she would do something to herself to die, or she would escape from the nursing home, and that we take her out and bring her home. She was giving the nurses a bad time, so father had to take her home. All this was probably due to the strokes that she had which affected her memory.

When mother was home already, she was making it hard for father. She was telling him to take her wherever she wanted to go and he was not getting any rest. She would only say: "I'll give money for the gasoline." She would tell him to drive her to a restaurant for french fries, to Prince Albert to shop, to Alice to see what she's doing, to Saskatoon to shop, to Oksana and other places. The doctor had told mother not to go farther away from home than twenty miles. We would remind her about that, and she would only say: "But what is the difference if I sit at home, or sit in the car and go? When I'm sitting in the car, I'm not doing anything." Still even with that condition father drove her as far as to Winnipeg to see Oksana; Edmonton to see John and other places. The doctor saw that her time was nearing so he told Alice not to stop mother from eating what she wanted or what she was doing. She was a diabetic and always loved ice cream and french fries. She always would give father $20.00 to take her to Crossroads restaurant in Wakaw for french fries or ice cream. We would tell her that she should not eat those things and she would only say: "But I don't eat a whole pail of it, just a little bit, and it won't hurt."

When we were ready to go home, we took another route home. Instead of going to Calgary as we always did before, we went north to Prince Albert and than west on to Glaslyn, Sask., because Marusia wanted to get some ostrich eggs. We heard there was an ostrich farm there and they sold ostrich eggs. We found the farm and bought six ostrich eggs at $50.00 each. Later Marusia resold four at the same price and kept two and wrote them into Easter eggs. From Glaslyn we kept going west to Cold Lake, Alberta to visit Marusia's nephew and his wife, Mike and Doreen Semeniuk. There we spent the night and left next morning driving farther west and north through Lac La Biche and unto Grand Prairie. We stopped at Bensenson, just east of Grand Prairie to visit Marusia's old friends the Antonio family. From there we headed out to Spirit River and stopped at George and Mary Zyha's place. On we went west to Dawson Creek in B.C., and spent the night there. Because Marusia had never seen the W.A.C. Bennet Dam at Hudson Hope, we drove there and stopped for a few hours and than continued south and unto to Prince George. At Prince George we stopped at Helge and Sophie Ludvigsen for the night and left for home the following morning. It was a long trip, but we stopped and saw many people, friends and old acquaintances.

Again things were moving along as usual, attending church, organizational duties, choir practices, meetings, etc., kept us busy and now that we were more involved in activities, we were kept hopping from one activity to the next. At one church meeting I made mention that Marusia and I are living in this area for two years and still don't know all the people in the three congregations. I said that maybe the church should make a church directory where we have pictures, names and addresses of all the members. Everybody thought that it was a good idea and because I had brought it up, now I was given that task to get everything organized and the books prepared with the Institutional Promotions of Canada Limited from Calgary. Than like everywhere else there were a few skeptical people when you give them something for nothing they ask: "What's the catch?" Everyone whose picture would appear in the book would get a free book, the church directory.

Now I had extra work. Organize all the people to have their picture taken. Get all the names, addresses, telephone numbers, etc. Line up the schedule who is to come to have their picture taken at what time. After all the work was finished and the printed pictorial directories were handed out to the people, many people later were saying: "This was the best thing that ever happened in our parish." Everybody was pleased and happy with the books. If you asked the same people today who were not in favor of such a book at the beginning, they were the first ones to say that such a book was very good to have. Such a book is good for about five years and than should be redone, because people pass away, new people move in, others move out, some change address and a book should be updated. Many churches have such pictorial directories.

ON THE MOVE AGAIN - TO VERNON

The wear and tear on us and the vehicle was getting to us. We made as many as eighty five thousand miles a year since we moved to Salmon Arm. As mentioned we made trips to Vernon sometimes three times a week and there were a few times that we even made five trips in one week for different things that were happening. There were times that we would go and attend as many as two and three functions in one day between Kelowna and the Vernon congregations. With all the traveling we were doing we decided it would make more sense to live in Vernon, where we would have so much less traveling. We put our house up for sale after having set everything up only now just live and enjoy. In the meantime we gave a deposit on a town house in Vernon. There were thirty two town houses being built in the west end of Vernon. We bought the town house in Vernon, but the house in Salmon Arm had not yet been sold.

We had to go to the bank to get a loan to carry us through until the house in Salmon Arm was sold. Because Marusia had dealt with the Bank of Montreal for fifty years, she said that we get the loan there. We went and made an application for a very short term loan. The people at the bank told us to come back in two days and they will have everything ready. When we came to the bank two days later, the people told us that they could not loan us the money for there were some problems that they got from Better Business Bureau. Now what? They would not tell us, but I can only recall or guess of one incident that may have held this against us.

When we still lived in Salmon Arm, we made one trip to Saskatchewan and bought fuel at a Husky Station with their credit card someplace in the southern part of Alberta. Coming back home through Lloydminster we again stopped for fuel at the Husky station and used the card there also. As time went by, we did not hear from Husky about a statement. We waited another month and still nothing. The same with a third month and nothing. After that when we were now in Vernon, we called Husky headquarters and asked them what happened that we did not get any bills for three months. They started to check and said that we did not pay two credit card purchases and our name was written as "bad standing". I gave them two cents of my thought telling them that they are the ones that did not send a statement and I was the honest one wanting to pay what I owed them and now they put me on a black list. Marusia and I went to another bank and in two days we had a loan. Marusia than withdrew everything out of the Bank of Montreal and we never went near that bank again.

The day came to move our possessions to Vernon. We had packed box after box and each time we drove to Vernon to some meeting or something, we would always drop off the boxes in the house. When we took possession of the house, we would take a load of things with the car. Marusia would stay in Vernon unpacking, while I turned around and headed back to Salmon Arm for another load. By the time I returned in just over an hour with a load of more boxes, Marusia was finished or finishing empty the boxes from the previous load. I would make about four or five trips in a day. Finally on December 27th MacCosham from Vernon came and took the heavier appliances and furniture. After living for two years in Salmon Arm, we moved and 1991 found us unpacking our things in Vernon.

We are now living in Vernon and are Vernon citizens. The house in Salmon Arm was vacant and for sale. When we lived in that house the insurance was $125.00 a year. When we moved out and the house was vacant, the insurance people sent us a bill to pay $800.00 a year, because no one is living in the house. Moving to Vernon, we had nothing to do. We paid $55.00 a month for condo fees and that took care of everything, snow shoveling, lawn care, water, sewer, insurance, garbage pickup, etc. We also had a small garden at the back of our place and the whole compound of thirty two houses was fenced in. When we planted things in the little garden, we had no stairs, just open the patio doors and the garden was level with the house next to the patio. This was a good place to live to pay $55.00 a month and no work to look after the house. All we had to pay here was the phone and television cable.

Now that we moved to Vernon, we were close to everything. We were elected to executive positions in the church and organizations. Marusia became the vice president of the Ukrainian Women's Association in the Vernon local. I ended up wearing four hats, so that when I was going somewhere, I had to make sure I took the right hat. I was elected chairman of the Vernon Parish Committee which included congregations at Vernon, Kelowna and Kamloops. I was at the same time vice chairman of the congregation in the Vernon church. I had been elected president of the Ukrainian Canadian Congress in the Vernon local and president of the Order of St. Andrew in which the members of the Order belonged from any one of the three congregations mentioned. Having all these responsibilities and than singing in three different choirs in the area plus other functions kept us busy enough. At least we did not have the traveling we had from Salmon Arm. People knew we were retired, so they made "go-phers" out of us; go-for this, go-for that. When living in Salmon Arm, many times we used to come home at 11:00 PM after some function had taken place in one of the congregations. We stayed overnight and next morning we were back to some other function or activity that was taking place the following day.

As already stated above it is now 1991. Ukrainians in Canada are celebrating the centennial of the first Ukrainian settlers in Canada. There were two locals of the Ukrainian Canadian Congress, one at Vernon and one at Kelowna. Marusia and I were involved in both locals, but more with the one in Vernon. Many activities and celebrations had been planned in both locals with only thirty miles one from the other. In Vernon on April 3rd we planted two cranberry bushes in the city park to commemorate this event. In Kelowna there was a special program on September 8th and a program was also held in Vernon on September 28th.

WORK AND LONG TRIPS

This same year the congregation in Vernon was doing some remodeling of their church. The basement and kitchen was remodeled. The church upstairs was painted and prepared for the feast day of the congregation. The feast day, Dormition of the Virgin Mary, falls on August 28th of each year, Archbishop John from Edmonton was coming to officiate in the pontifical service and be a participant in the afternoon program. I was the MC for the afternoon program.

The year went by very quickly with many activities that we attended, yet we did find time to make two trips to the prairies. We attended my parents' birthday in April when father was ninety years old and mother her eighty fifth birthday. Their birthdays fell two days apart, so when the family gathered to celebrate this occasion, we celebrated both their birthdays on the same day together. A "Come and go tea" was made for them in the seniors hall where both parents and especially father liked to go and meet with the people. The only trouble with the "come and go tea" was that people came but did not go and made it a "come and stay." Our house in salmon Arm did not stay vacant very long. It was sold to a family from the Kootenays in February.

This year went well for Marusia and me and we did not have any health problems. The headaches and nose bleeds that I could not shake off and the doctors could not remedy what the problem was when I was in Hyas, were now gone. Hope and wish were that all future years for health would be as good. Maybe because we were so busy, we had no time for illness. But I had always been busy in Hyas, yet the headaches and nose bleeds prevailed. I believe it was the stress and the high blood pressure that were causing me the anguish, so why could the doctors not diagnose the problem.

When the birthdays were over for the parents, Marusia and I did not return home. We kept going farther east to Ontario to see Marusia's sister-in-law, Beth Kwasnicia and her a family in London, Ontario. Beth has three daughters: Gale Ann, Judy and Sharon. We visited Beth, her daughters as well as Beth's brothers and sisters. When Sunday came we went to our church were Father Metulynsky was the parish priest. We also visited Marusia's cousins Kay Thompson and Jean Worobel at St. Catharines and her cousin Jeannie and Jim Kuney at Woodstock and other family in the area. The time that we spent in Ontario, the weather was beautiful and it was nice and warm.

After we visited Marusia's relatives in the east, we took another road home, going through the USA. We drove and enjoyed the scenery. When I was in Lac La Biche in the 1960's Mary and I had gone to the Royal Gorge in Colorado. Returning from the east we drove this time to Colorado so Marusia could see the Royal Gorge. The story of this gorge is something to see and know. If you can't go there in person, get on your computer and type in Royal Gorge and you will see what it is all about.

It was either January 17th or 18th that one evening we got a call from my brother John, that Kay and him are leaving for Phoenix, Arizona on January 24th and Marusia and I are to go with them and they will pick us up at 9:00 AM. We were refusing to go, but John insisted that he needs a driver to help him drive. After coaxing us, we finely gave in and said that we would go. The company where John was working was sending him to Phoenix to take a one day course in mechanics. They were going to fly him, but he asked if he could have a few days off and he would rather drive to Phoenix. John and Kay left Edmonton on the 23rd and stayed over in Kamloops at her son's place in a motel. Early next morning at 9:00 AM as John had said, they appeared in front of our house. Marusia and I were ready, so just took our suit cases and we were gone in a moment's notice.

None of us had ever been to Phoenix before, so this was quite a trip. We knew some of our friends and relatives that went there every year because they had a trailer or house and spent the winter in Phoenix with other "snow birds" from Canada. John and Jean Sawchyn had a trailer there. Our cousin Alex and Sylvia Korzeniowski also had a trailer in Phoenix and Alex's brother Stan owned a house. Now that we have a chance to go south, this will give us a chance to visit these relatives and friends.

From Vernon we drove down to Kelowna, Penticton in Canada and across the USA border to Moses Lake and Pasco, Washington. As we continued our trip we passed through Pendelton, Oregon, down to Boise and Twin Falls Idaho. Farther and farther south we headed to Ogden and Salt Lake City, Utah. Still farther down south we continued until we arrived at Las Vegas, Nevada and stopped there for one night on a Sunday evening. At night we drove on the street to see lights. Lights and more lights and still more lights. How much electricity is used up on that street without any need. Why that many lights are needed, I personally don't know. Is that a waste of energy or what? Than we turn around and wonder why there is a shortage of power and also pollution. We stayed in one of the motels and as we were registering, the desk clerk told us that we were lucky and the four of us were awarded free supper that evening. Some in our group even tried winning some money, but they had no luck.

Next morning we left for Phoenix stopping here and there to admire the scenery and take pictures. We arrived in Phoenix at supper time and found a Motel-6 and stayed there overnight. There were many orange trees around the motel. I thought if I take one orange and have a taste of a fresh orange, no one will even know that I took one off the tree. When we got to the rooms, I peeled the orange to have a bite of a fresh orange. Oh did it smell sweet as I peeled it. Than I sank my teeth into a fresh orange, and I could see all the way back to Vernon. The orange was so bitter I thought my mouth would become paralyzed. I did not know that those type of oranges were used only for decoration and for making marmalade.

Next morning we phoned Alex and Sylvia Korzeniowski and told them that we were in Phoenix. They told us to come and visit them and how to get there. We found our way to their place and they asked us where we stayed. We told them and they said that we probably did not have a good night, because we were in a red light and roughest area of the city. Did we know? That was our first time in Phoenix and you stay where you see a good looking motel. That same day we got another place, a motel, just skip and a jump from Alex and Sylvia. That morning Alex and Sylvia drove us around to show Phoenix and we went to find the place where tomorrow John is supposed to go for one day schooling. Next morning when John went to school, Alex, Sylvia, Marusia, Kay and I went shopping. I did not shop for anything, but was more interested in sight seeing and comparing the beautiful warm weather with the cold Canadian winter. When John returned from his course we had supper at Alex and Sylvia's place in their trailer in the camp ground.

After supper we went to the motel which was just a stones throw away from Alex and Sylvia. When we were in the motel we got a phone call from Alex to come the following morning to their place for breakfast. When we arrived next morning, we came to a surprise. There at Alex and Sylvia's place were two of Alex's brothers whom we had not seen as they say, "for ages." Joe and Marlene from Calgary and Stan and his wife right from Phoenix. After breakfast we went to see John and Jean Sawchyn in another camp ground, just around the block from Alex's place. We had lunch with them and than they drove us around and showed us different places in Phoenix. Next day we had lunch with Paul and Anna Stelmaschuk from Kelowna who were visiting in Phoenix at that time. After lunch we started to head westward towards Los Angeles. It was not on the way home, even somewhat farther, but John wanted to go and see Los Angeles and to drive along the Pacific Ocean on the way home. We arrived in Los Angeles that evening. I knew a little bit of Los Angeles, for I had been there two times before when I visited George Alexandro at Porterville and once when Marusia and I stayed when returning from Australia.

We got our motel for the night and John asked if we were ever to see Universal Studios, to which all replied, "no." Next morning we checked out of the motel at 7:30 AM and drove to Universal Studios. As we entered the grounds, John put Kay's window down and paid the guard our admission. There we had a small breakfast and after went on a tour of Universal Studios. We spent the time on the tour till about 4:00 PM seeing all the sights and sounds of movie making. No they did not accept us to be film stars.

After we had enough walking and sight seeing for one day, we headed back to the car. John came to the passenger side of the car to unlock the door and says: "Oh, oh. Look our window is missing. Someone broke into our car and I bet our cameras and everything else is gone." We looked inside and everything was there as we had left it that morning. Than it hit us all. When John paid for the tickets through the passenger side window, he never raised the window up but just drove away to park. The car sat on the parking lot all that day with our belongings in it and nothing was touched. Where we lucky or what?

That night we stayed in a motel in Los Angeles and next morning went to a church service at St. Andrew's Ukrainian Orthodox Church. After the service we headed out north towards San Francisco. First we made a stop to visit George Alexandro at Porterville whom I already have met a few times previously. He had written to Marusia and me that he was going to visit Ukraine, so we wanted to hear from him, what he had seen and heard in Ukraine and tell us about his trip. We had sent him a Christmas card, but never received an answer from him. We thought that because of his age he could not write or maybe he is in some nursing home.

We arrived in Porterville and found his house very quickly, for I had been there a few times before. In front of his house we saw a "For sale" sign when we drove up to the house. I thought that he could not look after his house and yard, so he was selling his place. I knocked on the door, no answer. I tried a few more times, but there was no response. Then we went over to the next door to ask if they know where George is. Here we got a shock what the neighbor told us. George had passed away about a year ago when it was very hot. He got heat stroke and died.

Finding out the sad news, we then headed back to get unto the Interstate highway towards San Francisco. Before we got to the highway, we passed through orange groves, vineyards and orchards. As we were driving along, in one place people were just setting up tall ladders to get to the top to pick oranges. We stopped and had a chance to talk with the owner of the orange grove to find out what we can about the growing of oranges. The owner even picked some beautiful oranges and gave them for us. Were those oranges ever good, fresh from the tree and into our mouths. You could sit in that grove and eat oranges all day long to your heart's content.

We got back on the Interstate and drove that day stopping here and there along the Pacific Ocean to wet our feet in the water and take a picture or two. That day we got to San Jose and stayed in a motel. Next morning we continued our trek north and stopped at San Francisco to see the famous bridge. We also saw the strange, dirty and scary people on the streets. People begging for money, others sleeping on a piece of cardboard right on the sidewalk beside a wall of a building. We picked ourselves into the car and headed straight out and over the Golden gate Bridge northward closer to home each mile as we drove. John wanted to see the Redwood forest, so he drove off the Interstate and took a road that went through the Redwood Forest. We drove and it was already getting late, late in the afternoon. The fuel gauge was beginning to dip towards the "E" mark and darkness was beginning to settle in the forest. Finally somehow we got out of that forest and found a small town, first filling up the tank with fuel, something to eat and than a motel.

Next morning we continued our journey north along the ocean and saw many large waves come crashing to the shore. We stopped at Crescent City, had lunch and than kept going north to get closer and sooner to home. We went through Grant's Pass, up to Eugene and on to Salem, Oregon where we spent the night. Next morning we passed through Portland and took the road to Biggs, north to Washington to Yakima, Wenachee and into Canada. We asked John and Kay to stay over night, but they insisted going on to stay at Kamloops at Kay's son's motel.

This year we are also preparing to go to a wedding in Winnipeg. My niece Kathy Foley, Oksana's daughter is getting married on February 22nd. Before we left for the wedding, we planted some garlic and onions in the garden back of the town house. We left on February 19th and got as far as Swift Current, Saskatchewan. A blizzard was already in the area when we got there. We had planned of getting to Moose Jaw that day but the blizzard beat us and we had to stop in Swift Current. Next morning we left and arrived in Winnipeg at 3 00 PM. We had called my parents from home that we would pick them up, but they told us they would go with John and Alice. As it later turned out they went with neither, because they said they did not want to be a bother anyone, so they decided to go themselves with the car. It also happened that if we ever tried this again a million times it would not repeat. John and Kay were in Thompson, Manitoba visiting her son. What will never happen again is that Father and mother from Cudworth, John and Kay from Thompson, Marusia and I from Vernon all three vehicles arrived nearly at the same time, less than in a fifteen minute span of each other. If it was tried to be so again, it would never work in a million times.

NEWS FROM PHOENIX COMES TO US

About a month after we arrived home from Phoenix with John and Kay, we got a phone call on March 3rd from a congregation in Phoenix, Arizona asking me to come and serve the congregation there. Had I known something like this would happen, I would have at least looked where the church was or someone from the church, but I knew neither. Not knowing anyone there and no one knowing me, yet I get a call to come and serve the church there. How did people know about me? It was about the same time when we were in Phoenix, the late Father Mykola Stetzenko from Vernon was also in Phoenix for holidays. He had been in the church on Sunday and told someone about me not serving and they should get me to come and serve them. I did not know anything about this, until Father Stetzenko returned home and told us that he was talking to some people in Phoenix and told them that I could come and serve there. He never asked me if I would go but said I could serve. How did he know if I could or not? The priest that was in Phoenix at that time was old and could not serve anymore.

At first I did not know what to tell the people in Phoenix. I told them, that if the Primate of the USA gives his blessing that I can serve, I would consider it. It happened that this was a long drawn out affair. The people from Phoenix had asked me to call Father Nestor Kowal and tell him that I am willing to come and serve. I knew Father Kowal from St. Andrew's

College Seminary in Winnipeg. We studied at the same time. I called Father Kowal and he said to write a letter to the Consistory in the USA to ask for their blessing to come and serve in Phoenix. I wrote a letter and was waiting for a reply. Before I received any reply from the consistory, other people in Phoenix having heard about me, began calling me and asking the same thing: "Would you come to help and serve our parish?" I kept giving them the answer that I had written to the Consistory but have no answer from the Consistory. The people told me they would be putting pressure on the Consistory, because Easter was coming and they needed a priest.

I again called Father Kowal and told him that I am getting calls from Phoenix, I wrote a letter the to Primate already and have not received any information. Father Kowal asked me to get a release from the Primate in Canada. I wrote a letter to the Primate in Canada asking for a release. Very soon after, I got a letter from the Primate in Canada, that releases are only given to clergy in good standing and he cannot give me a release because I broke a canon law by marrying a second time. Thus I lost all my privileges of ever serving again.

The congregation in Phoenix was desperate. They kept calling and begging from time to time asking me to come and serve them. I would not go and told them, until I had a letter from the Primate of the USA that I could go and serve. If I went without the consent of the bishop or Consistory, I could be charged for serving in the church at the Altar without proper authorization. I was hesitant to go until I received permission that I could come and serve there. On March 27th, I sent another special delivery letter to the Consistory in the USA which cost me $18.00. The people needed a priest because Easter was around the corner, asking me to come, and I would not go until I had permission to do so. It was now already past Easter when I finally got a letter from the Primate in the USA, Patriarch Mystyslaw who said that I cannot serve in the USA., because the canon laws in the USA are the same as in Canada.

By now I had already gotten up enough courage and enthusiasm to go and serve in Phoenix, but when this letter arrived, I lost all hope. It was some time later that I had learned that the Primate in the USA himself had performed a second marriage of a priest and had given him a parish to serve. I also learned later that there were other clergy in the USA that had been married twice and were serving on parishes. Later when we did arrive in Phoenix we learned that there were some priests who were married three times and they were serving in the church. I was getting the intention to write to the Primate to explain why some were married twice and were serving, while people are begging me to come to Phoenix and I am denied to serve them. People are "crying in the wilderness" to come and help them, and I cannot do anything. My hands were tied. Anyway that was the decision that the Primate made and that was the end of story. The Primate Patriarch Mystaslaw passed away before I had the time to write and ask him about this situation. As you will see, this story unfolded differently later on.

I am still hoping that before God calls me, I will have time to sit down and go through the canons of the Rudder and show the church how many other priests in Canada have created graver sins than me for marrying a second time and they are still serving. I broke a canon law and am prevented from serving. God willing, I hope to go through the canon rules one day. The Primate and the church look at me and have me as a grave sinner, but yet they cannot see what the Bible says: *"For all have sinned....."* (Romans 3:23)

As all this was going on between the church, the Primate in the USA and me, we got a phone call from mother that father was in the hospital in Cudworth and she is alone at home and can't look after herself or go anywhere she needs. We quickly packed everything we needed and headed out to Cudworth to stay with mother while father recuperates. Arriving in Cudworth and visiting father we soon learned that he has shingles, one side of his face is all swollen and red. His face seemed infected and the infection was heading down from his head. It was later that the doctor discovered it was not shingles, because he was treating him for shingles and yet the illness was not being controlled by the medication.

What really had happened as we learned later was, that when father was getting into the car, he hit his head against the sun visor. He hurt his head and an infection set in. What else was the matter, was that he always generously used a head cream and probably never washed his head with shampoo so all that caused the infection. He was afraid that he would lose his eye, because the infection was causing problems to his eye. Thank God, that with medication it was cured even though he never wanted to use any medication but when he saw what was happening, he used medication.

When we had returned back from Cudworth after father came home, Marusia had to take me to emergency in Vernon one day. My face had become swollen, red and I was sweating something terrible. The doctors did not know what was wrong and for a while they thought I was getting a heart attack, for I was sweating badly. The tests showed negative. I came home from the emergency and next morning the swelling and redness from the face were gone. Till today never did learn and know what it was, but only guess that it must have been some allergy attack. In the Okanagan there are thousands of orchards. The fruit trees and other plants are sprayed with pesticide and insecticide as much as three and four times a season. Maybe I got a sniff of one of the sprays that was used and that caused a reaction.

One day we got a phone call from the public health nurse from Prince Albert, Saskatchewan who said that the parents are both old, their health is failing and mother should be in a nursing home. We knew that mother would not go to a nursing home, so what can we do if she does not want to go there. All that mother wanted was to stay at home, so that father could drive her where she wanted to go for french fries or shopping.

One other thing that happened this year was that Andrew Antony told us that his family was having a "family reunion" in Saskatchewan east of Yorkton, at McNutt. The family wanted to have a thanksgiving service, but they cannot get a priest anywhere to come and serve for that day. The family was wondering if I would come and have a service for them. I told them the church regulations do not allow or permit me to come into a church to have a service otherwise I could be charged for that. The family asked me if I could serve in a hall. I told them that a hall or private home is not a church and anyone can come from anywhere and have a service in a hall or house. I agreed to their proposition to have a service on a Sunday morning in the curling rink hall at McNutt. On Sunday morning the family met in the curling rink hall and I had a service for the family.

Another happy Occasion this year was the conclusion of the celebrations of the Ukrainian Settlers coming to Canada. The Ukrainian Canadian Committee in Kelowna was having a special celebration and had invited the Ambassador from Ukraine to the United Nations, Victor

Batiuk and his wife to attend. I was given the job to video-tape the celebrations in Kelowna. Another celebration took place on September 26 - 27th in Vancouver. This celebration was held by the Western Diocese of the Ukrainian Orthodox Church of Canada. Present were all three bishops of the church, ten clergy with many people in attendance. Marusia and I attended this event.

I had been elected as a delegate to the Ukrainian Canadian Congress Convention in Winnipeg on October 8 - 11th. We left for this convention some time in advance and drove to Edmonton to see John and Kay. Than we stopped in Cudworth and also made a trip to Saskatoon. We were going to Winnipeg traveling through Yorkton, Sask. Conventions to me are a hectic time. You sit and sit and sit and listen. Yes you learn, but if you had a blood clot, sitting so long does not help a person. After the convention was over we returned for in six days we will be welcoming a law professor and me being president of the local Ukrainian Canadian Congress, I have to be home to welcome the quest and see that the organization of the program is going well.

WHAT - ANOTHER MOVE? AGAIN?

When Marusia and I were on our way to Winnipeg, to the convention we began discussing that we are spending too much time traveling between Vernon and the prairies. So going along we were discussing that maybe we should move back where we would have less travel than we had till now. We drove to Winnipeg, came home and in a month leave again for Dauphin, Manitoba, where the congregation is celebrating the twentieth anniversary of their Auditorium and I have been invited to be the guest speaker. We also knew that we would be making another trip to Yorkton towards the end of December to take part in the celebration of Father Nicholas Rauliuk's twenty five years in the priesthood. So we just go back and forth, back and forth. I did not mention that one year we had three weddings to attend in Saskatchewan of Marusia's family and each wedding was two weeks apart. Too long to be away from home and too short to drive back and forth. We returned home after each wedding and than drove again to the next one. We knew the Trans Canada Highway to Calgary by memory, just like the truck drivers who are on that road day and night know each and every curve and bump on the road.

So as we were on our way to Winnipeg to the convention, we discussed that we should move back to the east side of the mountains, (to the prairies) closer to family, but where? It would be better on us and the vehicle so we would not spend so much time on the road. We had calculated that in the five years we lived in British Columbia, we made nineteen trips to the prairies, that's like nearly four trips a year, any time of the year. All our families are on the prairies and they will not move to be closer to us, so if we want to be closer to them, and there are only two of us, so lets move back. We had already talked about this in August when we attended the Antony reunion in McNutt, Sask. When we were coming back from the Antony reunion we had already turned into Wynyard, Foam Lake and other towns along the road checking the residential areas if there were any houses for sale and what the towns looked like. In Foam Lake there wasn't one house up for sale. In Wynyard there were a few houses for sale but the town did not appeal to us.

Now as we were traveling to Winnipeg to the congress convention we talked about the same thing to look and check to see places as we passed through. Only the question was where? Alberta, Saskatchewan or Manitoba? We thought of different places as we drove. As we were driving through Yorkton, we stopped and checked with a real estate firm but there was nothing that looked interesting to our taste. As we were leaving Yorkton on to Dauphin, on the east side of Yorkton we saw new houses that were built and ready to move unto the foundation. We passed that place and than on the first turn off we turned back to go and check out what those houses were. They were all very appealing to the eye. It was Deneschuk Homes. It was exactly October 6th, my birthday. We stopped and went to look at the new houses that were standing on the lot ready to be moved.

We were shown some beautiful houses and there were a few that we fell in love with at first sight. We picked out a house that we liked which was sitting on the lot and than went inside checking for more information. As we were making this move the people told us that we should go out with them and pick out a lot where we want the house to be moved. We were taken to see some empty lots and picked a lot that had the front street and one back and one side lanes. When we came back to the office with the salesman we found out that the house we had chosen would not go on the lot we picked because that lot was too small. So now what? We started again from scratch. We looked at the designs of the houses in a book, checked, asked, looked, checked and finally came to the conclusion which house we wanted that would fit the lot we picked out. We signed an agreement and made a down payment. The wheels were set in motion for a brand new custom built house. Now we drove on to Winnipeg to the convention.

When we told people we were moving to Yorkton, people began to question us, why Yorkton, and not Saskatoon, Regina, Dauphin, or some other place, but Yorkton? We told them that we did not want a place crowded with traffic, yet where there was everything people needed. We also said that Yorkton would be a hub for us. Two hours to Dauphin, two hours to Regina, three hours to Saskatoon, only five to six hours from Winnipeg, all within a few hours to any place. This would save us so much time in traveling.

When we had arrived home from Winnipeg in October, we immediately put our house up for sale. We also began to pack things now and than. We were told by Deneschuk that the house would be ready for occupancy by the middle of February. Somehow we could not believe it but took their word for it. Another question: How will we move? A moving company? U-Haul? But than we put this on the back burner for things are not ready to be moved. We have to think of two more trips to make to Saskatchewan and Manitoba. We also had to see that our house in Vernon sells.

We packed here and there, now and than when the time was getting nearer to move out. We decided that we would take a U-Haul truck and move things ourselves. I said that I would drive the truck and Marusia could drive the car behind, but she said that she did not want to drive in the mountains in the winter time. We would have to take a trailer and put the car on the trailer.

Than came November 8th and we headed out to Dauphin where I was the guest speaker at the twentieth anniversary of the auditorium. After the event in Dauphin, we drove to Benito, Manitoba to visit our friends Emil and Mary Rubashewski. We spent the night there and next day drove to Yorkton to see the progress on the house. We were very surprised to see that the wooden basement had already been completed. At this time we gave more money towards payment for the house and we were told the house would be ready to move in by mid February. From Yorkton we headed out to Cudworth to see the parents and tell them the news about the new house in Yorkton and that we will be so much closer to them now. It was while we were at Cudworth that we received a phone call from the

Real Estate in Vernon that they have an offer on our house and if we would accept that offer. We were not even at home yet, when our house was sold in Vernon on November 13 - 1992. Coming home we knew that now we had to step on it to start packing because the people want possession of the house in Vernon on January 31st. We were not worried if we had to wait for a few days before the house was ready to move in, in Yorkton. We had family and many friends that we could stay with before the new house would be ready.

On December 24th we once again headed for the prairies, this time to Yorkton to attend Father Rauliuk's twenty-fifth anniversary of his priesthood. Before we left home, we called Deneschuk homes and asked in we could bring some perishable things to leave in the basement of the house. They said it was okay. When we arrived at Yorkton we stayed at a motel and the temperature that night had dropped down to minus thirty, but we had unloaded the perishable things into the house when we got to Yorkton. Even though it was that cold, it did not feel so, because it was a dry cold, not like in the Okanagan where it is a damp cold that goes right through your body. Only times it is cold on the prairies is when there is a wind chill. We were very surprised that the house was all finished and painted walls inside, but there were no carpets yet. Deneschuk also told us that the house would be ready to move in at the middle of January. This is about a month ahead of what they had promised us. Returning home from Yorkton, we had one more day left of 1992. Everything was ready for taping the Ukrainian program for Ukrainian Christmas Eve. I had prepared everything before we left to Yorkton. When we arrived home, we just went to the radio station and recorded the program on tape on January 3rd, to be played on January 6th - 1993. So now a new year has begun. The old year went by quickly, because of so many activities that had us on the go plus the trips back and forth.

The Ukrainian Orthodox Church has a tradition that every year after the Resurrection of Christ (Easter) and until Ascension, the priest and people go out to the cemetery where grave side services are held and graves of loved ones are blessed. We tried to go each year to Wakaw where Marusia's parents, brother and sister are buried.

VISITOR FROM UKRAINE

One other highlight of the past year was that in the summer a relative from Ukraine came to Canada to visit the Stefaniuk family. Who was he? Wasyl (Bill) Stefaniuk. Before our father came to Canada, he had married in Ukraine and had a son. He left his wife and son in Ukraine and himself came to Canada to make some money and than bring his family over. While he was in Canada, his wife passed away. His son was taken by father's brother and was brought up by him. When the situation in Europe was unstable with communism threatening from all sides, contact was lost with the family. Letters would not come to Canada and anyone writing a letter to Ukraine, the family never received the mail there. The mail was opened, read and destroyed and if anything bad was written about the communists, the family in Ukraine at times were taken to Siberia and perished there, while many other people were persecuted. Now this son that father had, grew up, married and he had a family, two sons, Wasyl and his brother John. This son that father had in Ukraine also had passed away, so only the two grandsons of our father are left. As mentioned earlier father, John and Kay had made a trip to Ukraine. Now Wasyl came to Canada to see our families.

He visited with father and mother than came to Edmonton to see John and Kay. John phoned us and told us that Wasyl is in Edmonton. Marusia and I made a trip to see him. We returned home and a few days later we got a call from John that Wasyl is on the bus coming to Kamloops to visit us and so we would pick him up at the bus depot. We drove to Kamloops and brought him to Vernon where he stayed a few days with us and than returned back to Edmonton, Cudworth and Saskatoon. When he was in Canada, he told us a lot of stories and many were harsh tales of the suffering of the Ukrainian people from the hands of the communists, but he also told us some humorous stories. I taped on video some of the humorous stories he told, where everyone was laughing until their stomachs were sore. I believe that they are all true, but the way he told them, even if you did not understand the Ukrainian language, you would still laugh.

When he was in Vernon, he noticed an old cordless telephone that we had in the basement. It was not working, so I just put it out of the way and was going to throw it out. He saw that phone and asked what it was. We told him what it was and said that we don't use it. He asked if he could have it. We gave it for him. What he did with it, he took it with him to Ukraine. There he repaired it himself, for he was an instructor in electronics. When the phone was repaired, he went outside to test and see if it was working. He was speaking on it to the neighbors or whoever. Some people who saw him speaking on the phone with no wires, began to look at him as if he was not his usual self. They said that something had gone wrong with him. When one neighbor got enough courage, he came to Wasyl and asked what he was doing. Wasyl told him, and gave the phone to the man to talk. That was the first electronic in their village.

When Wasyl was only ten or eleven years old, he was already electronically inclined. He had invented and built a radio that he could broadcast from it. One day he said that two airplanes came flying over their village and circled there during the day. The next day they returned and than the militia police arrived at their house. They said that there is a radio someplace in the house, so they started to look for it and found it. Wasyl was not hiding the radio. They asked who built the radio and they were told it was Wasyl's work. He told us that had he been an adult, he would have been executed, but because he was still a child they took the radio away, warned him not to do that again and left. This Wasyl and his brother John are both married and have their own children of which some are also married. The latest I heard was that one of John's daughters is married and she with her family live on Coney Island, New York.

So a new house is just about ready to move in and then the problem - how do we move? We began checking with moving companies, but they wanted an arm and a leg to move us. Prices were sky high. We checked with U-Haul and found that was our best deal. We arranged for a larger truck and a car trailer. Than another question. What are we going to move? The people that purchased our house also wanted the appliances. We sold the larger appliances and larger furniture and that gave us so much less to move. When we were in Dauphin in November we also went to Ruff's furniture in Dauphin and ordered our appliances for the new house in Yorkton. They said they would deliver the appliances for us which ever day we wanted. This company also had a store in Yorkton as we found out later. The store in Dauphin was operated by Peter Rauliuk, Father Nicholas Rauliuk's brother. They did delivered us the appliances on the day we had requested.

Since the house in Yorkton would be ready to move in on January 15th, one month ahead of the promised date, we decided we would leave Vernon on January 22nd. We had one more problem. If the weather will not be too cold, it would be all right, but if it will get cold, than what will happen with our preserves in the jars? But than came an answer for that too. Our good friend, Andrew Antony in Vernon was leaving for McNutt, Sask., to be for Ukrainian Christmas with his mother. He said he was leaving on January 4th. He was going with his station wagon and had lots of room and he could take our preserves(perishables). We told him that Deneschuk has the key to the house and that he get in touch with them when he gets to Yorkton and they will open the house. We called Deneschuk and told them that a man would be dropping some of our goods at the house and so they would open the house. It was also good for Andrew, because he had weight in his vehicle to travel in the winter on ice and snow.

Than came moving day and another question; who will help us load our things? People that knew us in Vernon knew the date when we were moving. On that day car after car began to appear and people came to help load the truck which I had picked up early in the morning. About eight to ten people came and in three hours everything was loaded on the truck. That morning Marusia and I had gotten up at 5:00 AM because there was still some last minute things to pack and do. When the truck was loaded, we drove to the U-Haul and had the trailer hooked up and the car driven unto the trailer. We are now ready and set for the road. Farewells were said and after two years of living in Vernon we were hopefully on our last move.

WHAT A DISASTROUS TRIP

Now as we know, every time a large truck goes on the highway they must report and get weighed at a weigh scale. Driving north and just out of Vernon there is a weigh scale. I believe but could be wrong, but when household moving trucks go, do they have to stop if they are hauling personal belongings? Me being an honest person turns in at the scales. They weighed the truck and motioned to move forward to weigh the trailer with the car. We were than waved to pull ahead and to come inside. We pulled off to the side and went in. It was just a few minutes before noon. When we went in, we were told that we were overloaded. So what do we do now? What do we throw out into the ditch? Do we throw out pots and pans? Maybe the mattress? The TV, or the clothing? How do you lighten the weight? The front part of the truck was ok, but it was the rear they said was over weight.

The man asked us what the weight of the trailer was. I went to the truck to get information, but there was nothing. The man called U-Haul in Vernon but could not get an answer. He than called somewhere in Eastern Canada and got no results there either. He finally faxed a letter to U-Haul headquarters in Phoenix. We waited patiently. We did not get angry, or anything, and held our cool even though we could see the man was not very polite but was rude and more like the thing that burrows and digs up your carrots in the garden. He thought we would become angry and would start swearing. We were quiet and even joked at times even though we felt uneasy, but did not want to show it. What do you do with an overloaded vehicle and where do you put your stuff off the truck? Which is the least important that we could unload?

Finally after one hour of waiting and it is now 1:00 PM, he comes and says that he can't get any information about the trailer, but what he can do, he can give us an overload permit to get us out of the province. We asked how much for the permit and he said $34.00. So why did he not do that or tell us that in the first place? He could have given us the permit, taken the money and we would have been on our way. Did he want to help us not to pay anything? He kept us waiting for over an hour at the weigh scale. We paid $34.00 and were on our way. He thought if we would have gotten angry and started swearing than he would have nailed us for something more or even call the police. He did tell us during this time that he had no use for the U-Hauls. We thought that maybe he would go out and check the truck, and find something else wrong and than he would nail us for more money. It never happened, because we were calm and collect during this whole ordeal.

So finally now we are on our way heading north. We could go to Salmon Arm and be on the Trans Canada Highway or we could take the short cut through Mara Lake and get on the Trans Canada at Sicamous. From there all we have before us is clear sailing and by this time we should have already been at Revelstoke, but because of the weigh scale, we are behind in our travel schedule. Just as we entered Enderby from the south, we heard a large BANG. Not paying too much attention we kept on going thinking that maybe something happened in town. I looked in the rear view mirror, but could see nothing, so we just kept on going. Now we are on the Trans Canada Highway and have passed through Revelstoke at 3:30 PM. Somewhere east of Revelstoke there are snow sheds, to keep the avalanches off the highway. Just as we were leaving the third snow shed, a canon like shot - BANG - rang out. I thought a canon had fired from somewhere that we did not see to get the snow off the mountain to prevent an avalanche.

As I was thinking of this the truck somewhat swayed when another thought hit me - maybe a tire blowout? I slowed down as we got out of the shed and pulled off to the side off the highway against the snow bank.

We got out and saw that both our tires on the right rear were flat. Both? Correct, both. Now it hit us. That bang at Enderby was a blow out, and now this second bang is the second tire blow out. Had we thought of it at Enderby that a tire may have blown, we could have had it repaired there and we would have no problem now. But going through towns, you hear all kinds of noises. So now what do we do in no man's land? Do we go back to Revelstoke, or do we go ahead to Rogers Pass? I thought that since we were going east, might as well look for help ahead of us and head for Rogers Pass.

It was now 4:00 PM. I put the four flashers on the truck. We locked the truck and stood by the side of the road, trying to see if we could get some type of help. About four minutes of waiting along came a large van filled with skiers from Germany. They picked us up and dropped us off at Rogers Pass service station. The service station was opened twenty four hours. We were about fifteen miles west of Rogers Pass as to the time estimated it had taken us to get from the truck to the service station.

At Rogers Pass, Marusia waited inside the service station, while I used a pay phone outside to call the U-Haul company for help. A lady answered and I told her the problem. I had to give her the number I was given by U-Haul people to call in case of problems. She asked me where I was. I told her I was at Rogers Pass. She asked me where that was and I told her about twenty five miles east of Revelstoke or some sixty miles west of Golden. She wanted to know if there are any crossroads or streets where we were. I told her we are in the mountains in no man's land with no street number where I was calling from. She said to stay by the phone and she would call me back shortly.

By this time it was about 5:00-5:30 PM. Large wet snow flakes were beginning to fall. It is now some twelve hours since we had something to eat when we had breakfast in Vernon. Half an hour went by and no phone call from the lady at U-Haul. Marusia comes out and says that the man inside said that if I was calling a toll free number, I could use the phone inside. That made me feel better, because I was already starting to get cold waiting for the phone call outside. We waited and when no answer came, I called again. This time another lady answered and I had to go through the whole procedure as I had gone the first time. After she knew of the problem, she said she would call back in a few minutes. Time was moving and when no call came in half an hour, I called again. The lady at the other end asked where we were. Again repeat the same story. She said to wait and someone will talk with me. I asked her where that person is and she said in Vancouver. Well do people in Vancouver not know where Revelstoke, Golden or Rogers Pass are in Canada?

I told the lady that I had already called two or three times since about 4:30 PM and it is now 6:00 PM and I still have nor heard anything from anyone. She tells me that the number I had called before was in Denver, Colorado, the emergency number. So then it hit me: Who the heck in Denver will know where Revelstoke, Golden or Rogers Pass are in Canada? That was the U-Haul emergency number. The lady in Vancouver started to apologize for taking so long and she said they are trying to locate someone to come and help us. I gave her the phone number where we were and she said she would call back as soon as she got something lined up. She said they were trying to locate someone in Golden to come and fix the tires. We waited. Still no answer. It was now 9:00 PM and pitch dark outside since about 4:30 PM. When I did not hear from her, I called again and she said that such and such a truck is already on the way and will pick us up at Rogers Pass as soon as he gets here.

It was 10:15 PM when the service truck finally arrived. The man that came with the truck, also brought along his wife, so Marusia had to stay back at the service station because there was no room for four people in the cab. We got to the truck and the flashers I had left on were not working now.

The service man tried to put the jack under the rear axle, but the truck was too low to the ground and he could not fit the jack underneath. I told him that we could take the ramp out from under the truck and place it under the wheels, drive unto the ramp and it will raise the truck about four to six inches above ground. We did that. We tried to start the truck, but there was no sign of life. The battery was dead. The flashers that were on from 4:30 PM drained the battery. The man said he had booster cables and we would boost the battery. No problem. We opened the hood, but no battery. We looked under the truck seat, but no battery. So where is the battery for this truck? We looked and checked and finally we found it underneath at the bottom of the truck on the passenger side. Heavy wet snow was still falling. The air was cold and damp. Large freight trucks keep flying past us going in both directions.

The service man tried to hook up the two batteries, but the booster cables were too short. The man said he would have to drive closer to the side where the battery was. He drove as close as he could to the U-Haul truck and just got the cables to barely, barely reach. When he tried to start the truck, one battery cable would jump off the battery post. I told him to hold the cable with his mitts and I would try to start the truck. It worked. We drove the truck up unto the ramp and than the jack was easily put under the axle. He lifted the truck with the hydraulic jack. He tried to take off the wheel rim, but it took a lot of pounding with the sledge hammer before the rust was loosened and he could take the rim off.

Than he tried to take the other rim off, and no matter how much he pounded and tried it would not loosen from the rust. I told him that maybe he should try to take the tire off where the rim is. He did and the tire came off very easily. He also installed the tire on the rim without taking the rim off. This was already luck. After the inside tire was installed and blown up with air, he started taking off the other tire that was taken off sooner. He tried and tried and it took a lot of coaxing and effort, but finally he got that tire off too. He installed the new tire, put it on the axle, tightened everything up and all was ready to go as soon as we put the ramp back under the storage space and I signed some papers for the work that was done.

As we were working on the truck, semi trucks kept whistling past us. As some of them drove by, they honked the horn that we get off the road. But how much more could I have gotten off the road? I had stopped against the snow bank on the passenger side. Past the snow bank was a gully of a few hundred feet deep and a river at the bottom. All the time as the service man was working on the tires, snow was coming down heavily with large wet flakes.

When all was finished we drove to Rogers Pass and I stopped at the service station to fuel up because it was midnight at this time and who knows where we may find another service station open. In that no man's land one never knows what could happen. Then Marusia and I headed for Golden and to Alberta eastward bound. About ten fifteen miles east of Rogers Pass we ran into a heavy snow squall. Snow was coming down so thick and heavy, that we just could not see the road. We crept along until about ten or twenty miles farther and we were out of this snow squall. Driving in that snow squall had made my eyes sore, because it seemed the snow was coming straight at us. It is now some eighteen hours since we woke up and haven't slept any since. I told Marusia to try and sleep and she would doze off for a few minutes here and there, but with the vehicle moving and uneven roadway surface it was not that easy for sleeping.

The rest of the road to Golden was no problem. Just as you leave Golden at the bottom of the hill there is a truck scale like the one in Vernon. I was not afraid that we would get held up because the man in Vernon told us that the overweight permit would get us out of British Columbia. Because we had pulled into the scale at Vernon, we pulled into this one at Golden also so that the police don't start chasing us. This scale is opened twenty four hours on the Trans Canada Highway. It was now 1:00 AM when we entered the scale. The lady took the weight of the truck and than waved us to move the trailer unto the scale. I was watching for the signal that she would call us in to report. Instead the lady waved her hands and said on the loudspeaker that everything was clear and to have a good trip. We did not load more things nor drop off things between the two weigh scales, so why did the man in Vernon say we were overloaded and the lady in Golden waved us through that everything is fine. What a difference between about a hundred and fifty miles at weigh stations. One friendly and kind, the other like a grizzly bear as if a fly had sat on his nose. The man in Vernon must have gotten up on the wrong side of the bed that morning. He had no friendliness, courtesy or kindness. Or, did he maybe have a hard time with some trucker head of us, so he was going to get even on us. After we left Golden we knew there were no more scales and if there were they were probably closed for the winter time.

The trip was now proceeding well. We had planned that if we leave Vernon at noon, we should be in Yorkton the following day before noon giving us twenty four hours traveling - taking our time. It was now 6:00 AM and we were just pulling into Calgary with still hours and hours of driving before us, but at least we were out of that no man's land in the mountains. We stopped in Calgary to refuel and while I was refueling, Marusia went to call my parents and tell them that we are late and will not be in Yorkton until sometimes much later this day. They were planning to come to Yorkton, meet us and help unload the goods from the truck, because we did not know anyone in Yorkton so that we could ask them to help us. As Marusia was talking with father, he told her that they were leaving for Yorkton in a few minutes and he hung up the phone. But they were only three hours from Yorkton and we are still ten to twelve hours to Yorkton from Calgary. There was hardly any traffic in Calgary at 6:00 AM.

It is now more than twenty four hours since we are up. After we left Calgary I felt tired and sleepy so I said that as soon as we find a place to pull over I will stop so I could have a little shut eye. About twenty five miles east of Calgary there was such a spot, so I pulled over, shut the engine and I fell asleep almost instantly. We had taken two pillows with us from Vernon and that pillow sure felt good and comfortable. In January the nights are long and when we stopped for a nap, the sun was just showing a bright haze in the east before it would rise. We had gone through enough in one day and now a little nap was the thing we needed. I slept for about ten minutes when suddenly I was awakened when some very noisy semi trailer flew past us. The noise woke me up. Now I already felt refreshed and we were on our way again. We stopped at Medicine Hat to refuel and to walk around, stretch our legs. After that short nap I had, I did not feel tired anymore. I told Marusia to take naps as we drove along and she did sleep for ten minutes here and fifteen minutes there. She may have slept maybe an hour on the whole trip.

Having refueled in Calgary and again in Medicine Hat, the road ahead of us was clear and dry like in the summer. The sun made the day so much happier. We have passed through Alberta and are now in Saskatchewan. A nice warm chinook breeze was blowing across the Saskatchewan prairie and our thoughts were saying that as we are clicking along we should be in Yorkton at or before sundown. As we were coasting along about 2:30-3:00 PM and about four or five miles west of Swift Current when suddenly another loud bang rang out. We couldn't have another blow out - could we? Anyway we had just passed under a railway bridge when we had to stop again. We pulled off the divided highway and stopped to check. Sure enough, the new tires on the right rear were standing up and well. Checking the left side, we found one rear tire was blown. So there goes our time to be in Yorkton before or at sunset.

The day was very beautiful, warm and sunny. The road was dry as the floor in a house. The highway was clear of snow. A very welcome warm chinook breeze wanted us to stay outside and breath in the beautiful warm fresh prairie air. We tried to hitch a ride to Swift Current which we could see ahead of us. A car came along, stopped and picked us up. An Electrolux vacuum cleaner salesman was driving to Swift Current. As we entered Swift Current from the west, there on the north side of the highway was a big U Haul sign on the building with trucks and trailers standing near it welcoming us. The man dropped us off in front of the door and we thanked him for the ride.

We went in and told the lady of our problem. She got on the phone and talked to someone. She came back to the counter and asked for the contract number and other information. Before we even got everything filled out, there was already a service truck waiting for us outside. We got in and headed out to the truck. The service man jacked up the truck, had the wheel off in no time and we were heading back into Swift Current with the flat tire. A new tire was replaced and we were driven back to the truck on the highway. The wheel was replaced and we were on our way, all this in probably an hour or less. This was service. We started the truck and drove to Moose Jaw where we refueled again and by this time it was about 6:00 PM and we were at least three hours from Yorkton. It will be dark and night before we get to our destination. So what else can happen before we get to Yorkton?

As we drove through Regina, it was already completely dark. The rest of the trip went well and I knew the road from Yorkton to Regina, for I had traveled on it many times when living at Hyas going to see doctors in Regina. A few minutes after 9:00 PM we pulled into Yorkton in front of our new house. We will not unload anything tonight, but are going to sleep and have a rest. We were thankful that after the experience we had, we finally arrived in one piece. We had the keys to the house, because when we were in Yorkton in December we got a set of keys from Deneschuk homes. We went inside the house and before we had a chance to look and see how the house was finished inside and check things out, the door bell rang. Marusia and I looked at each other more in surprise than anything else. Who knows that we are here and already coming to see us at this time of the night? We were not even sure if we should open the door, but we did. We opened the door and on the steps standing is Andrew Antony and his brother who had come to help us unload the truck. We told them we would not unload anything tonight, because we are too tired and we will unload tomorrow after we had some rest. It was now forty hours since we got up and we needed rest. Andrew and his brother took us to Holiday Inn and we had something to eat, when the place was just about ready to close for the night when we came in, but they still served us.

Andrew Antony had moved from Vernon to Yorkton before us, so at least now we knew two men who are willing to help us unload next day and than if father comes that will be enough men. We had the air mattress in the house which we had left when we had come to Yorkton in December to Father Rauliuk's anniversary. I pumped up the mattress and at least we could have something to lay on and rest. This was our first sleep in the new house and it was on the floor. We slept like dead people, for it has been hours since we last had a decent sleep and rest.

Next morning we were up at 8:00 AM somewhat refreshed and looking forward to another busy day ahead of us. Marusia found something to eat which we had in the truck with us. Since I never eat in the morning, I decided to go out, get the trailer unhooked and back the truck in towards the house to be ready to unload when Andrew Antony and his brother come to help. The car on the trailer was so badly covered with black slush and ice that it was even hard to distinguish where the doors or the lights were or what color the car was. It looked like one large hunk of dirty black ice and snow.

I got the truck backed towards the house and pulled out the ramp to walk on from the truck to the house, when suddenly from nowhere as if they fell from the sky, men began appearing from here and there. Father and mother also came and now there was enough people to unload the truck. What had been on the truck, in one hour it was all in the house. It was nice and mild outside, so the front door was even opened and people moved in and out freely to carry the contents from the truck into the house.

After everything was unloaded, we found the box that contained some dill pickles. We got some meats and bread that we had with us. We had some paper plates and gave a bite to the people who helped to unload the truck. This had been all Father Nicholas Rauliuk's organizing to see that when we arrived in Yorkton, there would be someone to help unload the truck.

EUGENE STEFANIUK

When everything was unloaded and the people left, I got the trailer hooked up. Than I drove the car off it. I took the truck and trailer to the U-Haul depot which was about two blocks from our house. When I returned from the depot, Father Rauliuk had already come by and brought a large tray of food. It was just about noon now and we were just getting ready to have something to eat. Andrew Antony was still helping to set up the beds and was still with us. Before we sat down to eat the door bell rang. Marusia answered the door and there in the doorway stood our new neighbor with a hot jar of soup for dinner. Was that soup ever good after all the experience we had been through the day before. We were so thankful and grateful to the neighbors and all the people that in one way or another helped us move into the new house.

It took Marusia and me about a week to get everything unpacked and organized. The house was beautiful, nice, clean, and neat. Deneschuks did a good job in building the house. Because the basement was not finished, we just left many things in boxes. If we needed anything we would go into the basement and get it from the box, since all the boxes had been marked what was in them. Later with the big, kind help of William Semeniuk, a church member, we got the basement completed. We also had to finish the basement, because each time we went into the basement for something, dirt from the concrete floor would always be brought with the shoes. The furnace was also blowing dust upstairs, so we had to finish the basement. After the basement was completed we had the blessing of the house on May 30th. We invited all the men and their wives who had helped us unload the truck when we arrived from Vernon. We are forever thankful and grateful for the people who helped us load in Vernon and unload in Yorkton. May God grant them good health and if God has called anyone to the other world, may they inherit eternal life in God's Kingdom.

A NEW LIFE IN A NEW PLACE - YORKTON

On February 22nd about a month after we arrived in Yorkton, we got a call from mother with some bad news. She said that father was in the hospital and she is alone at home. What a relief compared to when we were in Vernon, since it would have taken us a whole day to come to Cudworth, about twelve hours or more. Now we are only three hours away. Immediately we got into the car and were in Cudworth in no time. Father was still getting some tests done, so we decided that mother would come and stay with us until father gets better. He was worn down since mother was always telling him to take her here, there or wherever she wanted to go. We brought mother home to our place in Yorkton. Father needed some rest. Even when father was already home from the hospital, we still would tell mother that he was in the hospital. We wanted him to have a good rest and recuperate. This way mother did not pressure us to drive her back home.

In the evening we would be sitting and watching TV or talking and mother would say: "Eugene, mother will give you money for gas, if you would take Marusia and me for a ride to town." We three would get into the car and go downtown. She was saying that Yorkton was a very large city with many lights. As we would be driving, she would take out a

$20.00 bill and give it for Marusia. Marusia would take the money, for we had talked about this before, that we take the money and mother would be pleased and happy that we obliged her wish. Later when mother went to the bathroom or already was in bed sleeping, Marusia would walk in quietly and put the money back in her purse without mother knowing. This was happening each night, and each day she asked when she can go back home. We would tell her that father is still in the hospital (even though he was already home), and she can't be home alone so she has to still stay at our place.

Finally after we thought father should be feeling better, we drove mother back home. What a difference that made. We left in the morning and were home that same day in the afternoon. Going to Cudworth when we neared St. Gregor, Sask., we got a flat tire. I changed the tire and put the small spare "donut" tire on. We drove to Humboldt and stopped to get a tire. No such tire in the tire shops and service stations in Humboldt. We also asked for the same tire in Cudworth and nothing there either with the same size tire. On the way home we stopped at Lanigan, Wynyard and Foam Lake looking for the same size tire, but no one had such sized tires on hand. Next morning even in Yorkton, we could not find the right size tire. It was such a queer sized tire that people said they never heard of such a tire. Today I don't even recall what kind of tires and size they were. So what do we do? We replaced all four tires with new tires all the same size and kind. I can't recall what make of tires those were which we had a flat tire.

On March 22nd we got some bad news. Father called and said that mother was not feeling well and he took her to the hospital at Wakaw. For years mother was getting heart attacks and strokes and only God knows how many of those she had. She told father that she had a hard time breathing. When she would become ill any time of day or night or as soon as she was not well father would take her straight to the hospital at Wakaw where she could get help.

Mother had spent two weeks with us when father was in the hospital and she was always telling us that she wants to be at the house blessing when we bless the house. When we had the house blessed she did not come because she was in the hospital at that time. Father came with John and Alice to the house blessing. When mother was in the hospital, father or Alice would take her out on a day pass and bring her home to Cudworth for a few hours so she could see her house. The last time she was taken home, they had to use a wheelchair to move her around. It was sad not to see mother at the house blessing, because she always liked to be at things where the priest was having some service. She liked to attend marriages, anniversaries, birthdays, house blessings, graduations, etc. I don't even know if father or Alice ever told mother that they were at Yorkton to our house blessing.

Three days after the house blessing which was on May 30th, mother got another stroke while she was in the hospital. She was failing fast and the doctor said that she could go anytime. We drove immediately to Wakaw to see her and had to return that same day because we had company from Kelowna coming to see us, our very good long time friends, Tony and Elsie Burkowski.

Mother kept getting weaker each day and we could see by her condition that she would not last very long. But Marusia and I had another event to attend at Kamloops, B.C. Previously we drove from B.C., to the prairies for events and now we have to drive from the prairies to B.C. We left for Kamloops on June 17th to attend a fiftieth wedding anniversary for Walter and Lena Kucharek on June 19th. I had been asked to be the M.C., for their anniversaries. On the way to Kamloops we stopped at Wakaw to see mother in the hospital. She looked frail and weak and was losing her strength to talk. Marusia took her pulse and said it was weak, so she might mother may last another week if that. Marusia one time worked as a nurse's aid in the institution in Moose Jaw, Saskatchewan.

We arrived at Kamloops on June 18th and the following day everything went as it had been planned by the family. On Sunday we drove to church to Vernon and after that visited a few friends in Vernon, Winfield and Kelowna and stayed overnight at Tony and Elsie Burkowski's. Next morning we headed back home, because we knew mothers condition was worsening and we wanted to see her again. We arrived at the hospital at 4:00 PM and the door to her room was closed. We knew that something was not well. As we were going to knock on the door, the nurse came out and said that she'll be another minute and than we can go in. We walked to the end of the corridor, turned around and there coming towards us are Alice and John.

We greeted each other and started talking when the nurse came out and said that we could go in and see mother. Mother could not even lift herself anymore, no strength and energy. The nurse had to use a lift to put her into a chair where she was strapped in, so she would not fall off the chair. We began to talk to her, but she had no strength to talk. We asked her who each of us was and she only nodded her head that she knew who was who. As we were talking in the room, father also walked in.

We began to talk that she would not last very long with her condition. Getting worst each minute and hour. Father, John and Kay are to leave for Ukraine on June 27th. We talked that maybe we should go and see doctor Cenaiko so he would write a letter for father that father cannot go to Ukraine, because mother was very ill. Than we would fax the letter to the travel agency. We waited for the doctor in the clinic, but he was very busy that day, so we went back to the hospital which is across the road from the clinic.

The staff had brought supper for the patients. Mother was not eating anything, for she could not even lift up her arm and her head was tilted to one side. Marusia started to feed her and she sipped some soup from the spoon. As this was happening, the nurse came into the room and took over the feeding of mother and telling us that mother had not eaten anything for a few days, but at noon she had eaten all her meal. When the nurse started to feed her, we all walked over to the doctors office again. We told the doctor why we came and he said he would write the letter tomorrow morning and father can come to the hospital at 9:30 AM and it will be ready for him. We went back to the hospital, stayed for a few more minutes and bid mother farewell feeling that this may be the last time that we will see her.

Because Marusia and I had not been home for a week, we were anxious to get back and see how everything was. We left for home at 5:30 PM and were home at 9:00. We found things in order as we had left and the neighbors had been looking after some things for us. Being tired from the trip, we turned into bed just after 10:00 PM, not even unpacking our suitcases, because we were tired. This was June 22nd.

A BROKEN CHAIN LINK - MOTHER'S PASSING

Now June 23rd will be a day that will never be forgotten. There were six of us in the family, father, mother, Eugene, John, Alice and Oksana. It was on this day at 3:30 AM, just two days after summer had begun, in the wee hours of the rising sun, when we got a call from Alice that the hospital called her and said that mother was not responding. Alice called father in Cudworth and they rushed to the hospital. When they arrived at the hospital the doctor was there, and at 4:00 AM mother took her last breath and was gone from us. This day will always be remembered, because on this day the chain link that had held six people together for all those years was now broken. Mother had celebrated her eighty six birthday in the hospital on April 13th and left this world, making us children orphans. She left the world at the age of eighty six years, two months and sixteen days.

    As soon as mother passed away, Alice called us from the hospital and told us the news. We immediately called Oksana and John and knew that there will not be anymore sleep that night. We threw things together, took the packed suitcases and headed out to Cudworth. The doctor now would not need to write a letter for father. Mother beat the fax machine by some six hours. We left home at 6:00 AM and went to Cudworth for Alice said that they were going to Cudworth from the hospital. We arrived in

Cudworth shortly after 9:00 AM. Alice was at father's place and now we had to make the funeral arrangements. The funeral director arrived from Humboldt. The date and time for the funeral was being set and we had to get in touch with the priest yet. The prayers would be on Friday June 25th and the funeral on June 26th, both in the Ukrainian Orthodox Church in Cudworth where mother was a member.

Arrangements as to flowers, food, hall, lunches, priest, grave diggers, etc., all had to be looked after and taken care of. Than the pallbearers. Who would they be? It was talked that brother John and I the two sons. Than who else? There was in no way that it was working out, because there were grandchildren and their husbands, sons-in-law and others. If some one would not carry his "baba", while others did, there could be hurt feelings, because all loved their baba and wanted to serve for her. It took us the whole day to think and try to combine things about pallbearers. In the evening we all went to Alice and John's place on the farm and there again the topic of pallbearers was discussed. Than a thought came to me. How many granddaughters are there? We checked and found out that there are eight. One was in the hospital and would not attend the funeral. We talked and asked which ones will attend. We now have seven granddaughters that will be attending the funeral. Why not have six granddaughters be pallbearers and the seventh be the cross bearer? Those that were present said they would be pallbearers and those who were not present, we called to see if they would be a pallbearer. The weakest granddaughter would be the cross bearer and the other six stronger ones will be the pallbearers. The rest of the family spouses could be honorary pallbearers.

On the day of the prayers the family was to meet at the Cudworth funeral home to view the body. We all met in front of the funeral home and it was a heart wrenching and heart breaking experience for all with grief and sorrow on every face could be seen. When we talked to mother, she would not answer. That evening the prayers were held in the church in Cudworth. After the prayers there was lunch in the church basement and after that we all met again at father's place. That evening father said something that has much meaning and stuck to me to this day. Father said: "Funerals are nothing, until it strikes your family."

When mother passed away on the 23rd day of June, it had begun to rain that morning and it rained the day after and the day after that. It did not rain on June 26th, but it was a heavy overcast with hanging rain clouds and cool outside. When the funeral service was going on in church, at one time even the sun smiled when the sun rays came through the window and shone on the casket and on mother's face. The sun shone on mother saying: "Well done my servant." After the service we went to the cemetery for the burial. If it had been a hard time till now, well this was even more heart wrenching to see your mother who bore you, fed you, gave what she had and now going into the earth. After the service at the cemetery, everyone walks away, leaving mother alone without her family beside her. A sad day it was for the family, relatives and friends.

After the funeral on June 26th we had a full course meal in the Cudworth Community Hall in memory of our mother. Many relatives and friends gathered at father's place after the funeral for support of each other over the loss of a wife, mother, grandmother, great grandmother, relative and friend. That afternoon Marusia and I left for home as did John and Kay. Tomorrow John and Kay are leaving for Ukraine from Edmonton and father will be leaving from Saskatoon. They will meet in Toronto and than board a plane for Ukraine together. There was nothing more for Marusia and me to do, for Alice will drive father to the airport tomorrow morning, so all we can do is go home.

Father, John, Kay and Kay's sister returned from Ukraine on July 29th after a one month holiday. On this day Marusia and I could not be there to meet them, because the two of us had left for Spirit River, Alberta. We went to Canora and together with the late Father Hryhorij Udod and Dobrodeyka Lesia, the four of us were heading out to a church blessing in Spirit River where I had served many services in that church in the past. That first day we got to Smokey Lake. At that time the parish priest in Smokey Lake was the son of Father and Dobrodeyka Udod, Taras Udod. We had some supper and spent the night in the motel and what an experience that night we had. We were going to go to a motel near the RCMP detachment, but because there was paving going on near there, Marusia thought the noise would keep us awake, so we went to another motel. Marusia must have had a premonition to go to the other motel. Why? We were fortunate that we did go to the other motel. That night we went through a scary time.

PEACE RIVER COUNTRY AGAIN

At 1:20 AM a tornado hit the area. Damage was done all over and the motel we were thinking of staying had the roof torn off and sent it on the RCMP lot. The place where we stayed was constructed of strong concrete and we were safe. Shingles were torn off roofs, gardens were flattened, trees uprooted, power was off, etc. At 8:00 AM the following morning there were still six inch piles of hail sitting beside the west wall of the motel. That morning we left Smokey Lake and arrived at Spirit River in the afternoon.

On July 31st there was a memorial service for the late Mrs. Mary Zyha a long time supporter of the church. The Zyha family had been living in Spirit River area for many, many years, and many times I spent a day and night there when I had services in the peace River area. I was the first priest to serve in that church which they had bought from another denomination at Rycroft, moved it to Spirit River and remodeled. Now the time had come to bless this church and we were asked to come and attend. On August 1st the blessing would take place, with Archbishop John of Edmonton and the assistance of two priests, Father Hryhorij and his son Father Taras Udod. Father Hryhorij Udod served this area before this church was there and Taras was the present parish priest living in Smokey Lake, but looking after the Peace River area. In Spirit River I met up again with some old acquaintances I have known for many years. It was good to think back of the days when there was no church and services were held in the theatre, where Sunday mornings we had to get up early to go and clean the theatre and prepare everything for the service.

After the memorial service on July 31st we were taken to see a museum and many articles of history of Spirit River from the "olden days." Than we drove some fifteen miles north of Spirit River to see the Dunvegan area. There is an old Roman Catholic church near the Dunvegan bridge. We were very surprised to see that on July 31st so far north there were red tomatoes and corn ready for harvesting, while at Yorkton our tomatoes had just started to bloom well. Rows and rows of huge red tomatoes just waiting to be picked. Corn stalks six and seven feet tall with big cobs ready for picking and also many other vegetables that were been in that garden.

That evening we all had supper in the church basement where the blessing of water took place minutes earlier in the church upstairs. The following morning services started at 9:30 AM with the greeting of Archbishop John. This was followed by the blessing of the church and the Divine Liturgy. None of the people had seen a blessing of a church take place, so it was interesting for them. This also was only the second time that a Ukrainian Orthodox bishop had a visitation in the Peace River area. After the service and because it was the feast day of the church (August 2nd - St. Elias), a banquet was held in the Legion Hall. After the meal greetings and best wishes were extended to the congregation from different people. After all this was over the four of us headed back to Smoky Lake where we arrived at 10:00 PM, just as dusk had fallen. Next morning we motored to Downing, Alberta where again father and son had a service together at this church, for it also was the feast day of this congregation. From there everyone went to Vilna for dinner and from there we started to head for home, because Dobrodeyka Udod was not feeling very well. She had a very bad cough so we rushed home so she would see the doctor next morning. Marusia and I arrived home at midnight.

On August 5th father came to our place to tell us of his trip to Ukraine. He also brought $3000.00 for me that I had given him to purchase the house. I did not borrow him the money, but donated. He would not hear of it. John did not get his money back until father had passed away. Father told us that Ukraine and people are poor and living conditions are very low. They have no running water in the houses, no gasoline for vehicles and equipment, and the Canadian dollar was worth twenty five hundred coupons in Ukrainian money. A pound of butter cost twenty thousand coupons. Father said that he would not give them another penny of help. When they were in Ukraine the orchards were loaded with fruit. In one place they stayed, the family had just received nine large bags of sugar from the place were they worked. Some places did not pay the people with money but with products. Father told them that the orchard crop is good, they have sugar and they can make jams and preserves for the winter. They told father they have to save the sugar for making whiskey. Because of that father said he would not give them anything more, since they only think about drinking and not about the future.

Brother John also has twelve hours of video he shot during their trip. It shows an old truck that comes each morning and picks up the women from the village who go to work on the gardens to hoe vegetables. The men stay home, than go to the park to play cards and drink. John also has on the video how the cruel communists from Russia came into the Ukrainian villages and tortured people. Some were shot on the spot, they raped the women and pounded nails into the heads of the people. After all, father and John said they would not go back to Ukraine for many years unless they took with them bathrooms and rolls of toilet tissue. In five weeks being in Ukraine they had only two baths.

On August 14th, the family again met in Cudworth for a memorial service for mother. The service should have been on July 31st, but because father, John and Kay had only arrived back from Ukraine on July 29th there was no time to prepare anything and than Marusia and I were in Peace River area at that time. The priest was also away on holidays, so the service had to be put off when it was a more convenient for all to get together. There were about seventy people at the memorial service and a full course meal in the church basement. That is how things came to the end of August 1993.

Our father is now ninety two years young having had his birthday on April 15th of that year. All those whom he knew from the past have passed away and now with mother also gone, he was left alone and somewhat lost at times. When he was ninety two years old, he was still planting his own garden, cut the lawn, shoveled snow in the winter and did things around the house and yard. Marusia and I had asked him a number of times to come and live with, but he said he is alright where he is. Many times Alice who lived only fifteen miles from him, would come and clean the house for him inside. That feeling of being alone, I know just too well, after Mary had left and later passed away. At times things get to you and at times you have moments when you don't want to see or hear anyone, while at other times you just have to leave the house and get out among the people. A person struggles alone in their grief, sorrow, sadness, hurt and pain. I have learned from experience that once your spouse passes away, people don't seem to know you anymore as much.

On September 1st father gave Marusia and me a surprise. He was on his way to Winnipeg to visit Oksana and some friends, so he stopped in unexpectedly to see us since it was on his way to Winnipeg. Things for Marusia and me had been going on routinely like for everyone else. Than on September 11th at 10:00 PM we had a severe thunder and lightning storm pass through Yorkton. This was the beginning of worst things to come. Why? Because after the storm went through the night and next morning it was still raining. By afternoon the rain started turning into a snowy winter blizzard and throwing a shock into everyone. People at this time of the year are not prepared for such things from "Mother Nature." Maybe God dishes out for people like my late mother used to say: "How we give to God, in the same manner God also gives back for us." Later the snow melted and people had a chance to gather up their crops. Around Hudson Bay, Saskatchewan, many crops had to winter out in the fields, because the farmers could not get unto the fields because of too much moisture and the fields were soaking wet. They did not harvest their crops till the following spring.

On September 25th, Dobrodeyka Jane Luchak from Winnipeg came to Yorkton to conduct a workshop on religion. Marusia and I with Father Rauliuk and about thirty other people attended that workshop in the church basement in Yorkton. We did not get home till about 9:30 PM that night. As we were driving home, Marusia suddenly had a sharp attack in her chest. I was going to drive her straight to the hospital, but she said the pain was gone and she felt okay again. We went to bed and early next morning is church service and we both sang in the church choir. This night we slept very little. We were already in bed when at 11:30 PM Marusia wakes me up and says to take her to the hospital because she is not feeling well and has a pain in her chest again. We were in the hospital in no time. The doctors at the hospital determined that she would be admitted for observation and tests for the coming days. I did not get home until 1:00 AM and after this incident I hardly slept.

Next morning I went to church and than to the hospital. Marusia stayed in the hospital for three days and was told that she had an angina attack. She would need more tests and would have to see a specialist. She had been born with a leaking heart valve and heart murmur and the doctors came to the conclusion from the tests that there was a problem with her heart.

It is now October and there had been organized a bowling league of church members to bowl each Friday night. Marusia enjoyed bowling but she did not know if she would be able to bowl with her condition. We asked the doctor and he said that she can try and see if nothing happens, she can bowl and she can tell herself how she feels if she will be able to handle the bowling. So we bowled with other members until we left Yorkton later that year.

This same year the Ukrainian Orthodox Church of Canada is celebrating its seventy fifth anniversary. Congregations and parishes across Canada are holding celebrations. The congregation invited the Primate of the church from Winnipeg to come to the Yorkton celebration. The highlight was that on October 10th at the Pontifical service, Eugene Maximuk who was from Yorkton was ordained into a Deacon during the Divine Liturgy service.

In 1968 when I first became acquainted with Peter and Doris Chaykowski in Dauphin we became good friends and Doris and I even became God parents for Corrine Hnatiuk, John and Alice's daughter. Peter and Doris retired from farming, sold their land and moved to Vernon, B. C. Anytime whenever I was in the Okanagan Valley, I never missed their home and we always had good relationship and very much to talk about the church. When Marusia and I moved to Salmon Arm, Peter helped us build a shed and also helped to put the ceiling in our house. After we moved to Yorkton from Vernon, we kept in touch with each other by telephone and mail.

It was sometimes in 1993 that Peter, Doris and their granddaughter Kim took a trip to Ukraine. Upon returning from Ukraine Peter began to feel somewhat ill. On October 15th Doris called and said that Peter is not very well and he keeps saying that he would like to see us both. This was the first time that we had heard that Peter was ill. Yorkton to Vernon is nearly a thousand miles one way (923 miles). It is a two day trip one way. We sent Peter a get well card with our prayers for a speedy recovery. Later towards the end of this month we got another call from Doris saying that Peter is very ill and still wants us to come and see him before he passes away. Now we knew that for sure this was a grave illness.

We decided that we would go and see Peter, but in the Canadian Rockies at this time, the weather in the mountains is sometimes unpredictable as we learned this from our past experiences. We would go south from Yorkton, cross the USA border take highway number two and go through there with better roads and weather conditions. The first night we stopped at Browning, Montana and next morning continued on north into Osoyoos, Penticton, Kelowna and to Vernon.

We left home on November 1st and spent over a week away from home. We saw Peter and he was very sick and had lost much weight and was not even getting out of bed nor eating anything. His days as we would say, "Were numbered." When he saw us when we came to see him at home, he really changed and perked up after that. While in the area we visited a few more friends and were in church for the service on November 7th at Vernon. We also took in a bazaar and a few other activities while in the Okanagan. We returned home on November 9th, after nearly being killed by some one about sixty miles from home, west of Yorkton.

As we were traveling east on highway number fifteen, near Semens, Sask., we noticed a white car coming towards the highway from our right from a side road and seemed like it was slowing down to stop. As we got closer to the intersection, the car did not stop, but just kept going straight out across the highway. I had to swerve to miss that car and by inches just passed in front of it. Had I stepped on the brakes, I would have hit that car broadside on the driver's side and there would have been a very serious accident. By swerving to the left, I had just enough to get past and ended up on the shoulder on the opposite side of the road. I know there were two people in the car, whether male or female I don't know because it all was happening so quickly, that there was no time to see who they were. They were either blinded by the setting sun, or maybe they just had one or two too many in the bar and could not see the stop sign or us coming on the highway. Whichever it was, I don't know, but I should have just turned around and followed that car to see what was what, but after getting into such a shock, one cannot think or act as quickly. This was a very serious offence that the driver of that car had committed for not stopping at the stop sign, because had I not missed him, there could have been four people killed at that intersection. It was a shock but we made it home still trembling and shaking from the effects.

On November 17th we got another call from Doris telling us the sad news that Peter passed away and she wants us to come to the funeral. Only eight days when we came from Vernon and a thousand miles away, we now turn around and make another trip to Vernon. Prayers for Peter were held on November 21st (St. Michaels Day) and the funeral the following day. Fathers Mykola Stetzenko of Vernon and Isidore Woronchak of Surrey B.C. conducted the funeral service in the funeral chapel. I had been asked by Doris to give the eulogy, which I did. After the funeral we stayed with Doris overnight and left back for home early the next morning arriving home in Yorkton on November 24th after those sad days.

Meanwhile when we were gone from Yorkton, our good friend Andrew Antony had the key to our house and we told him to check the house and pick up our mail. Andrew did not want to go to the funeral, even though he knew Peter very well, because he said it would be too hard for him to face the situation. When we arrived home after the funeral on November 24th, we called Andrew to come over for supper for we were having varenyky for supper and we would tell him about the funeral. Andrew came over and we told him about the funeral. As we were having supper and Andrew was with us, another thing changed Marusia's and my life again. Since we have been married for the past five years we have already moved three times. From Moose Jaw, Saskatchewan to Salmon Arm, than Vernon, British Columbia and now Yorkton, Saskatchewan Now another historical event was on the horizon.

A HISTORICAL MOVE - PHOENIX, ARIZONA

As we were having supper, the telephone rang. The church executive from Phoenix, Arizona was calling me to come and serve their parish. This is not the first time for we well know that Phoenix had been in the process of getting me to come and serve their parish. The first time I heard of Phoenix that I had anything to do with it, was still back in Dauphin in 1974-75. The late Bill Perepeluk of Dauphin and earlier from Flin Flon, Manitoba, had traveled all over the USA and had spent many winters in Phoenix many times.

In Phoenix he had found the Ukrainian Orthodox Church and attended their services during the winter months. The congregation was small and poor. They had an old priest who served them. When Mr. Perepeluk came home, he asked me if the church in Dauphin had any old vestments that were not used, which can be donated to Phoenix to help the small congregation. At a monthly meeting we brought up this topic and the congregation in Dauphin obliged and we sent two pairs of used vestments for the Phoenix congregation. I never dreamt that some twenty years later I would be wearing those vestments serving in Phoenix. If someone would have told me than about this, I would have told that person they did not know what they were talking about or would have asked them what they were smoking.

As mentioned previously while we lived in Vernon we already had received a few phone calls from Phoenix asking me to come serve the church there. Each time I tried asking the Primate of the church in Canada to release me from church duties, but the answer was always the same: "nyet," because I remarried and broke a canon law. The people in Vernon and Kamloops had also asked the Primate to reinstate me so that I would serve the Kamloops congregation. People were saying that I was too young to retire. The congregation in Kamloops had never even asked me if I was willing and agreeable to serve them but they took upon themselves and asked the church headquarters in Winnipeg about reinstating me to serve them.

When the congregation in Kamloops received a negative reply, they mailed me the copies of the letters telling me what they had done and asked what I will do. When I received the letter from Kamloops what they had done, I also wrote a letter to the Primate, only he did not answer me, but the chairman of the presidium wrote back that I cannot serve anymore. This was somewhat queer to me. I wrote the letter to the Primate, but received a letter from the chairman of the presidium of the Consistory. If I want the chairman to write to me, I will write to him, but when I write a letter to someone, I want that person to write to me. I want the person I wrote to, to answer me. If the person I wrote to can't read or write than tell me and I can phone him.

I had asked the primate of the church three times to bring me back into the service again, and each time the answer was always the same. They were glad that they finally got rid of me, because now the clergy can go easy and don't have to work like Reverend Stefaniuk had done. The people wanted me to serve, but the few people at the top of the church would not permit it. I had a good life with Marusia. My headaches were now gone. The nose bleeds stopped. We had a roof over our head, a bed to sleep on and a piece of bread on the table. I was not looking for any work, but the people were after me to get back into service. Marusia and I had enough church work. What else did I need? It was the people who wanted me to serve them. The people asked me and I asked the Primate to permit me to go back to serve, but I was denied each time. The people from Kamloops,

Kelowna and Phoenix, Lac La Biche, Oakburn, and Prince George were denied their request each time. The people's wishes should be fulfilled. Each time the people asked me to serve them, I would turn around and ask the Primate and each time I received a negative answer.

So when we got the phone call from Phoenix, (from Mr. Bilyk,) on November 24th, and Andrew Antony was present, I did not hesitate anymore to ask the Primate if I could go to Phoenix. Time and again I was refused and denied in Canada, but when the cry came from, " the wilderness" from Phoenix, I accepted and did not ask anyone anymore. Andrew Antony heard the conversation, because I had the speaker phone on. We asked Andrew not to tell anything to anyone what he heard of the conversation on the speaker phone and to keep it a secret until we learn more what will be transpiring. In the meantime I had told Mr. Bilyk that I would need permission from the primate in the USA to come and serve there. Mr. Bilyk said that a letter to me would be in the mail tomorrow because everything had been taken care of with their Primate, Metropolitan Constantine. He also said the Consistory in the USA gave their consent that I could come and serve. Mr. Bilyk said they are asking me to come serve them for six months during the winter season. With this communication, the wheels were greased and set in motion. Now we need to pack again. But what do we take with us? Mr. Bilyk told us that they have a residence for the priest and every thing in the house that we would need.

We had a 1992 Pontiac Grand AM, but what can you put into that sized car to take with you for a few months from home and some two thousand miles from our house in Canada. We need a bigger vehicle to take some of our personal things with us. I will need some books and take the computer for I will need that and our clothing. We went to our friend Evan Ortynski at Key Chev in Yorkton and told him that we wanted to trade our car and a small Ford Ranger truck for a van. We made a deal and bought a brand new 1994 Lumina Van.

We had decided that we would tell no one anything that we are leaving Yorkton for the winter and heading south to Phoenix. Andrew Antony knew what was happening and we asked him not to say anything to anyone until we break the news ourselves. We thought that if anyone should ask us why we traded our car and truck for the van, we would tell them that we did not need two vehicles. We would not say anything to anyone until a day or two before we leave for the USA. My mother used to say: "We make plans and God changes them." That is what happened to our plans of retirement.

Father N. Rauliuk and I were members of the Order of St. Andrew and we were in the process of setting up a branch of the Order in Yorkton. We agreed before hand that I would take the position of the president and than we would elect the rest of the executive at the first inaugural meeting which was yet to have a date set up. One day Father Nicholas Rauliuk phoned and said that the meeting was going to be on such and such a date. When he told me the date, I knew I would not be there since we would already be in the USA by that time.

Instead of making it hard for the organization and not telling the truth, I had to tell Father Rauliuk that Marusia and I will not be in Canada on that day during the winter, because we are leaving Yorkton to warmer climate in the states. He asked and wanted to know where we were going. I had to tell him the truth and when I did, I did not know what was happening at the other end. For a while I thought he had hung up the phone, for there was no answer at his end. I guess he was in shock to hear the news of what was taking place. Finally he began to ask, how, when, what, etc. I told him that even Andrew Antony was at our place and heard the conversation on the phone when we got the call to go to Phoenix.

We thought everything would go well, but than Marusia thought that maybe we should get in touch with the USA Immigration Department to ask if I can serve in the USA. We called the USA Immigration in Calgary, Alberta a number of times and each time we were welcomed with a recording. We left the message, but never got any answer back. Marusia got a phone number for the customs at North Portal, south of Yorkton where we had decided that we would cross into the USA when we leave for Phoenix. We called there and they said that we would need a letter from the congregation in Phoenix showing that they have no priest and are asking me to come and serve there. They would also need proof that I have been a clergyman for a minimum of two years. When we heard this, we knew at that time there was a letter on the way from the congregation, but it was in Ukrainian, so what good would that do at the border if no one can read in Ukrainian. Because it was Christmas season drawing near, it would take a letter longer to get to us.

We called Mr. Bilyk in Phoenix and told him the circumstances and asked that the congregation write a letter in English and mail it to Father Rauliuk on the fax number we gave him. We talked with Mr. Bilyk in the morning and that same day afternoon Father Rauliuk called and said that there was a Fax message for us at his place. We were now busy packing and getting ready to leave for the USA. In the evening we went to pick up the fax. While there as we were talking, Father and Dobrodeyka Rauliuk told us they were somewhat concerned about us leaving because health care is very expensive in the USA and what happens if we get to Phoenix and the bishop will not permit me to serve. Our trip to Phoenix would than be in vain. When we got home we decided it would be better to call the Primate in the USA and ask him if he would give his blessing for the congregation in Phoenix and for me that I go and serve them. I knew the Primate, Metropolitan Constantine, because we both attended St. Andrew's College Seminary in Winnipeg at the same time.

Next morning we called Metropolitan Constantine and told him what was what. He said that he knew about that situation. I asked him if he will give his blessing that I go to serve in Phoenix. He said that he had nothing against that and said to call Father William Diakiw at the Consistory in South Bound Brook, New Jersey and talk to him about this matter. We called Father Diakiw and as soon as I said who was calling, the first thing he asked was: "Are you already in Phoenix?" I told him that we are still in Canada at home. Than he says: "I thought you were already in Phoenix, because they are waiting for you there." He said everything was okay and I could go and serve that parish. He also wanted to know how long we would stay in Phoenix. I told him that the congregation asked us to come for at least six months. Having this assurance that I can serve in Phoenix, we were now ready to leave and were more at ease.

Before we left for Phoenix, we purchased some health insurance. We bought six months of health coverage and paid $1600.00 for it in Yorkton. Why it was so expensive is for the reason that I was going to work there, not for leisure or any holiday as tourists go for the winter season. We were not "snow birds", but I was going as a working person. We would be returning back in the spring, but it never worked out that way as we will see when the story unfolds.

When we purchased the van, that same day we went to have it registered to have a licence on it. As the lady at the counter was filling the form, she asked if our address was still the same. We told her that in a few days we will be leaving for the USA where I will be serving a church but we do not know the address where we will be staying. She told us that when we get to the USA and know our address, to write to the Government of Saskatchewan and the Government will refund us the Sales Tax on the vehicle which was about $2000.00. She gave us the address in Regina and told us to do that as soon as we get to Phoenix and have our new place of residence. So we are leaving Canada for six months, but now what happens with our custom built house for the next six months? We can't take it with us in the van. What should happen if the furnace stops when it is minus forty below and the water pipes freeze? That would cause a lot of damage later. Once again we turned to Andrew Antony our life saver. We asked him if he would be able to check from time to time to see that everything is all right. He agreed to do so and said it would not be a hindrance for him. With all things (hopefully) in order and cleared up as best we knew, we left Yorkton at 6:00 AM on December 7th and headed south in a winter snow storm. Our van was taking us south away from the cold Canadian winter and into a new life. What awaited us at the end of our journey, only God knew.

We arrived at the border some three hours later and the man that had talked with me on the phone a few days earlier recognized my voice and took us into his office. He asked us how long we plan to stay in Phoenix and we told him six months as far as we know. He checked over our papers and than went to check something with another person in another room. He came back and said that we can stay up to three years on the permit that he issued for each of us. On the back of my permit he stamped: "EMPLOYMENT PERMITTED." Marusia's permit did not get that stamp. He also told us to check in with the Immigration Department as soon as we get to Phoenix.

After we were through with the Immigration, he told us to go to another counter and check with the customs people who were across from him. The man from the customs said that he wanted to see our vehicle. We went outside which was cold and blustery with swirling snow. He checked under the hood, than the door of the van and said that we will have trouble, because our van does not conform to USA safety standards. We went inside and he looked at some books and than he said that he does not know what kind of regulations Arizona has, so he will let us go after having spent an hour at the border.

As soon as we left the border crossing and drove for half an hour or so, the wind had stopped, the skies were clear and sunny like in a different world. USA was greeting us with beautiful sunshine. That day we got to Spearfish, South Dakota in the Black Hills about which you have previously heard about the Passions of Christ. Next day we left early, still in darkness, and for about fifty miles traveled on packed snow which was ice and slow traveling. Winter days are short and in two weeks it will be the shortest day of the year and you cannot make as many miles in the winter as in the summer in one days travels. We traveled to Trinidad, Colorado and spent the next night there. The rest of the way to Phoenix, the road was clear and dry.

The third day we arrived at Flagstaff, Arizona which is about three hours north of Phoenix and we could have driven to Phoenix, but did not want to arrive at night. We could have driven all the way to Phoenix that day, but decided it was better to spend the night and arrive in Phoenix in the daytime where we will be able to find addresses and better to see where we are. We were to stop at Mr. Bilyk's place when we arrive in Phoenix, because he is just two blocks off the highway on which we would come in from Flagstaff.

On December 10th we left Flagstaff and arrived in Phoenix at 10:00 AM having found Mr. Bilyk's residence. Coming off the I-17 Freeway it was easy to find his place. We got acquainted with Mr. Bilyk and Mrs. Shultz. Mr. Bilyk called someone on the phone telling them that we had arrived. In a few minutes Mr. Mykola Kushtch arrived and we were introduced. Mr. Bilyk and Mr. Kushtch drove ahead and we followed them to the residence where we would be making our next home for a while. After looking at the residence we drove to see the church. We looked at and in the church and then followed them to a restaurant called: "Country Harvest" where buffet meals are served. At this same restaurant were a number of Ukrainian Catholic church members who were having a memorial dinner after they had a service in their church. We got introduced to them. After dinner we were given the keys to the condo and the church.

Sunday December 12th is my first service in Phoenix. After not having served for five years and in a different country, one is somewhat rusty at the beginning. Many unexpected things could jump out: how will the cantor or choir sing? How will the elder brother assist me in the Sanctuary? How will the service go? How many mistakes will I make? Every priest when he comes to a new parish is always uneasy at the first service. After the last Amen was sung, I was wet as if I had come out of a shower. I knew after the service ended that things would be okay because the first service went well as if I had been in the congregation for a number of years. The only difference was that I had to pray for a different bishop and the government leaders of the USA.

WORK IN A NEW COUNTRY

At this service and the following ones, we met many people. That was not unusual, because when a new priest comes into a new parish, people flock to his first service. They want to see and hear the priest. What kind eyes, does he have? Are his ears large and protruding? Can you hear him when he speaks? Can he sing and serve well? What is his sermon like? Can you understand him or does he mumble and slur words? People come to judge the priest on his first service. The following Sunday we met even more people, because many "Canadian snow birds" came to the service. The phone messages went all over Phoenix that the congregation has a priest and more people attended the service. "Snow birds" is a name given to those people from Canada, that come to spend the winters in Arizona. The second service I had was on December 19th and after the service I had a baptism, baptizing a child, Larysa Petrenko.

The first two weeks were heavy and hard for us. It was lonely. We saw our members only in church on Sunday morning. We did not know the city yet and suburbs of three million people. At times we were lonely for the families and we were ready to pack up and go back home from where we came. When we heard of all the homicides in the city of some two hundred and some people murdered in a year in Phoenix in 1993, that was not encouragement to stay. But slowly, slowly we got to know more people and started visiting them, getting to know the city, we began to feel more relaxed and at home. And than when we thought of winter back in Canada, the cold, snow and storms, we began to talk and feel that it was much better in the warm climate. Now came Christmas and no close family. But what kind of Christmas is this? No snow, everything green, flowers blooming, and where is the snow in the winter? We finally began to realize that this was a winter where we needed no snow shovel or heavy winter clothing. We began to feel that we could live with this kind of winter.

Next came Epiphany. The service was held in church and the water is blessed. Now we go and visit the parishioners to bless their homes with holy water and prayer. We did not go to bless houses, for a house is not what a home is. A house is a building, a home is a family even though some people do call a house a home. We drove and visited the people and things began to change and we began feeling better. Driving around on January 19th and 20th, we had to turn on the air conditioner because it was so hot. As we drove around thoughts came to us how in Canada God was turning on the air conditioner with cold, cold winter weather where a person at times could not stay outside for more than a short time or stay out and get frost bitten. Thinking of all the cold and snow in Canada, maybe this place in Phoenix is not so bad after all. At least the heat, we don't have to shovel and if it gets warm, we turn on the air conditioner for comfort and stay inside.

After we also met more "snow birds" from Canada we began to feel more comfortable and at home. They came to church every Sunday, many driving as far as twenty and more miles. Than my cousin Alex Korzeniwski and wife Sylvia from Kelowna were there every winter and we could phone or visit them. There were some "snow birds" from Canada whom we had known personally from earlier times. The parishioners began to make us feel more like at home and this eased our loneliness for home. When you get a cold shoulder from people, than you know you are not welcome, but when the people showed their warmth and hospitality, we felt welcome, comfortable and being wanted. We became acquainted with the new city, new country, new people and life was becoming more normal.

On December 24th Marusia and I were invited to supper with Alex and Sylvia. The following day we again were invited to supper at Alex's brother Stan and his wife Ellen. Now the new 1994 year arrived. Those adhering to the Julian Calendar celebrate the Nativity of the Lord on January 7th on the Gregorian Calendar. On January 6th it is a strict fast day and there are twelve lenten dishes for this meal. Because we had known John and Jean Sawchyn before and they came to Phoenix for the winter months, they invited us to have Christmas Eve Supper with them. Marusia had met John and Jean Sawchyn years earlier before we were married when she went on a trip to the Holy Land with a tour. After two weeks, comes another lenten supper on the eve of Epiphany. On these two days the family always tries to be together for supper.

FAMILY FROM CANADA ARRIVES

My sister Alice and her husband John had left St. Benedict, Sask., and were heading south to the USA as far as Phoenix. We were expecting them to be in Phoenix for January 18th and we would have supper together. We were in touch with family in Canada and knew they were coming. We had called father one day and he says: "Tomorrow I am leaving for Edmonton and than with John and Kay we are going to Phoenix." That made us feel good. Some family will be together. We wondered how father would make it sitting in a car for three days to travel at his age of ninety two. Anyway we were awaiting John and Alice along with father, John and Kay on the 18th of January.

Then things went from bad to worse. When father had arrived in Edmonton at John's place, there had been a winter storm outside. Next day John went to clear the sidewalks and father went with him, but what did father do? He went outside into the cold frosty and windy air without buttoning his jacket up. He said and thought it was warm outside and he said he felt warm. Next morning they were leaving for Phoenix with father already somewhat not feeling well - "under the weather". They traveled three days and father's condition was not getting better but worse. Kay also had not been feeling too well and they all should have stayed home until everybody was well. Father had caught a cold and it must have effected his prostrate. He must have had prostrate trouble from earlier, but never mentioned anything to anyone because he was embarrassed. We knew of a person in Canada, that when he caught a cold, his prostate inflamed and he suffered terribly. This must have happened to father because he had problems going to the bathroom and water was retained in his bladder, but he would not tell anyone what problem he had.

Marusia and I were waiting to hear the door bell ring, because we knew that Alice and John were already in Phoenix by now. On January 17th the door bell rang. We were sure it was Alice and John. We opened the door and there in the doorway stood father looking half alive with John and Kay who looked as though they had gone through a wringer washing machine. It wasn't until the following morning that Alice and John arrived at our place. They had spent a few days in Las Vegas. On January 18th, we also had Alex and Sylvia for supper joining our family.

On the 19th of January we are having a service and blessing of water in the church. Everybody was up and preparing for church when Kay said that she was feeling sick and would not be going to church with us. Seeing the condition of father and Kay, Marusia says: "John, you better pack up father and Kay and head back for home as soon as you can before something worse happens." At 9:00 AM, John started his car and with the two patients on his hands started the trek back for home to Canada. We asked John to keep in touch with us from the trip how things will be going for them.

When father had arrived on January 17th, he never went outside until January 19th when they started heading back for home. That was not our father, for our father could not sit still for five minutes, but always on the go unless he was asleep. The whole time long he would not touch anything to eat and stayed in bed. We knew he was not well, but he never told what was bothering him. So the three of them came to Phoenix and didn't see anything, didn't go anywhere and didn't buy anything because of the illness.

That evening John called us to tell what was happening. He said that when they got to Las Vegas, father told him that he would not make it home to Canada. So what did John do? He put father on a plane to Edmonton and called their son-in-law in Edmonton to pick father up at the airport and take father to the hospital. Alice, John, Marusia and I were sitting on pins and needles all this time wondering what is happening.

Each time the phone rang, we jumped and always feared that the worst had happened.

In the meantime father got to Edmonton on the plane. The late Peter Onyshko picked him up and took him to emergency. They checked father over and would not admit him to the hospital because he was out of the province even though he had health insurance covered by the Canadian Health System. Peter Onyshko brought father to his place and there father stayed until John returned home. When John arrived home and learned what had happened, he filled the car with gas, put father in the car and headed out with him to the Cudworth Hospital where father would be only two blocks from his house. After we learned that father was safe in Cudworth, Alice and John left with the plane to Corpus Christi, Texas on January 22nd for a five or six day holiday.

In the meantime Alice and John's daughters back home knew that father was in the hospital in Cudworth, so they went to visit him. The granddaughters visited father(dido) in the hospital. Later that day Pat Walker their oldest daughter called us asking if John and Alice were at our place. We told her they went to Corpus Christi for a few days, but we don't know where they are staying. Pat got on the phone and through police channels located John and Alice and told them: "If you want to see dido(our father) alive, you better come home quickly." John and Alice called us to pick them up at the airport next morning in Phoenix. We picked them up, they had dinner and they left immediately for home. That day they drove all the way to Salt Lake City where they stopped, because they were tired and it was past midnight. Kay also was not feeling well. She had surgery on January 28th. There were now two people, family members in the hospital. We were keeping in touch with the people back home to know what was happening.

After John and Alice arrived home, they kept us informed as to what was happening with father. She said the doctors could not find anything wrong, because they were doing all kinds of tests and nothing was showing up that was wrong. Why? Because father was not telling them what was bothering him. He did not tell the doctors that he could not urinate. His prostate had become enlarged so much that the water could not pass through from the bladder.

One day John and Alice went to Saskatoon. Coming home they had met an ambulance going to Saskatoon. They came to Cudworth, and stopped at the hospital to see father, but he was not there. The nurse told them that the ambulance had taken him to Saskatoon. They turned around and headed back to Saskatoon some fifty miles. In Saskatoon with special doctors and instruments, they very soon diagnosed what the problem was. After that they sent him back home to the hospital in Cudworth. Later we learned they had drained over seven hundred and fifty milliliters of fluid from father's bladder. During that time we also called from home to the Cudworth Hospital asking about father's condition.

After Marusia and I arrived in Phoenix we went to see the immigration department. It also became evident to us in a few days, that we will stay longer than six months in Phoenix. The people were already beginning to tell us that they want us to stay on and they would keep us in Phoenix for a longer time. We learned that our stay would be indefinite. Knowing this and having gotten acquainted with the people and the city, we decided that we would stay as long as the people wanted us or something unforeseen should come up. Having learned of this, we called Andrew Antony in Yorkton and told him what was what and asked him to put up a "For Sale" sign in the window of our house. We knew that we could not have someone looking after our house when we are away having firstly promised that we would be back in six months. One other thing was that when we return back to Canada we may decide to settle someplace else and will need to sell the house in Yorkton anyway.

At the end of January our custom built house in Yorkton was already up for sale. It did not take long to sell the house. In less than a week after the sign was put up, we got a call from Andrew Antony that there is a buyer for our house. He wanted to know if we would accept the offer. I was not even home when he called. I was at a church meeting. Marusia called me at the church and told me the news. When I came home from the meeting we called Andrew Antony that evening telling him that we accept the offer and the house was sold. At least now we would not have to worry that someone may break in, or the furnace may stop in the middle of winter time and damage could be done, or involve someone to look after the house for months on end.

When the house was sold, we had to go back to Canada to close the deal and move our things out since the buyers wanted possession of the house at the end of February. After the church service on February 6th (six years after our betrothal) we left for Canada, going through Globe Arizona and stopping at Grant's in New Mexico for the night. The next day we got to Spearfish, South Dakota and on February 8th we arrived in Yorkton at 6:00 PM. Immediately we began packing, because the buyers wanted to move in and we wanted to get back to Phoenix as soon as possible. When the people in Phoenix heard that we sold our house, they were very happy, because they knew we would be staying longer than six months with them. What a hectic time we had that week. Pack, get the services disconnected, change of address, etc.

Having been in Phoenix for some two months, we now knew more less, what we needed to take back with us from Canada, but than what happens with the rest of the things? We were fortunate because the buyers also purchased all the furniture and appliances. That was a big relief. We phoned a few people that we had some smaller items for sale - like a garage sale. People came from everywhere and many things were bought by them and some things we donated to the church and organizations in Yorkton. When we were already leaving Yorkton, people were stilling coming to the house wanting to purchase things, but there was nothing left to sell.

So we packed everything we needed to take with us, but what about the rest of the things that we do not need? We were in touch with Alice and John and John asked what we will be doing with our things. We said we would put everything in storage, but John said to bring the things to their place and put it in the empty granaries on the farm. When we had everything packed, John and Alice came with their van and a Toyota truck to help bring things to their place. We packed both their vehicles and our van and headed for St. Benedict, Sask., on February 13th. We unloaded the two vehicles and had supper. After supper we went to Cudworth Hospital to see father. He looked much better than he did when he had come with John and Kay to Phoenix a few weeks earlier. We also told him that we sold our house and we would be staying in Phoenix longer than six months. The money from the sale of the house we invested in two banks.

On February 16th we left John and Alice's place at 7:30 AM on our trip back to Phoenix. We stopped at the hospital in Cudworth to see father on our way home. Leaving Cudworth we drove to Alberta and down to Sweet Grass, Montana to cross the border into USA. At the border we encountered a problem. Customs people would not let us enter the USA because our vehicle did not conform to the USA safety standards. The vehicle was probably built in the USA and now they would not let us cross into the USA with it. The customs officer then said that he would let us in if we signed a paper, that would permit them to come and forfeit our van if we do not have it registered in the USA. What else can one do in a situation like this? We signed the paper and told the custom officer that we had already started the registration process in Phoenix to register the vehicle. He looked at us and said that the Federal law is greater than the state law. He was also kind enough to tell us what to do. He told us to do three things:

1. He told us to write a letter to General Motors in Detroit for information to see if our van conforms to the USA safety standards.
2. When we get a letter from General Motors, than write to the Department of Transport in Washington to get permission to bring our vehicle into the USA.
3. After the above two have been done, send copies of that correspondence to him at Sweet Grass, Montana for approval of the papers.

Having signed the papers and told what to do, we continued on our trip spending nearly an hour at the Custom Office.

After leaving St. Benedict that same day we reached Great Falls, Montana where we stopped for the night. Next morning we continued our trek south and got as far as St. George, Utah. This was a nice place with red rocks in the area and later we learned that the area is prone to earthquakes. On the third day February 18th we arrived back in Phoenix just before the sun set, both tired and somewhat worn out from the whole ordeal. We unloaded the van, but did not unpack anything until the following day. We were just to tired to do anything more.

From now on we both got involved in the church even more, knowing that we will be there for an indefinite period of time. We wanted to get more acquainted with the parishioners. We spent more time visiting people in their homes, getting to know them better and to see what activities we could have in the church. We had visited a few families when we arrived in Phoenix, but when Epiphany came on January 19th, we visited thirty eight homes of parishioners blessing their homes with holy water. It was at this time that I was also asked to teach religion in a Ukrainian hall. The local Ukrainian Congress of America had a hall which was a few blocks from where we lived. One lady taught Ukrainian language and I taught religion once a week. The hall was just a few blocks away. To church it was about five or six miles. And so our work in the church continued. We visited people during the day and at night we tried to stay home. We were not at ease to travel at night, because there was just too much crime at night.

Now Easter (Christ's Resurrection) was coming and there are many more different services during the lenten period. Before Easter, we learned that one church in Phoenix had a seating capacity of six and a half thousand people and they were putting on an Easter pageant. Marusia, two church members and I took in the performance one day. To say the truth, the performance itself is worth seeing, but where and how it is held is another story. The pageant is held inside their church. The altar is moved or taken away for the performance. Inside into the church they brought camels, donkeys, sheep, doves, etc. Animals inside the church? The pageant takes place where the altar stands. We were told that one year during the pageant a camel had a nature call, and so it did its thing where the altar usually stands. Is this sacrilegious or what? What would Jesus say if He walked into that church and saw what was happening? Would He take a rope and chase everybody and everything out as we read in the Bible, like He did to the money changers?

It is written: "....*He drove them all out of the temple, the sheep and the oxen, and poured out the changers money, and overthrew the tables........*" (John 2:14-16) Is that pageant dishonoring His Church? To me that kind of pageant should be held outdoors or in theatres, not in a church. Can anyone say that such a building is a church? The animals do not know the difference between holiness and sacrilegious, so people should know better. Jesus chased the: "sheep and oxen" out of the temple, and here in the twentieth Century we see people bringing animals into a temple (church) opposite to what Christ did when He came to the temple when He was on earth.

But let's go back to our van. When we arrived in Phoenix, we immediately started to get our van registered in Arizona. We wrote a letter to General Motors and in one week we had a reply that our van conformed to the USA safety standards. Having that letter, we wrote a letter to the Department of Transport in Washington and sent them a copy that the van conforms to the safety standards of USA. We waited. And we waited some more. After five weeks we finally got a reply from the Department of Transport. When we got letters from the two places, we made copies and sent the originals to the customs at Sweet Grass, Montana. The letter from the Department of Transport said they had nothing to do with registering the vehicle in Arizona. This was contrary to what the man at the border had told us, that the federal law was greater than the state law. In just over a week we received the copies of the letters from the customs at Sweet Grass, all stamped and okayed. Now we knew that the van would not be forfeited.

As soon as we got the clearance from Sweet Grass, we went to get the van registered. The people at the registration told us, that before they can register our van, they have to have proof that we have insurance coverage on the van and also have an emission test. In the meantime we had called about twenty to thirty insurance agencies inquiring about the insurance. We finally settled on AAA because for an extra $4.00 we had better and more coverage. With the insurance at hand, we went to get an emission test and came out with a clean slate. Now we went and had the van registered and received the licence plates. The registration and plate for one year was $387.00. Insurance cost $526.00 for six months. When we had registered the van in Yorkton, Saskatchewan, the registration and plates cost $469.00 for a year. We can see the difference in costs between one country and another, or one state and another. We were told and shown on a map at AAA, that had we lived just four blocks farther away where we were living, our insurance rates would have been very much reduced. We lived in a high accident and crime area, so the rates were so much higher there. But than the coverage in Saskatchewan was still much lower than what we got from AAA in Arizona.

The cost of gasoline in the USA was also so much cheaper than in Canada. When we first arrived in Phoenix in December 1993, the unleaded gas was selling anywhere from $1.09 to $1.15 a gallon, not a litre. Later prices slowly increased and for super unleaded gas the price was

$1.31 a gallon. We also learned another thing, that in Nevada there are no self service stations, because that is their law.

After we got our van registered, the following day we went to get our drivers licences. It was not hard to get that either. When we went to get the licence, I told Marusia that she wait until I get the licence. Suppose we both would have went and failed, than what? How would we get around without a driver's licence? I passed my written exam, but did not have to take a driver's test. When I got my licence, than Marusia went and she passed her written exam with even a higher mark than I had, but the questions were different when we asked each other what the answer was for such and such a question. In a few days we got our driver's licences in the mail. The cost was $10.00 for six years. I remember father saying that the driver's licence in Saskatchewan was $25.00 per year. In Arizona $10.00 for six years.

We are now holding choir practices to the middle of May, because on May 14th there is a marriage in our congregation. George Cooley who lived some hundred miles north of Phoenix was getting married. His father is a priest in our church in eastern USA. George is marrying a young lady from Ukraine. Both the bride and groom are choir conductors. Archbishop Anthony from South Bound Brook, New Jersey will perform the marriage, because Archbishop Anthony knew George since he was a small boy and was his Altar server. George wanted the Archbishop to perform the marriage for that reason. The marriage was held in the Greek Orthodox Cathedral in Phoenix, because our church was too small for the people that would attend. The reception was held at the Hilton Hotel at the airport.

Next day being Sunday, we had a Pontifical church Service in the church. Archbishop Anthony, Father Victor Cooley(the grooms father) and I served in the Pontifical Divine Liturgy. The bride and groom were also in church and the groom conducted the choir, singing responses in the Liturgy. Archbishop Anthony had come to Phoenix on May 11th and stayed until May 17th spending that time to relax from his busy schedule.

BACK TO CANADA?

It was in May when we received a letter from the congregation at Kamloops, B.C., tellingus they completed their new church and are asking us to come to the official openinand blessing. They asked me to be the MC for their afternoon program. We started making plans to attend this function. When we lived at Salmon Arm and Vernon, we never missed any services that were held in Kamloops and had many friends there. Now we would have a chance to visit and see many of our acquaintances. The church blessing is to take place on June 26th.

Another small problem came up. Mother passed away on June 23rd 1993. My sister Alice and father had booked the priest, hall and ladies to have a memorial service for mother on June 25th, the day before the church blessing in Kamloops. We wanted to attend the memorial service, but how can we be in two places one day after the other with some seven hundred miles apart. We thought we could take a flight to Saskatoon from Kamloops and someone could pick us up in Saskatoon. We could leave Kamloops Friday and return Saturday after the service. We checked the airline schedules. The last flight leaving Saskatoon for Kamloops on Saturday June 25th was 1:55 PM. When you fly, you have to be at the airport at least an hour before flight time. It takes an hour to drive from Cudworth to Saskatoon. That would mean we would have to leave

Cudworth at 11:55 AM. At 11:00 AM, the service in church would still not be over.

The other thing was the cost. Air Canada wanted $699.00 return fare per person from Kamloops to Saskatoon. In the USA you fly for half the cost. In June 1994 Marusia and I flew from Phoenix to Newark, New Jersey and return for $632.00 return for both of us. That is just about from coast to coast of a few thousand miles and non stop. In Canada Air Canada wanted more money from one person and travel was only a quarter of the distance. We flew to South Bound Brook, because it was a one year anniversary that Patriarch Mystyslaw had passed away. The church had a sarcophagus built and he was buried inside the basement of the memorial church at South Bound Brook, New Jersey.

Before we left for Canada, things went along with always something doing just about each and every day. We are preparing to leave for Canada on June 19th. In the meantime the temperature was getting hotter and hotter. How hot? Too hot. How we survived that summer heat, I still do not know till now. Anyway the hottest it had reached was +46 C., or 114 F. There was one incident which was reported on Television. A mother and her child were walking on the sidewalk. The child tripped and fell. The child got burned so bad on the hot sidewalk, that she had to be taken to the hospital with second degree burns. The temperature of the sidewalk was taken and it showed +77 C or 171 F. That is just too hot.

Even though it gets that hot everything is still green in the city. Why? They pump water from the Colorado River near Las Vegas about a hundred and seventy five miles to water the crops, gardens, orchards and lawns. There are large gardens here and there. Garden crops are ripened and harvested. Anything that is left over that is not needed, they announce on the radio that people can go and help themselves to the crop on the fields. Help yourself to onions, grapes, watermelons, etc. Onions people picked for free about the middle of April. We picked all the onions we wanted and already had them in our shed in April. Grapes, you pick and pay twenty cents a pound.

Anyway back to our trip to Canada. We left on Sunday June 19th after the church service. We took a different route going west into Las Vegas and than on to Beatty, Nevada where we spent the night. Before we reached Beatty, it was already dark and the lights were on. We could see many and all kinds of lights in the distance which looked like a town and we asked the people in the motel what those lights were because there was nothing on the map showing any town. We were told that no one knows what those lights are and what goes on around there because it was a restricted area. We were told that day or night there is always a lot of activity going on there and the place is known as area 51 a top secret location.

Next morning we left Beatty and were going through Tonopah. We were going down a long curved hill and watching for the highway junction that we were to turn to. We must have been going too fast, for lo and behold all of a sudden a sheriff on a motorcycle is behind us with red lights flashing. We stopped and he came over and said that he was trying to slow us down because we were going over the speed limit. I told him that we may having going to fast, because we were looking for the sign of the highway where we have to turn off. He checked my drivers licence and the registration with his radio on the motorcycle by phoning some place. He never gave us a ticket and was friendly and told us where to turn off to catch highway #376. He wished us to have a good and safe trip.

What a trip traveling through Nevada. You go for miles and miles and miles without seeing or meeting anyone in that semi desert land. At times we traveled even for fifteen miles before we met a vehicle. Nothing but desert with just a lone tree here and there. A very destitute area. The road is straight and you travel for fifteen or twenty miles in places, before you come to a curve in the road. That is how straight and flat Nevada is in places. That day we stopped at John Day, Oregon at a motel beside a gurgling brook. The following day we crossed the border at Osoyoos and stopped at Peachland where we stayed at Alex and Sylvia Korzeniowski's place. We spent two days at their place and visited other friends in Kelowna. Leaving Kelowna we stopped at Vernon to see Doris Chaykowski and than left for Kamloops on June 23rd.

The blessing of the church was a historical event in the lives for those people. It happens once in a person's lifetime. The church is beautiful. Not only parishioners can be proud of that accomplishment but also the city of Kamloops is now having such a beautiful edifice in their city.

On Saturday June 25th after supper, the blessing of water took place with some seven priests and Archbishop John of Edmonton and hundreds of people present from Alberta, Manitoba and British Columbia. Sunday morning at 7:00 AM a thunder and lightning storm rolled over the city with pouring rain. People looked saddened to see their day darkened by the dark hanging clouds. But, by 8:00 AM the clouds had moved away, the sun came out and the rest of the day was just what the parishioners had been praying for, a warm, sunny day. The official ribbon cutting took place on the steps of the church before the service started. That was followed by greeting Archbishop John, blessing of the church and the Divine Liturgy. Following this there was the procession around the church, for it was also the feast day of the congregation - All Saints.

After the service everyone went to the congregation hall just two blocks away. The church services used to be held in their hall before the church was built. A banquet fit for a king and queen had been prepared by the ladies. After the banquet was the program of which I was the MC. Everything was completed by 3:00 PM in the afternoon. The congregation sold their hall in 2013. They have a hall for their use under the church.

One thing I must mention here. Father Mykola Stetzenko told us that the chairman of the Presidium of the Consistory from Winnipeg will not be attending, because he will be with the Primate attending a special day at Saskatoon blessing the Ikonostas at All Saints congregation. He said that there will be five priests in attendance, but come Sunday, there were seven priests. On the Saturday afternoon we had gone to the church with Archbishop John joining Marusia and me for we were staying in the same motel in Kamloops. At the church when we arrived there were a few parishioners still doing odd things here and there getting everything ready for the evening to bless water and for tomorrow to bless the church.

We looked over the church and than two parishioners say: "We have to go to the airport to pick up the Chairman of the Presidium of the Consistory." We were surprised, because Father Stetzenko said that the Chairman of the Presidium was not coming. The chairman of the congregation before he went to the airport asked me if they should pay the Chairman of the Presidium for coming. I told him that if they invited him, they should pay, but he looked at me and says: "We are not going to pay him, because he gets paid by the Consistory to do this."

They went to the airport and shortly were back again with the chairman of the Presidium with them. The chairman of the Presidium went to Archbishop John and asked for the blessing. Than he went to the other people who were gathered in church and shook hands with them. He did not shake hands with Marusia and me, he only said: "Oh, and the Americans are here too." He had learned that I was to be MC and that I will be attending, so did he come to make sure that I would not be serving. I don't know what I ever did wrong to him or the church, but even during the program whom ever I called to speak, everyone in their remarks including Archbishop John respected the chairman by saying: "Reverend Father Chairman......" The Chairman of the Presidium did not even acknowledge the MC.

Following the blessing of the church on Sunday and with the longest days of summer upon us, we headed north on highway #5 heading towards Jasper, Alberta. We got as far as Valemount, B.C., that day and stopped there for the night. Remember when I was in Prince George I had sold a vacuum cleaner to a family who asked if I was God. Next morning we left to Edmonton where we stopped to see John and Kay. We spent the night with them and the following morning we left for Cudworth. John and Kay had been at the memorial service for mother a few days before we came to their place. They told us that father was not looking well at all and they were wondering how long he will last, a month or two. We arrived at Father's place on June 28th and as we were told, he did not look well at all and was not very stable. When he tried to get up from the chesterfield, he would rock himself two or three times before he got up, he was weak. We stayed with father on and off while in Saskatchewan from where we visited family and friends at Saskatoon, Regina, Dauphin, Yorkton and other places, but always returned back to Cudworth to be with father as much as possible.

Before we left back for Phoenix, we noticed a big change in father's health. He was starting to eat more and better and seemed to be getting his strength back. When we returned back to Phoenix, John called one day and said that he had visited father and that father had improved greatly from the last time he saw him at mother's memorial service. What had probably happened was that father had worried himself sick because of mother's memorial service. He always worried about everything and that service probably made him sick. Because everything went over well at the memorial service as we were told, he began to bounce back. Whenever we called him from Phoenix, his voice sounded stronger and he was telling us that he was thinking of joining the old and aged people. Father will be ninety four in April 1995. He had served in the First World War and was severely injured, but survived to his old age.

Then Sunday morning we bid farewell to father and went to the service in Saskatoon. From Saskatoon we drove to Regina to visit and stayed overnight with our friends John and Jean Sawchyn. We reached Regina that afternoon and that evening had supper at Jean's niece.

Next morning we left Regina and headed out to Plentywood, Montana. This day we drove until evening and we reached Red Lodge, Montana not too far from the Yellowstone National Park. We stayed at a cabin and was the fresh mountain air ever fresh filling up our lungs. The following day we drove into Yellowstone Park and toured in the park until late afternoon when we drove heading east to Cody, Wyoming to spend the night there. At Cody we were charged an arm and a leg for the motel. There were no rooms available because something was going on in the town, so we had to take what was left. It was the last room that this hotel had. As we were filling out the motel register, two more people came for a room, but were told there were no vacancies left. It cost us $69.00 for a tiny, dirty and filthy room with holes under the door and around the windows. The mattress was old, sagged and the bed creaked every time you turned in it.

The following morning we headed south to Thermopolis where we saw beautiful canyons. Down south we headed to Rock Springs and than into Utah to Vernal. Our van took us farther south and down to Price, Green River and stopped over night at Moab, Utah. Next morning we went to see more red rock canyons, arches, hills and valleys. We left Moab and stopped some fifteen miles south at Moab, Utah to see the "Hole in a rock" house. The Christian (surname) family who built that house have passed on, but the place is now used as a tourist stop. Girls from Moab come out and make jewelry, selling it and looking after the gift shop. The Christian family are buried just a few steps from the entrance of the "hole in the rock" house.

Stopping in the campground near the "Hole in the Rock", we had lunch and than headed out south to Monticello, Bluff, Mexican Hat and into Arizona. When we drove into Arizona, we thought we were already home. It seemed like we would still have to spend another night on the road, or if we head home without stopping we will get home very late. We took the chance and drove on reaching Phoenix at 9:00 PM that evening, just as the sun hid its face for this day behind the mountains.

The weather had been hot, that is spelled H O T and dry. No rain had fallen in Phoenix and they tell us on the news that this year Phoenix is two inches below normal rainfall. Than on July 28th something changed and the normal caught up. At 6:30 PM a storm came and lasted till 9:00 PM and it was a STORM. Power was out, thunder and lightning rumbled across the sky. The clouds opened up and poured out rain like from a pail. This was what they call in Arizona, "the monsoon season". On September 2nd another huge storm came along and this time it was even worst than the one before. It was a long week-end when this storm arrived. Power was out to some places from Friday to until Tuesday. In one hour two inches of rain poured into the valley. Streets became rivers and some roads were closed because of flooding. One man was killed by lightning when he went to close the windows in his car in the parking lot by a mall. On the radio and TV they kept telling and warning people that the best place during a thunder storm was to stay inside a building. There are many bridges in Phoenix that cross creeks or rivers, but there is no water in those rivers. When the monsoon comes the water comes and fills with overflowing some streets. In some lower spots where there is no bridge the road could be flooded and there are signs saying: "Do not enter when water on the road." Yes they have fines if you cross the river in the water. That is why there are no basements in Phoenix under the houses, because when the monsoon comes and the rain pours, it looks like all the buildings are in the water, because water is rushing in all directions to get to the lowest spot, the river or creek.

LIFE GOES ON IN PHOENIX

Marusia and I were praying that things would work out and be better for the congregation. Some members wanted to have a church in another area and a better building. At present the church and hall are one building without even a wall between and is very inconvenient. Another thing is you don't know what you may encounter when you come to church in the morning in that area. During the summer we started the services at 9:00 AM to beat the summer heat build up. On August 7th when Marusia and I came to church, on the west side of the church parking lot, in the shade a man was sleeping beside the wall. On August 19th we came to church and see only traces and marks left on the parking lot that some vehicle had burned there. On August 21st when we came for a service, on the same parking lot in the shade a young couple were sleeping. Another time we came and a man was sleeping on the south side of the church between the church and the shrub of bushes.

You don't dare wake anyone up, because you don't know who they are. He can have a hand gun or a knife and could attack you for disturbing him. Or they could come back later with a gang and attack the people in church during the service or when people are walking in or leaving the church. Unclear and unknown what such people can do. Call the police? Later they could take revenge against you and burn the church down, cause vandalism or whatever. At that time some members of the congregation were already looking for a better place where the church was located. Where the church is situated, there are drive by shootings, drugs in the building next door to the church, prostitution, vandalism, muggings, etc. The congregation owns a piece of land some ten miles north west of the present church. Maybe the time will come that this would be a better place for a church where it is more peaceful.

It is now September 21st 1994 and fall is just around the corner. In the morning we have a service for it is a Holy Day dedicated to the Virgin Mary, Her birth date. Afternoon at 2:00 PM I had the privilege and honor to go to the Phoenix City Hall to give a prayer for the opening of the Council meeting. A prayer to start a council meeting for such a huge city like Phoenix? Where in Canada does anyone hear of the city or town council have their meeting started by a member of the clergy? To offer prayers to God to start a council meeting in today's times is something else. Look around you and see how many empty churches there are on a Sunday morning. When you see a city begin their meeting with a prayer to God, than you know that city must also be blessed by God, a city of over one million people. How wonderful it would be if other cities and towns followed the example of Phoenix, to start council meetings with a prayer. Maybe some councils in Canada do open their meetings with regular council members saying some kind of a prayer or something. But how many councils have a different clergyman come each time to say a prayer or blessing to start a council meeting?

This same day in the evening the Ukrainian community and area played hosts to a group of performers from Ukraine, "Karpatsky Vizeroonok." This group put on a show of Ukrainian dance, song and music. We had seen this group previously in Canada at Dauphin, Manitoba in November 1992, when I was the guest speaker at the Auditorium's anniversary about which it has already been mentioned. After the performance in Phoenix we had the privilege of hosting two members of that group who stayed overnight with us. Performers were billeted out to Ukrainian people's homes in Phoenix. Those that stayed with us told us of the bad conditions in Ukraine. One of them made a phone call to Ukraine and the call at that time cost twenty dollars.

This year in October the congregation celebrated its Feast Day on October 16th. It's feast day falls on October 14th, but because it is a week day the feast day is celebrated on the closest Sunday to the 14th when more people can attend. It is a Holy Day "Protection of the Virgin Mary." At the feast day there were many people in church. This was the first chram I was serving in this congregation because we did not arrive in Phoenix in 1993 until December.

As mentioned earlier, when I was in Dauphin in the 1960's and 1970's the congregation from Dauphin had sent two pairs of used vestments for the church in Phoenix. Is that God's will or what that some twenty years later I am once again serving in those same vestments that I had served in Dauphin? When those vestments were sent from Dauphin, I never dreamt nor knew that one day I would be serving in those vestments again. God sure works in wondrous ways. If someone at that time in Dauphin would have told me that some twenty years later I would be serving with those vestments again, I would have looked at that person and thinking they were talking nonsense and did not know what they were saying. But only God knows how and why He does things as He does.

Wherever I served in any congregation, I had many friends in each area. When we moved to Phoenix, many of our Canadian friends came to visit us. They wanted to see for themselves if it was true that I was serving again because in Canada I was not permitted to serve. On October 28th, Tony and Elsie Burkowski from Kelowna arrived in Phoenix for a one week visit. In the spring of 1955 they will be celebrating their 50th wedding anniversary. They brought us an invitation to attend their anniversary and asked me to be the MC at the reception. They stayed for a week and went home with what we thought were colds they picked up in Phoenix. It was later we learned, they did not have colds, but allergies. There are flowers blooming in Phoenix year round. The pollen is in the air the whole year. When Tony and Elsie arrived we had another group from Ukraine come to perform in Phoenix on October 28th. "Lviwyany" from Ukraine put on a program. After the performance this group also played for a public dance in the Suma Hall.

In 1994 when we had returned to Canada as already it has been mentioned, we visited a number of friends and attended the church blessing at Kamloops. One of the friends we visited was Stan and Minnie Andrechuk of Dauphin. While visiting them we got a surprise. They donated a large wooden engraved Ukrainian photo album. They donated this to the church in Phoenix so the congregation would sell tickets and use the profit towards the building or purchasing of a future new church. When we returned home and showed the album to the people, some people wanted to buy the album right there on the spot for the price it cost. I had to explain that the people who donated it, their wish was to make raffle tickets and have a draw for the album. But one prize was not enough to have a raffle. This album would be the first prize. The second prize was donated by Mrs. Kowal, a Ukrainian embroidered cushion. The third prize was a donation by Mykola and Tamara Burda, a cuckoo clock and the fourth prize was an Easter Egg donated by Marusia.

Everything was arranged and the draw was set for March 5th - 1955. I made seventy nine raffle books and later had to make more for those were all sold. Marusia herself sold over a thousand dollars worth of those tickets. I don't recall who won what, but the album was won by Sophie Hamar of Lac La Biche who came to Phoenix every winter. Her family owned a store in Lac La Biche and when I lived in Lac La Biche I used to shop there. Sophie Hamar is the chairperson of St. Demetrius Ukrainian Orthodox Congregation at Craigend, fifteen miles south of Lac La Biche.

After living in Phoenix for a year Marusia began to say that she was getting pains in her chest. Was it pollution in the city? Was it allergies? Was it some other disorder? She saw the doctor a number of times and was put through different tests. On November 14th she had a tread mill test. The test revealed enough that she was sent to a cardiologist. She had an angiogram and it showed that she had two blocked arteries, one fifty percent and the other ninety percent. The doctor said that the next step was an open heart surgery to do a by pass. She was sent to see a heart surgeon and an appointment was made to have the surgery at 7:30 AM on December 14th. Exactly one month from the day she had tread mill tests, surgery was already scheduled.

During all this time a number of parishioners with Marusia and me were preparing to go to Los Angeles for December 11th to the feast day celebration of one church, St. Andrew. When the surgeon said that Marusia was to have surgery on the 14th of December, he also told her to have complete rest and not to exert herself before the surgery. Our trip to Los Angeles was thus canceled. We were to have gone with our van which seats seven people. Things did not plan out as we had planned. My mother my times said: "We make plans and God changes them." On December 12th the doctor called and said that the surgery has to be postponed because the Medical Insurance Company does not want to pay for the surgery. The congregation had been paying our medical insurance to the tune of $472.00 each month.

As we know from earlier in this biography father had come to Phoenix with John and Kay, but he never saw anything because of the illness that struck him and the three of them had to rush and return home suddenly. Plans were now being made that father come to Phoenix for a while to spend some time with us because he was feeling so much better. On December 17th he arrived on a direct flight from Saskatoon to Phoenix. We went to the airport to pick him up. Because it was an international flight, the passengers had to go through customs. We saw him and other passengers when the plane came in and we could see the passengers as they walked past us, but behind a glass wall. We could wave to them, but could not talk because of the glass wall that separated us.

People arriving from Canada were all dressed differently for the summer like weather in Phoenix. Some only had sweaters on. Some had light jackets. Others were in T-shirts. But father was dressed in a white shirt with a tie, a black hat and suit and carried a trench coat on his arm. As we were standing and watching, there were people standing behind us watching and waiting for their company. Looking at the passengers through the glass wall, we heard someone behind us say: "Look at that man dressed up. He must be some kind of a politician coming on this charter flight." Whoever it was that said that, they were saying it about father, because no one else was dressed like father was. So father came and stayed with us for six weeks and that is how the year 1994 came to an end.

We have now lived for over one year in Phoenix, surviving the summer desert heat. If anyone has never gone through a desert area in the summer time, than they don't know what heat is. First we survived +47 C., and than +49 C., or 120 F. The desert sun burns everything up from the scorching heat. Yet if you go up to the tall building in Phoenix or look out of the airplane, you see a lot of greenery which looks lush with tall Palm trees, other kinds of trees, flowers, grass, etc. From the top of the skyscraper the city looks like it is built in a small forest, everything is so green and tall. Water is the life in the desert and is brought to Phoenix from far away places to feed the vegetation. If the water did not arrive in the desert, the city would die. Thus if there is water, no matter what kind of a desert it is, life would survive. No water, no life.

Towards the end of January we had an unexpected guest in church. Archbishop John of Edmonton had come to Phoenix for two weeks of relaxation. He was in church two Sundays at the Liturgy, but did not serve only sat in the Sanctuary. At the end of the service I welcomed him and told the congregation: "I don't know why his Grace has come. Maybe he came to take me back to Canada, or maybe he came to stay here and be our bishop." The people got a chuckle out of this, for they knew neither would happen.

LOOKING FOR BETTER CHURCH PROPERTY

One day we had a funeral in Phoenix. As we were riding with the funeral director to the cemetery, he said they were selling one of their funeral homes. I told the church executive and a few members became interested in maybe purchasing the building for a church. The members looked over the building and it looked like a good proposition and might be realistic. When we came out of the funeral home, we saw three young people, sitting on a fence, next to the property of the funeral home. They were sitting on the wooden fence like crows sitting on the power lines. We could see that the place would not be any better than where the church is now. Another thing was that Marusia and I had gone to the city hall to inquire if it was zoned that a church could be located there. We were told we would have to have washrooms equipped for handicap people. We would need to have so many parking stalls. There would have to be parking for handicap people. The kitchen facilities would have to be to regulation specifications. After listening to the information, we knew that place was out of the question to be converted into a church. The only thing that was good about that place was that it had a chapel that could seat a hundred and fifty people. When we learned of the price for the property and the regulations from the city hall, the decision than and there was, no go.

I ALSO WALKED ON THIS EARTH

Even though the funeral home property was now shut down the drain, the idea to move out of the present place did not go away from **some** members. Some members wanted the church to stay where it was. Tickets were being sold on the album and other prizes to raise some finances for a future church. On the day of the raffle, March 5 - 1995, we had a church service in the morning as usual. The dinner was held at the SUMA Hall. After dinner Mrs. Ann Chold of Saskatoon, an RN, spoke about the experiences she encountered going to hospitals and clinics in Ukraine. She had been going to Ukraine to help train medical staff.

When we learned that the funeral home was out of the question for a church, Marusia and I went to the City of Peoria to enquire about building a church on the land of nearly two acres, which the congregation owned. We discovered that a church cannot be built on that property. The city regulations were that a church must be built on a thoroughfare street. The church property was located at a dead end street. So now that option was out. So maybe the next thing was to sell this property and buy land where a church could be constructed or buy a building and remodel it into an orthodox church.

Marusia and I spent oodles of time driving many, many miles looking for property that was for sale. We crisscrossed street after street, hundreds of them in different directions looking where land was for sale. As I drove Marusia would take down the phone number and the street name or number. We drove through Phoenix, Peoria, Sun City, Youngtown and other suburbs. When we had about fifteen places of land for sale on paper, we would drive home. At home I would get on the phone to enquire about the land. Prices for the land ranged from $6.00 to $15.00 a square foot. That's right a SQUARE FOOT. Not an acre, but by the square foot. So how many square feet are there in an acre? I learned that roughly there are about 43,000 square feet in an acre. At $6.00 a square foot, the land would cost $250,000.00 dollars. For land that was $15.00 a square foot it would cost nearly three quarters of a million dollars. Later we learned that the land the church owned, nearly two acres, they were asking $50,000.00 for it and no buyers.

MARUSIA'S HEALTH PROBLEM

With all this on our minds, this did not help Marusia's health situation, for suddenly on March 24th at 1:00 AM she got a severe chest pain. I was going to call an ambulance, but she said she did not want to go to emergency. Finally at 2:00 AM she gave in and asked me to take her to the Good Samaritan Hospital which was just across the freeway from our church. We got to the hospital and she told the nurse she was having chest pains. IMMEDIATELY from nowhere, five doctors and nurses appeared. Very soon they found that she had a blood clot in her heart. They pumped hundreds of units of heparin into her to dissolve the blood clot. As this was going on, she got a heart attack in the emergency room. I was with her all this time.

    I knew something serious had happened. All the while she had been sitting on the bed with nurses and doctors present. Suddenly she seemed to loose her balance and her head began to sag to one side. I was asked to step out of the room. I stepped out and the next thing in my mind was, that I had now lost her forever. A few minutes later a nurse came out and told me in saying that I could come in and stay with her. I was in the hospital until 5:00 AM when she said her pain was gone and she was tired and sleepy. I left for home, but at such a time who can sleep?

    Later that day Marusia was taken to ICU where she spent the next ten days in the hospital. What happened next was the doctors knew she had blockages in her arteries. The doctors told me that she would not go home until she had her surgery. When she was in the ICU she had another angiogram done to see where the blockages were. On March 28th, I received a phone call from the hospital who told me that my wife was in the hospital and already there was a bill for $20,000.00, but because she needs surgery, that will probably be another $40,000.00 and on top of what the doctors fees were and other costs. We had medical insurance but the company said they would not pay for the surgery, because it was a pre-existing condition.

When we had applied for medical insurance, we filled out forms and had to put in our medical histories. Marusia wrote that she had a heart murmur. Because of this the insurance company would not agree to pay for her surgery. You also had to be covered for one year before the insurance kicked in. We were in a bind. The heart surgeon and other doctors began searching for records and statistics. They found a law which stated if you had a heart murmur for fifty years or more it had nothing to do with heart attacks or clogged arteries. Marusia was born with a heart murmur and she was past her sixties which was well over fifty years with a heart murmur. After the doctors dug up this information, they told the insurance company that they will have to pay. The insurance company did pay.

The church members knew what had happened and from time to time were calling to enquire how Marusia was. I was telling them that the insurance company was not willing to pay for the surgery but no one said nothing. One family that attended our church every Sunday, but where not even members heard what happened called one day saying: "Father, my husband and I talked about your situation and we agreed to mortgage our house to get money to pay for your wife's surgery."

When the matter was settled with the doctors and the insurance company, the doctors scheduled surgery for Marusia for March 30th at 2:30 PM. I was in the hospital that day and went with her to the pre-op room at 1:00 PM. We were waiting when at 2:30 PM the nurse came and said that her surgery is canceled because the doctor is held up at another hospital on an emergency case. Marusia felt, saddened, discouraged and disappointed. I tried cheering her up saying that maybe it's better this way. God knows what He is doing and wants it done His way. I told her it would be better if the surgery is in the morning when the doctor is not tired and not in a hurry. If the doctor was tired and rushing, he could make an error and results could be worst than they are now. That is exactly what happened. The surgery was rescheduled for next day at 7:30 AM. The day before surgery she said she would like confession and communion. At this time in Phoenix lived another Ukrainian Orthodox priest, Father Hryhorij Wolkowinsky. I called him up and told him what was what. I went and picked him up and brought him to the hospital and then took him home again. We had visited Father Wolkowinsky many times when we lived in Phoenix.

On March 31st at 6:00 AM I was in the hospital. Marusia was taken to the pre-op room again as was yesterday. When the time came to go for surgery, she was taken to the operating room and I was told I could go to the waiting room and there I will get results about the procedure of her surgery. In the waiting room there were about forty or fifty other people waiting to hear results about their loved one's surgeries. From time to time someone from one of the operating rooms would call a receptionist and tell her what was happening. She in turn conveyed the message to the family and told them about the procedure of the surgery.

I was sitting in the waiting room when the surgeon, Doctor Selsky, came in to see me at 7:45 AM. He came to ask on which leg Marusia had her varicose veins removed when she was still working in Moose Jaw. I told him it was the left leg and he left back to the operating room. At 9:00 AM the receptionist called me and said that Marusia's heart had been stopped and she was now on a heart machine and breathing with a machine. This was a very hard experience for me. The heart has been stopped. What if it does not start after the surgery is complete? I was all alone and no family. The chairman of the congregation Serhij Kowalchuk had said he was going to come and be with me, but I said so he would not bother. That was a good gesture on his part but he was not family. It's different if it's family member. I was lost like a seagull over the ocean. Our families were in Canada miles and miles away. I prayed quietly and thoughts ran through my mind: Will her heart restart? About two hours later the receptionist called me again. She informed me that Marusia was now breathing on her own and all they have to do is sew her up. Her heart was working and the chest has to be closed up. When I heard that news, I thought a new world had been born. I don't know how many prayers I said in that waiting room, before, during and after surgery.

At 11:30 doctor Selsky came to the waiting room to tell me that the surgery went over very well and that she had five by passes. He said that in an hour or so I will be able to see her in the ICU room. At 1:15 PM the receptionist told me that I could go and see her. As I came to the room and was about to enter, I noticed a nurse sitting by the door with a little table but she never looked up but having her eyes peeled on the machines that were hooked up to Marusia. There were all kinds of tubes with her, some in her mouth, some in her nose, some in her arms, etc. The place looked like a space satellite. I asked the nurse if I could take pictures and she said yes, but she never even looked who I was. Her eyes were watching the monitor like a fox watches a rabbit. I took two snapshots. She had a towel over her head. She was sick, but I do not know if she knew I was there. I saw I could do nothing for her at this time, so I went home to have something to eat, check the phone and to come back in the evening.

When I returned in the evening at 6:00 PM, she was beginning to open her eyes, but could not speak because of the tubes in her throat and nose. The nurse gave Marusia a pencil and told her to write what she wanted to say. Her writing was limited, because her arms were still tied to the bed. She wrote she was thirsty. The nurse dipped a piece of sponge on a stick into the water and wet her lips with it. I stayed a few minutes, took another picture and left for home. What else could I do for her at this time? She is tied down to the bed and the nurse is there the whole time beside her. I also was tired and needed a rest. I have been up since 5:00 AM this morning.

Next day I had a memorial service in the church. After the service I went to the hospital which was across the freeway from the church. There is a foot bridge to go over the freeway. Today Marusia looked more alive. She is awake and the tubes from her mouth have been removed and she is talking. When I came back again in the evening, she was already sitting on the side of the bed having her supper. This is only twenty eight hours ago since she had surgery and already sitting up and eating. What recovery.

Before she came home on April 4th, I came to visit her on the 3rd of April. When I came into her room she was getting a blood transfusion. The nurse said she had lost two pints of blood and they don't know why and where. How? why? where? Marusia was shivering and shaking very bad that even the bed was moving. The nurse brought a few more blankets and covered her up. The nurse said it was the blood making her cold, because the blood she was getting was from a refrigerator and when it goes into the body it makes the person feel cold. But I was now worried. She lost two pints of blood. Why, where, how? So where the blood disappear? I began to think maybe she will have to have another emergency surgery to find out what happened. Did something inside break and she is losing blood? Was she cut someplace accidently and blood is being lost? The nurse said the blood was not leaving her body and she is not hemorrhaging the blood out. If not where than is the blood disappearing?

After a while she began to feel warmer and felt somewhat better. I stayed till visiting hours were over and than went home. At the back of my mind the question remained: Where is the blood disappearing? What is wrong? Why did she need a blood transfusion after surgery was over three days ago. Transfusions are usually given during surgeries. Thoughts were racing one ahead of the other. What is wrong this time? Why a blood transfusion?

Just five days after her five by pass surgery, Marusia is released from the hospital on April 4th at 5:00 PM. But all the problems were not over yet. We lived in a two story condominium. The bedrooms are upstairs. The doctor said she cannot walk stairs. So what do we do? We decided that she would go up the stairs, very slowly and only one foot at a time and stopping to rest after each step. Once there I can bring her meals. There is a bathroom upstairs , so she will only need to move upstairs once and wait until things heal up and she will be able to move around more freely.

As mentioned, Marusia was released from the hospital on April 4th. Next day I had to take her to emergency, because her leg where the vein was taken out was bleeding. She was checked over, given medication and sent home. The story does not end there.

On April 11th I took her to the surgeon because her leg was still bleeding. Doctor Selsky immediately saw the problem. Marusia had gotten hematoma, a clotting of the blood in her leg. The blood she was losing was going under her skin and where she had her veins taken out. Her blood was thin after she was given heparin and other medication to prepare for surgery. When the vein was taken out, the blood did not clot, the veins did not close and the blood was going under her skin.

Doctor Selsky, right in his office, with his hands opens up the wound on her leg where she was cut and starts pulling out globs of blood from her thigh where she had the veins taken out. The blood was coming out in chunks like jello, a deep purple reddish color. Marusia was left with an open wound about ten inches long, two inches deep and two inches wide. Her thigh was like a piece of raw meat just hanging unto the bone. I told the doctor to sew up the thigh and he said that if he did, she could get an infection and than more problems may come. "But she can't be like that," I told him. He said that the nurse will show us what has to be done.

The nurse brought out a salt solution. She wet the gauze in the salty solution and put it inside the open wound. She filled the wound with the salty gauze and told us to do the same twice a day and have a shower before the gauze is put into the wound. This way the wound would start to heal from the inside and will not cause an infection. Can you imagine the pain putting saline (salt) solution on an open wound? You can imagine how much pain Marusia went through this before the thigh healed up. The doctor also got a nurse to come to the house to do this, but the nurse never showed up. I believe it was the Easter week end or something and people were off work. But the wound had to be looked after. When the nurse finally did show up, she asked us where we learned to do that. Marusia said she at one time was a nurse's aid and knew. What we had been doing was shower the wound in the morning, put in saline gauze into the wound and than wrap it up so that dirt did not get inside. This we did morning and night. The wound was starting to heal from the inside.

Something happened on April 27th. My ankles including the toes became all red, inflamed and hot. It looked like a string had been tied around my ankles and the redness only went so high. It was a perfect circle around the ankles. A few days later this redness moved away and the toes were clearing. Slowly all the redness disappeared but there had been no pain during all this time. It was not itchy and I could not even tell it had been there. It must have been some allergy.

It is now two months since Marusia had her surgery. Last October we had company from Kelowna, B.C. Tony and Elsie Burkowski had asked us to come to their 50th wedding anniversary on May 27th. I was asked to be MC for that event. But how can Marusia travel with only two months after her surgery. We had seen the cardiologist and the family doctor and they both said she can travel, but not by car. We flew from Phoenix to Vancouver non-stop by America West Airlines on May 25th. In Vancouver we rented a car and drove to Kelowna. The anniversary went over well and than we returned back to Phoenix on May 30th.

Than more problems appeared about health. On June 15th I got red blotches appearing on my body. This was somewhat different. The blotches seemed to have white scales which could be scrapped off. Because it was not getting any better I went to see a doctor. The doctor sent me to a specialist on June 26th. The specialist said it was a fungus and gave me some salve to put on the blotches. In a day or two it was improving, but than new blotches would appear in different places. Slowly by applying the salve, everything cleared up. But that was still not the end of the problem, for on July 13th I was sent to see a dermatologist because I had a rash on my back. Another kind of salve was given and things cleared up. The little red blotches still appeared from time to time, but the salve would clear them up. Either the climate or allergy effected me. We were using a lot of citrus fruit for consumption. Was the body overloaded with too much citrus, acid? People who had orchards, came to church, brought bags of oranges and grapefruit and those who had no fruit like both of us, we just helped ourselves to that fruit. I had eaten more citrus fruit in Phoenix in three years than previously in my whole life.

Like everyone else we were told to take holidays. I would rather keep working than go for holidays. But because the law is the law, we had to go away and this year we are going back to Canada. We took in the Dauphin Festival and visited family and friends while there. I had not been at the Dauphin Festival for a while since I left Dauphin in July 1977. We returned back home to Phoenix on August 10th.

While in Dauphin we visited many friends and one was Fred Chaykowski. He had been chairman of the congregation for a number of years when I lived in Dauphin. Fred Chaykowski was ill, not feeling well, for he had cancer. Fred asked me to come and take part in his funeral when he passes away. I told him that I cannot do that without the permission of the Primate of the church. Fred said that he would write a letter to the Primate to get the blessing so I may participate in his funeral. When we arrived back in Phoenix, we received a letter from Fred Chaykowski who wrote and said that the Primate was going to Sheho, Sask., and he stopped in and saw Fred Chaykowski. The Primate told Fred that I can take part in Fred's funeral service when that day comes.

On September 4th I got a phone call from Chaykowski's daughter who said that the Primate of Canada wants to talk to me and so that I would call him in Winnipeg. When she said this, I thought that maybe the Primate wanted to give me some instruction of what I can do or not do at the funeral. I called the Primate on September 5th. I told him who was calling and asked what he wanted to tell me, because Fred Chaykowski's daughter called and said that he wanted to speak to me. The Primate says: "What kind of a deal did you make with Chaykowski?" I was shocked. I told him that I made no deals, but said that only with the permission of the Primate would I take part in the funeral service. I told him that we talked about the old times and how things were going in the congregation. We reminisced about the past. Than I asked the Primate if I can take part in the funeral service. He says: "You may come to the funeral and stand somewhere in the back of the church, in a corner, so people wouldn't even know and see you there." I asked him if I may wear any part of the vestments and the answer was: "Absolutely not."

Than not only that, but he says, he was talking to the Primate of the church in the USA and was told that I was not accepted by the church in the USA, but came to Phoenix and took over the congregation. This is sure different from what I heard from the Primate in USA when I was still in Yorkton, Sask. I had called him and he said that he had nothing against me going to Phoenix to serve. There must have been something cooking already. Why? Because next day on the 7th of September I get a phone call from the Consistory in the USA in South Bound Brook asking me not to go to Canada to participate in the funeral. This was also the year of the Sobor of the church in the USA and they told me not to attend the Sobor. I was also asked if we were leaving back to Canada and when. I told them that at the present time we were still staying in Phoenix. I did not ask why all this was happening.

This year the congregation in Phoenix will be celebrating its thirty-fifth anniversary. Archbishop Anthony will visit the congregation for its celebration on December 3rd. Because of the anniversary coming up, I had asked the congregation to elect a committee to write a very brief history of the congregation. The committee was elected at the annual meeting in 1994. The year is running to the end and I asked if anything had been written. Two months before the celebration, nothing had yet been done. The committee had not even met together and had not yet done anything and not even one word of anything was written.

I knew that if I didn't do something immediately, there would be no written history for the up coming celebration. The only thing the committee was worrying about was that to publish a book it would cost money and would be costly. Anyway I started to look for information in the church record books that were in the church. I put down a few things on paper that I gathered from here, there and everywhere. Than another week was lost in getting this written and prepared when Marusia and I had to leave for Canada to be at John and Alice's fortieth wedding anniversary. We drove again to Canada and than had to rush back home to get things organized for the book and the celebration. Now there was only one month left before the celebration when we arrived back in Phoenix on November 2nd.

It was around the middle of October when we received a letter from the Canadian Government that because we were residing outside the borders of Canada we will have to pay a Non-Resident Tax on all income starting January 1st - 1996. This tax would be collected every month depending on the type of income we had each month and it could range as high as twenty five percent each month. We called a few times to Canada to get more information about this tax, but we got nowhere. Why? The person in Canada that was trying to help us could not speak good English. She would only say: "I help you. I help you" We could not understand her what she would be saying, so we gave up on getting that information. We waited to see what would happen, what kind of percentage on money we would be losing each month.

When we had sold our house in Yorkton, we invested the money along with other investments that we had in Canada. We waited for several monthly bank statements to see what effect if any there was on our investments. We found out from the bank statements that we were losing more Canadian funds than we were getting in American funds that I was serving the congregation. At this time we were trying to decide what our next step should be that we were losing so much money.

RETURNING TO CANADA

I was still not getting Canadian Old Age Security Pension at that this time. One elderly gentleman from the Ukrainian Catholic Church who was living over twenty years in Phoenix told us that he was losing twenty percent of his Canadian pension each month. He said that I hurry and get back to Canada, because I have to live in Canada for one full year before Old Age Security starts, otherwise I will lose twenty percent of old age pension each month as he is. Seeing and hearing all this, we saw that we should start packing and head back to Canada. Had it not been for all the money we were losing, we may have still been in Phoenix till today.

All these listed below items made us decide to return back to our native land. They were:

1. Non-Resident tax.
2. Some congregation members not interested in another church building.
3. Three water breaks in the manse with no water for days.
4. Another priest was willing to come and serve in Phoenix if I left.

Let us glance briefly at each of the above reasons that were helping us make up our mind to move back to Canada.

I have mentioned the Non-Resident Tax which was being collected from our income each month by the Canadian Government starting in January 1996.

Some congregation members were not interested in another church building, but there were some members who were really looking forward to move out of the arae where the church was. As Ihave already been mentioned earlier in this bio it seems people want something for nothing. No one seemed interested to get on the phone or into the car and check out some places if there was any possibility to get another church building in a better location. One day as Marusia and I were driving looking for vacant land for sale, we came upon a sign beside a church that the church property was for sale. We took the telephone number and later when we arrived home we called the Realtor. We met the Realtor at a designated time by that church to have a look and get some information. It was better property than what our church had at that time. There was a new three year old hall at the back of the church. There was a paved parking lot for twenty five cars. A man that was using the church driveway to get to his property paid for the use of the water that the church used. One thing was missing - there was no sewer hookup, but a septic tank. The Realtor said that the sewer would be coming within three years because the city of Peoria had already passed a by-law to have sewers installed in that area. Price for property - $128,000.00. I thought that was a real bargain.

The congregation had over $60,000.00 in the bank account. They had a piece of property that they could have sold for a minimum of $50,000.00. They could sell the present church for let's say $50,000.00. You already have $160,000.00. The congregation could buy this church, pay for it and still have some $32,000.00 remaining. There would also be no shootings, prostitution, vandalism, drugs, etc., as there was by the present church in downtown Phoenix.

It was arranged that the church members should come and have a look at the building one Sunday after the service. Most of those seeing the property said it was much better than what they had now. BUT, one church member quickly ran around the church building and than says: "This is no good, because if a flood comes, these bricks will get wet and the building will collapse." The building sat through the 1982 flood in Phoenix in that area and it did not collapse. Why would it collapse for the orthodox when it never collapsed for the other denomination that was selling that church. The reason they were selling it was because it had gotten too small for their congregation.

But Marusia and I did not give up. We kept looking and searching for properties. One day as we were driving through Sun City with a population of over thirty-five thousand where only seniors of fifty five years and older lived we saw a sign which said that the bank building was for rent. The bank had closed because there was an amalgamation of banks and this bank was left sitting vacant. We called the Realtor who looked after that building. We met at a designated time and saw the beautiful building. There were two buildings with a rotunda between the two. Big white fancy posts at the front of the building made it rich looking. The building was in the middle of a shopping centre with a large paved lot. The Realtor said the property was for rent for $1800.00 per month. I asked him the value of the building and he said it was assessed at one million dollars.

I told the Realtor that we were not interested in renting, but to purchase it, but the price was too high for us. We asked who the owners were and he said they lived in California. Than just to get the Realtor to forget about this I told him to tell the owners we will give them $300,000.00 for the property. If the owners accept the offer we will put a plaque on the wall, saying that this church stands here because of the generosity of such and such a family. A million dollar building to buy for $300,000.00. No way will such an offer fly. Who would sell a building for one third of its value? About a week later we get a telephone call from the Realtor and he says: "Bring your deposit for the bank building." You know that the telephone just about fell out of my hand when he said that. Someone accepting an offer of one third of the building's value. Is that possible? Is it real?

So now that this story is beginning, what is next? I told the church executive about all this and we made arrangements that people will come on Sunday after the service to see this building. The same person that had turned down previous offers that we looked at, here again he ran around the whole property, looked and than says: "This is not for us, because we will not be able to upkeep this building." That was it. Such a beautiful building that looked like a palace worth one million dollars and getting it for a third and the answer is negative, this broke the camel's back. Buy it for that price and then resell it and make money. Other people that saw the building were much in favor of that building - two buildings. After this Marusia and I quit looking for any more buildings or properties. After spending all the time, traveling, searching, fuel, viewing, checking and the result was always negative, without sitting and discussing the topic. Marusia and I gave up and never did anything else about this matter. It was only later that we learned from others there was one or two families that were dead set against another church building in another place. Why? Because they said they built the present church and they did not want to give it up. I guess they did not want progress. You try to do good for people and one or two will always put out their foot to trip you up. We quit and let the people do what they want.

3. Water breaks in the manse (condominium). One November night on the 14th Marusia awoke and went to the bathroom. She thought she heard the sound of running water as if some tap is not closed someplace. She woke me up and sure enough you could hear water running. We checked all the taps, but everything was shut off, so where is the water running. I opened the front door and on my knees I closed the water tap coming to the apartment. We listened and no running water. I opened the tap again, and you can hear the water running again. I turned the tap off until morning when it will be daylight and maybe we will be able to see better to find the problem.

When we got up in the morning we started to check for leaks. There are no basements in Phoenix homes. Since we could not find where the water was leaking, we closed the tap and called the church chairman and told him what was happening. He said he would get his plumber to come and have a look. The day went by and no plumber came and we have no water in the house. In the meantime Marusia had met a lady a few houses down and told her of our problem. The lady said that she had the same problem and a plumber had come, fixed the problem and it was for a reasonable cost and she was satisfied with his work.

Next day the chairman of the congregation calls and says that his plumber has no licence to come into Phoenix to do jobs. Again later he called and said that he called two other plumbers and had the same answer. On the third day he calls and says to get the plumber that had fixed the next door ladies problem. Marusia got the phone number from the lady and we called the plumber, but he said he was busy and it would take a few days before he would be able to come. We waited for those few days, but no one showed up. Than it was the Thanksgiving week-end in the USA. In the meantime we have no water in the apartment and I only would open the water when we needed to use the bathroom, shower or get water for cooking and washing dishes. We would fill up pails with water and keep the water line shut to our condo unit.

Since we are not getting any results from no one we called the chairman again and told him we have not seen any plumbers and we have no water in the residence. He said to call anyone who would come immediately. I looked in the phone directory and found more plumbers than people in Phoenix. Within an hour after I called two vehicles with plumbers from the same company had arrived. They came and checked the problem and said it would cost $800.00 to locate the water leak someplace under the concrete floor. The total cost for all repairs would be $2800.00. The plumbers called the "leak detector" and he was there in a few minutes, checked the place over and said the leak was under the floor in the main floor bathroom.

They took the floor tiles off, brought in a jackhammer and started to tear up the floor in the bathroom. When they finally had the concrete torn out and found the water lines, they saw that they were in the wrong place and would have to get the "leak detector" again. The "leak detector" was going to come after midnight, but we told him not to, because there are working people in the condominium and they need their rest and sleep. The plumbers were going to work after the leak was detected. We asked them to come back the following morning and they did.

The next day they tore up the floor between the kitchen and the bathroom, under the stairs and about five feet from the first place they had ripped up the floor. The problem was the copper pipe had a pin size hole in it and there was mud all over under the cement floor. This was repaired on November 28th. We had no water for two weeks, from November 14th to the 28th. Now everything will be ok and back to normal.

But it was not to be. Lightning does strike in the same place twice they say, but on January 7th - 1996 the same problem occurred. We could hear water running again, but where? It was not in the same place, because that place was still open left to dry up the mud. So where is the leak this time? This time the church members decided they would do the repairs themselves because the plumbers were too expensive. Later the congregation got back half of the cost for repairs through the condo insurance.

When the members came to do the repairs, they soon discovered that the problem was in the same place as the first one was. They began to break up the concrete. About a foot from the first place they found the same problem - a pin hole in the copper pipe. We kept the water shut off. This second break occurred on January 7th and was not repaired until January 15th. Again one full week without water in the house.

People say that lightning does not strike twice in the same place. How about it striking three times? That is exactly what happened. On March 30th about 3:00 AM we again heard water running. We would keep the water shut off and only turned it on when we needed water. This third break was repaired on April 9th. Again eleven days without water.

This third time the plumber did not repair that problem. I suggested that they put a new copper water line to run along the wall on the floor of the condo. When the second break had come, we had decided that we just about had enough of all this. But when the third break came, our mind was now made up that we are leaving and heading back to Canada. How many people wait for weeks to get water restored. We waited patiently and never complained to anyone only asked when the repairs would be done.

4. Another item: "There was a priest who wanted and was willing to come to Phoenix to serve." It was a few weeks before Easter, on March 4th that I got a call from Denver Colorado from a priest that had arrived from Ukraine and he wanted to come for Easter to Phoenix and have a service with me. I said it would be fine with me, because the second Sunday after Easter we were leaving for Canada and he could take over the congregation if the congregation wants him and if the bishop gives his blessing. I told the priest to call the chairman of the congregation to get his permission if they would accept him as their priest.

When I hung up, I called the chairman and told him that a priest is ready and willing to come and serve when I leave. The chairman says: "Well, no. Maybe better after you leave and than he can come and we will see him." Now what kind of talk was this? I told the chairman that it would be good if he came and we could serve together and in an official way with the blessing of the bishop, I would pass the congregation over to him. The chairman said that they would have to pay his airfare from

Denver to Phoenix. I say: "So what is a $75.00 airfare, doesn't the congregation have $75.00?" He replies: "Well you know that summer is coming and maybe we will close the church for the summer months, because few people attend church on Sunday in the summer." I still kept insisting that they let him come and they could see what he is like. Following this, I kept asking the chairman if that priest will be arriving and he kept saying that most likely they will close the church for the summer time after we leave for Canada.

What really hurt was when the day BEFORE my last service in Phoenix, I had a memorial requiem service on one cemetery (provody) for one family. After the service on the cemetery this family says that they are getting a new priest from Denver on Wednesday. We are leaving on Monday and the new priest is coming two days later. Why could he have not come and taken part in the Easter service as I had suggested? This priest could have stayed with Marusia and me until we left and it would not have cost the congregation anything but the airfare. Why did they not want this priest to come when I was still there? Was the chairman afraid that I might tell the new priest something about the congregation? Why did they not let me know what was happening in the congregation? Why? All these reasons helped Marusia and me make our decision to move back to Canada. Yet we could have stayed on in Phoenix until today, had the non-resident tax and other reasons mentioned had not come along.

Another thing was the 35th Anniversary of the congregation. I had been writing, checking and searching for information about the congregation for a **brief** outline history to print a booklet. I had done everything and it did not cost the congregation one red penny. The printing was paid for by the people for the ads that were sold to put in the booklet. In fact the congregation even made a few dollars on that booklet. The executive had always been worried that they would have to pay to publish the booklet. I had made it so each family who attended the anniversary got the history booklet for free. Books that were left over were sold and the congregation made a few cents from that.

After the books were printed and the anniversary was over, one member comes up to me and says: "You know we could have gotten those books printed for nothing, because where I used to work, they said that if the church ever needed any printing they would do it for nothing." After all was over than he says that the books could have been done for free. Why did he not tell this at any of the meetings we had when we talked about printing the booklet?

But let me go back a few weeks to December 1995 when Archbishop Anthony was visiting the congregation for its 35th anniversary. On Saturday December 2nd, before the anniversary, a member of the congregation and I were setting up the tables and chairs in the Suma Hall for tomorrow's banquet. The ladies were busy in the kitchen preparing the meal. The two of us set up the tables and chairs that they had in the hall. We could have used a few more tables and chairs. I told the man that we go to our church and we bring two or three tables and chairs. The man looks at me and says: "No, we don't need, because even these tables will not be filled up tomorrow." I tell him: "We don't have enough tables and chairs, and better to have more than not enough." He kept insisting that we did not need any more. I did not want to argue with him, so kept quiet and let it be his way. The whole while I had the feeling that we did not have enough tables and chairs.

Everybody went to the hall. Archbishop Anthony and I stayed behind to give the people the chance to get ready in the hall before we arrived. When Archbishop Anthony and I arrived at the hall I went inside to check if everything was ready while Archbishop Anthony waited outside in our van. As soon as I walked into the hall, the man who helped with the tables and chairs yesterday comes running to me and says: "We don't have enough tables and chairs." I just answered him and said: "I told you yesterday that we need more" and just turned around and walked away from him not paying attention to him. When you receive such cooperation from a church member, maybe it's a sign that you are not needed anymore, so best pack up and get out as soon as possible.

The church was jam packed for the anniversary service. Father Stephan Holutiak and his wife from Los Angeles were also present. The "snow birds" from Canada that came to Arizona for the winter also helped to fill up the church for the service. The hall also was filled to the full with many Ukrainian Catholic people attending. People who had lived in Phoenix for many years later told me that they had never seen so many people at our church function as they saw that Sunday of the congregation's 35th anniversary.

After the service was over in church, Archbishop Anthony and I were coming in the van to the hall, we talked about different things and I mentioned to him that Marusia and I will be leaving back to Canada because of the non-resident tax placed on us by the Canadian Government. Archbishop Anthony looked at me and says: "We don't want you to leave here, but we can't stop you either and we hope that what you do is the best for you. We would rather have you stay here, because we hear there are miracles happening in this congregation since you arrived." When the time came to leave Phoenix, there was no way we were going to stay on because of the non resident tax we had to pay. As this is written in 2016, many "Canadian snow birds" have already sold their mobile homes in Arizona and are not going back to spend winter in the south.

With 1995 drawing to a close and the anniversary of the congregation was now history, this gave us a minute to relax after a hectic year. Now we can again spend more time to visit with parishioners and the "snow birds". Summer and fall were over and the days were starting to cool off and Arizona winter was just around the corner. It was on December 8th that we turned on the furnace for the first time since early spring. During the summer the air conditioner is on but in the spring and fall neither furnace nor air conditioner was required.

In January 1994 sister Alice and her husband John had come to Phoenix the same time as brother John, Kay and father had come. At that time no one had holidays for John had to rush back to Canada with father and Kay who were ill when they had arrived in Phoenix. Now in January Alice and her husband John once again came to Phoenix for holidays to get away from the cold winter in Canada. When they were visiting us, they also came to the church service on Sunday. They had their fifth wheel and did not stay at our place, but would go back to the trailer park. We showed them around Phoenix and than slowly on January 28th they started to head back for home.

MY ILLNESS AND HOME TO
CANADA - CALGARY

Days are slowly rolling along. We have now received a few bank statements from Canada and we see that each month we are losing fifteen percent of our Canadian Income to the non-resident tax assessed on us. We will wait for another month and see if it is the same. Losing too much money is what we were seeing before us. With all the above things happening in the congregation and the plan to move back to Canada, I started to get pains in my chest. For one week the pains would come, stay for a while and go away. On March 10th while serving the Liturgy in church at the Altar, I felt as if someone or something heavy was sitting on my chest. On March 11th in the morning everything was fine, but afternoon the pains started to come back again. Marusia seeing what was happening tells me to go and see the doctor.

But to see a doctor you need to make an appointment and it may be a day or two to wait to get in. Marusia insisted that we go straight to the clinic and will see what happens. It happened all right. We came to the clinic and parked on the third floor parking lot. The clinic was full of people waiting to see their doctors. We came to the receptionist and she asked how she could help us. Marusia tells her that I have been having pains in the chest for a week. At that same moment I was taken to an examining room and was told to lay on the table. The nurse was there already when we walked into that room. She asked a few questions, wrote something down and left. Very soon she was back again and said that the doctor had called for an ambulance. The hospital from the clinic was only more than a block away and we could see the hospital from clinic. We told the nurse we could drive to the hospital, but she told me to lay still.

Suddenly we heard sirens outside. We thought maybe a fire broke out someplace and the fire trucks were going by. In a few winks six firemen rush into the room. I looked around thinking maybe there was a fire around us. One firefighter begins to give me oxygen, another starts taking the blood pressure. The third is taking the pulse, the fourth listening to the heart with the stethoscope. Another one was asking questions and writing down my answers. I looked at all the firefighters and say: "Hey you good people, I'm not on fire." They put me on a stretcher they had brought and whisked me downstairs. Outside a fire truck and ambulance were waiting. They take me to the hospital and I spent three days there going through a series of tests. After being released I was asked to return in one week for a stress and thallium test. The young lady cardiologist checking things said things looked fine. She left and than came back, sat at the side of the bed and says: "If you want, I'll bet you $100.00 that you had no heart attack and everything looks fine." When all this episode was over, I later sat down and thought: "When you are sick, firefighters come and if the house was on fire, would you call an ambulance?"

Living in Phoenix and being only four hours away from Oracle, Arizona, why not go and see the Bio-sphere? One day we picked up my cousin and his wife, Alex and Sylvia Korzeniowski and went to Oracle. Once there we learned that eight people were locked up inside the oracle for two years and never came out until the two years were up. Scientists tell us today that the world needs ten to twelve acres of land for survival of each person on earth. The experiment at the Bio-sphere was to show that eight people could live on two acres of land. The eight people lived and survived in the Bio-sphere having their own food produced inside. The Bio-sphere was covered with thick dual pane glass. Inside the Bio-sphere they had animals, salt water fish, chickens, grew their own grain, etc. Not one person who had lived in the Bio-sphere for two years even had a cold during that time but when they came out of the Bio-sphere, their skin was very pale white.

Time is slipping by. We received another bank statement and again fifteen percent of our Canadian income was deducted for the non-resident tax. Seeing this, we are leaving back home to Canada, but the question stood before us - when? We could have left at the beginning of March, but fast(lent) was just a few days in and than Easter - Christ's Resurrection. Maybe we should at least stay for this period and leave after Easter. We told the parishioners that we would leave after Easter, so that would give the people time and opportunity to come to confession, communion and have their paska blessed. The parishioners begged us to stay another week after Easter so that we could all have the communal dinner and have blessing of the graves. We agreed to do this, because what is an extra seven days this way or that after spending two and one half years in Phoenix. One day sooner or later will not make a difference.

There is a Ukrainian organization in the USA called YKKA, similar to what there is in Canada the Canadian Ukrainian Congress. A few days before we left for Canada, this Ukrainian organization in Phoenix was having a picnic in March. Marusia and I attended this picnic in a park some ten miles north of our church after the church service was over. There were more Ukrainian Catholics than Orthodox at this picnic. Present also was the president of the Ukrainian Catholic parish. He comes up to Marusia and me and says: "I hear that you are leaving back to Canada." We told him we were leaving in a few weeks. Than he says: "Well let me tell you something. You forget about Canada. Our church will make a deal with you. We will sign a contract with you for four years to stay in Phoenix and serve our parish. We will pay you $2,000.00 a month American money plus all the expenses that you would have serving our parish." That was a good idea, and my mind was saying to take the deal, and my heart was saying to go back to Canada as we had already planned. We were by now at this time past the "point of no return."

In the meantime we had already been packing our things in boxes and placing them on the main floor to see how much room would be taken up. We still had not made up our mind how we would move back. When we lived in Phoenix, we had made a number of trips to Canada and each time brought back some things from Canada which we needed in Phoenix.

Now the van would not have room for all those things. We had to find another way to move our things back home to Canada. We thought to take a U-Haul truck which I would drive and Marusia would drive the van behind, but she said she did not want to drive all the way back herself. We could take a U-Haul truck and a trailer behind on which we could put the van on. We were told that the smallest truck which could be used to pull the van was a sixteen footer. U-Haul would not allow for a smaller truck to tow a trailer with a vehicle on it. Another thing was, we could rent a U-Haul trailer to pull behind the van, but we had no hitch on the van.

When we started to check out other ways of moving, the prices were just out of this world. Everybody was going to charge an arm and a leg. The cheapest way after investigating moving ways, was still to move with a U-Haul trailer. A few days before we left for Canada we went to the closest U-Haul dealer and had a hitch and transmission cooler installed for $250.00. The trailer we would pick up early April 22nd for $110.00 when we will be ready to load and move.

My last service in Phoenix was April 21st, Marusia's birthday and our anniversary. The service went over well in church. We had told the parishioners in advance not to give us any going away gifts, because we did not need anything. After dinner different people were praising us for our work with the church for nearly three years of our stay in Phoenix. Many spoke publicly that they would never again have a priest like me. I also had closing words thanking them for their work in the church, and also reminded them of some things they should change. I never liked to be praised by people, but if I need any praises, let God praise me if I'm worthy of praise.

On April 22nd early in the morning we went and picked up the U-Haul trailer, brought it home and started to load it. Around 10:30-11:00 AM a few parishioners showed up because we had to give them the keys to the church and the condo. Some came just to personally say farewell. At 11:30 AM we left Phoenix in ninety degree Fahrenheit temperature. We knew that the farther north we will go, the cooler the weather will get. Phoenix is one thousand feet above sea level and Flagstaff some one hundred and fifty miles north is seven thousand feet above sea level. We will have to climb uphill for one hundred and fifty miles. That will be a test for the van and trailer. Whenever the road was an incline uphill, the van would slightly heat up, but as soon as we leveled off, the temperature would return to normal.

That first day we got to Panquitch, Utah where we stayed at a motel. The kind lady at the motel told us to park our van and trailer at the back where it was dark, so that young people driving on the front street would not see it and break into it. Next morning everything was all right with the trailer. This second day we left early in the morning and got to Great Falls, Montana. As we were traveling we talked that we would have to stop at Helena Montana for gasoline. We drove and it was already dark when I told Marusia that we have to turn in at Helena, but she kept saying that Helena was still a long way down the road where we could see many lights. I drove through where I thought it was Helena. When we got closer to the lights, she realized that it was not Helena, but some factory or manufacturing plant. We were now some ten miles or so past Helena and the fuel gauge was resting on the "E" - empty.

It was now complete darkness and we still had mountains before us which we had to climb over before we got to Great Falls. There are probably fifty miles or more before us to get to Great Falls and the fuel gauge is now below the "E" and the light for "low fuel" came on. Maybe there will be a service station along the road, if not we will be stalled somewhere in no man's land in the dark of night. We saw a place with a gasoline station, but it was now closed. A car came along and we asked if there were any service stations down the road. The man said there was one about fifteen miles away and they close at 8:00 PM. The watch showed us it was ten minutes to eight. Ten minutes before closing and fifteen miles to go. We will never make it Great Falls.

We are past the point of no return to Helena, so we must forge ahead with: "whatever will be, will be." We came to the other service station, and sure enough it was closed. We kept pushing ahead with the thought: "Whatever will be, will be. - kay sera, sera" We kept going to our set destination. As we drove along we see a sign saying how far Great Falls was, and we knew we would never make it to any service station. Then far away in the distance we can see a brighter sky - a glow from the lights of Great Falls, but still many miles away. The "low fuel" light flickers on and off warning of low fuel. We keep driving on an empty gas tank in night darkness. As we moved along, the miles slipped under us. Finally we are at the top of the hill and city of Great Falls lights are down below before us. We now are cruising downhill and getting oh so much closer to people. Even if we ran out of fuel now, we could coast downhill the rest of the way into the city.

The first service station we see we turn in, before we start looking for motels. The engine was still running as I turned off the key. There may have been a cup of fuel left. I opened the door to get out and the wind just about took the door off the van. Now I knew why we had made if to where we are. The wind was in our back and was pushing us, thus using a small amount of fuel. Had we been traveling against the wind, we may still be sitting at the side of the road in the mountains today. Surely God was traveling with us this day and evening.

The van was fully loaded as was the trailer and with the weight we could not feel the wind when we traveled. After filling with fuel, the next step was to find a motel for the night. We are not far from the Canadian-American border, maybe an hour or so. Next morning we went to see if there was anything we needed to buy and check the prices. We walked around the mall, but there were no bargains. As we are leaving Great Falls, a strong west wind is blowing and throwing up dust and papers into the air in the cloudy sky. We arrived at the border around 10:00 AM. We had a list of all the things we had purchased in Phoenix when we lived there. The Canadian customs officer looked at our list and said that because we had been residents of USA for nearly three years there was no duty on our items. He said the only duty would be on items if we purchased anything visiting the USA for two or three days. They also took away our permits which we had received when we first entered USA nearly three years ago.

Before we had even left Phoenix, we were already discussing where we should settle in Canada. We had been to the Okanagan. It was good. But too far away from all the family that lived on the prairies. There was too much pollution of orchard spraying with chemicals. Than father was still living, so we did not want to be too far away from him, to have more opportunity to visit with him. From the Okanagan it was just too far. We had made some nineteen trips from the Okanagan in five years when we lived there and that was just too much traveling. We also had lived in Yorkton for some eleven months. We had a new home, the city was beautiful, and everything was good, with the exception of the water which was not the best in the world.

Another reason we did not want to return to Saskatchewan, because as we could say we were "robbed" by the Saskatchewan Government of over $1,500.00. How? Remember that we had purchased a 1994 Lumina van when we were going to Phoenix. When we went to register our van in Yorkton, the lady told us to apply for a refund on the sales tax on the van. The van cost $22,000.00. The Provincial sales tax was seven percent which was nearly $1,500.00 and had not been refunded back to us. Twice we had applied to the Saskatchewan Government for the rebate and were denied both times. They said we did not qualify because we were still Saskatchewan residents. How could we be Saskatchewan residents when our address was in Phoenix, our van was registered in Arizona and we had Arizona drivers licences. How could we be Saskatchewan residents? For this reason, Saskatchewan was deleted from our list, otherwise we would have gladly returned to Saskatchewan. We lost nearly $1,500.00, so how could we go back there?

It looked like British Columbia and Saskatchewan were out. That left us with Alberta and Manitoba the two possibilities of settlement. Manitoba also has provincial sales tax, while Alberta does not. We decided we would stop in Alberta, but than the question, where? There were many places we could have stopped in Alberta to make our home. After weighing and checking out things, we made the decision to settle in Calgary. Calgary is farther south, Chinooks come through often bringing warmer temperatures and the Canadian-American border is only a few hours away.

When we were still in Phoenix, a family from Brooksby, Saskatchewan, Mr. & Mrs. Cipywnyk were in church one Sunday. After the service we were talking with them telling them we will be moving to Canada and maybe will even settle in Calgary. They told us in the conversation that they had a relative in Calgary who was a Realtor. They did not have his address, but promised us that when they get back home to Canada they would see to it that we get the address. One day when we came after visiting parishioners homes with holy water, there was a message waiting for us on the answering machine. Nestor Papish, the Realtor from Calgary had called and wanted to know what kind of a house we were looking for. We called him and gave him some information. A few days later in the mail we received a package from Nestor Papish with the houses for sale in Calgary.

When we arrived in Calgary on April 24th we found a U-Haul depot to drop off the trailer. First we took all our things to Sentinel Storage and had them stored. Next we took the trailer, dropped it off and than off to a motel for the coming night. From the motel we called Nestor Papish and he said to meet him the following morning at his office. We did and for two days he drove us around and showed houses for sale. Finally we found the house that we liked, a condo unit. Here we made our home for the next three years. We bought a condo for $145,000.00. The basement was still not finished, but we will look after that later. The following day from the motel we called my cousin and his wife, Joe and Marlene Korzeniowski to say hello to them and that we are in Calgary and bought a house. They asked us to come and stay with them until we move in. In one way it was wonderful, because now we had a chance to catch up on talking and reminiscing for all the past years that we never had an opportunity to get together.

After we made a deal on the condo unit, we knew we can get possession of it on May 3rd. So what do we do from April 27th to May 3rd? Well, lets head out to Saskatchewan and visit family, father and Marusia's family plus many friends. On the way back to Calgary we can bring some of the things that have been stored at John and Alice's place on the farm. We left all the seats of the van in Calgary at the storage place and went to Saskatchewan. First we went to Edmonton to see John and Kay and tell them the news that we purchased a house in Calgary. From there we motored to Cudworth to see father and other relatives in Saskatoon and around the area. We loaded the van with things we had stored on the farm and returned to Joe and Marlene's in Calgary for the night. The loaded van sat on the street for tomorrow we take possession of the house and will unload the van into our new house. We also went to Brick and ordered furniture and appliances asking them to deliver the goods in the evening on May 3rd.

Only five days after we moved in and still not even unpacked, on May 8th, John and Kay arrived to see us. They were more interested to see the place that we had bought, than to see us, because we had just visited them a week earlier. They stayed and in the evening returned back home to Edmonton.

On May 22nd father ended up in the hospital. The following day we left for Regina to see friends and than on to Cudworth to see father in the hospital. When we were at Alice and John's place on May 25th, we helped Alice put in her garden, because she was not feeling well, having back pains. On the 26th we went to the service at Wakaw and to the grave side services after lunch. Marusia's parents and other members of her family are buried at Wakaw. Was it ever cold that day on the cemetery - May 26th. After the services, Marusia and I went to our home place at Tarnopol which we called Ponderosa, and there we picked two pails of morels - mushrooms. Next day father was released from the hospital and we also planted his garden. In the evening we went to John and Alice's to the farm and loaded up the van for the trip home next morning.

The 28th of May we leave for Calgary and father also comes with us, because he wanted to see our new place. He stayed with us for two days and than we drove him to John and Kay's place in Edmonton, because tomorrow is their wedding anniversary. We returned home and father stayed in Edmonton and John drove him home to Cudworth. After this we made one more trip to Saskatchewan and brought the remaining things we had in storage. Now all our belongings were in Calgary in the new house.

Having all our things in Calgary, we decided that we would not need a van any longer, so we made a decision to trade it for a smaller vehicle, a sedan car. After shopping around we found a new 1996 Buick Regal which we purchased on June 20th. We only had it at home for three days and than left with it for a trip to Saskatchewan and Manitoba. We stopped at Regina Beach to see Father Michael Zaleschuk and family. From there we motored to Yorkton and Dauphin to see many of our friends. Whenever we visited Dauphin, our home away from home was always at Stan and Olga Saramaga's place, very good friends from a long time back.

THAT BUICK CAR TROUBLE

We arrived in Dauphin on June 25th and the following day we left for Benito, Manitoba to see Emil and Mary Rubashewski, our good friends. Because Marusia had never been to Flin Flon, Manitoba, we took the trip up north to see friends Fred and Rose Maluta who live in Calgary, but have a summer home in Flin Flon. I had known Fred and Rose Maluta since the 1960's when I used to serve in the Flin Flon congregation. From Flin Flon we motored down to Melfort and to Cudworth, Saskatchewan for we wanted to be in Cudworth at the service and the grave side services where mother is buried. Here in Cudworth the brand new Buick car gave us problems.

We came to church and everything was fine. Coming out of the church to go to the cemetery, the brand new car would not start. Completely dead. No lights, no horn, nothing. No time to play around why the car would not start, so we went to the cemetery with John and Kay who also had come from Edmonton to be at the grave side services. From the cemetery everyone returned back to the church basement for lunch. After lunch John is going to have a look what the problem is with the car. Him being a mechanic, it was no problem for him to find the trouble. He soon discovers there is no power, so must be the battery, but why would it be dead? He checks the battery cables and they are loose. The new car we had bought, had been in the showroom and there the battery had been disconnected.

When we bought the car, they just put the cables on loosely and never tightened them. What would have happened if the cables would have become loose half way between Flin Flon and Melfort in no man's land in the bush, where there is nothing and no one for miles and miles and miles around?

So what happened to the loose battery cables? The electronic system had to be restored and reset again through machines in a service shop. We could still drive, but the rest of the electronics had to be reset. We returned to Calgary on July 1st and the following day we went to the dealer where we bought the car and told them of the problems we had. They set everything back in order. The very next day we were going downtown to pay some bills. Right on Centre Street and 14th Avenue SW., the car stalled. This time the engine would turn over, but would not start. After trying over and over again it started and seemed like it ran on two cylinders like an old two cylinder John Deere tractor.

We had just enough power under the hood to turn off the main street and unto a side street. We called the GMC hot line and had about a forty minute wait for the tow truck to arrive. When the tow truck arrived, I tried to start it and it did start. I told the truck driver to follow us in case it stalls again on the way to the garage, but he said that once it started it will run. We went straight to the dealer and said that we paid such money for the car, and told them we want our old Lumina van back, but they said it had already been sold. They checked the car over and said there was nothing wrong. If there was nothing wrong, why did it stall in the middle of the street?

But that was not the end of problems with that 1996 Buick Regal car. Always there was something wrong with it. One time we were driving along and a funny scratching noise began to come in the steering wheel. We were not too far from where we had purchased the car so we pulled in and told them the problem. Nothing wrong. Next time we are driving the ABS lights come on. Drove in, checked, nothing wrong.

On September 20th we left for Prince George to attend the twenty-fifth anniversary of the church where I had served. Everything went well and fine at the celebration with a packed church and hall. We stayed at our good friends Sophie and Helge Ludvigsen in Prince George. Archbishop John was present as were the late Father and Dobrodeyka Mysroslaw

Kryschuk from Edmonton, the late Father Orest Hudema from New Westminster and Father Roman Szewczyk of Victoria, B.C. The choir from New Westminster sang the responses in the Liturgy. The ladies had prepared a meal that was fit for a king and queen.

After the celebrations in the church ended, and being in Prince George, and Marusia never being in Prince Rupert, we decided to take a drive to the coast. Since we were already half way between Calgary and Prince Rupert, might as well continue on to the coast. On September 23rd we left for Prince Rupert. We got there that evening stopping along the way to see Twin Falls at Smithers. The following day we toured in Prince Rupert and afternoon started back for Prince George and stopped at Smithers for the night. The next day we arrived at Prince George and stayed over night with Sophie and Helge. On September 26th we left for Kamloops to be in church there on the 27th. We got as far as Barriere, B.C., where we stayed in a motel.

The next morning we drove to Kamloops to be at the church service. We came to the church, but there was no life around. What, no service? We drove to the auditorium to check if there was anyone, and sure enough people in the basement preparing for the varenyky (pyrohy) supper that evening. They were getting ready for the evening, so there would be no one in church, and the service was canceled. We left Kamloops and drove to Vernon and visited with our "kooma", Doris Chaykowski and had supper with her. From there in the evening we drove to Alex and Sylvia Korzeniowski's at Peachland where we stayed until September 30th when we left for home.

The trip had gone well until we passed Canmore, Alberta, some sixty miles west of Calgary from home. There were some snow flakes flying around and we could see some patches of accumulated snow here and there in the dark. We were traveling at a hundred and ten kph the speed limit, but when we saw the snow, I slowed down to ninety, just in case we need to slow down suddenly. Cars passed us on the divided highway, but we drove slower. All of a sudden as a bolt of lightning, a deer from the right side flies out of the bush at full speed. It flew into the passenger side front fender. We stopped immediately and I went to check where the deer was and to pull it off the road, so that another vehicle does not get involved in an accident. I could not find the deer anywhere on the road. I checked the car, and the hood had been dented, the passenger side head light was smashed, as was part of the front right grill. The air bags had not gone off. I wanted to open the hood, but it would not open, damaged too much. The car was still running and seemed like nothing was damaged to the engine, no noises or anything rubbing. This was at Dead Man's Flats. Yes it was Dead man's flats on the Trans-Canada Highway.

We started to drive slowly, but than stopped, not knowing if we should continue to drive or stay where the accident happened. We were not sure if we would make it to Calgary for we could not see if there was anything else wrong with the car. We had a CB in the car and we got on it and asked if anyone could tell us what to do. Someone answered and asked if anyone was hurt, to call the police and tell them that a deer ran into the car. We drove slowly and came to a telephone near the road. I called the police through the telephone operator and a lady answered and asked if anyone was hurt. I told her no injuries and it was the police detachment from Canmore that answered to which we were the closest.

I told the police what had happened and I was told that if the car is drive-able and no one is hurt to continue on to Calgary and in the morning to report to the RCMP in Calgary. We started to drive and about three or four miles east of the telephone we spot an RCMP cruiser standing in the median of the four lanes of highway. I stopped and than backed up to the cruiser. I told the constable what happened and he said the same thing that if no one was hurt and the car is drive-able to report in the morning in Calgary. I went back to the car and started to pull away, when suddenly the cruiser came after us with the flashing lights. I pulled over and wondered what I had done wrong. The constable comes out and says: "I just remembered that tomorrow when you get to report your accident in Calgary they will send you back to Canmore because that is where the accident occurred in this detachment. I have forms with me and I can fill them out if you come to the cruiser and this will save you a trip tomorrow." I went to the cruiser with him and he took down all the information and gave me a sticker to put on the windshield. He also said that when we came over the hill, he was going to come after us, to tell us that we had only one working headlight.

Next morning we called the insurance company (All State Insurance) and told them what had happened. They gave us two auto body shops and told us we could go to any one we wish. We went to the closest one, Low Cost Auto Body. They looked at the car and said there was $3600.00 of damage. They gave us another car to drive while ours was being repaired. Later in the week we checked with the auto body and they said they found more damage and it will be $4200.00. In one week the car was repaired and was ready for the road. The only thing that was missing was the grill at the front and they had to wait for the part to come from the USA, because Canadian GMC people were on strike.

When we were at the repair shop they told us that they repair anywhere from twelve to fifteen cars a year that are hit by deer. This was only one little auto body shop, and how many auto body shops are there in Calgary that yearly repair autos from deer (animal) accidents. They told us that a police officer told them that on the old Trans Canada Highway from Calgary to Canmore over two hundred deer are hit each year on a stretch of highway about sixty miles.

Later when we had our car repaired I told the insurance company what to do. I told her that the federal and provincial governments plus the insurance companies get together and share the costs to build a fence six feet tall along the highways were deer are a nuisance. Why? If there are two hundred deer hit on that highway and if each accident is $4000.00 on the average, that means the insurance companies have to pay out $800,000.00 a YEAR for claims. How many fences for that money could be built on both sides of the highway to keep animals out and save money for insurance companies and car drivers. Besides that how many people will have jobs in the manufacturing of the fences and than putting up the fences along the highways. Besides the car damages how many people are injured or killed and with heavy costs that drive up the claims. Millions of dollars would be saved in car damages and injuries to people. Was anything ever done with this suggestion? She said she would bring it up at the next insurance company convention. Did she? I don't know. If she did, what was the response? Most likely some people would be opposed to it.

All this was happening with our 1996 Buick Regal to the end of September in just a few months of ownership of that car. All those problems with this one new car. When that car was being constructed, it must have been cursed in the factory when it was built. Someone must have put a curse on that car for we were having all those problems. Why in today's times should a brand new car give so many problems?

There were other things that were transpiring during the same time. In July we had taken a trip into the Okanagan because on July 24th the church in Kelowna was celebrating their feast day (chram) St. Peter and Paul. When we get to Kelowna we learned that a good friend of ours, Peter Harasym passed away suddenly and the funeral is to take place on July 15th. We stayed for the funeral and returned home the following day. Coming home and a few dozen miles from home we hear on the CB radio which we had in the car that there was a bad hail storm in south west Calgary. They had to get graders out to move the hail of the streets and open up the storm sewers. Truckers who had come through Calgary heard of that news and were passing it on to other truckers. Having a CB in the car, we sometimes learned and heard if roads are closed, if there are accidents, construction, etc.

After we got home we got a call from Alice that she had to take father to the doctor in Saskatoon because he had some skin condition. The result was that he was allergic to some foods like beans. He loved mashed beans and lived on them all his life, but whether that was the problem, we don't know, because later he still ate pounds and pounds of beans with no side effects. Maybe it was some allergy from some medication that he was taking or something else that did not agree with him.

While living in Calgary we were seven miles from church and the Orthodox Cultural Centre. There were times that we made three trips a day to the church or Cultural Centre. There would be something going on in the morning and that was usually a service. In the afternoon there may have been a meeting and that would end about 4:00 PM. Than another event would be in the evening starting about seven or later. Instead of sitting for a few hours at the Cultural Centre we would go home and than return in the evening. The most visiting we did was with our neighbors Bert and Ruth Paton who lived in the condo next to ours. We also visited Jennie Marchinko and her brother Joe and his wife Marlene Korzeniowski when they were in Calgary during the winter, because in the summer they spent most of their time in the Okanagan in British Columbia where they have a summer home.

Once in a while we would visit John and Kay in Edmonton because they were only three hours away. We would leave early in the morning, visit with them and be back home in the evening. Marusia always spent time sewing or embroidering and I spent time on the computer writing these words for others to read about my life. Very seldom we watched TV unless something very newsy or interesting was happening.

A BAD PAINFUL TIME

Then my problems began also. On July 22nd I get a large red swollen and painful left toe. Each day it seemed to be getting worse and the pain is unbearable. At 11:30 PM on July 24th the pain is so bad that Marusia drove me to the emergency. The doctor checks it out and says: "Gout." That's all one needs in their lifetime. If you never had gout, may God save you from it. Also on this same day we get a phone call from Marusia's cousin (Jenny Kuney) at Woodstock Ontario and we are informed that she is very ill in the hospital at London and she wants to see Marusia. We go to the travel agency and get tickets for Marusia to leave in the afternoon. We get to the airport and discover that the flight the travel agent booked Marusia on departed for London, Ontario the day before - yesterday. So what does one do now? They put her on a standby for a different airline plane that evening some four hours later. The travel agent had really messed everything up, or else she did not know that the plane had gone the day before. Maybe the travel agent was behind in one day at everything.

Marusia is in London and my foot (gout) is not getting any better at all. On July 28th, I went to church in Calgary to the feast day and service of the congregation. Right after the service I went home, because of the pain. There was still the procession around the church, the dinner and speeches, but because of the pain, that was not for me. The following day I drove to see the doctor again for nothing was improving. It was this same day that

Orest Fodchuk came to start completing the basement in our condo as we had previously planned. Pain did not stop, so the following day I again went to see the doctor and he prescribed for me Tylenol 333 with codeine for pain.

Marusia returns home from London on July 31st. My foot is still sore and with pain and maybe even worse than the days past. With pain not going away, Marusia again takes me to see the doctor. On August 15th I'm again at the doctor's office because pain is not letting up. The doctor gives me prescription to the tune of $210.00 and Alberta health paid almost all except I had to pay $12.00 for having the prescription filled. If these problems with gout were not enough, there is more to come.

On the night of August 17th-18th with pain in my left foot, I get out of bed at 4:30 AM to go to the bathroom. I know and remember I was not feeling very well, feeling dizzy and weak. I got to the bathroom and felt weak and seemed like things were turning black around me. I remember I sat down on the toilet seat and felt as if everything around me was spinning. I must have passed out, because the next thing I remember I was lying on the floor in the bathroom. Slowly I pulled myself up and bracing unto the wall I made my way back to bed. I lay on the bed for a while and felt thirsty, so I got up again to go to the kitchen for a drink of water. I recall that I got out of bed and was in the hallway going to the kitchen. After that moment I don't remember anything. The next thing I know and remember was Marusia was trying to lift me up and was asking if I have any pain anywhere. She asked if I can move my feet and if I can get up. Where was I? I was half way down to the basement lying on the landing on the basement stairs.

What I can relate here is what Marusia told me. She said she had heard a loud thump and was awakened by it. She felt the bed and I wasn't there. She heard me moaning and came to look for me, but could not see me anywhere. Than she heard the noise on the stairs landing going to the basement, and she came to help me get back up and see if I was okay. She could not lift me up, but with her help, she said I crawled up the stairs on my hands and knees. She said that when I got to the top of the stairs I passed out again. When I came to again(which I don't remember) she helped me get to the chesterfield and I told her that I was thirsty. She said she wanted to call the ambulance, but I had told her that I was tired and wanted to sleep. She told me that she helped me get back to bed.

August 18th is Sunday and on Sunday people go to church, or don't they? We got up and as always made the bed together one on each side of the bed. After making the bed, Marusia went to the bathroom and I began to feel dizzy again and I sat down on the floor. Here I passed out again. When I came to, I was having a nose bleed. Marusia said there was no way we were going to church, but to emergency instead. We got dressed and at 9:00 AM we were already at the emergency at the hospital. All this time I felt weak, dizzy and seemed like everything was turning around me. It wasn't until about 11:30 AM that things were starting to clear up and I began to feel myself again. In the emergency they checked me over and found out that I was low on potassium. I was given a glass of orange juice to build up the potassium. Because I was taking medication for high blood pressure, the blood pressure pills ate up the potassium. Why all this had happened was the doctor had prescribed for me medication of Tylenol 333 and than also gave me morphine to kill the gout pain. The combination of the two medications caused me to be dizzy because the blood pressure had dropped down very drastically as the doctor told me later.

After the fall into the basement stairs, I later found out why I had a nose bleed. I had bruised my nose when I probably fell against the wall or stairs when I passed out. The back of my head also had a lump and the back of my left knee was also painful and swollen. On August 21st I again saw the doctor about gout and pain. The pain at the back of the knee was now gone, but the knee cap was sore and I had a sore throat. The following day my knee cap is even more painful and Marusia tells me to put on a cold pack. I began to do that and each day the pain was subsiding and slowly went away.

Now with the pain getting less each day, I began to walk better and we took another trip to Saskatchewan on August 29th. We visited relatives and friends and returned back home on September 1st bringing back produce from the garden from John and Alice Hnatiuk and from father. One spring when we were visiting with John and Alice, we planted the garden for Alice, because she had a bad backache. Father and Marusia were planting the garden while I was rototilling. When we returned back home from Saskatchewan the following two days I felt very cold and shivered and just could not warm up. Slowly even this went away, but what the problem was, I do not know.

My foot by this time was again sore, but not as bad. A friend of mine from the church in Calgary, Walter Nychka, called on September 19th and asked me to meet him at the church in half an hour and he will bring me some things that will help my gout. I drove down and he gave me two packages of ground flax seed and said to take two tablespoons each day for two weeks and the gout will disappear. This same day John and Kay from Edmonton came to see us. Just like Walter said, in two weeks the gout pain was gone.

On September 20th we leave for Prince George with the hopes of stopping over in Jasper for the night which was more less half way of our trip. When we got to Jasper there wasn't one room available in the motels and hotels. All signs said there was no vacancies. We had to drive on and got to McBride, B.C. We stayed at a new motel that just opened up that week. Later we learned why there were no vacancies in Jasper. We thought as many other seniors did that summer holidays were over and motels would now be empty. We found out that older people put off their holidays after the summer season rush and now they filled up the hotels and motels.

The year is moving by quickly and it is already fall. On October 5th(day before my birthday), our neighbors Bert and Ruth Paton took us on a trip into the Kananaskis country to see God's creation, the beautiful fall colors. All the different colors of leaves that changed. You could not take your eyes off all those colors. It is eye catching in every direction you look. Next day my birthday John and Kay came from Edmonton for a brief visit and brought me a birthday cake.

October 16th came and again found us on the road heading for Saskatoon, because Marusia's great niece is getting married. We attended the wedding on October 19th and spent some time visiting friends at Sturgis and Yorkton, Saskatchewan and Dauphin in Manitoba as well as family and relatives around Cudworth and Wakaw. While in the area of that country, on October 20th the Town of Cudworth was honoring all those people who were eighty-five years and older. Cudworth was eighty-five years old that year. From a population of 1000 people, in Cudworth there were forty residents who were eighty-five and older. One lady was a hundred years old, another man was ninety-seven and our father was ninety-five, the third oldest. All others were younger. At this gathering in the Town Hall, the mayor of Cudworth, His Worship Peter Yuzik said that our father was the "George Burns" of Cudworth.

The basement in our house was nearing completion. By the end of October everything was done with the exception of the ceiling which we put off to another year for it will be a drop ceiling. On November 4th we had the carpet installed in the basement and the following day on November 5th furniture for the basement arrived.

As mentioned previously, we were having all kinds of problems with the Buick Regal. Each time we got into it to go somewhere we were always thinking: "And what else will happen with this car this time?" We decided to get rid of it. On December 21st we brought home a new 1997 Chevrolet Lumina which we purchased. On that same day we also bought a small 1987 Buick Skyhawk, so that we could have the small car to run around in the city and use the Lumina for longer trips. We did not want to use the Lumina car every day on the salty streets and roads. The little Buick Skyhawk we bought from the Summit Saturn dealer. At the time we were looking at the Buick Skyhawk, a sudden storm blew into Calgary catching us outside so suddenly that we never even had the opportunity to drive this little car. We just looked at it from outside, liked what we saw and bought it for $2750.00. Because it was already in it's eleventh year, later we had to add a few repairs to it.

Christmas is just around the corner. John and Alice wanted to go south to the USA for a while, but they did not want to leave father alone for too long a period. We made arrangements and on January 2nd 1997 so father would come to Calgary by plane from Saskatoon. The airfare was $170.00 one way. Had father said sooner a few weeks earlier that he would come to stay with us for a few weeks, the fare would have been $159.00. The trouble was that one day father wants to come to our place and the next day he calls Alice and says he does not want to go. He was putting this off until Alice went and bought a ticket for him and than he had no choice, but to come. On January 5th Oksana from Winnipeg also flew to Calgary to spend Christmas with us (January 6th and 7th). We took father with us and went to the airport but never told father who was coming. We said a friend was coming that he also knows. Father was surprised to see Oksana when she arrived at the airport in Calgary.

The Christmas Eve Supper on January 6th was held with family and friends. Father, Oksana, Joe and Marlene Korzeniowski, Jennie Marchinko and neighbors Bert and Ruth Paton. After supper we went to church and it was a very cold night, but still there were a lot of people in church for the service at midnight. Father stayed with us until January 10th and was getting restless, so we drove him to Edmonton to spend a few days with John and Kay. Later John put father on the plane to Saskatoon. He arrived in Saskatoon and one of John and Alice's daughters picked him up at the airport. Father had arrived in Calgary January 2nd and left January 10th - was that "quite a while" that father was at our place like Alice said.

OH THOSE BUICK CAR PROBLEMS

January 26th 1997 we left for Cudworth to pick up father to the funeral of Mary Yakubchak at Dauphin, Manitoba. This was mother's first cousin who passed away. When we left Calgary for Cudworth it was -38 C that morning. In the morning we went to church and after the service we drove to Cudworth. On January 28th Marusia was to have surgery for a trigger finger, but that had to be postponed, because we were at the funeral. She had her surgery later on April 23rd.

When we left home and got on the highway we heard a disturbing noise in the new car. Later we made two more trips to Saskatchewan with the Lumina and always heard the same humming noise which seemed to get louder each time. It was annoying to drive and have the humming sound mile after mile for the whole trip. When the car was standing and the engine running you could not hear that sound, only when the car was in motion. Before we made the trip to Dauphin to the funeral, I went to the dealer to have an oil change in the Lumina. The dealer told me they were too busy and maybe I can go to the Pontiac dealer a block away. After spending all that money on the car and they haven't got 10 minutes to change oil? All we needed was oil and filter and that is a ten minute job. We went to Cudworth as was and had the oil changed at Cudworth by a dealer who looked after GMC products. So do I feel like I want to got back to that dealer when we spend thousands of dollars and he says he has no time to change oil.

It was in 1996 that Marusia began to complain about a problem with her small finger. It was triggering and painful. She had to see a specialist on January 28th, but that was canceled because we were going to a funeral at Dauphin Manitoba. Later she had a day set for surgery, but again had to postpone the surgery because the doctor that was to operate on her finger did not know where he would operate because the hospital he worked from was closing down. Finally on April 23rd, just four days before Orthodox Easter she had her surgery.

Father had come to our place for Christmas in January. For Easter we are going to his place at Cudworth. Oksana also came from Winnipeg. It was a nice get together even though all the family could not be there together, for John from Edmonton was absent. We also visited mother at the cemetery during our stay there.

As mentioned above, we had the humming noise in the new car when you get out on the highway. Each time we drove on a trip the noise seemed to be louder. When we got back after Easter I made an appointment at the dealer to have the noise checked out. I was scheduled to be in the garage at 8:00 AM Wednesday morning. Marusia and I both went to the garage because something kept telling me that I will have problems at the garage. We arrived at the garage at exactly 7:48 AM, twelve minutes before schedule. The work order was written up and we were told to wait and we would go with someone for a ride to tell about the noise. We waited. Than we waited some more. And we still waited. It was 8:15, than 8:30 and now it is already 8:45 AM, we are waiting and still no one coming to tell us to go with them for a test drive. When we had come in they wrote up the work order, drove the car outside and were told to wait. We sat in the waiting room and could see our car outside but it had not been moved during all that time for more than an hour.

I tell Marusia that I am waiting till 9:00 AM. If nothing happens by then, I am taking the keys back and going to another Chevrolet dealer in Calgary. Other vehicles were brought in later after us, and they were being serviced and parked back outside. Our car has been sitting for an hour and no one has even been near it during that time. Finally after sitting and waiting for an hour and eight minutes, I says: "Enough is enough." One time they would not change oil. Now waiting for an hour and no movement at all. Well I'm ready to start some action. Marusia and I go to the counter and I say: "We've had our car in here for over an hour. You were to take it out on a road test and we were to go with you. Nothing has happened. I want the keys to our car and I'm going to another Chevrolet dealer." There were three men behind the counter and I heard one whisper to the other: "Give him the keys back." I told them that one time I wanted an oil change and they didn't do it and now this again. I told them that I want nothing more to do with their dealership either and they won't see me there again. We walked out and never set foot there again.

We took our car to another Chevrolet dealer. When we came there they asked us if they can help us. We told them the story. In about one or two minutes flat at the most, the manager or some mechanic was already talking with us. We went to the car and went with him for a test drive. We came back and the man told us to bring the car in on Monday, because the man that looks after the noise in vehicles is away on holidays. We said we would come back and told him that we will be able to leave the car with them even for a week, because we have another car with which we are leaving for Saskatchewan in a few days.

Going to Saskatchewan we took the little Buick Skylark. We went to father's place, than on to Benito. Driving to Benito, we heard a screeching noise in the car as if something was rubbing against something, metal against metal. From Benito we drove to Yorkton and then to Regina Beach and Saskatoon. When we got to Saskatoon we went to see Bill Meyer(Carolyn's friend. Carolyn is my niece). Bill listened to the noise and said it was the air-conditioner compressor that was gone. He sent us to another garage a few blocks away. They hoisted the car and found that the noise was coming from a pulley. They took the fan belt off and the noise disappeared. The car ran, but we had no air-conditioner. They also found that the frame which holds the air-conditioner was also cracked-broken. When we came home we had these things repaired and the car was working well again.

Having arrived home we went to pick up the Lumina which had been left to repair the humming noise. When we came to the garage, the service man asks: "Did you have damage on your left rear door when you brought the car in?" We looked at each other surprised, than at the service manager and say: "No the car was in perfect shape." We walked out to look at the car and sure enough the rear left door was damaged. The service manager says: "The City Towing must have backed into it, but we'll get it fixed for you." Again we left the Lumina for the repairs that had occurred. The service manager told us that the humming noise which had been in the car was caused by a faulty bearing on the front wheel.

Since we moved into the new house in Calgary it seems like trouble is always one step ahead of us with the cars. The new Buick Regal was giving us trouble. Than the Lumina had problems with the humming noise and than the damage to the door on the garage lot. The little Skyhawk also was bringing problems. I also had problems with gout setting in again. Marusia had the misfortune to have surgery on her finger. Than on March 31 as we both sat on the chesterfield watching the Ten Commandments on TV, the chesterfield seemed like someone jarred or kicked it. What is happening here anyway?

About the middle of April we got a phone call from Alexander and Nina Sahulenko of Phoenix that they are coming to Canada, because she is not feeling too well and they want to spend some time at Radium Hot Springs. She said when she lived in Minneapolis, she used to come to Radium Hot Springs every five years and that water was helping her. She has not been back at Radium Hot Springs for fifteen years. Later they sent us an itinerary that they will arrive in Calgary on June 28th. They want to spend a week at Radium and a week in Edmonton with their friends they know. They wanted us to reserve them a place at Radium Hot Springs for one week.

When we got their itinerary, we drove to Radium Hot Springs (one hundred and seventy miles) and booked them a cabin near the pool. We got to Radium before noon, found them a cabin, had something to eat and than went into the pool for awhile. We came home later that day and everything was fine. At 10:00 PM as we were watching the CBC news, I felt like something was crawling up my legs, and felt cold and shivering. I looked at my legs, and from the tip of my toes and all the way up past the knees about four or five inches everything was red like a lobster. It seemed like a rash. Was it some form of an allergy? I never went to see any doctor, and in about three or four days the rash disappeared. It left a mark as though the skin had been tanned or burnt. I was in the water at Radium up to my neck when we were there in the pool. Why was the rest of the body not covered in that form of rash, only the legs about six inches above the knees. Did it have something to do with the water at Radium Hot Springs. When we lived in Vernon one man told us that Radium Hot Springs is not good to go into that water because it has too much radium in it. Is that why my legs turned red like a lobster?

Everything looked well. Sahulenkos had arrived from Phoenix. We picked them up at the airport and they stayed overnight at our place. Next morning we drove them to Radium Hot Spring. That afternoon and evening all four of us went into the pool. The following morning we again went into the pool and left our company in Radium, while Marusia and I returned to Calgary. That evening the same kind of rash appeared on my legs in the same way it had happened the first time. The rash never went higher, just above the knees.

Anyway I should take you back a step to May and June. On May 17th we again had gone to Saskatchewan because on the 18th there will be grave side services where Marusia's parents, brother and sister are buried at Wakaw. These kind of services are held where ever Ukrainian Orthodox People live. The week following Easter and until Christ's Ascension the priest and people gather at the cemeteries, have services and the priest blesses the graves. Tropar of Christ's Resurrection is sung at each grave as it is blessed with holy water. The Tropar is: *"Christ is risen from the dead, trampling down death by Death, and upon those in the tombs, bestowing life."* A week later there will be the same service at Cudworth where mother is buried. John and Kay from Edmonton came to the service at Cudworth, but Oksana from Winnipeg could not attend this time. Instead of coming home from Wakaw, we stayed in Saskatchewan and visited our friends and relatives. During the time we were in Saskatchewan we heard on the radio and TV that Calgary and Edmonton were hit with severe snow storms on May 18th. This is already May and so is this spring?

While in Saskatchewan we also helped Alice plant the garden. Marusia, Pat Walker (Alice's daughter), father and I put in the garden for Alice, because she was complaining of back aches. I worked the garden with the rototiller. Father was making holes to plant potatoes (he is ninety-six years old). He also had already planted his garden at Cudworth when we arrived there. He still drove the car, cut the lawn, shoveled snow, worked on the garden, etc. He also looked after the house himself.

YELLOWKNIFE NWT - RAVEN MAD DAZE

It was sometimes in the past wintertime when I was reading the Ukrainian Voice, a weekly paper where I read an article about Ukrainians at Yellowknife in the N.W.T. Ukrainians in Yellowknife? And what are they doing up there? But than the other question: And where are there no Ukrainians? They are scattered all over the globe. Anyway the article said that they have their own group and participate in cultural activities during Raven Mad Daze that are held in June. Sounds interesting to see what this Raven Made Daze is all about. Would be interesting to go and also see the Ukrainian group. But there are no names, addresses or phone numbers where to get in touch about this.

We talked over about this Raven Mad Daze that it would be nice to go and see Canada up north. But where do we write to find out and get information? Oh yes, I'll write to the City Hall. Maybe they will send us some information. I wrote a letter and sure enough a few days later comes a package in the mail with details, pamphlets, road maps, etc., all about Raven Mad Daze and a letter from the City Hall thanking us for enquiring. Now we know that Raven Mad Daze is held every year in the month of June on the longest day of the year. Neither of us have been that far north before. Yes, I have been as far as Hotchkiss (north of Manning, Alberta) when I used to serve that area 1962-1967 and again 1977-1980 but not in the North West Territories.

So now everything is getting set and planned. We will leave in the morning of June 17th to be in Yellowknife in time for Raven Mad Daze. We left early and arrived that same day at High Level, Alberta about 9:00 PM. At 11:00 PM it was still daylight outside. We are not accustomed to go to bed in the daylight. We had curtains drawn closed, but still daylight was in the room as we tried to fall asleep. Finally we fell asleep. Next morning we leave and continue our trip north. We had planned that it would take us two and one half to three days to get to Yellowknife. We did not take into consideration of calculating the difference in daylight at this time of the year in the north country. We left High Level and got to Yellowknife the same day at 9:00 PM.

Once you leave High Level all you see and have along your way is bush, forest, more forest, lakes, rivers and more forest. The farther north you go, the shorter the trees become because of the short growing season. We arrive at noon at the sixtieth parallel(the border between Alberta and the North West Territories). There is an information booth at the border for summer months only. We got some information and kept on going. Bush, lakes, rivers, bush, lake, rivers for miles and miles and miles. All kinds of flowers are blooming along the roadside and in the ditches, but north of the Mackenzie River we see miles and miles of golden ditches. Dandelions from the side of the road and all the way into the bush, nothing but zillion golden yellow dandelions. The whole ditch is yellow. There are probably more dandelions there than in the rest of Canada put together. We come to Enterprise, N.W.T. and there the highway separates. One goes to Yellowknife and the other to Hay River. Seeing we have time on our hands, we turn off to go and see Hay River which is about twenty miles out of our way and than we have to return back to Enterprise to take the highway to Yellowknife.

Driving along to Hay River we stop to see two waterfalls, Alexandra and Victoria. We could not stop for too long outside, because the mosquitoes would eat you up alive. I guess they were tired of the northern blood and wanted some fresh southern blood for dessert. We came into Hay River and wanted to see Great Slave Lake, but did not see it because it was all fogged in. We were taken to the top of the 17th story building in Hay River and were told that was the tallest building in the North West Territories. After having our lunch which we packed from home we left Hay River and headed back to the junction to take the highway to Yellowknife. As we slide along the paved highway, all we see again is bush, swamp, rivers, lakes, sloughs for miles and miles with no end in sight. In places we drove for ten to fifteen or twenty miles before we would meet up with another vehicle on the road. As we drive along we see a sign that says: "Next service 212 kilometers." In another place we see a sign saying: "Next service 318 kilometers." When you go on that stretch of road, you must be sure to have enough fuel if you don't want to walk for miles or wait for long periods of time to get help. For miles and miles there are no services.

At Hay River gasoline was 58.9 cents a litre. At Yellowknife it was 73.9 cents. These prices were in June 1997. That is what it cost in Yellowknife some nineteen years ago. After we got back from Hay River, we had to cross the Mackenzie River. A huge river, about a mile wide and takes eight minutes to cross by ferry. This is the only road to Yellowknife. In the summer time, you get across with a ferry. In the winter time you cross on the ice - the frozen river. In the freeze up and melting periods the only way to get to Yellowknife is by plane or by boat from Hay River. As I write this in 2016, there is now a bridge across the MacKenzie River where the river can be crossed twenty-four hours a day year round.

After crossing the Mackenzie River, on the north side is a small Indian village of Fort Providence. Driving along we see a sign saying: "Mackenzie Bison Crossing." We were told that there are so many buffalo crossing at times, that traffic will be stopped on the highway for as much as fifteen minutes. We saw one buffalo going to Yellowknife and four when we were coming back home. After passing Fort Providence, we saw that it was 6:00 PM and we had another hundred and eighty miles to go to Yellowknife. The sun was up high, so we just kept on going. Even if we wanted to stop, there are no towns or motels along the way. We had a paved highway until about fifty miles from Yellowknife when it was gravel. There was also a stretch of about ten miles of road being constructed. We learned from the Mayor in Yellowknife, that in 2000 all the road will be paved to Yellowknife.

As we were driving along in the construction area at fifty kilometers an hour and in places at thirty, an Oldsmobile car catches up to us and is on our bumper and wanting to pass. When it was possible, we pulled over and let the two older gentlemen with British Columbia licence plates on their car go past us. We passed through the construction zone and than were on the pavement again. As we came over one elevation of the highway we could see a few miles down the road, that it looked like a car was on the opposite side of the road on the bank of the road. As we neared the place we recognized that it was the two old gentlemen that were in a big hurry. I guess they were in a hurry to get into the ditch. We slowed down to stop and possibly give a hand. We see one man is filling the car with gasoline from a Jerry can. I guess that was probably not their first trip, that they knew about having spare fuel.

The doors in the car are both wide open. The other man sitting in the drivers side shaking his hands trying to chase away the mosquitoes. There must have been a trillion and a half mosquitoes there. We stopped to help them and Marusia sat in the car because of mosquitoes. I came over and asked if they need any help. The man filling the car says: "It ran away on him and now we can't start it because not enough gasoline in the tank and not reaching the fuel pump." I stood beside him for a minute or two until he emptied the Jerry can. The other man started the car and I told him to drive out of the ditch before it stalls again. The ditch was about eight to ten feet deep and was at a sharp slant. The driver stepped on the gas and there was dirt and gravel flying in all direction, but he did get the car back unto the highway. When they were already on the road, I got back into the car and we drove off. We had left them behind, but about fifteen minutes later I see in the rear view mirror a car approaching. You guessed it, it was the same two gentlemen who were in the ditch just a while ago. They caught up to us, but never passed us, just stayed behind. We traveled like that until we reached Edzo a small village of the highway west of Yellowknife. They turned into that village and we never saw them again.

From Edzo to Yellowknife it is fifty miles and all gravel road. About ten miles before Yellowknife a highway truck was putting sodium or potassium chloride on the road to keep the dust down. For ten miles we had to drive behind this truck, because there was a sign on the back of the truck that said: "Stay back Do not pass." We drove the rest of the way to Yellowknife following that truck and splashing the fresh red salty mud all over and under the car. We arrived at Yellowknife and found our motel which we had booked from home a month in advance. When we got out of our car, we could not see what color the car was, for it was plastered with the red clay. Our motel was booked for the next day, but when we told the man we arrived sooner, he said there was no problem for our room was vacant. We spent three days in that motel as our home.

But than we also had a problem on our hands. We have to get rid of this red clay with salt before it eats the up car. We need a car wash. The man in the motel told us where the car wash was, so we drove there to get the car washed. When we got there they told us at the service station that the car wash is closed at 8:00 PM and will open tomorrow at 10:00 AM. It was now just somewhat past 9:00 PM when we arrived in Yellowknife. No car wash so we headed back to the motel for where else can you go after 9:00 PM.

We had something to eat which we brought from home in a cooler and were tired enough to go to bed, but the sun was still up and just did not seem to want to go down so that made it harder trying to fall asleep in the daylight. It was bright enough that we could sit outside the motel at midnight and still read the paper without lights. Anyway somehow we managed to fall asleep.

Next morning we went to get the car washed. During the night some mud had fallen and dripped off the car unto the parking lot where the car was parked. We went to the car wash and the sign inside the car wash says: "Minimum car wash $10.00." I had to look twice to see if I read correctly. The man came and I say to him: "How come so expensive for a car wash when you are sitting right on top of Great Slave Lake and have all the water you need?" The man answers saying: "You get a cheap car wash here, because other places will charge you as much as $40.00 for a car wash." So what does one do? Pay the man the $10.00 and wash your car if you want the salty mud off.

After washing the car we thought we should go and see the City Hall and tell the people who we are and thank them for the letter and information they sent us about Raven Mad Daze. We found the City Hall asked for the lady who had written the letter to us and she was called to the counter. We showed her the letter and she was very kind and thanked us for coming to Yellowknife. She told us to wait for a while as she went into another room. A few moments later she comes out with a man and she introduced him to us. He was the mayor of Yellowknife. The mayor called us into his office and we sat with him and chatted for about ten minutes. We could have been there longer, but the lady came back in and said that the mayor had a luncheon meeting and it was already noon. Before we departed the mayor gave us pins of Yellowknife, gave us a history book of Yellowknife, a commemorative coin and a few other smaller souvenirs.

We had called from Calgary a few times to make reservations in one hotel, but were told they book rooms for a month at a time not for a day. When we were talking to the mayor, he asked us where we were staying. We told him we were staying at the Northern Lights Motel and he said that was a good spot. I told the mayor that we will be going for meals to this one place, but he suggested that place was not for us.

From the City Hall we went back to the motel and had some lunch and afternoon we went to see the museum and the history of Yellowknife. A well cared for and beautiful museum it is. After that we drove around to see Yellowknife and Marusia wanted to go and visit the Wal-Mart and check on the prices. We were astonished to find that the prices for things in Yellowknife at Walmart were the same as in Calgary. In the evening (if there is an evening at this time in Yellowknife), we went to look again at the city. We saw beautiful homes of the Inuit or natives and they really looked after their homes and kept the yards neat and clean. We were driving on a gravel road, when suddenly we heard dogs barking. We slowed down and saw behind the fences all kinds of dogs each one in their one little fenced in place. When they all started to bark, we took off, for we were scared in case someone should come along and think we were harming the dogs.

In the evening we went to the top of the high rock in the city to see the "Midnight Sun." There are seventy steps to the top of the rock. We took some pictures of the sun as it was trying to set, but you could still see a part of the top of the sun as it was setting, but at the same time it was already also rising. You could still sit outside and read the newspaper without lights, but that is impossible for the mosquitoes would eat you alive without salt or pepper. Next day we called a few familiar Ukrainian names we found in the phone directory and learned that there were people living in Yellowknife who had moved there from Manitoba, Saskatchewan and Alberta.

Next morning we went back to see the dogs, hoping that we may find someone that will tell us something about the dogs. We found a man that was working in the kennels with the dogs and we asked if we could take some pictures to which he replied positively. When we first arrived there, the dogs started to bark and howl and we were afraid that maybe we were disturbing them. The man came out of the kennels and we started to talk while in the meantime he was trying to quiet the dogs down and after a short while they all became quiet. We asked him why the dogs were barking so loudly when we arrived and he told us that they were very happy to see someone.

The man said that he worked for the city and that the dogs were his hobby or sideline. He said that he has twenty-five dogs of his own and all the rest of maybe a few hundred belonged to other people. We asked how much a dog like that costs and he said it depends. His dogs he said were not the best so he would probably get about $2000.00 per dog. The better dogs go for $5000.00 and the super dogs as he said would sell for around $10,000.00. We did not see any huskies so we asked were the huskies were. He said no one raises husky dogs because they are not the best. He told us that a husky will run for two hours and he would be played out, while these dogs can run for eight to ten hours and when you stop they still want to run and have no side effects. We asked what they feed so many dogs with, and he gave us a surprising answer. He told us that they feed each dog with one chicken a day and the chickens are brought in from Alberta. The best food for the dogs he said was the chicken. After we left there we drove around and looked at the city and saw some beautiful enormous houses.

Now comes the Raven Mad Daze. It starts at 6:00 PM and concludes at midnight. The stores bring out their wares unto the tables on the sidewalk and street. The main street is all blocked off, so there are no vehicles only pedestrian traffic on the street. Dozens of barbeques and food booths are set up along main street. There are games for the children, street entertainment on large flat bed trailers. Just a fun time for everyone. Come Raven Mad Daze the whole city turns out for the fun and enjoyment. We were told that about eight to ten thousand people turn out on the street for the celebration. Children paint the street and faces with different color paint and chalk which is easily washed off. Yellowknife has a population of eighteen thousand people and more than half come out for the event each year as we were told. We just walked up and down, back and forth on the street and looked at what was going on, and here and there Marusia picked up a few things from the vendors.

A few times we stopped by the food booth that the Ukrainians ran on the street. They were selling sausage and varenyky (perogies). We bought some food from them and talked with a few of those that had a moment to talk. They told us that each year they have a parade in Yellowknife and each year the Ukrainians took first place for their float, but they don't enter a float anymore so that someone else would have a chance to win first place with a float.

Our motel was not even two blocks from the main street, so we had a chance to walk and see everything. We took some video and than went back to the motel for tomorrow morning we will be starting our trip back home. We also learned that at midnight there was going to be the start of a golf tournament as part the Raven Mad Daze. The sun does not set, so to play golf at that time of the hour is no problem. One thing I must add here. We saw on their streets from the Raven Mad Daze a lot of litter. Paper all over. Children painted the street with some chalk. Children shooting some kind of gum like substance at each other that looked like thick thread and of different colors. When we were leaving next morning for home, you would never believe that there was all that mess the night before. The streets had been cleaned, washed and were spick and span now.

We left at a quarter to seven in the morning. It was twenty-two miles of driving before we met the first car on the road. Since we had stopped and looked at things here and there on our way to Yellowknife, we can now head straight home and no stopping except for a few minutes to stretch our legs. We turned into Fort Providence since it was less than a mile of the highway. We stopped beside the river and were surprised to see and pick wild red strawberries on June 22nd. Is that not earlier than in some places on the Canadian Prairies? Going both ways we were lucky that we did not have to wait long for the ferry to cross the Mackenzie River. As we approached the river both times, the ferry was being loaded, so we just pulled in line and were loaded along with all other vehicles and passengers.

As we neared Manning, Alberta that late afternoon, we noticed something unusual. We could see that small creeks were filled with fast flowing muddy waters. We knew there must have been a heavy rainfall. We registered at a motel in Manning for the night and found out that on Thursday of that week the area received a little over three inches of rain. Even the river that runs through Manning was filled nearly to the top of the banks but there was no flood anywhere. Next day being Sunday we thought we would go to church in Manning to the Ukrainian Catholic church if there is a service there. We waited near the church till a quarter to ten and than drove away, seeing no action. Since there was no service we went to see Mrs. Slotiuk whom I knew since the 1960's when I used to stay at their place when I came to have services at Hotchkiss, north of Manning. Her husband had died about a year ago and she was very happy to see us. We did not stay long, because when we were there she got a phone call from some people that they were coming to pick her up to go to a picnic.

We left Manning just before noon and drove to Grimshaw which is some twenty miles west of Peace River and stopped to see Harry and Mary Kinakin, very good friends from years past. Mary Kinakin is the daughter of the late George and Mary Zyha whose names have already been mentioned a number of times. When we came to their place they had a big meal prepared. We spent some time at their place visiting with them and headed out on our way so that we can be closer to home, since tomorrow I have a meeting to attend at the church. This Sunday night we spent at Whitecourt, and Harry had told us to take highway twenty-two and it will be a short cut instead of going through Edmonton. Harry has been driving semi trucks all over Alberta so he knows the highways like the palm of his hand.

We left Whitecourt next morning driving through Drayton Valley. There we stopped and wanted to see some friends that I knew from the 1960's in Lac La Biche and later in Phoenix. These friends were not home, so we continued on our way home. We crossed a river and low and behold after driving for a while we noticed we were not on highway twenty-two, but some other highway leading to Leduc. Somehow we missed a sign, or there was no sign showing us where highway twenty-two was in a junction with another highway. So what do we do now? Just keep on going to Leduc and from there we will take highway two to Calgary. We believe that there was no sign showing where highway twenty-two was, for we told some people in Calgary what had happened and they told us that they had run into the same situation with that road. We arrived home at 3:00 PM in plenty of time for me to attend the meeting.

On July 27th the congregation in Calgary is celebrating its feast day(chram) of the church, St. Volodymyr or St. Vladimir as some say.

(Vladimir is the Russian version of the Ukrainian word Volodymyr). About a month or so before this feast day, Father Taras Krochak and Shirley Dinn the congregation chairperson, approached me and asked that I be the guest speaker at this feast day. Father Taras said that I can talk about vocations, the priesthood, since this year had been proclaimed as the year of the priesthood. I spoke on that topic, but also a week before that I was asked to be the cantor for the service, because the cantor would be away that day.

BUSY AT HOME AFTER THE TRIP

It was sometimes the first week in July Marusia had gone to see her doctor. She had blood work done and was told that her cholesterol was high. She was given a prescription, "Lipidil" to reduce her cholesterol. After taking this medication for a week or so, she got a rash on her legs. The rash looked like blood blisters. When she started taking this medication, I had a strange feeling as if someone or something was telling me: "Marusia is dying and needs help." I never told her about this feeling I had, because I did not want to frighten her since she already was having enough problems after the open heart surgery. She made another appointment to see a doctor about the rash. Our doctor was away, so a woman doctor looked after her. The doctor checked her over and said her liver is being damaged - holes are forming in her liver and the doctor thinks it's from the Lipidil. The doctor told her to quit the Lipidil. As soon as she stopped taking Lipidil that strange feeling I was having that she is dying went away from me. Was God or an Angel trying to tell me something? I do not know. What would have happened if she would have continued using those drugs? Would her liver have been completely damaged and destroyed? I do not know. I'm sure God knew.

On August 23rd the Ukrainian community in Calgary celebrated the Ukrainian Independence Day at the Ukrainian Catholic Church. Another Ukrainian event this year was the official opening of St. Stephan's

Ukrainian Catholic Church Hall on September 27th. This congregation had asked the other Ukrainian Catholic congregation and our Orthodox congregation to form one large choir to participate in this event. For this to happen, the three choirs got together for practices. The three choirs together formed a group of ninety people. We attended the choir practices and also the event on September 27th. The hall was filled to capacity. Later this year in December four Ukrainian Choirs in Calgary participated in a Ukrainian Carol Festival which was held in our church hall, at St. Volodymyr's Ukrainian Orthodox Cultural Centre.

We made another trip to Saskatoon to Marusia's great nephew's marriage - Allan Semeniuk on September 6th. Allan married Cynthia, a relative of Marlene Korzeniowski. Than again we left for Kelowna on October 10th to attend a 50th wedding anniversary for Alex and Vicky Kordaban which was held on October 11th. Another trip this year took us to Prince George, B.C. at the end of October where I showed slides of Ukrainian Orthodox Churches. We made another trip to Saskatchewan in November and attended the feast day service at Lepine, just east of Wakaw. Our last trip this year was to Winnipeg, Manitoba to attend a wedding of my niece, Gail Foley, on December 27th. We left home on December 25th in the morning. The trip was good, the weather was fine, no snow and also very little snow in Winnipeg with mild temperatures. Gail and Guy rode in a brand new Laidlaw bus. As they were riding in the brand new bus after the marriage in the church, the bus caught fire at the back and people were honking horns for the bus to stop and escape the fire. Guy worked for this company.

Before 1997 ended we attended two funerals in Edmonton in two weeks for the same family. My cousin Bill Derzak lost his wife. The funeral was on October 20th. Two weeks to the day on November 3rd the funeral was held for Bill. Wife and husband died exactly two weeks apart. It was very cold for the funeral in November, but the next day November 4th warmed up and it was a beautiful warm day.

After having moved from Phoenix and settled in Calgary, we attended church every Sunday and Holy Day, unless we were away, than we would attend church in the area we were visiting. It was more than a year after living in Calgary that we were invited to come and join the Golden Agers in the congregation, a senior Ukrainian club at the church. We attended the senior gathering about four or five times and than on December 2nd I was elected president of the club. Since I was elected president of the club, I was automatically a representative from the seniors to the church executive board. This would now involve me even more in meetings, activities and responsibilities. And thus 1997 came to an end.

The year 1998 started like 1997 ended. No snow and mild outdoors. But in Calgary things can change quickly. They say: "If you don't like the weather in Calgary, wait five minutes and it will change." That is what happened. We were planning to go to spend Orthodox Christmas with father at Cudworth. The forecasters began to say that a storm is coming. We called father and asked how the weather was in Cudworth and he said that it is very cold and said that we stay home and not venture out into the cold weather. My father used to say: "Don't look for trouble, trouble will find you itself." It started snowing heavily on January 6th at 2:00 PM and on January 7th at 6:00 PM it was still snowing and the temperature was -23 C. The snow did not stop falling until January 8th in the afternoon. January 10th brought a cold temperature of -29 C and the forecast was that it would even get colder. After January 14th, Orthodox New Years Day, the weather began to change with warmer temperatures and we became busy again with choir practices, meetings, weekly senior gatherings and other activities at the cultural center.

On February 29th, 1997 the congregation in Calgary hosted the late Father Peter Gillquist from the USA. Father Gillquist is an Orthodox priest who had been a Protestant minister all his life but became Orthodox. A number of his clergy friends and him, always used to discuss among themselves why there are so many denominations and that only one of them must be the right one. Each of the friends and him included had to study the historical aspect of each denomination. Later they met in an isolated place without daily interruptions to learn what each one had to say about his findings. They were always asking, "What happened to the early church that Christ had established?" After studying each topic they came to the conclusion that Orthodoxy was the true faith. They wanted to join an Orthodox church in the USA, but wherever they went, no one wanted to accept them. Finally it was the late Metropolitan Philip of the Antiochian Orthodox Church in the USA who accepted them under his wing. This is the same Orthodox Church that had ordained the first three priests for the Ukrainian Orthodox Church of Canada and looked after our church until we got our own bishops. Metropolitan Philip accepted a dozen of the clergy and hundreds of parishioners who accepted the Orthodox Faith. He accepted one clergyman and his congregation each Sunday until all were in the orthodox church. In 2013 Father Peter Gillquist passed away. Metropolitan Philip passed away in early 2014.

Time was running along and not waiting for anyone. Now Christ's Resurrection(Easter) was just around the corner on April 19th. Father's birthday falls on April 15th, so Marusia and I leave for Cudworth on April 16th, a day after father's birthday. The day we arrived in Cudworth we also drove to Melfort, Saskatchewan where Passions of Christ service was held that evening. The following day we went to Wakaw for the service of Bringing out the Holy Shroud. On Saturday the priest came to Cudworth to bless the Easter Paska. On Easter Sunday morning we went to church to Wakaw. The same day after the service we held a little birthday party for father at his place at the back yard. The day was beautiful, sunny and warm. All of us four children, plus most of the grandchildren and great-grandchildren were present.

On May 31st Calgary hosted guests from Ukraine. A dance group "Virsky" was traveling across Canada and performed at different cities. The performance was sold out at each place they went. Tickets for this event were $55.00 each and the performance was spectacular and without comparison. Marusia's nephew the late Mike Semeniuk and his wife Doreen from Cold Lake, Alberta were in Calgary at that time and they attended this function with us. The rest of the time was spent at meetings and getting more and more involved in various committees and organizations. Everybody wanted me to help them out with one thing or another and so a lot of time was spent away from home. Sometimes I was so busy that I had to be at the church for three different activities in one day. Later I will give you an example of time consumption with the various activities we were involved with at the church.

On June 21st at 7:30 PM we get an unexpected phone call from Phoenix, Arizona. The chairman of the congregation, Wasyl Szwez, was asking us to come back to Phoenix to serve the congregation. I did not accept the proposal because there was a priest serving there at that time and it is not right that I come and chase a priest out of the congregation.

I never did that to anyone before and I would not do it ever. I also told him that now we are both over sixty-five years of age, medical costs would be very high there. A few days later we get another call at 6:45 PM from the Duwirak family requesting the same thing to return to the parish in Phoenix. The following day, June 26th, the chairman called again at 9:40 PM begging us to return to Phoenix. They had a priest there at the time, but that priest had his mind set on another thing instead of the church. He had other interests instead of ringing the church bell he rang filled glasses.

MARUSIA - ANOTHER HEALTH PROBLEM

On July 5th we were on our way to church in the morning. Before we got to church, Marusia said that her left hand felt numb. Getting out of the car and going to church, she said she felt as though she had lost some control in her leg and that her coordination was not very good. I wanted to take her to emergency, but she would not go and would say that she will be ok. We sang in the choir and during the service I kept asking her how she was feeling and if I should take her to emergency or not, but she said it she was okay. After the service when we came home, she asked me to drive her to a walk in clinic not far from home. The doctor at the clinic checked her over, wrote a letter and told us to get to the emergency. We went to the foothills hospital and there she was again checked over and the doctors thought she had a TIA (Transient Ishmic attack), - which is a precondition to a stroke?

This same day when we got home we made a few phone calls to friends and one of them was Dr. Emil and Ann Cymbalisty at Yorkton, Saskatchewan. He is a chiropractor. We told them what had happened during the day and he said that Marusia immediately go to see a chiropractor in Calgary, Dr. John Liscombe. We made an appointment to see him. He took an x-ray and said to come back next day. When we returned next day, he showed the x-ray that Marusia's back was out of shape and he said that she has pinched nerves which will require about twelve treatments to put her back in better shape. She started those treatments and said she starting to feel better. Dr. Liscombe checked and found that one leg was an inch shorter than the other. She was seeing the doctor three times the first week and than less until it came down to once a month. During this time she got a phone call from the emergency room at the hospital that they made an appointment to have an MRI (Magnet Resonance Imaging) test the first week in November. During the period before the MRI, she had other tests the TIA, the scan tests, EKG, x-rays and other tests and they all showed negative.

July came and passed leaving Marusia with unstable news. August came and on August 3rd we take a trip to Cold Lake, Alberta to visit with Marusia's nephew Mike Semeniuk and his wife Doreen. We took the Buick Skyhawk car. Everything was going well until we came to Two Hills, Alberta. As we traveled along, I was taking slides of our churches here and there along the way. We were driving on a farm road to one church when suddenly the red light of the alternator came on. We drove into a farmer's yard and I asked if I could use the phone to make a call. The CAA people gave us a number to call in Two Hills. I called and told them what the problem was. The man said to come over and he would have a look. After checking the car, he said we can drive but not to use the air-conditioner, headlights, radio, etc. The battery was charged up and we could get to Cold Lake as things are. When we got to Cold Lake, Mike checked for the problem and found out that the alternator had gone on the blink. Next day for $160.00 we picked up a rebuilt alternator at Canadian Tire and Mike installed it.

The following day we left for home, but instead of going straight home, I decided to go to Lac La Biche and see our old friends, Bill and Sonia Balaban some twelve miles south of Lac La Biche. When we were coming from Cold Lake, the air-conditioner in the car quit working. When we got to Balabans, Bill said that maybe the air-conditioner froze. We had lunch with Bill and Sonia and than left for home. For a while the air-conditioner was working and than quit again, so we drive home with no air-conditioner on the hottest day of the year. When we were driving from Cold Lake to Lac La Biche, Marusia emphasized how beautiful the scenery was and that it would be nice to live in such a place. As we will see later, God works in wondrous ways.

Next morning in Calgary, I went to the garage. The mechanic checked and found that the air-conditioner was okay, but there was a loose wire connection underneath the car. That was repaired and the air-conditioner worked well after that. While we were in Craigend we reminisced about the 1960's, those "good old days." I mentioned for Bill and Sonia that I have over three hundred slides of our churches across Canada and they said it would be interesting to see them. Bill asked if it would be too much trouble to come in the fall to the feast day, November 8th and show the slides for the people. I said that it should be no problem to do that. So come November we make another trip north to the Lac La Biche country to the church feast day at Craigend. We left Calgary on November 6th and spent the next day with Bill and Sonia. On the 8th father Hryhorij Fil' had the service. Marusia and I helped the people with the singing-cantoring. After the service in the Craigend Hall there was a large meal fit for a king with many different dishes having been prepared. After the meal I showed slides and we left for home arriving home at 10:00 PM.

The rest of the month of August was pretty quiet until we got a letter from Phoenix, Arizona inviting us to come and help them celebrate their feast day (chram) on October 18th. We were also contacted by phone asking us to come and participate in their celebrations. We said that we would not be able to come because of Marusia's health condition. Now we get an invitation by mail (letter). Having received the letter, we thought it over and Marusia said that she felt well enough to go and we could see the people in Phoenix once again. We left Phoenix two years ago, so maybe it's a good time to make another trip for a visit, since it is their feast day. October 14th is feast day of the Protection of the Virgin Mary but the Feast Day was moved to Sunday so more people could attend.

But before October 18th rolls around, there are still things to do in September. In 1998 the Ukrainian Orthodox Church in Canada is celebrating it's eightieth anniversary and the congregation in Calgary its seventieth anniversary. It is also the fortieth anniversary of the establishment of the Ukrainian library at the church cultural centre. Mr. Mykola Woron has been the librarian from the day the library was established. This was also the Year of the youth in the church across Canada. The congregation decided to hold all four events on one day and to invite Archbishop John of Edmonton to attend. There was a committee of four people appointed to look after the program for this day on September 13th. The committee included Father Taras Krochak, the congregation past chairperson, the late Shirley Dinn, Larry Yuzda the congregation chairman and myself. We met a number of times to discuss the program and at one time the matter of the MC was brought up. Committee members looked at me and asked me to be the MC for the day. I told them that they should get someone else, because I'm not even a member of the congregation in Calgary. The three members of the committee insisted and I had to give in. There was three of them and I was one.

When Archbishop John came, he stayed at our place. On Saturday when he came, we had invited Father Taras with his family to come for supper. Reverend Deacon Zubrytsky brought Archbishop John, so he and his wife also stayed for supper. Next morning Marusia and I brought Archbishop John to the church where he was welcomed and greeted by the youth, the church chairman and the parish priest. The service went well and the program also. After the program many people came forward and thanked me personally for doing a good MC job even though I did not think that I did anything special that anyone else could not have done.

Before we left for Phoenix in October, we made another trip to Dauphin, Manitoba. Marusia had entered Ukrainian Easter Eggs in a contest at the Ukrainian Festival. She won prizes and now had to go and pick the prizes up. We also visited other family and friends along the way. From Dauphin we went to Cudworth to see father and with him attended a wedding on September 26th. Father Victor Lomaszkiewcz's daughter was getting married. There were seven priests taking part in the service and over four hundred people at the wedding. The bride, Anna, was born in Europe and she was left as an orphan at the age of four. Her mother had died when she went to a store to buy something. The wind came up, slammed a glass door, the glass shattered and a large splinter of glass pierced her chest and she died. It was a happy wedding which she had found someone to share her life, but the wedding participants sobbed when the bride spoke that her mother was not present.

When we returned from the trip we had the honor of another quest staying in our house. Mother Cassiana from Colorado Springs, USA, was with us for a few days. She was invited to come to Calgary as the late Father Peter Gillquist had come the year before. Everyone was afraid to take Mother Cassiana to stay with them, so Marusia and I were glad to have her stay at our place. We had met Mother Cassiana when we lived in Phoenix for she had been invited twice to come and speak to Orthodox people there during the lenten periods. It was at one meeting in Calgary that I had suggested we invite Mother Cassiana to come and speak to the congregation. Peoples eyed opened and they nearly fell of the chairs when I mentioned this. They said they wanted someone that is Orthodox to come and speak. I told them that Mother Cassiana was Orthodox and they said there are no nuns in the Orthodox church. Father Taras and I had to explain that there are nuns in the orthodox church. People came in droves to see and hear Mother Cassiana speak. There are many orthodox people in Canada that had never seen or heard of an orthodox nun. Yet when we look at the orthodox history in Europe, we see many monasteries(convents) for nuns. There are many convents built in Europe, Ukraine, Greece, Romania, etc. If there were or are no orthodox nuns, than why would convents be built for? Anyway after Mother Cassiana left many people learned something they never knew about. To Marusia and me it was a pleasure to have Mother Cassiana stay with us. We picked her up at the airport and took her back when she was flying back to Colorado.

MORE TRIPS

Now we are leaving for Phoenix. We left Calgary on October 15th and traveled to Pocatello, Idaho that day. The next day we could have easily made it to Phoenix, but we stopped at Page, Arizona. Being only some five hours away from the Grand Canyon and have never seen it before, we decided to turn off our way and see the Grand Canyon. After seeing the wonder of the world, we drove on and arrived at Phoenix at 4:00 PM at the home of Wasyl and Vera Szwez where we would stay for nearly two weeks at their place.

When Sunday came and we arrived at the church, I was asked and begged, "please, please, we are begging you........." to participate in serving with the parish priest, Father Mykola Mychaluk. Reluctantly, I participated and served with the parish priest. The service went over very well with a packed church and a beautiful meal prepared by the ladies of the congregation. Extra tables had to be added on to accommodate all the people for the meal. The following Sunday I was again invited by the parish priest to serve with him. When we had lived in Phoenix, I had baptized a child for George and Karen Szwez. They now had another child and it was baptized this Sunday after the service.

The next morning on October 26th we left for home in a thunderstorm and pouring rain. We could not even pack our car because of the heavy rain that was pouring, so we just threw things into the rear seat and trunk and left for home. When we got to Page, Arizona, it was a beautiful sunny day. We stopped by the large dam on the Colorado River and than we sorted our things in the car. This day we got to Ogden, Utah and stayed in a motel. The following day we could have easily made it to Calgary, but decided to stop at Great Falls, Montana and do some shopping. We did not buy anything, because the prices were the same as they were in Calgary. Next morning we left Great Falls and were home at 2:00 PM. The long trip to Phoenix and return cost us $131.00 for fuel. It was nice to have gone back to Phoenix to see friends, but I do not know if I will ever be back there again. My late mother used to say; "A mountain with a mountain will not meet, but a person with a person may."

In April 1999 father will be 98 years old. He tells us on the phone that his feet, throat and chest are painful. Marusia and I decided we would go to Cudworth to be with father for Orthodox Christmas on January 7th. Before we left for Cudworth we learned that Father Mykola Stetzenko in Kelowna had passed away. He was a good friend of ours and now we were making plans to go to his funeral in Kelowna. The day we were to leave for the funeral, we hear on the radio and TV that a huge snow storm was roaring through the mountains and the roads were closed to the heavy snowfall and avalanche near Revelstoke. We thought of taking a plane to Kelowna and someone would pick us up at the airport. But that also fell by the wayside for we learned from news reports that planes were not landing in Kelowna, because the city was fogged in. Because we could not go to Kelowna, we now are changing plans and going to Cudworth as was first planned. We packed and headed out to Cudworth. We left Calgary in drifting snow and it was that way until we got to Rosetown, Saskatchewan. From Rosetown the road and sky were clear all the way, but it was bitterly cold. This was on December 31st 1998.

We were going to have Christmas Eve Supper January 6th at father's place, but Alice phoned and asked that the three of us come to her place for supper and this way we will all be together. It is only fifteen miles to her place north east of Cudworth. Father, Alice, John their children and grandchildren, Marusia and I made up the unit of some twenty-three people around the table. John had bought a new natural gas heater for their garage on the farm. They took the vehicle out and put tables in the garage and even though it was -30 C outside, it was, cozy and warm for all in the attached garage. After supper we went to the church service at Wakaw. The following day on the 7th the service was at Cudworth. We went to the service. Following the service we had dinner with father and than left for home in very cold weather.

Here I have to say a word about what we heard on the radio as we neared the Alberta-Saskatchewan border. We were listening to the talk show on radio QR 770 from Calgary. The radio announcer was having an interview with a Roman Catholic bishop from Hawaii. He asked the bishop a few questions and than went to another topic. He asked the bishop if it were true what he had heard that in his church during the mass there were hula dances going on. He said it was true, but during the Lord's Prayer and communion the dances do not go on. The announcer than asked: "Your Eminence, do I understand correctly that the women hula dancers dance during mass with bare breasts? Is that true?" The bishop replied and said that was a normal procedure and that they dance in church during mass. As we were driving along and listening to this, I remarked to Marusia: "I wonder if Jesus came down from heaven today and went into that church during the service, if He would recognize it as His church which He instituted on earth two thousand years ago?"

Just to give you an example of what we did each day as retired people. They say that when a person retires, they don't work and have much time on their hands. Others that retired say they are bored. Well, I was bored, but bored from overload of work. For us to go to church in Calgary it was seven miles one way. At times there were days that we made three trips a day. That's right three trips a day. Our schedule for February 1999 looked something like this.

February 3th:	Choir practice 7:30 PM
February 4th:	Prayers Mrs. Ostrowercha 7:00 PM. (She was a member of Golden Agers)
February 5th:	Funeral for Mrs. Ostrowercha
February 6th:	Evening Vespers 6:30 PM
February 7th:	Church service 9:30 AM
February 8th:	Varenyky making bee 8:30 AM

February 9th: Seniors meet 10:00 AM - 1:30 PM.
February 9th: Church executive meeting 6:00 PM
February 10th: Choir practice 7:30 PM
February 11th: 55th wedding anniversary for Kindjerskis
February 12th: Church service 9:30 AM
February 12th: Leave for Dauphin, Man., for funeral Stanley Andrechuk.
February 13th: At Dauphin. (In Calgary Evening Vespers this day)
February 14th: Attended church service at Dauphin
February 14th: Prayers for Stanley Andrechuk at Dauphin
February 15th: Service at 9:30 AM (attended service at Dauphin)
February 15th: Funeral Stanley Andrechuk at Dauphin afternoon.
February 15th: Seniors meet in Calgary 10:00 AM - 1:30 PM
February 15th: TYC meeting at Calgary 7:00 PM
February 16th: Came home from Dauphin 4:00 PM
February 17th: Cultural Center monthly meeting 6:00 PM
February 19th: Ikonostac Committee meeting 7:00 PM
February 19th: Baba's Kitchen - supper at Cultural Centre 5:30-7:30 PM
February 20th: Evening Vespers 6:30 PM
February 21th: Church service at 9;30 AM
February 22th: Passion service 7:00 PM
February 23th: Passion service 7:00 PM
February 24th: Passion service 7:00 PM
February 24th: Town house (condo) meeting
February 25th: Passion service 7:00 PM
February 26th: Leave to Lac La Biche to visit Balabans

The above list is for the month of February activities. This type of schedule was for the whole year, with the exception of July and August when there were less activities because of the holiday season. The schedule is getting tighter and tighter each month, because I'm involved in more things at the church and cultural center. And I thought when one retires, they have lots of time. Not me. This shows how some people who are retired spend their time. With such a schedule one has no time to get bored, but can get bored from work.

We have a caller ID on our phone and know who calls us and when. When we returned home from Dauphin there were forty calls placed to us in those few days. When we are home, seems no one calls. As soon as you step out the door, than the phone starts to ring. There were two calls from the late Father Hryhorij Fil' of Radway, Alberta. We called him to see what message there was. He said that he would like us to move to Lac La Biche, so that I would be the cantor there since there is no one that knows cantoring in the church and there are eight congregations in the parish. There is no one that knows how to sing the troparee or other parts of services with changes when they occur or for other kinds of services.

This cantoring talk started when we were in Craigend for the feast day (chram) when I showed slides of the churches. We helped to sing at that time in church. After we got home from Craigend we got a letter from Bill and Sonia Balaban thanking us for coming to show the slides and helping to sing. They also asked us if we would not consider moving to Lac La Biche to make our home there. When we got that card, Marusia called Balabans and asked Sonia what kind of a joke that is to move to Lac La Biche. Sonia answered: "We never joke, we are always serious." When we heard this, we looked at each other and began to wonder, what they meant. We also had gotten two phone calls from the late Father Hryhorij Fil' about the same topic and we began to think, that maybe it really was not a joke.

On February 18th we received another call from Phoenix, and do I have to tell you why? Yes you guessed right. The news was that the priest that had been serving in Phoenix was given a notice that in four weeks he must vacate the parish. The parish will pay the priest a one way ticket wherever he wants to go, but he must leave. They are asking that I return back to Phoenix to serve the parish. The parish chairman said that one week is already gone and in three weeks there will be no priest in Phoenix to serve them. He also mentioned that the late Father Mykola Derewianka was in church on Sunday and he will be there again the coming Sunday.

After receiving pleadings from the north, from Lac La Biche, and now from the south from Phoenix, which way should we go? Go south to Phoenix, go north to Lac La Biche or stay put in Calgary? We talked about what to do. We decided that the first thing would be to put the house up for sale. If and when the house sells, than we will consider one or the other. On Saturday February 20th, 1999 we put an ad in the paper for one week that we have a furnished house for sale. A few people called to enquire about the house, but nothing else happened.

OUR FIRST COMPUTER - A NEW EXPERIENCE

When we had been living in Salmon Arm, I had started to write(handwritten) this autobiography, to put my life down on paper in word. Now had come the time to type this unto paper. I had already typed out a few pages when one day the doorbell rings. Sally Scales a close and good friend had stopped by to see us for a few minutes. She saw that I was typing something and asked what I was doing. I told her that I was typing out my life history. She looked at me and says: "That is not the way to do it." "Than how", I asked. She says: "You do it on the computer." We told her that we have no computer, but maybe someday we will get one when they are somewhat cheaper. Next day before noon, the doorbell rings again. We open the door and who do we see standing? There in the doorway is Sally Scales holding a computer in her hands.

She brings the computer in and puts it on the table saying: "Now you can type your life history." She plugged the computer in, pushed a button and says that when you want to shut the computer off, just press the same button again. I told her again that I don't know anything about computers and that if I start to type or work with it, I might do damage to it. She laughed and, said that I will learn, and said that I could not hurt the machine. With that she laughed and left on her way. Now what do I do? Where do I start? Which button do I press? What does this button do? What is this thing she called a mouse? What happens if I click on this? For a few hours trying to see what was what I sweated, hoping that I don't break something and damage the computer.

Slowly I learned what to do and how and than when I finished typing, we took the computer back to Sally Scales. After learning one or two small things about the computer and we would be in a store where computers were sold, we would stand and look at the screens with all the excited things moving about. We would look how some people were working with the computers. Then we moved to Vernon. One day as we were walking in the mall past Radio Shack(Source today), we see a sign in the window saying: "Complete computer set for $750.00." Complete - what does that mean complete? We went in and asked the clerk. The complete was, the computer, monitor, keyboard, printer and mouse." All for $750.00. It was a Tandy product. We asked the man why it was so cheap. He said they were not making those computer models anymore so they are selling them to make room for new ones. We decided there and than, that for us to learn how to operate a computer that was very reasonable. Now I can have something to do and play with another toy. Later when we moved to Yorkton, Saskatchewan, the computer went with us. It also made the trip to Phoenix and back again to Canada to Calgary. One day as I was typing in Calgary, that computer just froze up and nothing moved anywhere. So now what do we do? Do we have a funeral for the computer?

We had a good friend in Calgary, Mrs. Verna Paulencu who had moved from Kelowna to Calgary. One day when Marusia was visiting with her she mentioned that the computer had died. Mrs. Paulencu said that her next door neighbor fixes computers. We got the phone number and called Bohdan Maslak. He came over the following day, had a look at our old Tandy, shook his head and says: "It won't work anymore and it will be very expensive to repair it." I asked him what to do and he said that I would need a new computer. First thing that came to mind was: "How much?" He thought for a while and than says that it would be $1000.00 for a new computer. I thought for a while and said that I would let him know. The following day I called him and said that I would also like to have a Ukrainian program on the new computer. A few days later he came with a new computer. He had bought the parts and assembled the computer himself. He also brought a colored monitor with it and a large, heavy Hewlett Packard printer.

On February 23rd when Marusia got up she had another problem. Her left eye was bloodshot. She went to see the doctor and was told it was not serious and that was it. She made an appointment to see an eye doctor. When he looked at it, he said that a blood vessel had burst. He asked what medication she was taking. She told him that she was taking four aspirin a day as the doctors had told her to take since her open heart surgery. The eye doctor said that four aspirin a day was too many and so that she would cut down to only a quarter of an aspirin. Later her eye came back to normal.

MOVING - AGAIN?

On February 26th we again left for Lac La Biche to visit Bill and Sonia Balaban and just to go for a trip. While there, on Saturday we went to see if there were any houses for sale in Lac La Biche. We saw two brand new houses side by side that were being sold by Century 21. We went to see the two houses and made a $1000.00 deposit on one. The owner-builders(Charger Home from Cold Lake, Alberta) would have to accept or refuse our offer and we will not know until the 1st or 2nd of March. We also told the Realtor in Lac La Biche that we would buy the house if our house in Calgary was sold. On the 28th of February we went to church in Lac La Biche. After the service we returned back home. On March 1st we received a call from Century 21 in Lac La Biche, that our offer was not accepted.

On March 3rd in the morning we got a phone call from Century 21 people in Calgary telling us they heard we are interested in selling our house. They wanted to know if they could come and have a look at our house. We said, "Yes." They came and looked the house over and said they would like to list the house and to put up a sign that the house is for sale. We said we wanted to sell the house furnished. Within one week we got a call from Century 21 Terrace Realty that they have an offer on our house. The realtor brought the papers over to be signed if we agree with the offer. We were told what the offer was, we came down on the price a few dollars and a call by the Realtor was made to the buyers if they would accept the new price. The buyers accepted our lower price and the house was sold. We had put up the house for sale on March 5th and on March 10th at 8:00 PM it was sold. So now what? The people want to take possession of the house on April 15th. This gives us about one month to pack and get out of the house.

Next day early in the morning we were on the road once again heading for Lac La Biche. We arrived in Lac La Biche shortly afternoon. The two new houses side by side, that we had seen in February were still for sale. We went to have a look at them again. This time we chose the other one and made an offer. On March 12th we signed the papers purchasing the house on ninety-fourth Avenue. The house in Calgary was sold with the furniture, so now we will need furniture for the new house. There was a nice furniture store in Lac La Biche, Lac La Biche Furniture Decore. It was owned by Bill and Sonia Balaban's in-laws(swaty). Billy Balaban is married to Koreen, the daughter of the store owners. We went in and ordered all the furniture we would need for the house. The furniture would be delivered on the day we take possession of the house on April 15th, father's birthday.

After business was taken care of, we returned back home to Calgary for another month's stay in our "old house." We have one month to pack and move out. The basement in the new house in Lac La Biche is not finished. We began to think that we should finish the basement before we move in and this way there would be less dust in the house. BUT, who can finish the basement for us? We phoned the realtor lady, Wanda Plamondon, to get the builders of the house to come and do the basement. We had marked the floor in the basement where we wanted what kind rooms. A few days later we called to find out if the work on the basement had started. Wanda said that she had not heard anything from the contractors. She called us back the following day and said that the builders would not finish the basement because it was too far for them to travel back and forth from Cold Lake and the expense for us would be too much if they charged us per mile for traveling costs. We asked if she knew anyone who did such work. She said her fiancé, Denis Rymet, does such work. We told her to get hold of him and to do the work and we would pay whatever the cost would be. Wanda got her fiancé and with her helping him together they finished the basement before we moved in.

Having traveled to Lac La Biche and returned home, we began to pack things when we had time. Before all this had happened, we earlier had made plans to go to the Okanagan Valley in British Columbia. We left for British Columba on March 26th, 1999. Before we left for the trip we wrote a letter and left it with the secretary at the Cultural Center to pass it over to the church chairman. We wrote that on March 23rd we were relinquishing all our ties with the congregation and all its affiliated organizations. We told a few people at the congregation and the Golden Agers club, that we were leaving for the Okanagan to visit some friends.

Just as were about to walk out of the house we got a phone call from Kamloops, B.C., that a good friend of ours, Walter Kucharek passed away. The family was asking us to come to the funeral. The prayers were on March 28th and the funeral the following day. After the funeral was over, and people returned from the cemetery to the hall for a memorial dinner, a family member comes to me and says: "Reverend would you please be the MC, after people have lunch?" I had known Walter since 1977 when they resided in Prince George.

We arrived back from our trip on March 30th. Having a caller ID on our phone, we checked to see if there were any calls. The caller ID was loaded. It showed that dozens of people had called in the few days that we were away. When we are home we would get one call a day or every second day. When we leave home everybody calls. We knew who had called us from Calgary, so we did not want to answer those calls. When we were home and the phone rang, we looked to see who was calling. If it was someone in Calgary we would not answer the phone, so the people thought we were still in B.C. In the meantime we were packing and getting boxes from different places for our packing. By this time we had also made arrangements with the U-Haul company to rent a truck for moving. On April 6th we made a trip to Edmonton to tell John and Kay the news that we will be moving. On April 7th there was a service in Edmonton which we attended and after that drove to Lac La Biche to do a few more things and apply for services to the house. We wanted to see how the basement was coming along.

After checking things out in Lac La Biche, we left for Cudworth on April 9th to spend Easter with father. We headed out to Saskatoon, because sister Oksana was also coming from Winnipeg by plane. We had told her that we would meet her at the airport at 2:30 PM to pick her up. We picked her up and than headed for Cudworth. That same evening there was a service in the church where the priest brings out the Holy Shroud (Plashchanytsia). During the service heavy rain was pouring outside. I guess the world was crying that Christ had been Crucified. The following day at 2:30 PM the priest arrived to bless the Easter Paska in Cudworth. The church was filled full with the people from tiny tots in the arms of their mothers, to the elderly and the aged like father at ninety-eight years of age.

Next morning being Christ's Resurrection (Easter), we went to church at Wakaw and again the church was full. It seems that today there are two kinds of people the E and C people. Easter and Christmas the two times a year that these people come and attend church. I call them the E and C people

The following morning we left for home and arrived at 3:30 PM. Checking the ID we saw many phone calls that had come in since we left for the north and east. On April 13th we made a few phone calls to our relatives and close friends outside Calgary and let them know that we were moving from Calgary. We also let a few close friends in Calgary know that we were leaving the city in two days time. Everyone we talked to were very surprised and stunned. Everyone wanted to know what happened and why. People wanted us to come to their place for supper or for a meal before we left. We apologized that we could not come because next day in the morning we are picking up a U-Haul truck, loading and leaving Calgary as soon as we are loaded.

LAC LA BICHE - HERE WE COME

We left Calgary at 11:45 noon after we had a surprise first. As we were loading the truck with the last boxes we had, cars started pulling into the condo compound on the street. As people were getting out of their cars, they were also bringing containers of food with them. We had no dishes, cutlery, napkins, etc., for everything was packed in boxes and on the truck. People came and brought food with them so that we could have a meal with them. People that came were our closer friends: Malutas, Sydoruks, Chernetskis, Holluks, Patons. As the wives of the above were in the house setting up the meal, the men jumped in and were helping in finishing to load up the last things into the truck.

We had figured out the shortest route to travel and where there would be less traffic. I drove the U-Haul truck and Marusia drove the car with some few hundred yards behind in case someone was going faster and wanted to pass her. Everything went well until we came to the junction of highway #595, east of Red Deer, Alberta.

I had come to a stop sign and turned right. Marusia was a few hundred yards behind. I could see her in my rear view mirror. As I was turning to the right a car was coming towards us from the west and signaling to turn south. When I turned unto the other highway I did not see what was happening behind me, because I was already going in another direction - east. What happened was that as Marusia was coming toward the stop sign, the car coming towards her for some reason had turned into her lane and coming at her. In order to avoid a collision she had to take the ditch. In the meantime going in the other direction I kept watching the rear view mirror. I could not see her come, so I began to slow down. Nearly half a mile later when I looked and she still wasn't there, I stopped at a highway approach and was going to go back to see what is wrong. As I backed the truck into the driveway approach, I looked and saw in the rear view mirror that she was making the turn unto highway #595 from highway #21. I waited until she came up to find out what had happened that she was so much later in coming unto this other highway. She told me she had to hit the ditch to avoid a head on collision with the car that came from highway #595. I checked the car and everything seemed okay, with the exception of some gravel that had gotten between the rim and the tire thread bead. The rear wheel looked like it was somewhat low on air, but it looked like it could be traveled with.

After we hit highway #36 and highway #28, Marusia took the lead to Lac La Biche. She went ahead faster with the car to get to the Realtors before they close to get the key to the house. I could see that as she was pulling away farther from me, that the left rear tire was much lower with air than it was earlier. So I finally arrived at Lac La Biche at 5:30 PM. When we arrived we had another surprise waiting for us.

A number of vehicles were parked on the street in front of our house. Inside the house the furniture we had ordered was all in place with a bouquet of flowers on the table and a sign saying: "Welcome to Lac La Biche." Present were the Realtor lady, Wanda Plamondon, Bill and Sonia Balaban, their son Billy and daughter-in-law Koreen with their children Robyn and Jordan. All helped us to unload a few things from the truck that we would need for the night. After we unloaded more less what we needed we had supper together. The two Balaban families had brought home made food and there was enough for all. This indeed was more than we could have expected. The two Balaban families left for home living twelve miles south of Lac La Biche. Next morning they were back in town to help unload the remaining goods from the U-Haul truck.

After the truck was unloaded, I filled it with gas and took it to the U-Haul dealer. The dealer was happy to see a U-Haul truck in town because he said that people have been crying to rent a truck but there was non. Someone had seen the U-Haul truck during the night in front of our house and called the dealer to rent the truck. The dealer said that he had no truck, but they insisted that there was a truck in town because they saw it parked in front of a house. During the night the tire on the car had also gone down and was flat. We called a service truck and he came, filled the tire with air and told me to follow him to the garage to get the tire fixed. During the day we did some unpacking and in the evening we took in a music festival with the Balabans, where Billy and Koreen's children were taking part.

We were unpacking each day and putting up things where there was room. We needed shelving in the cold room, so jars and other things stayed in boxes until shelving was made for them. When Sunday came (April 18th) Bill and Sonia Balaban came to town and than together the four of us drove to a church service some seventy miles west of Lac La Biche to Richmond Park, north of Athabasca. The late Father Hryhorij Fil' was the parish priest whom I had known from the late 1950's-60's when I was still in Winnipeg.

On April 21st is Marusia's birthday and our anniversary. We had not planned anything special for this day, because we were still busy unpacking, but the Balaban families again had a surprise waiting for us. Koreen had baked a cake for Marusia's birthday and they brought it over to the house. Before we could have tea and cake, they said they are taking us out to supper. That was another surprise they gave us. What wonderful people with such beautiful thoughts of others.

Things rolled along from day to day. We still did unpacking and trying to get settled in. We would always need something for the new house, so we would have to run to the store to pick up this or that. On Sundays we would go to church where the service was being held. Sundays after the service, the priest visited the cemeteries and had blessing of the graves. May 2nd the service is at Boyle, Alberta and grave side services following the Liturgy. Afternoon the same day there were grave side services held at Grassland, Alberta. When we came to the cemetery in Grassland there was a huge amount of people milling around on the cemetery. When they saw Marusia and me, many of them hurried over to us to welcome us and to say hello. They were very happy to learn that we had settled in Lac La

Biche and they looked forward that we would help them in the church with the singing.

With a new house there is always so much more work when you move in. Yard work. The place has to be landscaped. There are rocks in our yard that have to be cleared. There is no top soil, so once rocks are removed top soil has to be brought in. The sidewalk is of patio blocks. No deck or stairs to go down at the back exit. No paved driveway. No lawn. The basement has no carpet. The ceiling in the basement is not finished. There are oodles of work with a new house. Slowly we were doing one thing at a time. We had the lawn leveled off and top soil put on. After the top soil was brought and leveled off, on May 19th we planted a garden at the back of the house: radishes, onions, garlic, beets, peas, etc. On May 12th we planted two rows of potatoes.

We took time to go to church every Sunday and Holy Day in different communities. On May 8th we attended a concert of the Cerna Ukrainian Dancers in Lac La Biche. There were fifty-two dancers participating in the concert. Cerna in Ukrainian means a "little deer." On May 14th we went to Cold Lake to visit Marusia's nephew and his wife, the late Mike and Doreen Semeniuk. We also went to Zellers and other stores and picked up things here and there that we still needed for the house. Lac La Biche has a population of three thousand and Cold Lake has fifteen thousand people.

Things and time moved along as well as they could. We made a trip to Edmonton to see John and Kay and to get some things for the house. Going to Edmonton, we'd leave early in the morning and be home before dusk for it was only a hundred and twenty-five miles one way. On May 28th we left for Cudworth to be in church and be at the grave side services on the 29th, where mother is buried.

Because the house we bought was new, there were no steps at the back of the house. If you opened the door there was a five to six foot drop to the ground. In order to avoid an accident we had to get the deck built. We applied to the town for a permit to construct the deck and the permit cost $20.00. We also had to apply for another permit from the Safety Board of Alberta at Fort Saskatchewan and that cost $60.00. Things today have to be done to codes and specifications. When this was in place we asked Denis Rymet if he had time to build us the deck with a roof. Building the deck, we made provisions for a door to be under the deck where we could store the lawn mower, the tiller, and other items. We wanted an open deck, but we soon found out that it was not very practical without windows. Why? Because when rain and wind came, the rain came unto the deck and ran down unto the stored things under the deck.

Having windows installed, we encountered another problem. When it was winter, the sun shines unto the deck and warms the place up to be very cozy some days. With the windows closed on the deck, frost forms on the windows overnight. In the daytime when the sun shines again, the frost melts and runs down the windows and the walls. We solved that problem, by keeping the screen windows opened an inch or two during the night. Now the windows stay clear overnight. The enclosed deck with windows is very useful. We could use it three seasons of the year. Even in the winter time on some days when the temperature outside was zero, the deck would warm up to +10 or more where it was very comfortable to sit and read.

On September 8th we went to Edmonton. Coming home along the way we stopped at Bon Accord , Alberta and picked up a Norland apple and Rescue crab tree to plant at the back of the house. The Norland apple looks exactly like the Red Delicious apple, only somewhat smaller. We planted them, but did not know if fruit would be produced so far north. Let me jump AHEAD for one second at this time. Those trees both rooted well and in the spring of 2000 the Norland had nineteen blossoms on it. As summer progressed the blossoms began to fall off and than there were only five apples left and by the time fall came along one apple had reached maturity. In the spring of 2002 both trees were covered in blossom and it looked like there would apples galore and there were.

Fall was now just around the corner. We still had no lawn and were waiting with it till spring. On September 10th we did seed a little patch of lawn at the back of the house where the two fruit trees were planted. Because there were still many warm days that fall, the grass was up in five days. It grew so well that fall, that I had to cut it twice. I wanted to put up patio blocks on the back to have a patio, but Marusia said that she wanted some green, because later if apples fall down they will bruise to the concrete. So we had a small lawn at the back of the house next to the garden.

November 19th we made a trip to visit and shop at Cold lake. This day we should have stayed home and not ventured out even though it was a beautiful day. It was an unfortunate day for us. As we were leaving Cold Lake at approximately 4:30 PM and turned west out of town, I saw two deer in the field not too far from the road. I told Marusia that we will have to drive slower because there might be more deer on the road. I put the cruise on at eighty-five kilometers an hour instead of one hundred as the speed limit sign indicated. We knew what a deer had done to our Buick car a number of years back near Canmore, Alberta. That memory flashed back and so we took precautions to drive slower.

As we left Cold Lake behind us, it was already getting dusk because of the short days of sunlight at that time of the year. About twenty-five miles west of Cold Lake as we passed the little Sandy Rapids Ukrainian Orthodox Church and just east of Sand River, coming around a curve, a deer flew into us from the north, the passenger side of the car. We did not see the deer, but all we saw was her head as it slammed against the windshield. Thousands of pieces of glass flew in all directions and left the windshield with a two inch hole on the passenger side. Glass flew in all directions, into our clothing, the hair, floor, seats. Marusia was still combing glass out of her hair a few days later. The outside right rear view mirror was broken off and landed somewhere in the ditch or road. The right side of the fender and both right side doors were damaged from the impact of the deer against the car. We were coming around a curve turning to the left and the right side of the road was about four to five feet above the ditch. That is where the deer flew out off. Total damage to the car was $4200.00.

We stopped immediately when the deer hit us. There was a vehicle coming behind us and it also stopped. The man came out and asked if we hit a deer, because he said he thought he saw fur flying from the lights of his vehicle. We both looked for the deer on the road, but no where could we find it. It either flew back into the ditch or it was not badly injured and just ran away. The right front door could not be opened because of the sustained damage, so that Marusia could not even get out of the car. Forcefully I pulled on the door to get it opened. We were not hurt and the air bags were not deployed. As I drove the rest of the way home (some fifty-five miles) Marusia held a cushion against the windshield because air was coming through the hole into the car. We came home somewhat shaken up and wondering what awaits us next and where. This northern part of Alberta is a bad spot for deer. Many cars run into deer and deer into the car at this time the year and as you travel you will most often find a road-kill animal. This year there were a few pictures in the local paper showing damaged vehicles from run ins with the deer. Even a police cruiser picture was in the local paper with a picture of a deer stuck in the grill of the cruiser.

We are entering a new day, new week, new month and new year. At the same time an new era, a new decade and century are starting. It is not even quite a year since we moved from Calgary. We found Lac La Biche beautiful and easier to live in than in the rushing city of Calgary. We can go downtown and park wherever we want or need and do not have to walk back three or four blocks to get what we came for. Calgary with nearly a million in population was just too big for us, yet living in Phoenix with three million population it was easier to get around and not be lost. Lac La Biche was quieter, more relaxed and easier to get about and yet we had everything we needed in town.

One other thing to mention here is something I have seen on TV, but never in live action, and that is the Polar Dip. Yes people across Canada take Polar Dips, but in Lac La Biche it is different. There was a story in the paper that a Polar Dip will take place on the lake on Churchill drive. I took the video camera and went to see what will happen on the frozen lake. A hole about eight feet by eight feet was cut in the ice. Some twenty brave souls only with their bathing suits plunged into the icy water and popped out again. The depth of the water was about four feet deep. The people on the east and west coasts of Canada go for a Polar Dip in the Pacific and Atlantic oceans, but the water in the ocean is much warmer than the water in Lac La Biche Lake in the winter time. Cold north winds blowing across the ice don't make the place more pleasurable for the skinny dippers. We can say that the Polar Bear Dippers in Lac La Biche are more hardier than those on the coasts.

We had been planning to go for Orthodox Christmas(January 7th) to Cudworth to spend with father. We called him that we will be leaving to Cudworth and he said to stay home because the weather is very cold and bad. He said that he would rather see us in the summer when the roads and weather are much better. Thus we spent Christmas at Lac La Biche. For Christmas Eve Supper we were invited to Bill and Sonia Balaban some twelve miles south of Lac La Biche. Twelve miles is not four hundred miles out in the open with cold temperatures and blowing snow in the winter.

Just a week into New Year, I had to make an emergency trip to the hospital on January 9th. I felt dizzy and had a headache. I checked the blood pressure at home and it showed somewhat high. At the hospital they took a test and it showed 214/110. That is high blood pressure that could lead to a stroke. Somehow it eventually went down by itself, but why it had run up so high, I do not know.

Just before Orthodox New Year (January 14th) we heard from Alice that father is very ill. Alice said that he can't walk and is in bed, does not eat anything and when he drinks anything, he throws up. We headed out to Cudworth on January 13th. We arrived and found out that father can't even sit in bed or have a drink of water by himself. Talking over with Alice, we found that there is a respite bed in the nursing home in Cudworth and father can spend a few days there until he is better. We were told that they could take father in anytime. The thing now was to convince him to go there for a few days until he is better. He had mentioned to us children that he would never go to a nursing home, because he wants to die at home.

January 14th is Orthodox New Years Day. That day early in the morning father seemed somewhat better. He got out of bed in the morning and lay down on the chesterfield. At about 8:00-8:30 AM there was a knock on the door. I opened the door and two small children about five-six years old with their mother stood in the doorway. They brought grain to sow for father in the house and bring him good heath and wishes. Father gave them some money, they thanked father for it and he thanked the children for coming. The wheat they sowed, I swept up, brought it to Lac La Biche and sowed it in the garden in the spring. I have been harvesting that wheat year after year since then. When I had it planted in Osoyoos, the birds beat me to it before it even ripened.

We finally convinced father to go to the nursing home for only a few days. On January 15th he agreed to go. We stayed another day in Cudworth, visited him in the nursing home, saw that he was beginning to be more relaxed, feeling somewhat better and looking more chipper, a day later we returned back home.

We arrived home and found everything was fine. Because of the mild weather in the winter the lake did not freeze very thick. On January they were to have dog races to start a new millennium, but because of the thin ice the races were canceled. It was held later on January 22-23 when there was more snow and thicker ice conditions. Anyone who has not seen a dog race, should make an attempt to see it, if it is still held. They have races in the North West Territories, Alaska, Yukon, etc., but those are different. There they last for a week or more and a thousand miles or whatever. There you see the start of the race but you don't see the rest of it until it ends. In Lac La Biche it's different. Trails are made on the frozen lake and the races are held there. The lake is huge, some twenty miles long and ten miles wide. You can stand on the shore of the lake on the ice where the race begins or you can sit in the City Hall of Lac La Biche and see the whole race from beginning to end. Bring a pair of binoculars and watch the race begin and finish. The trails zig zag and when the dogs start off, you watch them as they get smaller and smaller as they get farther away. Than you only see a black speck on the lake and soon that speck gets larger as the dogs are returning back to the finish line.

All the dogs with sleds do not start at the same time. They are let at intervals and than timed to see which dog sled can run the course in the shortest of time. The dogs themselves are something else. They howl, bark and jump to get going once they are hooked to the sled. It takes three men and the sled brake to hold the dogs from starting to run before the "go" signal. You see a different amount of dogs hooked to a sled. Depends what category one is in. You may see anywhere from six to sixteen dogs hitched to sleigh. As soon as the man gives the signal "go", the brake is released and the two men let the dogs go. All you hear near you is a "s w i s h" on the ice and they are gone as the sleigh skims over the ice and snow. Once they start running they bark no more, but are really happy just to get going.

A NEW WORLD? - 2000 MILLENNIUM YEAR

This is a millennium year. The parish of Lac La Biche decided to hold special celebrations and projects for this year. There is to be a service held in the oldest congregation in the Lac La Biche parish, that being Sarrail. Than the program moves to the youngest congregation in the parish, namely Grassland. Another project the parish decided on was to print a history book including all the congregations in the parish and there are nine of them alphabetically: Athabasca, Boyle, Craigend, Grassland, Lac La Biche, Noral, Richmond Park, Sarrail and Wandering River. Each congregation is to write the history of their congregation and than pass the material over to the book committee which included Mel Kuprowsky, Irene Luchka, Mary McNamara and Eugene Stefaniuk.

Because I had been doing an amount of writing and typing of different things, I was chosen to type the material into the computer since I had a computer. I had to write some of the general history myself because some congregations prepared only a general sketch of the congregation. Archbishop John had been invited to come to this celebration, but he did not come because he had been called away for that time to attend a special meeting in the USA. Starting on January 25 _ 2000, people from each congregation were meeting in Lac La Biche for choir practices learning songs to sing at the church service and the afternoon program at Grassland on August 13th.

All this time we were still in contact with Alice as to what father's condition was. He had already come home from the nursing home after spending a few days there, but you need a chain to tie our father down, for he would not sit still for five minutes in one place. He thought he was well enough, so on February 6th, he went to see Alice and John out on the farm near St. Benedict, some fifteen miles north east of Cudworth. While at Alice's place he tripped and fell down. He went home, but on the eighth of February he again ended up in a convalescent place because it was discovered that he had a broken knee cap. He stayed at the nursing home for two weeks before he was released to go home on February 18th. The nursing home is just across the back lane from his house in Cudworth. Father was wearing a special plastic cast on his leg to help him get up and give a chance for the knee to heal. During father's recovery period, we also had gone to visit him.

While visiting father we had the opportunity to attend a 70th wedding anniversary at Wakaw, Saskatchewan on February 19th. It was Metro and Mary Ostafichuk's anniversary. Marusia had a God parent the Ostafichuks, - and their children were making an anniversary for them in the form of a come and go tea. Metro Ostafichuk's birthday fell on the same day as their anniversary. We stayed for a while at the reception and than left for home arriving home at 9:00 PM.

Choir practices were held in Lac La Biche each Tuesday, and I was also asked to teach religion in the church basement at Lac La Biche. I started these classes on March 6th on the topic of "The Divine Liturgy." I explained the Liturgy from the day before the priest serves it, how he has to prepare and explained almost word for word the whole Liturgy from beginning to end. These lessons continued on until June and I was still not finished with the Liturgy. In the fall these lessons were prolonged.

One year in the 1990's father had taken a flu shot in the fall and he said it had made him very ill so he does not take any more flu shots. Maybe father had picked up a flu bug that he had been so ill during the winter. Why? Because Alice called in March and said that father was ill again, can't eat anything and throws up anything he eats or drinks. He must have weathered that flu, for later in March he felt so good that he even attended a birthday party for a friend, the late Mrs. Tina Kochan, John Hnatiuk's sister in Wakaw. We had been suggesting to father that we would make him a birthday party for his ninety-ninth birthday, but he kept insisting that he does not want any party. After he attended Mrs. Kochan's party, he tells Alice one time that such a party like Tina had, he would not mind having one. Communicating with Alice, arrangements were soon made to have a "come and go tea" for father for his birthday on April 15th.

Sometimes the problem with a "come and go tea" is that people come and forget to go. Anyway it was nice to see one hundred and five people attend the party for father on his ninety-ninth birthday. Usually no one makes birthday parties on odd years of their life, but father having reached such a milestone, it was good to make a get together each year, for who knows how many more birthdays a person that age will live to celebrate. How many more odd or even years of birthdays can one expect at that age. Next day after visiting and spending time with him, we made the trip back home some three hundred and ninety three miles.

Now came Easter on April 30th with a midnight service at Lac La Biche. After the Easter season I continued with the religious classes and also we attended the choir practices for the parish. The rest of the days we spent time doing things in and around the house and yard. Spring came and with it came garden time. We planted the early plants like onions, garlic, peas, radish on May 9th. It was one day earlier than we planted the garden in 1999. Again as already mentioned, weather in Lac La Biche may change quickly. Getting up on the morning May 17th, we were greeted with a new white coat of snow. It had snowed lightly overnight.

There have been problems in our church for some time now. Many smaller congregations were closing up or having a hard time to survive. The urban areas have larger congregations, but even those are not overflowing with people on Sundays. The north east part of Alberta has a large amount of Ukrainians residing there. There are many churches in that area, but attendance has dwindled down that some congregations are having only one service a year. Some parishes are having a hard time to support their congregation and the priest.

The Western Diocese of the Ukrainian Orthodox Church of Canada called a meeting for Smoky Lake, Alberta on May 17th to see if any answers could be found to help the dwindling membership of the congregations.

There were some hundred and fifty people attending. Suggestions were made, but nothing resolved. The people from Edmonton were asked to go back home, prepare a plan and return back to Smoky Lake on June 14th with a proposal. At that second meeting it was decided to disband the parish of Willingdon and turn those congregations to the parishes of Smokey Lake, Vegreville, St. Paul and Two Hills.

Having purchased our house in Lac La Biche, we also had a garden plot at the rear of the house. The problem here was that at times the wind and storms would batter the garden plants and cause damage to them, playing havoc with the plants. With the garden being at the back it was sheltered from the north by the house. On the south the neighbor had a house and fence. East and west sides were opened. When the wind came from one of these directions the plants had a hard time withstanding the battering from the wind. We decided that we needed to put up the fence on the east and west side of our property. On the west the neighbors already had a chain link fence, so we would just put up the fence on the east side.

On June 13th I started working on the fence. We purchased four by four treated posts and rented an auger to dig the holes. We bought lumber and I sanded the two by fours and the one by fours for the fence. Than I painted everything with two coats of paint. The two by fours are green and the boards are white. Now that the fence is finished, it looks like a knitted fence. I also made three gates. One more project to finish was to get latches to put on to open and close the gates. This was a few hours of work which was done later.

July 7th is a Holy Day, birth of St. John the Baptist. Misfortunes, grief and pain don't make it look like a Holy Day. On this day south east of Edmonton in the Pine Lake Campground around the supper hour a tragedy struck. Eleven people were killed by a killer tornado. It indeed was a tragedy that many people will remember the loss of their loved ones. Another tornado also roared through near Glendon, Alberta, south east of Lac La Biche, but no one was hurt or killed. It just ran through a six mile long stretch and a hundred yards wide, following a road running north and south. It bulldozed tall spruce and poplar trees as it swept along. The road where this tornado went through was closed because trees had been strewn all over the road which made it impassible.

COMPLETION OF AN EARLIER PROJECT

I had a computer and because I was retired, I was asked to do all the typing for the history of the parish church book. I typed everything and saved on floppy disks. Mel Kuprowsky took upon himself to apply for a grant for the book from the federal government to help defray some of the costs of printing. The committee met many times over and over again, reading, checking, correcting, changing of the material. We had to pick out the photos of the congregations for the book. We had to find out who the people in the photos were. We had to figure out a cover picture for the book. Finally after we had all this completed, Mel Kuprowsky and I made a trip to Edmonton with the manuscript to Quebecor-Jasper Printers to give them time during the summer to have the book printed and bound for the August 13th celebration.

There were times that many people from outside Lac La Biche and area came up to me and asked: "Why did you move to Lac La Biche, so far north?" As already mentioned, we wanted to get out of Calgary and into a smaller community. After I was elected to the book committee, it was then that I discovered why God sent me back to Lac La Biche, to complete a job that I was starting in 1966 but never completed.

The story goes back to the time when I was the parish priest in the Lac La Biche parish from 1962 to 1967. It was during the Ukrainian Orthodox Church of Canada fiftieth anniversary to be held in 1968 that this history period takes us back. When I was in Lac La Biche, it was in November 1966 at a parish meeting that a motion was passed to write the history of each congregation and the parish. Eight months later the church moved me from Lac La Biche to the headquarters in Winnipeg to be a missionary, to prepare the people for the church anniversary in 1968.

After ending up in Lac La Biche again some thirty two years later, I learned why I was once again in the place where I had my first parish. That project of 1966 had never gotten off the ground. There had been a start made, but when I left all things came to a halt. God works in mysterious ways. He brought me back to Lac La Biche to complete the task that I had started but never finished and which had sat undone for some thirty four years. Now I knew why I again landed in Lac La Biche, because it was "God's will" to come back and complete the project that had been stalled.

The book was not an easy task to do. Had it been written in 1967-1968 as it should have been, it would have been so much easier to do this book. Some thirty-five years later many of those who had started and built the congregations were now deceased and the history went with them to the graves. Just here and there we could find remnants of the earliest history. Some was gathered verbally from some of the living who had learned from their parents about the life of each of their congregation. We had to check at cemeteries, talk with those who were still living in the area, check with other local history books where each congregation was located.

But now the book was in the printers hands. They set everything up and made a "blue line" copy of what the book would look like. The printers sent the blue line to Mel Kuprowsky and than the committee got together again to check and see if there were any errors. Having done the corrections, Mel and I took the corrected copy to the printers on July 10th. This is a month and two or three days before the celebration for August 13th. The printers said that the books would be ready on July 21st.

This year because it was not hot but had enough rainfall, made a good year for crops of fruit, gardens and grain. Everything grew well this year. This year in a long time we had the opportunity to pick wild Saskatoon berries. One day Marusia and I both went out and in an hour we were home with two ice cream buckets of Saskatoon berries. Another day we went and again in one spot in the ditch we filled three ice cream pails of Saskatoon berries. We had enough berries to eat and also preserve in jars.

The mushrooms said they would not be left far behind the Saskatoon berries. In June there were dozens and dozens of people who came from British Columbia and from New Brunswick to pick mushrooms (morels) "smorzhee" about fifty miles north of Lac la Biche. A year before a huge forest fire had gone through the area and these people knew, so they rushed to the area and were picking mushrooms. We also went to see and check out, but you need an ATV to get around from place to place in the bush, because there are no roads. We went with the car and came home drenched in mud and water.

We went north from Steep Bank and the road there was not too bad. I asked the man at the lodge at Steep Bank if there was a road north to Conklin and he said there was. We took that road. When we hit the road a few miles north of Steep Bank, I thought we would spent the rest of the summer there in the wilderness, in the bush, stuck in the mud. It had been raining and began to rain hard when we were on that road. The farther we went north, the worst the road got. There was no way or place to turn around. It was a one lane road and bush on both sides with no gravel but a dirt mud road and that was for about fifteen to twenty miles. We traveled through that mud all with deep ruts and cuts in the road. How we did not get hung up in one of those ruts, well that is because God or the Guardian Angel must have been with us. When we finally reached the end of that road, I saw a sign pointing in that direction from where we came saying: "Winter road only." How we got through that mud, I still do not know to this day. That was the worst mud road I had ever driven on. I guess the man at Steep Bank wanted us to get stuck, because he knew what the road was like, so he could have told us that it is only a winter road.

When fall came, the other mushrooms (peedpenkee) kept shouting from the bush to come and gather them from the bush before it gets to cold for them. These mushrooms also were plentiful. We went to three different places to pick these mushrooms and each time we came home with full two eight gallon pails. The first time we went was about twelve miles north of Lac La Biche. Everywhere we looked, mushrooms were looking at us. When the ice cream buckets were full, we would go to the car and empty them into the larger pails waiting in the car. Than we would go for more.

One time as we came out of the bush, a man came towards us from across the road. He came with two large dogs and says: "What are you doing? Are you destroying the trees? This is my land." We told him we were sorry, that we did not know it was his land and that we were only picking mushrooms, and we can give them for him. We asked him if he was picking mushrooms and he said he was not because: he did not know what kind to pick.

The two dogs that came with him came across the road and ditch to us. One was a large German Shepherd and the other was a cross of pit bull terrier with something else. The pit bull had big powerful jaws and looked like in three or four swallows and I would be in his stomach. Even though they were large dogs, they were friendly. Marusia asked the man what the name of the pit bull terrier dog was. He said: "His name is Barney, He is very friendly and will even go into the bush with you." We both said hello to Barney, patted him and he was really friendly, wagging his tail having found new friends. The man told us that we could pick mushrooms as long as we did not do any damage. We asked the man if there are any bears in the area. He looked at his watch and says: "Yes there are. There is one that was shot near Lac La Biche and he is very mean and comes through this area each day at about this same time." He also told us that he saw a bear this year that had a white stripe on his back and must have seen about forty other bears this past season.

Anyway, we thanked the man for allowing us to pick mushrooms. He turned around and went home across the road, while we headed back into the bush for more mushrooms. As we were leaving Barney came and followed us. Now at least we will be safe if a bear should happen to come around. We started picking mushrooms again. Than a few minutes later we noticed that Barney was not with us. But where did he go? Than it hit me. Oh yea, maybe Barney found the scent of a bear, went to check out, than will arouse the bear and they will start running toward us. Barney will fly past us and go home and than we will be left to fight with the bear. As this thought came to me, I say to Marusia: "Lets get out of here as fast as we can, before Barney finds a bear and brings the bear to us." We both did not go into that bush anymore to pick mushrooms.

The second place we went was some seven miles west of Lac La Biche. We bought some meat from Scotts Meats and asked if we could pick mushrooms on his farm, a quarter of a mile east of his shop. He seemed scared that we asked this and did not know what to say. Eventually he said that we may go, because he does not pick mushrooms for he does not know what kind. This was a nice place to pick, because it was right beside highway #663. There were a lot of nettles in this place. We also picked two eight gallon pails of (peedpenkee) mushrooms here.

Our third stop that we went was about twenty-five to thirty miles north of Lac La Biche. This place was filled with mushrooms. This place was on the road to where people from across Canada had come to pick morels near Steep Bank where we had traveled the very muddy rainy road. The mushrooms we picked here were very beautiful. They had a small head on top with a very wide solid white stem. They looked so nice, that you could just about eat them there on the spot. This place was off the road about a good half mile. After we had picked two full pails, we found some bear tracks and an ant hill that the bear had dug up. When we saw the torn up ant hill, we immediately left for the car.

Quite some time before summer had come to an end we received notification that a family reunion on my mother's side was going to take place at Green Lake, British Columbia, near 70 Mile House on July 21-23rd. We had began to talk to take in this family reunion, like the one two years earlier at Tees, Alberta. We wanted to get out of Lac La Biche, because maybe it was warmer in British Columbia. We left home early morning July 21st and arrived at Green Lake just before sunset, and found the place where the reunion will be. Than we found a motel and still had enough time to have a rest from the trip. We enjoyed the beautiful scenery of British Columbia and the time we spent with the relatives. Some of the relatives that were here came for the first time, for they did not attend the reunion at Tees. After spending two days with the relatives, those present decided to have another reunion in 2002 somewhere in Manitoba during the Dauphin Ukrainian Festival if that would be possible.

It was on Sunday July 23rd in the afternoon that we left Green Lake and headed south to Kelowna and Vernon to see other friends. Marusia and I spent a few days in the Okanagan, picked some apricots with the late cousin Alex and his wife Sylvia Korzeniowski. After we had lunch with them, we left for home and got as far as Golden, British Columbia. There we spent the night and next morning we left for home. Our plan was to go the shortest route, from Lake Louise we would turn north unto the Jasper highway, head to the Saskatchewan River Crossing, turn east and head for Red Deer, Alberta. We drove a mile or two north of Lake Louise and the road was closed. Everybody had to make a small detour into a parking lot where there was a booth and everyone had to pay eight dollars to go through the park.

We told the lady that we are not stopping anywhere, just going straight through the park and on to Red Deer. The lady insisted and said all vehicles had to pay to go through the park. We turned around and went back on the Trans-Canada Highway to Calgary. Just west of Calgary near Cochrane is highway # 22. There we turned and headed north then east to Airdrie unto highway #2 to Edmonton and home. We by-passed Edmonton and arrived home at 4:30 PM. While we were away on July 23rd a severe thunderstorm with hail had roared through Lac La Biche. There was considerable damage caused to crops and gardens. People told us that the hail was the size of marbles.

This year Lac La Biche Parish had some changes. The late Father H. Fil' who had been serving the parish from Radway, Alberta for fourteen years was retiring. He said it was hard for him to drive all the distance from Radway each time for services or other needs. His last service was on July 30th of this year. He served the Divine Liturgy in Grassland in the morning and than in the evening he had a service at Athabasca where a farewell was held for him by the parish. The parish is getting a new priest, Father Michael and Dobrodeyka Theresa Domaradz. The parish manse that had been located in Lac La Biche will not be used anymore. It is too old and too much damage has been done to it by the renters. Father Michael had informed the parish that he would like to reside in Athabasca. But there is no manse for the priest in Athabasca. The parish was getting short of funds to purchase a manse, so a place had to be rented for the priest to reside in. An apartment had been found for the time being until some other suggestion comes up in the future.

Sometimes when things in a person's life go, they really go. There is a saying in Ukrainian that goes something like this: "When bad comes, you don't need to chase it along, but for a wealthy person even a rooster lays eggs." That is how it sometimes went for sister Oksana. At a very young age of her thirties she lost her husband who died from a sudden heart attack. Oksana was left with three girls and a son only thirty days old. She struggled in her lifetime to bring up the children the best way she could. She purchased a house so the children may have a roof over their head. She had to take out a mortgage and it was not easy.

Finally her children grew up and each one went their way. Oksana had worked in many places holding various jobs in her lifetime and at times even three jobs to support her family. She worked in restaurants, cafes and hospitals. She was bought out by the hospital and then left to get another job. She worked in a restaurant on the Trans-Canada Highway at Headingly, Manitoba just west of Winnipeg. She was coming to the time when she would retire and maybe take things easier after all the hard work of supporting and raising the family. She was going to retire on August 6th, just five days before her birthday. But as things happened that day, she fell at work and damaged her knee. She was taken to emergency and waited five hours and never saw a doctor. The nurses only came around and gave her aspirin to ease the pain. Waiting for five hours and not getting any assistance at the hospital, she left without seeing a doctor. She was driven to a walk-in clinic. There she was looked at and sent home. On January 3rd 2001, she was still at home and could not do anything because of pain. From August 5th to beginning of January nothing had been done, only that she was told that she would have surgery on her knee on January 29th 2001.

Finally came August 13th, the day of the millennium celebration by the parish of Lac La Biche. The little historical church in Sarrail was filled to capacity. People had no place to even stand in church, so many stood outside. Two priests, the late Father Hryhorij Fil' and Father Michael Domaradz served the Liturgy service. After the service everyone went to the Grassland Community Center for the banquet and program. The ladies prepared a banquet that was just soooooo delicious. Over two hundred people took in the service, banquet and program.

At one of the previous parish meeting I was elected to be the MC for this afternoon program. We had a program committee and with us getting together we got the program set up and I only had to carry out my duties on the day of the event. One thing we did about the history book was, that no one, even the book committee did not see the history books until the day of the program when the boxes were first opened and the books put up for sale to the public. Before the books were opened to the public, three books had been specially prepared. One was bound in blue with gold printing, another with silver printing and the third with bronze printing on the covers. What we did was put the three books up for sale by auction. The church member (auctioneer) from the Sarrail congregation, John Martyn, auctioned off the three books. The three books sold for over $1,000.00 which brought some money to help in the printing cost of the books. All other books were sold at $30.00 each. A few years later the books were put up for sale at $20.00 each, just to sell them off, so they don't stay in boxes in the church. In the program we also had Ukrainian dancers, a choir conducted by Val Pawlik of Lac La Biche, a fifteen minute history of the church. I spoke on the past history of the church for five minutes. The late Father Hryhorij Fil' spoke on the present time of the church while Father Michael Domaradz spoke on the future of the church.

After the late Father Hryhorij Fil' left the parish - retired, Father Michael Domaradz had his first service in Athabasca on August 6th. The following Sunday on the 13th was the millennium celebration where both priests served, because the late Father Hryhorij was invited to come and participate in the celebration after his official retirement.

On September 16th, when I awoke, I had a strange feeling in my right ear. It seemed like there was a drum in my ear and was pounding out one beat after another. Once it was louder, the next time quieter, but still the pounding was there till about noon and than disappeared. I was thinking of going to see a doctor in the afternoon had the pounding not ceased. This has occurred a number of times since then.

As mentioned above, the new priest, Father Michael Domaradz, came to the parish and settled at Athabasca. Since there was no manse for the priest in Athabasca, the parish rented out an apartment until something could be worked out to get a house. A few weeks after the priest moved into the parish some people began talking that maybe people should get together and purchase a house for the priest to live in. This idea materialized when Father Michael and Dobrodeyka Theresa moved into a house on the south west side in Athabasca. Eight people got together and purchased a house. The parish will pay rent to these eight people. Maybe in the future if things expand and grow the parish may buy this house or buy another one. Eight people each put in $5,000.00 towards the house. Alex and Helen Krawec of Athabasca put in $10,000.00, William and Olga Sworin of Grassland also the same amount as did Peter and Ollia Marchuk of Athabasca and Marusia and I the same amount.

In October we left for Dauphin where Marusia was to pick up her prize for the Easter Egg contest she had won. On the way to Dauphin we stopped at Cowan, Manitoba to see Mr. Chorneyko to pick up a few books called "Roll call", about the internment of some eight thousand Ukrainians and other peoples right here in our own country Canada, during the First World War. From there we journeyed on to Dauphin to see our good friends, Stan and Olga Saramaga, Minnie Andrechuk and others. We spent two days in Dauphin and then left for Yorkton, Regina and Moose Jaw.

ARE THERE FALSE RECORDS?

Being in Yorkton we traveled about thirty to thirty-five miles north to the area of Rhein, Saskatchewan. There is an old Orthodox church and cemetery. When we lived in Yorkton for some eleven months, we were in the church for a service in the spring when the priest had a service and was blessing the graves. I remembered seeing an old cross that someone was buried there over a hundred years ago. When we had some time, Marusia and I drove there at a later date. We found the church very easily and than went to look at the crosses.

Sure enough, there in the old section of the cemetery is the cross I wanted to see again to take a few snapshots of it. There is a puzzling thing about that cross, which letters and numbers are already not very legible because the concrete has started to wear away. Anyway on the cross is an inscription that says who is buried there. The name is Kasian Stefaniuk. It is not clear enough to see the birth year with a star (*) beside it and that number could be 1830, 1850, or 1880. The other year's figures are harder to decipher the year of death. The first two figures with a cross (+) are somewhat clearer showing 18. The last two figures are harder to define and it shows 1880,1888 or 1889. So the man died in one of those years, but figures are not very clear.

What is unclear and baffling to me is that if Kasian Stefaniuk had died even in 1889, than something has to be straightened out. In 1991

Ukrainians in Canada commemorated one hundred years of the first Ukrainians in Canada, Ivan Pylypiw and Wasyl Eleniak who came to Canada in 1891. If these two men were the first Ukrainians in Canada, than how come that a person by the name of Kasian Stefaniuk was already buried in the cemetery in Canada **at least** a year or two before the two Ukrainians are said to have arrived in Canada? Was Kasian Stefaniuk not sooner in Canada than the two men mentioned. God willing, maybe one day I will have an opportunity to be in that area again and than I will try to see if I can learn anything more about the man buried in that old cemetery north of Yorkton. Maybe there are some records that may show who that Kasian Stefaniuk was, what he did, and when he came to Canada. Maybe some Canadian and Ukrainian records may have to be straightened out and tell the TRUE story of history. Some say they go by the official recorded history of first Ukrainians in Canada. Well it is RECORDED on the monument that a man was in Canada years before the two men, Eleniak and Pylypiw arrived here. When these two men arrived, the man Kasian Stefaniuk was already deceased and only God knows how long he had been in Canada before the two men came here. Yes my surname is also the same, and I am no relative to the man, but if we are writing history write the truth and let's not falsify the history that tells us different. Let's not be like Russia, where Vladimir Putin, said on May 20 - 2009: "We have to counteract the attempts of distorting history to the detriment of Russian interests." this was taken of the Internet. We say Russia falsified Ukrainian history of Ukraine. And what are we doing? Is this also not falsifying history saying that Ukrainians were here at such a date, when we see a Ukrainian man was already deceased when the (first) two other men arrived in Canada. Russia wants history to be what Russia says not what history says, so let's not be like the Russians twisting history to their benefit, but let's say things as they are and not the untruth.

In Yorkton we stayed with our friends Andrew and Lena Antony. I knew Lena from Dauphin when she was living there with her husband Nestor. Her husband passed away some time ago and she married Andrew Antony. As for Andrew, we met him the first time when we lived in Salmon Arm and Vernon. We sang together in the church choir at Vernon.

Next day we left Yorkton and headed out to Regina to visit another couple, John and Jean Sawchyn. They were getting ready to leave for

Phoenix, Arizona for the winter months. We stayed over at their place and next day went to church service at Selo Gardens, a Ukrainian Senior Complex in Regina. It was October 14th a Holy day of St. Mary the Protectress. After the service we left for Moose Jaw where tomorrow the Ukrainian Women's Association of Canada (UWAC), Moose Jaw local, will be celebrating their fortieth anniversary. When Marusia lived in Moose Jaw, she was a member in the local. They had sent an invitation asking Marusia to attend the celebration.

When we got to Moose Jaw, I could not go to visit anyone with Marusia that evening. On the way to Moose Jaw, I was feeling nauseated. We came to Moose Jaw and got to a motel. I had to lay down because I was sure what the problem was - inner ear imbalance. I've had this happen to me before, so I knew what was coming. The only thing that helps me, is to lay down and be very still, try not to even move an eyebrow. I laid down on the bed and Marusia went to visit some of her old friends. I would have liked to go with her, but I knew I had to have the rest, otherwise things would get even worse. When Marusia came back from visiting, I was feeling much better after a few hours of stillness and being motionless.

Next day was the church service. There were about six or seven people in the choir loft. The church was not completely full, but there was a good crowd. After the service there was the banquet and program in the church basement. The presidents of the National and Provincial Ukrainian Women's Association were present as well as other dignitaries. The program ended at 2:00 PM and we immediately left for Cudworth to father's place. Why? Let me tell you the next episode.

SO WHERE IS FATHER?

October 15th is John and Alice's anniversary. Before we had left father's place for Manitoba, we told him that we would be at his place at 5:00 PM on Sunday and then together the three of us, father, Marusia and I would go to Alice and John's place to wish them a happy anniversary. Twice we had mentioned this to father before we left for the trip eastward. It was John and Alice's forty-fifth anniversary. We rushed from Moose Jaw to be on time, for we knew father well, that he would not sit in one place for five minutes.

When we arrived at Cudworth it was still daylight and still before 5:00 PM. When we drove to father's house, we saw a brown car standing in front of his house, so we knew that he was having some company. To get to the house, you had to go through the garage. As soon as we opened the garage door, we saw that father's car was not in, so we figured that he must have taken someone and they went for coffee or to visit someone else and leaving the guest's car outside on the street. We knew that if his car is not home, than he is not home either. Some company must have come and father took them out for supper to the restaurant. We went to the house, the door was unlocked, but he was not in. Then we went to the two eating places in Cudworth, but his car is not there either. We drove back to the house and called Alice to see if father had been talking to her today. Alice said that she had not seen father today. I tell Marusia to stay in the house in case someone calls and I will drive up and down every street in Cudworth to see if father's car is parked anywhere in town. You can drive up and down each street and cover the whole town in five or ten minutes.

I checked all the streets and his car was nowhere in town, so I drove back to the house. As I drove back to the house, I noticed that the brown car that had been parked in front of his house was gone. I figured that when I was driving around, I missed him and he came home with his company, the car is in the garage and the company is gone home with their car. When I walk into the garage, his car is not home and the brown car is gone also. Now what gives? It tells me that he is still not home. Now what and whose car was that in front of his house and now it is gone also? I come into the house. Marusia calls Alice again. Alice says she is coming right over because it's already dark and father does not drive anywhere after dark. It is fifteen miles of gravel road. Alice said to go over to Bill Trischuk's and ask if he saw father today. I walked over because it was only a block away. As I came near Trischuk's place, they also had just come home and were going into their house. I asked if they had seen father today and he says: "Yes, I saw him about 2:30 PM and he said he was going to John and Alice's place." W H A T ?

He was going to John and Alice's place at 2:30 PM and it is now about 6:00 PM and Alice has not seen him today. What is going on? What happened? Where is father? Is he someplace in the ditch? Is he killed in some accident? Is he lying injured? All kinds of thoughts are now racing through my head. What shall we do next? Best wait for Alice and than we'll decide what the next step will be. W o r r i e s.

Marusia and I started making some tea and toast because we haven't eaten anything since noon. We sat down and wondering what happened and what next to do. We are eating, but there is no appetite. Worries are bigger than the appetite. Suddenly the door is opening into the house. It can't be Alice yet, because it's fifteen miles by gravel road and takes longer to drive. We look and father is slowly dragging himself into the house. We look at him and together say: "Where were you? We are all worried that something happened to you, it's night time and you are not home." Just as he begins to speak, the door opens again and Alice walks in. She walks in and begins to laugh, and also asks him where he was.

Than father tells his story. "Well it's Alice's anniversary, so I thought I would go to her place and say Happy Anniversary. When I got to her place, I did not get out of the car, but blew the horn a few times and no one came out, so I knew they were not home. Than I thought they must have gone to Middle Lake, Saskatchewan, because Darcey is expecting a child, so they must be there. I drove to Darcey's place, honked the horn, but there was nobody home there either. By this time it was getting dark and I was hungry, so I thought I would go to Crossroads restaurant at Wakaw. I did not want to drive on the gravel road, so I drove highway #20 to highway #41 and than to Wakaw. When I came to the restaurant, Mr. Van Harachek was there. He came and asked me if I was in the hospital to see the granddaughter. I said no and asked if Darcey is there. Then I thought that is where John and Alice must be in the hospital so I go there. When I get to the hospital, Darcey was walking in the corridor, but no one else of the family was there. From there I went back to the restaurant, had some french fries, coffee and came home now."

As father is telling his story, Alice is having a good laugh and than she says: "I don't worry anymore, because he looks after himself." So that is the excitement we had that day on John and Alice's forty fifth anniversary. We never did make it to their place that day, for next morning we left for home to Lac La Biche.

In the summer time two ladies Mrs. Ann Zwozdeski and Mrs. Chernowski from Edmonton came to visit Marusia and me to ask if I would take upon myself to teach cantoring in the Lac La Biche Parish. Cantors are always needed in the church to help sing the service, funeral, marriage or whatever services are held. I told them I would help with what I know and could. So when we returned from our trip to Manitoba and Saskatchewan on October 16th, I started teaching cantoring on October 18th. The ladies from Edmonton had told me not to get discouraged if only two or three people would come for such courses. When I started teaching I had seven students coming to class each week on Wednesdays. So now on Monday I teach religious classes. Tuesdays nights is choir practice. Wednesday is cantoring lessons. Three evenings in a row are taken up and there is even no time to get bored. During the day, I usually prepare classes for the evenings.

I ALSO WALKED ON THIS EARTH

We have come through spring, summer and fall is upon us now. It is October, the time for goblins and witches. This is one day of the year I dread and never look forward too. Why? Because this is the night of yearly VANDALISM, as I call it. This is the night when youngsters go from house to house saying: "Trick or treat." This is the night when children are taught that the world owes them a living, that they have to get things for nothing, or else. They are taught from the youngest of ages that the world owes them everything. Why do you think there are so many homeless people on the street today? They are looking for handouts starting from a small age which they learned they must have everything given to them. Why else? They don't want to work, they just want handouts. Give us food from the food banks, supply us with free housing and don't give us any jobs. That is what they are taught and learn from Halloween time and its customs.

As previously mentioned, there was a manse for the priest in Lac La Biche and I lived in it for five years from 1962 to 1967 and other priests lived in it prior to me and others following my departure from Lac La Biche. The manse was now old and damaged by the renters. The renters instead of keeping someone's property in good care, they inflicted damage instead. They wrecked the inside of the house that would be too costly to repair. The parish wanted to sell the house and have it moved off the property, but there were no takers after they saw the shape the house was in. The manse belonged to the parish, but was situated on the property of the Lac La Biche congregation. In order to build a new house there today, the town would not permit that to happen. The garage was attached to the manse and it was sitting straight with the town property line on the back lane.

The parish asked someone to take the house for nothing, just to move it off the lot and fill in the basement. Again even for this there were no takers. Only thing left was to demolish the manse. This took place on November 6-7 of 2000, the millennium year. The house was knocked down and removed by Chwedoruk Construction of Lac La Biche. In the spring it is hoped that the dirt would settle in the basement and than a fence put up around the back of the church.

When we were in Phoenix serving in the church, we met people from Ukraine. A man with his son were there from Odessa, Ukraine. He has an aunt in Phoenix, so they came to visit her. The man has a son that was never baptized. Having lived under communist rule in Ukraine, people tried to hide their religion or stay away as far as they can, so that they not be sent out to Siberia into exile. Arrangements were made to baptize his son who was eleven years old. What a coincidence that was. The father's name is Eugene (Ewhen), the son's name is Ewhen and my name is Ewhen. God works in mysterious ways. The God-parents for the lad were Marusia and Yurko Illinski. Since that time we have been sending something for the family to Odessa each year during the Christmas season. We go to Edmonton and mail the gift through a company called "MEEST." Meest means bridge. A bridge from Canada to Ukraine. If you send parcels through the post office, the mail is opened and searched before it is delivered. Good things are taken out, and than the parcel is packaged up. When people come to get the parcel, the people in the post office in Ukraine say that the parcel was opened in Canada. We know that is not true. If you send parcels through meest, they deliver it to the door of the person in Ukraine. This year we mailed a parcel to Odessa on November 23rd. We were told the parcel will be in Ukraine the first or second week in January.

As mentioned many times earlier about the weather, one more thing about changing weather. On December 8th, one would think of a cold, frosty morning with Jack Frost nipping at the nose and ears. Not this year. On December the 8th it started to rain just before noon with a good solid rain. This day we have to go to Athabasca for prayers for a lady who passed away at the age of one hundred and two years. It is fifty-five miles to Athabasca. We were worrying that the road may be very icy and slippery if it should happen to get cooler and freeze. Black ice on the road could fling a car out of control and end up in the ditch. We left somewhat a bit earlier to get to Athabasca before it gets dark and to be there in good time. The road was wet but no ice. We returned home that evening and the road was just as good coming home to Lac la Biche.

Before the prayers for the deceased started, the family of the deceased was standing inside the entrance to the church and talking. I came down from the choir loft to see the priest. The son of the deceased says to me: "Are you related to the Stefaniuk that used to serve in this church?" I pointed to myself and say: "This is him." The wife of this man was standing about eight ten steps and heard what we were talking about, comes over and says: "Than you must have buried my mother." I asked her what year she had died and I said: "Yes, I was here during that period and must have done that funeral."

Next morning we again left somewhat earlier for Athabasca to be in church on time and expecting roads to be icy in spots after the rain last night. The gravel trucks had already been out earlier and sanded the road, so there was no ice, but lots of spray mist from passing vehicles. The funeral was held in Athabasca and than the body was taken to Coolidge for internment in the Orthodox Cemetery. After the funeral people met at the Forfar Hall in the Coolidge area for a memorial dinner.

Marusia and I sat with the family during the meal, and the lady whose mother I buried years ago pulls out two pictures from her purse and shows them for me. Yes, there I was in the photo leading a funeral procession to the cemetery where today we had a burial. Than she turns around holding the other photo and points to a man about thirty-five years old and says to me: "That is the man that you baptized, which you see in this other picture." It was also during this time that we learned from the lady that her father is still living in Athabasca Seniors Care Home at the age of one hundred and three. Two weeks later we learned that he also died.

The old year is slipping down to the end. Sister Oksana from Winnipeg had come down and spent a week with father. We thought we should go and also spend a few days with him. We left home on December 21st. The roads in Alberta were super like they always are, good and dry. When we hit the Saskatchewan border the Yellowhead highway #16 from Lloydminster to North Battleford was not too bad yet, but after we turned unto highway #40 to Prince Albert, the road was something else. The highway was all icy; no salt, sand or anything done to it. As it rained and snowed people just drove over it forming more ice and the road was a terrible rough skating rink.

From Blaine Lake, Saskatchewan to Waldheim the road again was much, much better, but down from Waldheim, to Rosthern, Wakaw and Cudworth the road was even more icy than previously that we drove on from North Battleford to Blaine Lake. You can't travel fast on ice and no work had been done to alleviate the icy problem. With such road conditions one loses much time in traveling. Just west of Rosthern the road is so terrible with ice and roughness that one is ready to break down and cry. You can only travel ten to fifteen miles an hour on the rough road covered with ice, pot holes, and lumps of ice around which we had to turn to the side not to hit the ice standing like a large bag filled with something. We were very lucky that our car held out in one piece. Today there are all kinds of machines available, why can't a grader cut the ice off or a sand truck put some sand on. How can one province keep its roads in tip top, while the other just neglects it all.

We stayed with father overnight and than went to Yorkton to pick up an Easter Egg marker for Dobrodeyka Theresa Domaradz. Andrew Antony makes such egg markers. When we came to Yorkton, did we get a surprise? There was snow galore. When you drive out of the driveway, you cannot see the street because there is so much snow, higher than the cars. The centre boulevards have so much snow on them that you cannot see the vehicles on the other side going by. We had lunch in Yorkton and were back at father's place before 5:00 PM that day. It is only one hundred and eighty miles from Cudworth to Yorkton.

On December 25th we went to Saskatoon. Marusia's nephews and nieces were meeting at Matt and Anne (Marusia's niece) Kawchuk's place for supper. When all the relatives and friends arrived, there were thirty-two of us that sat down to supper in the basement where tables were set up in two rooms. There was enough food that you could have feed half of Saskatoon. Food of all kinds that your heart desires. We stayed till about 9:00 PM and than returned back to Cudworth for the night. Cudworth to Saskatoon is some fifty-five miles. Next morning we leave back for home. Having left father's place about 7:30 AM and about three miles west of Wakaw a truck is tipped over on its roof in the ditch. Someone must have been going to fast on the icy road and ended upside down in the ditch. When it happened, we don't know. The road is straight and we did not see any traffic coming towards us. We arrived at home at 3:30 PM.

STRANGE BUT TRUE!

A strange thing happened before the end of the year ended. For many, many years I have worn a neck cross. When Marusia and I got married, Marusia gave me a new gold neck cross to wear because the one I had was wearing out. I never take that cross off and wear it under the shirt all the time. I had it off one time when the chain broke and it had to get repaired. What happened this one time (and happened again later) is strange, true and without explanation.

On the night of December 28th we went to bed as usual shortly after 10:00 PM after watching the CBC news. Everything was fine. In the morning when we get up, we make the bed together. I from my side and Marusia the other side and in one minute the bed is made up. This was happening the same on the morning of December 29th, only this time as I turned, I noticed on the night table beside me a neck cross and chain. For a split second I thought: where did that cross come from? Than I felt for the cross on my neck and it was not there. How did my neck cross end up on the night table beside the bed? I never took if off. How and WHO took it off?

I also remember when I was sleeping that night I was talking with someone. Who it was, I don't know and what we were talking about, I don't know. It was a mystery to me how my cross ended on the table. The first thing that Marusia asked me when we awoke was: "Who were you talking with in your sleep last night?" This was even more mystery, because she heard me talking with someone, but who or what, I don't know. What will become of this strange sign, I don't know. This is the year of Y2K. Is this the year when Y2K ends for me? What will 2001 bring? Later 2001 did bring me the saddest day in my life, just two days before my birthday. Someone took the cross of my neck during the night and talked with me. Ten months later God took away my joy and love - Marusia.

We are now in the new 2001 year. January 6th is Orthodox Christmas Eve. I don't call it Ukrainian Christmas, because there are other nationalities like the Russians, Bulgarians, Serbians and others that celebrate Christmas at this same time. I haven't heard anyone saying Serbian Christmas, or Russian Christmas or any other kind of Christmases. Those countries that are Orthodox celebrate Christmas on January 7th each year.

Marusia and I had been preparing to spend Christmas with father. He will be one hundred years old in April and we wanted to be with him, because who knows how many more Christmases he will celebrate. But as mother used to say: "We make plans and God changes them." What we had been planning for quite some time, again turned out different. The roads were like skating rinks in many places. Cars were reported in ditches after hitting icy patches from the freezing rains. We had to cancel our trip to Saskatchewan. But with good friends in and around Lac La Biche, they kept in touch with us, found out we were not going to Saskatchewan, so Bill and Sonia Balaban asked us to be part of their family for the Christmas Eve Supper on January 6th.

Christmas Eve for Ukrainians is very special. Usually people fast all day with the exception of the ill, aged and children. Twelve meatless and dairy free dishes are prepared for the special family supper. All family members try to be home for this special occasion. The first dish to be eaten is "kutia", boiled wheat with honey, poppy seeds, nuts and candies added to it. In one corner of the house the land lord places a sheaf of grain. This symbolizes the family clan of the generations of that family, so that is why everyone tries to be home this evening. We had an invitation to have supper with Bill and Sonia and their family. There were more than twenty-five people gathered around the supper table. After supper some caroling was done. Gifts were exchanged. After that we drove back to Lac La Biche to attend the midnight Divine Liturgy service. On January 8th the service was at Grassland and the 9th it was at Boyle.

The month of January seemed to fly through very quickly. Before we knew it, it was that time again for the priest to visit the parishioner's homes with holy water. Such an event took place at Sarrail on January 21st after the Divine Liturgy was served in the church. Bill Pisarewski, Marusia and I helped Father Michael Domaradz visit the parishioners homes with holy water in the Sarrail congregation.

In the fall of 2000 I had started teaching cantoring classes to seven people from the Lac La Biche and Craigend congregations. On January 23rd I received a surprise in the mail. A letter arrived from Edmonton with a cheque to help offset any financial costs that I had with the cantoring classes. I did not expect to receive anything because I always practiced that: "If my church does not cost me anything, than it's not worth anything," so why get paid. I did it for the love of doing it. I did not return the cheque but at year end I mailed a report and said that I would not accept anymore honorariums for the small contribution that I give for the church.

A few days later, end of January, we learned that brother John's first wife Doreen had passed away in Winnipeg. Her two sons(my nephews) Gregory lives in Edmonton and Philip in Austin Texas. She passed away on January 25th. Also this same day I had gone with Father Michael to help with the blessing of homes in the congregations of Noral and Wandering River.

In the Ukrainian Orthodox Church as in other Orthodox churches when people come to church to worship, many people buy a candle and light it in memory of their deceased relative or friend, or in some cases for the health of their family who may be ill. Marusia and I have been doing this from the time we were married. I put the candles for the deceased and would put a candle for good health for Marusia or other family members. This one Sunday in February of 2001 at the service in Athabasca I did everything as I had been during years before. About half way through the service, the candle that I had put for the health of Marusia, that candle burned down half way and went out. Just went out without any reason. All other half inch thick candles burned to the end, this time the candle for Marusia's health went out after burning only half way down. When I saw that it went out, I went and lit it again, but at the back of my mind there was a question: "WHY?" All candles burning, but one among them goes out half way burned. I knew which candle I had put there for there were not many people in church and few candles were put.

I know father had said many times that when mother was still living, he saw a the candle go out at a service. He later checked and found there was nothing wrong with that candle. That year mother passed away. I knew that something may be wrong with Marusia this year since the candle went out only half way burned. This year, before the year ended, Marusia's life was snuffed out like the candle. Believe it or not, but I know that twice I heard of this that happened for father and me, and we lost our spouses. A sign of an omen of what to expect that something will happen? Science would think of trying to find any kind of answer to this puzzle, but I know that God knows what is to happen and sometimes He shows us signs of things to come, but we don't understand them.

On February 9th Marusia's nephew, George Semeniuk, in Saskatoon got a serious heart attack. Marusia was always close to George for he had helped her a lot when her late husband Mike Paziuk had passed away at Moose Jaw, Saskatchewan. Since that time she was always grateful to him for his assistance in time of need. We called every day or they called us to keep us in touch with what was what. On February 14th, Valentine's day, Marusia left for Saskatoon to see George because we were informed that his condition was getting worse. I took Marusia to Vegreville where she caught the bus to Saskatoon. I dropped her off and did not stay to wait for the bus, because as we were approaching Vegreville, a snow storm was already in progress. I wanted to get home before the storm became more fierce.

Next day is February 15th. It is a Holy Day - Meeting of the Lord in the temple. It is now forty days since Christ was born and His Mother had not gone anywhere for the past forty days, obeying the Holy Law of God as stated in Leviticus 12 1-8. This day the service was at Craigend some fifteen miles south of Lac La Biche. There were ten people in church and the weather was cold with drifting snow.

On February 16th sister Alice and husband John Hnatiuk of St. Benedict left Canada for Arizona where they want to spend a few weeks in the sun, getting tanned and away from the cold Saskatchewan winter. Marusia did not come back home from Saskatoon until February 23rd when I again went to Vegreville to pick her up at the bus depot. In the meantime we had kept in touch with each other by phone to see how things were in Saskatoon with her nephew.

Fast(lent) in 2001 began on Monday February 26th. During the fast period there are more services held beside the Sunday Liturgies. There are memorial services. There are passion services where a number of clergy come together to have the special service, Passions of Christ, etc. More people attend these services because they come from the whole area of the Vegreville Missionary District where six priests meet in one church and have service. Marusia and I attended all the scheduled five services that were held in Thorhild, Lac La Biche, Vegreville, Myrnam and Borowtsi.

After Marusia returned from Saskatoon having seen her nephew in the hospital, we learned that George was flown from Saskatoon to Edmonton and had open heart surgery at the University Hospital. Hearing this we got into the car and drove to Edmonton to see him. After his surgery, he was again flown home back to Saskatoon hospital to recuperate. Later he was released from the hospital and said that he was feeling much better.

MARUSIA'S HEALTH BEGINS TO FAIL

This bad year began on March 16th. This was a sad day for Marusia. After having supper as we usually did about 6:00 PM, we watched the TV news and than I went back into the basement to work on the computer of what I was doing. I was typing the Epistle book into English to use at church services when needed. There was no Epistle Book in English in any of the Lac La Biche Parish congregations. As was the case when I was typing in the basement, Marusia was upstairs where it was warmer and she watched her favorite program on TV "Wheel of Fortune." Most of the times as she was watching she was at the same time doing some embroidering. At other times she may be in another room sewing her new wardrobes or doing something in the kitchen. As I was typing in the basement this evening, she comes down and she looks like something had happened. She tells me she was sick - threw up her supper. At this time we didn't think too much about it, because she herself said that maybe she is getting the flu or maybe ate something that did not agree with her.

If it was the flu, a few days later she should have felt somewhat better, but some five days later on March 21st, she was sick again, the same thing. The following day it happened again. It was then that I told her to make an appointment and see the doctor, because even if it's the flu, he may give her a prescription for it. She made an appointment and went to see the doctor. But what can a doctor do, he is not god. First he ordered some blood test work. Maybe things would have been different towards the end of the year had the doctor ordered **all** the blood works, but no, there were only a few blood tests. Why do blood tests a number of times? Take enough blood and do **all** the tests for everything at one time. The report came back negative on the first test. Then the doctor ordered more and different tests. Again negative results. Third time more blood tests. Each blood test that is done takes time for results. The blood is sent for testing. A person waits for the results. Results come in, the doctor looks at them and than calls the patient in. Then sends for more tests. Each time tests are needed time goes by. If one blood test was taken to be checked for everything, surely to God, the doctor would see in the first test what the problem may be. By the time all the blood tests were done it was too late for Marusia

Another thing that happened to Marusia this year was that her arms began to ache in early January. When she was going to Saskatoon to see her nephew George in the hospital, she already had painful arms. Her arms began aching so bad that at times she could not do things for herself and I had to help her get dressed or whatever. She could not put her hands to the back. The pain was getting worse and at times I even had to cut up the food for her on the plate, because of the pain she could not do it. She told the doctor about it, but he said it was arthritis. She was given medication and one day the pain was gone, but returned again in a day or two. Everyday she used to drive downtown to get the mail and get groceries or whatever while I was doing something else. One day after she went downtown she comes back and says: "You'll have to go for mail yourself from now on, because my arms ache so bad that I can't even hold the steering wheel." The doctors were still doing blood work at this time and said they hadn't found anything. Finally in April they sent her to Edmonton to see a specialist for arthritis. When the report came back, we were told by the family doctor that they want to check her for cancer in Edmonton. This same evening she was sick again as was previously a number of times from the first time till now.

This year, natural gas and gasoline prices were sky-rocketing. We were traveling to all services with our 1997 Chevrolet Lumina car. It has a six cylinder engine and is not too bad on gasoline, because it has an overdrive in it. But than it just happened. Looking through the local paper, The Lac La Biche Post, I noticed that Tarrabain Motors in Lac La Biche had a used

1997 Ford Escort car for sale. When we went downtown the next time, we went to see what kind of a car that was. It looked in very good shape and had only fifty-two thousand kilometers on it. Our Lumina car of the same year had a hundred and thirty five thousand kilometers. We asked the dealer how come only so few miles and he said the car came from Plamondon and the man who owned it, used it only to go to town for coffee. They were asking $11,900.00 for the Escort. I said it was too much. Marusia says that we will not give them more than $8,000.00 for it. We went into the office and the salesman wrote up an offer for it for $8,000.00. He took it to the manager, came back a few minutes later and says that they can't sell it for that price. He suggested we try for $10,000.00. It was getting near 4:00 PM and we were expecting company at home at that time. We were leaving for home and told the dealer that we will not give more than our first offer. We left for home to meet our company.

About a quarter after four the phone rang and the salesman asked if we will accept to pay $9,000.00 for the car. Marusia hearing what I was talking with the salesman on the speaker phone says: "Nothing more than $8,000.00", and at that we ended the conversation. We waited for our company that still had not arrived. About half an hour later the door bell ran. We figured that our company had shown up. Opening the door we see the salesman standing and the little Escort parked in the driveway. He says: "You are hard to bargain with, but we will let you have it for $8,000.00." So that day we bought the little four cylinder, four door purple Escort Ford car. Being a standard transmission, Marusia said that she would not drive that car, but I would have to drive it myself.

April 12th came. What happened on April 12th and 13th, I don't know. There was an evening Passion service (Great Thursday) at Boyle on the 12th. All went well until about half way through the service I seemed to be getting a hoarse throat. Seemed like less and less sound (voice) kept coming out. On April 13th (mother's birthday, if she would have been living) we were to leave for Cudworth because it was father's birthday on the 15th and also Easter Sunday. We did not go to Cudworth as planned. When we got up on the 13th, I could not even whisper out of my mouth. No sound was coming at all. I do not know what the problem was. On the 13th being Great Friday, the Holy Shroud (Plaschanytsia) is brought out in the church. I could not participate in any singing, for I could not even make a hissing sound. Lost my voice completely. In the late afternoon of the 14th, I began to get some voice returning, but it was already to late to make any plans to go to Cudworth, so we started to make plans to have Easter at home. We went to Bill and Sonia Balaban's place, they having invited us to come and spent Easter with them and their children who all had gathered there. So we never went to Cudworth in 2001 to be with father on his birthday, Easter Sunday or even Orthodox Christmas.

When we bought the little Escort car on April 9th, the salesman filled the tank with gasoline. I started to drive the Escort around town and to different places for church services and than filled the tank with gasoline again on April 14th putting in ten gallons of gasoline. During this time I had driven four hundred and thirty miles. Ten gallons of gasoline into that mileage gave us forty three miles to a gallon. Wonderful.

Brother John, sisters Alice and Oksana and I had been planning a birthday party for father on April 15th. But as mother used to say: "We make plans and God changes them." We all were planning to be with father on his birthday and Easter at the same time, but that never materialized. Some people around Wakaw and Cudworth heard of our plans and said it would not be good to have the birthday party that day since it was Orthodox Easter and many people and family would not be able to make it because they wanted to be home with their families. So the plans were changed to hold the celebration on April 22nd. Marusia and I left for Cudworth on April 20th to help get things ready for father's birthday.

Marusia and I had purchased some seeds from Home Depot in Edmonton to plant in the garden. Each year for the past twelve years of our married life, Marusia always would be outside in the spring puttering around in the garden or around flower beds. She would plant something here, dig something out of there, transplant something in a new place. It did not come to me that something was going to happen this year. She did not plant one onion, she did not plant one seed, she did not pull out one weed this spring. All she did was tell me what to plant where. Than we also purchased flowers for the front and back of the yard. She would say: "I'll pay for them." We would come home, but she would not plant anything. She only told me what to plant and where. It should have struck me at least once that something is not right, something is wrong, something is not natural that she is not doing anything in the garden or yard. Never did it strike me once that she must have felt that she would not see or taste any of the fruit from the garden. If she felt bad or knew something, at least she never told me anything. But I'll come to that later.

We could tell that spring was here. The big red flying ants are out. The ice on Lac La Biche Lake disappeared on May 1st. People who have lived in Lac La Biche for many years said that the ice goes out about the middle of May, but this year two weeks sooner. So all signs point to an earlier spring. On May 3rd I again planted some things in the garden: radishes, lettuce, onions, garlic, carrots and beets. Marusia did not help with anything. Other years I would make rows, she would plant the plants or seeds and I would cover the rows. This year she did nothing, but told me what to plant where. She only sat on the sundeck steps and looked. On May 14th I planted one row of wheat. I planted it too thick, and I put it all in one row. In the fall I gathered what I could and made a few small sheaves of wheat to have for Christmas the "diduch."

I can't remember when or where, but one day Marusia saw this beautiful rose in one store and said it would be nice to have this hardy Canadian Explorer rose in the yard. She paid for it, we brought it home and later I also bought a rose and said this one would be mine. I planted both roses the same way, the same day with some manure mixed with dirt in the bottom. Watered them the same. What happened was that my rose started to grow and flourish beautifully, but Marusia's rose seemed to have died. It looked sick, as if it had no hope and nothing to live for. It looked so bad that one day Marusia says: "Pull this rose out and we'll get another one, because this one will not grow." I convinced her to give it a few more days or weeks and maybe it will return back to life. Sure enough a few days later we could see her rose pushing out buds to bloom and tiny new shoots on the branches. Than it took off and did it ever bloom that whole summer long with a beautiful pink color. My rose on the other hand pushed out about half a dozen blooms all summer long and it was not half as healthy as Marusia's rose.

As you already know, Marusia is not feeling very good and well. Finally she gets an appointment to see a specialist in Edmonton in the afternoon on May 16th. God planned that day well for us, for we were at a funeral at Boyle in the morning and than left for Edmonton to see the doctor. After seeing the specialist, the doctor had another appointment made in

Edmonton for an MRI on May 25th. We made another trip and than there were more and more trips to follow. Returning home from Edmonton on the 26th of May I planted the remaining of the garden, cucumbers, beans, tomatoes, etc.

For quite some time Marusia had always been complaining of pain in her back. At times the pain was so severe that she would sit on the love seat and would cry due to pain in her back. She would take an aspirin or something to kill the pain and it helped for a while, but than the pain would return. In the evening of May 29th, she asks me to take her to the emergency because the pain is so bad that she can't take the pain anymore. The doctor on duty checked her and told her he could give her a shot of demurral and asked her if she wants to spend the night in the hospital or go home, because in twenty minutes she will be asleep. She thought for a while and said she would go home. The hospital is only two blocks from the house. The nurse gave her a needle in the hospital and we went home. She went to bed as soon as we came home and very soon was sound asleep. In the morning when she woke up she said the pain was gone and she had slept right through the night and had a very good sleep like never before.

Things for Marusia did not seem to go good or get any better. On June 4th we learn from the doctor that she has to go through some tests over again because some of the results of the previous tests are not clear. The doctor said that he thinks she has an inflammation or a tumor in the bone. We still don't know what is wrong.

The day June 4th is not only a bad day for Marusia and me, but also for father in Wakaw. He had filled his car with gasoline in Cudworth and than drove to Wakaw to get some groceries. He left his wallet on the seat in the car after filling the car with gasoline. He went to the Wakaw Co-op, got his groceries and went to the counter to pay, felt for his wallet and it was not in his pocket. He left the groceries and said he forgot his wallet at the service station in Cudworth, so he'll have to go and get it. He got into his car, started the car and began to pull away when the car jumped like a frightened rabbit and smashed into the car parked in front of his car. The police and ambulance came and the police took away his drivers licence. He only had a sore arm where the seat belt came around his shoulder. This was the last day that father had driven a car. What more bad news can one get in a day. Marusia has to go through more tests and father has an accident.

I know it was not father's fault with that accident he had. There was something wrong with his car which he had, a 1997 Plymouth I believe it was. What was wrong? A few times he let me drive that car when we visited him and I always told him there was something wrong with the accelerator on his car. You would step on the gas pedal and the car would jump like a rabbit. I told him that something was wrong, but he said it was okay and was good for him. Had the car not lunged forward as it did, he may have been driving yet for a while. John, Alice and I talked that we were always afraid that father would have an accident, and no one of us would tell father to give up his drivers licence. At times he would take a few older ladies to go shopping to Prince Albert or Saskatoon and we were afraid that if he ever got into an accident with passengers in the car, there could have been some dire consequences. We knew that if we told him to give up his licence, he would hate us for the rest of his and our lives. God works in wondrous ways. Father had the accident and the police took his licence away, so he could not be angry and hateful towards us.

Another bad event in the month of June. A small congregation of St. Demetrius at Craigend is to have Archbishop John of Edmonton come and bless the church, cemetery and the altar in the church. This was to have been done a few decades ago, but the late Metropolitan Ilarion of Winnipeg took ill and could not come to consecrate the church. Now the children and grandchildren of the founders of the congregation finally got everything ready to bless the little church on June 17th. This was also the celebration of the sixty-fifth anniversary of the congregation. Everything is ready to go. Than we find out the day before the celebration is to take place, that Archbishop John became ill and will not be able to come to the celebration. History repeats itself and the little church and cemetery are left standing unconsecrated. Is it a bad omen of some sort that the same thing happened again? The church service went through with the parish priest and the late Father Jaroslaw Puk of Vegreville officiating. The afternoon program took place at the Heritage center in Lac La Biche and I was given the chore of being the M.C., for the program as well as having the main address at the celebration. Twice the people prepared for this special occasion and both times it never took place. Reminds me of what mother used to say: "We make plans and God changes them." We can't fight and win against God to have it the way we want it, it will always be the way God wants. What He thinks and does, no one can outdo Him.

As previously mentioned, my hope and wish is that 2001 had never come, but jumped from 2000 to 2003, but it's not what we want, but what and how God does. June 17th in Craigend things did not go as planned. Now on the 18th of June Marusia gets a call from the clinic that the doctor wants to see her. We went to the clinic and the doctor said that she has a spot on her right breast, he also said that something is wrong with her right ovary and there are problems with the right kidney. How much more bad news in one day can a person receive?

One thing though seems strange here. The doctor tells her that there is a problem with her right ovary. What is strange about this is, that back in 1969 (some eighteen years ago and before we met and knew each other) she had surgery in Moose Jaw, Saskatchewan for a complete hysterectomy. She said the doctor at that time told her that both ovaries and whatever else had been removed. How come the doctor in Moose Jaw told her that the ovaries were removed and the doctor in Lac La Biche, some thirty-four years later, says the right ovary is showing a problem. The doctor in Lac la Biche checked her that day and said that the right ovary was still there.

Another thing happened this day. I cut the lawn and the grass clippings I always scattered the clippings on the garden and than in the fall rototilled everything into the ground. I finished cutting the lawn, put everything away and came to the house to clean up. I came to take off my watch, but it's gone. Where is it? I went back to look for it wherever I was on the lawn and the garden, but could not find it anywhere. I have two or three other watches, but the one that is missing is about thirty years old or more, so it's not a very big loss, but still so many things happening in one day and year, going wrong. This year father smashes the car, Marusia is losing her health, I lose my watch. Next day on the 19th of June I went to hill the potatoes on the garden and there low and behold, I see a piece of the wrist watch strap looking at me. I picked it up, wiped the dirt off and still wore it for years after that as an everyday watch.

Again this year 2001 is showing its stuff. Marusia has a biopsy on her right breast in Edmonton. This same day we learn from my sister Oksana in Winnipeg that her daughter (my niece) Gail is pregnant and will have to terminate the pregnancy because the baby is deformed. The doctor told her to terminate the pregnancy now, and the baby will only live an hour and will die. If the pregnancy goes nine months, the baby will live a week and will still die. She took the doctor's advice hard. When the pregnancy was terminated, the baby's body was deformed as Oksana later told us. Another thing that happened to Gail was a strange thing. Hearing the news, Gail was distraught and tired. She lay down on the chesterfield at home and fell asleep. She dreamt her that baba (my mother) came to Gail and told her not to worry and have the baby, for baba will after the baby. Is this a sign of a bad omen? And they say dreams don't mean anything?

Talking about dreams. Gail had a dream on June 20th. But than Marusia also had a dream on June 22nd, just two days later. What did Marusia dream? With all the bad news, she herself was tired because of her health. She lay down on the love seat (she always liked to curl up on the love seat) and she fell asleep. She dreamt that the love seat is not where it was, but was in the dinning room where the table is. She dreams that the front door opens. She looks and sees me walking into the house, but than she looks again, and it is not me but her father that came through the door into the house. At that she awoke and told me about the dream, but I did not say anything at the time. This stuck in my mind and heart. I could figure that one out - her father had come to take his daughter from this earthly life to eternal life. Some three months later the worst happened, Marusia left this earth, passed into eternity to be with her father and God. So again, do dreams tell of forthcoming events? Two dreams by two people and dreams are fulfilled.

Two days later we again receive unfortunate news. On June 25th the nurse called and said the doctor wants to see Marusia again. We went to the clinic and the report was that she has a spot on her right breast and that spot is cancer. He said it is bad news and also good news. The bad news is that it's cancer, but the good news is that it is the slow cancer with only one centimeter which would require two chemo treatments and it would be cured. This news hit us both very hard even though we may have been expecting something like that could happen. We came home, she sat on the love seat crying and saying: "Why me?"

After the shock somewhat was getting over, we went to say good-bye to our next door neighbor RCMP constable Murray Smith and his wife

Shelly who were moving to Airdrie, Alberta and were packed, loading the truck and ready to go. Marusia broke the bad news to them. Shelly was a nurse at the hospital and they talked for a few minutes. We bid them farewell and walked back to the house. We came to our driveway and beside the garage we were stunned again. On the sidewalk beside the garage we found a twenty two bullet. How did it get here and from where? We walked there a few minutes ago and it was not there. Was this another omen or what? I picked up the bullet and took it over to constable Murray Smith and he said that he has lots of those bullets. The thing is, how did it get to where we found it and why all these things happening?

The end of June has arrived. On June 29th we leave for Saskatoon, Saskatchewan to attend the wedding of George and Wanda Semeniuk's daughter Carrie. George had heart surgery in Edmonton in early March. The wedding was on June 30th. We spent the night at father's place and than on the 30th we went to the wedding. Marusia's side of the family were all there. It was an emotional day for Marusia and me, but I did not want to show that I was hurting inside. She must have had the same feeling, probably knowing inside that this may be the last time she would see her family on this earth. When the time for us came to leave, it was emotional. We all had tears in our eyes but at the same time all wished and hoped for the best. Marusia had told the family by phone a few days before we went to the wedding about the news from the doctor. We did not think it would have been a place at the wedding to break such news. We phoned one family member and told them to let the other family members know of the news.

Next day is July 1st. We went to church at Wakaw and than after lunch we went to the 50th wedding anniversary of Mr. and Mrs. Roman Skakun in Wakaw. We stayed there about an hour and left for home. Going to Saskatchewan and returning back home, Marusia slept half way each time because she was tiring out and feeling weak.

We returned home from Saskatchewan and waited for the doctors next step. It was two weeks on July 16th that Marusia had another appointment in Edmonton at the Cross Cancer Institute. There she also went through some tests at 8:00 AM. We went a number of times to Edmonton for different tests and they were always in the morning. We would leave the day before and stay at John and Kay's place so that we would be on time for the appointment the next day. Once the tests were over we would return back home and waited for the next step. On July 17th we again left for Edmonton, because she had tests the next morning. After the tests, back to Lac La Biche we go. Two days later on July 19th again for more tests the following day. Three times to Edmonton in one week. The thing is that people from the country (out of Edmonton) had to be in Edmonton for the tests in the mornings, while the city folk who live right in Edmonton would come for the tests in the afternoon. We know that the people from Edmonton came for the same tests later in the day, because we talked to a few and they said they were having such and such tests, the same as Marusia. Why do people from the country have to drive over a hundred miles or more for a morning test, while the city people come for the same test in the afternoon. I don't understand and do not think that is fair.

Again the doctor at Cross Cancer Institute said that the cancer in her breast is one centimeter long and two treatments of chemo therapy will get rid of it. But then Dr, Smylie says: "We know you have a small breast cancer, but why are you having back aches? Do you have another cancer in your body that we can't locate and detect?"

The tests on the 20th of July were for her kidneys. After the tests the doctors said they were looking at the right kidney, because it seemed like there is a blockage from the right kidney to the bladder. Later in Lac La Biche the doctor told us that he thinks the right kidney is dead because when she had her hysterectomy in 1969, the doctor at that time may have severed or cut the tube from the kidney to the bladder and that must have caused the kidney to die. Marusia had another test done on her bladder at the Grey Nuns Hospital on July 31st. After this test we waited for the next move

We waited ten days. Marusia is getting weaker each day and back pains are still on, even though she is taking Tylenol number three. Every second or third day she is sick again, throwing up. On August 10th after supper she was sick again and the back pain continued to be severe. She cried from pain and after throwing up her supper she says: "Maybe take me to emergency." I took her to the hospital at 7:30 PM and from that day she never came back home again. The on-duty doctor checked her over and said he would put her into the hospital if there is a bed available. He came back after a while and said there was a bed. She went into room number

MUO4, where she spent the rest of her life, to her last breath on earth, with the exception of ten days when she was in the Cross Cancer Institute Hospital in Edmonton.

Next day at noon I came to see her. Visiting hours are from 12:00 noon to 8:00 PM. I came when she was having lunch. As she was trying to eat, I saw that she could not even feed herself. The spoon seemed to be missing her mouth and would hit her chin or cheek and seemed like she had no power to control the spoon. She could not even feed herself. From then on I took it upon myself to be at each mealtime to help her with the meals. So three to four times a day I went to the hospital which was only two blocks away. Three times for meals and the fourth time after supper to see her and help the nurses tuck her in for the night. This continued for two months. Than came the point that she could not even hold a glass of water to have a drink because she was too weak. She could not comb her hair, so I helped her with that too. First few days she could brush her teeth (false teeth), but later she could not even do that. I would brush and clean them and she would put them back in.

The very next day on August 11th she was put on oxygen. She said it was hard for her to breath, so they gave her oxygen with the little tube in the nose. She stayed on oxygen from that day until she left this earth. Later she was put on oxygen that covered her mouth and nose and later she had a bag hooked on to the oxygen mask. This same day on August 11th her nephew Mike Semeniuk and his wife Doreen from Cold Lake came to visit her.

After she had been in the hospital a few days, she tells me one time: "Next time when you come, bring me some paper and a pen." I thought maybe she wanted to write a letter to someone, so I brought her a whole scribbler. When I brought this for her she says: "You write down what I will say, so you wouldn't forget, because I can't write." She told me what to write and it was as if she knew what was going to happen and she wanted everything arranged.

She told me that when she passes away to have prayers in Lac la Biche. She told me who she wanted for pallbearers in Lac La Biche, every congregation chairman from the congregations. The next day after the prayers in Lac La Biche, is the day for traveling to Wakaw to take her body there. At Wakaw she wanted her relatives to be the pallbearers. She also told me what to do with her personal things. "After I am gone, make a garage sale of all my clothes and give the money for the hospital here in Lac La Biche, because the nurses here look after me like my own mother did. They can buy something for the hospital with that money." She also told me that when she dies not to buy flowers even though she loved flowers, but instead give money to the hospital in her memory. She said that she would not see the flowers when she dies.

Marusia was a perfect seamstress. She sewed all her wardrobe. Nearly a year ago one day when we were in Edmonton, she bought some green material with green sparkling petals and sewed a dress. She had never worn it to any occasion and said that when she dies to bury her in that dress. She wanted her Ukrainian clothes to be given to the Ukrainian Women's Museum in Saskatoon. One thing she could not make up her mind about was her jewelry that she had. She kept telling me that she is thinking what to do with it. One day when I came to see her she says: "My jewelry, you sort it out and put each set into an envelope. Seal the envelope. Than in alphabetical order take one envelope at a time and give them to my nieces."

Another time when I came to the hospital she says: "Tell the funeral director, Derek Kruk, to come to the hospital I want to see him." I made an arrangement and Derek came to the hospital with books and information. She looked through the books at the assortment of caskets and picked out a white metal casket with flowers. Not to make her feel bad that she is arranging her funeral, I also picked out a blue metal casket for myself.

After being in the hospital for one week, my sister Alice and her oldest daughter Pat Walker from Wakaw came to see Marusia. They came on August 17th and left early next morning because they had to be in Saskatoon that day before 3:00 PM.

Another thing that happened and hurt Marusia was the mess up in the hospital in Edmonton. Our family doctor was away on holidays. The substitute doctor was on the phone when I was in the hospital and he said he made an appointment for Marusia to be at the Grey Nuns Hospital on August 21st at 8:00 AM. When I finished talking to the doctor (and the nurses heard me at their nursing station), they marked it in their chart that Marusia has to be in Edmonton on August 21st at 8:00 AM at the Grey Nuns Hospital.

When August 20th came, the nurse from the hospital in Lac La Biche called the Grey Nuns Hospital in Edmonton to confirm Marusia's appointment for tomorrow at 8:00 AM. Good. The ambulance was booked to be at the hospital very early tomorrow morning. Everything is fine. Everything is a go. The following morning I was up very early to go with Marusia to Edmonton in the ambulance. I came to the hospital and the ambulance was there already waiting to take her. Just before Marusia was to be put into the ambulance the nurse called the hospital in Edmonton to confirm that we would be leaving soon. For over twenty minutes the nurse was on the phone with Edmonton and they said they could not find any information record that Marusia is to be there that day. The trip was canceled. When Marusia heard this, she was very disappointed, upset and discouraged. You could see the disappointment in her eyes. The doctor had called and made the appointment. The day before Marusia was to leave for Edmonton, the nurse called to confirm the appointment for tomorrow. Everything was okay. Then the day she was to go to Edmonton, the nurse called that Marusia is ready to leave for Edmonton but now there was a problem because they have no record that Marusia was to be there for tests. The nurse called yesterday and confirmed the trip and now they say they have no record. Why? Who answers the phone at Grey Nuns Hospital?

It was after June 25th when we heard the bad news. Marusia one time had said: "I'll go to Edmonton, get chemo therapy and I'll be ok." Yet Edmonton messed this one up really good. Looks like they ran out of paper in Edmonton to mark down the appointment. The doctor from Lac La Biche made the appointment, called me at the hospital to tell about it, the nurses heard me talk with the doctor, and they made a note of it in their charts, yet no record in Edmonton? The day before the trip there was confirmation and now they say they have no record? ? ? ? Why? Why did the Grey Nuns Hospital not want Marusia to come for tests? Why? I wanted to know why this was a problem.

When this appointment did not get through that day, the doctor in Lac La Biche called again and made an appointment with the Cross Cancer Institute for the same test that was to have been done at Grey Nuns Hospital. The doctor made an appointment for August 23rd in the morning. Because Marusia is weak, she could not go by car, so an ambulance would have to take her there. She wanted to go by air ambulance.

A friend Peter Pysyk of Sarrail, had passed away and the prayers for him were held on August 22nd. Next day in the morning is the funeral, the same time Marusia has to leave for Edmonton. Again on this day somewhat a disappointment that I was not going to Edmonton. Going to Edmonton she had a good trip because she was given pain killers. But coming back, it was a different story and she said she went through hell. The early morning pain killer had wore off and for the return trip they did not give her any pain killer. Every bump and hole that the ambulance hit on the road, she said she felt that on the return trip. She said she would never go by ground ambulance again. Could they have not given her a pain killer in Edmonton for the trip back home? When she was brought back from Edmonton, I was waiting for the ambulance by the hospital. Once she was taken to her room, she told me to put a sign on her door so that no one would walk in because she was in pain and needed rest. She rested from 3:30 to 5:00 PM and had slept the whole while. When I came at 5:00 PM to feed her, she had just awakened a moment before that and said that she was feeling better and the pain had eased up.

Night came and went. Than came August 24th. When I came to see Marusia at noon, she said that she had slept before noon and dreamt of some kind of a wedding. She did not know where or whose wedding it was. I remember my late mother telling many times when you dream of a wedding, that is a forecast of an upcoming funeral. Did she dream of the wedding, and it was a sign of her own upcoming death and funeral?

After being in the hospital for some nineteen days, Marusia's niece Anne Kawchuk and her nephew George Semeniuk and his wife Wanda of Saskatoon came to visit her in the hospital. They stayed for a day and than left back for home. Marusia was having a good number of visitors. When George, Wanda and Anne left for home, sister Alice and her husband John came to visit her on September 1st. They left back for home on September 4th. During this time on the 2nd of September two more of Marusia's relatives came to visit her, Mike and Doreen Semeniuk of Cold Lake, Alberta and Mike's brother Bill and his wife Margaret of Saskatoon also arrived. They came around noon and left in the evening back to Cold Lake.

The doctors once again made an appointment for Marusia at the Cross Cancer Institute for chemo therapy on September 4th. The day arrived and the ambulance was waiting at the hospital. The nurse called Edmonton to confirm the appointment and the ambulance is ready to leave for Edmonton. So what happened? You can take a guess. They tell the nurse in Lac La Biche her bed in Edmonton has been canceled. How do you think Marusia felt this time? I also was upset like she was. No one can tell what feelings she had in her heart. Myself being upset, I went to the nursing station and said: "If I have to drag Marusia across the floor of this hospital I will. Somehow I'll get her into the car and will drive her to Edmonton. I'll call the TV and radio stations in Edmonton and tell them to meet me at the Cross Cancer Institute, because I will drive right up through the steps with the car and than we'll see if there is room for her or not. Why is there room for drug addicts, alcoholics, and other "good for nothing people", but no room for Marusia? She worked for twenty-six years in the hospital at Moose Jaw, Saskatchewan and now when she needs a little help there is non for her. Why do the rich, sports people and others get treatment right away, but not her?" I said what I had to say and walked away from the nursing station back to Marusia's room. I did not say it against the staff in the hospital at Lac La Biche, but at Edmonton. I sat down and we both were disappointed and discouraged. I told her what I had just told the nurses, but Marusia was disappointed with everything. That same afternoon the nurse brought her news that she is going to Edmonton on September 7th for chemo therapy. So once again Edmonton messed things up as they previously did at the Grey Nuns Hospital. It was not the fault and error by the people in Lac La Biche, it was the people in Edmonton that disrupted things for her.

The day September 7th came. The ambulance arrived and she was not very happy because she already had an ambulance ride before and she was not looking forward to the same ride again. The nurse gave her a pain killer in Lac La Biche and they took with her the thick mattress she was lying on. I went with her in the ambulance. The ride to Edmonton was good with no pain. The ambulance left early in the morning because we were to be in Edmonton for 8:00 AM. We arrived in Edmonton at 7:35 AM, some twenty five minutes before schedule. The paramedic and I went to the receptionist and reported who we were and for why we are there. The receptionist checked her list for the day, gave us a paper and said to report to the chemo therapy room. We reported at the chemo therapy room at 7:40 AM. There were two nurses there already. One nurse says: "Take any bed you wish." There were about ten beds in the room all made up and waiting for patients. We took the one closest to the nurses station. The paramedics left Marusia and me and they were told to be back about noon, because by then Marusia would be able to go back home.

    Marusia is lying on the bed. I'm standing and waiting beside the bed and giving her water to sip from time to time. She lay on the bed and I stood beside her till 10:00 AM. Other people came, got their treatments and left. No one comes and does anything with Marusia as if though she has some threatening or contagious disease and they are afraid to come near her. And yes the nurses see us because we are right in front of their desk. Shortly after 10:00 AM, on the sound system comes the announcement: "Mary Stefaniuk please report to nuclear medicine." Can someone tell me how she is supposed to get there if she can't even turn herself over in bed? I went to the nurse and asked her how Marusia is supposed to get to the nuclear medicine room. The nurse called for a person to come and take her and the bed to the designated room. All that was done there, was that some tests and x-rays were taken and she was wheeled back to the chemo therapy room.

    Dr. Smylie came to see her and said that he will check if there is a bed and she would be left in the hospital. After a while a nurse comes and says there is no bed available. When we were still waiting for Dr. Smylie to come back Marusia says that she is having a bowl movement. I got the nurse, they closed her off with the curtains and had to clean her and also all the bedding. All the bedding was replaced. A while later Dr. Smylie came and said there is no bed available, so she would have to return back on Monday to Edmonton and they will have a bed for her. The paramedics were back by this time and were waiting to take us back to Lac La Biche. Before we left I told the nurse to give her a pain killer for the road. They gave her an intravenous pain killer. The paramedics would not leave until all the medication had gone into her body. They said that the medication was a drug and they can't take a drug into the ambulance. So we had to wait a while longer before the medication went through and than left for home. So where was the chemo-therapy which she was to have received that day? Nothing. Why? ? ?

Monday came when Marusia is to go to the Cross Cancer Institute and have a bed ready for her. Before everything was ready to go, the hospital in Lac La Biche got a call from Edmonton, not to bring her because there is no bed. Again another strain on Marusia and me. We were ready to leave and here another disappointment. She took it hard that day, because it seemed like she did not want to talk to anyone, did not eat all day, just was sad and disappointed. Could I blame her for that? No. It is absolutely not her fault. You are told one thing one day and the next day you are told something else. Seemed like everything was working against us in whatever hope she had in getting better and that was being dashed day by day. That same day the nurse called me at home and told me that there will be a bed on the 11th of September around noon. The Lac La Biche people were doing their thing, but Edmonton was messing everything up each time and day.

It is now September 10th. Tomorrow Marusia is going to Edmonton for chemo therapy. On the 10th I came home at 9:30 PM from the hospital after the visiting hours and after the nurses had prepared her for the night. She was not feeling well today, because she was not in Edmonton as she had been previously promised. Can you blame her, no, but tomorrow she is going to Cross Cancer Institute.

At 2:00 AM in the morning I get a call from the hospital that Marusia wants to see me. I rushed over because I thought things had turned for the worse and that she may not make it before morning. The security guard was waiting by the door to let me in. I came to her room. She was very sick and weak. She had an oxygen mask on her face and was breathing very heavily. She looked weak and frail with no color on her face. The nurse came and said that maybe we should cancel the trip to Edmonton, because in her condition she might not make the trip.

I went back home. Now came morning. Marusia is weak. She could not talk because of the oxygen mask and she was very weak. Around 8:30 AM the nurse came and said that Edmonton called to say they have a bed for her and they wanted to know if she was still coming to Edmonton. I told the nurse that in her condition she maybe she should not go. The nurse said to think a minute and she'll be back shortly. I was telling Marusia that she is very sick and maybe she should not take the trip to Edmonton. The nurse came back and we talked that she is very weak for the trip, but Marusia was making signs to take the oxygen mask off. The nurse lifted the mask off and in a low whisper Marusia says: "I want to go to Edmonton." When she said that, I decided I would not stand in her way, but try to fulfill her wish. If she thinks she is strong enough to go, than let's go. The nurse went back to call Edmonton that the ambulance would be leaving about 9:30 AM from Lac La Biche. I could go with the ambulance. If I go with the ambulance, how will I get around in Edmonton without a vehicle? I have to take my car. The nurse came in again and said that I could go in the ambulance, but I told her that I will go myself with my own car. The nurse asked if I knew anyone that could go with Marusia. I said I could not think of anyone right now. In a time like this a person sometimes can't even think clearly.

I wanted to be in Edmonton before the ambulance will get there, so I would have to leave somewhat sooner. I don't speed, but the ambulance travels faster. I rushed home to get a few things for myself to stay in Edmonton. When I was getting my pills, I saw Val Pawlik's house across the back lane. Marusia and Val were always very close friends and they talked on the phone nearly everyday and visited each other across the back lane. Val is a sub teacher in school. Maybe she is home today and she might want to go. I called Val. She was home. I asked what she was doing and she said she was watching the news on TV. I asked her if she would like to go for a ride to Edmonton with Marusia in an ambulance. She says: "Give me fifteen minutes to dress up." I told her to be at the hospital at 9:30 AM. It was now 9:00 AM. I grabbed my things and headed back to the hospital. I told Marusia and the nurse that Val will be over shortly and she will go with the ambulance to the city. I left, got into the car and headed for the big city. It is September 11 - 2001 or as some people today know this day as 911.

As I was driving, I opened the radio and was listening to CHED talk show. I hear Dave Rutherford and someone else talking about a plane that flew into a Trade Tower Centre Building in New York and another plane flew into the Pentagon in Washington and a third plane crashed into the ground near Pittsburgh. What is this? Some story? Is this really happening or some re-enactment of a show? As the news kept on going,

I began to realize this was no joke, but true events unfolding before my ears. Everybody remembers this day as 9-1-1. I remember it as the day when John the Baptist was beheaded and services are held that day in our churches.

I got to the Cross Cancer Institute at 11:40 just before noon, just two and a half hours of traveling. Every time I went to Edmonton that is what it took me to travel one way. Ten minutes later the ambulance arrived at 11:50. They took Marusia to her room and left back for home. Val told me that they made it to Edmonton in one hour and forty five minutes because they did not leave Lac La Biche until after ten.

When Marusia was already in her room, immediately the nurses started to work and organize everything for her. Just a few hours later they found a problem with Marusia. She had pneumonia and her liver was not functioning. Finding this, they said she can't have chemo until the pneumonia is gone and the liver is functioning again. They began to give her some medication and a doctor came in and asked us some questions. She was a small doctor in size and the nurses called her: "The Little One." The doctor asked us one important question: "Should your heart stop, do you want us to bring you back or not?" Marusia and I looked at each other and I say: "Could we think about this for a minute or two?" The doctor said: "Yes."

I stayed in the hospital until about 8:00 PM. I asked the nurses what the visiting hours were and they said there are no visiting hours and you come and go when ever you wish, because there is security at the door after 8:00 PM. I went to John and Kay's for the night. When I came there, I told them what the doctor asked us about the heart stopping. John, Kay and I agreed that if we were in Marusia's position, we would say not to bring us back, but let God's will be done.

Next morning I was at the hospital at 8:00 AM so that I could feed Marusia. Today Marusia is feeling much better than she was last night. Color seemed to be back in her cheeks and she looked more lively. Just as I had come into the room, breakfast was brought for her. I brought up the topic about what the doctor asked us the day before. Marusia said that if her heart stops, let it stay and not to bring her back.

They were now getting her ready for chemo on the 13th of September. When that day arrived for chemo, another setback came. They found that her heart was uneven, weak, racing and beating unevenly. Again chemo is postponed until the heart is regulated. The "Little One" doctor came in and said they can't give her chemo until Monday, because they don't have the people on the week-ends who administer chemo.

During Marusia's stay in Edmonton, I was staying at brother John's place in Edmonton. Every second or third day I would run home to check the mail, news, the house, garden, etc. It is only a two and a half hour trip one way and nice to get out of the city traffic and noise.

On September 17th the doctor came and said everything looks okay and Marusia would be having radiation in the afternoon. Afternoon came and she was taken to the radiation room. I went with her, but only to the door of the radiation room and waited outside. In about an hour and a half she was out and she said that when they were giving her the radiation she thought there was a fire in her stomach. Next day she rested because on the 19th she will be getting her chemo therapy. I left for home on the 19th of September because there will be a funeral prayer service in Grassland for late Annie Federkiewicz at 7:00 PM followed by the funeral service the next day.

I came home, did a few things around the house, picked up the mail, checked the phone calls and in the evening went to Grassland for the prayers. The church was full of people and it was nice and warm in the choir loft. After the prayers the body was taken to the hearse. When we came out of the church it was raining and a very cold strong north wind was blowing. I was only in my suit and felt the wind and the rain go right through me from front to back. A shiver went through and I could feel immediately that I was going to get a cold. I came home after the lunch in the Grassland hall and could feel a sore throat coming on with a sniffle, a sure sign of a coming cold.

Next morning I had a running nose and a sore throat, but I still had to go do the funeral. The day was nice and warm compared to the night before. The funeral went over well. After the funeral I was going to go to Edmonton, but with a cold, some people told me to go home and get the cold over before I go to any hospital, because it's not a good thing to bring a cold to a patient in the hospital. That is what I did. I came straight home. Marusia already was sick enough and she didn't need me to bring her a cold. I remembered then that the doctor had told us that visitors with colds, flu or sore throats should not visit people who have chemo therapy, because the patients body is weakened enough from the treatments the patient is receiving.

This evening I called Marusia. John had a phone installed for her in the hospital. Marusia was not answering the phone. Maybe she can't reach it or maybe she is so weak she can't get it. I tried a few times more calling her, but no results. She was not answering. I called John to see how things were because he and Kay were visiting her every day. John answered and said that they were just leaving for the hospital. I told him that I would call there at such and such time and so he would answer when I call.

Time passed by. Then I called Marusia. John and Kay should be there now. Still no one is answering. I called again and still no answer. What has happened? What is wrong? Then I called the nurses station and said that I'm trying to reach Marusia on the phone and John should be there but no one is answering and if she could go and check to see what is wrong. The nurse says: "John is right here, if you want to talk to him." John tells me that Marusia has been moved to another room near the nurse's station and she will be coming home to Lac La Biche tomorrow. In that case I will not be going to Edmonton tomorrow but will meet her in Lac La Biche when the ambulance arrives. Before I had left for home on the 19th Doctor Smylie said that Marusia is slated to get another chemo therapy in Lac La Biche on September 26th.

September 21st came and there was a service in Athabasca, a Holy Day, the Nativity of the Virgin Mary. I came home right after the service to be waiting by the hospital when the ambulance arrives from Edmonton. When I came home the hospital from Edmonton called me and said the ambulance has left Edmonton at 1:00 PM. That told me that two and a half hours later anywhere about 3:00 PM, the ambulance should be arriving in Lac La Biche. I was waiting outside by the ambulance entry. About 3:00 PM, the ambulance arrived and I met them at the door of the hospital. Even though I was taking Tylenol, I still had a touch of a cold, and I did not want to come too near to Marusia, so that I don't pass the cold over to her. Marusia looked in better spirits. Maybe with God's intervention she will pull through this illness and will still come home. As the days went by my cold was starting to vanish. Again I was making three to four trips each day to the hospital. I was beginning to get worn out myself. I could not sleep very well and was getting tired as the days rolled on. Marusia's condition did not seem to change too much even though she looked somewhat better. She still had no appetite and at times wanted only ice. At times she could not even drink water, due to the weak condition and had no strength to even pull for water with the straw in the glass.

Another thing that happened which is unusual is that on September 25th I noticed that a bird had flown at the window on the sun deck. How do I know this? Well I saw a few feathers stuck to the window and it looked like something had marked the place where the feathers were. I went outside to look if I could find a bird on the ground, but there was non. Ukrainian people from ages ago used to believe and say that when a bird flew into a window that was a sign of news or death. Someone from that house or a neighboring house will die shortly. What happened a few days later tells me that this must be true.

When I was leaving Edmonton for home on September 19th, Doctor Smylie said that Marusia would get another chemo treatment on the 26th of September at Lac la Biche and that the family physician would administer the chemo. I asked the family doctor at home in the hospital if Marusia would be getting the chemo on that day, but he said he had no information about it from Edmonton. Two days later when I was in the hospital, the doctor came in to see Marusia and than says to me: "You are right. She was supposed to get chemo here, but Edmonton forgot to send it out." That is how things went for Marusia. It's either something canceled, they have no record of it, they forgot about it, no bed available, no appointment, etc. etc. During all this time Marusia had to suffer because of someone's mistakes. It was no error or mistakes on the personnel in the Lac La Biche hospital. They gave Marusia number one treatment like any mother would for her child. It was at the end of the line in Edmonton that caused all the confusion and hardships. I still think if Edmonton would have moved earlier and did as they should have done, Marusia would have survived longer or maybe even recovered from the illness. But than, who is to argue against God's will? Sooner or later we all must meet our Creator. Like the late Father Mykola Stetzenko used to say; "We all were not born at the same time, so we all will not die at the same time."

Anyway I could see that Marusia is now getting weaker and weaker as each day went by. On September 27th I was at the hospital about 5:00

PM and supper had come in. Marusia and I got another surprise. Sister Alice and her daughter Darcey with Darcey's children walk into the room. Marusia really got an uplift when they walked into her room. She looked like she could have jumped out of bed she was so happy to see them all. They stayed in Lac La Biche till September 29th and than left back for home.

Sunday September 30th is the service at Grassland, but I never made it there. At 2:30 AM the hospital called and asked me to come to the hospital because Marusia is very weak and her heart was getting weaker and irregular. From 2:30 AM to 10:00 PM this day I spent in the hospital. I took a ten minute break at 8:30 AM when I went home to call Father Michael Domaradz that I would not be in church that morning. That afternoon Father Michael, Dobrodeyka Theresa, William and Olga Sworin from Grassland came to see Marusia.

She could not talk by this time. When she was saying something, it was only a whisper and we could not make out what she would say or want. Than it hit me. Why does she not write what she wants? I gave her a piece of paper and pencil and she wrote: "Slush" on it. Slush is crushed ice mixed with some drink or juice. Another time I again gave her paper to write what she wanted. She wrote: "Fan." It was hot for her. She must have had a fever and was burning. Third time she wrote: "Sleep", because she was tired and wanted to sleep. The last time she wrote was :"Cold clots." I could not figure out what she wanted. What is a "cold clot?" The writing was getting weaker each time because she was losing strength in her hands. So what is a "cold clot?"

It was not until some time later when she was already gone, when I was writing this autobiography, that it hit me what she had wanted. She was hot and burning and wanted to have some cold cloths put on her arms. Today as I write this, my heart is still heavy and aching that I did not know what she wanted at that time and hour. For the life of me at that time I could not figure out what she wanted. I never even thought to ask a nurse if she knew what it was. The two things CLOT and CLOTH are different. She could not even spell the word correctly by this time, she was already so weak. I feel hurt to this day that I did not help her when she wanted the cold cloths on her arms.

Next day Marusia looked somewhat better. She even had some Ensure to drink, for she had not eaten anything for a few days already. Once in a while she would still have strength enough to take a sip of water. When she could not even do that, than I would dip a sponge and place it on her lips and mouth to keep her mouth moist. I was in the hospital and stayed there for a while and than went home. I picked a pail of cucumbers (October 1) and made five quarts of dills. The bigger cucumbers I kept in the refrigerator for eating and gave some to the neighbors. Still no frost in Lac La Biche and flowers (geraniums) are still blooming outside.

October 2nd as on other days, I was in the hospital most of the day, passing water for Marusia with the sponge. In the evening at 7:15 the doctor came with a nurse and brought Marusia her chemo. This was the chemo she was to have received on September 26th and which had never been sent out of Edmonton. As the doctor was administering the chemo, the nurse was standing near by and marking something in the chart, asking Marusia if she feels okay. All she could do was barely shake her head - yes. Marusia is nearing the eighth week in the hospital. It will be exactly eight weeks on October 5th one day before my birthday. All this time stress and pressure on me were also starting to take effect. Tiredness had caught up to me. Going to and from the hospital four times a day, the trips to Edmonton, the messed up plans in Edmonton were beginning to have a toll on me and worse on Marusia. Seeing Marusia suffer was not easy. Her legs were now twice the normal size. She is not eating anything.

My heart ached and was in pain to see her going through such trials. All her life no one did anything for her, she did everything for herself and for others, now **everything** has to be done for her. Today some nearly fifteen years after she is gone, I can still see her lying on the hospital bed, her eyes staring at me and wanting to say something and can't. Even now I still shed a tear as I am rewriting this in 2016 fifteen years after she is gone. I can see her staring at me with those grey eyes looking at me at times and not blinking once. I could feel her helplessness and I can't do anything for her. We would look at each other and when I felt my eyes were going to shed tears, I would turn away or walk away so that she would not see me crying. The heart ached and was with pain, but what could I do?

October 3rd I went to the hospital as I did every day. Marusia was sleeping most of the time, tired and hard to awaken her. I'd awaken her, but her eyes would just close again and she was asleep. I went home to do some work that was starting to lag behind. At 11:30 AM I get a call from the hospital, to come immediately, because Marusia is getting very weak. I rushed to the hospital and in her room on each side of the bed were two nurses sitting holding Marusia's hands. She looked like she was unconscious and in a deep sleep. When I saw what was happening, I began to break down because I could see that the end was coming for Marusia. The nurse asked me if I am okay, and I said, yes. After a short while the nurses left to their other duties. The rest of the day I sat beside the bed holding her hand and watched her hard, deep and heavy breathing, gasping for air even with the oxygen on and trying to pull in another ounce of air into her lungs. I left her bedside twice this afternoon. Once I went to check the phone if any calls had come in and the second time to pick up the mail. The phone had showed a number of calls, because people had been calling to ask how Marusia was.

It is now exactly twenty-four hours since Marusia got her second chemo treatment. It is 8:00 PM October 3rd and she began to open her eyes more and more. I thought maybe she had slept so hard having received the chemo and now she was beginning to feel better. She began to move her head from side to side. She began to move one hand at a time showing great progress from what it was a few hours earlier. Her hands seemed to be picking up energy. Looking at the improvement she had made by 9:00 PM that evening, I told her when a nurse came in: "That if you keep improving overnight the way you have in the last hour, you'll be able to walk by morning." For about the next hour or so she began to get better and better. My heart was beginning to feel better too. Maybe at last God heard someone's prayer and is going to raise her up from this dreadful illness.

I was beginning to get my hopes up as I sat beside her bed, holding her hand and watching the progress she was making practically each minute. Marusia is getting better, maybe in a week or so she will be home. Maybe the chemo is helping her and doing its work. By 9:30 PM she began to close her eyes again and she again seemed like she was tired and wanted to sleep. I asked her if she was tired and with her head she motioned that she was. I waited for a while more, sitting beside her as she kept falling asleep. When a nurse would walk in or some noise, she would open her eyes slightly. I stayed until 10:45 PM and told her I was going home to rest. I also was getting very tired after going through this whole day. I took off the mask of her face and gave her a kiss, replacing the mask back on. She responded with her lips when I kissed her.

At the edge of the bed I said "Good night" to her and "See you tomorrow honey." She opened her eyes and I waved my hand. She responded with the energy she had left and with her right hand slightly moving the three middle fingers she waved good-bye to me. She knew what was happening that I was going home and she tried to wave good-night. I told the nurse at the nursing station that I was going home to get some rest. One nurse says: "If you want, we'll put a special chair or cot in her room and you can spend the night here." Yes, it's possible and very kind of them, but I am too tired. Than what kind of a rest would it be if every few minutes the nurse will walk in or some noise will be made, than I would awaken each time. No I'll go home and it will be more restful and quiet there and I will rest better. I thanked them and left for home. Had I known what was waiting ahead, I would have stayed and sat up all night without sleep or rest. By the condition Marusia was in now after the chemo, it looked hopefully for a better tomorrow.

I left the hospital and this was the only time that I ran from the hospital when I went outside and it would seem that I was running away from Marusia in her greatest time of need. Why did I run? It was pouring rain outside and the parking lot is a distance from the hospital, so I ran not to get wet. Had I known, I would have stayed at the hospital and would have not even walked out of the hospital, not alone to go home. I would have sat the next few hours beside the bed had I known her end was so near.

MARUSIA PASSES AWAY AND FUNERAL

I came home and went straight to bed. I fell asleep immediately because I was just dead tired and was taking sleeping pills each night to get some rest that I needed. I was in a deep sleep when at 2:12 AM the phone rang. I knew that it was the hospital calling probably to tell me to come to the hospital for things were getting worse. I answered the phone and heard: "Eugene, come to the hospital right now." I knew by the tone of the nurse's voice that things were not good. It took me about two to four minutes and I was by the hospital. The security guard was already waiting at the door to let me in. I walked straight toward the nurses station and the head nurse was already waiting for me. She began to walk with me to Marusia's room, put her arm on my shoulder and says: "Mary just passed away."

At those words I thought a knife had gone through my body. We walked into the room. Marusia was lying on her back with the head slightly tilted to the left. The oxygen mask was already off her face. When I saw Marusia, I broke down and started to cry. I went over and kissed her and felt her forehead and arms and they were still warm. Another nurse walked in and asked me if I'm okay. How can someone be okay at such a moment? They were only doing their duty trying to help me at this trying hour. How else could they help? Maruisa is gone forever. I sobbed, but nothing helped. She was not moving, lying motionless. I told the nurse I would be okay and asked her to bring a black garbage bag so that I could take her things home. Marusia would not need them anymore. One nurse brought a black garbage bag and they helped me put things into the bag. Her false teeth were in a container in the bathroom. The nurse took them and said that she would try to put them back into Marusia's mouth. My heart and soul cried each time I put some item into the bag. A tear fell for each thing Marusia had owned which I was putting into the bag.

Thirteen beautiful lovely years have come to an end. The one I loved and the one that loved me maybe even more is now gone forever. So much we did together, never being without each other but three times in our thirteen years. We traveled together, laughed together, cried together, and now only memories left and things I have to do myself. I gave her one more kiss, took the garbage bag with her things and slowly and sadly with tears welling in my eyes hindering me to see where I was walking, I left her room which had been Marusia's home for the last two months. I left the hospital with a sad and broken heart. Never again will I see her smiling face or hear her special giggle when she laughed. It is all over. What will I do myself now? Who will help me in all that we did together? She did so many things. She taught others how to do things. She helped others whenever they needed help.

It was 2:45 AM when I returned from the hospital. I knew I would not be able to sleep now. I put a large candle on the table and lit it. I lit that candle each evening when I was home and even after the funeral until it burned to the end and went out itself. It was too early to call anyone and tell them the sad and heartbreaking news. I went into the basement, turned on the computer and started to write out Marusia's life history (obituary) as she had told it to me in our lifetime. The funeral director will need this for the record. My eyes kept filling with tears as I typed in her memorable life history. Grief, sorrow, aches and pain filled my heart and soul. By the time this night ended and a new day had begun, I had written out Maruisa's life history as I had learned it from her in our thirteen years of married life.

About 5:30 AM, I went upstairs and started making long distance phone calls, starting with Ontario which was already 8:30 AM at that time. I called Marusia's sister-in-law, Beth Kwasnica and told her the sad news. I asked her to convey the message to her three daughters (Marusia's nieces). Than I called Manitoba, Saskatchewan and down west. By the time the day ended I had made thirty-five long distance calls to family and friends. Everywhere I called I could hear by the sound of their voices that people were in shock, saddened, stunned and crying. Some seemed short of words to talk. The person that took this news the hardest was her previous hairdresser in Calgary, Julia Reynolds. When I told her the news, I could hear her cry and sob and she could not talk because of the shock.

It is October 4th, just two days before my birthday. What a birthday gift I received in 2001. As I have already mentioned, I wish that this year 2001 had never come, or that 2000 would have jumped straight to 2003. The whole day for me was sad. As I would go to pick out her clothes for the funeral from each drawer, tears would fill my eyes, so I could hardly see what I had in my hands. Finally I got all the things she had wanted me to have for her wardrobe for her last earthly trip. The day came and went. When evening came fifteen people had come by the house this day to bring comfort and some as far away as thirty-five miles.

At 11:00 PM snow flurries began to fall. The world was now crying for Maruisa. There had been no frost till now, but after the snow flurries came, next morning all the flowers and everything else froze. Maruisa passed away on October 4th and the flowers she loved so much also died the next day, the morning of October 5th.

It is October 6th, my birthday. No happiness. Every year for the previous twelve, Maruisa gave me a beautiful card and a small gift, but not this year and ever more again. No one to embrace me on my birthday and to give me a kiss. Even though it was my birthday, and Maruisa was now in the funeral home, I still managed to travel to Sarrail some thirty-five miles west to sing for a marriage ceremony in the church. The family had asked me to come for lunch to their house, but at a time such as this, who wants to eat or associate? They understood. Somehow now I felt like I did not want to be around with anyone. I had no appetite for food. This same evening I had an invitation to attend a surprise birthday party for William Sworin, but I passed over my card with others who were going to the party. I came home from church in Sarrail and was trying to get things arranged for the funeral.

Everything what I saw in the house, a pain would shoot through my body. Tears filled my eyes and I sat down and wept out my grief. Why? WHY? Jesus had said that whoever asks His Father for anything in His

Name, He would give it to us. How many people prayed and asked God to give Marusia her health back. Why did God not hear us? Why did Jesus say to ask and yet it never was fulfilled? Did I not ask God for health for Maruisa? Did Father Michael not have prayers along with other people? Was there not even one honest, sincere and righteous person asking God to send Maruisa health? Why did she not receive what others were asking on her behalf?

There were hundreds of prayers sent to God and heaven for Maruisa's health. Why did God not fulfill His children's requests? But then I would think of another way when people prayed and said: "THY WILL be done on EARTH as it is in heaven." God knows why He does not fulfill our petitions. My late mother used to say: "We make plans and God changes them." Marusia and I had made plans to go to Dauphin, Manitoba to attend Stan and Helen Malchuk's fiftieth wedding anniversary. We did not make it. Our plans were changed by God. We had made plans to go to the Dauphin Ukrainian Festival and while there to travel to Brandon and attend a twenty-fifth wedding anniversary of a couple that I had married in Dauphin twenty five years ago. Those plans also were not fulfilled. God's plans are different than ours. God's will is different than ours. Later in 2013 I even published a book entitled: "Whose will is it?"

Yes it is hard to go through such grief and sorrow losing your spouse. Yes, my mother died some eight years sooner, but that pain and parting was different. That loss was different. I have buried over five hundred people in my lifetime being a priest, from small infants to one hundred year old people, but that was all different. People at those funerals cried, but it seemed I had no feelings, because it was not a member of my family. When our mother had died and we had gone to the prayers, and coming home and our late father said a very wise thing. He said: "Funerals are nothing until it hits your own family." What true words those were and are. You don't know someone's grief and sorrow until it touches your own family.

October 7th came, the day after my birthday and there is a service in Lac La Biche, the first Sunday of the month. I went to church and knew it would be hard, and it was. At church services Marusia had always stood behind me while we sang. I could hear her soprano voice and it was easy to follow and sing. During our time in Lac La Biche we had sang this way in the Lac La Biche parish of eight congregations at Sunday and Holy Day services. Today the service started, but her voice was not there. From time to time during the service tears filled my eyes when a memory came that we sang together for the glory of God. Now here is an empty space that will never again be filled. After the service Father Michael Domaradz and the late Father Hryhorij Fil' had a panakhyda (memorial service) for Marusia. That was a hard moment. I did not sing that service. Other people sang, for I could not sing or even stand. I sat during the requiem service and my eyes were crying out my tears. I thought my heart would burst with the choking feeling I had in my throat.

After the service there was coffee served in the church basement and I was going there, because for some reason TODAY, I wanted to be with the people, opposite to the day before. As we were walking out of the church, a surprise and than a heartache again. My sister Alice was standing, waiting outside for me by the church gate. Again pain rushed through the body. She nor anyone else can do nothing to bring Marusia back. Alice and her husband John had come to ease the pain during this hard time. I gave Alice the keys to the house and told her to go there if she does not want to come down for coffee in the church basement. She and John went to the house to rest, because they had left home at 4:00 AM their time.

Coming home from church, after a while more family members started to arrive. Brother John and Kay from Edmonton came. Alice and John's daughters Corrine, Pat and Kathy with their families came. There was to be viewing of Marusia at the funeral home 4:00 PM, but the funeral director, Derrick Kruk, called to ask if we could come sooner because many of his family have come to be with him for a thanksgiving dinner. So we all went earlier to the funeral home. In the evening at 7:00 PM the prayers were held at the funeral home, because the church was too small to hold the prayers there.

When we went to view the body afternoon, I thought the end of the world had come. I thought I would die before I got to the casket. How could I go and see my love of thirteen years lying motionless and speechless? It was so hard, oh so hard to face such a moment in one's life. I thought my eyes would flow out with the tears. How come she is not answering me when I talk to her? My heart and soul cried inside and at moments I thought I would also want to die to be with her. I wanted to die to be together with my Marusia. I wanted to go and be with her to help her in the other world. Is she well there? Is she with God?

When evening came, it was time for prayers. I knew there would be many people, because she had many friends she met through the church and others outside the church. And they came, from near and far. All came to pay respects to her because they all loved her. Was there or is there anyone who did not love her? All those that came loved her as much as she loved them. A large empty space in my heart and soul was now established. The Mission View Funeral Chapel was full. The service was served by Father Michael Domaradz and the late Father Hryhorij Fil'. The place was full of people from near and far. I could not believe that Marusia is in the casket. If that is her, why does she not speak and come back home? After the prayers people filed past the casket for the veneration of the cross. Than it came for me to go to the casket to bid farewell to Marusia. I was shaking. My feet had no strength. My eyes ached from tears and were burning from crying. I remember someone was holding me, but I do not know who.

After the prayers people met at the Lac La Biche hall, McArthur's Place, where coffee (lunch) was served. Loveth Beniuk had come to the house when Marusia passed away to see me when she heard the news Marusia passed away and she asked if there will be lunch after the prayers. I said there would be and she said not to worry about anything and she will look after the lunch. She told me where the lunch could be held, at McArthur's Place or in the Senior Heritage Center. After lunch Billy Balaban read my prepared thanks to the people which I had written and Mary Pisarewski read a poem which I had written in memory to Marusia. This poem I wrote on the day of my birthday, two days after her passing.

TO MARUSIA - MY LOVE

More than thirteen years ago we met,

In November when a service was set.

A month later, through God's will,

I ALSO WALKED ON THIS EARTH

You saw me in church, that stands on the hill.

There was a service, where I gave a speech,

With two other priests, we came people to teach.

You asked for a copy, of what I had read,

So others could learn, of what I had said.

It was some three years, before we met,

I had some dream, that God had set.

Of a golden-haired girl, so brave and true,

When I met you my love, my skies turned blue.

In church on Sunday we were betrothed,

And waited for the wedding day to begot.

In April we promised, each other our love,

And the blessings came to us from above.

Twenty-six years in a hospital, you worked indeed,

For the young, the old, and all those in need.

Than saddened you were, when alone you became,

But God sent me to you, to help ease your pain.

We lived together, shared life and all we knew,

Until today I am again, so sad and blue.

EUGENE STEFANIUK

I loved you my love, with all my heart,

And that I did, from our life's start.

Together we traveled, near and far

By plane in the air, on the road by car.

To Australia, New Zealand, and the USA,

To tour and visit, our friends each day.

We lived in Salmon Arm, and Vernon, B.C.,

Than moved to Yorkton, near our families to be.

A call came to serve God, in Phoenix, USA,

We left in December 93, there we were many a day.

There you became ill, your heart was repaired,

During your illness, all the time for you I cared.

We returned to Canada, in Calgary to stay,

We prayed and worked, not only one day.

Calgary became to large, for us there to be,

We wished for a country, wide, open and free.

We moved to Lac La Biche, found many a friend,

Our voices and hands, to God and people we lent.

Than again my love, you began to feel ill,

I ALSO WALKED ON THIS EARTH

With your great illness, we climbed every hill.

To make you healthy, to be strong and well,

But now for me rings, again the sad bell.

You are gone my love, I am alone and sad,

For thirteen years, your love I had.

Now I am alone, so sad and blue,

How will I live and what will I do?

I'll pray to God, for your soul each day,

You to be in heaven, in my prayers I'll say.

Good-bye my sweet love, I loved you so,

Now in heaven, seeds of flowers you'll sow.

You did God's work, you loved to sing,

In the heavenly choir, much joy you'll bring.

Sing praises to God forever more,

With all the Saints, inside Heaven's door.

I miss you my darling, the pain already is great,

What will happen to me, in this world of hate?

Ask God to look after me, my sweetest love,

So He would upon me, send His Holy Dove.

My tears will fall, each day for you,

Because I am alone, so sad and blue.

Some day we'll meet, and than forever more,

We'll share our love, within God's Heavenly Door.

On my birthday October 6th - 2001
Lac La Biche, Alberta.
From your loving husband Eugene

The funeral director gave me the guest book which people signed when they came to the two prayer services and the funeral. I see that those who signed for prayers in Lac La Biche, there were ninety-three people plus the pallbearers. How many more there were that maybe did not sign I don't know. After the lunch in Lac La Biche, people dispersed to their homes. Next morning we have to be up early because we have nearly four hundred miles to travel. Marusia will be leaving for her last LONG earthly journey and ride. She will be going back to the place where she was born and struggled on this earth to make things good. She had frozen her hands in the area where she was born and lived when she was going to town to get some things. When she was working for Canada Packers, she burned her same hands with acid while testing cream. Life was not easy when you were born in the 1920's and 1930's. No wonder they are called: "The dirty thirties." Marusia had set a Canadian record working at the creamery by grading (candling) 1000 dozen eggs in one day all by hand

October 8th is Thanksgiving Day in Canada. Thanksgiving? Thanksgiving for what? So what have I got to be thankful for on this day, that my love has been taken away from me forever? Thankful that I will never see her again or hear her voice? Thankful. Yes - Thankful to God for having given me Marusia for thirteen years of love and joy. Anyway my sister Alice and her husband John left for Wakaw at 4:00 AM. John wanted to be back home before their son-in-law Vern Walker would start to dig the grave for Marusia's resting place.

Brother John, Kay and I left in two vehicles for Wakaw at 6:45 AM. We traveled through Cold lake, Alberta, Pierce land, Meadow Lake, Glaslyn, Prince Albert and unto to Wakaw in Saskatchewan. Marusia and I had traveled this route a number of times and it was the shortest way from one place to the next. Maybe the road from Cold Lake to Meadow Lake is not the best in the world, but at least it is paved. After we passed Glaslyn, John passed me and I never saw him again, until the prayers in Wakaw that evening. John does not like to drive the speed limit and I am different. I set my cruise at the proper speed and I don't worry about getting any speeding tickets.

I arrived at Wakaw at 2:00 PM and went straight to Dmytro Ostafichuk's place, Marusia's God father. There was no answer. Later after the funeral Mr. Ostafichuk told me that his wife is in the nursing home and he must have gone to see her. From Ostafichuk's place I went to the cemetery about 2:30 PM. As I came down the highway, Vern Walker was just pulling into the cemetery with the back hoe to start digging the grave. Brother-in-law, John Hnatiuk was there also. I was there from the beginning to the end of the grave digging. My heart cried to see such a picture before my eyes, where my love will be laid to rest. The day was very beautiful, sunny and warm all day long.

In the evening people gathered at the church of St. Mary's Ukrainian Orthodox Church for prayers at 7:30 PM. Two priests, Father Michael Domaradz and the parish priest Father Roman Kocur officiated at the prayer service. Again the church was filled with family and friends. People from as far as Winnipeg and Vancouver attended the prayers and funeral the next day. After the prayers there was lunch served in the church basement. I asked Mike Semeniuk from Cold Lake, Alberta, Marusia's nephew, to read my thank you to all who came. Mary Prefontaine, Marusia's niece, from Saskatoon read the above poem. The thanks and the poem were again read the following day at the dinner after the funeral service. After the prayers were over, I went to spend the night with Alice and John. Looking in the guest book I see there were one hundred and four people attending the prayers, but that is somewhat not right, because those of my family who had signed in Lac La Biche, they did not sign again in Wakaw. Marusia's body was left in the church overnight.

Next day was a hard day for the heart. This is the last time that I will see my beloved Marusia. The day was very beautiful, sunny, warm, clear skies and no clouds or wind. If anyone earned such a beautiful day for their funeral Marusia did for the hard work for God, church and friendliness to the people. This will be the last time I will be able to touch her and bid her farewell into the other world. This day I also got a surprise. There were three priests serving the funeral service. The late Father Mykola Derewinka and Dobrodeyka Janice from Dauphin, Manitoba had arrived during the night and participated in the funeral. When I served at Dauphin, Manitoba, Father Mykola was ordained at Dauphin. When I served at Hyas, Saskatchewan, Father Mykola was at Canora, just thirty miles apart. I am also the Godfather to their first child Pavlo. Many times I spent with Father Mykola at Canora when I traveled there for business or just passed through and stepped in to say, "hi". Father Mykola and Father Michael Zaleschuk had married Marusia and me at Moose Jaw, Saskatchewan. Father Mykola Derewianka passed away in the fall of 2013.

People started to gather at the church much before 10:00 AM. I remember seeing people that came from Winnipeg, Dauphin and Swan River in Manitoba. They came from Yorkton, Regina, Moose Jaw, Hudson Bay, Melfort, Saskatoon, Middle Lake and other places in Saskatchewan. They came from Calgary, Medicine Hat, Lac La Biche, Edmonton and places in Alberta. They came from Vancouver and all places in between. There appears over a hundred names signed on the day of Marusia's funeral, but this is not accurate, because many people that were for prayers the evening before did not sign again, yet they were at the funeral. It is hard to say how many people came, but the church was filled full with mourners. The choir at the prayers and funeral led by the late Roman Skakun and late Tony Bilokuray sang beautifully. I am sorry that I never had the service taped, but at such a time as this, one cannot recall and remember everything that has to or should be done be done.

It was a sad day for me. Three priests serving. Choir singing like in heaven. People filled the church in every space there was. Family and friends gathered to pay their last respects to Marusia. The service is now over. Now comes the last farewell, the good-bye for ever from this earth. People filed past the casket. Than came the relatives and my last moment to face the dreaded time. What pain, what heartache, no one knows except me who lost my everything. What agony for the heart, soul and mind. No one knows this pain, until they lose their spouse.

I thought my eyes would flow out with tears that day. They were burning and filled with tears. Slowly and sadly with hot tears flowing down my face, I say good-bye to Marusia. I will never again see her smiling face, hear her special laugh or hear her voice. I will never again see those beautiful grey eyes. Than someone pulls me away from the casket. As the casket is closed I catch the last glimpse of my love. Never again will I see her. I will miss her. How will I live without her. She was my right hand in everything even when serving the church at Phoenix, Arizona. She did so much. She cared so much. She loved so much and I loved her dearly. Who will care for me now and what will become of me? I learned from her to do so many things.

Everybody is now outside. Marusia in the casket is in the hearse. Now begins Marusia's last ride on this earth to her resting place, a land that was once owned by her uncle, John Kwasnica. The land where her uncle, parents, brother and sister all are resting, just steps away from each other. I lived on that farm in the 1940's and worked on it when we lived at Wakaw when I was about eight years old. We lived only half a mile east of where Marusia was laid to rest and she will be only about five miles south of the place where she was born some seventy-four years ago. The cavalcade is slowly beginning to move from the church. The RCMP are stopping the traffic on the roads not to interfere with the funeral procession. Half a mile of cars are following Marusia to the cemetery.

Everybody is at the cemetery. Now starts the last few paces for Marusia from the hearse to the grave. What a heartache. No. No. No, don't go, come back. Don't leave me behind. Take me with you. Who will be with me in the car when I travel to church or on some trip? What will I do by myself without you? Who is going to wash my shirt? Who is going to talk to me in the house? Marusia, please come back, don't go, take me with you if you must go. After the casket was taken to the grave, I seem to have lost track of what else happened. As I wrote this some fifty-five days later, I can only imagine what happened at the grave side. I remember the casket being carried, and than a blank spot remains until we left the grave and headed back to the hall for dinner.

After the burial everybody went to the Wakaw Recreation Hall for a memorial dinner. My sister had ordered food for 200 people. Alice and John did so much during this time to make all the arrangements in Wakaw for the funeral. THANKS are in order for John and Alice for all their work and support, because I don't who could have done all that work for Marusia. By the amount of food left it told me that there must have been one hundred and sixty people at the funeral for the memorial dinner. There were plates set at the table and by the number of plates used it tells me that it was about one hundred and sixty.

After dinner, George Semeniuk, Marusia's nephew from Saskatoon read my thank you to the people and Mary Prefontaine, Marusia's niece read the poem again like the night before. The late Father Mykola Derewinka also said a few comforting and soothing words, how we became "koomy", how we worked together for the church, that he had married Marusia and me at Moose Jaw, Saskatchewan some thirteen years ago. After singing "Vechnaya Pamyat" (Memory Eternal) people came forward to the head table to express their condolences to me. It was hard when the family and other people came forward to the head table and I shed tears each time. Together we would cry on each other's shoulder. I lost Marusia, my love, my spouse and they loved her and now lost an aunt, relative or friend, so we together shared our loss, but mine was the greatest. As people filed past they shook my hand and we hugged each other. Then the people dispersed to their homes or duties. After the people left I went to do some squaring up with the bills: clergy costs, cantors, the hall, church, newspaper, caterers, etc.

The day of the funeral was beautiful, sunny and shirt sleeve weather. I remember it was sunny when we were going to the cemetery and coming back. After I had paid and looked after the bills, I still had enough time to stop and spend a few moments at the cemetery. I still had some tears left over that fell on Marusia's grave. The flowers were on the grave. I kissed her grave, cried and slowly with a sad and heavy heart turned away from her and headed towards the car, to go and spend an hour or two with father in Cudworth.

Marusia did not survive that dreaded disease of cancer, yet she survived other dangers in her life. I do not recall what year, but she told me that one time when she was flying from Ontario back home, they had to make an emergency landing in Winnipeg. What had happened was that the landing gear on the plane had not come down. The plane circled Winnipeg for quite a while dumping fuel, than landed on the belly of the plane in the foam which had been spread on the runway. She said that the wheels of the plane had come through the floor of the plane when it landed.

Marusia had a brother who worked on ships traveling around the world. One year she and her brother went to Mexico for holidays. I do not remember where in Mexico. She had come down to the ground from the apartment waiting for her brother outside, when suddenly the lizards started screaming and heading for the ocean. Dogs started to howl and than an earthquake shook the area. She grabbed unto the handrail attached to the apartment and held on until the earthquake ceased. As previously mentioned, she survived the open-heart five by-pass surgery, yet the dreaded disease of cancer took her life.

Marusia had also planned three times to go to Ukraine and never got there once. She wanted to go and see the village where her parents had come. She said the first time she did not go was because her late husband had gotten ill and the doctor advised her not to go. She got her deposited money back. Than she was going to go another time and did not go because of the Chernobyl explosion and the tour was canceled. The third time she did not go was that not enough people had signed up for the tour and the tour never materialized. After we were married I suggested we go and visit Ukraine, but she said: "I was planning three times to go and never went. I guess God does not want me to go there." And so it was that she never did see the birthplace of her parents.

After the funeral I went to father's place, and we went to a Chinese restaurant in Cudworth for coffee even though it was later in the afternoon. We sat down and placed our orders with the waitress. Two people, John and Kathy Sholtar walked in, saw us and came over to pay their condolences. We told them that they could sit with us at the same table and they did. The four of us had coffee together. John Sholtar pulled out forty dollars and gave a donation to pass over to the hospital in Lac La Biche in Marusia's memory. We went back to father's house and sat for a while talking. I could see father was getting tired, because at the age of one hundred he also felt some of the pain that I was having. Mother has passed away and he went through what I was going through now. He said that he was tired. I said good-bye to him and left back to St. Benedict to Alice and John's place to spend the night.

Next morning at 8:00 AM I left for home on October 11th. Before I left Wakaw, I just had to stop once more at the cemetery and say goodbye to Marusia. I could have stayed there all day, but the sun will not be waiting for me. It is moving and time does not stand and wait. It is time to go, but oh so hard to leave my love behind. It was so hard, so hard to say the good-bye again. When will I come to see you again, my Marusia? Why did God have to take you away from me? Why did you have to suffer so much? The days are now getting shorter. If I want to get home before sunset, I have to leave now. Thank you Marusia for everything. I'll pray that God accept your soul into His Kingdom. I'll pray that God forgive you any sins you may have committed.

I traveled home the same way I had come to Wakaw. The trip home was sad, traveling alone. Traveling to Wakaw and back I did not even open the radio in the car. I did not want to hear anything only Marusia's voice and it was not in the car. I sang the same church hymn over and over and over again. "Holy, Holy, Holy, Lord of heavenly Hosts......." I arrived home at 4:00 PM just in time before the sun hid its face for the day. I also had stopped at Bill and Sonia Balaban for about fifteen minutes who live only twelve miles south of Lac La Biche. They also had been to the funeral at Wakaw.

Returning to Lac La Biche, I stopped at the post office to pick up the mail. I had not picked up the mail for some three days. The mail box was fully packed. Sympathy cards filled the mail box. I drove home and came into the sad, lonely and cold house. I turned up the thermostat to warm up the house and than carried everything from the car to the house. Food that was left over from the memorial dinner, Alice took some, other people took some and I brought some home and put it in the freezer. I unpacked the suitcase and than started to check the mail. It was now dark outside. Each letter as I opened and read, eyes filled with tears. I had a large candle that had been given to us one time, so I lit that, put it in a metal container and had it stay lit all night long. The last night that the candle burned at night was on October 17th when it was so low that it would not burn anymore.

The next day I spent at home. I washed the sheets from the two beds that company had slept on them, as well as any other clothing that needed washing. Each time I was doing that my eyes would fill with tears. Marusia loved to do the washing and ironing. She worked as a seamstress in the hospital in Moose Jaw. The evenings now became the saddest and loneliest. Still I would not open any radio or TV in the house. I don't want any music. I don't want to hear anything but Marusia's voice. The first time I opened the radio was on Sunday October 14th. On Saturday the 13th I was at Billy and Koreen Balaban's (twelve miles south of Lac La Biche) to their son's birthday supper. I accepted the invitation and took a small gift for Jordan. There were about fifteen to seventeen people, family and friends, that talked while the children played. I felt out of place. All came in pairs, I came alone. The heart ached being alone, but what can I do? After having supper and a piece of the birthday cake, I left for home because next day is Sunday and must go to church to Athabasca, fifty five miles west of Lac La Biche. There I have to give the main address about the Altar Servers who are being honored that day.

The service on October 14th went well, but again I felt the empty space. Marusia always stood behind me in church and she started to sing the melody and it was easy to harmonize. Now I can't hear her voice anymore. Dobrodeyka Theresa was not in church today, so it was somewhat harder with no soprano to start and lead. Marusia and Dobrodeyka sang together, but many times Dobrodeyka was not present if she had to work in the hospital that day. Marusia and Dobrodeyka would also read the psalms in the Morning Matin service.

After the service there was a Thanksgiving service and dinner followed in the church basement. There, certificates were passed out to the Altar Servers for their work in assisting the priest during services. Now another pain came to me. They give a certificate to MARUSIA and me for helping sing in the church services. That did not help the aching heart, even though the parish tried to make it easier. Her name is on the certificate. Can she see it now or read it? Tears welled up in the eyes again. After this I had to give my speech.

I also had been in touch with brother John in Edmonton about seeing a lawyer now that Marusia is gone. He made arrangements with his lawyer to be in Edmonton at a certain day and time. At the same time I would also have to go and see the Federal Government (Human Resources) about the change in my marital status. I went to Edmonton and John took me to see his lawyer. I returned home that day just as the sun was setting. When night comes I don't like to be on the road to chase wild animals away or them coming into the path of the car. That is why I always want to be home before dark.

When Marusia was in the hospital she must have known that her time on earth was approaching, because she told me so many things what to do when she passes away. She loved flowers, yet she asked me that people not give flowers for her for the funeral, because she will not see or smell them. She asked that the people make donations to the hospital in Lac La Biche in her memory. On October 17th I took to the hospital in Lac La Biche $1350.00. As this was written on November 26th 2001 I had another $545.00 on hand. I also learned that the hospital got money from people that did not send money to me, but straight to the hospital. So there could be about $2000.00 donated to the hospital in her memory. There is a small metal bar with Marusia's name placed on the wall in the hospital along with many other names who have made donations to the hospital. Marusia also asked that I have a garage sale of her personal things and the money to go to the hospital. I can't have the garage sale now, because it's too cold in November. This will have to be done in the spring of 2002. As this was later written, I personally passed over $2000.00 of donations to hospital in her memory.

I should also mention that the year 2001 was also not very good for the town of Lac La Biche. There was a water ban that we could not use for watering lawns, gardens, flowers, washing cars, etc. I had two large plastic barrels at the back of the house. They caught rain water off the roof. When one would go empty, rain came in the evening, just enough to fill the empty barrel. This continued all summer long in this way. God would send just enough rain showers to fill the barrel with water. So I had water for the garden and the flowers all summer long. When Marusia and I had lived in one other town after our marriage, that town situated on the shores of a large lake, they also had a water ban one year. A funny article appeared in the paper of that town which said: "If it's yellow, let it mellow, if it's brown, let it down." Every time I see a "water ban" sign, I would think of the article I had seen in the paper.

Now on October 22nd is Billy Balaban's birthday. I baptized Billy when I served in the Lac La Biche parish in the 1960's. I was invited to come to the supper on the farm. Billy's sisters, parents and other family members were in attendance. Again I felt out of place being alone. I had supper and a piece of birthday cake and left for home.

I had talked to father on the phone and asked how many children had come for Halloween to his place last year. He said that he had over one hundred. I made a decision that I would go on the 31st to his place and help him with the passing out of treats. He is one hundred years old and getting weak. By the time he gets up and sits down and up and down, Halloween will wear him out. I left early in the morning and went the same way I had gone to Marusia's funeral. Before I got to father's place, I stopped for a few moments with Marusia. The flowers were blown of the grave, so I replaced them and added a few new ones. From there I left for father's place to Cudworth after I had spoken to her and cried at Marusia's grave.

When I arrived at father's place it was about 4:00 PM, Alice was there also. I asked father when the kids would be coming for treats and he said they had already been around 2:00 PM. Alice had a problem with the truck because it was making a screeching noise. She called John to come and see what is wrong. John came and took the truck to the garage. A small rock had fallen into the wheel drum and was rubbing against metal making the shrill screeching noise. John and Alice went home and I was staying with father overnight.

Next day I took father and we went to Alice's place on the farm for dinner. After dinner we went to the cemetery again. From there to Wakaw where father went and got a few things in the store for himself. I took him home to Cudworth and myself left for Saskatoon to see Marusia's side of the family and fulfill one more of her wishes she left with me. She had asked that I give each of her nephews and nieces $100.00 for those who had come to see her in the hospital. I stayed over night at George and Wanda Semeniuk's place. Next morning George and Wanda were leaving early for southern Saskatchewan, so I had an opportunity to get away early for the trip home. This time I went from Saskatoon to North Battleford, Lloydminster, than up north to Cold Lake and home. I also stopped at Cold Lake and gave Mike and Doreen the small gift from

Marusia for coming to visit her in the hospital. I came home early today, well before sundown.

When I was in Edmonton to see a lawyer, he gave me forms to fill out and then bring them back in and they will see what has to be done to probate the will that Marusia had. When I came home that day there was a letter in the post office already waiting for me. It was from the Saskatchewan Government Employees Pension Benefits where Marusia had worked for over twenty-five years in Saskatchewan. There was a form that I had to get a lawyer to sign. So now, do I make another trip to Edmonton just to have a lawyer sign the form? Or, do I get a lawyer in Lac La Biche so that if I need a signature, I can have it in five minutes instead of spending a whole day going to Edmonton and back. So I decided to go and see a lawyer at home, Tom Maccagno. His father, Mike Maccagno, in the 1960's owned the theater in Lac La Biche and any clergyman that wanted to see some movie they were admitted free. His son is now a lawyer, so I took the will and the papers and went to see him instead of making the long trip to Edmonton.

In Ukrainian life when someone passes away there is a tradition that on the 40th day after the passing of a person people gather to have a memorial service for the deceased. Forty days after Marusia passed away fell on November 12th, the day after Remembrance Day. I asked Father Michael to have a memorial service for her on that day. People came from every congregation in the Lac La Biche parish. There were about forty to forty five people present. I went to confession and communion this day. The food that was left over and in the deep freeze from the funeral at Wakaw, I took out the day before to have it unthawed and used it for the memorial dinner. The day of the memorial service was just as beautiful as the day of her funeral.

Finally it came into being that Ukraine an enslaved country under Russian rule for four hundred years was freed from the enslavement in 1991. Father, John and late Kay took a trip to Ukraine in 1989 when Ukraine was still dominated by the Russian communism. They were not allowed to go into the village, but they sneaked out one day with a car that took them to late Kay's village. When the car arrived in front of her sister and brother's house, her sister came out to see who was looking for who. She came out near the car and asked who was there and who they were looking for. My late sister-in-law Kay said: "Hello, my dear sister, I'm Kay." The lady standing near her gate says: "I have no sister. I don't even know where she is or whatever happened to her. I haven't heard from her since she was taken away. I have held many memorial services for her." The late Kay comes out of the car and says: "Well I am your sister. What do you mean that you did not know where I was? I have been sending you parcels for forty years and you always wrote back that you received the parcels and thanked me for them." What happened to the parcels that were sent for four decades to Ukraine? My late sister-in-law received letters of thanks for the parcels. People in the post office or whoever was in charge of the mail would take the parcels for himself/herself and than write a thank you letter for the gifts, supposedly from her sister. How was she to know and find out what was happening? But God made it possible that this dark mark of communism be exposed in their system when my late sister-in-law had an opportunity to visit Ukraine and find out what had been happening for four decades.

On November 23rd the ladies from the parish were to meet at 9:00 AM in Boyle to start making varenyky for a supper and Search for Talent show, but this did not turn out, because there was a funeral being held in that hall in the morning. By the time the funeral was over, the memorial dinner and the hall cleaned up somewhat, it was not until about 3:00 PM when the varenyky bee started working. Three of us men rolled the dough and the ladies pinched the dough together. There were thirty-four of us working in that group. At 6:30 PM everything was finished for tomorrow's supper and the talent show.

Today is November 24th, 2001. This is the day of the first annual varenyky supper and Search for Talent Show. For a while when the people started coming, I thought they were coming from all Alberta. The chairs got filled up and supper took place. Everybody had lots to eat to their hearts content and much food was left over so the remaining food was sold after the program for $250.00.

Then the Search for Talent took place. There were eight contestants: singing, dancing and one contestant played the violin and a lady played the piano. Through this contest we raised nearly $2500.00 for the parish purse just from the pledges that evening. The meal tickets brought in some $2000.00, so when the evening was finished and the expenses counted up, the clear proceeds netted over $4000.00 for the parish. This whole day was cold and dreary and snow flakes were flying around, but the road was dry.

On December 4th, I went to Radway some seventy five miles south west of Lac La Biche to a church service. I had seen the schedule in the paper and knew there was a service there. I came to the church but there was no life, nothing. The sidewalk is not shoveled and no one around. I drove to the store in Radway and knew that the late Father or the late Dobrodeyka Fil' would know if there is a service or not. Dobrodeyka was in the store. I asked her why there is no service, and she said she did not know anything. She called someone and was told that the service in the morning was canceled because Father has funeral prayers that evening and a funeral next day. Where in the church rules or canons does it say that if you have prayers in the evening, you don't have a Liturgy Service that morning? December 4th is one of the large twelve Holy Days the church has during the year. It is the Entrance of the Virgin Mary into the temple.

December 22nd I again left for Saskatchewan. I visited John and Alice and stayed a few days with father. I also stopped to say hello to Marusia and put new artificial flowers on her grave. On the 25th I left to Saskatoon to Marusia's niece Mary and husband Denis Prefontaine. That evening the rest of Marusia's nephews and nieces gathered and we all had supper together. Because I had forgotten to take home a parcel from father, I returned that evening back to Cudworth and spent the night with father. Next morning I again visited Marusia and left for home, arriving home at 6:00 PM when it was already dark. It was good that I came back that day, for the following day it was very foggy and visibility was down to zero and traveling was very bad.

And so ended the year 2001, which I have mentioned and hoped that if would have never come for me. It was a year that will be remembered for always. That was the year that broke my heart and soul. Marusia and I had served God to the best of our ability as we knew how. We were very happy and compatible with each other, but God has His ways and His ways are better than mine or anyone's else. Marusia and I both had been married twice. Neither she nor I had any family from our marriages. That was God's will to be so. Because I have no family it is so much harder to carry on alone in life. One way looking at it, I feel happy that Marusia is not suffering anymore as she did in the hospital. The other way I am sad for I don't know where she is in the other world. But right now I just have to carry on with my life as best I can and know how until the day when I will meet her again in eternity.

On January 4th 2002 there were prayers in Boyle and a funeral the following day. Right after the funeral I left for Saskatchewan to be with father on Christmas Eve, January 6th. I went to Mundare, Alberta and picked up some Ukrainian sausage to take for Alice and the girls. I was going to have Christmas Eve supper with father, but Alice called father and said so we both come to their place for supper on the farm. We had supper at John and Alice's place. There were some thirty of us at the supper. It was not easy to be without Marusia. John had a heated garage attached to the house, and it was nice and cozy while outside it was hovering at -30 C. After supper I took father home and than went to Wakaw for a midnight church service.

Next day, January 7th is the Nativity of Christ (Christmas). I went to church to Codette north east of Melfort, Saskatchewan. On the way home I stopped at radio station CJVR in Melfort to talk with the program manager about starting a Ukrainian program on their radio each week. The manager was not in, so I left my name and phone number and asked that he call me in a few days when I get back home. On January 8th I stopped in church at Prince Albert for the service and after the service headed back home. The program director from radio CJVR at Melfort called at 10:13 AM on January 16th. He said that he had talked over my suggestion with the station manager and he said it was decided not to accept my suggestion, because their station is strictly a country and western music station. I did nothing more about this matter and that was the end of Ukrainian radio programs.

On February 2nd I went to Edmonton to be at the memorial service for Natalia Kryschuk. It was a forty day memorial service. It was warm and mild outside and the vehicles were just awfully dirty from the slush and salt on the streets. On the way home after the service I stopped at a car wash to wash the Escort car because it was so dirty that one could not even see where the doors were. I washed the car and started to drive home on the Manning Freeway when I noticed at the bottom of the windshield that there was like a thin string of ice. Not thinking anything I drove home knowing that warmer weather will melt that ice. Next morning there is a service at Lac La Biche. I drive out of the garage and noticed that the piece of ice on the windshield had not melted. Having a second and better look at the windshield, I saw that it was not ice, but a crack along the bottom of the windshield from end to end. I think I can only guess what had happened. When I went to wash the car in Edmonton, the windshield was cold and the warm water in the car wash cracked the glass.

FATHER ENDS UP IN THE HOSPITAL

On February 11th I got a phone call from Alice that father is in the hospital in Wakaw. It seems that he fell down on the floor and could not get up and must have laid there some twenty four hours. Mr. Bill Trischuk who always checked on father in the morning came to see him. The door was locked inside and it was already about 10:00 AM. Father was always up at 6:00 AM. Mr. Trischuk went home and called Alice that the door is locked inside and no one is answering. Before Alice got to Cudworth from the farm some fifteen miles away, some people had already broken a window in the door and unlocked the door to get in. They found father on the floor and called for an ambulance. When Alice arrived they were putting father into the ambulance to take him to Wakaw. The following day Alice went into the hospital at Wakaw because she had to have some surgery done. Both father and daughter are in the same hospital together at the same time.

Father stayed in the hospital a few days. As soon as he ended up in the hospital, brother John and sister Oksana arrived at Wakaw to see father. It seemed like there was no hope for father. A day or two later he felt much better, but told John, Alice and Oksana that he will not be able to go back home to stay by himself. He asked that John, Alice and Oksana look for a place for him where he would be able to stay. They found a place, St. Michaels Haven, in Cudworth which at one time was a hospital before the provincial government closed the hospital in 1993. John, Alice and Oksana took father out of the hospital to show him the place. He said that he would be able to live there since it was only a block from his house. Than they took father back to the hospital at Wakaw. In the meantime I was calling Alice every day to be updated as to what was happening.

On February 15th another great church Holy Day, the Presentation of the Lord in the Temple. The service this day is at Sarrail some thirty five miles west of Lac La Biche. After the service I came home and sat on the deck reading the newspaper. It was +6 outside and +20 on the deck. The deck was enclosed with windows, thus it made it a three seasonal deck.

February 21st the third draw for a monthly raffle that the parish had. The following day I will leave for Saskatchewan to see father. I did not go this time because a storm had come on during the night. I was all packed and ready to leave but had to cancel my trip. This same day father was released from the hospital and taken to Cudworth where he would stay at the St. Michael's Haven a senior residence place. On February 28th we had the final draw and now that this was over, I left for Saskatchewan the following day. I was in Saskatchewan till March 5th when I returned back home.

Since Marusia passed away, I have been going to bed at 10:00 PM. About 9:30 PM I would say my evening prayers. On March 14th is Alice's birthday. At 9:40 PM as I was reading my prayers in the bedroom, when someone or something lightly touched my right shoulder. I was startled and turned around to see what or who, but there was no one. I was somewhat uneasy over this event, and after getting into bed still shook up thinking who touched me on the shoulder. Was it God, an Angel, Marusia, who or what? This has also happened a few times in Osoyoos where I was living since 2006. At one time being alone at home, when Joyce was in the hospital, I was washing the supper dishes when someone called out: "Eugene." Yes you would get startled in broad daylight when you know there is no one in the house and your name is called or someone touches you on the shoulder.

On March 31st, Latin (western) Easter. A storm is raging outside, cold and some four to five inches of snow came with the storm. March went out like a lion, roaring away with the storm. Now comes April. Maybe now spring will be here. On the 2nd I get a letter - invitation from Dauphin, Manitoba to come to their service on May 12th which is their feast day(chram) and the 30th anniversary of the priesthood of late Father Mykola Derewianka and also Mother's day. I am asked to be the main-quest speaker after the service. During this same time April 1st to the 4th, John Hnatiuk spent time in the hospital. I believe he had a knee replacement.

Spring must be just around the corner, but spring forgot to close the door and old man winter slipped into our place again. On April 4th the service is at Sarrail. In the evening a Missionary service at Athabasca with six priests serving. This day when we came out of the church in Sarrail after 11:00 AM a storm was starting to form. Heavy snow was coming down with wind gusts. The road to Athabasca was already covered with wet slushy snow. At 5:00 PM the service started and snow was still coming down. After the service everyone went downstairs for lunch and the program that followed. When the program finished and people came outside everyone got a big surprise. There was about eight inches of heavy wet snow on the vehicles and covering the ground. The trip to or from Athabasca takes about fifty five minutes each way on a regular dry road. Today it takes more than two hours to get home. The windshield wipers were freezing and the windshield had to be scrapped by hand a few times during the trip home. In some places there was about twelve inches of snow because the car was pushing snow in front. Next day the storm passed over just before noon leaving some twenty inches of heavy wet snow behind. People could not get out of their garages, because of the heavy snow and the amount of it that fell. I had a snow blower, so I blew out the snow for the whole block on my side. A few days later it warmed up and the snow was gone.

On May 9th I left for Dauphin to be at the congregation celebration on the 12th of May. I left earlier so that I could stop and see father for a day or two and then continued on my way. I stayed at Stan and Olga Saramaga's in Dauphin, for as mentioned earlier this was our second home away from home when ever we visited Dauphin. The service in Dauphin went over well as did the program. There could have been more people in church, but because it was Mother's Day, less people showed up in church and the feast day.

When I returned from Dauphin Spring was already well on its way. On the 16th I planted part of the garden, the hardier vegetables: onion, garlic, carrots, radish, beets and peas. The following day I planted more garden, eleven potatoes and wheat. Today was a very windy day and a funeral was held for Mrs. Katie Tratch. The winds were coming from the south and because the ice on the lake had started to weaken, the wind drove the ice unto the north side of the lake, so that on May 18th the ice was gone from the lake but was pushed up on the shore on the north side.

This year was not a very good year. Last year it was pretty dry and 2002 was not any better. Because of the dry conditions, forest fires started earlier than normal. On May 19th highway #63 had to be closed from Grassland to Fort McMurray because of the heavy smoke. The traffic was then rerouted through Lac La Biche on secondary highway #881 to McMurray. There was also another fire about thirty five miles south from Lac La Biche. This fire brought smoke into our area. The doors and windows in the house were all closed and still you could feel the choking smoke in the house. There was only about a quarter mile visibility if not less due to the smoke.

Before the year 2002 ended I had made fifteen trips to Saskatchewan, Manitoba and British Columbia. I made another trip to Wakaw to the funeral of Roman Skakun. He was the cantor in church for many years and sang at the funeral when Marusia died. Also this year Marusia's God mother Mary Ostafichuk passed away at Wakaw and I also attended that funeral. From Lac La Biche to Wakaw it is some three hundred and eighty miles one way.

Because I sold the Lumina car (for $7500.00) which we drove for a number of years, I did not want to use up that money for myself, so I ordered a monument for Marusia's and my grave at the cost of $5300.00. I also paid the $1800.00 taxes on the house with that money. That made a total of $7100.00. The rest of the $400.00 I donated to the church and the children of Chernobyl Fund and the $7500.00 disappeared so quickly as if it never was around.

Than came the time for "Provody", grave side services after Easter. On June 7th I left to Saskatoon and spent the night with Bill and Marg Semeniuk, Marusia's nephew. They had bought a condo and just moved in, so I had a chance to see it. Next day I drove to Wakaw to John and

Alice's place and than went to fix up the grave and get ready for the service the following day. On June 9th in church before the service, I turn around and was surprised to see Bill, Sonia, Billy and Koreen Balaban entering the church. They came to the provody and to give me support in the hour of need. After the services I left for home.

Another strange thing happened to me during the night of June 11th. When I got up on the 12th in the morning, I was scared, afraid and did not know what was happening. My hands, feet, face and body were all swollen and puffed up. Why, I do not know to this day. I began to move around after I got up and was thinking of going to see the doctor, but as the day was moving along, the swelling began to subside and disappeared. Now, maybe once a month or more my left hand would become swollen during the night. Get up in the morning, start moving around and the swelling quickly disappears.

One day when I was doing something in the house, I could hear water dripping and leaking. I started to check where, what and why and found that in the bathroom there was the leak. I looked what was wrong and found that the flapper was not sitting properly on the toilet tank and so water was leaking out. I tried to fix it, but it would not work until I went and got a new flapper, installed it and no more leaks.

FATHER'S HOUSE IS SOLD

I talked to Alice a few times during the week and one time she says there is a man interested in buying father's house. June 27th very early in the morning I leave for Cudworth again. The weather is hot, +34 in Cudworth. Alice, her daughter Pat and I cleaned father's house, because the man that bought the house for $1500.00 wanted to move in shortly. We cleaned and washed and packed.

Someone may think there is an error in the price of the house mentioned in the above paragraph. No that is not an error. When the parents bought the house they paid $25,000.00 for it in 1982. In twenty years the house prices just tumbled and crashed into the basement. When the parents were looking for a house there were no houses for sale. Because of that the prices were sky high. Twenty years later one man in Cudworth was looking for a house and he said there was something like twenty three houses for sale.. If you wanted to sell, you put a lower price hoping it would go, a higher price it would stay. And since there was no one interested in a house we had to let it go at such a low price. Another thing that the house was old and needed some repairs. The roof had been leaking in one place and needed a new shingles.

I came home from Cudworth on June 28th in the evening. The following day I find out from Alice that Mrs. Mary Ostafichuk, Marusia's God mother passed away. The funeral will be on July 2nd. So the car did not even cool off from the trip a day ago when I turn around and head back to Wakaw to the prayers on July 1st and funeral on July 2nd.

One day in June I made an appointment to see a doctor for a prescription refill. When I came to the clinic, I was told my doctor was away and was asked if I would mind to see another doctor. I saw another doctor and he took my blood pressure. Than he asked me why I was taking this one kind of a pill. I said I was given that prescription by the doctor because I could not sleep. He told me that he did not want me to take that sleeping pill anymore. I responded that I can't sleep and need something for sleeping. He said he would give me something different, but so that I do not take those sleeping pills anymore. He asked me when was the last time I had a physical check up. I told him that it must be about ten years ago. He told me I have to get a physical check up. I went to the hospital and had blood work done. In two weeks I am to see the doctor for a physical check up. This was to be on July 3rd. Because I was in Wakaw at a funeral I did not know if I would be back, so I called and had the physical test postponed a day later on July 4th.

At 10:45 AM I had my physical check up. Doctor checked me over from head to foot. Than he asks me how long I have had a black spot on my right breast. I told him that I noticed it about two or three months ago. He said that he did not like the looks of that spot and that it would have to come off. He also saw a black mole on my back and said that would have to come off also. The receptionist made an appointment to have the surgery the following day on July 5th at the hospital. Two pieces of my body will be removed. This same day afternoon I made a trip to Vegreville because the Ukrainian Pysanka Festival will be taking place during the week end and together with the late Father Jaroslaw Puk and Dobrodeyka we are to set up a display for the festival. .

On May 16th I had planted some peas. I had two kinds of peas. I planted both varieties about four minutes apart. One was the Lincoln Homesteader and the other was the Alaska pea. On July 9th I was already picking the Alaska peas while it was about ten days later when the homesteader was ready. From the Homesteader you make one maybe two pickings in the summer and its over. The Alaska pea grows and grows and grows all summer long producing peas. The pods are much smaller but in the end they make up for the same as the Homesteader, only if you want fresh peas even in September, the Alaska pea still produces. It will grow up to seven, eight feet and maybe even taller.

To this time we have had no rain for quite some rime. Than it came all at once. On July 18th at midnight a storm came up and rain just poured from all sides and in the morning when I checked, two and one half inches of rain had come down. What was unusual about this thunder storm is the lightning. Lightning flashed at night non stop. We've all see lightning before. A lightning will flash across, than thunder and a while later another flash of lightning. This one was not so. This was non stop flashing, like light bulbs flashing from a camera. If there was any thunder that night, I don't know, because the storm made so much noise with the rain and wind, that you could not hear if there was any thunder. But that was not all. The following day July 19th another inch and a half rain came and on the 20th of July again an inch and a quarter and than finally on the 21st a fifth of an inch came down. On July 20th I had a garage sale of Marusia's things and did not sell everything because of the big rains those days. Later I had another garage sale.

The rest of the month went by quickly. Lots of work outside now after the rains. The lawn, garden and flowers all growing like being fed with yeast. I go to every Sunday and Holy Day services. Come August 6th I again left for Saskatchewan and Manitoba. A family reunion of the Chalupiak, Derzak, Korzeniowski and Stefaniuk families. This takes place at Clear Lake Manitoba on August 9-11th. After the reunion I left Dauphin on August 12th and arrived home the same evening.

When we purchased the present house in Lac La Biche, it was brand new. About a year ago I noticed that there was a crack in the ceiling. It looks like the middle of the house is settling down and a crack appeared. I will soon fix that. I need to take a big wrench, get up on the step ladder and crank up a few turns on the pole in the basement. Yes that is what I need to do. I turned once, but then could not get the wrench in to make another turn. Somehow I finally got the wrench in and tried to give it another turn. Sure, the ladder went one way and I went the other way. I fell backwards on my back and with the speed I fell, I rolled unto my back and ended up just about standing on my head against the wall. I shook that off, took another look, put the wrench and ladder away and that was the end of that job.

I ALSO WALKED ON THIS EARTH

On August 17th early in the morning I left for Saskatoon. Tammy Semeniuk is getting married to David Nahirniak. Tammy is the daughter of the late Bill and Marg Semeniuk and Bill is Marusia's nephew. I was asked by Tammy to take videos of the marriage like I did of her sisters marriage a few years earlier. She also asked me to say grace at the reception. Next day on Sunday I went to the church service at All Saints Ukrainian Orthodox Church, but there was no service there, so I drove over to the Holy Trinity Cathedral on the west end of the city. After the service I left for home.

August 20th I went to look for Saskatoon berries. Yes I found some, but they were not like the year before. This same day there was something unusual. Picking Saskatoon berries north east of the town of Lac La Biche, I could hear some kind of a noise. I looked up, but could not see anything. I came out of the bush and than noticed up high, oh so high, cranes already heading in a southerly direction. Could winter be just behind the cranes on August 20th? Cranes leaving for the south so soon? It was about this same time that I noticed there were no hummingbirds around also. All summer long they came to the feeder fighting and chasing each other. Now they are gone. Is that a sure sign that winter is not far behind?

I had received a phone call from Sophie Ludvigsen from Prince George, British Columbia that the congregation had received a large amount of Ukrainian books and they don't know what to do with them. She asked if I could come and sort the books out, which ones are good and which are not. I promised that I would do that but don't know when. After most things were off the garden, I left on September 1st going to Grimshaw, Alberta to visit good friends Harry and Mary Kinakin. Just south of McLennan, I had to drive off the road and stop because the rain was pouring so hard with hail that I could not see the road. I stayed overnight at Kinakins and left for Prince George the following day. Again heavy rain and hail north of Prince George that I had to pull over and wait until the storm cloud went through. For two days I was checking the books and sorting them out what the congregation can keep and others that they could give away to some other library. September 4th, I left going south from Prince George and stopped at Williams Lake for fifteen minutes and saw cousin Diane Russell and than kept on going south and got to Cache Creek that day. Stayed overnight in a motel and that is where I forgot my small alarm clock the next morning.

Next morning I left to Kelowna through Merritt, B.C. I called my cousin Alex Korzeniowski but there was no answer. I called Tony & Elsie Burkowski and there was no answer either. I still drove to Burkowski's thinking that they may be just outside of the condo where they lived, but not finding them anywhere, I turned the car north and headed for Vernon to see "kooma" Doris Chaykowski. I came to Vernon and Doris Chaykowski also was not home. Seeing that no one is around, I decided to keep going home. I got as far as Golden, B.C. and stayed in a motel. The following morning I leave early heading east to Lake Louise. There I turn north and to my astonishment I find snow on the highway just north of Lake Louise. I pass through the wintery stuff and head east towards Red Deer and get on highway #36 and than go north all the way home arriving in Lac La Biche at 6:00 PM.

In 2001 there was to have been a blessing of the church and cemetery at Craigend some fifteen miles south east of Lac La Biche. It did not occur, because Archbishop John became ill and could not attend. The congregation again made plans for the blessing to be on September 22nd 2002. This time the dream of the congregation was realized and fulfilled. Archbishop John and a sub deacon from Edmonton arrived on September 21st. They stayed with me. I also invited Father Michael and Dobrodeyka Theresa to come for supper. After supper we all went to have a service and confession in the church at Craigend while Archbishop John stayed at the house and rested. After the service we returned back to town and all stayed at my place.

Next day was the church blessing. After the service everyone went to the cemetery to have the cemetery blessed. As the blessing was going on, a cloud came along, shaded the sun, than a cold north wind with rain came upon us. Many people were not prepared for this cold wind and later a number of people ended up with colds. I also caught a cold and later as this was written I still had a tickle in my throat a few years later. After the service, dinner was held, and I was the MC for the afternoon program. When everything was over, my guests came back to the house with me to rest and after a while all dispersed to their homes and I was left alone by myself.

FATHER MOVES TO WAKAW SENIORS PLACE

To this day there still has not been any frost in Lac La Biche. The flowers and gardens are still growing. When we got up in the morning of September 23rd, the lawn was all white. Mr. Jack Frost paid a visit finding his way to Lac La Biche after having visited the people in the surrounding country two to three weeks earlier. Next day even a few snow flurries were flying around looking for a place to settle for the winter. The rest of the month flew by quickly and soon October was upon us. This month father also moved from Cudworth to Wakaw to the Millsite place. Here in this place he has to prepare his own meals, while when he was in Cudworth, he had everything. Father was saying that it was costing too much eight hundred dollars a month in Cudworth. He wanted something cheaper. I guess somehow from someone he found out that in Wakaw you can get a room for seniors for over three hundred dollars a month. He said that he would want to be there. Alice and Pat moved father to Wakaw to the Millsite, but there everyone had to prepare their own meals and clean the room.

As years and times crawled by, many things come into a person's life. Mostly when people age, illness of one form or another strikes a person. When I talk with my brother and say that this is hurting, or this is painful and he reminds me saying: "Eugene, that's the Golden Years coming to visit us." John has been having problems with his knees for some time, but when he was younger working in Manitoba, Alberta and the North West Territories, many a time he had to work in severe cold weather on his knees. Many times he lay on a cold winter cement floor to do mechanical work on his knees and that did not help, but work was work and it had to be done. Now for what happened then we have to pay with our health now. I myself was stricken with gout.

Gout is a form of arthritis as the Internet tells me. It is a form of illness when your body has too much uric acid. This acid forms into crystals and than settles in the toes, ankles, knees elbows and cause severe pain. Yes there is medication for it, but the side effects to me seem to be worse than the gout itself. I had three different forms of medication for the gout which the doctors prescribed, but I would rather suffer the pain than later go through the damage the medication can do to the body. I have found out that the best thing for me to reduce the amount of uric acid is to drink a large amount of water. I would drink a gallon of water in a twelve to sixteen hour period and flush out the acid. Then pain becomes less that I could tolerate it. The pain comes winter or summer and as the internet says the uric acid is caused from the type of foods we eat. According to the list of different foods on the internet, it tells me that there is nothing a person can eat to be free of uric acid. I also think that to a certain degree there must be some hereditary that goes with this gout and arthritis. It seems that sooner or later everyone has arthritis. Some is more severe than others, but we people just have to get used to it and know that we must live with it for the rest of our lives. In our family my older sister Alice and I have gout, and thank God others don't have it.

FATHER NOT WELL

October is the month of my birthday, but it is also the month of the saddest day of my life. Marusia passed away on October 4th - 2001. This year I have a memorial service for Marusia at Wakaw and following the service the blessing of the monument on her grave. I left for Wakaw on October 2nd, so that I could get the grave fixed up for Saturday and maybe help get things ready for the service and lunch.

The service was planned for October 5th at 10:00 AM. After the service everybody went to the cemetery for the blessing of the cross-monument. It was a cool day in the morning, but when we got to the cemetery the sun came out and it was a comfortable day outside, that one could stand outside and not get chilled. Following the service at the cemetery the people met in the church basement for lunch. Another surprise this morning. Before the service started who is in church this morning? Bill and Sonia Balaban from Lac La Biche along with Bill and Olga Sworin of Grassland. After lunch Bill Sworin asked me to go with them to show them the place where we used to live. We drove some twenty miles east of Wakaw and I told them information about the different things in the area.

On Sunday 6th is my birthday. This day the service is at Lepine, Saskatchewan about four miles east of Wakaw. Bill and Sonia Balaban with Bill and Olga Sworin also came to the church service that morning. They were very impressed with the church in Lepine because it is ninety five years old and will be celebrating its one hundredth anniversary in 2007. After the service there was lunch in the parish hall and after lunch we stopped at Wakaw to say good-bye to father and than headed out for home. The people from Alberta wanted to see which other way I go, so they followed me from Wakaw to Rosthern, Waldhiem, Blaine Lake, Shell Lake, Glaslyn and Meadow Lake, Saskatchewan. We stopped at Meadow Lake to fill up with fuel and Bill Sworin says that we will stop at Cold Lake for supper, because it's my birthday and they want to buy supper for me. We stopped at Cold Lake at a Chinese restaurant and had supper there. From Cold Lake they went ahead of me and I never saw them again until sometimes later that week.

I made four trips in four days to Athabasca October 22-25. There were eight of us that had purchased a house for the parish priest to live in. The parish was renting the house from us eight people. But there were things that had to be done from time to time to upkeep and maintain the house. For two days we were building a deck at the back of the house for the old deck had come to the end of its life, that it was unsafe to be on it. Two other days were spent repairing the bathroom, tearing out a wall and replacing it with new shower walls.

Towards the end of September our father had moved to Wakaw from Cudworth. He had lived at St. Michael's Haven but was unhappy there. He said it cost too much of $844.00 a month for food and room. In Wakaw he moved into a place that cost some $300.00 per month, but he had to prepare his own meals. He lived there for about one month maybe a bit more. On October 29th Alice and her daughter Pat Walker found father on the floor early one morning. Alice and Pat were only a block away from father and every morning they went and prepared his breakfast. John and Alice were already living in the town of Wakaw.

On October 29th when they came in, father was lying on the floor. I called father that morning to see how he was and Alice answered the phone at father's place. I asked what she was doing there so early and she told me what was happening. I told her not to do anything but call an ambulance and straight to the hospital. He went to the hospital that day and never returned home again. We learned that he a seizure or a stroke, because his speech was somewhat different and from that time on he never was himself again.

When this happened to father the medical staff at the hospital told Alice that if the family wants to see father to come because he could pass away any time. On October 31st I left for Wakaw. Alice and John had bought a house in Wakaw in town and moved from the farm at St. Benedict into Wakaw just a few days prior to this. I came to John and Alice's place and than we went to see father. He was ill and did not have much strength. He could not stand himself and needed assistance to stand or get up. That evening we went to see him again. When we came in Pat was already there and father was sleeping. We said to wake him up. We tried to wake him but he was not responding. We got the nurse and she could not wake him up either.

We decided to get the priest to come and give father Holy Unction. The priest was in the hospital within ten minutes. He started the prayers and the anointing. As he was doing this, father moved his left arm swiftly across as if to chase us away and says: "That is not necessary, that is not needed." He was still like in a coma. At this time Dr. Cenaiko had also arrived at the hospital. He took father's pulse and says: "The time has come. It's time." More family members of John and Alice also arrived at the hospital. The priest stayed for a while and said that he had to go home, so I walked him to the door of the hospital. When I returned, Vern Walker, Pat's husband says: "I think dido is opening his eyes." To the surprise of everybody, yes he started to open his eyes and than softly began to talk to us. His strength seemed to be getting stronger.

On the 2nd of November Oksana from Winnipeg arrived and John with Kay came from Edmonton. That evening as we were all in the room with father he was trying to talk and about 10:30 PM he says that he is hungry. Alice asked him what he would like to eat and he says: "Cornmeal with garlic." Alice and Pat were out of the room like lightning. A little while later they came back with what father has requested. Father ate everything. The door to father's room had been closed. After a while a nurse came in to check father's vital signs and when she opened the door, she says: "What's going on in here?" We told her is was the garlic because that is what father had asked to bring him. That night after he had eaten everything, I never saw father laugh as much and as hard as he did that night. We began asking him questions. At one time Alice asks if father had a tractor on the farm. Father says: "Yes with one tail." Everybody started to laugh and father laughed of that more than I had ever seen him laugh in all my life that I knew my father.

As the days were slipping by, it seemed like father's condition was better one day and worse the other. On November 11th, on Remembrance Day at Wakaw, Dr. Cenaiko made arrangements to have father brought to the Remembrance Day ceremonies in the auditorium. They took father in the handicap bus having dressed him up warmly. Father was introduced there. I believe he was the only living survivor in the district from the First World War. At this time father was one hundred and one years old.

I returned home on November 5th because on the 8th of November there is the last chram (feast day) in the parish district at Craigend. John and late Kay also left for home because they were getting ready and packing to leave for a wedding at Cancun, Mexico.

Something happened to me on November 15th and I don't know what. I was doing something on the computer most of the day in the basement. About 6:00 PM, I began not feeling too well. I felt nauseated and when I walked it seemed like I was drunk. I could feel that I was not walking straight and my balance was not very good. I thought I should dress and go outside for a walk that in case something should happen to me on the sidewalk, someone may come along and get me help.

I walked out and I could feel that I was walking as though I had a few too many. I was now safe, because I knew that if something happened to me and I fell on the sidewalk, a car would come along and someone would get me help. I walked north towards the police station and down the hill. I walked farther yet, down to the Tempo gasoline station. I turned left and kept walking in a state from one side of the sidewalk to the other. I got as far as the arena. I saw there was a hockey game going on because there were quite a number of cars there. I went inside and into the cafeteria area and sat down to watch the game. Most of the people were in the arena area. When I sat still, I felt that I was not nauseated and things were not turning or spinning around. The game ended and I started for home. Than it hit me. Again for the third time in my life I must gotten that inner ear imbalance.

Walking home I felt somewhat better, but still not myself. I got home and thought of taking my blood pressure. The meter read 189/101. Wow, that's a stroke level. I was feeling somewhat better now, but what about the time when I felt worst, what was the pressure like then? It must have been even higher. I took an aspirin and went to bed somewhat earlier than other nights. In the morning I took my blood pressure again. This time it read 140/70. Now that is like a young spring chicken, a teenager. What caused and did the shooting of the blood pressure so high and suddenly the night before, I do not know. That was November 15th.

In 2001 the parish held its first Search for Talent night at Boyle. This year the parish is holding its second Search for Talent again at Boyle on November 23rd. Again I was the M.C. for this event. On November 22nd about thirty five people gathered in the hall to make varenyky for the supper the next day. The crowd at the Search for Talent was good but the funds were not as good as the first year. Maybe the drought in the area had an influence or maybe people just held back with their pledges for the contestants. All in all, it was still a successful event.

JOHN AND KAY'S TROUBLE TRIP

John and Kay are to return today from Cancun, Mexico. They were in Cancun to a wedding. I never called them this evening for I did not know what time they were arriving. Next day on November 18th at 8:13 AM the phone rings. I answer, but I see the Caller ID showing: "Dr. Shmoorkoff." Who is this? Never heard of him. The doctor tells me who he is and than asks me if John called me to which I said he did not. Than Dr. Shmoorkoff says that John and Kay are at Sioux City, Iowa, because yesterday on the plane Kay got chest pains, hard breathing and the plane had to land to get her to the nearest hospital. I waited all day to hear from John, but than in the evening I called the doctor, the number on the Caller ID. The doctor's wife answered and I asked her if she also was on the plane last night. She said she was and that they landed at Sioux Falls, South Dakota. She said that John asked me to phone their son in Thompson, Manitoba.

Than it hit me. Doctor said Sioux City, Iowa and his wife tells me Sioux Falls, South Dakota. Soooooo....., where are they? Then I called Alice and told her what had happened so far that I knew. Alice got excited and said that they were probably kidnaped with the plane, like the terrorists over a year ago in the United States of America. I also called Oksana and told her the story. She said she would call Transat Airlines and find out where they had landed. After a while she calls back and says it was at Sioux Falls, South Dakota. She also called the hospital in Sioux Falls and they said that

John and Kay are not in the hospital anymore and they don't know where they went. What happened was - in the early afternoon when I was still waiting for word from John to see what is what, Kay was released from the hospital, they caught a flight and arrived home that evening at 9:00 PM while we were all worrying what is happening. Later we learned, that Kay had gotten pleurisy. The night before they left from Cancun they were sitting beside the ocean in an open air restaurant with a very cold wind and breeze from the ocean and she got chilled.

Father was not getting any better either. I called Alice just about every day to see what was happening. On November 27th I again left for Wakaw to see father, maybe for the last time - and it was. When I saw him, he had lost more weight and was much weaker than previously. We could now clearly see that the end for him was nearing, only no one knows when that will be, except God. I returned home on the 29th.

ANOTHER CHAIN LINK BROKEN - FATHER PASSES AWAY

Than came the sad news. God called father away at about 1:00 PM on December 3rd 2002. Marusia left this world on October 4th 2001. Times are hard in such happenings. Father said wise words when mother passed away: "A funeral is nothing until it happens in your family." How true that is. How many funerals you go to and it is nothing until it hits your own closest family. At such a time it seems that the whole world collapses around you.

    I left for Wakaw on December 4th to help Alice arrange everything. Alice had said she will be in Saskatoon and had told me to meet her at the funeral home. Alice said that the prayers were set for December 6th and the funeral the following day. Another hard time, but not as hard as it was with Marusia - my spouse. The funeral was like a funeral. Some one hundred and forty people were at the funeral. All the services and lunches were in Wakaw at the church in the parish basement hall. After lunch father was taken to Cudworth to be laid to rest beside his earthly spouse, his wife and our mother. Two priests served the services, parish priest Father Roman Kocur and the late Father Mykola Derewianka from Dauphin. After the services and the interment at the Cudworth Orthodox

Cemetery, I left back for home, for what else could I do for father or anyone else?

When father passed away, Alice said that I meet them in Saskatoon because that is where we have to make funeral arrangements at the funeral home. We met at a designated place and than John, Alice Pat and I went to stores to pick out clothing for father. When that was finished, Alice went shopping. Towards evening we had something to eat and than met the funeral director at Acadia Funeral Home giving him the information he needed about father. From there we left for Wakaw. That all was on December 4th. Next day I helped John and Alice to clean up little chores here and there for sadder days are yet to come. John and Oksana also arrived for the funeral. Oksana came with her two daughters, Gail and Kathy from Winnipeg. John's son Gregory from Edmonton also arrived with John. The late Kay did not come because she was still in bed with her illness which she had from the Mexico trip.

Viewing for the family was at 5:00 PM at the Cudworth funeral chapel. We all went there. Another heart wrenching experience for me with two family funerals in a year. After we viewed the body we returned back to Wakaw to have supper at John and Alice's place. Coming back to Wakaw, I told those present in the van the following words: "It seems that father is still living. Why? Because when today you go to a funeral, it is someone that is in their fifties, sixties or seventies maybe eighties that passed away. Here father has passed all those stages and lived through his ninety years of age and even one hundred was pushed past him. It seemed to me that he would never die and even though he is gone, it seems he is still here." When the time came God took him away at the age of one hundred and one. Mother had passed away in 1993 and father had lived alone another nine years after that.

We all had supper at John and Alice's and then everyone went to the church for prayers. Prayers were hard again, with hurt, grief and pain surrounding the family. Father being a hundred and one years old, you would think few people would come to a funeral because of the generations gap. How many are there living father's age that would have something in common from the olden days? There were many people at the prayers and even more the following day at the funeral.

After lunch I spoke on behalf of the family thanking people for coming to the prayers and giving support for the family at such a crucial time. Other speakers were Diane Russell (Williams Lake B.C.,) our cousin spoke from the Derzak family. Late George Semeniuk expressed sympathy from Marusia's side of the family. Rev. Michael Zaleschuk of Regina Beach recollected the time when he served in Winnipeg at the Holy Trinity Cathedral and father was the elder serving him in the Sanctuary. Pat Walker spoke on behalf of the Grandchildren and Great Grandchildren. Both serving priests Rev. Roman Kocur the parish priest and the late father Mykola Derewinka also spoke briefly extending their sympathies and saying that they very well remember the times when father and mother never missed a church service when they were living and traveled to every church for the services no matter whether winter or summer. A farewell song was sung at the cemetery beside the grave, "The cranes are flying away". Father is now with his life partner and our mother, in the hands of God.

On December 8th at Lac La Biche there was a carol Festival. There were some six to eight different choirs participating and it was held in the Roman Catholic Church. The organizers had contacted someone from the two Ukrainian churches, the Orthodox and Catholic churches if we could get together and sing a few Ukrainian carols.

On December 14th I ate the last tomato I had from the garden. Tomatoes were not a bad crop this year and they all had seemed to ripen nearly at the same time in the basement. I canned most of them, for I could not eat that many and those that were green just stayed on to ripen and I would use them one after the other.

The end of the year is just on the edge of leaving us. December 25th, I leave early in the morning for Saskatoon, because Marusia's nephews and nieces with their families all gather in one house and have a Christmas supper. I have been invited this year to be at Bill and Marg Semeniuks place. Bill and Marg bought a new condo and the condo has a large gathering room. Today every family that is coming will bring some food. Everybody eats, sings, plays cards, visiting, talking being together of about thirty five people.

The following day I visited Marusia's cousin Mary Burrell in Saskatoon. Somehow there is a coincidence to this story about this cousin. When I was still preaching at Dauphin, Manitoba I used to order things from a Mary Burrell who was an agent for Nature's Sunshine natural herbs. Later when Marusia and I were married, she says one time that when we will be in Saskatoon we will visit her cousin Mary Burrell. Than something clicked and I recalled the name and the herbs I used to order from Mary Burrell. Was that another of God's ways of learning about someone whom I had never seen before that are now related to me? Mary Burrell's father and Marusia's father were brothers.

After I visited Mary Burrell for an hour or so, I left for Regina Beach to visit another good friend, Rev. Michael Zaleschuk. We have known each other for many years, because many times we even served with each other at different occasions. When Marusia and I had met, he married us in Moose Jaw, Saskatchewan in April 1988. I stayed at Zaleschuks place overnight and next morning headed out to Regina to visit two more very good friends, John and Jean Sawchyn. I spent one day at their place and was going to stay until Sunday, but December 28th the weather forecast on the radio said that seven centimeters of snow was coming to Regina.

I got scared of the snow, so I grabbed my bags and headed north to John and Alice's place always to be closer to home and hoping to spend a day or two at their place. As I nearer closer to Wakaw, I heard on CKBI radio from Prince Albert that there is a sixty percent chance of snow for Prince Albert. I turned unto highway # 2 and stopped at Cudworth cemetery to say a prayer and hello to my parents. Than I went north and stopped at the cemetery at Wakaw to say hello to Marusia, shed a few tears and left to John and Alice's place. When I came to their place, John was not home. I had tea with Alice, left her a few things and headed out for home about 2:30 PM. I got home at 9:00 PM on a nice and dry road all the way from Regina to Lac La Biche. So where was that snow they were forecasting? I made as already you know many trips to and from Saskatchewan this year. Only one trip I made west to Prince George and Kelowna. The coming year I can see only one or two trips to Saskatchewan unless unforeseen circumstances may bring more travel there. The rest of the traveling should be around home and maybe a trip to British Columbia where relatives and friends keep calling to come and visit them. I do not want to head out to B.C. in the winter time because the roads in the mountains are something else when it snows and avalanches come down. Marusia and I sat one time for hours just east of Revelstoke, while the avalanche was being cleared off highway.

LIFE MUST GO ON

As 2003 approaches, I see three trips to Saskatchewan. One on January 11th for father's forty day memorial service. One on May 11th for provody at Wakaw, Saskatchewan and than one on Saturday June 14th provody at Cudworth. So far nothing else that I can foresee on the horizon for going east unless unforeseen things come up. I am planning to go to British Columbia in March or April to visit people who call me and keep asking when I will come to visit them. The rest of the year I should hang around home and catch up with some of the work that has set me behind somewhat. So ended 2002.

Everybody's life is always tied around their family. When you have a family and they may live far apart, God still provides that they meet for family occasions, funerals, weddings, anniversaries, reunions, etc. As for me I have one brother and two sisters and they have their own families and look after their own interests. Parents are gone. Two wives I had are also gone. No children. Left alone and lost as a lost sea gull over the vast ocean. I try to keep in touch with my brother and sisters and other relatives and friends as often as I have occasion. When it comes to important matters for deciding what is what, I leave that up to God to help me at those times.

The New Year started off like the old one left with no snow until January 7th Orthodox Christmas (Nativity of Christ). The parish priest had the schedule of services prepared in advance for 2003. Christmas Eve service starts at Athabasca at 11:00 PM on January 6th with the Grand Compline and then followed by the Holy Liturgy. Brother John had called some time ago asking me to come to their place in Edmonton for supper on the 6th. Drive a hundred and twenty five miles to have supper? But that is where I ended, because the family members all want to be together on January 6th. I went to their place for supper. After supper we sat, talked and caroled for a while until about 9:00 PM when I had to leave for Athabasca to be in church for 11:00 PM. After the service I came home at 2:00 AM on January 7th. I had some rest and than went caroling with the group for the Craigend church. We caroled in town and in the country and I was home about 9:00 PM. I had just come home when the door bell rings. The carollers from the Lac La Biche congregation came to carol at my place.

On January 8th the service is at Boyle. Today there was a very cold north west wind blowing but no snow in our area. This evening the sun was setting as usual, but something that I had never seen before. I have seen red sunsets, but never the color of the red that it was setting today. It was blood red and also looked like fire. I remember my late mother saying that such a sunset was an omen of war or unstable life in the world. Did the war in Iraq start this year after the terrorist attacks in New York in 2001?

The following day the service was at Grassland in commemoration of the first martyr St. Stephen. Right after the service I left for Wakaw. I drove to Mundare, Alberta and bought some sausage because on the 11th of January we have a fortieth day memorial service for father. It is already forty days when he left us and we became full fledged orphans. After the service on the eleventh I returned home and arrived at 6:45 PM. I don't like to be far from home in the winter time because should the power in the house go out or the furnace stops, there would be problems if the water pipes freeze. In the summer time I do what I do in the winter. What I usually do is shut the water off and drain the pipes

I had arrived home on the eleventh, because tomorrow the twelfth is a service at Sarrail. Had I known I could have stayed another day or two in Saskatchewan. When I came home in the evening, I got a call from Sarrail that the service there for tomorrow had been canceled because of cold weather. It was -26 and a cold, cold wind. The church in Sarrail is a historical building and they must keep it in the shape it is. They cannot put power in it, so the place is heated with a round barrel type wood stove. When it is cold outside with a strong wind, you just can't heat a building that has no insulation. Today the priests are canceling their services left and right. When I served in that parish in the 1960's, there was no such thing as to cancel a service even if there was a winter storm howling outside. I remember that in this same church it had been so cold that when I put the chalice to my mouth for Holy Communion, the chalice stuck to my lips and I had to wait until I could free the chalice.

Well those who think it is getting warmer should come to Lac La Biche when it is -32 C, take off their jacket, stand outside on the sidewalk for half an hour and than come back into the house and tell me if it is really warming up. I think they would change their tune on Global warming very, very quickly. It sure is good to sit in a warm house or office when it's -30 or -40 below outside and say that the earth is warming up. But come to Lac La Biche, Edmonton, Saskatoon or Winnipeg and stand in a shirt for half an hour outside in -30 C and than tell me if the place is really warming up.

Can these same people tell me why Greenland is called Greenland when it is ninety percent covered under ice. Yet at one time bananas grew in Greenland. So from that time till now has it warmed so much that Greenland is ninety percent frozen under ice? Today's young generation does not remember those olden gone by days, but what had caused the drought in Canada in the 1930's? Was it the green gases and global warming? Was it the from gasoline vehicles and tractors, when there were no such things? The only green gases that came then was from the horses pulling the ploughs and binders on the fields, yet there was that terrible drought which was named: "The dirty thirties." Surely no one can say it was from green gases that we had that weather. They keep telling us that the ice is melting in the Arctic. Does someone think the ice never melted before. It has melted for thousands of years. And what happened to the Titanic? Where did that ice come from, fell off the moon?

This year as in the past year, the parish held its annual calendar draw in February. I made all the tickets and never charged one single red penny for the paper, ink, work, etc. Yet the parish made a good penny to have coffers to help pay for all parish costs. The draws were held once a week at Wally's Fast Foods at Grassland. The first draw this year was on February 7th.

Maybe the year started out not bad, but than it turned bad. Two months into the New Year, I had an accident. I had prepared a meal to cook for noon, put it in the oven to bake while I went into the basement to do some work on the computer. After some time I thought I should go upstairs and check how things are doing in the oven. I walked up the first flight of stairs from the basement unto the landing where the door leads to the outside and to the garage. Then I turned and headed the second flight of stairs to the kitchen. As I reached about the third step from the top, my hand slipped of the spindle staircase, I lost my balance and fell backwards head over heels ending up on my back with the legs in the air. I got up somewhat shaken but nothing seemed broken. The marks are still on the spindle from the finger nail scratches. In the evening I was very sore and everything was hurting. It wasn't until Valentines Day that my left side of the hip, leg and under the knee, everything was black, blue and sore. The pain was not letting go. Everything was becoming stiff on my left leg. I took a few photo shots of my left leg and thigh. Because the pain was not letting up, I went to see a doctor. The doctor ordered x-rays, so I went to the hospital and had that done. Nothing broken only a lot of bruises.

One morning when I woke up, I had a problem. Maybe it was good that a church service was canceled on February 15th , because had the service been on and I went to church, people would have thought I was involved in a fight with someone. When I got up this morning, my nose seemed as though it was bruised with over an inch long red bruises. When I saw that mark, I took a picture of myself to show for others.

More trouble started on March 9th. I had a gout attack. It did not last for a day but for many days before it left me. That is painful and I have been having a number of gout attacks. Just a few days later on the 13th of March another thing happened. The ring of my finger just slipped and fell off all by itself. How? Why? Since Marusia and I have been married I had not taken my ring off my finger. As I was typing on the computer keyboard the ring just came off by itself. How come this just slipped off by itself without me even touching it. Why? Why? Why?

March 17th brought us a huge amount of problems. Cars were in ditches and people could not even get out of their garages because ice formed from the wet snow and cars had to push snow in front of them because so much snow had come down. I started up the snow blower, but it would not blow the snow, because the snow was too wet and it clogged up in the pipe with ice. This day there was to be a service at Craigend. The service was canceled because Father Michael Domaradz ended up in the ditch west of Lac La Biche. I had driven out of the garage and gone to Craigend but about two miles from church Bill and Sonia Balaban were returning from the church and said they just got a phone call that the service is canceled. I turned around and started to head back home following Bill and Sonia. Bill and Sonia had gone ahead and were about a quarter of a mile in front of me. But before they got home they ended up in the ditch about one mile from home. When I returned home, I began blowing the sidewalk and people's driveway so that they could get out of their garages, but this was causing problems because snow was forming into ice in the pipe.

When the sun begins to climb higher, people begin to think of spring, even though we know it is not spring yet for a long time. On April 12th I seeded some onions, tomatoes and cantaloupe so that I could transplant them later into the garden. As for the cantaloupe, it grew that year and was the size of a baseball and had not grown enough for maturity. Maybe another month more of growing and it may have been larger and mature. God willing, some day I'll start them even sooner in the future and maybe will have cantaloupe.

April 24th we saw rain arriving in Lac La Biche at night and stopped the following afternoon. During this period also my friend, Mr. gout had come back to see me again. The pain is dreadful, worse than a toothache, so I made an appointment to see the doctor. The doctor gave me a prescription for two kinds of medication and said: "You have to take both of these because if you just take the one it will eat your stomach." Yeah, that's all I needed to hear. So which is the lesser evil, have the pain or have your stomach eaten up? I only took the prescription once or twice and than took no more unless the gout returned and the pain was very severe. This I continue to do till this day. When gout comes, and pain is unbearable, I'll take the pills for a day, two or three at the most otherwise I try to flush out the uric acid with water.

As mentioned previously, it happened again this year. On April 30th the big red flying ants appeared. Many years ago in some parish people told me that when the large flying ants appear, than it's safe to plant your garden because spring has arrived and frosty days are over. Even though the big ants were back the ice on the lake did not leave until May 13th. When ice starts to break up and there is a strong wind, it will push the ice up the banks of the lake forming huge piles of ice. When the ice left, the following day on the 14th I rototilled the garden and planted a few things: peas, onions, garlic, carrots, radishes and beets, because these guys are not afraid of the cold. Next day a cold north wind would come that chased people into the house to put on a warm jacket for outside venture.

When I served the parish of Dauphin in the 1960-70's, I became acquainted and knew many people. A number of people had moved to Kelowna many years previous and as you have read. I visited some of them whenever I traveled through that area. When Marusia and I lived in Salmon Arm and Vernon, we visited back and forth many times with one family, Tony and Elsie Burkowski. Marusia and Elsie became like two sisters. When Burkowskis celebrated their anniversary, I was always asked to be the MC for this occasion. We were living in the Okanagan, when they celebrated their fortieth anniversary. When they were celebrating their fiftieth we flew from Phoenix to their anniversary and I was again the M.C. When May comes I know it is their anniversary. They called me to ask if I could come and be at their anniversary, because there will be nothing large, but about ten people, the closest friends and that will be in a restaurant. I had been planning to go to the Okanagan, so now I will have that chance and reason to visit a friend in Penticton. I left on May 20th for Kelowna to be at their anniversary. It is a number of years since Tony went blind and can't see anymore.

I visited them when I arrived in Kelowna, but stayed at my cousins place, Alex and Sylvia Korzeniowski the while that I spent there. I also attended church at Vernon when I was visiting my "kooma", Doris Chaykowski. After I had lunch with Doris, I left for home arriving home the following day at 3:00 PM and still having time to plant the garden before sunset.

Then in Lac La Biche the heavens opened up on June 2nd and 3rd. Rain came down in barrels and it came non stop. Over five inches of rain fell. At first it started small and increased on June 3rd to trainloads of water. From 10:00 AM to 3:00 PM that day in the five hours, five inches of rain came upon us. Some people had their basements flooded. The sewers could not handle that amount of water so fast so the water started to back up on the streets and driveways of some houses. My house was spared, but had it rained for another two or three hours, I may have had to get scared and concerned that the water could have come up my driveway as it did on the neighbors driveways and yards. I took a number of pictures to show what was happening from that downpour.

When I was in Wakaw earlier in the year, the church executive said they received some money in a grant to paint the small church east of town where Marusia is buried, and they were worrying that there is no one to paint that church because everyone is afraid to crawl up ladders, since all members are in their older years. When I heard that, I told them that I would come and paint the church. Why shouldn't I? I prayed in that church and lived only half a mile away from it in the 1940's. When I had finished my garden, I left for Wakaw on June 9th. Brother-in-law John Hnatiuk, who was the chairman and the late Tony Bilokuray the treasurer of the church helped me spray paint the lower part of the church. Than I went on the ladder and did the upper part of the church and around the peaks and did the dome. When the white was finished, I painted the trimming in green. I finished everything at noon on June 13th. The following day there was a grave blessing at Cudworth where our parents are buried. I attended those services and left for home at 1:30 PM arriving at 8:30 PM. I had to be back because next day there was a service at Boyle and their chram - feast day of the church.

Things just went from day to day with always something to do. I had to hoe the garden and get rid of the weeds blown in from neighbors lawns. I cut the lawn, did typing on the computer, went to church services, looked after housework, etc. There was always something to do and no time to get bored like some people say they are. The only people who are bored are those that don't **want to do anything**, because one can always find something good to do. On June 25th we had a tremendous thunderstorm roll through Lac La Biche. The storm brought only two tenths of an inch of rain, but there was enough thunder and lightning that it could have caused a flood. The clouds were dark, rolling and twisting in the sky. Tornado and severe thunderstorms were issued on the radio for our area that day. Near Wasketenau on June 30th a tornado had touched down, but no damage was done. In Lac La Biche at 6:30 PM (the longest day of the year) people were already turning their lights on because it became so dark with the low hanging black clouds. At Grimshaw, Alberta, north of Grand Prairie also a severe thunder storm and wind went through the area and caused damage.

On the prairies in the winter time, it is snow and cold winter storms. When summer comes different kinds of storms come with it. Thunder storms and sometimes they are something. As previously mentioned, one storm rolled through at night where there was a non stop flashing of lightning. Other times big heavy, strange and scary clouds come, but all you would get is a lot of lightning and thunder and no rain. In the Ukrainian there is a saying that says: "From a large cloud, small rain." That is what happens sometimes. A dark rolling cloud comes along which is dangerous looking and you could look for a tornado forming from it, thunder makes a lot of noise, puts some fright into people and moves on. That's what happened in Lac La Biche in June 2003. I stood on the deck and watched the clouds in case a twister or tornado would be forming from those clouds, and I would rush into the basement.

I had a bad day on June 28th. Was very depressed and everything I did or touched it went wrong. Today I also see Marusia's rose has buds on it ready to start blooming. Her rose that seemed it had died some time back blooms each year. Mine on the other hand which had a good start, died the following year and to date has not even left a mark where it was planted.

My garden is somewhat protected from the north winds, because it's on the south side of the house. On the east side I have a picket fence as well as on the south side. The west side has a chain link fence and that does not stop much wind but the garden survived the storms and on July 12th I already had fresh Alaska peas in the garden.

When summer comes all congregations have their feast day (chram) except Craigend which comes in November. The feast day in Athabasca was on July 13th this year. Also at the same time they celebrated their fiftieth anniversary and I was asked to be the main speaker at the feast day. After the feast day service and program, I still had four hundred and fifty miles to drive to Wakaw, Saskatchewan for a funeral the following day, for Metro Ostafichuk, Marusia's Godfather.

Another strange thing happened to me at 3:30 AM on July 17th. I was asleep and got up to go to the bathroom. I got out of bed like all other times, but I could not find the door entrance out of the bedroom. I was lost in my own house in my own bedroom. I was feeling the walls trying to find out where the doorway was. Finally I felt the dresser, stood for a while and thought which way I should go to get out. The door was never closed and I could have walked out, but for some unknown reason, I walked into the wall inside of the door and could not locate it where the door was. I was lost in my own house in the middle of the night.

On July 25th my cousin Alex and wife Sylvia Korzeniowski from Kelowna arrived at 3:30 PM. It was so wonderful to see them and have them for a visit. On July 27th we three went to Vegreville, some ninety miles south of Lac La Biche to the church service and their feast day, St Volodymyr. Alex and Sylvia left my place on July 29th at 8:45 AM going to Wakaw to stop at Alice's place. Before they left Alex had been outside by the garden and he had found a dead bird on the sidewalk that probably had hit a window and died. Many people have told me time and time again that when a bird flies into a window, it means you will receive some news. If the bird dies, there will be news of a death in that house, or some close family or friend.

Summer is really here. The days of the 1930's and 1940's are here. July 30th and 31st the temperature had reached both days at +31 C. Hot, really hot. Rain is already needed. The grasshoppers are increasing daily and are having their picnics in the gardens, the lawns, the fruit trees and some flowers. Rain is needed to drown them out.

Again another feast day, this time in Wandering River some fifty miles north of Lac La Biche on the way to Fort McMurray. Here again I was asked to be a speaker on this glorious occasion which took place on August 2nd. On the 5th of August I leave for Calgary. A Ukrainian organization Ukrainian Self Reliance League of Canada is holding their convention. I have a chance to see some of the friends we had in Calgary before we moved out to Lac La Biche in 1999. Have not been to Calgary since we moved.

The humming birds have been coming to the house and it looks like the same ones come back each year since we moved to Lac La Biche and put out the bird feeder. This year on August 31st I have not seen anymore of the hummingbirds, so I presume that they have taken their flight back to the warmer climate. At times we hear people say that the humming birds come hitch hiking a ride with the Canada Geese by hanging on to the geese as they fly north or south. This I cannot believe. The geese come to the north country when at times there is still no open water and snow on the ground. The humming birds don't show up until sometimes in May or June when flowers are already in bloom. The geese fly south some years after the snow is starting to fall, but the hummingbirds are long gone south by that time. If not, would the hummingbird survive that cold weather so early in the spring or late in the fall? Of course not.

A funny thing happened on September 6th. At 2:00 AM at night while I was asleep I heard some bird chirp somewhere in the house. I got up looked around, nothing and went back to bed. A few moments again the chirp. There has to be some kind of a bird in the house, but probably in the basement. I started to check around to see what and where. As I was checking the basement, there it goes again up in the basement ceiling somewhere above. Can't see no bird there, so I waited to see if it would come again. Sure enough, there it goes again. It was the smoke alarm chirping to replace the battery. The funny thing was that there was no battery in that smoke alarm and it was not in the basement but upstairs in the hallway. That smoke alarm was without a battery, but worked off the power - electric.

Next morning I started to call around and ask what it could be since the smoke alarm upstairs had no battery in it and yet it was chirping. Finally someone told me to call Bernie Romaniuk. I called him and he said to take a towel or something that makes wind, to wave it near the alarm and it will stop. He said that sometimes those things are so sensitive that anything will turn them on even if you have too much stale warm air in the house. I did as he suggested and later sold the house and no more birds were chirping in that smoke alarm.

I got a phone call that George Zyha at Spirit River passed away. This was a family that when any priest came to have a service in Spirit River this was the place where the priest would stay. They looked after the clergy. Mary Kinakin from Grimshaw called that her father passed away and I said that I would be there, because I had spent many a night and day at their place when serving or just passing through the area. As we were talking on the phone I say to her: "My both parents are gone and now both of your parents are gone also." She replies and says: "That's right Reverend, and we are the next generation to go after them." How true. The funeral was at Spirit River on September 9th. After the funeral I took the longer way going home, going south to Grand Prairie and through Grand Cache staying overnight at Hinton. I came home the following day at 5:00 PM.

Again another incident in July. When I went out into the garden, I found a dead bird on the sidewalk. It looked like a sparrow. The older people have told me many times that you can expect news of a death in the family or of some grave illness. Sure enough, when I look at the next day, what did I hear and learn? My niece Carolyn Hnatiuk had the West Nile illness. So does a bird that flies into a window and die, bring bad news? I guess it does.

A SCAM AND NOT A SCAM?

While watching the news on CFRN on September 16th, I learned something new. When Marusia passed away in October 2001, the following year in 2002 in April some man had come to the house and sold me a Gold Medal Card. By showing this card to certain merchants who support it's organization, you get discounts on purchases. I paid $40.00 for the card and put it my pocket and the book with names of sponsors in the glove compartment of the car. In the book were business sponsors from British Columbia, Alberta and Saskatchewan. The problem was I forgot and never used that card.

When I was traveling in British Columbia this year I stopped at Sicamous to get an ice cream cone. As I opened my purse there was also this card. I took the card and than went to the car to look at the book where I would be able to get discounts in B.C. There I find that Dutchman Dairy of Sicamous gives ten percent on sales. I went back to the store, and picked out some cheese to purchase. I gave the girl the card. She looked at it and than says: "What is this for?" "What is this?" I told her what was what and she said she never heard of such a thing or company. The girl still gave me ten percent on my purchase. I went to the car, took the book and brought it to show the name of their dairy. She was surprised and said it was the first time she had seen and heard of this kind card and company.

When I got home and watching the news, sure enough this Gold Medal problem surfaces on the news that someone is involved in some fraud with a company. Valerie Osctzowski had mentioned on the news, that anyone who has this card to get in touch with the police because they would want to speak to that person. Next morning I took the card and the book and went to the RCMP in Lac La Biche. Staff Sargent Colin White took interest in this. He called CFRN, but the people he needed to talk to were not in. He left a message.

Next day Staff Sargent White calls and asks me to come in to see him. He told me that I am to call a certain number in Edmonton and the people there would like to speak to me. When I got home I called the number a few times, but there was no one there so I left a message. Maybe a month or so later I get a call from Edmonton from the Consumers Complaint Department. The people wanted to know how I was involved with the Gold Medal card. I told them all I knew and they said my card was valid until April 2004 when it expired and it had been sold to me properly. There were however cards sold in Edmonton by a certain company and those were fraudulent. After that I never heard anything more from anyone about any card.

TIME RUNS ALONG AND WAITS FOR NO ONE

Time never waits for anyone. It goes by and each year seems to slip by faster and faster. It is now September 20th and Mr. Jack Frost has visited some areas in the province, but he still had not found his way to Lac La Biche. On the 20th of September I still picked half an ice cream pail of cucumbers and made dills. Other people in the surrounding areas had even forgotten about gardens, while in Lac La Biche town flowers were still blooming. The days are now shorter and it is starting to get cloudy and dreary outside. This day, I don't know what or why, whether it was the weather outside or what, but my day was sad and depressed. Finally the following night in the darkness on September 24th, Jack Frost found my garden during his visit to Lac La Biche. It was -2 this morning. From then on, Mr. Frost kept visiting Lac La Biche and the whole province and later even the whole country.

After Jack Frost made his appearance in Lac La Biche, the skies cleared, the sun was out and the temperatures hovered in the mid twenties for a week. Is this Indian summer or "Babene Leeto" - Grandma's summer? In Ukraine this warm spell is called, "Babene Leeto" which means Grandmother's summer. It was at this time of the year that old grandmothers gathered together, prayed and sang that the warm weather would return before the snows come. The warm weather usually returned and people rejoiced over the sunny warm days of fall before the snow arrived.

On October 4th it was +24 C. It was two years ago today that Marusia passed away. John and late Kay from Edmonton came to visit me today because my birthday is in two days. On October 5th there was a service in Lac La Biche and after the service Father Michael had a requiem service for Marusia. John and Kay also were in church. Monday is October 6th and my birthday. John and late Kay were still with me until noon when they left for home. John had said that he never was in Athabasca and wanted to go home that way to see the place. They took the longer way, but they saw Athabasca down in the river valley and on the hills above the river. Another strange thing happened on the next day. Frost had come and killed everything, but on the 7th of October Marusia's rose began to **bloom** again.

When Marusia and I had bought the house in Calgary in April 1996, we had the basement completed. Orest Fodchuk did the work. He had a man from Ukraine who was helping him. When they finished the basement, Marusia and I asked this man from Ukraine, his wife and son to come to our place for dinner. They came and brought us a cyclamen plant. That plant started to bloom in Calgary and than October 8th 2003 it started to bloom again in Lac La Biche. Did it ever bloom? It was all covered in blossoms with pinkish flowers so thick that it was even hard to count how many flowers were on it. It bloomed like that from October to the end of April the following year. Later this same plant bloomed in Plamondon and at Osoyoos, British Columbia as you will later learn how and why.

Now comes October 12th and it's Thanksgiving Day in Canada. Every year Bill and Olga Sworin from Grassland invite me to come to their place for Thanksgiving dinner. All their family gathers of about twenty people. Olga's two sisters from Kelowna, British Columbia come each year at this time and we have a chance to exchange news and views. This year we had dinner about 3:30 PM and then I had to go to Sarrail where there was a baptism. Than what happened on October 25th at night I do not remember, but when I awoke it was already 8:30 AM. I do not remember when I slept so long, but I felt embarrassed of myself for sleeping so late. Usually I am up at about 6:30 or 7:00 AM. As mentioned above, Marusia's rose started blooming on October 7th, it is now October 21st and the rose is still blooming. It was a hardy rose.

In 2000 I had started teaching cantoring classes. Cantors are always needed in the Orthodox Church. The following year I was going to continue, but when Marusia became ill and passed away on October 4th, I didn't want and didn't feel like I wanted to go out and be with people some days. The year passed and than I said I would go and teach cantoring in Grassland-Sarrail congregations. I started those classes on October 27th in the Grassland church. After classes, Olga Sworin says: "Why don't you come to our place and have the classes in the house. It is always warm in the house and there is enough room." After that we met most of the time at Sworins, but we also met at Bill and Mary Pisarewski's and once or twice at Alex and Pauline Tymo and Alex and Emily Kononchuk. Once they all came to Lac La Biche to my place. These classes continued that winter into spring in April just before Resurrection of Christ (Easter). So every Monday during the winter time I was away from home.

When Father Michael and Dobrodeyka Theresa moved into the parish they lived for a while in an apartment building. As already mentioned there were eight people who put some money together and bought a house. Later the priest moved into this house. Things went well and at one meeting it was decided to sell this house. When this was made known, Father Michael and Theresa decided to buy their own private house. They purchased a house in Athabasca and on October 31st they moved into their own house. The house they had lived in was put up for sale.

It was sometime in the summer that Bill and Sonia Balaban came over one night, and they visited me more often than anyone else in the parish. They said they will be celebrating their fiftieth wedding anniversary this year and asked me to be the MC for their anniversary. I told them that they have children all married and one of the children or relative could be the MC. Sonia says: "It's our anniversary and we take for an MC who we want." After that I had no more say. This anniversary took place in Craigend some twelve miles south of Lac La Biche. In the church in Craigend there was a Molebien service, a service of thanks to God and to ask God's blessings for years to come. The meal and the program followed in the Craigend hall and this took place on November 1st.

This year in 2003 the Ukrainian Orthodox Church of Canada is celebrating its eighty-fifth anniversary. Congregations held small celebrations in their parishes and than the Vegreville Missionary District held the huge celebration at Smokey Lake, Alberta. Archbishop John celebrated the Divine Liturgy and was assisted by the clergy of the Missionary District. They were:

Smokey Lake Parish	Father Benny Ambroise
Vegreville Parish	Father Gene Maximuk
Bonnyville Parish	Father John Lipinski
Lac La Biche Parish	Father Michael Domaradz
Radway Parish	Father Alexander Palamarchuk
Two Hills Parish	Father Wasyl Sapiha
Retired priest	+Father Jaroslaw Puk

A few weeks before this event took place, I was asked by Father Gene Maximuk if I would be the guest speaker for this occasion. I accepted the invitation and began to prepare what I would have to say. There were over two hundred people in attendance. This event took place on November 15th.

That same afternoon from Smokey Lake I traveled straight to Boyle. Yesterday some thirty people met and we made varenyky to be for the Third Search For Talent show on November 15th. I again was the MC for this as was for the previous two events. In July of 2004 the parish voted not to hold anymore talent shows in the future. Two days later winter arrived with about four to six inches of snow. It turned cold after this and was dreary outside with low hanging clouds and days getting shorter and the nights getting longer.

This year of 2003 there was still one more trip to make to Wakaw. On November 22nd we will be having a one year memorial service for father. It could not be held any other time because the priest was already booked for other activities. On November 21st I left for Wakaw at 5:30 AM in complete darkness. At Wakaw at this time it was already 6:30 AM. The memorial service was held on November 22nd. After the service and dinner I left Saskatchewan at 1:00 PM for home and arrived home at 7:00 PM Alberta time. Next day there is a service at Sarrail. When I got home I learned that the service in Sarrail was canceled because the snow plow did not open the road to the church. Had I known, I would have stayed another day in Saskatchewan and would not have had to rush home. On November 26th at 3:28 PM, I got a call from Athabasca that we have an offer for the house. The other people who had money tied in the house all agreed to sell for the best offer. This same evening I got a call from the Alberta Lung Association asking me if I would be willing to canvass for them again. I have been doing this for the last four years, so why not do it again. If I can help with anything, I am willing to do that.

It was one day in December that I received a phone call from one of the schools in Lac La Biche if I could come and teach the children to sing Silent Night in Ukrainian. On December 5th I held the first practice with the children and than another practice on December 8th. I would have loved to hear Silent Night sung in four languages. I went to the program, but before they sang Silent Night I was gone, because I had to be in Athabasca that afternoon for special prayers and then a supper followed by a meeting by the Ukrainian Women's Association local..

I was having problems with that gout again, when my toes ached with pain and the toes were beginning to change color. When my toes were not getting any better, I went to see the doctor. Doctor sent me to the hospital for blood work. At the hospital they took three vials of blood. They were not the regular vials, but one ounce bottles. They did not take full bottles. The other thing this time was that they had to take blood from both arms, two bottles from one and the third from the other arm. The doctor had told me that I have a blood clot in the toe. But that was not the end of the blood works. I had to come back to the hospital for the next two days and again taken as much blood from both arms. I thought something must be wrong since so much blood was needed for testing.

I did not have in mind making many trips this past year, but when the year ended I added another ten trips to my record. The list below shows where the ten farther trips took me this year. It's not how we think or plan, but how God has planned things out for us, without us knowing. I did not have any thoughts of going anywhere farther this year, than probably Edmonton the farthest, yet when the year ended I had made more trips as some would says: "That I bargained for." Anyway the trips were made and all things turned out and I was pleased with all that had transpired this year. Where was I this year

I ALSO WALKED ON THIS EARTH

Early in the morning of 2004 in the new year, gout found me again. In January gout started and continued for a number of days. On January 10th between 10:30 AM and 4:00 PM we got over two inches of snow. This same day John and late Kay left for Florida for two months, driving with the car. Late Kay has a sister in Daytona Beach and they had flown there before, but now John decided to go there by car so that they may see more of the country. Later when March comes, I will tell you what happened to them on their return home trip.

MORE HEALTH PROBLEMS

I noticed that on January 30th my toes were turning reddish blue, so I went to see the doctor. I did not know what the problem was. The blood results that were taken of three bottles each for three days showed negative, nothing wrong. Why then are my toes turning red and blue? There is no pain, itching or swelling, normal, only skin color. When the doctor saw my toes, he made an immediate appointment with a specialist Doctor Russell in Edmonton at the University Hospital. Doctor Russell checked and looked me over and said that he would let my family doctor know what the results are. After I saw Doctor Russell I left for home.

Next day I got phone call from Doctor Russell who said: "Start taking aspirin immediately, right now." I told him that my stomach is bothered by aspirin, so he said to take a quarter coated aspirin a day. That I started to do. The doctor from Lac La Biche had also made an appointment to have an ultra sound for the heart and stomach. That took place in Edmonton. When the results came back. Doctor Lindsay said that everything was ok, but that I had a gall stone that showed on the ultra sound. He told me to let him know if it bothers me and they will get it out.

Things were starting to bother me. The toes were not improving and now another problem. My fingers were becoming sore. For a while I thought that something was happening to me like it did to Marusia. If you recall she had said many times that her arms were sore and many times I had to help her dress up and help her with food because her fingers were painful. Now am I getting the same thing? My fingers were sore on both hands that I had to use my palms to button the shirt, etc. When this happened, I did not wait, but went to see the doctor. The doctor looked and did not know what the problem was. After I had seen the doctor, it seemed that my hands and feet were starting to heal, get better. When I had seen Doctor Russell the last time, he asked me to come back and see him again on March 11th. I saw him that day and he sent me to a dermatologist, Doctor Lin. Doctor Lin checked things over and than wanted to know about the black spot on my left finger. They cut a piece of the spot out for a biopsy and put three stitches on the finger.

I cannot let another important thing slip by without mentioning it. As you can recall in December 2000 I had dreamt that I talked with someone during the night and someone or something had taken my chain and cross of my neck during the night. Well let me tell you of another similar incident that happened the night of February 21st to the morning of the 22nd during the night.

I had gone to bed as usual at 10:00 PM. Need some rest because tomorrow on the 22nd is a service in Boyle. I fell asleep and things were all right. During the night I felt that I was wrestling with someone and I was the loser. I thought that I was at the bottom and someone else was on top of me wrestling me to the ground and holding me down. Sometimes during this time whoever or whatever it was left me and I had to go to the bathroom. It was 3:13 AM when I awoke from the wrestling and went to the bathroom. When I returned to lay down in bed, I felt for my neck cross. I always put it to the side, so that I don't lay on it and so it would not pierce the skin during the night.

I felt for the cross and chain, but it was not there. I thought that the chain must have broke and is on the bed. I got up again and put the light on. As I turned towards the bed to look under the covers for the cross, there right before my eyes is the cross and chain lying to the side of the pillow on the bed sheet. I was shook up and goose pimples rolled over my body. How and when did that cross come off my neck? Who took it off? It is the same unanswered riddle as of December 2000. The chain was not broken. When it happened the first time, ten months later Marusia was gone, and over a year later father passed away. Now that this has happened again, will someone else of the family be gone in ten months, maybe sooner or later? What is the meaning of this? Who came and talked with me in December 2000? Who came and was wrestling with me last night and both times took the cross off my neck? Who? What? Why? An unanswered puzzle till today.

Before I get too far away, I must say what happened to John and late Kay. They had left January 10th for Florida for two months and were now on their way back home. They wanted to be back before March 10th because that is when their medical insurance expired. Everything seemed to be well, fine and dandy until they hit Regina, Saskatchewan. They had stayed over in Regina and left in the morning. As they later told me, a very sudden storm from nowhere came up a few minutes out of Regina. They said the storm came up so suddenly that no one could see anything and seven vehicles piled into each other on the highway. John ran into a car ahead of him and another car ran into him from behind and made his car look like an accordion. The car was totaled. The late Kay was taken to the hospital and spent two days there while John stayed in a motel. Late Kay was bruised where the seat belt was and also her knee had been injured. John had his forehead scratched by the air bag. Later they caught a plane from Regina and flew home to Edmonton. The insurance company paid them for everything and later even paid John for the Mercury Marquis car that had been demolished in the accident.

More problems came to visit me in March. It was a nice sunny warm day so that in the morning I sat on the deck and read the paper where it was +20 C and +4 C outside. At noon I had lunch and than went into the basement to do some work with the computer. As I was typing, at 2:30 PM a funny pain came up in my stomach. It was a pain that I had not felt before. I knew something must be wrong, so I shut down the computer and went back upstairs. The pain was not letting up, but increasing. I felt nauseated and was sick, threw up. The pain continued and I lay on the floor, than on the chesterfield, tried standing on my head by the chesterfield, but nothing helped. I suffered all afternoon. In the evening there was a choir practice in the church basement in Lac La Biche. I went to the practice with pain.

After the practice the ladies were talking what they will prepare for the missionary service that coming Sunday. My pain was not easing up and I decided to go home. Going home, I made a decision to stop at the emergency at the hospital. The doctor on duty checked and said it was gall stones. Now I knew how gall stones give pain for a person. My mother suffered many times with such pain, before she had her stones and gall bladder removed, when they still lived in Winnipeg. Than the doctor at the emergency says: "I'll get a bed here in hospital, because you can't go home. You will be unable to sleep at home." I was admitted to the hospital.

Next morning the pain was gone after I had been given medication during the night and put on intravenous. When the doctor came in to see me in the morning, he said he will get me to see a surgeon in Edmonton. After that he released me from the hospital. I was tired. I came home and went and lay down on the deck in a beautiful sunny and warm day. I fell asleep probably for an hour until the phone rang and woke me up. Now there was no pain and I was getting back to be myself. Remember that I had three stitches on my finger in Edmonton. Well at that time I was told to get them out in ten days. I went to the clinic. There was no doctor at the clinic. One had gone to South Africa for holidays and another was in Grand Prairie. The nurses at the clinic would not take the stitches out, but said that only the doctor can do that. They advised me to go to the hospital and there will be a doctor probably from the other clinic. I went straight to the hospital. There was no doctor present at the hospital, but the nurses in the emergency took the stitches out.

Like many other parishes in Canada, the Vegreville Missionary District was holding missionary services during the Great Fast - Lent. Such a service this year was scheduled for Lac La Biche on March 21st, first spring day. People from all over the north eastern part of Alberta came to the service. One priest had a sermon in church during the service. Than followed lunch and after that another priest had an address. The lunch was not held in the church basement but in the Heritage Seniors Centre in Lac La Biche where there is more room and more convenient. There were some ninety two people present, attending this event.

Doctor Lin in Edmonton, when I saw him the last time made another appointment to see him at 2:00 PM on March 25th. When I had the gall bladder attack (mentioned above), the doctor also made an appointment to see a surgeon Doctor Schiller at 11:00 AM in Edmonton on the same day. Two doctors on the same day. I saw Doctor Schiller. He said that from what the results showed, I need to get the gall stones out and the lady would schedule a surgery date for me. The lady checked the schedule and said that I am slated for surgery on April 30th.

From there I went to see Doctor Lin. He with another young doctor checked me again and saw a black spot on my left arm about an inch or two above the wrist watch. He asked how long that mark had been there and I told him as long as I remember. Doctor Lin looked at it with a magnifying glass and than told the nurse to cut it out into two pieces for biopsy. Again stitches were used to close the wound. These stitches I later had removed in Lac La Biche hospital on April 5th. Doctor Lin said that the symptoms of my toes and fingers were that they had been frozen. Frozen? How? When? Where? How could they have been frozen, when I know they never were. He also said that such symptoms sometimes come and go without explanation. After this I went to see John and late Kay.

On March 28th there was another missionary service, this time in the parish of Bonnyville, in the St. Paul congregation. This was the first service being held in the church that had been brought from Willingdon, remodeled and now it looks like a cathedral.

Now came the Resurrection of Christ (Easter) April 11th. This year the service is in Athabasca at 8:00 AM. During the Liturgy service I was beginning to feel that there was something wrong with my stomach. I was hoping nothing would happen so that I can get home as soon as possible. Next day the service was in Sarrail. I could still feel my stomach was not itself so I hurried home as fast as I could. That afternoon I visited the bathroom seven times. Maybe the gall bladder was giving me problems? On April 17th I again had stomach problems.

On April 18th the service was in Craigend and than grave blessing followed. Afternoon a service in Lac La Biche and blessing of the graves. At 5:00 PM there was a baptism at Lac La Biche. A busy day and the stomach is still not right, something wrong, but somehow I survived the problem this day.

SURGERY TIME

I ended up in Edmonton again to see the doctor . Doctor Lin made an appointment for me and asked that I bring all my medications when I come in. Now Doctor Fischer checked me over and told me the same thing that my toes and fingers have symptoms that they were frozen. How could that be? I know my hands and feet and I know that they were never frozen.

It is getting near April 30th when I go for surgery. Before I go, I should plant some garden, for who knows if I will be able to do anything after surgery. April 26th, four days before surgery I plowed the garden and planted some onions, radishes, lettuce, garlic and carrots. I had to do this now because I was told that I have to be at Royal Alexandra Hospital on April 28th at 11:00 AM. Some pre surgery tests are to be done and information about the surgery was told to me and some other eight or nine patients. After this I went to John and late Kay's and spent the rest of the time there until May 4th after surgery, before I came back home. But let me tell you about the surgery.

When I was in the hospital on April 28th, I was told to be in the hospital for surgery at 6:30 AM. John brought and dropped me off at the hospital at 6:00 AM. I had to go and report on the floor where the surgery would take place. When I arrived, the nurse said that my bed was ready and waiting. I had to undress with nothing on, except the hospital gown they gave me to put on. The gown was already waiting on the bed as was a small paper cup with a pill and intravenous to be hooked up. My bed was number one of the four in that room and I was the first one there. When I had changed into the gown, I was lying on the bed and the surgery was slated for 8:30 AM.

Shortly after 8:30 AM a nurse came and told me to take the pill that was waiting for me and than she took me with the bed to the pre-op room. In that room there were many other patients waiting for surgery. Than came a doctor and was looking over my files at the foot of the bed and said that he would be putting me to sleep. He checked the papers over and left. A minute later another nurse came and wheeled me into the operating room. I noticed there was a clock on the wall and the time on it was 8:45 AM. The people in the operating room told me to slide over unto the operating table. I did. The operating table was narrow, so I put my hands on my chest after I had moved to the operating table. A nurse told me to move up, so that my head would be over the edge of the bed. Another nurse told me to put my arms on the arm rests. I put my right arm out, and sure enough there was an arm rest. What happened after that I don't remember a thing. I thought the doctor would come with a needle to put me to sleep, but when all that happened I do not know. I don't even remember putting my left hand on the arm rest, that is how quickly I was knocked out.

The operation went through and I was taken to the recovery room, which I do not remember. The next thing I do remember is someone asking somebody else what time it was. I recall the other person replied that it was 11:00 AM. I thought I was still in the operating room waiting for the surgery to take place. But as I began to open my eyes more and more, I realized I was not in the operating room, it was another room. A thought came to me was that I was still waiting for the surgery. What a surprise, when I later realized that the surgery had been over and I was in the recovery room. About 11:30 AM the nurse again wheeled me with my bed to the room where I had first been when I arrived at the hospital. At 12:00 noon a nurse came, looked at me and took my blood pressure asking me: "When are you going home?" I said: "I don't know, because I have to have surgery and no one told me anything and maybe go home tomorrow or in a few days." The nurse says: "You can go home now." W H A T ?" I say: "What about surgery?" She said that the surgery was over and I can go home now. "Surgery is over, and I can go home now?" I say to her: "I don't know when my brother will come here to pick me up, so maybe you phone him to come and get me now." A few minutes later she came back and said there was no answer at John's place.

The nurse told me that I could change into my clothes and lay on the bed to wait to go home. That I did. I waited and also waited when the pain would come, because all this time I had felt no pain anywhere. About 1:30 PM John and late Kay come into the room bringing a potted rose. When they came into the room they saw me all dressed and thought I was still waiting to have surgery. They were surprised that the surgery was over and I was ready to go home.

As we were leaving, the nurse gave me a prescription for Tylenol number three for pain. On the way home John stopped at the Safeway pharmacy to pick up the prescription while Kay and I waited in the car. At 3:00 PM, I was already in the house at John's place. Only six hours ago I was on the operating table and now I am already at John's place. When my mother had surgery for her gall bladder she spent two weeks in the hospital in Winnipeg. What an improvement in medical treatments for the ill.

It was a beautiful warm sunny day on April 30th. The late Kay was doing something in the garden and around the yard and John was fixing something on a car at the back of the garage. I was walking around outside and after a while I thought pain was starting to come on, so I went into the house, took a Tylenol pill and lay down on the chesterfield. Some time later the pain was gone, so I was up again and wandering outside in the beautiful sunlight looking for some kind work to do, but no one offered me any work.

Things went well until about 7:30 PM on May 1st. John and I were walking around in the house and it was still daylight. But in the darker hallway, I saw a flash of lightning and say to John: "I think it's going to rain because it's lightning." John looks at me and says: "How is it going to rain when there isn't even a cloud in the sky?" Than another flash of lightning came. Than it happened again, and than again. Each time I moved my head there was this flash of lightning like a half circle, just flashes. When I was still and no head movement, no flash, but as soon as the head moved there was that flash again, just like lightning in the sky.

On Saturday May 1st, since there was no pain I was thinking of going home on Sunday afternoon, but John and late Kay insisted that I not go for another day but wait until things are maybe a bit healed inside. When we got up on Sunday morning, I felt I was bloated, but no pain. I took a Tylenol and than went and lay on the chesterfield. John and late Kay had gone to church. When they came from church, we had lunch and I was feeling much better by afternoon. I told them that I am well enough to take off for home tomorrow. John said that I am not going anywhere until we see an eye doctor and see about the flashing light. I stayed that Sunday in Edmonton. As this was written in 2014, (checked in 2016) ten years later that flashing light still flashes from that time.

Come Monday morning John takes me to his optometrist, eye doctor at Bonnie Doon. Even though there were patients already in the office, John told the receptionist what was what and they took me ahead of time without any appointment. The receptionist thought it was an emergency case. The doctor checked things over and said there was nothing wrong with the eye that he could see. He said that the only thing he saw was the retina had separated, but it was coming back together again. I had told him that I had surgery on Friday and he thought that maybe it was some side effect from the medication during surgery which could do that. The rest of the day I spent in Edmonton. Tuesday morning came and I felt fine and said that I will be venturing back home. Have not been home since April 28th a full six days. When I got into the car, I put a cushion on my stomach and than the seat belt over the cushion so that in case of a sudden stop, I don't feel the jar and get an injury to the cut where the surgery was. What kind of a cut? I had only four small holes cut into my stomach. I came home on May 4th at 12:30 noon. The ice on the lake was gone and this was very early, because it usually does not go until the middle of May.

This same day after I got home in the evening I always like to call those where I left for home from and notify them that I was already home. When I called this evening on May 4th, John told me some bad news. Vern Walker, Pat's husband and John and Alice Hnatiuk's son-in-law passed away suddenly. His funeral is scheduled for Friday May 7th. How I wanted to go and be there, but a week after surgery and everyone is telling me to stay home and not look for trouble, but to recuperate. Vern had dug the grave for Marusia and that was the first grave that he had ever dug.

He owned a back hoe and did many jobs around the area. After he dug the grave for Marusia, he was probably digging graves for all funerals in the area.

I called Pat when I heard the news. She said that Vern had been in the hospital in Wakaw the week before for three or four days and had an appointment to be in Saskatoon the following week for heart tests. He never made it to those tests. On the 4th of May 2004 he and son Jordie went to Prud'homme, Saskatchewan to haul and crush rock. Vern was on the front end loader loading the truck. Jordie saw that something was wrong with his father. First Vern took of his cap, than his jacket, his shirt and than even his T-shirt and he was sweating. When he saw what was happening, he called Pat (his mother) and she started to drive to Prud'homme. She called the ambulance and the ambulance was following her to the place where the men were. When they got there, Vern was not talking, but still breathing. The ambulance took him and started on their way to Saskatoon, but called Saskatoon for another ambulance to meet them because they had no life saving support equipment on their vehicle.

Pat and Jordie in the meantime raced to the University hospital in Saskatoon to have all the information and be ready to meet the ambulance when it came in. They gave all the information and than started towards the emergency room when they saw the doctor come out and they meet him in the hallway. "We tried to revive him, but were not getting any pulse, so we pronounced him dead," said the doctor. What a shock to the family and all those who knew Vern. I could not go to the funeral, so what did I do at home? At the precise time the funeral was taking place at Wakaw, I read the whole funeral service at home at the same hour. Was there not a bird that flew at the window at my place a few month ago?

Back to more about surgery. When my mother had surgery to remove her gall bladder, she was cut just about in half as she later showed us her scars. For me my surgery for the same thing was different. The surgeon told me when I saw him the first time, that they will make a small incision, put a light inside the body. Than they cut two more holes where two knives or scissors are inserted to cut the bladder off. One more incision they make at the belly button to pull out the gall bladder. Now after the surgery some three months later, you cannot even see where the incisions were made. Just like a miracle.

When I arrived home I spent very little time doing anything. I either sat or lay most of the time, to give a chance for things to heal inside. The Tylenol I was given for pain said on the label: "Take one or two tablets every four hours for pain." The nurse in the hospital had warned me twice that Tylenol may cause constipation. Instead of taking the dosage as the label said, I used only two Tylenol a day, one in the morning and one at night and there was no pain whatsoever during the recuperating. There was no problem with constipation either, did not cause any problem.

Before I had my surgery, it was a few weeks prior, I was talking with a friend from Manitoba and he told me that if the gall bladder is removed one may have a running stomach(diarrhea) for the rest of their life. Two weeks later on May 13th, my stomach became loose for the next two days. So maybe this friend of mine was right? Will I have to live with this condition for the rest of my life?

When I was coming home from the hospital, the nurse told me to make an appointment with Dr. Schiller, the surgeon, in about three weeks for a check-up. I called from John's place and made an appointment for May 17th. Later the receptionist called and asked if I could come on the 19th, two days later. To me it did not matter whether sooner or later. I saw Dr. Schiller at 1:00 PM. He checked me over and said that everything seems to have healed well and he told me that now I can eat whatever I wish and like. He also warned me that should I ever notice a little bubble forming around the belly button to come and see him or another doctor immediately, because it could be the start of a hernia and they would fix that up. Before I left, I told Dr. Schiller thus: "Doctor, if all surgeries are like this one, you can cut me every second day if need be because I have had no pain." He just chuckled and said that now I can eat whatever I wanted.

Now another problem showed up before me. A loose stomach was hindering my progress in what I was doing, and every second or third day I would have a loose stomach. Than more loose stomachs followed in June. A family reunion had been planned for Sudbury, Ontario for August 6-7-8 of this year. How can I go to such an event with stomach problems I was having? Will probably have to miss this family reunion this year, unless some real changes take place with my health.

The things I had planted before my surgery were already up and growing well. The following day we got the first good boomer of a thunderstorm over Lac La Biche at 1:40 PM with strong winds and large heavy raindrops. This evening again I had a loose stomach. On May 27th I went to Grassland to Bill and Olga Sworin's because Olga's two sisters and their husbands from Kelowna were visiting and they wanted to see me. There we had a barbeque and I had to be careful and watch what I was eating, because I did not want to get caught with stomach trouble. The following day, rains came for three days bringing us two inches of rain. On June 2nd another thunderstorm rolled through at 2:00 PM bringing with it hail the size of marbles. Had it hailed for another ten minutes everything would have been white like snow in the winter. The hail came down from the roof in drainpipes and at 7:30 PM there was still a pile of hail on the grass where the drainpipe came to the ground.

When I had seen Dr. Fisher before my gall bladder surgery, he said to go ahead and have my surgery and than after that he will want me to have an echocardiogram of the heart. His office made an appointment to have this test on June 7th at 12:30 noon. This morning I woke up with a sore throat, headache, somewhat of a fever and had a sleepless night. Is this symptoms of West Nile illness? I had the tests done and after that went to see John and late Kay and came home well before sunset. The following day I was very ill. I have not slept for two nights already. I felt nauseated, headache, fever, cough were all with me these days. I thought that if things did not improve the following day I was going to go and see a doctor at the emergency in the hospital. This morning when people arose from sleep all the roofs on the houses had been painted white. Jack Frost had come for a visit to Lac La Biche. Probably his last visit until fall. On June 11th Dr. Fisher called and said that the tests which I had showed negative.

Like Dauphin, Manitoba, Vegreville in Alberta each year also hold a Ukrainian Festival. The late Father Puk from Vegreville called me if I would bring some items for display at the Festival. We had a display two years ago. I agreed that I would bring the items on July 1st in the afternoon. Canada was celebrating Canada Day, but I was on the road to Vegreville this day. I would have to pick up the displayed items sometimes on Sunday afternoon July 4th.

On July 4th there was a Feast day service at Noral and this was followed by a semi-annual meeting of the Lac La Biche Parish. I had something to eat, but was careful what I ate and than I had to leave for Vegreville to pick up my things from the Festival. I did stay for part of the meeting, than was excused and left. Gout had also come to visit me again. I thought that maybe he had forgotten me and would give me peace of mind, but it was not so. I arrived at Vegreville and the display was not to be taken down until Sunday 5:00 PM. Because the turnout at the Festival this year was poor, for some reason the people did not come to view the displays until Sunday afternoon. After that I went and had some supper at late Rev. and Dobrodeyka Puk's place and left for home shortly after 7:00 PM. This day I had a bad experience coming home. I felt that my stomach was beginning to act up and not normal as it should be. I kept driving, but felt that I had to stop for a bathroom rest, but where do you stop, when there are no rest areas. I turned off the highway unto a gravel road and stopped near a bush, but I never made it. The stomach beat me. I arrived home and had to take a shower and wash all the clothes. Now for sure I'm not going to go to the family reunion, not with this kind of a stomach. The following day I still had trouble with my stomach.

On July 12th Sarrail congregation is celebrating its seventy-fifth anniversary. I got together with Bill and Mary Pisarewski on July 8th for a practice to sing and set up the program since the three of us were chosen to prepare a program for the day. I was also asked to be MC for the day at the program. The little historical church was packed with people for the special event celebration.

After this celebration, Father Michael Domaradz took a few days off for holidays and will not be having any service on July 18th in the parish. Where can I go to a service the coming Sunday? I heard on the radio that there will be a Ukrainian Day at the Heritage Village some thirty miles east of Edmonton. Maybe that is where I'll go. Than two days before this the radio weather forecast said it would be in the +30 C range. In such heat there will be no place to hide at the Heritage Village which will be filled with thousands of people for that event. No I'm not going there. Than it came to me. My late mother would say: "We make plans and God changes them." That is what happened this week-end. I'm not going to the Heritage Village, no service at home anywhere, so I started to look around where the priest from Smoky would be having a service that Sunday. Oh yes, I found it, and it will be at Borowtsi.

But where is Borowtsi? Who can I call? Who do I know in those areas that could tell me? Oh yes, I know, Nancy Shysh the choir conductor for that area and she will know. She lost her husband a year ago and had invited me to come to the year memorial service. Two days before that memorial service I had to call her back and tell her that I would not attend, because we have a funeral the same day in our parish. When I called to ask where Borowtsi was she said it was only two kilometers north of Willingdon. Oh, yeah, I've seen that church a mile east from the highway but never knew what it was. She said you have to go to Willingdon and than take the road north. She asked if I will be at the service and I said I am planning to be there. She said it would be nice because than I could help sing. So all is set. I have not been at Borowtsi before, so this will be something new and a chance to see the little church.

Sunday morning comes. I am ready to leave about 7:30-7:40 AM. Just as I am putting on my jacket to leave, the telephone rings. Father John Lipinski from St. Paul is calling and says: "I know you are getting ready to go to Borowtsi to the service, but could you instead come to church at Kyivski Hjay, because I have no cantor. My cantor can't come because she has a funeral in the family and I've been calling since 6:30 this morning and I can't get anyone." I looked at the time and asked what time the service starts and he said at 10:00 AM. I told him that I would have time and would be there. I had made plans to go to the Heritage Centre, but I did not. I made plans to go to Borowtsi, but I did not. My mother's saying was: "We make plans and God changes them."

The last time I had a loose stomach was on July 6th. Because time has gone by and things seem normal, maybe I can go to the family reunion. I had called and told Diane Russell, cousin at Trail, B.C., that I would not be going and the reason why. Now that the stomach problems have somewhat eased off and settled, maybe I can go. Later I called her again and told her that things are looking up and maybe I'll be able to make it. But gout has now grabbed my left foot and invaded the right one and is very sore. On July 29th I called the clinic to see the doctor about the gout, but was told there were no openings until Tuesday morning. But how can I suffer so long? Early Friday morning with great pain in my right foot, I went to the emergency. The doctor looked at my foot and gave me a prescription.

At 9:00 AM I was at the drug store to get the prescription filled. I came home and took the two kinds of pills that I got.

Today it is Friday and the start of the Pow-Wow in Lac La Biche. Father Michael came from Athabasca at 10:30 AM and with s few thousand other people we stood on the sidewalk and watched the parade. As we stood there, I could feel the pain decreasing in my left and right foot. After the parade we went to the shore of the lake to see the water bombers flying over the lake displaying how they put out forest fires. Following this we came home and had some lunch. After lunch Father Michael went to visit some people and than about 4:30 PM we left for Stry south of Vilna for a marriage rehearsal. We returned home and Father Michael stayed overnight at my place. On July 31st around noon we left for Stry for the marriage ceremony at 2:00 PM. After the marriage we returned home because tomorrow is a Feast Day service at Wandering River.

FAMILY REUNION AND GOUT PROBLEMS

As time was flying along, I noticed I was having less trouble with my stomach. If I have no more problems, I can go to the family reunion at Sudbury, Ontario. From first I was planning to drive there and back as this reunion had been announced two years previous. I was thinking I would drive to Wakaw the first day, next day to Winnipeg and than another day or two to Sudbury. But as mentioned many times my plans were not as good as God's. Whether we make plans or not, they are useless, only God's plan is final and the best.

When the days were getting closer to the reunion, I started to think seriously to go by plane. I checked with the travel agent Ukaan in Lac La Biche and the fare was $1137.00 return to Toronto, Sudbury and back. I also had talked to my cousin Jennie Marchinko of Calgary and she said that she with her daughter Edele are flying to Toronto and renting a car to Sudbury and back to Toronto. She said it was costing them only $500.00 each for a return trip to Toronto and back. When I heard this, I thought: "Why can't I fly to Toronto and rent a car?" I went to the travel agency again and asked for a return trip from Edmonton to Toronto. The cheapest fare she could find was for $460.00 return plus taxes which came to $580.00 in total. Well at least it's not $1137.00. I saw the travel agent on July 27th and she said that airlines usually put up their seat sales on Wednesday morning. I told her that I would not be able to come Wednesday morning but in the afternoon. That day there was a service at Boyle and than a service in the seniors villa, so I did not get back home until 3:00 PM that day.

I stopped at the travel agency and she said there was nothing else that she could find that was cheaper so she booked a flight for me to leave Edmonton on Friday August 6th at noon and return on Monday at 11:00 AM. The cost was $582.00 return. When I learned of this that I was now going, I called Lisetta Chalupiak in Sudbury and told her to book me a motel near the place of the reunion. She asked when I was coming. I told her that I arrive at Toronto at 5:40 PM and would be taking a car from Toronto. She said that her brother from Toronto will also be coming on Friday after work and I may be able to catch a ride with him. I told her I have to be back in Toronto Sunday evening because my plane leaves at 9:00 AM on Monday morning. Lisetta said that her brother would be going back to Toronto on Sunday afternoon because he has to be back at work on Monday morning. She told me that she would get in touch with me one way or another if I would be able to come with her brother.

After I had a seat booked in row twenty three, I knew I was on my way to Sudbury. When I was coming home from Wandering River from church on August 1st, I was listening to CHED radio from Edmonton. An ad by Jetsgo airline was on the air. It said: "Fly Jetsgo to Vancouver for $29.00, to Winnipeg for $59.00 to Toronto, Montreal, Ottawa, Halifax or St, John for $89.00 one way." W H A T? And it costs me to go to Toronto for $250.00 one way with the same airline? I went back to the travel agency and told her what I had heard on the radio. She checked and said that the sale for those seats went on July 31st and she had booked my flight on July 28th. With these seat sales you had to take your trip anytime before December 15th. I guess for a poor person the wind is always blowing in their eyes.

So worrying was over for travel. Now just to get to the airport on time. When I got up on August 5th, I was listening to CHED radio and the news was that it was very foggy in Edmonton and around the area. Than it hit me. I have to be at the airport in Edmonton at 10:30 AM. If I leave home and hit a heavy fog, travel will be slowed down and I may be late for my flight. I called John and asked him if I could come to their place the day before, stay over and if he would drive me to the airport. He said that I could come, stay over and leave the car on the street in front of their house.

I went to Edmonton on Thursday, stayed over night and next morning John drove me to the airport.

I had no breakfast this morning, for I was afraid if I eat anything, I might get stomach problems on the plane. The plane left at 11:00 AM. I flew by Jetsgo. They were the cheapest to fly from Edmonton to Toronto. The plane was full both ways and it was one of those planes that was long and narrow and looked more like a torpedo or a rocket. The plane was full having twenty seven rows of five seats in each row. What I learned in Toronto at the airport before we took off for home that there are : Air Canada , Jazz, Air Alliance, and Tango. All of these planes are Air Canada. Why? Because under the names of the three planes Jazz, Air Alliance and Tango are smaller letters printed saying "Air Canada."

When I had come to stay with John and late Kay I had not heard anything from Lisetta as to when her brother is leaving Toronto and if I can catch a ride with him. From John's place I called Lisetta to get some information, so I would know what to do tomorrow when I get to Toronto. Lisetta told me that her brother had already left for Sudbury because he left a day earlier. So now what? Do I walk, hitch hike or how do I get to Sudbury? John gets on the computer and we start looking for car rentals. We found some but it took time, so I got on the phone and started calling with the toll free numbers in the book. I called one company and they said all their cars are booked for Friday. I called another and they wanted and arm and a leg. That was also out. I called National-Tilden. I told them when and where I was going and what I needed. They wanted $121.00 for the whole time. I said I wanted a car with unlimited miles. John and I both agreed that it was a good deal, so I booked a car and told them I wanted the smallest car, because I'm a small man. The lady chuckled and said there would be a vehicle waiting for me when I get to Toronto. And she only wanted to know what time I will arrive. I told her and she did not even ask for my credit card number to book the car.

The plane left Edmonton on time. Now when you want to eat on the plane, you have to pay for what you want. I did not have breakfast, but I bought a bagel on the plane and that cost $2.00. That was my dinner for that day. When we arrived in Toronto, the plane touched on the runway on time at 5:40 PM. Than you walk, and walk, and than walk some more to pick up your luggage. Finally we get there and the luggage is coming in.

Some people got their luggage and were gone while Eugene is standing and waiting, and waiting and waiting. Finally it is the third or the fourth from the last. I pick up my suitcase and asked the security person where the car rentals are and he told me to follow the signs. When I get to the car rentals, there are lineups at each car rental office. So Eugene waited for his suitcase and now has to wait for the car, because people that got their luggage sooner came to the car rentals sooner. So I stand and wait in line. By the time everything went through and I got the keys to the car to leave, it was already 7:05 PM when I got on the road. Now I have three hundred and eighty eight kilometers ahead of me to Sudbury.

The car I received was a Chrysler PT Cruiser. It had sixteen thousand kilometers on it. I was given a map of Toronto, took a look and saw the easiest way to get out from the airport to the highway to Barrie. When I got on the freeway, I see the speed limit is one hundred kilometers an hour and cars are passing by me like rockets. Than I sped up to one hundred and five and cars are still passing Eugene. I sped up more to a hundred and ten and they are still flying past me. I did get up to a hundred and fifteen kilometers an hour and they were still passing me. No I'm not going any faster because I don't want to get a speeding ticket. Later after the freeway ends north of Barrie, Ontario and we are in a ninety kilometer speed zone, I see the following in both English and French:

Speeding 100 - $100.00 fine
Speeding 110 - $153.00 fine
Speeding 120 - $295.00 fine

Now you know why Eugene did not want to take a chance and get a speeding ticket in Ontario. When I got to Parry Sound, it was already dark and had to use headlights. I arrived at Sudbury at 10:25 PM. I was wandering and thinking all this time where and how will I find the motel in the dark not knowing the city. I knew that Lisetta had booked the motel called Richards Lake Motel. As I come within a few miles of Sudbury, what do I see looking at me - yes right in front is Richards Lake Motel. I pulled in and walk in to register. The lady immediately asks me: "Are you Eugene?" I told her I was, registered and got the keys to the room. I bought a bottle of juice and a bag of potato chips to have my supper. My room number was six.

Next morning when I got up, Jennie Marchinko and daughter Edele were already outside getting into the car to head to the reunion. Since I did not know the way where to go, I followed them to the Ukrainian National Community Park called "Zaporozha." Zaporozha is a place on the Dnieper River in Ukraine where the Kozaks at one time had their fortress. That place was later destroyed by the Russian princess Catherine the Great. How I got back home, will come later when the reunion is over.

One word about the family reunion.

Our first family reunion was held at Tees, Alberta in 1998 with about twenty people. Two years later the next one was at Green Lake, British Columbia with some thirty people showing up. The third one in 2002 was at Clear Lake, Manitoba with about forty people present. In 2004 the reunion was set for Sudbury, Ontario and forty seven people attended. The next reunion is scheduled to take place in Saskatchewan in 2006 with the place and dates to be announced when arrangements will be made. The people from Regina will look after the arrangements. Most likely it will be the first or second week of August. Time will tell. Reunion started in Alberta, and then they went alphabetically by the provinces: Alberta, British Columbia, Manitoba, Ontario, Saskatchewan and then started the rotation again.

When mother was living she used to tell us many things about the family, who was who, but when we were younger we took no interest in that and it did not stick to our head. Now that we are somewhat more mature and know what is what we would like to find out some things, but there is no one to ask and get that information from. It is the same with the other families, Derzak, Chalupiak, Korzeniowski and Stefaniuk.

The family reunion started out with our three closest families at Tees, Alberta: Derzak, Korzeniowski and Stefaniuk. There was a Tillie Korzeniowski and Mary Derzak the two sisters who came to Canada and were living at Grandview and Ethelbert respectively. My mother was a first cousin to them. The Paul Chalupiak family from Pittsburgh, U.S.A. attended the reunion in Sudbury. Paul also was a cousin to my mother for she would always say: "pervay bratt", meaning a cousin. What we did learn at this gathering was that the grandmother of all four, Tillie Korzeniowski,

Mary Derzak, Paul Chalupiak and Mary Stefaniuk was a grandmother to all four of our parents. When the next reunion takes place, I believe that there will even be more information uncovered about the closeness of these families and their generations.

It was Saturday morning when I arrived to meet with the rest of the clan at the camp. Later there were three families who arrived from Pittsburgh. They were the grandson of Paul Chalupiak and they arrived with two great grandchildren. I have mentioned a few times at our reunions that today if only one of our parents were still around we would have found out much more who, what, where, how, etc.

People mingled around with each other and talked about who is who and the relation to each other. In the evening the ladies a prepared banquet. Beet leaf rolls, cabbage rolls, meat balls, potatoes, turkey, salads, etc. etc. After the meal we had a gift exchange. You picked a wrapped gift which was wrapped in newspaper and you opened it up. The next person to take a gift could either take your gift away or open another gift from the pile of gifts. Than on another table there were other gifts and these were for the "silent auction." You bid for the article by putting down your name and bid for the article; at the end whose bid was the highest you purchased the gift for that price. On Sunday morning at 7:30 AM all bids were closed and the highest bidders purchased their product.

Sunday morning everybody met again and had the whole group picture taken as well as of each separate family. The people from Pittsburgh were leaving early in the morning because they wanted to get to Niagara Falls for the night. Next morning they wanted to leave early again because some had to be back at work in the nursing home at 3:00 PM on Monday. Lisetta took me in her van and we went to the cemetery to see where her husband was buried. We said a prayer, I took a picture or two and we returned back to camp. It was now shortly after 10:00 AM. I was also leaving for Toronto today and was hoping to get away somewhat earlier to avoid the evening rush into Toronto. I stopped and filled up the rental car with gasoline in Sudbury. When I got nearer to Toronto I wanted to fill the tank again, but could not find a service station anywhere.

What I had seen around Sudbury and for about fifty miles south were cars standing on either side of the road with signs saying: "Blueberries for sale." There were many of these cars just outside of Sudbury. I was going to get some for the reunion, but learned that the ladies had blueberries for they made blueberry varenyky and ice ream for dessert on Saturday night. I was curious of how much the blue berries were selling for. I asked someone at the camp and they said that a two liter basket was selling for $10.00. I told them that Extra Foods and AG grocery stores in Lac La Biche were selling two litre baskets of blueberries for $4.88 and $4.98 and they are the big blueberries from British Columbia from home grown blueberry orchards.

I got to Toronto to the airport to return the car at 3:30 PM. I had looked for a service station before I got to the airport to fill up the car but no service station along the route. I told the lady at the office that I could not find a service station and that there is only three quarters of a tank of gas. She calculated how many litres of gasoline would be needed and said it was fourteen litres. I figured fourteen litres at eighty cents a litre would be about $10.00. She calculated everything together and said the whole sum was $151.00. What increased the price was that the fuel tank was not full. Do you know why? Because they charged me $2.25 a litre for fuel. That's right, $2.25 a litre where at the service station it was only eighty cents a litre at that time. So fourteen litres at $2.25 a litre and that makes $31.00 for fourteen litres, just about three gallons. I learned my lesson. But if you ever rent a car fill it up before you take it back, or you will be charged an arm and a leg.

WHAT A NIGHT AT THE TORONTO AIRPORT

I turned the car in, so what do I do from now until tomorrow morning? It is 4:00 PM and my plane don't leave until tomorrow morning at 9:00 AM another nineteen hours. What does one do for nineteen hours at the airport? If I take a taxi downtown to some motel and than the taxi back next day, than pay for the motel, that will be a little too much. Oh no, Eugene will be wiser and stay right here at the airport in the hotel and no need to pay for a cab there and back. I walked into the hotel then to the counter to register. The lady at the counter asked me is she can help me. I asked her if they have a small room with a small bed for a small man and she hands me a the paper to fill out the registration. Before I start to fill anything I ask: "How much is the room?" She says: "The rooms are $349.00 a night." That's right, that's what she said. I asked her if there are any cheaper rooms. She looked at me and than asks to see my drivers licence because they have discounts for seniors. She looks at the licence and says: "So you are a senior. For seniors that will be $295.00." I thanked the lady, turned around and went back to the airport terminal. I told her that I only wanted to rest on a small bed and not buy the hotel.

So now what? I'm going to spend my night at the airport. Sometimes I've seen on TV that hundreds of people stay at the airport when planes are canceled. There are numerous doors at the terminal for people to enter in and exit the terminal. I sat on a chair opposite one entrance, watched and counted people moving around. I calculated them every five minutes. In one five minute period, one hundred and thirty people moved through. In another five minute period ninety people moved through. In the third five minute period one hundred and twenty six people moved by. If you take the smallest figure of ninety people per five minute intervals and there are twelve five minute periods in an hour, so in one hour the least people that would pass through this one door would be one thousand and four people. This is only one entrance, and how many other entrances are there in that one terminal which may even be busier?

I sat there with a hot swollen gout foot. I took my foot out of the shoe and tried to be comfortable, but there was no comfort from the pain. Till 6:30 PM I sat there and than decided to go up on the escalator to see where I would be boarding my plane tomorrow morning. When I got to the top of the escalator, I got of the escalator and just stood there. No way am I going to go anywhere. The crowd of people on that floor was like a wall and nothing was moving. There was no room to move in the terminal which was about a quarter of a mile long and probably forty or fifty feet wide. I slowly pushed my way down to the other side of the escalator, stepped on it and went down to the main floor where there was an abundant room to sit, stand and move around. About two hours later I once again chanced the escalator trip upstairs. When I arrived at the top, the place was empty like a drum. All those people cleared through and probably many more in such a short time between 6:30 and 8:30 PM. What a people mover that place is. Thousands of people moved out in such a short while. What a place. Just to sit and see it and all the activity is enough to keep one thinking.

So I spent my night at the airport terminal. My plane does not leave until 9:00 AM tomorrow, August 9th. I sat and watched thinking, maybe, maybe I would recognize someone in all this crowd, but no, not one person. Than my gout was not helping and seemed to be more pain as time went on. I already had this gout problem before I even left home for Toronto and Sudbury. I could take a pill, but my pills are in the large suitcase, because I packed everything in the morning thinking that I would be in the motel and have my suitcase handy. So do I open the suitcase in the middle of terminal to get my pills? I had seen that there was a little cubby hole to the side of the entrance of the building and that security people would sit there and watch or talk in there. I thought that place was reserved for them but there were no signs. I went up to that place and asked the security guard if that place was reserved for them. He told me anyone can sit there. There I opened my suitcase and took my pills out. I went and bought a bottle of water and took my pills for gout.

I would have tried to sleep on the chairs like some other people were already doing, but there were a lot of people moving and milling around. Why not go upstairs where it is quieter? Ah, Eugene is going to be the wise one now. I went upstairs and there were two or three employees cleaning the place. I asked if I could lay on the chairs to sleep. One person told me to go to the far end where it will be quiet all night as there will be no planes for boarding in that end of the terminal. I took his advice and found a place at the end of the building, lay down and tried to fall asleep. B U T then a thought came by. I fall asleep. What if someone quietly comes by while I'm sleeping, quietly picks up my suitcase and leaves. Than Eugene will go home without a suitcase. I pulled the suitcase closer to me and stuck my hand through the lower handle. Now if someone wants my suitcase, he will also have to take Eugene.

My feet were now tired and the pain from gout was not letting up. I had seen in the lower level of the terminal that some people were laying on the chairs and had taken their shoes off. So why can't I take my shoes off? I did. Than another thought came again. I'll put the shoes under the chairs, this way I may be able to hear if someone comes and I will wake up. B U T what if someone tip toes up to me while I'm asleep and takes my shoes, than tomorrow morning Eugene will have to go home without shoes. No let the shoes stay on, but just loosen the shoe laces. This way I did manage to get forty plus winks of snooze during the night. Later on the plane I caught a few more winks.

Finally daybreak had arrived. I had awakened about two hours earlier and already come back down to the main floor. I was also wishing that the plane would already arrive so that we could board and get some shuteye. I was the first one to get the boarding pass at 6:30 AM because there was an attendant already at the counter waiting for passengers to book their seats. Our Jetsgo plane was one that arrived from Newfoundland and it was fully loaded. People disembarked the plane and the crew were preparing the plane for the Edmonton trip. Finally came the call to board the plane. We are aboard and awaiting for clearance to leave for the runway when just as 9:00 AM came, the captain comes on and says: "Ladies and gentlemen, we have some problem with the oxygen. We need a new tank and it will take about five minutes to get the tank and five minutes to replace, so we will be somewhat delayed to takeoff." Now what else can go wrong after the night I had?

After some time we could hear some people working at the bottom of the plane and it was already 9:30 AM and we are still at the terminal now half an hour late. As if that is not enough of a delay, I see a tractor pulling a wagon with suitcases. They come and stop right underneath our plane under my window. I could see what they are doing. They are loading luggage into our plane. I do not know what happened, but I saw the luggage being loaded unto this plane when we were still in the terminal. We could hear noises as they were loading the luggage. Suppose we would have left on time, what would happen once we landed in Edmonton? LUGGAGE LOST? So where was this luggage till now? Because we were late in leaving, the luggage was loaded. Had we left on time that luggage would not have been in Edmonton on that plane. Then sometimes we wonder why people loose luggage. Than two men come out from underneath the plane laughing and joking and one was glancing at me to see if I was watching them. Finally when everything was ready we left the tarmac, but as we were taxing out, I counted eleven planes ahead of us on the taxiway lined up preparing to take off.

We left Toronto exactly one hour late, but arrived in Edmonton only twenty minutes late. When we left Toronto it was nice sunny and clear for about twenty minutes. When we got above the clouds we did not see anything but clouds, until about five or ten minutes before we landed in Edmonton when the plane had descended lower. John was at the airport, picked me up and we went to his place. Than we picked up late Kay and went together and had dinner, came back to their place and I left for home arriving just after 5:00 PM. I was dead tired from all the experience and the sore gout with a swollen foot. I am usually in bed at 10:00 PM after saying my prayers. Today my prayers were said just after 8:00 PM and 9:00 PM I was already in slumber land as soon as my head hit the pillow.

When I arrived home I stopped at the post office to pick up the mail. The box was full but mostly of flyers. There were two bills and also a letter from the Alberta Benevolent Association. They knew that I had been teaching cantoring in the Grassland-Sarrail area in the past winter and they wanted me to send them a report how many hours so that they may have them for their records. I wrote a letter back the next day and thanked them for thinking about an honorarium for me, but I said that I would not accept any. If I can't do anything for my church, than I shouldn't do anything. The last year income tax I had just come under that I did not have to pay any income tax. If I accept money from and for everything than I will have to pay income tax so that the government would have enough to give to the lazy bums on the streets for not doing anything. No I don't want to make money, but just so I can get enough from year to year not to starve. If I make more and save it, will I take it with me to the other world? I wrote in the letter that I don't want any honorarium, but let them pay for the books for the students that I was teaching.

So far this year I have made only one trip outside the province and that was for the family reunion in Sudbury. People I phone to talk too, or they phone me always keep asking me when I will come out to visit them. Well I don't have any trips planned this year to go anywhere even though I still have to make one trip to Saskatchewan to visit Marusia, Pat Walker and see John and Alice's new house in Wakaw. The farthest trip so far this year by car has been about ten times to Edmonton to the clinics, doctors, hospital, surgery, etc.

EUGENE CAUGHT IN A SCAM TRAP

I must now mention also another incident that happened this year. Sometimes towards the end of April I had received in the mail a small catalogue from the Canadian Mail Order Exchange Inc., from Hawkesbury, Ontario. The catalogue looked like any other small mail order catalogue I had received many times before and ordered things from them. There were a few items that I ordered and sent the order away on May 10th with a cheque for $43.70. I waited for the order to arrive. I waited some more. Nothing. I had ordered a small owl that hoots when there is motion. I wanted that owl for the garden to keep the cats from coming to use my garden as a bathroom. And I waited some more and no parcel comes in. On August 17th I wrote a letter to the company asking about the holdup of my order, what happened to it?

About two weeks after I wrote that letter, my letter was returned to me with a yellow Post Office sticker on it saying: "Moved - address unknown." W H A T ? Moved and address unknown? What about my goods that I ordered three or four months ago. Will my money be returned? I came home and dug out the canceled cheque I had mailed to the company. The cheque had cleared the CIBC bank in Montreal on May 14th, just four days after I had sent in the order. On May 17th the same cheque cleared through the bank in Calgary and at the end of May I had my canceled cheque back with my bank statement. But where is my order?

Come Monday morning at 10:00 AM I was already standing in front of the CIBC bank in Lac La Biche waiting for the bank to open. When the bank opened I told them the problem that I had encountered and asked that my account be closed and another one opened. The bank was understanding and helped me with advice and they ordered me a new set of cheque books so that the old ones be thrown away.

Then I took the canceled cheque, letter and the catalogue and went to the post office to get some information about the company moving away and if they can trace it to the new address. They said they can't do anything. The postmaster took the yellow label of the envelope. Since I have been whitewashed I than walked across the street to the Lac La Biche Post newspaper to tell them to put information in the paper about this fraud that is on the loose. The man took the catalogue and typed in the name of the company on the computer, checks it out and says: "This company has over one thousand claims against them and they also have different names for that company." He said that one could get information on this company on the Internet under the title, "Rip Off." W H A T ? So now what? If the crooks cashed my cheque, they will also have my bank account number and that is not good. So what will happen if they get my account number and clear my bank account? I checked the bank statements and did not find any irregularities. Thank God for that so far, but what about the future? My bank account was canceled and a new one assigned, so that should be all right. My next stop was the RCMP. I explained what happened and the constable said, there is nothing they can do, unless the claim was over a $1000.00.

So that is how the smart people make a living. When all this happened and I learned that I will not see the $43.70 again I began to tell the people in each congregation after the church service during coffee time how I got ripped off, so they would watch that it not happen to them. I showed them the catalogue and the cheque and told all to be aware of the crooks. One man in Grassland congregation said that is how "smart people" make money. They set up a company with a post office box number. People order goods. They take the orders by opening the letters, taking out the money and cashing it. They throw the orders into the garbage. When they picked up a pile of money, they close the post office box, move to another town, start another company, open a new box number at the post office and wait for more money to come in. That is how they catch fish like me. I learned that if I need anything to buy, buy it at Zellers. When I told Marusia's nephew in Saskatoon what happened, he said if I get anymore such catalogues, just to cross off my name and mark on the envelope: "Return to sender." At the other end they will have to pay the return postage. This was not the first time that I had ordered something from such a catalogue and never had any problems until now, when - Eugene got caught in a scam trap.

The RCMP could not help me much either, but I had one other thing to do. I have to write to the Ontario Provincial Police in Hawkesbury, Ontario and let them know what happened. Later this matter was somewhat checked when it ended in a court case some nine years later.

On August 22nd was the time when I noticed there were no humming birds around anymore. In the summer they fought at the feeder and now haven't seen one for a while. It was also cold this day even though it was the middle of summer. Seemed like it would surely freeze overnight, for even the furnace kicked in because of the cold. Than come August 27th in the evening, a storm ripped through Lac La Biche at 6:30 PM. Wind, hail, thunder, rain, lightning, whatever you wanted the storm brought. In ten minutes of that storm, half an inch of rain came down. As soon as I saw the storm approaching and hail began to come down, I quickly lit the "Thunder Candle" and said a prayer. As soon as I finished the prayer the storm began to subside and only rain came down. All this in ten minutes of time.

The year 2004 saw more action in the church congregations. A year or two ago there was nothing only the regular service on Sundays and Holy Days. This year more action. Funerals, a few marriages, baptisms, memorial services and this made me somewhat busier now than in the past four years.

. There were other months with less activities, but there may be others with more church work. It was a summer of go, Go, GO. Had no time to think about such things as rest or holidays or to be bored.

This year I planted a different variety of potatoes - KENNEBEC. When I dug them up, I could not believe what I was digging out of the ground. I took a few larger potatoes to show around town. I had pictures taken at the Lac La Biche Post paper holding three potatoes. I had one weighed at the post office and it showed 1.4 kilograms, which is something like three pounds. You could make a lot of french fries from that one potato.

My dear and good friend Mr. Gout just loves me so. Only thing with this friend is that when he comes he does not know when to leave. I had severe attacks with gout during the year. Try and stay away from certain foods but still nothing seems to change or help. On October 9th and 10th the pain was so severe that I cried and could not move a step. Usually the pain is greater at night. Two days in a row the pain was so severe that I cried myself to sleep. If you ever had a toothache, gout pain is worse. The pain comes and is so painful that it makes you feel chilled, cooled and shivering inside the body.

Time does not wait but rolls along. October 16th brought white roofs in the morning when snow came overnight. This day I went to Cold Lake usually when I needed anything, I'd go to Zellers in Cold Lake which was the closest. There I also stopped in and saw Mike and Doreen Semeniuk (Marusia's nephew). I came home before dark and in the evening I get a call from George Semeniuk (Marusia's nephew) from Saskatoon that his brother Bill in Saskatoon is in the hospital. George himself was having problems with his heart, had surgery and now he himself is in and out of the hospital.

On October 18th I made a trip to Athabasca for a memorial service and it was what you could say good luck for that trip, because the following day we got dumped six inches of heavy wet snow. How the trip would have been in that kind of snow, I don't know. In the meantime my friend gout was still with me but he would give me some relief now and than until on the 26th of October he went into my left knee and that was even worse than in the big toe. At least when it's in the big toe, you can still walk somewhat, but the knee has to bent and turn and that is worst than terrible. I cried from pain and trying to do whatever came to my mind to get rid of that friend. I should call him my foe not friend, maybe he will get angry at me and leave me alone. Later I tried to drink as much water as I could handle to flush out the uric acid.

So it's that season once again when all kinds of classes and schools start. On November 1st I started the cantoring classes again in the Grassland-Sarrail area. The miserable weather had come and gone, changed to much more to my liking that on November 2nd I could sit on my deck and read the paper, while people with open air decks could not, but had to sit in the house. Every year Athabasca congregation has a fall supper. This year that took place on November 4th. But this day before I left for the supper, my right foot was starting to swell with pain. Oh yes, that foe did not forget me, so he thought he would go from the left to the right foot and I might accept him. No way. The pain was not getting less, but more, so on November 5th I went to the emergency. This afternoon it also started to rain. I have found out that gout is a form of arthritis and arthritis loves cool wet days, so now he will probably sit and wait with me till summer when it warms up.

DAY TO DAY LIFE GOES ON

November 8th and it is the last Feast Day of the year in the parish. The congregation of St. Demetrius in Craigend have their service and dinner to follow. Usually during the summer after the service a congregation goes outside and makes have the blessing of water, then three processions around the church. The first circle, the priest censes the church. The second time around, the priest blesses the church from all four sides with holy water. The third time the congregation stops on each side of the church and the priest reads a Gospel passage. After the service and dinner everyone went back to their homes and in the evening there was a memorial prayer service for Anne Lobay of Lac La Biche and the funeral the following day.

Recall back a few paragraphs about the thieves that stole $43.70 from me when I ordered goods from a mail order catalogue? Yes, when I returned from Craigend, I stopped for mail and a letter had arrived from the Competition Bureau wanting me to write and sign a complaint about the company. How did they get my name? Yes, when I had written a letter to the Ontario Provincial Police, they passed my letter over to the Competition Bureau. Will I be in more hot water just for notifying authorities of what had happened? We'll see what happens. I wrote a letter and send it to where I was asked to mail the complaint.

Every year the country celebrates Remembrance Day. Each year in Lac La Biche at the Cenotaph wreaths are laid in memory of the fallen service people. This year at one gathering the Lac La Biche and Craigend congregations decided that they should get a wreath and have it placed at the cenotaph. But who will do that? Oh yes, they know of a person, so they appointed me to do this. But it was terribly cold to stand near the lake and the breeze from the lake went through the clothing the skin and came out the other side, for the following day ice was already beginning to form on the lake and the day after the whole lake was a sheet of ice.

Since 2001 I have been canvassing for the Alberta Lung Association. On November 18th the association called from Edmonton asking if I could help them out again with the canvas in 2005 which would be from April 15th to May 2nd. I volunteered as I did other years. It is for a good cause, for they say: "When you can't breath, nothing else matters."

December 19th is St. Nicholas Church Holy Day. This day I went to church to Luzan. Have been there before for missionary services. Coming home from the service, I came through heavy rains and wind. I was listening to CHED radio and they were telling people that the winds in Edmonton were one hundred to one hundred and twenty five kilometers an hour. This wind was also in the area where I was coming home, but because there is more bush around this northern part of the province, the winds are not as noticeable. Even so it is still cold when you have such forceful winds blowing.

Everyone has been hearing about same sex marriages. What a shameful disgrace in the eyes of God. The Government of Canada is in favor of this demoralizing act of nonbelievers. They say they are believers in Christ. Where in the Bible or when on earth did Christ ever speak in favor of this? No where, but the opposite is true. Christ condemned this kind of behavior. Canada says it was built on Christian principles. Where in the Bible in Christianity can one find same sex marriage? No place, for there is no such thing. We know what happened to Sodom and Gomorrah. That will also happen to Canada. On December 27th I wrote a letter to the Prime Minister of Canada stating my objection to such a law. How many other people did the same thing. They talk about it with friends, but that is as far as it gets. They say same sex people are also people of God. Not in my book. Because nowhere in the Bible can I find such cases, but yet it speaks against such acts. Such acts are the work of the devil. Read the Bible from end to end and you will see for yourself.

And so another year has come and gone. And what has it brought and left me with. Left me with much gout pain. Left us with a cold, cold temperature. Left us with unforgettable memories from two and three years back. Left us with different kinds of work and activities. But all in all the year came and went and we are still here.

Time rolled along and I was planning and getting ready to take a trip to Saskatchewan in the middle of February to see sister Alice and husband John as well as Marusia's side of the family in Saskatoon. But the plans I had made and was looking forward to going did not materialize, because God had other plans and I had to be around because on February 12th there was a funeral in Sarrail. "We make plans and God changes them" as my late mother used to say. I was going to go to Saskatchewan because Father Michael was on holidays. When there were no church services in the Lac La Biche Parish I check the area where there was a service, so I went to Luzan again which is south of Willingdon about sixty miles south of Lac La Biche. So I did not go to Saskatchewan until February 15th and returned home on the 18th at 3:30 PM. I had gone all the way to Nipawin and brought home over one thousand dollars worth of beeswax candles for the congregations in the parish.

Than a Canadian tragedy hit us on March 3rd, 2005. When something like this happens and hits closer to home, than it is so much more painful. At Mayerthorpe, Alberta, about a good hundred plus miles west of Lac La Biche, a crazed man took the lives of four Royal Canadian Mounted Police officers. This was a shock not only to the town of Mayerthorpe, Alberta or Canada, but to the whole continent and probably the world. The police had gone to search the place for drug grow-up. It looks like the work shift was changing with four police officers when somehow the crazed man snuck into the place during the night and fired fatal shots killing the four constables. He also took his own life. The father of the crazed man later told on TV that "He is not my son and I don't even want to know him."

As the TV media and others told us there were ten thousand police officers from around the world attending this funeral service. The following day there were funeral services in the homes of the fallen Mounties. One of the fallen was a twin brother of a Mountie of the Johnston family from the Lac La Biche area. The funeral for Constable Johnston was held in Lac La Biche the following day in the largest church, the Evangelical Free Church with over two hundred police attending plus many, many hundreds of people. There were police from New York City and Border Patrol Officers plus many other places across North America.

On April 8th I received bad news from John that their son-in-law, Peter Onyshko passed away suddenly. Peter was a school teacher in Edmonton for a number of years and had problems with his marriage and also with liquor. He was only sixty years old. Prayers for him were held in Edmonton, but I could not attend, but I did go to Glendon, Alberta for the burial because the body was brought to Glendon. And boy, oh boy, was it cold that day. A cold north wind on the open cemetery with rain mixed with snow flurries made it colder than bone chilling. Over an inch of rain fell that day in the Glendon-Lac La Biche area.

Again it is that time of the year when families visit the graves of their loved ones and the priest blesses the graves. This year I leave on June 3rd for Wakaw. Tomorrow I will check and fix up things on Marusia's and her parents' graves. Sunday the service, blessing of the graves and I return back home 9:30 PM, still in broad daylight for in this northern country when June comes along you can still read the newspaper outside without lights at 11:00 PM if it is a clear day. The long daylight hours make the plants grow much faster. What I noticed was that Marusia's rose and mine also somehow revived and both were showing buds to bloom.

Like people, congregations and organizations have anniversaries. This year the Lac La Biche congregation is celebrating its fiftieth anniversary from the inception of the congregation. Much water has gone under the bridge since the beginning of the congregation and now was the time to celebrate the achievements. It was some time back that at one meeting it was decided to put up a large cross outside on the church yard. It was left up to Orest Bereska and myself to look after the design and construction of the cross. We both met a number of times to check, look and correct before the cross was constructed. Gladys Bereska was elected to prepare the program for the day and to make table centers. The official celebration and blessing of the cross took place on June 26th with many people from around the area attending. After the service, dinner was served in the

Heritage Senior Citizens Centre and a program followed. I had again been asked to be the MC for the program for the afternoon.

July is upon us and summer time is a time of festivals, parades, sports, etc. In the last few years I have been going to Vegreville to take a Ukrainian display for the Ukrainian Festival. This year again I was asked by the late Father Puk if I would bring my display to help the set up. I said that I would and early on the morning of July 1st at 7:00 AM I left home with my display in the car and headed out to Vegreville

My late mother had always told us since I can remember never to do any work on Holy Days Rest, pray and take it easy was her moto. There are a few Holy Days in the Orthodox Church during the summer that people should refrain from doing things on those days. Why? Because as our mother taught us, that the Saint whose Holy Day it is may send down thunder, send down hail to destroy crops, send down wind, etc., to damage people's property for not obeying God's Commandment that one ought not to do any work on the Sabbath. What is a Sabbath? It is not Saturday as some people believe, it means Holy Day and that includes the Christian Sunday. *"Remember the Sabbath day, to keep it holy. Six days thou shalt labor and do all thy work; but the seventh day is the Sabbath of thy Lord thy God: in it thou shalt not do any work, thou, nor thy son, nor thy daughter, thy manservant, nor thy maidservant, nor thy cattle, nor thy stranger that is within thy gates. For in six days the Lord made heaven and earth, the sea, and all that in them is, and rested the seventh day: wherefore the Lord blessed the Sabbath day, and hallowed it."* (Exodus 20:8-11)

In the evening July 19th at about 7:00 PM I was watering the flowers at the back of the house and the two apple trees that I had. All of a sudden from someplace a wasp came and attacked me - stung me. I dropped the hose and hurried to the house. I went to the old recipe my mother had taught us. We had bees on the farm during the ration years in Canada in the 1940's and did not need to buy sugar which was rationed, for we had our own honey. When a bee would sting us, mother would grab a stainless steel knife and place it over the bee sting. The pain would be lessened as would the swelling. Till today I don't know what and how it works, but it worked for me each time I pulled out the wasp sting and applied the stainless steel knife. The pain and swelling were not as bad as they otherwise could have been. I made nothing of that sting, because bee and wasp stings can occur many times in the summer time.

Again a few days later the same thing. Two wasps stung me this evening. I repeated what I had done to the first sting a day earlier. In my head it started turning the idea: There must be a wasp nest someplace that I can't see it. This time I had to check out where the nest was. I left the watering, the hose and from far started to look at the apple trees from different angles. AHHHH, there you are. I found you. A wasp nest on one branch of the apple tree among the leaves that one could not see it. The nest was just a little smaller than a gallon size pail or container. I could also see two guards sitting near the entrance to the nest. Well you, guys, you have to wait until it gets dark, than I will come to visit you. When it's daylight you make war with me and when it gets dark I'll make war with you. Because in July the sun does not set till late, I had to wait until dusk fell. When it was dark enough, I took a plastic shopping bag and went outside. Slowly without moving or disturbing the apple tree, I got the plastic bag over nest and quickly shut the top with the nest in the bag. Any guards or fighters there are, they will stay in the bag with the nest. I squashed the bag until I was sure there was nothing moving in it and threw it beside the deck. Tomorrow it will go into the garbage bin.

UNEXPECTED EVENT AT A CHURCH SERVICE

On July 12th is St. Peter and Paul Holy Day, two of great Apostles of Christ. I wanted to go to a church service, but all priests were in Winnipeg attending the Church Sobor(convention). I looked at church schedules of surrounding priests and saw that Father Benny Ambroise had a service at Andrew and he had said once before that he was not going to the Sobor. I knew from previously seeing the late Father Jaroslaw Puk at the Ukrainian Festival in Vegreville, that he would be having a service at Nova Bukovina a few miles south east of Glendon because he was not going to go to the Sobor either. I got dressed and headed out south still not knowing where I was going. When I neared the junction of highway #55 and #36 twelve miles south of Lac La Biche, I slowed down not knowing where to go, but at the last minute, I turned to go to Nova Bukovina because in the 1960's I served that Bonnyville-Glendon Parish.

I turned left and headed out east. I came to Glendon, but not knowing where to turn after I passed Glendon going south, I took a chance and turned left on a country road. I remembered that I had to go east and then at the next crossroad I turned right, and sure enough here is the big gully or ravine and the church is on the other side. I came and parked where there were a few cars. I went into the church, said my prayers and sat at the back. Not long after, the late Father Jaroslaw Puk and Dobrodeyka arrived. Since there was no cantor, someone came and asked me to be the cantor. I had to get out books and find what was what as to the service for that day. Now everything is at hand. The late Father Jaroslaw was now vested and the service ready to start. The service started and everything went well. Great Litany, small Litanies, Lesser Entrance, Epistle, Gospel, sermon, Great Entrance, other Litanies, The Creed, Lord's Prayer. Where I was standing I could not see the late Father Jaroslaw because I had part of the Ikonostas between us. Dobrodeyka was standing behind me and more to the left and she could see the late Father Jaroslaw at the Altar.

After the Lord's Prayer and before the Communion, I could hear Father Jaroslaw's voice was different as if he was slurring. A moment later the two men that were helping Father Jaroslaw in the Sanctuary rushed towards him from both sides. I knew something was wrong so I rushed to the Sanctuary to see the two men holding up Father Jaroslaw and were asking to get a chair to put him on it. The congregation was on edge. What happened? Did Father get a stroke, a heart attack? Someone asked if anyone had a phone and asked that they call the ambulance. In the meantime Father seemed to have been somewhat revived that he was now sitting. After the excitement settled down somewhat, Father Jaroslaw kept saying that he is okay and wants to have Communion. How is he going to have Communion holding the chalice in his hand when he can't even stand up? I kept telling him not to have Communion, but he insisted. What else could one do? He began to take the chalice, but I supported the chalice from the bottom, so that if anything, I could hold on to it so that it would not fall on the Altar or the floor.

Just a question: What would or should happen if a drop from the chalice, or the whole chalice should be accidently dropped and spilled? Yes there are rules and regulations for that too, but how many people know what to do, God forbid for it ever to happen? Because the Orthodox Church treats religiosity seriously, therefore serious consequences could follow after such a catastrophe. Should a drop or contents fall on anyone's clothing or on the floor, the place where the drop fell it is to be cut out, burned and the ashes buried outside the church on the side where the Altar is. We recognize that the Blood of Christ must be respected and everything to be taken seriously about it. If the chalice by chance was spilled before the bread and wine were Body and Blood of Christ, no problem, the material can be washed and reused - B U T when the elements are all ready consecrated, that is another serious and different matter. That is why usually two people hold a piece of red (or other color) material when someone is receiving communion, so that should a drop fall it will fall on the "eleton" the red cloth. That cloth is never washed, but it too is be disposed off by burning it and digging the ashes into the ground against the church foundation on the side where the Altar is.

Than father turns to me and says, you help me finish the service. I said no, but he said I have to help him. I did what he asked and after the service he said he wants to have the blessing of the water. We brought the chair into the middle of the church in front of the service table and sitting on the chair he began the service and asked that I help him to read some parts of the service. During this time the ambulance was on the way coming to the church. Before the finishing of the blessing of the water the ambulance arrived, but Father Jaroslaw insisted that he is not going with the ambulance and that I finish the last page or two of the water blessing. People began to tell Father to go with the ambulance to the hospital and when Dobrodeyka said that he should go and get checked out, he said he would go. The paramedics put Father on the stretcher after he was helped to remove the vestments and they took him to the ambulance. Dobrodeyka said she would take the car and follow the ambulance, but we told her to go with the ambulance and someone will bring the car for them to Bonnyville to the hospital.

The ambulance left and the people came to have a drink of water and than all went to the hall for dinner somewhat shaken with the incident that happened a few moments earlier. I was asked to say grace at the dinner which was more like a banquet, and at the end I was called upon to say a few words. Having finished dinner people began to disperse to their homes or wherever. I also started to drive for home. Having driven half a mile north of Glendon and before turning left for home, something kept telling me to go east to Bonnyville and see what is happening there at the hospital. I turned and went to Bonnyville.

I arrived at the hospital and went in. I asked the receptionist to see Father Jaroslaw, but the she said no visitors. I knew that eventually I would see what is what. As I was sitting and waiting, Dobrodeyka came out of the emergency room. We met and she said to come and see Father, but I said the receptionist told me no visitors. Dobrodeyka says: "It's okay, I'll tell them you are my brother." We started towards the room again and a nurse said we can go in. Father was dressed laying on the bed. We started to talk and Father said he still hadn't heard anything what was wrong. Than a woman doctor came in. She began to tell us that they can't find anything wrong, except that Father is a diabetic. Another doctor came in and than began to tell Father what is what. He said that his blood sugar had dropped drastically and because of that he was passing out. He asked Father what he had for breakfast that morning and Father told him he does not eat breakfast before the service. The doctor looked at him and than says: "From today you will always eat breakfast, every day and you can't skip it because you are a diabetic and you must have breakfast every day." The doctor said that Father can go home, after giving him a prescription. So now I can drive them both back to where the church is and they can pick up their car.

Just as we were walking past the receptionist the phone rang and she says that it's for Father Puk. People from the hall were calling to inquire if they can come and bring the car for them to Bonnyville. I told Father to tell them that I am going to bring them back to the church. We left the hospital but had to stop across the street at a drug store to pick up a prescription for Father. While traveling back to the church which was about twenty some miles west of Bonnyville, I mentioned to Father that we have to call another priest to come and consume what is in the chalice. When we got to the church Father said he wanted coffee, but he said that he will first consume the Holy Gifts in the chalice. We went to the church while a few people in the hall put on the water to boil for coffee. Father consumed the Holy Gifts and than we walked to the hall for coffee. After they drank their coffee, everyone was ready for home. Father said he was going to drive home, but we said that Dobrodeyka should drive. He insisted that he was okay and he would drive home to Vegreville. A man who was from Edmonton whispered to me that let Father drive and he will follow behind, because he is going that way anyway. That is what happened this day at Nova Bukovina.

Some time ago I had received an invitation to attend a fiftieth wedding anniversary for Morris and Shirley Buchy in Kelowna on July 16th. I have known this family and their parents from the time I was serving at Dauphin, Manitoba. Because there was no service anywhere during that time because of the Sobor in Winnipeg, I made plans to attend. I left for Kelowna on July 14th and stayed with Alex and Sylvia Korzeniowski in Peachland. Following the anniversary I left early on the 17th and stopped in to see Joe and Marlene Korzeniowski on the west side of Vernon and Okanagan Lake. I spent a few hours and than left for home stopping in Vernon at Mike's Fruit Stand to get some fresh fruit. Having bought what I needed, I left and stopped at Red Deer, Alberta for the night. Next morning I was up and arrived home at 1:00 PM. This day I still preserved fourteen quarts of cherries.

The summer is rushing by. Chores in and around the house and the garden keep me busy. Gout comes and stays for a while and than leaves. Than on August 4th I had to make a trip to Edmonton to get some ink and paper for the computer. After I had done my business I stopped to see John and late Kay and left for home. Later that evening when I called John to tell him that I was home and the trip was okay, John told me that at 4:00 PM he was taken to emergency because he felt dizzy and nauseated. Whatever had happened I don't know to this day. Maybe he had an attack of the gall bladder because of something he ate?

When we had bought the house in Lac La Biche, later we had the deck constructed. But every time it rained we had a problem that water was coming down between the eaves troughs and the roof. Why? I don't know. Finally I had enough of this water dripping when it rains. I had the man come and do the eaves trough on the deck and south side of the house. The man said that whoever did the eaves troughs, did them wrong. After this was repaired, there was no more dripping between the roof and the eaves trough. This work was done on August 9th. The following morning the temperature in Lac La Biche was only 4.5 C, pretty cool for this time of the year.

My foe, gout returned again and with pain being as severe as it was, I knew I had to do something. Yes I had medication for gout, but some pills may bring more harm to a person than the pain itself. One kind of pill has side effects on the kidney. Another pill destroys red corpuscles and a third causes damage to the bones. So which in the lesser evil of all? I would rather have pain than damage to parts of the body. So I started to look on the Internet about gout and found more than I thought there would be. I found one firm of herbal pills and I ordered them. I used these pills for nearly a year, but when nothing helped I did not reorder them anymore. The following night I went to bed at regular time, but did not fall asleep until 3:00 AM because of the pain when I finally cried myself to sleep.

JOYCE

What God does, He does in wondrous ways. It was sometimes in September that I got a call from a lady. I answered the phone and she asks: "Is that Reverend Stefaniuk?" I said I was and she asks: "Do you still translate letters from Ukrainian into English?" I said I do if I can read the writing. She said she would bring me a letter from Ukraine to translate. She told me when she would come, but somehow I had gone to town to get the mail or something and when she came I was not home. I did find her letter stuck in the doorway with a phone number on it to call back when I did the translation. I translated the letter and when it was finished I called the number. It was not a Lac La Biche number, it was from Plamondon, some twenty miles west of Lac La Biche. The lady answered and said she would be in Lac La Biche on a certain day and would stop in to pick up the letter. When the lady came, I did not think that I had seen her before, but I had. When Marusia was still living, this lady and her late husband had come in the spring of 2001 to have a letter translated.

Anyway when she came she said that she had been to see us before with the same petition. She asked where my wife was, and I told her she had passed away just about four years ago. She was stunned and surprised for she said she never heard of it. Then she told me that her husband had passed away that spring. We started talking and as they say: "The farther into the bush, the more wood there is." One thing lead to the next and I learned that Father John Lipinski buried her husband Bill Babenek at Elk Point, Alberta that spring.

I learned that she and her husband had lived at Fort McMurray and they attended the Orthodox church there. They later moved to the Plamondon area and went to church at Elk Point some one hundred and twenty miles south of Plamondon, because that is where her husband was born and came from. Also I discovered that her husband had visited his family in Ukraine and she would like to go see and visit his family there. We talked about Ukraine and I gave her two videos of Ukraine to take home and look at them and she can bring them back when she is in town sometime later.

Time went by and I never heard or saw Joyce until one day about a month later she called if I would be home and she would bring me the videos back. She came the following day and I made some tea and we sat at the table and talked about different things. Before she left I gave her two other videos about the Orthodox Church so that she could look at them and be more acquainted with the Orthodox Faith. I told her that there are churches closer than at Elk Point and she could attend one of these. She thought Grassland congregation would be the closest for her. After saying good byes, she left for home.

About six or eight weeks later Joyce called again and said she would bring me the videos back. When she arrived, I made some tea and we sat and chatted about the videos and other things. She asked about grave markers and how long it takes to get them installed, etc. Maybe a week or two later I called Joyce and said that there was a church service in Lac La Biche the coming Sunday. She said she would not come there because she did not know anyone and she would rather go to Grassland because it was somewhat closer for her from Plamondon.

DAY TO DAY ACTIVITIES CARRIED ON

For the last fifty years John and Alice had remembered their anniversary was always on October 15th. Their daughters wanted to make them a fiftieth wedding anniversary on the 15th, but the halls were booked so they had to set the celebration for October 22nd. I left October 20th going to Saskatoon to visit some of Marusia's family and especially her nephew George Semeniuk who was not feeling well at all. On the 21st I went to Wakaw hoping that I would be able to help the girls get things ready, but when I arrived there, they had everything under control, planned and ready for next day's celebration. One of the daughters, Carolyn, was not feeling well and after the party which ended early, Carolyn was rushed to Saskatoon to emergency to see what was wrong. I never did learn what really the problem was.

The year is rushing to the end but before that on November 2nd I had one of the bad days. I guess everybody has those from time to time. It seemed that everything I did or touched this day it went wrong. I have met people who also told of the same thing, that no matter how or what, they had problems all day long. The following day I canned pears and tomatoes and in the evening drove to Boyle to attend a parish meeting.

On November 6th Vegreville was having a special celebration. The congregation of St. Volodymyr was having the blessing of their Ikonostas. I received an invitation to attend, because Archbishop John will be there and me being a member of the Order of St. Andrew, along with other members from Vegreville we formed the honor guard for His Eminence Archbishop John. Next day we woke up to a quarter of an inch or less of snow and on November 8th the last congregation in the parish at Craigend celebrated their Feast Day, St. Demetrius.

As mentioned earlier I had gone to Saskatoon to visit Marusia's nephews and nieces on October 21. On November 10th I received the bad news that George Semeniuk passed away. Now I get ready to go to the funeral which was held on November 14th in Saskatoon. At the same time I again saw Marusia's relatives and saw that George's brother Bill was not very well and he said that he did not feel well.

Like people when they get older, they wear out and the same with everything else. I had bought a printer for the computer and had been using it for a number of years and I did a lot of printing books for the congregations for different services, etc. On December 8th the old printer told me it had enough of me and said it would not help me anymore. I picked it up and took it to be repaired. It would cost $120.00 to repair it. WOW. That much to repair? Yes you can buy a printer for $49.00, but than you are charged an arm and a leg for the ink. So hearing about the cost of repairing the old printer, I purchased a new one for $189.00. This one was better. It had four color cartridges compared to the old one that had only two.

December 13th is St. Andrew's Holy Day. This day the service was in Lac La Biche. After the service I left for Vegreville because there will be a service around 5:00 PM and than members of the Order of St. Andrew get together. This day also had a small winter storm with some blowing snow. I was afraid that when I get into the open prairie closer to Vegreville the storm may be really bad, but it was not because the winds this day were not as fierce as some other storms are. The trip coming back was tougher for it was night time, but I made it home just fine.

During this time Joyce and I would call each other once in a while to see what is new in each of our worlds. It was luck in one way, because we would be on the telephone at times for an hour at a time, and luck because it was not long distance calling. Joyce had mentioned a number of times that she will be going to Fort McMurray to spend Christmas with her son Robert and his wife Kim and their two daughters Erin and Ashley. I kept thinking at times how that trip would be, because too many times the road there was not in the best of shape for winter driving and than big heavy trucks are always on the highway accidents happen on that stretch of highway..

On December 28th I received more bad news from Saskatoon. On November 10th George Semeniuk had passed away. This time Bill Semeniuk, George's brother passed away on December 28th just over a month with two family members, brothers, gone to the other world. So now I make another trip to Saskatoon to attend the funeral that was held on December 31st. Hopefully that this past year now has ended on this sad note and maybe we can look forward to better things in the New Year just ahead of us.

When I returned from Saskatoon, I called Joyce on January 1st to ask how her trip was to Fort McMurray. She said the road was good and she was happy to be with her family. I asked her what she was doing and she said it was a sad day for no one had called her and this was New Years Day and she had no one to talk to. I told her that if she wants I can drive out and talk with her to make her day happier. I asked for directions how and where to get to her place and told her that I could be there at 1:00 PM. Where she lived it was a beautiful scene. She lived on the west side of lac la Biche lake and you could see the lake all the way to the east end. She lived on three acres of land and her son had a summer cottage next to her property also on three acres. I stayed till about 3:30 PM and left for home after we had some tea.

On the 3rd of January I was doing something in the back room of the house. Later that morning I glanced out the front window and saw a large collie dog lying in the driveway of the neighbor across the street. It was a black and white large collie dog. Was the dog hit by a car and than dragged itself up the driveway? The neighbor across the street was at St. Paul for the Christmas school break, so he was not around to see what was happening. About an hour later, I glanced again and saw the same dog still lying there. So what can I do now? Call the town or the police to go and investigate the situation. I called the police and they said to call the town and the dog control people would have to look at that. I called the town and told them what I was seeing from the window of my house. After I called, I sat in the front room, turned towards the front window and reading, keeping one eye open on the dog next door and reading the paper with the other.

The funny part was the dog had not moved at all after having sat their for a few hours, but I thought that surely the dog must have a broken back or something that he hasn't moved and is lying in the same place and position all this while. Some time later two town crew men arrived. They stopped in front of the house and both talked to each other and than slowly one began to move towards the dog on the long driveway towards the back of the house. I could see the man walk slowly and keeping an eye on the dog. Than he stopped and said something to the man by the truck, he turned around and came back to the vehicle. What was it? It was a large **toy** collie dog that some child must have taken and left it there. It was embarrassing, but yet if it had been a live dog the man would surely have needed help, but I took it upon myself to let someone know. I did not know if the dog was alive and friendly, so I was afraid to go since I was not prepared to handle a hurt dog if that is what it was.

Nativity of Christ came and for three days of January 7th to 9th services were held in three different congregations: Athabasca, Grassland and Boyle. During this period of time a sad time hit the congregation in Lac La Biche. Julia Homeniuk who was the main soprano singer in the church passed away. It was sad for the family and church members to go with this sadness during this period of time. The funeral for Julia was held in Lac La Biche on January 10th and the body was taken some sixty miles south of Lac La Biche to Wasil for burial near the Saskatchewan River.

On January 11th I took another trip to Plamondon to visit Joyce. Joyce had a large black Labrador dog named Cleopatra. Each day about 1:00 PM Joyce would go with the dog for a walk along the frozen lake even though the dog was free and ran loosely on the six acres of open field, still the dog liked to run on the open frozen lake. I drove out and together with the dog, Joyce and I, we walked about a mile and than a mile return trip. Returning back to the house, we had some tea and I left to be home before dark.

It was on January 8th that Joyce drove to church in Grassland. She felt more comfortable to go there than in Lac La Biche, because she knew a few people in Grassland. At the service she had a surprise, because there was a family she knew that also came to church to Grassland but lived in Plamondon. During the service no one said anything and only one person had approached her to ask where she was from and who she was. Isn't this a problem in many, many churches? When some new person walks into a church for service, how many parishioners would show concern to a new person in church? And then people wonder why the church is not growing and less parishioners each year.

On January 20th is John's birthday. As mentioned earlier we would go visit each other on our birthdays a day or two sooner or later or on the day of the birthday. I could not go to Edmonton on the 20th, so I called John that I would come the following day. I had mentioned to Joyce that I was going to Edmonton and asked if she would like to come or needs anything from Edmonton. She said she would go for the ride and get some sewing material that she needed. So on January 21st I leave in the morning, picked Joyce up and we go get some ink for the printer and Joyce got her material. Following that we went to see John and late Kay. They were surprised and they were happy.

Some time earlier Joyce had called and said that her brother Marvin and wife Pat from Fort McMurray were coming to Edmonton and would stop in to see her. She asked me to come for supper. I came that day for the time she said and we sat and waited, and than finally she got a call that her brother would not be coming, because something came up and they would not be able to come. We had supper together and I left for home.

BETROTHAL (ENGAGEMENT)
JOYCE AND ME

Joyce and I had now been acquainted with each other since September. One day talking on the phone Joyce says: You know maybe we should get together and get married. She said we have two differnt residences and if were married we would have only one house and one house expenxes and cost. We began to talk on the phone and make plans how and what. We decided to go and see Father Michael Domaradz in Athabasca about having a betrothal (engagement) service in one of the congregations after a Sunday service. We drove to Athabasca and talked with Father Michael and Dobrodeyka coming to the conclusion that we be betrothed at Craigend this coming Sunday on January 29th. We asked Father and Dobrodeyka not to tell anyone anything until after the betrothal service. After we visited Father Michael, I brought Joyce back home to Plamondon and I went home.

    Now that we have taken these steps and life is beginning to change faster than I can dream, I called Royal LePage in Lac La Biche if they could come and give me an estimate value on my house, since sooner or later I will sell the house and move to the farm where Joyce is living. Tracey Thompson and her father, Roy Worthington came to the house and looked at everything and took down information and said they would let me know when they have the figures worked out.

Having made these arrangements and getting ready for the betrothal service, we needed rings. So on January 26th we make another trip to Edmonton to buy rings for this coming Sunday. We purchased the rings and shopped for other things we needed and also stopped in to see John and late Kay. They were surprised and very happy what we told them about the upcoming betrothal service on January 29th.

On January 27th, Royal LePage called and asked me to come to their office for they have an estimate on the house. Joyce had come to town for some things that day and I asked her to meet me at the Royal LePage office so that both of us can hear the news. The news was more than I expected. Marusia and I had bought the house in 1999 for $110.000.00. The estimate of the house now was $239,000.00. That is $129,000.00 increase in just seven years. That is how much the house prices have gone up in Lac La Biche in the last few years. When Joyce and I were with Royal LePage, we also looked at some houses for sale at Osoyoos, British Columbia. Now let me tell you why we were interested in Osoyoos.

It was sometimes the first or second weekend of August (before Joyce had come with the letter to translate) that she with her two sons was in Osoyoos. Her son Robert from Fort McMurray had some property in Osoyoos and was planning to move his construction company from Fort McMurray to Osoyoos. Joyce's other son Kevin from Ontario was participating in Penticton's Iron Man Marathon. Joyce being alone at that time for having lost her husband, also at that time bought some property in a seniors compound in Osoyoos where she would have a house built like other condo owners. After she had purchased the property, she was getting mail from the Condo Association as to the progress of the condo community. What she was reading in the minutes, she saw that there was a lot of dissatisfaction, confusion and things not in harmony. After we had met, it was in the spring in March that her son called from Fort McMurray and told her to take a trip to Osoyoos and see what is happening with the condo community. Later this will be explained what happened. But now since we were in the process of being betrothed and later married, we were planning to move to Osoyoos and build a house on the property that Joyce owned supposedly in a year or two.

Now being at the Royal LePage office we told them that we were planning to move to Osoyoos and would need a house there. They pulled out on the Internet the houses that were for sale in Osoyoos and we looked at a few of them. There was a house that we fell in love with, but since we were miles away from seeing the real thing, we were also deciding that we should go and see for our self what there is. We made a trip to the Okanagan, but this will be told later what transpired.

When we were at the Royal LePage office and received the news of the value of my house, I was going to go home and think about what next to do. As we got up to leave, the realtor asked if I would like to list the house for sale and if so they would like me to list it with them. I thought for a second and then say: "Well do you have a buyer for my house?" The father and daughter Realtors both answered saying: "Yes we do." What? I can have the house sold without any advertising? Why not sell it if there is a buyer. There and then I had the realtor fill out the forms to sell the house. I signed the papers. Now what? Things moved pretty quick. There were three showings of my house on January 28th and I had an offer for $230,000.00. This was on January 28th.

Next morning January 29th I called Bill and Sonia Balaban and asked her to bring a camera to church for the service. They wanted to know why and I said that she will want to take some pictures. After the Liturgy service, the betrothal service for Joyce and me took place. There was shock in the church. Some people did not know what was happening. Some later said that we were married. Some were in tears for they had met Joyce before in Lac La Biche in stores and other businesses.

On January 30th I had the cantoring course at Grassland. This evening we were meeting at Bill and Olga Sworin's place. I asked Joyce to come also. I traveled just three or four miles past her place, so it was just not that much to turn of the highway and pick her up. When we came to Sworin's, Bill and Olga were surprised and shocked to see us. When the rest of the people arrived for the singing, than we made an announcement what had happened. They had not heard of what happened in Craigend after the church service, so they were somewhat shocked and surprised.

On February 3rd Joyce picked me up at home and we drove to Bonnyville to see the doctor with whom she had an appointment for her knee surgery to take place on February 7th. When we returned home I had a call from Royal LePage on the caller ID. I called the office and they said they had an offer of $234,500.00 for the house. I accepted the offer and the realtor came to the house to have me sign the papers.

Again on February 7th Joyce and I were in Bonnyville for she had surgery on her knee scheduled before noon that day. While she was in surgery I sat and waited until she would be ready to go home, because the doctor had said she would be able to go home the same day after surgery. It was in the late, late afternoon when dusk had fallen when she would be able to leave the hospital. She was moved by wheelchair to the van and was placed in the rear seat where she lay all the way home. Today she says that she does not remember being taken to the van. As we drove along in the dark of night I would say that we are at LaCorey, or Iron River, or Craigend, etc. We got home and I helped her out of the van and with crutches in her hands I was helping her up the steps to the house. On the last step, she somehow stumbled and lost her balance and both of us fell on the steps and than I had to help get her back up and into the house.

On February 16th Joyce had an appointment with the doctor in Lac La Biche to check the healing process of her knee. On this same day I also made an appointment to see Doctor De Ritter to have my prescriptions refilled. We both saw the same doctor at the same time. Following the morning appointment we left for Vegreville. The congregation in Grassland had an icon that the late Father Lawrence Kubin had painted when he served the parish here. The congregation wanted the icon to be somewhat redone, so we took the icon from the church in Grassland after the service on February 15th, and took the icon to Vegreville because Dobrodeyka Maximuk wrote icons and she said she would restore the icon.

During the rest of the time, I was at home packing and cleaning out the house. Joyce by this time towards the end of February was well enough with the knee that she could get along herself and drive to Plamondon a few miles to get what she needed, mail, groceries, pay bills, etc. I still went and held cantoring classes when Mondays rolled around. Later when Joyce was more mobile I would pick her up and she would come to the classes also.

Now the Fast-lenten period had come starting on March 6th. This evening the service of the Great Cannon by Andrew of Crete was held in Grassland and than the following night again in Grassland. On Wednesday this service was held at Athabasca and on Thursday at Boyle. Thursday was not a very good day for traveling. We were going to Boyle and I gave Joyce the keys so she could drive. About eight or nine miles north of Boyle as we traveled in the dark, we could see that something was wrong. We came to were the highway went through a swamp area and slowed down when we saw a vehicle in the ditch. An SUV vehicle traveling at a high speed ahead of us stepped on the brakes to slow down and before the driver could count to two he was sliding across the highway, into the ditch, the wire fence and landed in the spruce trees. Joyce had slowed down and we were okay on the icy road. There was also another car in the ditch. After the service I drove home but taking the road from Boyle to Caslan, than north to Plamondon. Here the roads were not as icy, but there was more fresh snow on the road.

Now that our plans were beginning to come together we knew that two households had a lot of things. Everything was doubled up. Three bedroom furniture in one house and three in the other. Dishes, bed sheeting, towels, smaller kitchen appliances, etc., was going to take up space, so where do we put all this? We need a garage sale, but in the winter time in -20 or -30 C weather? We decided that we would need to store some of the things in storage. Joyce had earlier called the Atlas Van Lines in Cold Lake and they said they would store our things there until we were ready to move to British Columbia. In the meantime I was moving all my things from Lac La Biche to the farm north of Plamondon to Joyce's place and stored my things in the garage attached to the house. Joyce also has a lot of carpentry tools and machines; lath, planner, saws, drills, etc. When all my things were moved to Plamondon, the moving people from Cold Lake came with a truck, loaded all of the carpentry machines and some of my things and took them for storage.

Than came some sad news. My cousins husband Stan Malchuk passed away in Dauphin. So now we need a few days to go there and back. We leave on March 27th for Dauphin. We stop at Wakaw for the night and Joyce had the opportunity at this time to meet my sister Alice and her husband John. Next morning we left for Dauphin, but had called Andrew and Lena Anthony in Yorkton that we would stop for lunch at their place. They were very happy to see us and we had lunch with them and we left for Dauphin for the prayers are on the 28th in the evening. John and late Kay and Oksana also came to the funeral. Alice and John could not come because they had some people coming to do something for their new house that they had purchased. The funeral was on March 29th in a full packed Ukrainian Catholic Church. Stan had sang in the Dauphin Ukrainian Festival Choir and was involved with the Ukrainian Festival. He also made thirty six sets of "Tsymbaly" - Dulcimers, so he was well known in the long time that Helen and he had resided in Dauphin.

After the funeral we had to rush right back home, because the people are taking possession of my house on the 30th of March. The house had been empty by now, with the exception of the last few things that I had left to the end to use for making tea, some rags for cleaning, some clothing, etc. This was loaded into the van and taken to Plamondon with the rest of the things.

During the weeks that sailed by, Joyce was receiving updates and minutes of condo meetings in Osoyoos. As they say: "The farther you go into the bush, the more wood there is." Each time she received the minutes the more baffled she was with what was happening. Finally her son Robert in Fort McMurray tells her to get on a plane go to Osoyoos and find out what is happening. Robert made the plane arrangements and on April 3rd we flew to Kelowna airport. We arrived in Kelowna, rented a car, a 2006 Ford Taurus, and drove to Osoyoos. We arrived at noon, had something to eat and than went to see the condo place. There was a lady walking in the condo complex. We stopped and Joyce talked to her. The lady said, had they known at the time they bought the place, what they know now, they would not have settled there to retire. Than someone else came along the way and told something different and finally Joyce stopped at the treasurers place to pay for her monthly condo fees on the land.

HOUSE HUNTING IN OSOYOOS

From there we went to see the realtor in Osoyoos and Joyce told them to put up the condo lot for sale. At the same time we said that we would like to see some information on houses for sale in Osoyoos. They said they would drive us and show us a few houses in the price range we were looking for. First they took us to a brand new house that was not even completed and it would be ready in another two weeks to move in. We fell in love with that brand new house and wanted to buy it, but there was one thing holding us from purchasing it. Behind that house stood a mountain wall of rock about seventy five feet high with houses at the top. What if some of the rock hanging there should happen to break off? Would it end up under the table in the kitchen or on the bed in the bedroom? We learned that to put a retaining wall the cost started at $18.00 a square foot and we figured that would set us back most likely another $100,000.00. We decided to by pass the beautiful new house. As this is written in January 2014 that house had been sold before and it had been on the "For Sale" block again. I guess no one wants to look at a rock wall at the back of the house.

Having left that house we were shown another house. Something was not to our liking so we went farther on. We looked at a few houses and finally we stopped at the one on, 12101 Pinehurst Place and just a stones throw from the golf course, or as we could say, across the street. The price of the house $420,000.00. This house has a three car garage. A two car for vehicles and the third is a work room for carpentry. When Joyce saw this house, she said she is not going any farther to look at houses because this house has a work shop, exactly what she wants. We looked at the house inside and out. The only thing we saw was that the roof looked like it could use new shingles, but with time that will probably be done and it was. The house has three bedrooms, room for an office, three bathrooms, living and formal dining room upstairs with an eating area beside the kitchen, a family room in the basement and a large area for her sewing room.

Joyce needs a large area for sewing. She has as much sewing material and fabric in the house as Fabricland have in their store. Joyce also has five sewing and embroidery machines and she did much sewing as a volunteer for the Royal Alexandra Hospital in Edmonton. She also sews customs for her grandchildren for figure skating or other activities. She donates all her labor and material and not charging anyone for anything. All volunteer work. She belongs to a club in the U.S.A. who send out greetings, best wishes and sympathy to people around North America and this also is volunteer work for buying paper, envelope, ink, stamps, your time, etc.

After we saw the house and it looked adequate for us, we went to the Realtors office to write up the purchase contract and sign it. Possession day would be July 4th. Today is April 3rd when we purchased the house. That gives us exactly three months time to pack, sell Joyce's house in Plamondon and move to Osoyoos. Things were happening so fast that we could not believe how it all occurred. Anyway after signing the purchase agreement we had time to drive around and look at the house a second time. Next day we once again went to see the house on our own to find out what we would need to bring from Alberta. The owner was home so he told us a few things how things work. Like for instance, there is a water softener in the house, and the town gets underground water which it is hard. The salt we have to use in the softeners is Potassium Chloride and not Sodium Chloride. Why? Because the west side of the town where we bought the house there is a golf course. The water collected from sewage is treated and than used for watering the golf course. If Sodium Chloride were used the salt would kill the grass on the golf course and people don't want that to happen to the fourteenth best golf course in Canada. I could not believe that of the thousands of golf courses in Canada this one where we live only a block away is the fourteenth best in Canada as we were told at that time.

We returned back home on April 5th. Next morning Joyce called the paper in Fort McMurray and put an ad in the paper that she has a house for sale in Plamondon with property going to the lake - waterfront. We also made a sign and put it up at the entrance to the yard, hopefully that someone will be interested and will buy it.

After a few days when there was no reaction from buyers about the ad in the paper, she called the Realtor in Lac La Biche and they listed her house to sell. It was after their sign came up, that a man from the area stepped in one day to inquire about the house. We told him that he has to go to the Realtor and deal through them. He was not very reactive to deal with the Realtor. We told him that if he did not want to deal with the realtor, he should have stepped in and bought the property privately when it was for sale before it went to the Realtor. It was less than a month on April 27th Joyce sold her house for $420,000.00 the same amount that a house in Osoyoos was purchased for.

Now that we sold our houses we both became "homeless." Neither one of us had a house. Byers were already living in my house in Lac La Biche, and in Plamondon the house is sold and belongs to the new people and we are just living in it until he takes possession. But now the packing and the moving has to take place as well as our marriage which we had planned for May 28th in Lac La Biche. We made our own invitations and mailed out twenty one invitations to farther away relatives and friends on May 1st, giving people a months notice and time to make their plans to come and attend. But now problems started. We had talked with Father Michael Domaradz about our marriage plans and told him of the date and he said that the marriage would be after a service. We would come to confession and communion in Lac La Biche, be at the service and than get married and have a small reception someplace in town

PRE-MARRIAGE PROBLEM

Everything was going well until the service at Craigend on May 7th. After the service everyone gathered at the Craigend Hall for coffee. During the lunch, Joyce went to get some coffee for herself and Father Michael went to fill his cup also. There by the coffee pot, Father Michael tells Joyce that he can't marry us. Joyce comes back somewhat disappointed and tells me not to make any announcements. I was going to announce to the people of our up coming marriage and that all are invited to attend. Leaving the hall after lunch, Joyce tells me what Father Michael had told her. We were shocked, surprised and wondering why, since he was the one that did the betrothal (engagement) service in Craigend a few weeks ago so why not the marriage?

When we got home we were still somewhat disturbed. Invitations had already gone out to people of the day and place of our marriage because we had made these arrangements with Father Michael and all was a go. Than we had to call those people who received the invitations that the marriage is off. We called Father Michael and wanted to know why the change. He would only say that we call Archbishop John and ask him for the blessing that he marry us. Why should we call? You are the one that will perform the service so you call. We told him that we wanted an answer the latest Monday at 7:00 PM, if he will marry us or not.

Next day around supper time, Father Michael called us and said that the church would not marry us and the bishop does not give his permission for Father Michael to perform the marriage. He said that because it was our third marriages, (we both had lost our spouses through death), and the church would not perform the third marriage. SO NOW WHAT HAPPENS?

Yes we had called the day before and told our relatives and friends of what had happened. I have friends across Canada and we keep in touch with each other from time to time. Monday night I called the retired Reverend Michael Zaleschuk at Regina Beach to see how things are with them because we call each other every second of third month to keep in touch. During our conversation he asked how everything was and I said: "We are having a problem. Joyce and I met, were betrothed in the church, but now the church would not marry us." I told him that after giving thirty some years of my life for the church, of preaching, cantoring, belonging to organizations, etc., and now when I needed the church, I get a kick in the teeth." I told him of our dilemma and he says: "Go to Saskatchewan, get a marriage licence and I will marry you anywhere in Saskatchewan for I am a marriage commissioner in the province of Saskatchewan."

"Well now, just a minute, maybe we can do something yet. Give us a day or two to see if we can make any arrangements and are you free on May 28th, than we will let you know." Now what is the next step after hearing this? Joyce and I decided that maybe things will work out somehow. We could go to Wakaw, Saskatchewan for the May 28th service and the provody at the graves. We can be at the grave where Marusia is buried. Joyce also said that one time she was in Saskatoon at the Saskatoon Inn and there is a nice spot with water fountain and plants and maybe we could get married there after the service and grave blessing at Wakaw.

We got on the phone and started calling. Saskatoon Inn was gracious to provide us with the space to be married and than to serve a supper after the marriage. We booked a room for about 20 people for a reception. Where are we going to find twenty people for that day? Anyway we called my brother John to stand up for us and Joyce called her niece Beth in Saskatoon if she would stand up and both agreed. Now maybe things will get together yet. Than we called Reverend Zaleschuk and told him of what had transpired during the last twenty four hours and asked him again if he was free for May 28th. He said he would be there. We had not intended to be in Wakaw on May 28th, but God works and changes our plans. God planned that we would attend the service at Wakaw, attend the grave blessing, be married at 5:00 PM and have a small reception.

Now we had one other thing and that was getting a marriage licence. The closest point in Saskatchewan is Pierceland some thirty miles east of Cold Lake, Alberta and it is some ninety miles to Cold Lake. Joyce and I leave early on the morning of May 11th to get a marriage licence. We go through Lac La Biche, Iron River, La Corey, Cold Lake and into Saskatchewan to Pierceland. We stopped at the village office to inquire if they have marriage licences. No. The lady calls Good Soil farther east of Pierceland to ask if they sell marriage licences. No. Than she says there is a man and wife who issue licences just out of the village but they are gone to Ontario. The lady phoned the place, but no answer. So now what? The next nearest place is Meadow Lake, Saskatchewan and that would be at least another hour if not more to drive. But we had no other choice. We get in the car and head to Meadow Lake.

We get to Meadow Lake just at noon and find the City Hall. We go to inquire and learn that they do not sell marriage licence. What? A town of probably five thousand people and no one sells marriage licences in this place? Don't people get married here? But another lady overheard our conversation and came to the counter and said there is a store in town that issues marriage licences. We took the name and address and drove to find the place. Ah, there it is. As we park in front of the store, right in front of our eyes in the store window a sign says: "Issuer of marriage licences." We found the right place. The lady that was looking after us, said that she also performs marriages and if we wish, she could marry us right then, and she would find two witnesses. We told her that our plans are all set for May 28th and it will be in Saskatoon. She sold us the marriage licence. Than we went to have some lunch and after that started back tracking for home.

Things were working out as well as could be after what has transpired as we were getting nearer May 28th. One thing before that was that on May 18th Joyce had an upset stomach. I thought that she had picked up some virus or something, but later found out that when she begins to worry, her stomach becomes upset because later that happened a number of times before we had to go somewhere and leave home for a few days. We left for Wakaw, Saskatchewan on May 26th one day to travel there. The following day we had time to go to the cemetery and get the graves ready for next day. Than we also helped Alice in the house to get things ready for the meal in the church basement after the service. In the evening we relaxed more awaiting for the next day. So far it looked like only John and late Kay from Edmonton were going to be at our marriage, because John Hnatiuk will have to go with the priest to two other cemeteries after the cemetery in Wakaw. Anyway we invited and asked them to come to Saskatoon and be with us if they can make it, but they did not think they would come, but they did come after all.

On May 28th the service went well in church. The church was not as crowded like it was other years. Why? I don't know. Some of Marusia's family from Saskatoon also were in church. Her two nieces and niece-in-law were in church, lunch and at the cemetery. We kept quiet about our marriage and told no one anything. At the cemetery the service took place as usual each year. The priest had now gone past the final graves, Marusia's nieces were getting ready to go back to Saskatoon. Joyce and I came up to them and say: "What are you doing at 5:00 PM this afternoon?" They looked at us and thought we were inviting ourselves to come and visit them. Than we say: "We are getting married at 5:00 PM at the Saskatoon Inn and we are inviting you and husbands to come to the marriage and reception." Well they were stunned. They said they had to go home and get dressed, but we told them it was an informal dress.

They did come and one funny thing was that when they got home one of the women told her husband, that they have to go to a wedding. The husband asked when the wedding is and she said: "In two hours at the Saskatoon Inn." They all were somewhat shocked not knowing who, what, where or when, but they came. There was the late Matt and Ann Kawchuk, Mary and Denis Prefontaine and Marg Semeniuk. Than Alice and John did come as were John and Kay. There was Reverend Michael Zaleschuk and Joyce's niece Beth with her friend Phil and their two boys Martin and Dane, Joyce and myself. After the marriage we met in a room that the staff of Saskatoon Inn had prepared and we had a meal served each one ordering what their heart desired.

Following the reception people retired to their homes. Joyce and I spent the night in Saskatoon as did John and late Kay. The following morning John and late Kay left early in the morning for Edmonton. Joyce and I left somewhat later after we had looked after paying the bills for the event. We arrived back home on May 29th at 5:30 PM.

Before I go to another topic, one more thing about the marriage. Father Michael had talked with Archbishop John and the answer was that Father Michael cannot marry Joyce and me because of our third marriages. But is there not something wrong here? Is marriage not a Sacrament? Did Christ not attend a marriage in Capernaum where He performed His first miracle? Is the church against the marriage Sacrament? If we were divorced, yes I could see maybe a difference, but we were both widowed. Yes later Father Michael told us that Archbishop John may have permitted the marriage, but he had received too many complaints to allow us to marry for the third time. So instead of bringing members to the church and having the church grow and expand, the church was helping to get us out of the church and go somewhere else. But let me direct you to a few places that tell us about marriage in the Orthodox Church.

A. We must remember one thing here. The Ukrainian Orthodox Church in Canada started when the first three priests, the late Fathers Dmytro Stratychuk, William S. Sawchuk and William Sametz were ordained priests by the Antiochian Orthodox Bishop Germanos at Minneapolis-St. Paul, Minnesota, USA. This same church (Antiochian) has printed a service book for the Orthodox Church that many Ukrainian Orthodox priests use today from time to time for reference for services. The book is called: "Service book of the Holy Orthodox-Catholic Apostolic church." This book as it says on the first page is: "Compiled, translated, and arranged from the old Church-Slavonic service book of the Russian church and collated with the service books of the Greek church" by Isabel Florence-Hapgood.

At the bottom of the page we see: "Syrian Antiochian Orthodox Archdiocese of New York and all North America. The blessing for publishing this book was given by Antony Bashir, Metropolitan-Archbishop of New York and all North America.

Now let us look and see what we read in this service book about marriages.

On page 605 in the Appendix B we read: "This second Order of Marriage is used only when both bride and bridegroom have been previously wedded. When either is now married for the first time, the preceding Order is used. **The holy Church permits second and even third marriages, but unwillingly.** Nicephorus, Patriarch of Constantinople, commanded that persons who entered into a second marriage should not be crowned, and should be deprived of the Holy Communion for the space of two years. Persons who entered into a third marriage were debarred from Communion for five years. **This rule is not observed at the present day,** but explains this separate Order for Second Marriage." (Underlined and bold is mine)

So according to the Holy Orthodox Church second and third marriages are permitted. Why was it not permitted for me after all of my life was spend in and with this church? Could I after this, still stay, carry on my life in this church? I had given faithfully and one hundred and ten percent of my some thirty years for this church and in the end when I needed the church, I got a kick in the teeth for giving half of my life in service for this church.

B. But that is one example that we have read above about the third marriages of people in the Orthodox Church. I did find an articles on the Internet about marriages. A Greek Orthodox Church of Greater Omaha issued a notification about the Sacraments in their congregation. There is information about the Divine Liturgy, Baptism and Christmation, fasting, Funerals, memorial services and marriage. Under the Marriage item are a number of requirements for a person to be married and at the bottom of the requirements we read: "**No individual may marry more than three times in the church.**" Now is the Ukrainian Orthodox Church not part of the Orthodox Church worldwide? The Greek Orthodox Church and the Ukrainian Orthodox Church of Canada fall under the same Constantinople Patriarch. So how come in one church it is permitted to be married maximum of three times and in the other (Ukrainian church) it is not. Why the difference in the same faith? Today on the Internet there are tons and pages of this information. I just took four other examples from the Internet to show the hypocrisy that dwells in a church.

C. In the Pastoral Guidelines in the St. Vasilios Greek Orthodox Church in Watertown, N.Y., USA I read in the third section: "No person may marry more than **three times** in the church with permission for a third marriage granted only with extreme Oikonomia." I think this is plain to see.

D. Another example: From the Internet taken from St. Paul the Apostle Orthodox Church on Oakley Drive in Las Vegas, Nevada. "Those who enter a **second marriage** are not crowned and are noted admitted to receive the most pure mysteries for two year - those who enter a **third marriage** are excommunicated for five years." So one can be married the second and third times, but they cannot receive Holy Communion for two and five years respectively, but still the second and third marriages are permitted.

E. One more example from the Internet: taken from St. Peter Orthodox Church Naples, Florida, the church serving the southwest Florida area. I read: "Orthodox Canon permits a **second or third marriage**, but more than that is strictly forbidden." I think that this is clear and needs no further interpretation.

F. Lets have one more example also from the Internet: Taken from the Greek Orthodox Archdiocese of America. I read: "The church will permit up to but not more than **three marriages** for any Orthodox Christian. If both parties are entering a **second or third marriage**, another form of marriage is conducted much more subdued and penitential in character."

G. Now there is also another canon (law or rule) in the Orthodox Church that a priest must be married to be ordained a priest. If a man wants to be a priest but not married, he can be ordained a priest, but once he is ordained, he cannot get married. Now we would think that a canon is a canon and must be abided by it. But I want to take you to another example that this was not abided by. A Ukrainian person, according to records in North America, there was a priest by the name of Father Ahapy Honcharenko. In a book entitled "" (Memoirs) in the Ukrainian language for the period of 1892 to 1942 written by Wasyl A. Chumer and he very briefly mentions the life of Ahapy Honcharenko. On page 15 we read one sentence: "Рукоположення доконав на нім єпископ Мелетій Ловцов на Кореї, дня 25-го січня, 1862-го року." The translation for this says: "The ordination on him was performed by bishop Meley Lovtsov in Korea on January 25 1862." On the following page we read: "У вересні, 1865 року Гончаренко одружився: взяв собі за жінку Альбіну Цітті італійку." Translating this means: "In September 1865 Honcharenko got married, taking for a wife Albina Tsitti, an Italian." So here we see another canon that was disregarded and Honcharenko having been a priest for more than three years, later becomes married.

H. And lastly one other thing. What and who is older, Christ or the Church? Yes we know that Christ is older because it was He who instituted His Church which we have to this very day. So as to marriages in the Church, we know that Christ upheld marriage, because He Himself with His Mother and the Apostles were at a marriage feast in Cana of Galilee. *"And the third day there was a marriage in Cana of Galilee; and the Mother of Jesus was there: and both Jesus was called and His Disciples, to the marriage."* (John 2:1-2) Did you notice where they were? It does not say they were at the wedding, but at the "marriage." But being at the marriage they also attended the wedding feast because they ran out of wine and there Jesus performed His first miracle.

But there is also another important item mentioned in the Scriptures about marriage. Remember the Samaritan woman and Christ meeting at the well as we read in chapter four of John's Gospel. One interesting point in this chapter is Jesus meeting the woman from Samaria. After some conversation between the two, Jesus tells the woman: *"Go, call they husband and come hither."* (John 4:16) "And what does the woman say? *"The woman answered and said, 'I have no husband.'"* (John 4:17) Jesus tells the woman: *"Jesus said unto her, Thou hast well said, I have no husband: For thou hast had five husbands; and he whom thou now hast is not thy husband: in that saidst thou truly."* (John 4:17-18) Did Christ condemn the woman for being married five times? Absolutely not? So why does the church think it is greater than Christ and condemns the second and third marriages? Christ did not condemn the woman for being married five times, yet today we have laws made against what Christ was doing. He attended a marriage but did not condemn the five marriages of the Samaritan woman.

So how come Orthodox churches can and may perform second and third marriages, but not the Ukrainian Orthodox Church in Canada? It is a part of the same Orthodox Church as the ones I mention above and there are tons of other information stating the same as the examples given. So why was I denied the Sacrament of marriage in the church I gave most of my life too?

Than we wonder today why the church is losing members. Instead of helping and assisting people and bringing them into the church, the church chases people away from herself as if though I or others have some contagious disease and the church does not want anyone to be contaminated. Yes, Christ blessed seven Sacraments including Marriage, and yet today the church would not permit the Sacrament of Matrimony to be performed for me.

Joyce having sold her house, we next put up signs near Robert's (Joyce's son) cottage that it was also for sale. Because no one was calling, Robert got a Realtor in Lac La Biche to sell the cottage. They brought and put up signs and before we left Alberta the cottage was also sold. In the meantime Joyce's lot in Osoyoos which was in the hands of the Realtors was sold on June 1st.

On June 3rd Joyce and I leave to Fort McMurray to a retirement party for son Robert from the Fire Department. Robert had been with the Fire Department for some eighteen years and was now retiring and will be going into construction only. We spent the day in Fort McMurray and returned back home the following day. Robert had purchased thirteen acres of land on the east side of Osoyoos and would build a house there. But before their house would be built, they also bought a brand new house so when they move from Fort McMurray they would have a house where to live, before they build their own house.

When I got up on the morning of June 7th, I was not feeling to well after breakfast. I felt dizzy and threw up my breakfast. I felt nauseated and everything seemed to be turning as I moved around. At first I could not get the handle of what may have been wrong. I lay down on the chesterfield and slept for an hour. When I awoke, I felt better and than began to wonder what could have been the problem. Oh, I know what. I must have been getting another attack of the inner ear imbalance like I have had at other times.

GARAGE SALES AND MOVING

Because of all the events happening till now, we had accumulated many things and began to find out that we had a lot of things that we don't need. So what do we do with those items? Yes, we'll have a garage sale of two week ends. The first sale will be of the "loonie and toonie" sale on June 9th and 10th. We got rid of some things, but than for the next week-end sale a week later we got rid of more items. On this second sale we put up a sign in the garage that after 3:00 PM everything that is left goes for free. People came after 3:00 PM and helped themselves. Take everything but only leave the garage. During these garage sales I also put up my small car the 1997 Ford Escort for sale. A few people inquired about it and finally before we left for British Columbia I sold the car for $3000.00. We had bought it in 2001 for $8000.00. After I sold the car, Joyce was going to Lac La Biche and I gave her the cheque to put in her account until I need it and than she can return the money later.

Joyce had two animals on the yard, a cat named Keyano which is strictly in the house and does not go outside and a big Black Labrador Dog weighing eighty pounds. Now that we are moving, the cat will move all right in the van, but what about the big dog? What do we do with Cleopatra? We had noticed that when spring had come, she would always run and hide in the shade where it was cooler. So if the temperature for her is too hot at plus twenty some Celsius degrees, what will happen when in Osoyoos the temperature will go up into the thirties and higher day in, and day out? Cleopatra had nine acres of place to run around here by the lake. Where will she run on a little lot about the size of a house?

But than it happened. During one of the garage sales, a family came to the sale, saw the dog house and asked how much for the dog house. We said: "If the dog house goes, the dog goes with it." The family came to pat Cleopatra, who was on a chain, and they made good friends. They went home and a while later they came back with a small dog. We let Cleopatra loose and there was more fun watching Cleopatra chase the small dog and then in reverse, more fun than a barrel of monkeys could provide you with. The people agreed to take Cleopatra.

Just a few days before we left, the people did come for Cleopatra. Because we had not heard from this family, we were planning that Cleopatra will now be coming with us to Osoyoos. But just the following day at noon two vehicles pull into the yard. One was towing a trailer behind. Yes they came for the dog house and Cleopatra. Our hearts broke. We could have said that we are taking her with us, but the promised word we had given the people to take her, we had to keep our word. As the trailer moved near her house and which was being lifted unto the trailer, Cleopatra lay under the trailer as if to say that she is not letting her house go. When the dog house was loaded, the man that was taking Cleopatra opened his truck and we were standing and talking with him. Than what happened, happened and why? Cleopatra jumped into the truck, into the back seat sitting and waiting of what will happen. Joyce and I tried persuading her to come out, but to no avail. We took a bone and her food and asked her to come out, but she would not move. Why? It was as if she knew that her place is in Alberta and she is not going to British Columbia. As the two vehicles pulled away, our hearts broke and we could not stop the tears.

Will she be free on the farm with all the horses that the people owned? The wife where Cleopatra was going, worked in the Veterinary clinic in Lac La Biche, so we knew that she would be cared, loved and looked after. That was the last we saw of Cleopatra. Later Joyce e-mailed the people to see how she was doing and we waited for quite some time before we heard from them. We found out that Cleopatra and the horses did not get together too well, so they gave her away to another family with children.

Through the Internet we learned from this family that Cleopatra is doing very well and likes the new home.

The movers from Cold Lake told us they would come to pack the glassware about the 24th of June. Than they would come and load the moving van with everything on June 28th. That did not happen. The people showed up ten days earlier on June 14th to pack the glassware. Than they came back on June 22nd and finished the packing and labeling. Joyce and I also packed many of the things and were so busy at times that we did not stop to eat or rest because we were notified that the movers will be loading our things a week sooner than scheduled, on June 23rd. They loaded everything and took it back to Cold Lake where it sat until they were ready to haul it to Osoyoos for July 4th possession day of our house.

On June 21st, the parish made a farewell for us at Grassland, Alberta. We had told people we do not want any parties or gifts and so they would not do anything. We even had suggested that we would not appear at such a gathering. We were still hurt that we could not get married in the church in which I served for thirty years plus years. As for gifts, we have so many things that we have no place or use for them. Why do you think we made two garage sales? Yes, to get rid of things we did not need. Anyway we thought it would be better on our part that we show up. We went. People from each congregation were there. A large supper was served and than each congregation had the chairman or representative speak on behalf of the congregation expressing their best wishes and thanking us for all the work that we had done. At the end they presented us with a beautiful wall picture that was painted by a lady from Edmonton and only so many copies of it were made - limited edition.

Because we got another extra gift from the parish, that made the need to bring one more item with us to the west. We had everything packed and ready to roll and when the movers came, they packed everything into the largest trailer they had and everything just fitted in with about five feet space left at the back door. When the man first saw all the boxes packed and what had to be moved he said that he would be able to take everything. I could not believe it, but I was telling him that he would have to go back and bring another truck. How right he was. Everything did fit in as he had said it would. They took everything to Cold Lake and it sat there for about a week before it was moved to our new place in British Columbia.

One thing that I have to mention about this evening farewell is that Father Michael was not the same person I had known for the last six years. How many times he stayed at my place overnight when he had services in Lac La Biche and it was too far to go home to Athabasca and return next morning. Every time there was any kind of a service I was there to help him out. At this farewell they had a head table with Gloria Shewchuk, parish chairwoman, sitting at one end, Joyce next to her, than me and Father Michael at the other end. Father Michael in his address which he gave, never ONCE thanked me for everything that I helped him in six years or even the furniture I donated to them when they moved into their own house and they had no furniture. And while sitting at supper, he sat with half of his back to me as if he had nothing to do with me. I asked Father Michael where Dobrodeyka was and he said she was working. She had a job at the hospital in Athabasca. Later when we were already in Osoyoos, people called us and told us why she did not come, because no one invited or asked her. After everything was over, there was a group picture taken. They put Joyce and me in the middle and asked Father Michael to sit beside me, but he would not and did not. He went and stood at the end of the group photo.

Because Joyce does a lot of sewing and some of the things are done from the computer, we decided to get a lap top from Smiley Furniture and Appliance store in Lac La Biche. We bought the top of the line laptop that has so many gadgets that we don't even know what it is for what or what it does. That is the computer for Joyce to use. We bought it in 2006 and it died in 2013, serving seven years.

On June 30th very good friends, William and Olga Sworin asked Joyce and me to come for supper to their place on the farm. We were stretched for time, but because of their generosity and kindness that we have known, we went to their place.

During this time there was no furniture in the house, so we slept in the summer cabin that Robert owned next door. That cabin was also sold but possession date for it was later, so there were beds in there and we stayed there during the night. This same day on June 30th, the man who purchased Joyce's house took possession of the house. We have everything packed, loaded and ready to leave for British Columbia tomorrow morning.

We left Plamondon with a loaded dodge van about 9:00 AM on July 1st heading for Claresholm, Alberta where Joyce's brother Marvin and wife Pat move on this same day into their house that they bought. We stayed this night at their place and everyone slept on the floors in the bedrooms, because their furniture does not arrive until the following day. That evening we hear some loud bangs outside and thought that someone must be shooting, but than it sounded different and we went outside to investigate and learned that it was the Canada Day July 1st fireworks at the end of the street.

When we left Plamondon, Joyce put Keyano in a cage for traveling with us to Osoyoos. For some eight hours, all we heard was meow, meow, meow. When we arrived in Claresholm we put her in the house, but she would not eat or drink anything, but would try to find a place to hide. The following day again, Keyano goes into the cage and for about four hours all we heard was meow, meow, meow. Joyce did the driving both days. After listening to Keyano, I said that I will let her out and see what happens. She can't run away because the van is moving and the doors are locked. After I opened the cage, she came out, said a few more meows, walked around in the van over the packed things and than lay down on the floor at my feet and stayed there the rest of the way to Osoyoos

SETTLING IN OSOYOOS, BRITISH COLUMBIA

We left Claresholm July 2nd at about 9:30 AM. We traveled south on #2 highway until we hit the Crowsnest highway #3 and headed west into the mountains. We arrived at Osoyoos 8:30 PM and met Robert with the family who had arrived a day earlier to buy their new house in Osoyoos. We stayed at the motel in Osoyoos, because we don't take possession of our house until July 4th. On that day the movers brought our things from Plamondon and before they unloaded they asked for a certified cheque which was in the amount of $18,000.00 for the moving, storage and packing. The house has a three car garage. What was for the kitchen, living room or bedroom, went into such room, but anything else was stored in the three garages with boxes piled one on top of the other up to the ceiling.

On July 7th with two vehicles (ours and Robert's) we drove across the U.S.A. border to buy a few things we needed because we were told that groceries there are much cheaper. Joyce and I went with the van, while Robert with his family went with their truck. Yes groceries are much cheaper there even if you take into consideration the exchange on money. One time Joyce and I went to Omak, we bought a gallon of milk for $1.98. Two pounds of cheese for $3.29 or skinless and deboned chicken breast for $1.29 a pound, butter at $2.00 a pound and so forth. We live only about one kilometer from the U.S.A.- Canada border.

Next day Joyce and I drove to an orchard and bought eight pounds of cherries for $8.00. Those cherries were consumed and the following day we went and bought another full shopping bag of cherries. They say cherries are good in preventing gout. I'll see how true that is. We bought cherries every second day until the cherry season ended. Than it was other fruit. One place north of Osoyoos we bought peaches, apples and other fruit at twenty five cents a pound, all these prices in 2006. Since then prices have risen higher.

On July 16th early in the morning Joyce and I go to Kelowna to the church service. It is their feast day service of St. Peter and Paul which falls on July 12th. They celebrate the feast day on the closest Sunday to July 12th. There we met many people and old acquaintances from the years when Marusia and I used to attend every service. After the service, dinner and speeches, we went to visit Tony and Elsie Burkowski.

I must also mention that we took possession of the house on July 4th. There is a place for a garden, but no one has done anything with that garden since who knows when. The weeds were two feet tall and cramped into every piece of the ground. On July 11th I took the rototiller, tilled the garden and planted some vegetables; peas, carrots, beets, etc. Yes we still had a garden even though it was planted so late it still produced. On July 22nd I planted some onions and of all the onions only one came up and those were going to be a good onions, only that the quails got to the onion greens before we did and they chopped of the green, so that onion did not grow after that. Why the rest never came up, I don't know, but maybe the onion was no good. Sometimes you have onion growth started while still in the container, but these onions were not like that, they showed no life. I must also mention when I rototilled the garden, the ground was just like powder and you sank up to your ankles in the dusty powder, that is how dry it was.

On July 29th I had an experience. I had hoed the garden and was going to water the rows of beets, carrots etc. I turned around from the garden towards the garage, when low and behold crawling along the wall of the garage a four foot long and probably a good two inches thick, a snake. I stood frozen for a second. I would like to chase it away from here, but how close can you come if it is a rattlesnake? The snake crawled along and than I could see that it was trying to crawl up the tire and the car shock absorber under the van. Now that's all we need, is a snake in the van someplace where we can't see it. I quickly slipped on the other side of the van and went into the house and told Joyce to go out on the deck and see a snake. Quickly I went out again and opened the water house. The pressure is very good here at the house and I was trying to wash the snake down the driveway unto the street. The pressure worked but the size of the snake was not as strong as the pressure. Slowly, slowly I began to move it down the driveway when the driveway was wet and in that manner I got the snake off the property unto the boulevard on the street. Whatever happened with it I do not know. It was later we learned from people in one store that if there is a snake, there is a number to call and someone would come, pick it up and take it away.

Robert and the family left back for Fort McMurray a few days later. On July 31st they arrived again for a months vacation this time. It was good that they came, because a few days later Joyce and I leave for a family reunion in Saskatchewan. At least there will be someone staying in the house. But on August 2nd it was so smoky outside that we could not see the town down in the valley. There were two forest fires burning in the U.S.A. and the wind was just right to blow the smoke in the direction of us and pollute the air. At one time there were twelve hundred firefighters fighting those fire.

On August 3rd Joyce and I leave for the family reunion at Fort Quapplle, Saskatchewan. This same day when we left, Robert's friend from McMurray with his wife and family came for holidays to the Okanagan and they all stayed in our house. That day they had an incident. They all went unto the deck and closed the sliding door behind them. Somehow the door got locked and they could not get back inside the house. They had left all the keys inside the house. They went to a neighbor and called the locksmith. The locksmith man could not open the door either because of the special lock that it is. The only way they got inside was after the locksmith got a drill and drilled away the lock and than could take it apart. Robert had tried to break the glass on the front door, but he said that he pounded all he could, yet the glass would not break. Another incident that happened was with the grapes. The grapes on the fence had a heavy crop.

They were hanging over. One morning when they awoke, the weight of the grapes had bent the steel posts damaging the fence. It wasn't till later in the fall after the grapes were ripened when I straightened out the fence posts.

The family reunion was held with about sixty to seventy people attending. When our reunion started, there were the four families, Derzak, Korzeniowski, Chalupiak and Stefaniuk, on my mother's side of the family. Now we have more people coming to the reunion because they have the same surname and people we never knew of or heard of before from our parents. At this reunion everyone is trying to figure out how who is related to who. The reunion was from August 4th to the 7th. We left for home on August 6th and stopped at Regina for the night. Next morning we stopped at the hospital in Regina and saw a good friend, John Sawchyn who had, had surgery for his hip or knee and was recuperating. We left Regina just before noon and got as far as Fort MacLeod, Alberta. Just before that we stopped at Taber and bought a sack full of Taber corn. We left next morning and arrived home at 6:00 PM. That evening we still blanched the corn and put it in the freezer.

The garden that I planted on July 11th grew. On September 15th, we picked, blanched and froze peas this day. The earlier variety of peas, the "Alaska" we had been eating for about ten days earlier. The carrots and the beets were still growing and there had been no frost till now. This same day there was a big, big golf tournament for there were cars parked all around the street since the parking lot was too small for all the vehicles. We live just about across the street from the golf course and can see it from our east window

This same year we make another trip, back to Alberta. Joyce's niece Jennie Burk at Okotoks is getting married on September 30th. Joyce had been making table centres for the wedding all summer long and now we had to deliver that and also she is to adjust the brides gown the day or two before the wedding. We leave September 27th to Okotoks and spend the next few days there. The marriage was held in the Anglican church and when I first saw the marriage in the church, I thought it was a marriage in the Orthodox Church for some things were similar. The wedding reception was held at the golf course in the club house with some hundred or more people.

EUGENE STEFANIUK

After the wedding on Sunday morning October 1st Joyce left with Robert, Kim and the girls to Fort McMurray and I was left home. Joyce will be baby sitting the girls for a week or so, because Robert and Kim are leaving to Prince Edward Island to buy some property for investment. Joyce returned home from Fort McMurray on October 11th. I was at home doing what had to be done and I even cut the lawn the second time since we are here from the beginning of July. On the first weekend in October (Joyce was still in Fort McMurray), I was to have gone to a fiftieth wedding anniversary for Mike and Ann Derzak at Kamloops, but that had to be canceled, because Anne was not feeling that well.

On October 9th the man that looks after the underground sprinklers came to blow the water out of the underground pipes and shut the sprinklers for the winter time. In the spring time he will come again and turn them on. I thought he did that only for us, but later I learned that he was doing that to other houses in the area. We thought this was a quiet neighborhood, until this same morning when we got up, we saw one of the neighbors golf carts someone was trying to steal during the night, but they pushed it part way down the hill and could not get it started and left it sitting against a street light.

We have had no rain in Osoyoos since July 7th yet everything was green and lush. The underground sprinklers watered our lawns every morning at 2:00 AM for half an hour or so. The garden we watered whenever it was dry. Than on October 16th we had a rain shower come and everything was so well refreshed. We were in Kelowna one day and had bought three roses. On October 17th we planted two at the back and one in front of the house. The following day on October 18th we turned on the furnace for the first time just to kill the chill in the morning because it was beginning to get cool. The following day on the 24th I dug out the beets and the carrots and rototilled the garden the day after. Now winter can come if it wants or if it finds its way here.

As the year was coming to the end, we were doing what needed to be done from time to time. I would do some small things outside while Joyce was in the house sewing most of the time. She had head bands to sew for the granddaughter in Fort McMurray and head bands for the granddaughter in Ontario to sell for figure skaters and beside that, sewing volunteer work for the Royal Alexandra Hospital in Edmonton. While sewing she said that someone had touched her on the shoulder on October 28th. That is the same experience I had two or three times when I was still living in Lac La Biche and later in Osoyoos.

Having moved to Osoyoos, the closest Ukrainian Orthodox Church is at Kelowna some ninety miles away. Depending on road conditions it may take you to get to the church anywhere from an hour and forty five minutes and up. It also depends on the traffic and the time of day. We have been a few times to Kelowna and it took us closer to two hours each time to make the one way trip. Because of the road conditions (heavy fog) on October 29th we went to the Anglican church service in Osoyoos. We were treated like royalty. We had our picture taken in the church, invited to come down for coffee. The minister came, sat with us and we had a chat. Other people came and introduced themselves to us. It sure sounds and feels different than what I have known or seen in the orthodox church in some places.

Mr. Frost did find us after all. Waking up October 30th it was -4 C outside the first killing frost. Than come November 2nd, it began to snow and the whole countryside turned white. But, by 5:00 PM that afternoon the snow was all gone, the road was dry and it was once again black like no snow had fallen. When November 27th came, outside we had a full blown prairie winter storm. Blowing snow and cold wind made it better to stay indoors than to venture into the cold stormy weather outside.

On November 5th the Dneipro Choir from Edmonton were having a concert performance in Kelowna at 2:00 PM. We left before noon to be on time, because we had no tickets and we wanted to assure ourselves that we get the tickets at the door. The following day Robert from Fort McMurray arrives to take possession of his new house in Osoyoos. We said we would pick him up, but he said that he would take a rental car in Kelowna and drive in himself. That he did. On November 10th Robert left back for home. The next day we both went to the Remembrance Day celebrations that were held in the Elks Hall with a full house of people with even the standing room filled.

November 12th we went to the Anglican church service again and than afternoon drove to Kelowna to pick up Robert and two of his men who are coming to Osoyoos to start putting up walls for his house that he will build on the east side of Osoyoos on the mountain. They arrived at 9:30

P.M. Robert drove us to the Dillworth Inn where Joyce and I spent the night and Robert with the men drove on to Osoyoos, so that tomorrow they may start on the construction of the walls. Why did we stay over in Kelowna? Well the next morning Joyce and I are taken to the Ford dealership and Joyce buys a 2006 Mercury Grand Marquis car. We drive the car home and park it in the driveway until we can make some room in the garage to drive it in.

Come November 15th a friend of ours Derek Arnold brought a truck load of horse manure and dumped it on the garden. I had a bout of gout at that time and it tied me down so I could not go and help with the unloading. Anyway on the 17th I felt somewhat better with less pain and I spread the manure on the garden and the next day on November 18th I rototilled the garden again. You sure can't rototill anything on the prairies at this time of the year unless it's an exceptional mild time going into late fall.

The new year has become old and is slipping soon into oblivion. December is now upon us and the very next day brings us bad news. Oksana had been feeling ill and at 3:00 AM on December 2nd she called her neighbors to call the ambulance for her. She was rushed to Grace Hospital where at one time she was an employee there. What is wrong? All kinds of thoughts race through your mind when you hear of something like this you ask yourself. "Is it serious?" But if an ambulance has to pick you up at 3:00 AM, than you know it is not very good. Gail, her daughter kept us informed what was happening with Oksana. She was taken to Health Sciences Centre for tests, than for a cat scan and than an MRI, before it was discovered that she had a blockage in the bowel. A blockage, that could be caused by a tumor that grew in there or some other thing. More tests revealed that she had scar tissue blocking her bowel. She did have some surgery earlier in her life and when the healing process came, it started to heal and grew causing the blockage. On December 7th she had her surgery. I do not know when she came home from the hospital because we were away at that time.

Joyce has a son in Barrie, Ontario who is married to Cathy and they have two children, Connor and Courtney. Connor is interested in hockey and Courtney is doing great in figure skating. Joyce had been talking with Kevin and he asked that this year we come out to their place to celebrate Christmas. Since Kevin has been away from home after marriage, Joyce said that she had never been for Christmas with him and his family. Joyce lived in Fort McMurray as did Robert with his family and so they always had Christmas there together.

We talked things over and decided to go to Ontario to be with Kevin and the family. Now we have to get a date and how we are going to go. We could go by plane, but Joyce is not very good for flying. When the plane banks while turning, she grabs a seat or someone next to her and tries to straighten the plane out. I said that we could drive. We could drive into the U.S.A., and drive out at Detroit or Chicago and we would miss most of the snow and cold. Joyce said not to drive in the winter time. Okay. Than we thought about taking a train. There we could relax, take our time and enjoy the scenery. We went on the Internet to book seats or a room with a bed to leave from Kamloops. We checked and the following day we received an email from VIA that the trains for the Christmas season are full, booked for two years. That cut the train and the car transportation out. Two more choices, by bus or by plane. Checking into the bus lines we found out that we would have to transfer a number of times and it would take longer. The only way left would be to go by air. We started to check the different airlines and there are only two that we could fly out of Kelowna to Eastern Canada and that is Air Canada and Westjet. Checking into the cost of the fares there was quite a difference. Westjet was the cheapest and so we booked two seats for us on December 14th and return on the 26th.

LEAVING FOR ONTARIO

A few days later I was checking something again about airlines for a trip to Ukraine and a WestJet pop-up ad came up on one of our searches. Not thinking too much I just clicked in again for the trip on the same day to Toronto and find out that they put on a seat sale and the tickets are less than what we had booked. When Robert was here in November we told him about this and he got on the Internet and soon we got the cheaper tickets but lost only a few dollars for cancelling the first tickets. For the return fare I paid $1300.00 with all taxes for both of us. We left home at 7:30 AM on December 14th. Coming to Kelowna we stopped at Dillworth Inn and made reservations for December 26th, because we would be arriving from Toronto at 9:30 PM. By the time we get the baggage and leave Kelowna it will be late and we do not want to travel at night when drunk drivers are on the road or deer trying to beat the traffic. We left our van in the parking lot where you may park for a number of days or weeks at a time. The parking place is huge and there are hundreds of vehicles parked there.

The plane leaves on time at 11:35 AM and in Toronto it is already 2:35 PM and we should arrive in Toronto at 6:45 PM. Everything went well and we touched down exactly at 6:45 PM. We waited for over an hour to get our luggage, I still do not know why it took so long. People were already getting impatient to wait for luggage so long. Joyce's son Kevin met us at the airport and than we had an hour of travel to get near Barrie. When we arrived the family was still up and waiting for us. After a short meeting and greetings, all went to bed, for some were going to school in the morning and others to travel to Toronto to work.

The following day Joyce and I had the house to ourselves to rest. When the children came home from school we had an opportunity to talk with them. They were very glad to see us. That evening we all took things easy and relaxed. Come Saturday morning, Courtney was off to the skating rink for figure skating practice. Kevin and Connor were the sales people selling head bands that Joyce had made and brought to help raise money for the skating club. In the evening it was another entertainment. Kevin and Connor took us to the arena to see a hockey game between Barrie Colts and the Kitchener team both of the Ontario Hockey League. It is a beautiful arena seating four thousand people and it was filled to the top. The game was fast and exciting and the home team lost by a score of four to two. They were missing their star player who was on a trip to Europe to play in the Junior world championships.

Sunday morning Kevin, Joyce, Connor and I were up early, because Connor was to have hockey practice in an old arena at 6:00 AM and there was about a twenty minute drive to get there. After the practice we came home and rushed to get to Toronto because Kevin had purchased six tickets for the matinee to see a live performance of Aladdin. What a live show that was. It was held in a large theatre downtown. After the performance we returned home stopping at Swiss Chalet for supper. No one stayed up late because everyone has their thing for tomorrow.

On Monday morning December 18th Kevin gave us his car to go to Windsor. Joyce has a brother and sister-in-law, Howard and Janet Burk, who live there and that was Joyce's old stamping grounds for she was born there and attended school. Joyce is a transplant from Ontario into the west where she started her western life in Grand Prairie, Edmonton and later in Fort McMurray. We found our way out to Toronto very easily for Kevin and Cathy had prepared us a map and it was no problem at all. On the way to Windsor we stopped at Paris, Ontario because Joyce wanted to get a few things from the Mary Maxim store. We arrived at Windsor in good time and found a motel where we spent the next three nights.

After getting into the motel, we went and got a plant and some other things and drove to see Joyce's very good friends from their school days. Joyce was going to play a good trick on Bill and Carol Scase, but we forgot the phone number in the motel. We were going to stand near their house and make a call asking what is new in Windsor. As Joyce would still be talking on the phone we would knock on their door. This did not happen because Joyce had no phone number with her so we just came up the steps and rang the doorbell. Bill answered and opened the door. At this time it was already dark about 6:00 PM. When the door opened, Joyce without saying anything just walks right in and I follow behind. Carol was in another room. Bill seeing someone walking into the house without saying anything says: "Hey who are you coming in here like that?" Than Joyce asks: "Is Carol home?" Than it all broke out. It was a surprise meeting and a good time. Than together the four of us went out and had supper. After that Bill drove us around for about an hour showing Windsor and all the old places that the three of them used to roam around where they lived. I still could see before me and haven't gotten over it, seeing Detroit across the Detroit River at night. Another sight to behold was at 9:00 PM where there were rows and rows of semi trucks lined up on a one mile bridge going into Detroit. It was a sight in itself.

The following morning we got a plant and than Joyce drove out to meet her brother before noon, because afternoon he was going to work at the Ford Motor Company. We visited with them and Howard went out and brought home a take out meal for each of us. Janet, sister-in-law, made some tea and we had a good lunch and chat. Howard showed his stamp collection that he has and it is some collection. After lunch and good byes, we left because Howard was going to work. Joyce drove out to the Times Magazine that is published about Walkerville where Joyce went to school. Today Walkerville is part of the city of Windsor. Why was it called then and still even today is mentioned as Walkerville? This was something I did not know. Did you ever hear of Hiram Walker? Yes the place where all the stuff is prepared for parties. Hiram Walker distillery is in Windsor and it is like a town in itself along the banks of the Detroit River. Joyce stopped to pay her subscription to the paper and met an old acquaintance. We also bought a book about Walkerville which has many, many pictures and stories.

Than Joyce drove to show the place where she lived and the house is still standing as she remembers from those long ago days. We also went to find Joyce's aunt Elsie. We stopped along the way to get some wreaths to put on the graves of the family members at the cemetery. While there in La Salle, Joyce found out where her cousin lived so we went and spent some time with Marlene and Ron Tann. From there we went to Joyce's aunts place, (nursing-seniors home) and brought her a plant for Christmas. Being just about supper hour, we had to leave but we went to see her other cousin Carole and Dave Hutchinson. By this time it was already dark. We started to look for the street where her cousin lives, but got lost and had to stop and ask where and how to get to such a street. It is different in the daytime than at night to look for an unfamiliar place.

We found the place, had some tea and also chatted with them for a good hour and than left back to the motel. That was a learning day in Windsor for I had never been there before. I liked the city both at night and in the daylight. No hills, straight streets and well laid out and even a river separating Canada and the U.S.A.

Next morning the first thing we did was go out to the cemetery to see where Joyce's family members are buried. We placed the wreaths on the graves of Joyce's parents Warren and Dorothy Burk, step mother Margaret Burk, aunt Shirley and uncle Lloyd and grandparents, the Howards. The cemetery itself at that time of the year is something else. Flowers and wreaths cover the whole cemetery and it looks like a field of flowers. We stopped at the office to ask about the plot where Joyce will be buried and she paid for the opening and closing of the grave. The day was sunny, but the wind from the north west blew right through you at the cemetery. From there we went to Tim Horton's and had coffee and hot chocolate after the cooling off on the cemetery. While at Tim Horton's the semi trucks coming from Detroit came in one and two lanes of trucks, coming non stop. I told Joyce that if my mother was alive and sitting in Horton's with us, she would be crossing herself and saying: "Eugene, where are all those trucks coming from? Where are they going?"

Next we drove around and Joyce showed more of Windsor, the school where she attended and the shopping places as well as drove along the Detroit River once again to see Detroit in the daytime. It was not as spectacular as it is at night with thousands of lights. The river itself I was told is a mile across and you could tell it's deep because you could see the water in a rolling and churning movement as it flows by. We went back to the motel in the afternoon and rested before we drove out to Bill and Carol's place once again. This evening we took them out for supper and returned back to their house chatting for a while before going back to the motel.

The following morning we got up, packed and checked out of the motel and started our trek back to Toronto. We wanted to be in Toronto before 4:00 PM because Kevin would than leave the car he was using while we had his car, and he would be able to drive home with his own car from work. He showed us where he works and we met a few of his co-workers and left for home. Next day on Friday December 22nd we stayed at home while Kevin went to work and the children to school. Cathy also was home today, but she had gone to do some errands and to the gym with her friends. On Saturday it was again to the arena where Courtney was practicing and learning figure skating. Connor had to go for hockey practice on Sunday morning at 7:00 AM. Joyce and I got up and Kevin had already awakened Connor, so Joyce and I drove Connor to the arena for his practice. After the practice we stopped at Tim Horton's and had coffee and some sweets.

The rest of Sunday we spent relaxing, taking things easy and even reading. Sunday was Christmas Eve. Joyce and I were not in church in the morning, but we knew that the Anglican church, just about five or ten minutes from Kevin's place, was having three services that evening, one at 4:30 PM, one at 7:30 PM and one at 10:30 PM. We went to the 7:30 PM service. The church was packed. The lady minister said that they had a packed church at 4:30 with two hundred and fifty people attending that service.

On Monday the 25th of December, Christmas Day, Kevin, Joyce and Cathy were in and out of the kitchen preparing for the meal, cooking the turkey, etc. I spent most of the time reading. Joyce and I had been thinking to take a trip to Ukraine in 2007. People in Ukraine invite us to come and visit them. Kevin has a book entitled: "The Sink." I was looking through it and what I had seen I made up my mind that I would not go to Ukraine, because there is still too much mafia stuff going on. We had a huge supper and than took it easy the rest of the evening. Joyce and I had even started to pack a few things because we are leaving back for home tomorrow afternoon.

On Tuesday around noon Kevin and Connor drove us to the airport in Toronto. Driving on the Freeway 400 from Barrie, we passed through Vaughan. We could see the parking lot was so full around the mall, that people parked on the approaches to the freeway and even in the ditches. As far as the eye could see it was cars parked filling the parking lot. We arrived at the airport and wanted to check in our luggage so that we don't have to drag it around with us, but the lady at Westjet told us they do not accept the baggage but two hours before flight time. We had about three hours plus to wait before we take off. Kevin, Connor, Joyce and I had coffee and than we said our good byes and they left back for home because they have to pack also, to leave on a ten day cruise and they are also leaving home tomorrow.

HOMEWARD BOUND

The plane left on time from Toronto at 5:45 PM. The flight was good but this time we had to stop in Calgary. When we flew from Kelowna it was a non stop flight, coming back there was one stop over. We found out from the girl that sat next to us, she was coming from St. John's Newfoundland on this same plane. She said they had stopped (I believe she said) at Halifax and than Toronto, now Calgary and Kelowna. We asked the attendants if they are going farther west from Kelowna, but they said Kelowna was the end of the trip.

When we landed in Calgary, there was a change of crew for the plane. After the plane was cleared up, we boarded and ready to leave when the captain's voice comes on and he says: "Good evening ladies and gentlemen. I have some good and some bad news. The bad news is that you have to listen to me for forty five seconds and another bad news is that the airport in Kelowna is closed due to heavy snowfall. But the good news I have is that the people in Kelowna promised us they would have the airport open when we arrive." So now what? With heavy snow, how will the landing be? Anyway we took off and waited as to what will be, will be.

We arrived in Kelowna on time at 9:30 PM. The Kelowna Airport will be getting a hundred and forty million dollar expansion. In 2006 over a million and a quarter passengers went through this airport and they did not expect that many passengers to go through for another six to eight years. It was in one of the magazines somewhere I had read which said Kelowna is the fastest growing city in North America, yes in North America. We landed in a snow storm and just about five minutes ahead of us another plane had landed which had been delayed because of the heavy snow but circled until the runways were cleared.

When we got off the plane we had to wait for the luggage. I told Joyce to pick up the luggage when it comes and to wait while I go and locate the van in the seven inches of snow. People were walking around like lost sheep looking for their vehicles under the blanket of snow in the dark even though the place was lit up. When you have acres of parking and it is all filled with cars, and than covered with snow, try to find a vehicle in the dark. Joyce knew where we had parked the van and when I found it I cleared off the heavy snow and that took time. When I had gotten out of the terminal, a front end loader was clearing the road near the terminal. It was dark and all I had on was a pair of slippers with no grip on the soles. Yes, I slipped on the ice that was formed under the snow where it was cleared and down I went crashing to the bottom, falling on my left side and elbow. No I did not hit my head to the ground and nothing was broken.

I had started the van while I cleared the snow off and than got in and drove so it would be closer to the terminal and not to carry the four suitcases too far. I could not find a place nearer, so I drove around in another lane and found a parking spot closer by. I went inside and the luggage still was not out in the terminal while hundreds of people from two planes waited for their luggage. Finally the luggage arrived and would you know it, everyone is taking their luggage and we are waiting and waiting and waiting for ours until near the very end comes our luggage.

We picked up the luggage and brought it out near the entrance where Joyce would wait with it while I went to get the van. Before you get the van out of the parking lot, you must pay. You pay with your credit card, but you put the parking ticket into the slot of the machine and it tells me that it will be $65.00 for the parking and than says that you can pay by cash or credit card. After the transaction went through, a receipt comes and it tells you that you have ten minutes to get your vehicle out or after that the gate will not open. Everything went well. I paid with the credit card, drove out, we picked up the luggage and drove to the motel. We were lucky that we had booked a motel before we had left for Toronto. How would one travel the ninety some miles in seven inches of snow in the dark. When we arrived at the motel, we turned on the TV to see the weather and there was a warning that if you don't have to travel, stay off the road.

From the motel we also called Martin Dubyk and Mary to see if Bill and Olga Sworin from Grassland are still there. We were talking with Olga Sworin before we left for Toronto, that they were coming to Kelowna before Christmas and will come and see us. Because we would be away at that time, she said maybe at least we could see each other when we come back from Toronto. We made plans that when we get back on the 26th, we would come and visit them at her sister's place, that evening because next morning on the 27th, they will be leaving back home. We called a few times and there was no answer. We went to bed after the day and the trip had made us tired. Next morning we again called Martin Dubyk and they answered the phone. It was now about 9:15 AM. Sworins were to be at the airport by 10:00 AM. There is no time to stop in to visit, so we talked for a few minutes with Olga Sworin and we left for home. The farther south we came the less snow there was. When we got home at 12:30 noon, Derek Arnold was just finishing to shovel our driveway which had about two inches of snow. That evening as we listened to the news, we heard that Kelowna was in for another four inches of snow on top of the seven that they already had from the storm the day before.

Next day when we got up there had been about an inch of snow overnight. I wanted to shovel that, so went outside and was moving the snow. I slipped on the driveway and down I went with a thundering crash, on the same elbow and left side that I had fallen at the Kelowna airport. Only this time when I fell, it was harder and I think there was even a small earth tremor caused by my fall. Again I did not hit my head, but my left hip and elbow were now even more sore.

If you recall when I had surgery for the gall bladder, I later had a problem with the eyes that a light keeps flashing on the side of my eyes. A half circle of light would flash like lightning each time I moved my head. In the daylight I can not see the flashes, unless I'm in a dark room. The first time that the flashes started was after my gall bladder surgery. So the year ended with flashes of lightning. Now another new year is just unlocking the door. What will it bring?

LIFE GOES ON IN OSOYOOS

The New Year 2007 also brought more pain. Mr. gout returned and was giving me a bad time. While we were in Ontario, I ate anything and everything and had no problem with gout and thank God for that. Now come home and a week later gout finds me. Is it the food, the water, the weather? The men from the Anglican Church had asked that I come and join them on Thursday mornings at 10:00 AM for perk-a-tory. They sit at the Rattlers coffee shop and talk about different things that are happening around. I went there and they sit and drink coffee. I had hot chocolate.

January 6th is the Orthodox Christmas Eve. Joyce and I are preparing our supper for tonight. We cook the wheat and everything else that we need for our twelve meatless dishes. We tried to make cabbage rolls, but were unsuccessful. The cabbage would not go soft to roll. When it finally got soft, it would tear apart, so instead of cabbage rolls, we made lazy cabbage rolls. At 6:00 PM we had our supper. Gout was with me. Tomorrow January 7th is the Nativity of Christ. Gout is very bad and I would like to be in church, but the service is at Vernon which is about a two and a half hour drive. But even if it would have been in Kelowna, I would not have gone, because gout was very painful. Joyce did get up, dressed and went to the Anglican church for the service, while I stayed in bed until noon when she came back. Pain was just too great to move around.

By evening the pain became somewhat less. On Monday the 8th of January, a Holy Day in commemoration of the Virgin Mary, we go to Kelowna to the church service. Gout is still there but at least it's walkable and I could stand the pain. After the church service the late Tony and late Elsie Burkowski come to us and ask us to follow them to the Swiss Chalet for dinner. Just as Elsie turns away, the late Emily Chanasyk comes and says that she is taking us out to dinner. We thanked her and said that we already have an invitation. After the veneration of the cross, we come outside and getting into the car when Morris and Shirley Buchy ask us to come to their place for soup. We thank them and say that we have already two invitations. So we follow Tony and Elsie and have dinner at Swiss Chalet. We wanted to go and spend some time with them at their place in the seniors home, but they said that no one is allowed to visit, because there is the Norwalk virus in their building. People don't even go to the dinning room to eat, but meals were brought to the rooms to stop the spread of the virus.

After we left Swiss Chalet we stopped in to see Alex and Sylvia Korzeniowski at Peachland for it is along the way home. We stopped for about half an hour and than left wanting to be home before darkness. We try to stay away from driving at night.

I have heard that Lake Osoyoos is the warmest lake in Canada. If that is true, than why it did freeze on January 13th? Till now the ducks and geese were swimming about, but this morning they would have to put on their skates to move around on the ice. We learn from people that have lived here for many years that it's ten years ago when the lake froze here the last time.

On January 18th is the Epiphany Holy Night, the day before Christ was Baptized in the River Jordan. This evening again there is a meatless supper. In Kelowna they will have the blessing of the water at 4:30 PM and supper will follow. I was thinking that maybe even if we go we can stay overnight or drive back slowly and carefully. That did not come about. Snow was coming down all day. I went down to meet with the men from the church for coffee and Rev. Patrick Reid also came from Oliver. We asked how the road was and he it was deteriorating very badly. Than I knew that Kelowna would be out for us. So Joyce and I again prepared our supper, but not as much as the last time for January 6th..

If you remember in 2005 in November and December there were two funerals in the Semeniuk family in Saskatoon. George Semeniuk passed away on November 10th at Saskatoon and the funeral was on November 14th. Just about six weeks later George's brother Bill passed away in Saskatoon and the funeral was on December 31st. Two brothers in six weeks are gone. But another brother Mike Semeniuk from Cold Lake had not been feeling that well and was losing his battle to cancer. On January 30th, 2007 we got the sad news that Mike had passed away in Cold Lake. I wanted to go to his funeral but God had other plans. My gout had acted up again in the left knee and right elbow. Than listening to Edmonton Global news we heard the police were asking people to stay off the roads because they were in very bad shape for driving in the storm So out the window goes our plan for attending that funeral. There was one more avenue open. Take a plane. That might be okay in the summer time, but during that time the Kelowna Airport was also going through its own problems.

Joyce was to go to Fort McMurray to baby sit the two granddaughters. She had her ticket and everything booked and reserved to leave on February 9th at noon. This morning when we got up there was some fog hanging around, but we left well ahead of time just in case of some hold ups on the road. We passed through Penticton and there was some fog and a plane was just leaving the airport when we went by. As we headed farther north towards Peachland, the fog was becoming heavier - thicker. We had the radio on listening to the news, but nothing is mentioned about the airport.

There was fog in Kelowna and at the airport when we arrived. We arrived at the airport and there are cars galore. We took the suitcases and headed to the terminal to check in. And what do we find? Yea, people, children, pets and more people and still more people that you can't even walk through. What in the world is going on that there are so many people here? When we finally get to the counter to check in, we find out that the plane to Edmonton and Fort McMurray is canceled as are all others. Yes we saw that on the monitor that it was canceled, but still we went to check in. The girl says that the flight is canceled and asks that we come back the following day and Joyce would be able to fly out to Calgary and than wait till Sunday evening to fly out to Fort McMurray. So what kind of deal is that? She has to be in Fort McMurray before Saturday.

What we learn is that the instruments for flying in the fog were down. The plane to test the equipment was to fly in from Ottawa, but they could not land because of the fog. So two days no flights came in or out and that had the people backed up, EVERYBODY wanting to get their flight and fly out, but nothing was moving. We find out that Joyce can't leave until the following day and get into Fort McMurray on Sunday night, that did not work. Robert and Kim were leaving for Thailand on Saturday morning and Joyce was expected to be there on Friday evening. Now that this did not work, Joyce got on the phone to Robert and told him what was happening. He suggested that we get out to the Greyhound bus lines and maybe they can get to Edmonton sooner than the plane. We left the airport and headed out to the bus depot. As we neared the bus depot, Joyce's cell phone rang. It was Robert. He says: "Mom, I got a flight for you on Air Canada from Penticton to Vancouver to Edmonton and than Westjet to Fort McMurray Saturday morning."

We make a right turn at the next corner to get out on the highway and head for Penticton having enough time to be there for the 4:30 PM flight and it is only 12:30 noon now. It is only a forty five minute drive to Penticton. We get to Penticton in plenty of time and wait for the plane to arrive and leave for Vancouver. We waited. Baggage was checked in and than we learn that the plane from Vancouver to come in is late fifteen minutes. Than they tell us the plane is late half an hour and that was already past 5:00 PM. How much later will that plane be. Outside among the mountains the sun was getting ready to go to bed and it is dusk. I do not want to travel in the dark, so I tell Joyce good-bye and leave her at the airport and myself get into the car and head for home before it gets really dark.

I arrive home at 6:00 PM and it is now dark, but I made it safely. Later Joyce calls from Vancouver and says that the plane was an hour late leaving to Vancouver. In Vancouver she had to catch a flight at 11:00 PM to Edmonton, but that plane was not leaving until 1:00 AM Saturday morning. She got to Edmonton and waited a few hours before she left on WestJet at 7:00 AM for Fort McMurray. She arrived at Fort McMurray at 8:00 AM and Robert and Kim were already at the airport because this same plane that she just disembarked from, they are taking to Edmonton. They exchanged words of what was what, who, where, etc., and they left.

Joyce took their van from the airport and drove to where she would make her home for the next month until March 6th.

Robert and Kim had gone to Thailand because their friend had bought a resort and were having the official opening and they wanted Robert and Kim to be there. They stayed there until the 3rd or 4th of March and left back for home. Joyce picked them up at the airport in Fort McMurray on March 5th in the late afternoon. Next morning they take Joyce to the airport and she flies out at 8:00 AM to Edmonton. There she changes planes and the plane arrives at Kelowna some fifteen minutes ahead of schedule at 11:58 AM. We had lunch and than we went to see the late Elsie Burkowski for a few minutes and than headed out for home.

While Joyce was in Fort McMurray I received sad news that Tony Burkowski passed away in Kelowna on February 14th. Tony was in the hospital and was to leave for home in two days, but he got a massive heart attack in the hospital and passed away. This same day on the 14th of February the Town of Osoyoos had the street sweeper cleaning the streets. One golf course opened its doors for another season of golfing this day. The other golf course opened on February 21st. I made a trip to Kelowna on Saturday February 17th because a long time friend Joe Luchka was celebrating his 90th birthday on that day and I received and invitation to attend. Joe Luchka is Olga Sworin's brother-in-law. This evening the party was over at 7:30 PM, but I spent the night at Dillworth Inn. Next morning there was a church service in Kelowna. After the service I came back home. Monday the 19th I returned back to Kelowna for the service of the Canon of Andrew of Crete at 5:00 PM and than prayers for Tony Burkowski at 7:00 PM. Again I stayed at Dillworth Inn and the following morning attended the funeral. Elsie had asked me to give the eulogy about Tony after the funeral luncheon in the hall. Following this I returned home.

It looks like Osoyoos spring will be a little sooner than spring in Lac La Biche. On February 21st I raked the lawn and now just waiting for some rain to come so that I can put some fertilizer so the grass may have some nourishment for the summer. The gout had so far given me some peace, but it showed itself in my left foot again on February 27th. As usual the foot is painful, sore, red and swollen.

Near Oliver some ten miles north of Osoyoos is a lavender farm. The owner, a lady from Canmore, Albert sold the farm because she has no time to spend with the work at the farm here. The people that bought the lavender farm will be tearing up all the big two and three foot lavenders and planting the land into vineyards-grapes. So the new owners put an ad in the paper they are selling the $29.99 lavender plants for $9.99 each and you can come and buy as many as you want. I had told Joyce on the phone at Fort McMurray about this and she wanted me to go and get a lavender plant so we would have one in our yard. I went and brought home the large plant and planted it in the garden on March 3rd.

On March 6th I make another trip to Kelowna to pick up Joyce at the airport. As mentioned above the plane arrived earlier than was scheduled. Joyce said that the pilot had made an announcement that all the passengers on the flight to Kelowna were on board, so instead of sitting on the tarmac in Edmonton, they were leaving fifteen minutes earlier. The weather from March 6th for a few days has been really beautiful in the +10 to 12 C. Snow is gone. People are golfing and I'm ready to get going in the garden.

People tell us that Global warming is ensuing us. I wonder how. When we got up on January 13th, Orthodox New Years Eve, Lake Osoyoos was frozen over. Did it freeze from Global warming? I doubt it. If the earth is warming up, there should be no ice. I know for a fact that the lake in Osoyoos did not freeze from Global warming. People who have lived many years in Osoyoos, tell us that it is the first time in about ten years that the lake froze.

Fog again was coming into the valley practically each day. Some days it was very bad, that we could not even see the golf course one block from the house as it was so foggy on January 25th. Other times we can't see downtown and other times the fog is lighter that we can see the town down below. Many times we could see the clouds are lower than the mountain tops. We could see the town below, than a layer of clouds and than above the clouds the snow covered white peaks of the mountains.

When Joyce arrived home from Fort McMurray and saw the lavender plant, the first thing she said was: "We should get a few more lavender plants." Okay. When Saturday comes we will go and get a few more plants. We went the following Saturday on March 10th and bought four more plants, brought them home and planted them on the edge of the garden. Now we have five large lavender plants and that should make a sweet smelling garden. Later we dug one plant and gave it for Joyce's brother in Okotoks. They planted it in the fall, but they said it did not weather the Alberta winter and died.

So spring comes somewhat earlier in Osoyoos than it does on the prairies. I had checked the garden and it looked like it was dry and warm enough to rototill it. Come Monday after noon I haul out the rototiller, start it up and rototilled the garden. After that was done I planted carrots, onions, beets, radishes and head lettuce. This was on Monday March 12th. Other vegetables will be planted later. Our garlic that was planted last fall in October is already three inches high as of March 12th. I know that we need rain, because the place is starting to dry up. There is so much rain on the west coast around Vancouver that the Trans Canada Highway has been covered in many places by mud slides. On the local news from Kelowna on March 13th it was mentioned that the highway may be closed for up to two weeks before the roads could be cleared and in some places the large washouts repaired. Here we could use half of that rain. They forecast that showers or rain are in store for Osoyoos, but none come.

Lately on the news we hear that the bones of Jesus and his relatives have been found in Jerusalem. When I first heard this, I thought: "What nonsense." How could bones of Jesus be found when forty days after He Resurrected, He ascended to heaven. This Ascension is not a myth, because the Apostles where with Christ when He was ascending to heaven. They were adult men and saw what was happening, so how could Christ's bones be found in some box? Do you know what this hoax is about? It is some people that do not believe in Christ, God or Christianity want to destroy Christianity so they keep finding things year after year trying to prove their "unbelievers" point of view. But Christ Himself said that His church, His Name, His deeds will never be destroyed. What He did and still does, will never be lost. *"On this rock I will build My church, and the gates of hell shall not prevail against it."* (Matthew 16:18) Don't let anyone fool or betray you that bones of Jesus were found. This is a hoax and Christ will destroy that as time will go along. Remember this and stand up for what is right, what the Bible tells us.

BUSY DAILY LIFE

We have three computers in our house. Joyce has a regular one and also a laptop which we bought in Lac La Biche, Alberta in 2006. I have just one regular - tower computer. We also have three scanners at the present time. But prior to this we had two scanners, but on January 18th, Joyce's scanner decided that it must retire, so it gave up and quite. So we went to Staples in Penticton and she got a new scanner, copier and printer, all in one. Now everything is working just fine, like new.

Some time ago my printer also decided to retire and go on pension. If you need to print something, you need a printer. I started to check for a printer on KIJIJI, where people put their ads on for free, and I found that there is a printer in Calgary, one that has four colours of ink. I answered the ad and two days later the printer arrived on the bus. It was what I wanted, and it worked good until one day something clinged like a spring where the paper goes through. Now to repair that it will cost more than to buy a new printer. So now that printer goes to the recycle depot. Eugene has no printer again. I thought of something. Let me bring the one in the garage that has been sitting in a plastic box for a few months when it did not want to work and now was getting cold. I brought it in, hooked things up and - zippo - the thing works. Yes it worked for a few weeks but then died again and went to see its friend at the recycle depot. The rest of the story about printers will come a few pages later.

I ALSO WALKED ON THIS EARTH

On February 5th the Anglican priest Rev. Patrick Reid came to see us. He came to ask if we have any icons, because they need icons for a lenten service. They will have a lenten service in Oliver together with the Lutheran church. The Lutheran and Anglican churches have reached some consensus that they can attend each others services and take communion.

On February 29th - Leap Year - Joyce and I are going to a funeral to Kelowna. Dobrodeyka Diane Woronchak's mother passed away and the funeral is being held today. Going to Kelowna north of Oliver, about three or four miles, a man was working, discing, on the field. At this time of the year the prairies some years are still frozen solid. If people are out on the field already, than the golf courses are not far behind and on March 5th of 2008 the golf courses opened and people were now starting their golfing season. On March 16th, Joyce's son Kevin arrived in Osoyoos from Ontario. He took two weeks of holidays and came to help his brother Robert with the construction of homes. He stayed until April 3rd when he returned back home.

On March 22nd I took Joyce to Kelowna to the airport. She flies today to Okotoks (Calgary) for the baptism of her great niece. Over a year ago we were at the wedding of her niece and now the baptism of her great niece. She had spent weeks and weeks of sewing a baptismal gown for the great niece to be baptized in. The baptism is on March 23rd, Western(Latin) Easter day. Joyce returned home from Okotoks on March 24th. Going to Kelowna and back we saw a number of people working on the fields, preparing the land for planting, or maybe some seeding. The only seeding in this area now is the seeding of vegetables in the garden. We don't see any fields of crops here like on the prairies except fields of orchards of fruit and vineyards.

March has arrived and it's warm enough that we can walk around in shirts and need no jackets. On March 31st when spring goes out like a lion or lamb, I go up the hill to help Robert with the construction of his house. Yes Robert and family lived in the town of Osoyoos for a year or so, while their permanent house was built on the mountain. I don't go outside too much in the winter because from about October to end of March or April, my hands get cold and I can't even hold anything. But now March is ending on the last day and I head out to the mountain and start helping Robert with his construction work. What we did today was the cement trucks brought a few loads of cement and that was poured on the floor of the house. Two inches thick. Later eighteen by eighteen concrete tiles will be laid on the floor, but that will come later. That is where I will be found for the rest of the year - half way up the mountain on Hallis Road. Robert will be laying the tiles and I will be helping bringing tiles, cutting tiles, mixing mortar, etc. There we will spend the rest of the summer finishing the house inside and out. The previous year I had helped Robert with the start of the construction of their new 5000 square feet house. I started to help when he was digging the basement, then putting up forms for concrete and everything from the basement up to the top of the roof, I was there each day helping. On April 3rd Kevin went back home to Ontario.

On April 8th in the late afternoon I rototilled the garden, but did not plant anything, because it was already to late to start planting that day. Most of my day is spent on Anarchist Mountain at Robert's house. It was not until April 12th that we put in some garden. Onions, carrots, lettuce, watermelon. We planted three rows of carrots and only about fifteen to twenty seeds germinated. It was the same thing with some other seeds that we planted later. I'm just guessing I know the answer to this riddle. We bought the seeds in packages at the hardware store. What happens to the packages of seeds that are not sold, I asked one person in a store. The lady told me that the seed company takes them back. Am I wrong to assume that the left over seeds are mixed with a FEW new seeds, then repackaged and sold again? Am I correct? If that is the answer, then what happens is, the seeds get old and they don't germinate. Vegetables are not wheat, where seeds will stay for decades and when planted it will sprout and grow.

I was helping to put up the cabinets in the house, and putting on tile on the floor. Robert also started to build another house higher up the mountain on a lane called Bull Moose on Regal Ridge about six miles east of his house. There are a number of lots in that area on Bull Moose, Wapiti, Cougar, Raven, Eagle, Sasquatch sub-divisions, etc. The area is 10,000 acres large. So at times I would even go and help with the house that is being built there to sell. There is always so much work with building a new house. An older house can be remodeled easier because the footings, foundation, walls, roof are already there. A new house you start from scratch and do everything step by step, from the bottom up and that is why there is so much more work on building a new house.

May 5th on a Monday, Joyce and I went to Vernon. A special event is taking place today. In 1932-33 Stalin with his henchmen and regime, eliminated anywhere from seven to ten million Ukrainians off the face of the earth. He forcefully wanted to impose collectivization on the Ukrainian people. People did not want that and resisted. What Stalin (Communists) did, was take all the food away from the people, so people would go hungry. And they went hungry because over seven million died of starvation. All kinds of food was taken out of Ukraine and shipped out to other countries. There were as much as twenty-five thousand people dying of starvation each day. Wagons came through the villages in the mornings and took all the deceased people and buried them in mass graves. Some people were still breathing, but the henchmen driver would say: "Bring them out too, for they will die and we won't have to stop here again the next day to pick them up."

There are people today who try to cover up this artificial famine of eighty years ago. But check the history of Ukraine. Check the population figures and you will notice that in a five year span or so the population dropped by nearly ten million people. One time as the famine came to an end world leaders met for a meeting and told Stalin they heard there were seven million people in Ukraine that died of starvation. Stalin lifted up both hands extending his fingers saying: "ten million." I guess he knew what he was doing so he corrected the person who had said seven million. But there are others that say that the population did not shrink in those years. If it did not shrink, do you know why? There was train after train hauling Ukrainians out of Ukraine, out to Siberia to be executed or put to hard labour. When the trains were returning back to Ukraine, they brought loads of Russians to fill in the space of the deceased Ukrainians. That is why there are so many Russians living in the Eastern Ukraine today, because they were transplanted from Russia into empty Ukrainian houses, yards and towns where people had perished.

In order that the world knows what happened to the Ukrainians, the year 2008 was proclaimed as a year of remembrance of the "Holodomor" famine, the year of hunger-genocide. A survivor of the Holodomor, Mr. Stefan Horlatsch traveled across Canada carrying a torch in remembrance of the famine. The torch was carried in thirty-three countries around the world. Governments around the world recognized the famine as one of the great tragedies of the world against humanity. Holodomor means starvation by famine. Joyce and I attended the gathering in Vernon, the only stop in the Okanagan. The torch was carried through the streets of Vernon to the city hall where dignitaries assembled and heard messages from those gathered on the city hall grounds. There were older people, younger people and children. Mr. Horlatsch presented the torch to the mayor of the city and to the present people. This event took place in Vernon at 4:00 PM on May 5th the only stop in the Okanagan .

We planted our garden and then snow covered it, but green onions and radishes were already up and we had them from our garden for supper on May 16th. Yes I know that on the prairies people, some, just start to put in their garden. Maybe in the cities on the south side of the house where the garden is shaded from a building some people could put their gardens in sooner

On May 6th I was again at Robert's house helping him. We spent much time on the floor installing 18"x18" tiles. The house is five thousand square feet. That required a lot of tiles and mortar to lay the tiles. Then a number of tiles had to be cut when you came to doors, corners or walls. It took much of the spring to do the ceramic floor tiles. May 6th also a special day for me. It was on May 6th 1962 that I was ordained a priest at Fort Frances, Ontario by the primate of the church and my seminar professor, late Metropolitan Ilarion. That happened nearly half a century ago.

On May 20th we had a good downpour of rain in Osoyoos. When heavy rains come we get a problem. We get water in the shop attached to the house and also in the storage shed. Twice already we have had water in the house. When heavy rains come, the eave troughs cannot handle all the water so it runs over the eave troughs unto the ground and then along the wall of the house, finds a crack and into the basement of the house. Another problem is that our one lawn is six inches lower by the wall of the house then it is by the city sidewalk. So naturally when heavy rains come, the water cannot all soak into the ground, but runs downhill and that would be in our case, towards the house and into the basement. That we hope to remedy in 2009. One other thing that helps for the water to get through into the house is the sandy soil in this area. Water here seeps into the ground like water going through a sieve.

The place where Robert built his house they have Geo-Thermal heating. No furnace needed. There were six wells dug near Robert's house of over three hundred feet deep each one. Then into those wells we put in black plastic pipes. The pipes are then filled with a special solution. Then around the outside of the pipes also a mixture like mortar is filled into the wells to keep the pipes warm - insulation type. This keeps the house warm in the winter and cool in the summer. The cost is not small for this, but then you need no fuel only the liquid inside the pipes is circulated and keeps the temperature at what the thermostat is set for.

Robert, Kim and the girls are living in a new house they purchased on Oleander when they moved to Osoyoos. They lived on Oleander until their house was completed on the mountain east of town and the lake. So some days I was at three places something to do. Do something at the house on Hallis where they will live now. Then sometimes would go to Bull Moose where the house for sale is being built to do something there, and then even sometimes had to come back down to Oleander to do something like landscaping or moving things from Oleander to the shop on Hallis. Sometimes deliveries were made to Bull Moose or Hallis and someone had to be there to accept the goods. Some times concrete was brought to one place and that took two or three hours work, and after that we would go to the other place to do something while the concrete was drying..

So spring is here and summer is right on the heels of spring. On the 13th of June just before summer begins, I have a problem with the 1996 Ford Contour. I had bought the car in December 2006 and in the spring of 2007 I had to get the air conditioning repaired because it was not working. I took it to the garage where I bought the car but he said they don't do air conditioning and sent me to his neighbor Hilltop Auto body. They checked it out and found that it was low on Freon or whatever they use for air conditioning in cars now. They fixed it and it worked good all summer and winter long until it came to June 2008 when I again had no air conditioning. I knew then that there must be something more than just to refill the compressor with Freon. At the same time you could hear some screeching and funny noises when you start up the car and drive it. Every day it seemed to get worse and worse.

On a few occasions driving the car it would make all other kinds of noises. One day Joyce and I started to go to town and drove the car with the noise that we were already accustomed too. But just past the stop sign on the corner the car stalled. It started again and we drove a few feet more and it stalled again. We started it the third time and I made a U-turn and drove back to the house. We called BCAA that we have trouble with the car and they sent down a truck to pick up the car. It was towed to the garage where I had purchased it. Later in the day I went to the garage with Robert. They had found the problem. The shaft in the air conditioning compressor was gone. It was metal rubbing against metal and I recall that even a number of times the car would smoke from under the hood. All in all I asked how many loonies it would cost to repair and the garage man just showed me 5 fingers, so I knew it was a five hundred dollar job. I told them to repair it. But Robert interjected and said that they give the bill to him for payment. When later the car was repaired and I came to pick it up, I asked how much is the cost and asked for the bill, the owner said that it had already been looked after. After that, the car worked very well the rest of the summer when air conditioning was needed. This had happened on June 13th. Is that superstitious or not?

The whole summer long, day in and day out, with the exception of Sundays I was up on the hill working at Roberts house. The most time was taken up by the floor tiles. We spent many, many hours leveling the 5000 sq. feet of floor with concrete and laying of the tiles. There were a number of times that I was all alone measuring and cutting tiles because Robert and family had visitors coming from Fort McMurray, Edmonton or other places each week to see them. I would measure and cut the tiles, having them ready that when Robert found some free time, he would come and lay the tiles. I mixed all the mud (mortar) for the tiles and helped to get the floor finished. It took a long time to complete, remember it is 5000 square feet of floor.

Besides the tiles there were also times when concrete was brought to be poured for the front steps. There was time that trenches had to be excavated for the Geo-Thermal heating pipes to be installed. At times we would also go to Bull Moose if some help was needed there or even to Raven, another sub division, where Jack McEvoy, was building his house and needed some help. I would help to install insulation in the walls, or have insulation blown into the attic, help to unload large, huge windows for the houses, etc. A lot of times I also spent installing rock on the outside walls of Robert's house, the house on Bull Moose, on the fireplace on Robert's gazebo and later on Kevin's house on wapiti.

One day we had a storm in Osoyoos. And it was a storm and a half or two storms in one. We got a downpour of everything. Rain, hail, wind, thunder, lightning and everything in between. The storm came up at 7:30 PM and everything became dark outside at that time. The water coming down from the mountain on the Fair Winds Street past our house looked like waves on the lake. We did get water into the shed at the back and some into the workshop but none had come into the basement of the house. The storm that came caused damage to many orchards because the storm was about a six miles wide strip. Fruit was damaged in some places up to 100% by the hail and wind. Other people that did not have the full force of the storm also had some loss but they still salvaged part of their crop. Any crop that is damaged by hail, the SunRype company in Kelowna buys that fruit and uses it for making juices, jams, etc.

As mentioned a number of times the seasons in Osoyoos come sooner and last longer than on the prairies. On July 5th we picked the first crop of cucumbers from our garden. The cucumbers were not started in a house and then transplanted. Seeds were sown directly into the garden from the package. At that time we also had the second crop of radishes ready to pick, but the only problem with radishes is that they are good not only for humans to consume, but also maggots like them and they usually get them before we can. Oh yes, there is a way to keep the maggots out by using different chemicals in the ground. I do not like the chemicals, so when we pick the radishes we check them and which are good, are good, and the ones that the maggots got, we discard it or cut the bad piece out and still save the good part. Some people say to put coffee grounds in the rows where radishes will be sown. I tried that when I lived in Lac La Biche in Alberta, but I found no difference. Maybe the maggots even enjoyed the radishes more with a different coffee flavor added. But I think I will have a solution for maggots. I know that when maggots get into the onions in the garden, use soapy dish water and water the onions with that. The next day or so the maggots are gone. So if it works for onions, maybe I could put soapy dish water in the rows and then put the seeds in. After the plants come up, water the radishes again with soapy dish water. Just a few days later on July 16th we picked the first red (ripe) tomato from our garden. On July 18th we made four jars of dill pickles of the cucumbers we picked from our garden.

The days are moving along and so are the floor tiles in Roberts house. After a long tiresome day after day of tiling we finally finished laying the tiles on the floor on July 8th. On July 9th I had other work to finish. I cut the tiles for the trim around the bathtubs. Robert was not in this day because he had more company again so he was away. After the tiles were laid one more tile job had to be done - grouting. A mortar type of cement is mixed and then the spaces between the tiles are filled in and the floor washed a number of times to clean everything up. Outside around the shop and the house I also did the parging. This is putting a coat of thin coat of concrete like mortar around the bottom of the building of the house and shop. As for the shop, I was there also from the day when it was started. When the foundation was poured, walls and roof came on, Robert and his men returned back to McMurray, and I was left to tie up the rods on the floor when the floor will be poured with concrete. The day when I was tying the bars a rain cloud came and since there was only the sheathing on the roof, but no tiles, water was coming down in the cracks where the sheathing was and I was soaked like a rat that day.

In the spring we planted our garden. I have mentioned that only a few carrots germinated from two packages of seed. On July 17th we planted three packages of beets the ladies from the church in Kelowna had given us to plant in our garden. One package was not bad, but the other package had enough seeds germinate that we could have counted them on the fingers of one hand. Why? As I have already mentioned earlier, the seeds are probably too old and do not germinate. Later whatever those beets grew we picked them and delivered them to Kelowna to the church ladies. The ladies at the church use the beets to make borsht for luncheons and meals that are held in the hall after services or for other occasions. It looked like our soil for the beets was not good, because all the beets seemed to have a form of scabs on them.

July 21st I had an appointment to see a surgeon, Dr. McIvor in Penticton. When I had my gall bladder surgery in Edmonton a few years back, the surgeon at that time told me that if ever I see a little bubble forming on my belly button, to go and see a doctor, because that could be the start of a hernia. Well a little bubble had formed on the side of the belly button, so I saw my doctor in Osoyoos, and he made an appointment to see Dr. McIvor. The doctor asked me if I have any pain and I told him I did not. He said that the little bubble is a formation of fat not a start of hernia. He said that if I want he could operate on it, but that if it don't hurt or bother me, than I can leave it as is. I told him there was no pain, but if I see the bubble getting bigger, than I will come back and see him. He said that is good because no need to operate if it is not giving any pain or bothering me.

The days are hot. There is still work to do at Robert's house. Robert wanted to do some work on the outside of the house, putting on rock. We started putting the rock on the house on July 24th. When cool weather came in the fall, we stopped that work, because the mortar would be too cold and would not hold the rock. When it was hot with the sun shining, we would work in the shade. When the sun moved over where we were, then we would move to another place where there was shade. If the wall was too hot, we would not work on it because it dried the mortar too quickly.

On August 12th we learned of problems that were starting to flare up on Regal Ridge, where the house on Bull Moose was being built. Robert lost a pile of lumber that had been sitting by the house on Bull Moose. Other people in the area also lost tools and other equipment, trailers, air compressors, etc. These thefts kept happening from time to time at different locations on Regal Ridge Mountain subdivision. We already had the Jacuzzi installed in the house on Bull Moose and thieves came one night, cut the pipes and took the Jacuzzi. One man could not do that, there must be a gang working on these thefts

After the middle of August I left to Alberta to a family reunion. This was now the sixth family reunion we were having. Our first reunion was held in Alberta, followed by British Columbia, Manitoba, Ontario and Saskatchewan - alphabetically by provinces. This year we once again start in Alberta near Stettler beside a large lake called Buffalo Lake. The next reunion will take place in British Columbia in 2010 and Diane Russell said that it will be not far from Vancouver near Chilliwack or Abbotsford. She will look for a place.

Joyce was to come to the reunion, but her grandchildren were coming from Ontario at the same time, so she was staying home to be with the two grandchildren. Later things changed and only the grandson came. It was also in June that Kevin, Joyce's son, also moved from Ontario and is staying with us. He is an RCMP officer and came to help Robert with the construction. He was hoping that he could get an RCMP posting in Osoyoos, Oliver or Keremeos, but that did not work out. He was thinking of retiring from the RCMP. It was later in November that he got word that he can work with the RCMP again in Kelowna.

ANOTHER FAMILY REUNION AND CAR PROBLEM

Back to the family reunion. Because Joyce will be home, I left for the family reunion early on August 21st going to Edmonton. I wanted John to have a look at the Ford Contour and see if anything needs fixing. I arrived at John's place at 8:30 in the evening and John was just having his supper. He is alone at home. His wife late Kay has been in the hospital in Edmonton since late June. She was always in pain and when she could stand pain no more, John took her to the hospital. She stayed in the hospital until the middle of December. When she came home, she was still in pain, and while she was in the hospital she had two surgeries and neither helped her. Her pain was in the head which the doctors diagnosed as shingles. Kay passed away in 2016.

    The following day on the 22nd John took of the wheels of the car and found that the rear brakes had to be replaced. We went and picked up the brake shoes and put new brake shoes on. He also checked a few other things and about 5:00 PM I left for Buffalo Lake to the family reunion. When I was not too far from where the reunion was, I remembered that I forgot to take my prescription pills. So now what do I do? Turn around and go for the pills or keep going to the reunion first and show up that I have arrived? I decided to go on and at least leave things that I brought for the reunion and than go back in the evening to John's place and spend the night there again. It was one hundred miles one way.

Returning back to Edmonton, it was already dark about half way to go. Between Camrose and Edmonton I was traveling when the sun was already set and it was dark. I could see that there were a number of bigger vehicles coming towards me and a semi truck coming from the left towards the highway. At night even with lights on, you cannot see as well as in daylight. Because there was a cross road ahead of me, I slowed down some, because the large semi truck from the left was clipping at a good rate of speed and it looked like he may not stop. I knew it was a truck because many lights were on. And if he don't stop he could make a flat pancake of the car and me, so I went over to my right as far as I could see that it was safe to do. But then all of a sudden one great big BANG. What happened? Oh yea, one large pothole on the right side of the road and I had to hit it in the dark.

What had happened is that someone must have being digging a well to strike oil on the side of the road. After I hit that pothole I could hear and feel that in my car somewhat was vibrating. Now maybe something gone wrong with the steering. Anyway I kept going and got to John's place later at 10:30 PM. We sat and talked for a while and went to rest. Early next morning at 6:00 AM I left back to Buffalo Lake. My car must have a wheel alignment or maybe balance the wheels because I could feel the vibration in the steering wheel. John said that he had wanted to check a few more things on the car, but because I was leaving, that would have to be done some other time.

I drive back the same road I came the night before to Edmonton and kept my eyes peeled to the left side of the crossroads which I approached to see if I could locate the hole that I hit the night before. No, I did not see or find it. Must have missed it someplace. Got to Buffalo Lake just before breakfast was finished. Spent the rest of the day, talking with family members catching up on the latest news. This family reunion is from my mother's side. In the evening after supper there was a gift exchange with those that were present.

I stayed Saturday night at the camp where all others were staying. There were a lot of cabins, so I was alone in one cabin. Next morning we had breakfast and then had a service which I had prepared. There were about

50 people at the reunion and the service. During the service I also had a memorial service for all our deceased family members of the four families: Chalupiak, Derzak, Korzeniowski and Stefaniuk. Following the service we had lunch, cleaned up the camp and started to disperse for our homes. Because I knew that I would not be able to get home that day, I decided to go back and see John. Maybe stay overnight there and leave next morning for home. I arrived at John's place and we went to Canadian Tire and got a new fuel filter for the car. He replaced that and it was 6:30 PM when I left John's place heading south. It will give me about four hours to drive and then I can stop at Clareshome for the night which would make it about 10:30 PM. I would stop at Marvin and Pat Burk's place, Joyce's brother and leave for home next morning. Driving on highway #2 from Edmonton all the way to Clareshome, I could feel the vibration of the wheels and was thinking that I have to stop at a tire shop along the way and have the wheels balanced. Maybe when I hit the pothole the lead weight came of the wheel, if there was one, and that is what is causing the vibration.

Anyway when I got Clareshome it was just about 11:00 PM with a few minutes to spare. I drove to Marvin and Pat's place, but there was no light in the house. Well now, how would that look for someone to go about waking people in the middle of the night as if though some bad news is about to be told. No, I'm not going to wake up the people, let them have a good night. I drove back to the highway to find a spot where I could pull over, fold the seat down in the car and spend the night there. Just on the outskirts of town on the north end I found a place where a few semi-trailers were already parked for the night and also a private bus. That is where I spent the night.

I'm up at 5:30 AM next morning. I could go and visit Marvin and Pat, but to wake people up at that time of the morning? No, I'm heading out for home. The sooner I leave, the sooner I will get home. Along the way I stopped to fill up with gas at Crowsnest Pass and bought a few things so that I would have something to nibble on as I drive. I drove for about an hour and a half or two and came into Sparwood. Going through Sparwood I caught the sign of a tire shop. Oh yea, that's as far as I'm going. I have to get the wheels aligned or balanced. I pulled in and told them I wanted the wheels checked because I have a bad vibration. They took the car in and in a few moments call me to the back of the shop. They don't tell me any good news, but bad. The right front tire has a bulge to the inside the size of a chicken egg. Then the owner also tells me that the rim is bent. Now that is what the pothole did to the car. If I would have stayed over at John's place and next morning gone to a tire shop, I may have been able to get the Department of Highways to pay for a rim and a tire. But here, now in British Columbia, how do I confirm that what happened, happened between Camrose and Edmonton. Maybe I would have to go back to that part of the highway, drive up and down and see if I can find that pothole.

I can't drive with that kind of a tire, because it might blow up on the road and then what will I do if I'm maybe in no man's land? When you go through mountains, there are many places there is nothing around, but forest. I had one experience driving in the winter through the forest highway in January 1993 moving from Vernon to Yorkton. Well I need a new tire, but how will that be, having a brand new tire on one side and an older one somewhat worn on the other. I need two new tires for the front wheel drive car. The people replaced the old tires. I took the one that was still good put it into the trunk and brought it home. It still has many good miles left on it, so maybe someone some day may be able to use it. The man tried to straighten out the rim somewhat and said that I get a used rim someplace from auto wreckers because this rim will also cause a vibration. I came home as was and had not replaced the dented rim. Later the story will be told what happened to the Ford Contour, where it is and what it is doing. Just a hint - it is resting. I arrived home at 5:00 PM that day all in one piece.

I guess with the weather in the desert you can do many things. But Osoyoos is supposed to be the only proclaimed desert in Canada. I lived in the desert in Phoenix for nearly three years but this is not the same kind of desert. A desert is supposed to be warm to hot nearly all year long. Osoyoos has frozen lakes, snow, cool temperatures, so it's a different kind of desert. Anyway on September 6th we planted a row of radishes, just to see if we would still have radishes from the garden that late. And, yes they grew, and on the 10th of September, just four days after planting they were up, but like other times, the maggots got most of them first.

Previously I mentioned that problems were starting on Regal Ridge. Someone was stealing things from places that were being constructed. On September 18th when Jack McEvoy went to his house where he is building on Raven Road farther east from Bull Moose, he got a surprise. Tools had been stolen during the night and also a number of pellets of floor tiles. The tiles alone were worth ten thousand dollars. Other places had also been robbed and no one has been caught. People were trying to find and figure out who is all behind the thefts. Later it was mentioned in the paper in December that over a hundred thousand dollars of items were stolen on Regal Ridge from various places.

It was this same day that Joyce left for Vernon. She went and will stay over at Roman and Gail Chez's place. Tomorrow morning the two ladies are leaving for Bragg Creek where an Orthodox Women's Retreat will be held during the week-end. Joyce returned home on the 23rd of September all full of enthusiasm and talking already about the next years retreat for the year 2009.

Joyce returned home on the 23rd. The following day (24th) as usual I was up on the hill with Robert when he gets a phone call that Joyce fell down and broke her wrist. Now that's all we needed to hear. I left everything and rushed home. I changed and we went to Oliver to the hospital, for Joyce had called the clinic what happened and they said that she go straight to the hospital. Well what happened was that Barbara Ann Scott does not compete in figure skating anymore, so Joyce thought that maybe if she takes figure skating lessons she would compete in the winter Olympics in Vancouver in 2010 in place of Barbara Ann Scott. What happened she lost her balance, fell down and broke her left wrist in three places. She had a cast put on and a few weeks later it was bothering her so she had that one removed and another one put on. Later when the wrist healed somewhat she wore a wrist support.

The days are now shorter and the nights longer. The days don't have as much time to warm up, but still in October we were putting rock on the outside of the house. Once the rock is all installed on the wall, it gets a muriatic acid wash to preserve and give it a finishing natural look and touch. But I could already begin to feel the coolness in my hands. For many years now as soon as October comes my hands become cold and stay that way until sometimes end of March or April. Even though I was wearing gloves it was already cooler, and the hands were still cold. On October 9th we picked and brought in tomatoes and cucumbers from the garden. Yes they were still growing, but really slowing down with the growth. On the prairies some years at this time there may even be snow on the ground already.

This year in 2008 there were two weddings in the family. John and Alice Hnatiuk's grandchild Tanya Wehage of Saskatoon got married on October 4th. Oksana's first and oldest granddaughter Stacey got married in Louisville, Kentucky on October 18th. We thought we would be invited to the weddings, but neither of the families invited anyone except John and Alice in Saskatoon, and Oksana and family from Winnipeg went to Louisville for the wedding. I guess because of the cost of travel and other reasons only the closest family was at the weddings. If we would have had an invitation to Louisville, we would have made an attempt to go, since we have never been there before. But as things went we did not go anywhere. Joyce went the farthest to Okotoks to her great nieces baptism, the women's retreat near Calgary and I went to Edmonton to the family reunion. The rest of our travels were spent the farthest to Kelowna and Vernon church services.

On October 30th, Robert and family left for Vancouver. I was then alone installing rock on the house. On October 31st, I was working with the rock when at 11:00 AM it began to rain. I could see from Roberts place that far to the west some mountains were already looking grey and others white from snow. I knew that the rain would turn to snow and then all the outside work would be over for this year. When November came, I stayed home and did not go to help Robert anymore with anything, unless it was inside work, where it would be warm. We learned from my brother John via email that our brother-in-law John Hnatiuk of Wakaw, Sask., had knee surgery in Saskatoon on November 9th. We tried calling Alice a few times to learn what is happening, but she was not home. She was spending time in Saskatoon close to the hospital to be with John. I never did ask her where she stayed, but I presume she stayed at her daughters place Cathy Wehage on the east side of Saskatoon.

Now comes November 12th. On this day I rototilled the garden. It still had plants growing, but everything was now over with growth. So I picked all the rest of the beets, onions and tomatoes from the garden and brought them inside the garage. Later this day we got email from John from Edmonton that Alice was in the Wakaw Hospital.

ANOTHER CAR ?

Joyce and Robert have been somewhat after me that I buy a newer car than the 1996 Ford Contour that I have. It is an older car, has less miles than some much newer cars and it was still working okay. Yes I put two new tires on it, had a new air conditioning compressor put in and a brand new battery. The rest of the car was in sound condition. But I had thought that an older car gets older and repairs may have to be added, so I thought to check and see what I could find. I wanted an automatic transmission, four cylinder engine, power steering, air conditioning and cruise control. If any other equipment will be on a car, that is so much better, that was already a bonus, but at least these things I want on a car. I found such a car in Vernon. I believe it was a 2001 with low kilometers on it. So on November 14th Eugene is going to Vernon to buy that car. It was a Chevrolet Cavalier. The first car that we ever owned back on the farm in the 1950's, was a Chevrolet, so I can get another Chevrolet. With my age and the sun beginning to set for me, this might be the start and finish with a General Motor Product for my cars.

So off I go early in the morning to Vernon. I find the car dealer and yea, there it is that car sitting. Is it waiting for me to take it home? The saleslady comes to help and I asked her about the car in the newspaper I had found and she said that car was just taken into the garage to be inspected before it is sold. I said that the car is on the lot, but she said that is not the car that is advertised. But very quickly they made changes. They got the car out of the garage, brought it to the front, put on dealer plates on it and said: "Go try it out." Eugene gets in and heads out of Vernon to the north. I get out on the highway and everything is working well, but I can't find the cruise control. I stop on the side, check the paper where the car was advertised in and sure enough it says that it has cruise. Well I don't know where it is, but I think I know enough about cars what a cruise control is. It will not be in the trunk of the car, or in a tire, but somewhere on the steering wheel.

I turn around and head back to the dealer. I come into the yard and still sitting inside looking at the dashboard, but how come the engine stalled. I can't hear the engine running, yet I look at the instrument panel and there are no lights on, that the engine is stalled. I step on the gas pedal and now the engine I could hear. Now that is my car if it is running so quiet that I can't even hear it. But one thing, where is the cruise control? I shut the engine off and go inside. The sales lady meets me and says: "How is the car?" I tell her everything is very good but where is the cruise control on it? "Oh it's on the steering wheel or on the windshield washer handle." I told her there is none. So she goes out to check and sure enough there is no cruise. Then she says that they can install the cruise, but I would have to come back tomorrow because they need time to install it and they have to inspect the car before letting it out. I told her that I would not come back because it is too far for me to come over a 100 miles to get a car. That was the end of that Chevrolet Cavalier.

We again learned from John by email, that on November 19th Alice was rushed to Saskatoon by ambulance. The doctors in Wakaw had checked her and said that she had symptoms of a heart attack. Because they don't have all the services in Wakaw as they have in Saskatoon, the doctors did not want to keep her there but sent her to Saskatoon. Now what is wrong? She was nauseated with dizziness and weak. The doctors said it was signs of a heart attack. Later when Alice was sent back home we found out that she had an inner ear infection and imbalance. Now they have to send her to higher up doctors to check out why she has inner ear imbalance. I guess Alice must be related to me, because I also have the same problem. In our family only Alice and I have gout, no other family member had or has gout

November 22nd, Robert, Kim, Joyce and I go to Kelowna. The ladies went shopping and Robert and I went looking for a car. We looked at cars at a few dealers but there was nothing that was appropriate for me. I want a small car with a small engine, so that we can run around town and not spend too much on fuel with the price of gasoline high as it is. The cars were small but had bigger engines, or it had no equipment that I was looking for, so we had no luck in finding anything. Two days later Robert and I went to Penticton to check out the cars there. Better to get a car that is closer to home than far away in case something goes wrong and then farther to travel to get it repaired or checked out.

Three days later Robert took his truck to Penticton to Sentes, General Motors to have it checked as something was not working too well. While there we also looked at some cars. We test drove one car. It was what I wanted in a car and it also was Chevrolet, a 2006 Cobalt, four door, light brown color with more equipment than I was even thinking of. The car was one that was used by Sentes people as a courtesy car. The price $8900.00. One thing was that they would not have the car ready until the following day after they made a complete checkup of the vehicle. So Robert's truck will stay in Penticton until it is repaired with whatever is wrong and this car is not ready until the following day. The company gave us another courtesy car which we drove home and then back next day to go and pick up the car I purchased.

CATS

When we moved to Osoyoos from Alberta we had a cat Keyano moved with us. Well after a little more than a year Keyano died. Joyce wanted to get another cat. She found a breeder in Kelowna and we went and picked up a cat. We called him Julius because he was born in July. But Julius always seemed lost being alone, so we got another cat from the same place. The cats are the ones which some people say that the cats ran into a wall and their faces are flat. This second cat an orangish brown we called Timmy. Those two cats gave us more laughs than two dozen barrels of monkeys. Anyway Timmy had to be neutered. When we picked him to take home from the vet, he was not the same cat. He could not run or walk straight as normal, but he staggered from side to side and had no balance. When we saw something was wrong with him, Joyce took him to the vet hospital in Penticton. There they discovered that he was blind on one eye and that he had, had a stroke.

He lived with us and we saw that he even had problem to eat or drink. Anytime I went to get a shower he always wanted to get into the tub and we would have to open the taps at the slowest to let water run. He would stand under the tap, let the water run down his face and then into his mouth. He could not drink water out of a bowl with his tongue like other cats and when I think of it now I see that it was because the stroke must have affected his tongue. Anyway to make a long story short we saw that he was getting worse and worse as time went by. On the morning of December 9th we found Timmy had died during the night beside our bed. Joyce says that she was up at night to the bathroom at 4:00 AM and Timmy was in the hallway in the house. When we got up that morning just before 8:00 AM, Timmy was already not alive. Timmy died early in the morning of December 9th 2008. We buried Timmy next to Keyano in the corner of our garden. We think of it now that he starved to death. We know now that he never seemed to eat his food, but it was pushed around the plate. When we think of it, we remember that he never licked his mouth which tells us that he must have been paralyzed, - his tongue also. So he only lived on water.

Timmy wasn't even with us for a whole year. He must have suffered because now that we have another cat in Timmy's place we can see how the two cats eat food or drink water, that tells us that Timmy must have had a hard time eating and drinking. We never saw him drink water lapping it up like we see the cats doing now. All he did was pushed food around with his face. When we gave Julius and Timmy baby food for a treat, Julius would lick up his plate clean. Timmy only pushed his food around the whole plate. Both Julius and Timmy as long as he was with us gave us enough laughs and enjoyment that you could get from two barrels of monkeys. That was before Timmy began to wobble around and without balance.

After Timmy was gone, we saw that Julius was not the same cat he was when Timmy was around. Don't tell me that animals don't understand things going around them or what is happening. Julius knew what had happened. After Timmy was gone he would come to the place where Timmy died and sat near the bed or by the door as if waiting for someone or somebody. We would see tears in his eyes so we knew that he knew what was going on. Joyce says that we need to get another cat, a friend for Julius because he will not be the same.

Joyce made arrangements with the people we got Julius and Timmy f rom. The lady said we can have a cat from a litter that there is in Victoria, B.C. But to drive in the mountains in the winter time, we said, no. The lady from Victoria was going to bring the cat to Kelowna, but then the avalanches closed the highways and no one could get out of Vancouver to the east. What happened after the phone calls and emails was that the lady would put the kitten on a plane in Victoria for a direct flight to Kelowna.

We would have to meet the plane to pick it up. The plane was late at arriving in Kelowna on the 13th of January 2009, but anyway we got him and brought him home. Keyano when we were bringing her to Osoyoos from Alberta she cried, meow, meow for a whole day of traveling. The next day we let her out of the cage and she would sit on the floor of the van and was quiet. Julius and Timmy were the same, only this was a two hour trip instead of two days.

Another very touching thing that happened with Timmy was, when we came to pick him up. Just before we took him, his mother nursed him. Then she washed him with her mouth, tongue as if to say: "Okay son, you are now leaving your mother and going away. Be a good kitten (boy) where you will be, because I will not see you again." It was sad to see that animals act as Timmy and his mother did. Don't tell me that they did not know what was happening.

Anyway, when we picked the present kitty up, he looked bigger than some normal older cats do. He was grown for being a kitten eight weeks old. Anyway when we picked him up, he was also meow, meow in the cage coming home. I told Joyce to take him out of the cage and let him loose in the car. When she did that, he became quiet all the way home. Bringing him into the house we thought there would be some incidents between Julius and him. We called him Tommy. But it was not so. From first Tommy had to go to every place in the house looking someplace to hide. He was frightened and would not come to eat or drink for over twenty-four hours. In the meantime we would look for him and take him in the arms for a while and slowly he began to get used to Julius and Julius to him. Now a week later in the house, he is giving us more laughs than one barrel of monkeys could. What happens next only time will tell.

As previously mentioned Joyce had a misfortune when she was skating, fell down and broke her wrist. Being in the hospital on that day after she broke her wrist the doctor put a cast on her wrist. I know that casts were put on limbs, where they mixed a plaster and put it on the cloth where the limb was broken. I got a surprise when I saw the new style of casts. It is nothing more than a material like cheesecloth is, wound up in a roll. There are different colors too. The doctor wets the roll in water, wraps it around the limb, give it a few minutes and the plaster is as hard as any other plaster would be. About two weeks later Joyce started to say that the cast was too tight and hurting her wrist. We went back to the hospital and it was cut and a new one replaced. Cutting the plaster was another modern invention. The doctor has a small round electric hand saw and cuts the plaster. The saw would not cut you, because it's made not to damage a person's skin. The cast stayed on until November 18th when it was removed. In place of the cast Joyce bought a wrist support to use when doing anything. Slowly the wrist healed and it is normal again.

By the Julian Calendar December 13th is St. Andrew's Day. An organization that was already mentioned was started in Winnipeg in the late 1960's called "Order of St. Andrew." I have been a member of this organization since the fall of 1967. It was started with the hope that we could get one thousand men across Canada to become members and each one donate fifty dollars a year to help out St. Andrew's College financially. The College on the University of the Winnipeg Campus had a mortgage and also needed more finances to help the college continue its work to teach and train young men for the priesthood for the Ukrainian Orthodox Church of Canada. Later branches of this organization were established in bigger centres across Canada. One of those branches is located at Kelowna, and includes members in Kelowna, Kamloops and Vernon congregations.

Each year on the 13th of December a service is held where there is a local, then a luncheon and program or annual meeting of the branch. In 2008 there was a service planned in Kelowna. We were planning to go that day but a day before we got a call the service is canceled. A sweeping snow storm rolled into the Okanagan Valley dumping in places as much as five to six inches of snow. Roads became treacherous, so things were canceled and we stayed home. The following day, 14th of December the temperature dropped and another two inches of snow was plummeted into the valley and the temperatures began to drop even more. On the 15th of December it dropped down to -13 C on our thermometer. It was colder from the cold east wind than from the snow itself. Snow came every day following the storm. Finally it stopped and the temperatures started to drop. The lake began to freeze and I guess the Global Warming froze the warmest lake in Canada, Lake Osoyoos, for the third straight winter.

BITS AND PIECES

Sometimes in the winter you never know what the road is going to be like. It may be nice, clear and sunny at home, but drive twenty miles or so and you could be caught in freezing rain, snow storm, accident and then you can't get to the church in Kelowna. In the summer of 2008 the government started to widen the highway #97 just north of Summerland. They drilled the mountain, closed the road and blasted the drilled part. You never know when you can be stopped for road construction and for how long. In the winter time the road was closed for two weeks because there appeared a crack in the mountain and their concern was for the safety of the traveling public. So the construction people shut the road until it was safe again to travel then they opened it up. They are widening the highway to a four lane road for about five-six miles. A few years ago we heard on TV that the Canadian and the USA governments talked about making Highway #97 a four lane highway from Alaska to the Mexico border. Now that would be a long, long four lane highway. It would go through Alaska, Yukon, North West Territories, British Columbia and the USA to the Mexican border.

Something unusual again happening to me. On January 17th we went to bed as normally, between ten and eleven at night. I put on a two piece pyjama on every night, summer or winter. We fell asleep and during the night at 3:30 after midnight, I got up to go to the bathroom. What a shock and surprise. Where is the lower part of the pyjamas? The top, shirt part, is on, but what happened to the lower, pants part? Where is it? I looked, and there where the pajamas stay in a drawer during the day, the pant part of the pajamas are folded and placed on the shelf. How? When? Why? What? Who? What is going on? How did one part of the pajamas come off me? I asked Joyce if she heard or saw anything during the night and she said, nothing. I knew that I did not see or hear anything either, but then this mystery still comes to mind from time to time. What and who, I don't know what to make of such unexplained mystery.

The devil keeps doing his work. We got a phone call from our friends in Dauphin, Manitoba, Stan and Olga Saramaga on January 25th and they wanted to share with us a story about the church in Hudson Bay, Saskatchewan. When I resided in Hyas 1980-1988, I served the congregation at Hudson Bay. It was one hundred and nine miles one way. When I had a service in Hudson Bay I had to be on the highway, sunshine or winter storm, at 7:00 AM. Much depended on the weather how long it would take to drive to be in church an hour before the service. I have been only once to Hudson Bay since 1988 and that was for a marriage.

We got a phone call from Dauphin that the Ukrainian Orthodox Church in Hudson Bay was broken in and vandalized. Yes, the devil is still doing his work. I recall that the same thing had happened to another Ukrainian Orthodox Church at St. Julien, Saskatchewan about ten or fifteen miles west of Wakaw. If I recall I had heard that there was over $10,000.00 dollars damage done to the church at St. Julien. I don't know how much damage was done to the church in Hudson Bay, but in the Ukrainian Voice newspaper of February 9th, 2009 there are three pictures of the damage to the church. The pictures resemble what we see on TV after a tornado or hurricane passes through leaving destruction everywhere.

Robert is building a house to sell on Bull Moose Road on Regal Ridge east of Osoyoos. Bags of mix was made up and holes, scratches and joints were filled in. The house has 3600 square feet, including the full basement, so there is a lot of work to do. When this will be finished, then comes the sanding of the wall and ceiling and finally the painting. When the painting is finished then we can start laying ceramic tiles on the floor. After that there will be rock put on the front outside wall and the landscaping.

Kevin, Joyce's older son, has been in the RCMP for some twenty plus years in Ontario. The RCMP finally gave him a transfer to British Columbia after he had told them he was quitting and retiring. I guess they did not want to lose a good man, so they transferred him to British Columbia. He started work in his new place on February 2nd, a day after his and Robert's birthday. He also thinks that he will be involved in one way or another with the 2010 winter Olympic games in Vancouver.

On February 4th we got a phone call from a very good friend, Olga Sworin, at Grassland, Alberta, notifying us that her husband William (Bill) passed away. We knew that Bill had been sick for nearly a year or more and Joyce and I talked that if he should pass away we would go to his funeral. But as my mother said many times: "We make plans and God changes them." A week before this Joyce had the flu and then Kevin was hit with it also. I got hit with a flu and cold. I got a sore throat on the fifth and the flu bug on the 6th. I did not go to help Robert at Bull Moose, because not feeling well. I finally started to lose the cold on the 9th and began to feel better on the 10th of February. Because of this we could not attend the funeral which I would have dearly loved to. Because I had known Bill and Olga for years, and it made me feel more like family. When I served in the 1960's in the Lac La Biche Parish, Bill and Olga Sworin were living in the interior of British Columbia. One year they came back home to Grassland area and while they were visiting I had the honor of baptizing their daughter Gloria. I would have wanted so dearly to be at Bill's funeral, but I guess it's not want we want, but what and how God wants.

AND STILL WORKING DAY TO DAY

Last year on February 23rd, Home Hardware in Osoyoos had already put out their garden plants outside the store to sell. The town was also sweeping the streets for a few days. Looking at the same day a year later, the lake is still frozen, snow is still lying all over on white mountains in every direction you look. Is that a sign of Global Warming. If it is, I would sure like to see where it is warming up. The prairies are again shivering in a deepfreeze cold spell that has invaded them from the north. I have told others, how could it be Global warming when temperatures seem to be colder this year than they were years back. The other day a friend told me that he cannot find an answer to the question of Global warming. He says that dinosaurs lived near Drumheller, Alberta millennium years ago. It means that they did not live in the cold place. If it was -20 or -30 in Drumheller the dinosaurs would not have lived there, so it goes to show that the earth was warmer at that time, than it is today. I say that ice in the Arctic Ocean melted before and is still melting today. First we were told there is "Global warming." Now they changed the name to "Climate change". What will they think of next to give a new name to their invention? I don't care how much one wishes to talk about Global warming or Climate change, they will not be able to do nothing about it, because this world in is God's Hands not ours. He has been looking after it for millennium years and He will still look after it but whether it will be for the good or bad, that will depend on how people live and thank God for what they have.

Sometimes I sit and wonder at God's great marvels and Wondrous things and the ways He does. When I was on my first parish in Lac La Biche in Alberta 1962-1967, one year I had taken a vacation (holidays) in 1964 or 1965. So where did I go? First time into the mountains and down into the Okanagan Valley. There was no one that I knew in those areas but to get acquainted with the mountains that is where the car carried me. I very well remember going through Kelowna on the "old floating bridge" and down through Penticton and into the southern Okanagan. I went as far as Osoyoos, and then turned east unto highway #3 the "Crowsnest Highway" towards Cranbrook. I very distinctly remember Osoyoos as I stopped on the side of the road on the east side of Osoyoos on the mountain top and from the viewpoint admired God's beauty, lake, trees, mountains, blue sky, Osoyoos in British Columbia and Oroville in Washington USA.

Had someone in the 1960's told me that one day I would live in Osoyoos, I would have told the person they did not know what they were talking about. What would I have to come to Osoyoos for? What is there in store for me in Osoyoos? But as we see God does things His way and differently from what man thinks or does. Not only that I lived in Osoyoos, but the road that leads east out of town up and hundreds of feet overlooking the town, just a stone's throw from highway #3, I have spent the last few years every summer helping in the building of a five thousand square foot house for Robert Burk, Kim his wife and their two children Erin and Ashley. As I toiled there during the summer months I could see thousands of vehicles, cars, trucks, motorcycles, buses, cyclists, etc. on that highway just above where I toiled. That is how and what God does in His Wondrous ways. Robert's house is only a hundred yards from the highway on which I drove some nearly half a century ago.

My thought always was, that as the years rolled unto my shoulders, I would retire someplace not too far away from where I was born, so that I could rest the weary bones in my homeland. Like my father he would say many times that he would like to go back to Ukraine where he was born and to die there at his birthplace. But it was not to be, for God had completely different plans than what he have. No, plans just don't happen.

God causes them to be and happen. He only has to think and it will be done. Do we not say in the Lord's Prayer: *"Thy will be done on earth as it is in Heaven?"* So how can I or for that fact anyone else say and think that they do as they want or please. No my child, you can't do it without God's will. I never thought or knew that one day I would end up in Osoyoos to spend my last years which I have remaining on this earth. But why things happen as they happen, only God knows, because His will and plans that He had, has and will have for every being on earth are different than our wills, wishes or dreams.

Spring must be slowly waking up to the warm sunshine. On March 4th it was the first time that this spring I saw a man on the field. Where? Not far from our place and across from the High School in Osoyoos. Yes he was tilling the field and getting ready to plant grape seedlings. Yes between Kelowna and Osoyoos there are tons of wineries. There is something like over twenty wineries between Osoyoos and Oliver in a distance of about twelve miles. The fruit trees are being ripped out of the ground and everyone is going into vineyards-grapes. What happens if there will be too many wineries and not enough fruit? The liquor prices will have to drop and the fruit prices will go up.

As I have mentioned before that when heavier rains come, the neighbors and we get water in our basements. Well this year in 2009 we had made plans to do something about it. On April 3rd the neighbor with his help and Robert with his crew got together and we pulled out fourteen gorgeous beautiful healthy green cedars between our houses. We moved the crushed rock to the side. Then Robert brought thick basement wrap about three or four feet wide. We made a little channel like, and put the basement wrap one on top of another, and covered it all back with rock. Now if water comes it will run down the gully and into a four inch white plastic pipe. Ray our neighbor made a hole in the concrete wall while I dug a trench from ten inches deep to four feet deep under the lawn and garden and put the pipe in. We covered it with dirt and now any water that will come will come down on the basement wrap, will go into the pipe and out to the sidewalk and street.

The following day on the 4th I still pulled up and cleaned up the roots where the cedars had been planted. I also rototilled the garden and planted some early and hardy seeds and plants: carrots, onions, garlic, beets, radish and lettuce. When the plants did start to come up, another foe showed up. I noticed that the beautiful lettuce about two inches tall was chewed-eaten by something. Oh it's probably those quails coming and eating the garden before I get up in the mornings. But then one day as I was doing something on the side of the house, what do I catch in my sight? Yea, I see a chipmunk standing on his hind legs beside a lettuce leaf and is having a picnic. Oh, so it's not the quails, it's the chipmunk. A day later or so the neighbor is outside and tells me that there is a chipmunk running around our area and they feed him nuts. So they feed him nuts, but he is also coming over to our garden for his salad.

For about a month I have nothing marked in my diary. There was always something to do at home and finding work around the yard. It was not until it got somewhat warmer in May that I finally ventured out with enough faith that my hands will not get cold and I started to put rock on the outside of the house on Bull Moose. I started "rocking" the front of the house and it took quit a while to do it. I was doing that myself, while Robert, Kevin and David they were always doing something else or working at Roberts yard on Hallis building a swimming pool and gazebo. There is a high peak on the front of the house on Bull Moose, so I had to use a ladder to get to the top. You have to measure a rock, cut it, go up and try if it fits, come down and go up with the mortar with the rock and carry some mortar to put on the wall. So it was a lot of ups and downs the ladder, but that was good, because it gave me a chance to burn off some of the stored winter fat I had on my "table muscle".

When Robert and Kim are away, Joyce goes to stay with the girls at their place. In the morning she brings and drops them off at the school and then comes home. Afternoon she would pick them up at school and go back to Hallis to stay with the girls overnight. This one morning she comes home and says that she left the car at the garage. What happened? When the car sat still it was okay, but when she would press the gas pedal and the pressure comes up, gasoline starts to leak someplace under the car. I went to the garage and the people said they need a part that would cost about $150.00. I looked under the car and say: "Why don't you put on a clip like on a rubber hose and tighten it and see what will happen." I guess they would not make too much money that way. But they did as I suggested. The car has been working like it should ever since.

July was hot and we worked when it was cooler in the morning and quit earlier in the afternoon when it got too hot. In July we were now building an outdoor swimming pool at Roberts place. Also the gazebo was being built near the house and the swimming pool. A lot of concrete was brought in and we made all the patios on the back side of the house and around the pool. We also built a pump house for the swimming pool. Yet all the work was not finished because it began to get cool in the fall and we had to leave things for next spring. A fence or wall still has to be built around the swimming pool. The fireplace in the gazebo still has to be finished with rock. The bar and counter top in the gazebo need to be finished. So all this was left to spring 2010. At the same time when some of the work around the pool was being done, I would be at Bull Moose putting on tile around the tubs and the Jacuzzi tub in the washrooms and splash guard tiles on the kitchen wall.

In October we received some bad news. A very good friend of ours, Sonia Balaban, passed away. She had lived in Lac La Biche with her husband Bill. Years ago Bill had a stroke and Sonia was Bill's third arm doing everything for him. Sonia sang and cantored in church. With Bill (she was also his chauffeur), they went to church services in the parish and to many services outside the Lac La Biche Parish. Sonia also helped in the hall whenever there were any functions. She was involved in many other church activities. She had been ill with cancer for over one year. They even made one trip to see us in Osoyoos, but we did not see them, because we were away at that time.

When Marusia was still living in Lac La Biche, every year during Orthodox Christmas Eve we would be at Bill and Sonia's place for Christmas Eve Supper with all their children and grandchildren. We were like family. When Marusia passed away we still visited often back and forth. They lived twelve miles south of town. Now that she passed away Bill called so we would come and sing at the funeral. When we arrived we learned that the parish priest would not be doing the funeral service, but another priest from Edmonton will be the celebrant. Marusia died in 2001 on October 4th and Sonia on October 3rd of 2009.

Prayers for Sonia were held on October 8th and the funeral the following day. The service was in All Saints Ukrainian Orthodox Church in Lac La Biche and the funeral at St. Demetrious Ukrainian Orthodox

Church at Craigend, so we left for Lac la Biche on October 7th and got to John and late Kay's place at 7:30 that evening and stayed at his place. Next morning we left for Lac La Biche. Traveling to Lac La Biche we encountered a number of snow squalls along the way and the weather was cold. I guess I forgot that we were back on the prairies, but we were prepared because we had thrown parkas and winter boots into the car, so we were not worried about freezing. When the funeral was over, lunch followed in the Craigend Community Hall and right after that everyone began to leave for their homes. We arrived back in Edmonton at 4:30 PM at John and Kay's place and stayed the night there again. Next morning we left Edmonton, drove to Airdrie, by-passed Calgary and were home at 8:45 PM. The highways were good to Lac La Biche and back.

Spring had come and gone, then summer came for a visit and it also left on its way and following it, fall arrived for a visit also. Since we moved to Osoyoos we had our boxes and things stored in the two car garage. Because of the space taken up with our possessions there was room only for one car. I kept saying that we need to have a garage sale and get rid of things we will never need. FINALLY - after many times of talking about a garage sale it was held on November 7th. Things were sold and there were still things left over. So what do we do with the rest of the things? Put them back in to take up space or what? We knew that the Kiwanis club in Oliver took in things and then sold them to the public. So one day we stopped in Oliver and talked to the people about what we have. They said they will take anything we have. A lady from Osoyoos who helps in Oliver said she would come and take the things. One day she called and came with her small car. We loaded her car, but there were still things left, so I loaded the big car Marquis, and with the two full cars we took things to Oliver. The Kiwanis club sell the things and then turn over the funds into local projects. That way they help the community.

Robert purchased a house on Bayview downtown on the shore of Osoyoos Lake. As for other days, I just did what had to be done in the remodeling of the house on Bayview. Robert would be there helping or showing what to do. I spent the time in cutting tiles and tiling the bathroom walls with 8"x8" tiles. Then the kitchen wall were the sink (splash guard) was also tiled with smaller tiles that were left over from other cuttings. Granite counter tops were installed. Walls removed. Floor covering was removed and hardwood floor put in. Ceramic tiles put in the bathrooms and kitchen. Tiles were put on the walls and floor, then grouting was done and washing. New shingles were replaced on the roof. The whole house had a good changeover.

Now came the time to look at the garden again. Being busy, the days are shorter and working each day, did not give me the chance to rototill the garden this year. On Saturday, if I wasn't working, than maybe it was raining or some other thing that I did not have the time to do the tilling, so first time ever since who knows when I did not have the garden tilled this fall. Maybe it will now be as an experiment to see how things will grow when the garden was not tilled in the fall. At last on December 1st I dug out the carrots. The beets were dug out much sooner, because when I was at work, Joyce dug them out and made borsch.

When December 3rd came, Joyce, Robert, Kim, Erin and Ashley all left early at 5:00 AM to Penticton. They are off to Thailand for a week where Robert has a house and from there they fly out to Australia for a ten day cruise along the east coast of Australia. They will be gone for three weeks until December 21st. They left in the morning and the following day we got about half an inch of snow but it was all gone by noon.

Now problems are starting for me. I was starting to get a backache. Also the optometrist office had called earlier to tell me that I need another eye examination and they scheduled that for December 7th. Because of the backache, I had also made an appointment to the clinic to see the doctor about the backache. This same day I went across the border to pick up a parcel for Joyce's niece in Okotoks, Alberta. When I came home from the USA, I stopped at home addressed the package and drove to Penticton to send it by bus.

Some time earlier I had been having problems with the printer. Everything would be open and always a message comes on the screen that the printer will not print because the door is closed. Now I know if the door is opened or not, because it was working before and now it quit. The old printer I had put in plastic and threw it outside in the corner of the garage. When I had been in Penticton a month or so earlier, I had bought a new Brother printer. Brought it home and hooked it up but never used it for about two or three weeks. When I did use it for the first time, I printed about 35-40 pages and a sign comes on that no more black ink in the cartridge. What, just 40 pages printed and no ink? I had bought another cartridge, put it in and this time printed only eight (8) pages and again it says that there is no ink in the cartridge. Well this printer is going back where it came from, back to Staples in Penticton.

So when I took the parcel to the Bus Depot in Penticton, I also took the new printer back to Staples. I told them what happened. They plugged in the printer, pressed a few buttons and asked me if I wanted my money back. Yea, I want my money back, but I also need a printer. So they credited me and I went and picked out another printer.

When I came home I put the new printer with the box under the desk and it's sitting there, not even taken out yet. I went and brought in the old Canon one IP4300 that was sitting in the cold garage and plugged it in and hooked it to the computer. I knew that it will tell me that the door is not open. I turned it on, punched in what I wanted to print and ZIPPO, away goes the printing. That old printer has been going since. The new one is sitting in the box, unopened. So I figure that when the old printer sat outside in the cold with -12 C temperatures, it changed its mind and wanted to be in the warm room, so it started to work and has been till now.

HEALTH PROBLEMS AGAIN

On December 7th I saw the eye doctor and I had an appointment with the doctor for a prescription refill. When I saw the doctor, he said my blood pressure was high, but that could partly be because of the fact that I had a backache and blood pressure will go up when a person is not well. Even though the backache was there, I was still going to Bayview to work in the house, but did not do much on December 8th because ran out of tile adhesive. The pain was getting worse so that I had to use a cane to get around.

My backache was getting worse. On the 12th of December I drove to emergency to the hospital in Oliver. My doctor was on duty that day and I had a chance to see me. They took x-rays of my back and the doctor said that I had a Sciatica problem. Now I have heard of that Sciatic, but did not think about it, until it came to visit me and showed me how much pain it could be. Since my blood pressure was still high, doctor Van Der Westhisain put me on nitroglycerin patches to put on each day. He said to keep track of the blood pressure and see what happens. When the pain was not going away, I went to see the doctor again on December 19th. Oh yea, this is St. Nicholas Day in the Ukrainian Orthodox Church.

When I saw the doctor he said I may need some therapy to relieve the Sciatica pain. I asked him about a chiropractor or a massager, if that would help. He said that I can go and see a massager and he gave me a paper to go and see Greg Inkster. I went with the cane because of the pain. The massager massaged my back and leg and when I was leaving him, I carried the cane and did not use it. I felt good. For some time now I have been getting from time to time a blood like patch on the top of my left hand. The massager asked me what that was and I told him that it happens a few times during the year. He started to work on my left hand and said that by Sunday the spot will be gone. And by God, as he had said, it happened. When Sunday came I got up and sure enough there was no spot on the hand.

So the back pain was gone for a day, but then came back again. No help. So now what? Go back to the massager? I decided to try one more thing. Go and see a chiropractor. I went and was taken in to see Dr. Martha Collins who took x-rays of the back and neck. She spent some time with me and explained what the Sciatica is. She said a person's Sciatica nerve is as big as a person's thumb. She said that Sciatica can be healed for some people in two or three treatments and for some it may take from four to six weeks before relief will come. I had a treatment this day and the following day I had two more treatments at 9:30 AM and at 12:00 noon. And true to behold, the backaches had stopped.

That is how the old year ended. But then the New Year 2010 started like the old one ended. It snowed two inches overnight and than in the afternoon it started to rain on January 1st. When it snows one has to shovel the snow off the side walks and the shoveling really does not help when you have a back ache. In Osoyoos in the Anglican Church there are three of us families that are mixed marriages. There are Harold and Audrey Cox, Ian and Helen Ritchie and Joyce and I. Last Year Helen Ritchie wanted to do a Ukrainian Orthodox Christmas Eve Supper, but it was too late by the time anything was to be done. So when the New Year began, the three of us families met to plan this supper. We met on January 2nd. We decided who would do what. For the last two Sundays they announced in church that who would like to attend to put their names down so that we would have a more less figure of how much food to prepare. When January 6th, Ukrainian Orthodox Christmas Eve came, the three of us families were busy getting things ready for the Holy Supper in the evening. Some things had been prepared a day or two prior to the 6th. But then on the sixth, tables were set up and everything else prepared at home and then brought to the church basement for the 6:00 PM supper. Forty-five people attended the supper. For almost everyone this was the first time they had seen this kind of due. It was weeks later when people were still meeting us in church or on the street and thanking us for what they had experienced. Yes we had, kutia (boiled wheat) and kolachee, and fish, and varenyky and borsch, etc., etc. After the meal one lady comes and says, "I never knew there could be so many foods without any meat or dairy products in them."

Robert and Kim had purchased a house in Las Vegas, Nevada in the December 2009. They left for Las Vegas beginning of January to buy furniture for the house and do some work that had to be done and maybe even rent the house out if possible. In the meantime on January 12th I went back to Bayview to finish the tiles in the shower room. I had everything finished except two inches from the top. I cut twelve tiles of eight inches long and two inches wide and attached them to the wall. Then I took grout and grouted the walls and the floor in the shower room. That completed the tiling work. There is still some touch up things to do and then finish painting of the walls.

As I have mentioned previously I had purchased a small car, 1997 Ford Contour. That is the car that was in Edmonton and John replaced the brakes and then at night I hit the hole on the highway between Edmonton and Camrose and damaged the tire. Well that car went around town each day, many times to Penticton and Kelowna. But as you read earlier, Joyce and Robert were saying to get a newer car. So I bought a 2006 Chevrolet Cobalt.

Now the Ford Contour, I was going to put it up for sale. But Robert wanted to buy it and then sell it to one of his workers. I took the Contour to Robert's place and it sat there for a few weeks. He made arrangements and gave the car for his worker and the man was to pay Robert for the car. Well the story is different. The worker got the car and drove it to work and back, and wherever he needed. Then one day he was going to work and going up the hill he passes an RCMP cruiser. As I heard the story, the police pulled him over and when they came to check on the driver, he was smoking a toxic cigarette. The car was impounded for a day and later he got it back. Sometimes later yet he was driving it and I guess the engine just blew out and that was the end of that car as I understand.

I PUBLISH A BOOK

I know that all these pages have a lot of reading in them. But this is not the only thing I wrote. I have other material that I have written that could be published. But today to publish a book takes a lot of money. I know there are other kinds of books now, because Joyce has one. I believe they are called e-books. You buy yourself a unit about the size of a paperback, but only about half an inch thick or so. In that e-book you could install hundreds of books. So that is now the latest kind of books that have been invented. So if a person buys one of these he can have hundreds of books in it, so who will buy the book that is printed on paper? So I guess my work that I wrote will stay unpublished.

 Time does not stand still. One day on the computer a pop-up ad jumped on the screen. It was a printing company West Bow Press advertising to self-publish books. I clicked on the ad to get some information and before I knew it I had things filled out to receive more information. As time would have it, I did publish one of my books, "Whose will is its." It is a book on spirituality or religious topic. I ordered fifty books so I could sell them. It is now some three years plus and in that time I have sold thirty books. Yes I gave away some as advertising, but sold thirty books in three years? I have advertised on the Internet on KIJIJI in twenty cities across Canada. As of January 2014 there were 2297 people who checked about the book, and you know what - not one book ordered and sold. At the same time I see that there are twenty-three different places on the Internet that my book is advertised for sale all around the world. Yes these twenty-three places advertising my book in the USA, Great Britain, Australia, Poland, India and China. One would think that at least one person would buy a book. I could say that of those twenty-three places, I would assume that a million people have seen the ad and would buy a book. And do you know what, to date from all the Internet advertising, not one book has been sold. The company West Bow Press also did some advertising of my book, but how many books were sold, I have no idea or record.

I have also sat for about forty to sixty hours at Coles Book Store in Penticton with my books to sign as people would buy them. Yes I sold two books there. I have told people that had it been a book about pornography I would need police to control the crowd for people would come running to get such a book. But because this is about religion, people are running away from God and the religion and nothing is selling. What a world we are living in today. But the time is coming and each day closer to the day when this world will receive what Sodom and Gomorrah received millenniums ago.

I also made a video at home in Lac La Biche of the Ukrainian Orthodox Churches in Canada. It is not a professional work, but at least it is on paper, on slides and a video. All the churches are not on it, but only those that I had a chance to serve in, drove buy and stopped to take a picture. Some are both interior and exterior pictures. If I was serving, I was inside so had a chance to take a picture of the interior. Otherwise when I drove by, the church was locked, so I only took a picture of the exterior. I can say that I did not waste time watching TV, drinking, partying, etc. When I had a few moments of free time, I was busy with something else that is worthwhile. And we know that winters on the Canadian Prairies are long cold and dark, so there is some time at least to do something extra and worthwhile.

We are now nearing to the end of the year as we say, "up to date." This work you are reading was rechecked in in early 2016. Because my age is getting up, I felt that sometimes I am not as fast as I was when I was fifty, when I have been helping Robert and Kevin as much as I did earlier. I did help finish Kevin's house with him in 2012. I felt that because I am older, my response is not quite as it was during younger years, that I should not work with them, because if anything happens that I may fall or trip and then they would have a problem about safety at work. So instead of going and helping in the construction I would go help them to finish Kevin's house. I will mention now and then what I was helping them with. What Robert was doing now, he would build the walls for the house in his shop and then we would transport the walls and set them up where the foundation was poured for the house.

Imagine - a decade has expired in this century. Osoyoos started out when on February 4th the golf course opened so the golfers can start to shine their clubs to start hitting and chasing the little white balls on the green fairways. I have still been seeing the chiropractor from time to time. When I first went to see Doctor Collins, she had me come in twice a day. Then she made it every second day and then once a week. When I felt good and back pains were gone I still had to go and see her, but in January 2012 I had an appointment for another checkup, but it happened that on the same day that I was scheduled for a treatment, we had to leave home in the dark, because Joyce was scheduled to have knee surgery in Penticton. This will be mentioned again later. That day I did not get a treatment.

Yes I helped here and there with the footings and the foundation and then later with the interior of the construction of the house. When concrete was brought in, I helped with that also. With the help of Kevin's house there were also times that we worked at Robert's house putting tiles on the patio at the back of his house. When there was the pouring of the basement at Kevin's house on April 16th, I was hurrying not to be late because cement trucks will bring the concrete and they charge for waiting if the place for pouring concrete is not ready, and as I was driving past the school in our area when low and behold I was stopped by the police for driving too fast. The police had no radar, but he gave me a $138.00 ticket for going too fast in the school zone and it says on the ticket that "in the opinion of the constable" I was going to fast. Maybe I was, it's his word against mine. Anyway the constable checked my records and I think he saw there were no blemishes on my driving, so what he did, he wrote across the ticket: "Warning." So I did not have to pay a fine, but do you know what? Even at night when I drive past that school I drive at 30 km/hour. Why? Well I have talked to two town councillors about the sign by the school, but nothing has been done.

Go to another town or city and they have school zone signs and it tells you that from 8:30 AM to 4:00 PM the speed is 30 km/h. In some places they say the speed is 30 km/h during school days. By our school there is a sign and all it says is "30 km/h". So does that mean that the 30 km/h speed zone by the school is 24/7 , 365 days a year? When I get out on the highway there is a sign that says 80 km/h and I understand that it is such a speed 24/7 at 365 days a year, day or night. When I see the sign by the school in our area and there is a picture of children on the sign and then below it says 30 km/h, so what am I to understand that at this particular school the 30 km/h speed is 24/7 the whole year through?

This same year Robert got another job to frame a house on Sasquatch subdivision. So at times we would do the same thing that Robert and I built the walls in his shop, mark them which is where, pile it outside and cover with a tarp. So I was helping along where help was needed and what I could do. We did the framing in the shop and then hauled all the walls to Sasquatch. The house on Sasquatch was huge, looked like a three story building. Trusses were brought but because of the size of the trusses, the truck that brought the trusses could not get near the house, so the trusses had to be carried from the road to keep the road open. So there never was a dull moment in the construction. But this one day when we were working on that house the temperature on June 15th was only +4 and it was snowing. So one can imagine how high up we were building that house.

Again the same mystery as before that happened a few times. This morning of May 16th when we got up, my cross and chain were on the floor beside the bed. Yes this suspense is still unsolved. Who, what, why the questions still unanswered to this day. Another unsolved question is the wedding ring. The ring is on my finger day and night. But one day after awakening I felt something that my ring was different. I looked at it and sure it is different. Instead of being round like a ring is, the ring on my finger was square, yeah that's right - SQUARE. This occurred 24th of October 2011. How did it become square overnight. I know I didn't squeeze it into a square. I tried to make it round by squeezing it, but I could not. I pressed and tried to squeeze the ring back into a circular, but I could not do it. I did manage after trying different ways to round it out a bit, but it is still not round like it was or should be. So how did the ring become square overnight?. Who, why and what is the unsolved mystery?

Another family story would be better told by my brother John than by me, for it was him that had the misfortune of what happened. On July 26th John and another friend got into the car and drove east of Edmonton towards Vegreville to look for and pick red top mushrooms. They found some bush and went looking for the red top mushrooms which we call: "kozaree" I believe in was in the Mundare area. As John was walking, he tripped on a wire fence which was in the ground and in the brush which he did not see. He fell and broke his ankle. Now he could not walk because of the pain. He had a cell phone and called for help. He asked that they send a helicopter to fly him out because he was in the bush and quite some distance from the road and his car. What happened was that an ambulance came to his rescue, but he insisted that they get a helicopter because they can't drive in with the ambulance into the bush. The paramedics said that they will carry him out on a stretcher. They brought the stretcher and carried him out to the road, put him into the ambulance and off to Edmonton they went. John spent a week in the hospital and finally he had surgery to place his ankle into position. To that time they did not do nothing to his ankle because it was swollen. Finally in the surgery they put a stainless(?) steel (?) rod in his foot from his heel up to near the knee. Yes John has recovered and I always forget to ask him when he is going to go pick mushrooms again. He keeps telling me that if we need anything, go to the store and buy it. But John, they also have mushrooms in the store, so why did you not buy those mushrooms, but you went looking for them in the bush.

And so the days come and go. And it is now two years since the last family reunion and in 2012 we meet once again. This time it fell to have the reunion in British Columbia. Diane Russell living in Delta, B.C., near Vancouver took upon herself to make arrangements. She found a place at White Rock, B.C. which was very nice and convenient because it was inside the city. We had sleeping quarters, there was a space for games outside on the yard, there were meals prepared by the caterers of the owners of the place. So all in all it was a very good spot. The nest reunion is scheduled for Las Vegas, Nevada. Yes we would like to go, but Joyce was waiting for the hospital in Penticton to call when she is to come in for second knee surgery. So that reunion was missed, for I would have liked to go and see the place in Las Vegas, because I had passed near it and only stopped once when John, late Kay, Marusia and I went to Phoenix for John's one day course that the company from Edmonton had sent him to attend.

During all this time, the time slips by and waits for no one. I was still helping Kevin and Robert at construction. Oh, there is so much work on a new house before one can see the finished product. I helped with what was needed and when needed. But I spent much time in "rocking." I never did this before, but at Robert's house, the gazebo and Kevin's house I did most of the rock work, installing rocks on the outside of the house. It is time consuming. You mix the mortar, have the rocks near you, put mortar on the wall and the rock and apply the rock to the wall. Many times rocks do not fit, so you need to find one that would or get a bigger one and cut it. When all the rock is finished then comes the muriatic wash of the rocks. I found out also that if there is too much humidity, the rocks do not want to bind to the wall. If the wall is too hot from the sun, then also the mortar on the wall dries up too quickly and it will not bind as it should.

This year in the fall, eyes and ears of the people in the world were glued to their televisions in their homes. A tragedy had struck in Chile. There was an explosion or earthquake and miners were stuck in the mine and could not get out. A hole had to be dug to where the miners were. There a cage was built to fit the hole. It was sixty-nine days later that the miners were finally pulled out of the mine one by one and I sat and watched until the last miner was out and free. A special cage had been built and was let down into the mine and one miner at a time was pulled out in that cage. Emotions ran high as the last miner was finally freed. This was indeed a miracle. Think for a minute that you are locked alive in the earth for over two months. What would you do? What would you think? It is a real test for one's nerves. Being buried alive in the earth's crust for over two months? ? ?

The year is running to the end. Many things happened in this past year, but before the last month flew away more bad news arrived. Sophie Kozushka from Sturgis, Saskatchewan called and said that her husband Eddy was not well. She said that he was in the Yorkton Hospital. This news came by telephone on December 1st. It was a few months later on February 20th, 2011 that Eddy passed away. You may recall that when

Marusia and I got married, Eddy and Sophie were our attendants at our marriage in Moose Jaw in 1988. How I wished that I could have attended that funeral, but a few days before I had the privilege of having a bad cough and a cold. When Sophie had first called that Eddy was not well I had already been figuring out how I would go to the funeral. I would fly either to Regina or Saskatoon and rent a car. But mother used to say: "We make plans and God changes them." Why did that cough and cold not come a week before or a week after his funeral, but exactly at that time? But even before Eddy passed away Oksana, my sister also ran into trouble. On February 2nd she was taken to hospital by ambulance in the middle of the night and on February 5th she had surgery. We never did find out what the surgery was, but she recovered from what ever had been the problem.

WINDSOR, ONTARIO AND HOME

Each year after Easter (Christ's Resurrection), the priest and people visit the cemeteries and have grave blessing. In 2011 there will be grave side services in Wakaw on May 15th. Joyce and I leave for Wakaw on May 13th. Is this Friday superstitious? Well lets see what happens. We drive to Kelowna and leave our car in the parking lot. We leave by plane from Kelowna and fly to Saskatoon, through Calgary. In Calgary after we are ready to leave the terminal we get a very bad smell of fuel in the plane. I wonder what would have happened if a spark would have happened inside the plane at that time. Anyway as we are thinking what is happening the captain comes on the intercom and says: "Ladies and gentlemen. We are having a little problem. One of our engines does not want to start." What? And we will fly in a plane that one engine is a problem? Anyway the door to the plane is opened and two service people come into the cockpit, look at something and went out. A minute or two later they come in again and do something and leave. Next we hear that there is some noise on the engine where we are sitting, but we can't see what they are doing, because the cover of the engine was opened towards us. After what they did, they came back into the cock pit, went out and the engine started. When they left and the door of the plane was closed, then the pilot comes on and says. "Ladies and gentlemen. We had a little problem with an igniter. We will be pushed away from the terminal and will try and rev up the engine and see if it will work. If all is well, we will be taking off." Yes we did take off and arrived in Saskatoon, but at the back of the mind there was: "one of the engines does not want to start." I guess technicians knew what they are doing. We arrived in Saskatoon, got a rent a car and drove out to Wakaw to John and Alice's place where we stayed for the week-end. The rental car that we were given I had seen on TV the ads that those certain cars were giving good mileage. No they don't. I was disappointed with the mileage I made with the car we were given. On Saturday I washed the grave stone of Marusia, her parents and put some new flowers on the graves. Sunday was the service in church and a meal in the church basement and then services on the graves. Following the grave services, we drove to Saskatoon and rented a motel near the airport. Tomorrow morning we are leaving Saskatoon.

Come Monday morning Joyce leaves at 6:00 AM to Windsor, Ontario where she will visit family and friends and also take in the convention of the quilters guild. I also wait at the air terminal because I will be flying west to Kelowna at 8:00 AM. If I had to drive to Saskatoon it's a two day trip one way. I leave Saskatoon at 8:25 AM., change planes in Calgary, arrive in Kelowna and I am at home at 2:00 in the afternoon. In six hours I'm home but by car I would still be someplace in Alberta. By car about fifteen hours of driving one way. Joyce arrived home a few days later after she visited with her brother, her friends and was at the quilters convention.

Being in Saskatoon I had an opportunity to fulfill another part of Marusia's last wishes before her passing. She had asked me that if and when I sell the house in Lac La Biche, she wanted me to give each of her nephews and nieces $5,000.00 from the sale of the house. She had five nephews and nieces in Saskatoon, Anne, Mary, George, Fred, Bill and Mike in Cold Lake, Alberta. I had finally scraped up enough dough that I could give those in Saskatoon of what Marusia had wanted. George, Bill and Mike has passed away, so I gave it to their wives. Now I am still trying to save up another $15,000.00 because Marusia had three nieces in Ontario. I finally managed to save up $15,000.00 to give her nieces the money in Ontario. I was looking that I may have to borrow some money from a bank if I need, but I wanted to fulfill Marusia's last request. With God's help I did manage to get enough funds to pay the three nieces, but there was one problem. Two of the nieces are living in Ontario, but their sister had not been heard from for quite some time. I checked on the Internet for people search but could not find their sister. I went to the RCMP in Osoyoos and asked them to see if they can locate her, but they said they could not help me with such a request. So what happens after you have no contact with someone for so many years? Are there any laws or rules about such an incident? The third niece did finally notify the family where she was and so I also sent her the $5000.00 like I did for her sisters.

Time is moving along and never waits for anyone. Things are done when and what is needed from day to day. Then we get surprised visitors stopping in for a few moments to see us. Fred and Lorraine Waskowicz from Prairie River, Saskatchewan stopped on their way home to say hello. They were in the Okanagan Valley visiting friends and where on their way home traveling east to Alberta and Saskatchewan to see their family along the way home. They lived about thirty miles west of Hudson Bay, and when I served that church in Hudson Bay they never missed a church service. Yes how many people live a block or two from their church and you seldom if ever see them in church. Why? Because they are the "E" and "C" people who come to church at **E**aster and **C**hristmas.

OSOYOOS LIFE GOES ON

The Chevrolet Cobalt was starting to pile up more miles each day and the fuel price is not going down but up, so I decided to find something with a smaller engine that uses less fuel. One day being at the Hyundai dealer in Penticton for an oil change, I saw a beautiful bright blue 2009 Kia Sentra car. Yes I made a deal and bought the little car. After having driven it for a few months I realized that the mileage I was getting from driving it did not change much from the Chevrolet Cobalt. I drove the Kia until I saw in the paper that Hyundai dealer in Kelowna was selling 2010 Accent cars for a lower price then regular. I went to check out what was what and found out that they had purchased a bunch of cars from a car rental company and were able to sell them cheaper because they bought the whole group of those cars. After a check of the cars and discussion, I purchased a 2010 Hyundai Accent in June 2012. I believe that Hyundai owns 40% of Kia, or I could be wrong, maybe Kia owns 40% of Hyundai. Yes, this car has a better mileage, but I still want something to get even better economy. Somehow all vehicles today seem to be overpriced, and the mileage they are said to get, does not add up.

When July ended and August came, again I got caught up someplace with the inner ear imbalance. Again the nauseated and dizzy feeling. I had to stop and recuperate before trying to do nothing, but lay still. Three days came and went before I saw some relief from this imbalance and to get back to the mountain to help Kevin finish off his house. I did the tiles in the house in the bathrooms and then grouted the walls and the floor. In November it is already cooler but there was heat in the house, so it was warm enough to do what had to be done. But again that inner ear gave me that same problem it has given me in the past. For three days I tried to cure that imbalance but on the fourth day I asked Joyce to take me to emergency on November 14th at 9:30 AM. Came back home at 2:30 PM. The doctor at the hospital made an appointment for me to have a cat scan in Penticton the following day, for he thought I had a heart attack. The cat scan showed negative.

Then came November 18th and the earth had a heart attack. At 5:09 AM as we were sleeping we heard the rattling of the shower doors in the bathroom. Now who would be in the shower and if someone is in the house, how did they get in? In was later during the day we heard on the news that there was an earthquake about forty miles south in the USA not very far from Omak, Washington and it is thirty miles to Omak from our place. We never felt the house move, but only the shower door in the bathroom rattled. Gave us a scare thinking someone had crawled into the house without us hearing him.

On November 19th I got a strange phone call from Ukraine. Some man by the name of Fedorowich called asking about Marusia. He said he was in Edmonton in the summer and got my phone number from people in Edmonton. He said that Oleksander Fedorowich was his grandfather and somehow that was tied to Paziuk who Marusia had been married to. He said he wanted information about Marusia, because they were writing and working on a history book about the family. I could not understand him very good what he was saying, because half of his speech was Russian. He also wanted photographs of Marusia, which we sent him through email. After that, never heard from him anymore.

When Joyce was not feeling too well one day she went to see the doctor. She was checked over and some tests were done and then given a prescription. On December 19th Joyce gets a call from the hospital so she would quit taking aspirin, Lipitor and Celebrex. This was the hospital calling, but we never did find out why she had to stop using those prescriptions. Was someone just experimenting with these drugs on her? I know that Marusia had been on Lipitor when we lived in Calgary and she was told to stop taking them immediately because it was causing holes in her liver. Did the tests find something wrong that Joyce was taking them and now told to stop.

As you have probably already noticed that as the years crawl up on one's back, and there is less being written for each year. Yes I had a good memory at one time, until I was put on blood thinners when I had gotten phlebitis while I was in Dauphin. I was told by some medical people that the medication I was on had a side effect of memory loss. And nowadays they call memory loss, "dementia." I know myself that at one time in younger years and not using any medication my memory was much, much better than it is now. How do I know? When I was in the RCAF, twice once in St. Jean, Quebec and once in Winnipeg I was asked to go into air crew in the RCAF. Now do they put people who have poor memory into air crew? The military will not take you even into the military if your memory or mind are not normal. Today as this is written, it is written according to my records that I have kept from 1961 to the present time. Had I not put down on paper, these events would not be as thorough as they are, or this book would not have been published.

Now the clock has struck 2012. Starting off the New Year, it started on the wrong foot for Joyce. She had been complaining of aches and pains in her knees for a number of years. Finally 2012 starts out with Joyce going under the knife for knee surgery on January 9th. We had been told that she would probably be in the hospital for three, maybe four days, but she spent a week, returning home on January 16th. Why longer, because they discovered that she was low on blood and they had to give her four pints of blood because the hemoglobin was very low. When she did finally come home, she needed help in everything, for she could not walk and she could not drive the car for two months. Besides that I had to drive her for physic-therapy to the hospital in Oliver every second day for a few weeks. I did the cooking, washing and helped her dress and everything else.

Then I had an experience on January 11th, two days after Joyce's surgery when Joyce was still in the hospital. I was home having come from the hospital in the evening, had my supper and started to wash the dishes at 9:00 PM, yes late this day. As I was washing the dishes, someone in the house startled me by saying out loud and clear: "HI." startled I turned around but there was no one in the house and yet so clearly this came out of nowhere. Who was it? It sounded like a woman's voice. Joyce has told me of an episode that she had one time when she was sewing with the machine in the basement. She said that someone touched her on the shoulder. She was startled when she turned around and there was no one. And not to be out done, I had the same feeling twice that seemed like someone touched me on the shoulder and do you get startled. What are all these things happening around us from time to time? Who is doing all this? Angels, God, the devil, and why? When Joyce was in the hospital we also had to install a new furnace because the old one was not breathing anymore and was dying a slow death. Robert said that he will get the furnace looked after getting a price through a contractor. We had applied for two grants, Federal and Provincial, for installing a new furnace. The two grants that came I gave to Robert, but I never received any statement how much the furnace was or labour costs. So when Joyce came home the new furnace was already installed and working. It was also on January 20 that I took Joyce to the clinic because she had to have the staples removed from her knee following the surgery.

A while back I mentioned that an earthquake had taken place about forty miles south of Osoyoos. Another earthquake occurred again on January 17th that measured 2.8 on the Richter Scale. This time the earthquake was NE of Osoyoos and SE of Oliver which would in my estimation be about where Baldy Mountain Ski resort is. This time we hear no noise or felt anything like the first time.

LIFE MOVES ALONG

Come January 18th is the day before Epiphany, Baptism of Jesus in the Jordan River. This is another Epiphany Eve Supper that the family tries to be home together. But it has also been known that the church is a family of many people. So there is a meatless supper after the water is blessed in church. In some congregations they have the supper on the 19th of January where all kinds of food are served. This day I go to Kelowna for the 4:00 PM blessing of water and then supper. Joyce is at home and Arlene Grieg came over to stay with her for a few hours before I return home. But the road was something else. Three to four inches of snow had been coming down all day so the road was wet and slushy. Yes in some places the plows had cleared the road, but as they cleared the snow, more came down so it is hard to keep up with the snow in some places. The following day another five inches of snow fell and that took three hours to clear the snow off the driveway and sidewalks.

Gold and silver prices are going up, yes up, but for how long, we don't know. Some people were coming into Osoyoos for the weekends at a hotel and were buying gold and silver. People were bringing all kinds of money. The buyers told me that one day a man brought his coins in a wheel barrow because it was too much and too heavy to carry. I took a pocket watch that I have. The people said they don't buy pocket watches, but told me that if I go to Vernon to an antique dealer I should be able to get $450.00 - $600.00 for the watch. It is a year now since that happened and the pocket watch is still in the drawer. I did go to Vernon one day in 2014 and took the watch. The man looked at it and said that it would be worth about $300.00. He said he did not want to buy it, but took my name and phone number that in case someone would be interested and would want such a watch, he would know where I live and have such a watch.

Back to the computer printer story again, yes again. On February 8th of 2012 the printer died. Well, I will not bother with it, but go get a new printer. I got more than I bargained for. I went to Penticton and bought at Staples a Brother printer. Good. I brought it home hooked everything up and away we go. After printing about thirty to forty sheets of paper, the screen tells me that no more ink left. I had bought an extra cartridge of ink, so I install it and keep printing. About eight sheets printed out, the sign comes on that there is no ink. Now that can't be. Something wrong with this machine. It goes back into the box and back to Staples. Then I went next door by Staples to Zellers and bought an Epson printer. Brought it home, hooked everything up and each time it pushes the paper to be printed on, there is a noise like a car running into a building. Bang-crash-bang-crash. Loud crashing noise each time a sheet of paper is fed. This won't work either. Back it goes to Zellers. But I need a printer. So as Joyce is at physic-therapy in the hospital at Oliver, I go to Source (Radio Shack) and buy a nice Lexmark printer. Same as with others, I hook it up and it works good, but one flaw. It was a demonstrator and I guess it demonstrated too much and had a little problem. Each time a printed sheet came out, it had a small mark at the beginning of the paper, that the paper was catching some object and the paper was bent up. Well that is no good either. So a day or two later it also goes back where it came from. But I need a printer and I don't have one. I'll look on KIJIJI again and maybe I'll find something. I sure did. I found a canon MX510 that a person was selling in Kelowna and he wanted $75.00 for it. The ad said that this printer cost over $200.00 when it was new. I answered the ad and next time I was in Kelowna I went to the address to pick it up. It is more elaborate for it had a scanner, copier, Fax, printer, all kinds of trinkets. I asked the man why he was selling it and he said that he changed his courses at the University and does not need it anymore. I paid him what he wanted and he gave me $60.00 worth of ink that he purchased for the printer, so I can say that I only got the printer for $15.00. That printer had been working pretty good. I would say that this printer is somewhere between a regular and a commercial type printer. It has three ink colors, so that when one color runs out, I only refill the color cartridge and keep printing. All in total there are five cartridges. Two black, one for printing and one black for photographs. Three colors are Magenta(red), Yellow and Cyan(blue). That MX510 worked until it died in 2016. It went to the recycle depot and I purchased a new one from Source and it works just fine so far.

Not only the printers were not practicing what they are supposed to be doing, but also the computer decided that he had enough of me. I had bought it in Lac La Biche, I believe it was in 2005. I have a nephew in Austin Texas who works on computers and knows them as well as his own palm on his hand. When we were talking one day on the phone, I told him that my computer has fallen asleep and I told him that I had it at the computer shop and they said that the capacitors are gone and that it will cost more to replace than to buy another computer. But Philip in Austin, Texas said he would send a computer. Good! That is what he did. He put a number of new parts in it and brought it up to grade and shipped it out to Oroville, Washington where I went to pick it up. Coming home across the border I told the customs people that my nephew in Texas sent me a computer. In turn I was asked to bring the computer in. They took it to some room and I guess they were just making sure that there wasn't anything coming into Canada that should not be here. I did have to pay $59.00 of duty at the border. The computer has been working well, except now and then when I maybe hit a wrong button on the keyboard when something goes wrong and then I can't do anything. I call Philip and we get on our computers, me here is Osoyoos and he in Austin Texas, and he gets connected to my computer and I just sit and watch how a few thousand miles away he is roaming all over the screen on my computer and fixing up the problem.

This was the year that Joyce went through two surgeries. She had first knee replacement surgery for her left knee on January 9th 2012. We were told that she would be in the hospital about 4 days. Her second surgery for the right knee took place on August 23rd of this year. This time she spent less time in the hospital but still was given two pints of blood. Things were looking good, until in 2013 something happened that she was starting to get pain again in her left knee. She saw the doctor and then had x-rays taken in Oliver, but has been referred to have x-rays taken at the Kelowna Hospital. We are waiting when she is to have this x-ray but she feels that something is broken in the knee, whether the bone in the knee or the metal part. After time passed by, the doctor said that everything with the knee was okay, but it was in her mind that something was wrong.

On May 2nd we received some bad news. Joyce's brother Howard in Windsor Ontario called in the evening that his wife Janet passed away. Joyce wanted to know when the funeral will be and she would go to be there. Howard said that the body was already cremated. Joyce felt bad about that. But as the days rolled along, Howard later sold his house in Windsor and moved to Sarnia, Ontario where his daughter lives. Joyce is planning on going to visit Howard in Sarnia and also at the same time to attend the graduation of her granddaughter Courtney near Barrie, Ontario. Kevin and Joyce are both going to the graduation leaving at the end of June 2014.

Another sad news item came in the email from Swan River, Manitoba from Emil Rubashewsky telling me that Peter Kurkowsky from Stenen, Saskatchewan passed away. Peter and Mary Kurkowsky have been members of the church in Stenen and many times when I lived for eight years in Hyas, I stopped at their place for tea and many times invited for meals on special days. Peter helped me in the Sanctuary when I served there and Mary had been the president of the Ukrainian Women's Association in the Stenen local for probably as long as the local has been in existence. Later that year Emil Rubashewsky in Swan River also passed away.

I guess it tells and shows how well a person is known or what things they do for the community in which they live. When I served Lac La Biche, one day I had a funeral in Lac La Biche. A man had passed away and his family lived in Lac La Biche. When I got the news that he passed away I went to see his wife about the funeral arrangements, but she said she has no dealing with the funeral and she is not going to attend his funeral. I somewhat pleaded with her to change her mind, but she would not. When the day of the funeral came there was only the funeral director, his helper, the cantor and me. So the cantor and me were also pallbearers. In 2012 the same scenario was replayed twice but I was the cantor this time not the serving priest. Once in Kelowna there were only four people and some time later in the summer the same thing happened again in Penticton. It looks unnatural when in a family there are two, three, four or more children and the parents looked after all the children, from birth until they flew away from their nest, but when the parents get old, no child wants to take the parent into their home to care for them. What a pity in the world today to see this, but it's true. There is no space in care homes or nursing homes for aged people, but the children whose parents are in those care homes have their large homes with room for everybody but no room for one or two parents. Hey what's wrong with this world?

Towards the end of July and beginning of August more bad news. First on July 18th brother John was taken by ambulance to the hospital, because of severe pain in his back. Diagnostics showed kidney stones. He had no surgery, but was told what to do so as not to have the pain reoccur. On August 7th we get a message that sister Oksana in Winnipeg had fallen down the stairs. A day later on the 8th of August John took late Kay to the hospital because she had an attack of pneumonia. Then for me the computer would not open (start up), so afternoon I took the computer to the computer hospital in Penticton. One other thing in August before the month disappears, Joyce had her right knee replaced on August 23rd. We never counted the staples in her left knee, but the right knee had 44 staples to close the wound. The family doctor took the staples out at the clinic.

SPEED LIMIT AND HELEN MALCHUK FUNERAL

/

Sometimes it's good and at other times it is not good to reach the age of the big eight zero - 80. In British Columbia they have a law that once you hit the 80 mark, every second year the senior has to go and get checked if he/she can still drive and operate a vehicle. I got a letter of notification that I have to go and see the family doctor about my ability to drive. I went. The receptionist checked my vision where I read the letters on the wall. The doctor checked my hearing and gave me some questions that I answered orally to the best of my knowledge. Then I went home and was told I will be called to go and have a reaction test. Yes they called from the hospital in Kelowna to appear on such and such a day. I went. The man told me what will be taking place. On a monitor screen I was to do certain things to see how fast I react to things and how much I remember. Having passed things so far, I was called again to Penticton to go for a drivers test. I guess I passed everything because later I got a letter in the mail which said I can still drive. Come 2014, Eugene will go through the same thing again, this comes every two years. When 2014 came I was not called in until 2016 in August when I received a letter to repeat the performance to be able to drive. Yes I know there are senior people that should not be driving, but then what about the youngsters in their teens and even folks if their thirties and even older that drive as though they own the roads, also just showing off they can drive and you better get off the road if you don't want to end up in road rage. So 2014 passed and I was not notified to come for a test that year but in 2016.

Yes they are talking in British Columbia to increase the speed limit on the highways. First I am against that. First let the people show that they follow and obey the signs and speeds that are posted now. People today are speeding and you put up the speed limit higher, do you mean to tell me they will not speed after that. I have cruise control in my car and set the cruise at the speed limit. I see no one behind me as I travel at eighty or ninety kilometers an hour when all of a sudden from nowhere a car appears behind me. If that car was going the speed limit he should not be able to catch me. It shows that drivers are not obeying the speed limit signs. The government either has to put on real penalties on speeders or else put the speed limit slower than it is now. How many people are killed each year due to speeding and the government wants to increase the speed limit so even more people get killed? It seems to me no matter how much you talk and educate the public, they do not listen.

To have people drive according to the speed limit there is only one way to teach the people and that is through their pocket book. This thing the government has today about penalties for speeders, this is just a big joke. So the man pays $75.00 fine for speeding. He goes to work and in half a day or a few hours he earned back what he paid. Why not make a penalty be a penalty, so the person would squirm when he gets a ticket. The penalty should start with a $500.00 fine because the person was speeding, but on top of that add $100.00 fine for each mile over the speed limit. So if someone goes ninety kilometers in an eighty kilometer speed zone, his fine would be $1500.00. If he gets caught once he would have learned his/her lesson in driving and obeying laws. If the person is caught a second time double the penalty for each speeding infraction. I'm telling you that in four five years death due to speeding would be nil. And to top everything else, I suggest that each vehicle, except ambulance, police and fire truck, should have a governor installed on their car. Anyone dismantling or tampering with the governor cannot drive for a year. You will see how fast people will learn to obey the signs, and you would be greatly surprised.

Come October 1st in British Columbia people must have winter tires on for if they have an accident, they get no insurance coverage. I had a set of four brand new tires installed on the car on November 6th. Then that same day we get a call that Helen Malchuk, my cousin, passed away in Winnipeg. I called the airlines to fly from Kelowna to Regina but I had to be in Regina before 2:00 PM. There I would rent a car and drive to Dauphin for prayers that evening. The funeral would be next day. There were flights into Regina but later on in the afternoon and that would not work. I tried the bus companies and that did not work, so I guess I don't go to the funeral. But then Joyce says: "Why don't you drive with the car?" I did not think long, for she said that about 11:30 before noon and half an hour later I was on the road heading to Dauphin. I can go through the mountain passes because I have new winter tires. The first day I got to Cranbrook about 5:00 PM. In the summer time there would still be four to five hours of driving, but in November days are getting shorter and I don't want to drive at night when wild animals are on the road.

Next morning I'm up and at the break of dawn, I'm on the road heading east. This day I got to Moose Jaw, Saskatchewan. The next day I had only about four to five hours of driving left and made it to Dauphin in plenty of time. Prayers were held in the evening and everything was fine. After prayers people went to their homes or to motels who stayed in the motels. When I went to bed about 10:00 PM, the night was nice and clear and not much cold outside. But then during the night, Mister Storm got enraged and he came to Dauphin. The storm with winds and one foot of snow was dumped on Dauphin. The priest was having a service in the morning, so the funeral was not held until 2:00 PM. I had some time to visit a few people. I visited Stan and Olga Saramaga for a while and then went to see the late Father Mykola Derewianka who was ill with cancer and was living in Dauphin. Father and Dobrodeyka Derewinka and I were close friends. He was ordained in Dauphin when I served there. I also visited them whenever I was in their vicinity. Now he has that dreaded foe which everyone hates and in 2013 in the fall he passed away.

The funeral for Helen Malchuk, my cousin, was in the afternoon in the Ukrainian Catholic Church. The storm by this time had somewhat subsided but it was still there. At the cemetery we were also somewhat lucky because the grave was shielded by the bush, so it was not as bad as in the open field. Then lunch followed in the church basement. The priest was to have been the MC at the lunch, but he left because he had other duties, so the family asked me to thank the people on behalf of them and I also called a few other people to say a few words and we dispersed back to the motel rooms. The storm was still blowing but not as it had during the night before.

I spent the night in the motel and since tomorrow is Sunday, I will stop in church for the service and then head out for home. I came to the church. The sidewalks are all covered in snow, No life around anywhere and it is already 9:30 AM. So I guess they must have canceled the service because of the storm. Later when I got home I called Saramaga in Dauphin and they said there was a service and there were only nine people in church. I guess they must have come after I had passed by the church earlier. This day there was still blowing snow when I got out of Dauphin. Just west of Grandview there was a snowplow to the side of the road, the hood over the engine was open. There was a half ton truck in front of the snow plow and two men were checking something under the hood. At the Wroxton, Saskatchewan corner there was a snow plow in the ditch and another snow plow was already hooked to the one in the ditch and they were trying to pull the one out back unto the highway. I did get to Yorkton and as I turned south there was a car in the ditch that had been there for some time because only the top part of the car was visible. When I head to Melville on the railroad overpass in Yorkton, a semi truck was off the bridge in the ditch and it was running. I guess they were waiting for someone to come and help him get out. Where there was an open space the road was clear, but where there was some bush there was packed snow with ice. When I got to Melville, there was no storm and the road was dry. I drove to Swift current that day.

Next morning I left and when I hit the Alberta border, the road was wet and slushy, but there was no snow on the road. When I got into British Columbia the road was dry. Farther west yes there was snow in the higher up passes and one mountain pass had snow on the highway that was not yet plowed and I was glad I had good winter tires on. I had to make one more stop at Trail, B.C., for the night. It was already dark when I got there so I stayed over night and got home the following day at noon.

This old year is running to the end. Before it ended, I got one more big surprise. Before the year ended I got a phone call from Quebec from lawyers that I will have to appear in court. And what did I do when I haven't been in Quebec since I was in the RCAF in the 1950's. The lawyers reminded me of what happened when I ordered things from a catalogue and never got my goods. The lawyers said that I will not have to come to Quebec, but will probably have a teleconference to testify from near home. They said I will hear from them later as to what and when.

But early in the New Year of January 8th 2013 one evening there is a knock on the door. Now who would be coming to see us at about 7:00 PM? We open the door and there is a man standing and saying: "I have papers for you to appear in court in Montreal." I signed a paper that I received the papers and he left. On January 21st I get another call from the lawyers in Montreal asking if I received the writ about the upcoming court case in Montreal scheduled to start on February 5th and will last for ten days. I said that I did get the writ. I had to drive to Penticton to testify by web cam. I saw the lawyers on the screen and the judge, but I did not see other people. When the lawyers finished with me asking a few questions, the judge asked the defense if they had any questions and they said no. I was thanked and it was over. The court was from February 5th to the 15th, ten days. Later the lawyers called again and I asked the lawyers if the people got jail sentences and they said the court is not finished because they ran out of time and the trial will resume in September. It was in April that I got $97.00 for testifying in that trial. This is now the end of December 2013 and I never heard anything more of what happened or will happen.

On January 15th now in the new year we also received news from Saskatoon that on January 8th Matt Kawchuk passed away. We asked when the funeral will take place and we were told it was on January 11th. I checked my schedule during that time and see that I could have went to the funeral. Matt was married to Anne who was Marusia's niece. The same thing had happened to Marusia when her cousin passed away in Woodstock, Ontario and we didn't find about until everything was over.

Joyce has been telling me that I am going deaf. Well I can hear this keyboard clicking, so I can't be death. I have been having some problem with my throat for about two years. As soon as I start to sing in church or read loud, I become hoarse. My voice runs into some baritone of which I am not acquainted, with because I had a tenor voice. I went to see the doctor about my throat and he sent me to a specialist. I had a hearing test and found out that I have a loss of thirty percent of my hearing. The doctor checked my throat and he said that it's "acid reflux." He gave me a paper of what to eat and what not and to raise the bed four to six inches higher where the head is. The same thing as before and not too much difference to what it's been before. Since I did what was advised, nothing has changed much, except I don't get the heart-burns or acid reflux as they say, like I used to get sleeping on a level bed.

Time runs and waits for no one. To stop for a minute and think it seems like yesterday we entered into, and celebrated a new century, but it is not so, for we have already used up more than a decade of this century. We even have one foot inside the door of the New Year 2014, for in one wink of the eye we will find ourselves in a New Year and nearly half of the second decade of this century. So in all this time what have we learned? Speaking from myself of my profession a clergyman, I have learned that man has made himself a god and forgotten Who his Creator is. I have seen and learned of many churches becoming emptier year by year, month by month and day by day. Older folks are passing on, and the younger generation have forgotten who they are and why they are living on this earth.

Life moves along. Some days are better, some not so good. During all the while Joyce is always saying that her knees are painful. She goes to see a doctor, but is told arthritis is setting in. When medication was not helping she would again go to see the doctors. Finally the doctors ordered x-rays to be taken of the knees. When the results came it looked that it was not arthritis but worn out cartilage and bone is rubbing against bone and that is where the pain comes in. Then she was sent to a surgeon about having surgery for the knees, one knee now and later the second.

Joyce and I had lived for a few months in Plamondon before we moved out to Osoyoos, B.C. Things were going well for us. I was helping her sons in their contracts of building houses while she was at home doing her thing. We would go to church in Kelowna when services were held and I was asked to be the cantor to lead the singing in the church. Paul Malysh, from Vernon, who had been the cantor resigned from that position because he was not feeling very well and his age was catching up and thirdly he could not drive. When there was no church service in Kelowna, we would attend the Anglican church in Osoyoos.

OSOYOOS "KOLOMAYKA" STARTING

Get ready to dance. Living in Osoyoos Joyce began to complain about painful knees. When she was having these pains she started to talk that we should order a chair that would take us downstairs and reverse. I kept saying when things get so bad that we will not be able to walk up or down the stairs, then we will check into it. One day we went to see the surgeon, Dr. Taylor, in Penticton and she brought up this same subject to the doctor. Doctor Taylor looks at her and says: "And how are you going to get your exercise?" After that I never heard anymore about a chair lift.

There was also another thing. Everything was working fine in the house. One day she says that we should get a new dishwasher. I asked her if the one in the house was broken and she said no. I said why then do we need a new dishwasher when the one we have is working. One other time she mentioned we should get a walk-in bath tub where she could soak in the tub. I told her that we have three bathrooms in the house and one has a bath tub. If she can't get in we can get a little step ladder with one or two steps which sits over the bath tub side and it would be easy to walk in and out of the tub.

One day we were going someplace and when we got into the garage, we noticed the deep freezer was not working. The orange light was on, and it was not running. Seeing what happened we called a man to come and have a look to repair it. The man checked it over and said it will be too costly to repair and cheaper to buy a new one. Two hours later there was a new freezer in the basement. If something is not broken, why fix it or throw it out. My philosophy is: "Do you want it? Yes. Do you need it? No."

After hearing all this sort of: "We need this, or we should get this.... etc." one time I told her that if she wants, maybe her son Robert could buy out my half of the house and I can live in it but I would have no say in anything, since it would not be my house. I told her this way the house could stay in their family. When the house will be yours, you can do as you please with it and I will have no say in whatsoever you do with it. This thought was not much with Joyce, so she went to see Robert about my suggestion. She came back and says: "Robert said so we would give him this house we are living in, and we could move up the mountain (12 miles east) and we could get Kevin's house on Wapiti because the renters will be moving out in two weeks." That house they were offering us was worth $689,000.00. Our house what we had paid for it was $420,000.00. So what happens with the difference of over $260,000.00? Where is Joyce and me going to get that extra money to pay for the difference. I am eighty years of age, where can I go to work now to earn the money to pay the difference.

Robert, Kevin and friends on Anarchist Mountain are partying people. Every second or third day they would have a party. If it wasn't a birthday, than some anniversary, or some occasion with old time friends showing up, or any other get together so it was party after party, after party. Liquor and food flowed like water in a river and following most times poker card games. I told Joyce that the liquor they pour into their bodies has hampered their brains to some degree and they do not know what they are saying. Next time Joyce was up the hill to see them she mentioned to her sons what I said about liquor. She comes home and says that they don't want to see me on their property again. In the Ukrainian language there is a saying: "The woman off the wagon, easier for the mare." Since that time I have not even been near Anarchist Mountain.

I did not agree to that proposition because I also have an obligation to the church in Kelowna. I was asked to be the cantor for the congregation. I would leave for the 10:00 AM service on Sundays at 7:00 AM. I never knew if there may be an accident or get tied up in traffic and then be late for the service, funeral or whatever. There could be a snow storm and the switch backs on Anarchist Mountain of which some are only 20 kph coming down the mountain could get a car crashed on that road when snow of six or more inches will fall during the night. When the town of Osoyoos gets inches of snow, Anarchist Mountain can have a foot of snow, so how do I get to Kelowna? I did not agree to their proposition. I told her that today animals, coyotes, wolves, bears, cougars, bob cats and others are leaving the forests and are coming down into communities, and why should I do the opposite? One day she went out by the garden and she saw a bobcat behind the house. She said the cat stared at, so she backed away slowly and went into the house. I did not agree to their proposition. I guess they thought had I gone for it, then they would take this "old man" and throw him out on the road and that would be good riddance of me.

Because Kevin had started his own company they now they had two companies, they had to get it registered and have officers or directors on the board. They said they have to put Joyce as one of the directors of the board. That was very fine and dandy and I was glad that Joyce was going to be on Kevin's board of the company. Things rolled along and on January 9th Joyce had her first knee surgery in 2012. Following her surgery I did everything in the house and time after time helped dress her for she could not dress herself. Every second or third day I drove her to the Oliver Hospital for her physiotherapy until two months later when she could drive the car herself. Then came August 23rd 2012 and she had her second knee replaced, so once again I was looking after her as I did the first time. But now at this time things started to turn around. One day she comes from visiting her sons and says: "Kevin said he is giving me the house on Wapiti." Oh, "giving for you", so that means Eugene has to find a place for himself, because no one is giving Eugene a house.

I guess Joyce was having some problem after her knee surgery. Some time, maybe two months or so, she tells me one time that she thinks that the replacement knee she had must have broken, because she felt different and something was wrong. Off to the doctor goes Joyce and already she was having second thoughts that the knee will have to be operated and replaced again. When she came home she said she will have to go and get an x-ray taken of the knee. She went. A few days later the clinic called for Joyce to go and see the doctor. I don't know who she saw, but when she came home she told me that the x-rays did not show anything wrong and the doctor said it was only in her head what she was thinking and saying.

One evening in September of 2012 (it was about September 8th) when we were already in bed, I was turning over in bed and accidentally with my leg hit her sore leg on which she had knee replaced surgery. She screamed from pain and that even hurt me. When this happened I told her I will move to sleep on the chesterfield so I would not hurt her again, so that she could have time to heal and recuperate after the surgery. Another reason to move was that a number of times she would tell me I was snoring during sleep and kept waking her. Me sleeping in another room (on the chesterfield) would give her more comfort to sleep and from disturbing her sleep and she could sleep more peacefully. As this prolonged from one week to one month and more, Joyce tells me one day: "Why don't you sleep on the bed in the spare bedroom instead of the chesterfield?" I took her suggestion and moved into the spare bedroom.

But then came another reason why I ended up in the spare bedroom. I have been having trouble with my throat for a number of years. I saw my doctor about this and he sent me to see a throat specialist, Dr. Vilas Prabbu in Penticton. I was checked over and told to raise my bed at the head about four to six inches higher than the feet end of the bed. I did that. I bought a two by six inch boar and raised my bed higher at the head. Even today to this very day I still have the head position of the bed raised as the doctor instructed me to do. So there were two medical reasons why we ended up sleeping in two separate rooms Joyce's knee surgeries and my throat problem with the raised bed at the head position.

Life carried on. One day Joyce says that her sons are picking her up and they are going to Penticton to the lawyer to sign papers because they are putting Joyce, their mother, as one of the directors of the board of the company Kevin started. Robert's company is called "Kerin Construction." Kevin called his company "PLS Construction" which means Plumber-Level-Square. What transpired on that trip started this whirlwind of events that happened when this Kolomayka started. I believe the day was March 12th - 2014. I don't know if both sons had taken her to Penticton or only Robert took her there. When they arrived back home in Osoyoos, she was dropped off at house and the son(s) went their way. Joyce came to the house and says that she saw a lawyer and she wants a divorce. W H A T ? I kind of heard that in one ear and none with the other, and did not pay any attention, but somewhat shrugged that off. It was later when she said because we had not been sleeping together so she is asking for a divorce. She said the lawyer told her when people don't sleep together they can get a divorce. Has anyone ever heard of such a ridicules law? My parents never slept for years together unless they were traveling or visiting people. They lived together for over sixty years and in their later years slept on and in different rooms and beds, but never applied for a divorce. How many other people I knew that also slept and even today there are people who sleep on separate beds maybe even in separate rooms, but they don't ask for a divorce. Who set up such a law that gives permission for a divorce for not sleeping together? Joyce and I lived in the same house, ate the same food, drank the same water, traveled together, and here not sleeping together (because of medical conditions) and we can apply for a divorce? Has someone's head got twisted around setting such a ridicules rule for a divorce? I shrugged off such rules and let things be as they are.

Time crawled along. One day on August 18 - 2014 Joyce says that her sons (and friends?) are going to international dinning, going to the USA for supper. At 6:45 PM the doorbell rang. Joyce and I had our office in the basement. I ran up the stairs, opened the door and a man saying he is the bailiff and has some papers for me and I have to sign that I received them. I signed the paper and the man left. I opened the envelope and began to read that Joyce is applying for a divorce. Oh so this is for real? This is serious. Now I had to start putting two and two together. When Joyce arrived home after their international supper, I told her what happened an hour or two ago. The paper stated that we had not been sleeping together since March 2012 so Joyce is applying for a divorce. Well something smells fishy here. She had her second knee surgery in August 23rd in 2012 and we slept together until September 8th or 9th 2012 when I accidentally hurt her knee while turning in bed. It was September 2012 but the legal paper I received says March 2012. Hey - there is six months difference here what she says and what had actually occurred since I went to sleep on the chesterfield and then the spare bedroom. You know, I know, and the world knows what things are called when they are not true - correct.

If such is the case, then next day I go to Penticton to find a lawyer, because this is serious. The paper says she is applying for a divorce because we have not slept together since March 2012. Before I had gone to find and get a lawyer. I had asked Joyce at five different times if she still was serious and wants to go through with her plan and her answer was affirmative each time. Come September 2014 Joyce brought me papers to sign for separation. I assume that paper was drawn up with her and her family. She had signed a copy, but to this day in 2016 I have not signed anything. It was in October 2014 I had gone to see the lawyer again, because the lawyer called and she wanted to see me. The lawyer said she talked with Joyce's lawyer and they decided that Joyce, the two lawyers and I, just us four people meet together someplace and try to work things out, maybe settle this matter without a court. I said I was ready and willing to do so, but later the lawyer called me and said Joyce was not in favor of such a meeting. She knew that without her sons present she had nobody, to have support her and her sons' ways. So this plan the lawyers had suggested was shot down the drain. Who was it, Joyce, or her son(s) made up the story that we had not slept together since March 2012. As mentioned above one can see there is a six month discrepancy between what Joyce and her sons have to say and between the truth. Her knee surgery was on August 23rd, and I went to sleep on the chesterfield in September 2012, but the paper saying March 2012. Something does not smell right here.

    Another thing what the paper says is when Joyce and I got married she said it would be her third marriage. Well on this paper it says it's her fourth marriage. Something does not jive here. She said she had been married twice, before we got married and now it says that I am her fourth husband. What gives? I had been married twice before. Mary Olinec was my first wife married in June 1960 and she died in March 1982. My second marriage was Mary (Marusia) Pasiuk married in April 1988 and she passed away in October 2001. Now I learn from this paper that I am her fourth husband. Had I known this information before hand this marriage would not have taken place. Who were her three precious husbands? I knew of her last husband Bill Babenek. Where are the other two? What happened to them?

    I'm sure her son(s) had made up the paper for our separation. The paper stated that our house will be put up for sale. Eugene will stay in the house and look after it until it is sold and expenses will still be the same as they were previously, Joyce paid the city taxes and insurance and I paid all the utilities. Joyce will move out of the house on November 1st, 2014. On October 20-2014 we signed the agreement with Realtor Alina Lovin to sell the house. As of January 29th there had been nine showing, two had made an offer, but pulled out of the deal at the last hour.

When November 1st arrived it was a rush period. Joyce's granddaughter came with her car and Joyce with her car. They loaded both cars full of Joyce's belongings and took them to Roberts' (Kerin Construction) vacant house on Bayview in town. They made a few trips picking up things and delivering them to the Bayview house. The house on Bayview is small, so many of the things Joyce had of her personal and other belongings were only taken from the house from time to time. The paper said the locks on the house could not be changed. They were not, except the lock on the garage side door broke and I had to replace another lock and gave Joyce a key to that lock. The paper said Joyce was to call Eugene twenty-four hours in advance when she will be coming to pick up her things, but this never happened not even once. She came whenever she wanted.

Two sons and look what they put their mother through for a few months. As Joyce told me before we went different ways that she stayed in the house on Bayview for one month. There she had no land phone, computer nor television in that house. After one month they moved their mother up the mountain twelve miles east of Osoyoos, into Kevin's house on wapiti which was vacated by renters. She started to set her things up when suddenly and unexpectedly people came with a cheque and bought that house. Joyce had stayed a few weeks in it and then had to vacate it and be moved again this time as she told me she was going into the area of peregrine. In early 2016 I had received a few items from Joyce which I guess she had taken unexpectedly with her belongings, and I believe that after some months later when she discovered them she mailed them to me with the return address of her younger son Robert's address at Hallis Road. So is she living with her son now? ? ? ?

Her sons and her friends really treated their mother well, a seventy three year old woman, sending her from one house to another and no place to settle. I told Joyce that at her age she should be living in town where there is an ambulance, police and fire protection. Being twelve miles up in the bush is no place for a seventy-three year old woman to live by herself without the protection of police, fire and ambulance service. But our house did sell and we had to vacate the premises. I did not know where I will end up and what I will do. Seeing how things were heading in which direction I had to get out and find a place. I started looking. In the meantime before vacate date came, I took my belongings and put them into storage in Osoyoos for a few months until I know where I will be.

I had my life set to go back to my stamping grounds, back to Saskatchewan where I was born, where Marusia is buried and I have my "homestead" right next to her. I had a place selected. I will get myself a modular home in a modular home park just a few miles east of Saskatoon. From there I will be only some fifty miles from where my "homestead" is at Wakaw, Saskatchewan. But as this was all taking place through the Internet I got calls from people in Yorkton, Saskatchewan and Dauphin, Manitoba to move there because they need a cantor in those congregations. But my kin started to get after me to stay in British Columbia where I have been for the last eight years, because it will be too hard on my eighty-three year old bones on the prairies when winter comes along with minus thirty and forty below. I have a niece and her husband Corrine and Allan Olynuk at Middle Lake, Saskatchewan who are both Realtors in Humboldt, Saskatchewan and they told me not to get a modular home in Saskatchewan for when cold winters come, some people have problems with freezing water lines. I was left half way between Saskatchewan and British Columbia.

When the house was sold, I did not know what my share of the house would be, because there were lawyer fees, Realtor fees, taxes and all, so how much will be left so I can purchase something to rest these bones of mine before the good earth will take them back. Because I had been cantoring (singing) in the church at Kelowna, I wanted to be in the area not too far to the church. Yes I looked for places in Kelowna at modular homes, but if it was something cheaper, it was in a condition that some people would not want to live in it. If it was something better than the price was also better. Since I had lived in Salmon Arm and Vernon with Marusia 1988 to 1993 and I knew people from the church in Vernon, I started to turn back to Vernon to see what I could find. I had found a place through Century 21 just south out of town, but it did not appeal to me too much. Finally through Century 21, Nathan Sulz guided me to the Big Chief modular home park and RV centre where I purchased my present dwelling. The day I purchased my present place, the weather was terrible-horrible. A cold, cold north wind, snow and rain, clouds hanging low nearly touching one's head that day.

What I bought was not the most modern unit. It was built in 1977 which is somewhat older than some others, but then I am also not a young spring chicken. Yes I had to put some money and time to fix the place up because people who lived here did not look after maintenance of the place. I had to repaint the interior and exterior of the place. Each room in the house was of a different color. The outside was probably the only modular home in that camp that was a darkish greenish gray color while everything else in the park was a bright color. The deck at the back I had to tear down because it was rotten and unsafe to walk on it. I had to replace the posts that hold the car port because they were rotten at the bottom. One think I have noticed in the year I have been here is that everybody sticks to themselves. There are 139 units here and there is a small creek that runs through here year round. It is very quiet and peaceful here. This place is for people 55+ of age to reside. No pets, so no barking dogs to keep one awake, no cats tearing up the flowers. As long as I can still drive, do my own snow shoving on my driveway, cut the lawn, I can stay here. If worse things should come and get my health, than I will have to think of different things. Do I then move to a seniors home where I may have to be looked after? Will I have to move to Saskatchewan and find a place to rent where I would not have to do anything. I don't know, neither do you, but only God knows what is awaiting me. What is my future?

This divorce thing is not settled yet and what will the outcome be when it does come? The sun has already started to set for me. At the age of eighty-three there is no time to start a new race now. So from one day to the next I await the mail to see what it will bring for this separation and divorce. Yes I still sing in the church in Kelowna and in Vernon. Being over a year in Vernon, I have not been to anyone's place yet and had less than a dozen people visit me, who? Roman and Gail Chez visited me in July and brought over some cherries. On March 13th Hennadij Boyarskay and his wife Natalia Boyarska (choir conductor in Kelowna) visited me because he came to take measurements to built me steel steps where the deck was. And then on April 25th I picked up Paul and Ann Malysh to come see where I live. They can't drive and have always been asking me wanting to see where I live. The Parish Priest Father Roman Trynoha has spent a number of times over night here. He lives in Kamloops and when he has a service in Kelowna or Vernon he comes the day before the service to spend the night so he would not have to travel the winding mountain road early in the morning in case the weather would be bad. Then near the middle of August (7-9) Father Roman called me twelve times in two days. I was at a family reunion in White Rock, BC. When he could not reach me, he called Sophie Kniaz from the congregation to come and check if anything happened to me. Sophie did not know where I live, so she asked someone and she finally found my place and came. A moment later another person from the compound came to see what had happened to me. On August 28th Father and Dobrodeyka Isidore and Diana Woronchuk along with Harvey and Ollie Yule stopped in to see where I live. These last four were in Church in Vernon (Feastday) and they came to see me. So I had a few visitors, But I have not visited anyone yet.

Now a few last things that have transpired in 2016 in the first half of the year. I will start with my brother John who lives in Edmonton. He had been complaining about the pain in his both knees. Finally after seeing doctors and tests it was determined he needed knee replacements. On April 7th of 2016 he had his right knee replaced. His late wife Kay has been more in bed in the last eight years or so than on her feet. John looked after her and himself. Then on July 12th John had his other knee replaced, so now he is half bionic. But Kay's condition became worse and she was rushed to the hospital and on July 19th gave up her soul - passing away. John is on crutches just a week after surgery and Kay passes away. The funeral for Kay was on July 29th. My both sisters with some of their families members attended Kay's funeral. But when Alice and her husband John returned home to Saskatoon, John was driving with his truck one day when he got a heart attack, the truck was damaged and he ended up in the hospital.

Myself, I also had a few run ins with my health. I am coming eighty-four this fall. My teeth have been with me all those years, but then suddenly I get a few toothaches. I go to see a dentist. She says two teeth must be extracted because they can't be repaired. I had two teeth removed when all of a sudden another tooth on the other side of the mouth starts to ache. I go see a dentist and she looks at it and says it will cost over $2000.00 to repair. I though for a moment and say: "You know these teeth are just about eighty years old. I think it's time for them to go on pension. Get it out." So I have had three teeth extracted in a month's time.

If you remember 2004, I had my gall bladder removed in Edmonton. Today when the gall bladder is removed it is taken out through one's belly button. The surgeon at that time told me that if I ever see a bubble forming to see a physician. I have had a little bubble for a number of years but then noticed in the spring of 2016 it was getting bigger, so I saw the doctor. He sent me to a surgeon who said they can repair it because if an intestine ever gets caught in there, then it will be a serious problem. So come August 16 of 2016 I had surgery for the hernia. Two weeks after that surgery I am mentioning this in my bio.

CLOSING WORDS

I wish to end this bio with a few unexplained events from my life and to let today's generation know that they nor anyone else have no explanation for these incidents. But I have an answer to the unexplained events in my life. Everything that happens and comes, comes from God or the devil. There is no in between. A person is either with God or against Him. Miracles have happened, they are happening today and they will happen tomorrow, the day after and even after you are gone from this earth. Science tries to explain things, but they have a hard time. I know that for sure, because a few decades ago science came up with the term" Global warming." When things did not go the way they thought it would the "Global warming" became a new name called: "Climate Change." Wait a few more years or decades and science will also change "Climate Change" to something else and that will be after I am gone from this earth.

Do you know what will happen tomorrow? An honest person will probably say they don't know. Well neither do it and no one else does. So as I put down these last few lines in August 2016, I want to say that things are happening at this moment and will happen. I have been suffering with gout for some time. My both knees were very painful that I could not even walk across the room without a cane. Most nights are sleepless because of pain. I do have one medication that takes away the pain but the doctor says it is harmful to the kidneys. It will kill the pain for about twelve hours, but then the cycle begins again. I have come to the point, I don't even know what to eat anymore, because as you can see on the Internet the reasons for gout is dependent on what foods we consume. The more purine in certain foods, the worse the attack and pain are.

I am not the only one going through these days with this pain. I am the oldest of us four siblings. My brother John, who comes after me had a knee replacement on April 7th and July 12th in Edmonton.

My older sister Alice in Saskatoon is also having her problems. She has been hit with gout like me for a number of years. But the last year or two she has not been feeling too well and the doctors are telling her she has some women problems with her health. The last time she was for tests and checkups the doctors found another problem. They say it looks like she has a problem with her heart. She has some appointments made for more tests to check and see what is what.

The younger sister Oksana in Winnipeg is not short of her problems. I don't know if even she herself knows how many surgeries she had so far and for what. Her latest bout is with her goiter. Is goiter the same as thyroid? She had surgery and removal of her goiter on June 7th in Winnipeg. Tests have shown that her goiter is cancerous inside, but they don't know if it has spread outside.

My other item on the list is I'm awaiting to hear the outcome of the "Osoyoos kolomayka." As you read above, Joyce has applied for a divorce and I don't know anything what is going on, so I'm sitting and waiting from day to day when I will get some news of what is taking place. We have been separated for over a year, since April 1-2015, even though she left the dwelling on November 1st 2014 and I stayed in the house until it was sold.

Putting all these last few lines together you can see that our family is going through a number of health related problems, each one having their own aches, pains and worries. What will happen in days to come, only the Good Lord knows what will be. If this project does go to print before the divorce comes, there will not be any information about it, but should the divorce come before the printers get this book to print, there will be some information about the divorce happenings mentioned here.

DO YOU BELIEVE IN MIRACLES?

I did, do and always will. Miracles have been on earth since the creation of this earth on which you and I walk. Is it not a miracle that we can put a few seeds in the ground and later harvest a crop form it. I remember reading one time that science had taken a kernel of wheat, analyzed it, found all the ingredients it contains and then made a kernel with all the same material as the regular kernel. Then they planted their kernel and a regular kernel of wheat and waited for results. In a few days the regular kernel sprouted and grew. The kernel which science had made did not sprout and they were somewhat disappointed their kernel did not germinate. They had the exact same ingredients in their kernel but it would not grow. So each year when a farmer plants two bushels of wheat and a few months later he threshes twenty-five or more bushels from the two bushels he planted, is that not a miracle?

Now there have been miracles since the creation of this earth. Was it not a miracle the Hebrews came to the Red Sea, the sea divided and they walked across to the other side? Today they are finding pieces of articles at the bottom of the sea which took the lives of those who came after them. Is it not a miracle that Christ was born of a Virgin Birth? Was it not a miracle that Christ Resurrected after being dead for three days in the tomb? Were those not miracles where Christ made blind men see, deaf men hear, lame people walk, evil spirits chased out of people, etc. etc.? Yes miracles occur even today but science has no answer for them so they say they are "unsolved mysteries." Did you hear about the forest fire at Fort McMurray, Alberta in the spring of 2016? Over two thousand houses were destroyed. Over 80,000 people were evacuated, and yet there was a miracle that happened in that "beast of a fire." Six years ago a young 23 year old man, Michael Leclercq, was killed in a car accident south of Fort McMurray. The family made a wooden cross, put his picture in plexi-glass and put the cross where Michael lost his life. Do you know what? There was a picture of the cross near the road. The forest fire burned buildings and melted steel in the city and then went across the road and to where the cross of Michael's memory stands in the bush where he died. And do you know what? Yes, the fire burned all the grass, burned and scorched the brush and trees all around, but the cross was never touched by the fire. Why? You can see on the picture that was on the Internet how everything burned around, but the cross stood in tact. Why? Is that a miracle or an "unsolved mystery?"

I believe in miracles. Man cannot create a miracle, only God does that, but God uses man as an instrument to create miracles. I a sinful soul have been an instrument in creating God's miracles and I mention a few of those miracles ("unsolved mysteries for science) which God used me to do His Will. Here are a few of them.

ONE: It happened in one congregation when I had just sat down to dinner(noon lunch) when the phone rang. I answered the phone and the doctor was calling from the hospital that there is a woman was on her death bed with her last breath just moments away and he asked if I could hurry to the hospital to have some prayers. I asked who the lady was and hearing the name I knew I did not have such a person as a member in one of my congregations. I said that maybe they should try calling a Ukrainian Catholic priest, but the doctor said they did and there is no answer, so he called me. I left my meal and grabbed my belongings and rushed to the hospital. I knew that I may be late, but knew at the same time that at least I would make an effort to help the dying person. I arrived at the hospital and hurried to the intensive care unit. There was the doctor who had called me and a few nurses were assisting the doctor in his effort to help the dying person. I put on the stole and got the prayer book and items I needed for Holy Unction. I did what I had to do and told those present that I did what

I could and the rest is now up to God. I don't know what they thought of these words but I knew I had done what I could and I knew that the doctor had done what he could to the unconscious and unresponsive woman.

I returned home and then finished my cold meal, for there were no such thing as a microwave in our house. I was sure that the lady had passed away. Next day I drove to the hospital to visit my parishioner that were in the hospital recuperating. I got the names of Orthodox patients from the receptionist and then room by room I checked in to see my ill parishioners. I walked past the intensive care unit and the door was opened. I glanced into the room, the beds were made up and no patients in them. There was one patient yesterday, and she passed away, so the beds are now empty. I strolled down the corridor to see the parishioners and as I walked past this one room, I turned my head for a glance to see how many beds are occupied with patients. As I walked past this room and glanced from the corridor, somehow something struck me. A lady reading a book look familiar. I took a few more steps past the door and stopped. Is it true? Am I seeing something that I don't seem to understand? Slowly I turn around and go towards that room to the patient that looked familiar. Slowly I walk up to the bed and I see it is the woman I gave Holy Unction to yesterday. Maybe it's just someone that looks like her. I looked at the name tag on the bed, and sure enough it is the same name. I looked at her and stepped up closer to ask how she is feeling. I told her who I was and then asked her a few questions and finding out that it is the same woman, I asked her if she remembers me giving her Holy Unction and prayers the last day. She said she did not hear or knows anything about it. That lady stayed a few more days in the hospital and was discharged to her home. Months later when I was still in that parish I would meet that woman on the street, in a store or at some community gathering she would always come to me give me a hug and thank me for saving her life. I told her I did not save her life, but God did. So where was the science, where was the medicine, where was the faith and God in this case? It was God who restored the woman's life, as Christ had done many times during His life on earth. The doctor was there and he saw there was no hope for the woman, so he called me.

TWO: In one congregation we had an early morning (6:00 AM) Easter service(Christ's Resurrection) followed by the blessing of Easter Paska (food baskets) that the parishioners had brought to be blessed in ending the forty day fast. A youth group in this congregation went with a basket to collect Easter eggs to be taken to the hospital to give to the patients and staff. I had told the youth to collect the Easter eggs and wait for me either in church or at the hospital and then we would go and pass out the Easter eggs to our church members who were ill in the hospital. When the service was over people dispersed to their homes. I had to take off my vestments and clean things at the Altar and then headed to the hospital. When I arrived at the hospital, the youth were already coming out of the hospital. I thought they were coming to join me and we would walk in, but they tell me they already gave Easter eggs to everybody and they still had some left. They also told me that the nurses at the intensive care unit told them they should not have come into the intensive care room without permission. I told them that they could go home now since they had passed out the Easter eggs. But I knew I may have a problem on hands if I walk into the hospital again. So I decided to go and see the intensive care unit and apology to the staff there for what the youth had done.

Yes I went in. Instead of finding fault and having to apologize on behalf of the youth, I heard a different story from the nurses. They began to tell me of this one patient who was on his deathbed and they were sure and positive that he would not survive till noon that day. He was not responding to them. The girls had left him an Easter egg. He was unconscious and death was immanent. I still apologized to the nurses and left for home. That day towards evening came a phone call. A nurse from the hospital was calling and I was sure she was going to tell me that the patient on his deathbed passed away, but she told a different story. She said that after the girls left, the patient seemed to be miraculously improving every minute and that same day in the late afternoon they called the doctor in, they examined him and discharged him for his condition was very good and he was cured enough to go home. Yes I later visited that man at his home of the farm. What has an Easter egg to do with medicine? Who cured that man? Did I? Did the doctor? Faith and work in God always does what is impossible for man.

THREE: In one congregation towards evening a young couple came to see me. The husband knocked on the door and when I opened it, I could see distraught on his face that something was wrong and the first thing that hit me was that someone in the family had passed away. The husband said they would like to talk to me and I waved my hand that his wife come from the car. We began to talk and they start to tell me their problem. They said that one day they went to their neighbors' place with their little two year old daughter for a visit. The neighbor had a large huge dog. As they were standing and talking outside, the dog barked very loudly and the child started screaming. They came home with her but her screaming and crying continued. Not knowing what to do they took the child to the hospital and told what happened. They said the doctor gave the child a needle, the child started to calm down and they left for home. I guess when the medication wore off the same thing returned to the child, the screaming started again the next day. The parents were desperate and someone suggested they go and see one lady who would melt some wax, say some words and pour the wax into cold water. The wax would harden and form the shape of what was bothering the person. Witchcraft? When they did go and see the lady, they found that the wax formed into a dog. That was all the lady could do for them. The child carried on in screaming and crying day after day.

Having found no help and cure, in the last stance they came to see me, if I could help them. I put on my cossack and said so we would go to the church. Before we entered the church I stopped on the steps turned to them and said: "Do you believe that I can help you?" In just about a crying plea they said "yes." We walked inside the church. I put on the stole vestment, read a prayer and gave the child some Holy Water to drink. I gave them some Holy Water to take home and asked them to give the child Holy Water to drink once a day. I told them that if this does not help, that they come see me again and we will have a service, will bless Holy Water and they will have to have the child drink that water for twelve days. They thanked me for my time and left for home. I did not see the couple for a few weeks and somewhat had forgotten about that incident, but I had a marriage ceremony and then to attend the wedding. When I arrived at the wedding reception, there in the hall in one corner were sitting the two parents with their little child. I hurried up to them to ask of how things were coming along with their daughter. They looked happy and told me: "Father when we came home that day from church, we don't even know that she is around. She has been sleeping very well and is quiet that we don't even know that she is in the house. We thank you so very much for what you have done for us," Now is there a scientific answer to this? Did medicine or the woman (witchcraft) help? What is the answer? Only one answer and that is from our Creator - God who can only do this. God used me as an instrument to do His work.

FOUR: My mother immigrated to Canada in 1929. She left in Ukraine one sister (my aunt). There came the Second World War. The war came into their village and surrounding areas. People in Ukraine grew corn for their use and used the stocks of corn for cutting it up and feeding it to the cattle in the winter time. In the 1950's we brought mother's sister to Canada to Winnipeg where she lived. When she arrived in Canada she told us of a story that happened to her personally. One day she was going through the corn field, after a battle had taken place there. As she walked among the rows of corn stalks she stumbled upon a soldier who was killed in that field. She said when she first saw the soldier his eyes were open and she was horrified from the scenery. She told us that day after day wherever she turned and looked she saw the face of that dead soldier with his eyes open and staring at her. She wanted to find relief from that incident and went to a few different doctors but no help came. Wherever she turned there was no aid, but the same face of the soldier appeared each and every day. She told this same story to one older woman in her village and that woman told her what to do. She told her to go to the place where that soldier had died and say a prayer for his soul. She was terrified to walked to that area but with trembling and not knowing what to expect she walked to that spot. When she got there, she fell on her knees and said a prayer for the soldier's soul who she never knew and do you know what happened? After she returned home and to this very day she has never seen that face of that soldier again. So is prayer a medicine? Of course it is and it helps everyone who gets on their knees and prays with great faith and humility. Why could the doctors or anyone else not help her, but the simple little Lord's Prayer gave her peace and tranquility after she had prayed?

FIVE: In one congregation there were the Royal Doors built and installed in the church but they needed to be painted. One day I went to the church and started to paint the doors. A while later my wife came to tell me there are some people that want to see him. I left the church and went to the manse, cleaned myself somewhat from the paint and went to meet the people. There was a young couple and one older lady, the mother of the young man. First thing that came to my mind was that the young couple wanted to get married so they came to see me about that. I took the young couple into my office and asked them what they wanted to tell me but neither one or the other would say anything but they would say to each: "You tell him." After some more prodding and asking they finally started to open up and tell me their story.

They had been going around for a few months and would go to dances or movies and then returning home in the middle of the night they would see a ball of fire following behind them as they drove home in their truck. They were afraid. Another time when they arrived home they sat in the truck at the lady's residence and they saw a black cat come along and go into a wooden box that was beside the house and tipped over with the open end to the ground. The young man got out of the truck and went to check on the cat, but when he turned the box over the right way, there was absolutely nothing. Still another time as they were sitting in the truck they could see a fireball in the sky coming down toward them in a bouncing way. When the fireball came nearer they were frightened and the fireball fell on the roof of the house and looked like sparks scattered in all directions. Another time they were coming home from a movie and they could see a huge bird the size of the their truck flying in front of them. Again this brought fear into their life. If I would have heard this from one person, you know what I would have thought, but two people seeing and living through the same thing telling me their fears, that means there is more problems than just in the mind. I put on my cossack and the two people came with me to the church. I read some prayers over them and blessed them with Holy Water and gave them Holy Water to drink. The mother of the young man says: "Could you also please bless the truck inside and outside?" Jesus told us: "By your faith let is be so."

Having heard this I asked the young lady where she lived. She told me the place and I said that I would like to meet her mother and father and have a talk with them. I told the young lady that on a certain day I would be in her town and will be teaching religion after school and will take her brother and sisters home so they can show me the way to their place. I picked the three children after school and they told me which way to go. Must have been about three or four miles.

When I turned off the road into the driveway about a hundred yards from the house, I felt a strange feeling come over me, why and what I did not know. I stopped by the house and went in with the children into the house. The young lady was home with her mother. After talking and inquiring about what was what the lady of the house tells me: "Father please do something because I can't stand this talk about what they keep talking about each day." I had brought with me a stole of the vestments, Holy Water and a cross. I asked the lady if I can sprinkle the house with Holy Water and she said to do whatever I can to help them. The house had four rooms, two downstairs and two bedrooms upstairs. I sprinkled the two rooms downstairs and was on my way upstairs to do the same. As I stepped off at the top stair, a strange thing happened. I felt like something or someone grabbed me with its hands or whatever and was squeezing me. I felt I was in a strap being tightened around me. I got a shock and then I had a thought come to me and I said to whatever it was that was holding and squeezing me: "What am I afraid of, I have a cross and Holy Water." As I whispered this, immediately I felt that whatever was squeezing me, let go as if nothing had happened. I sprinkled the two rooms upstairs, came down and went and sprinkled the house outside from all sides and then came back into the house.

I asked the lady where her husband was and she answered that he passed away some two years ago. I asked where he was buried and she said it was in the cemetery across the road from the church. Because the Ukrainian Orthodox church has special graveside services after Easter and blesses the graves of the deceased, I told the lady of the house to clean up the grave of her husband and Sunday after the service in church we will bless the graves and the grave of her husband. She said she has no way of getting to the cemetery and the church. I told her to ask her daughter's fiancé to pick her up and go check the grave and come to church on Sunday.

Coming home and driving right next to the cemetery I stopped to see if I can see the grave of her husband. Yes I found the grave and it was caved in and weeds all over and around it. When Sunday arrived I had the service in the church and then blessing of the graves. The lady with her brood of children was in church. We came to the cemetery and blessed the graves and we came to the grave of her husband. It was different than I had seen it a few days ago. The grave was leveled with new fresh dirt over it, some flowers on it and I blessed it as I did other graves. After all was over I went home. About a month later I had a marriage in that congregation and then attended the wedding reception. At the reception the two young people who were having these terrifying experiences were also at the reception. I went over to them and asked then how things were with them. They replied that after I had visited the family of the young lass and had the blessing of the grave, they had not seen nor heard anything more to that day. Now, why did peace not come to the family before I did what I did? No explanation? Well God can do what man cannot and He can explain it was His Hand in this help for the young couple.

Now these are just a few examples of what transpired right in front of me where I had taken part in the aid of those who were in dire straights for help. Why did the medical and scientific world not help the above named people in their circumstances? Yet God had His hand in helping out the people who were "crying for help" in their own way. After my participation in trying to help the affected and they received help, they had a completely different outlook on religion. The young couple in the fifth example above were later married by me and already had a child which I baptized and another child was on the way, but I was moved from that parish, so I don't know what happened after I left. The couple with the child screaming and could not sleep, (item number three above) later moved far into the northern part of a province where they are living to the present day and that child grew up, is now married herself and no more screaming and sleepless nights. No answer for these incidents by science. Probably the only answer would be unsolved mysteries.

HOW I HAVE ESCAPED DEATH FIVE TIMES

(1)

Now you may wonder what all this is about. You may wonder how can someone escape death when everyone must die who is born into this world. After reading these five incidents, you may recall that you may have had very close calls to death yourself, but in one way or another you escaped death as I did these five times I want to tell you about.

My first recollection of death goes back to about 1951-52. Father had purchased a car, so now we could go and visit people who were farther away. My mother had two cousins in Manitoba, Tillie Korzeniowski at Grandview, Manitoba and Mary Derzak at Ethelbert, Manitoba. One day the parents decided to go and visit these two cousins of mother. Fine and dandy. John, Alice and Oksana will be home for three or four days before we return. I was delegated to go with them because I knew English and would be the navigator which way to go. Father was the car operator - chauffeur.

We left on our designated day and drove from Tarnopol to Clair, Saskatchewan. At Clair on the farm, there was a couple living which mother knew from her home place in Ukraine, the Yuzdepskis, so going through Clair, we have to stop in and see them. We found the place and after our visit we were ready to leave when they said they would like to go to see mother's cousins because they knew them from Ukraine when they lived there. They said they have never been to see them because they have no car to go. There were three of us, father, mother and I, so there was still room for two more people, so the parents asked them to come along with us. They gladly accepted the proposition and before we knew it all five of us are on our way to Manitoba.

After a few hours of traveling we arrived at Meharry, near Grandview, Manitoba and found the place where Korzeniowski lived. We stopped there for some time and people not seeing each other for a few decades had somewhat of a party style meeting. Yes there was some liquor served and Mr. Yuzdepski had one or two more shots so after we left the place we headed back unto the highway towards the east. Father was driving, I was on the front seat the navigator. Mother with Mr. and Mrs. Yuzdepski sat on the back. Mr. Yuzdepski having a happy feeling fell asleep on the back seat behind the diver, mother in the middle and Mrs. Yuzdepski on the right.

Fine. We are skimming along the highway at nearly fifty miles an hour as the speed limit was at that time on gravel highways. Now we pass Gilbert Plains and as we are coming down a hill I notice a sign pointing to the left showing: Ethelbert. I tell father we have to turn left. It was too close to turn left, but father made that turn. There could have been a catastrophe on that corner. Instead of father to go straight, slow down, turn around on the other side of the raven and come back to the Ethelbert turn-off, he turned sharply and we just about ended up in a ravine probably forty feet deep. Later father himself said it was Mr. Yuzdepski who save us all, because he had been sleeping on the left side and his dead body wait held the car from flipping over and rolling a number of times into the ravine. After the dust settled from the gravel we all got out somewhat shook up and noticed we had a flat tire on the right rear wheel. The tire had come off the rim. We changed the tire and traveled the next twenty some miles to Ethelbert and had the tire repaired there. Following the visit we returned back home the following day.

I beat death there for the first time that I can remember. Had we gone down rolling over with the car into that ravine, there could have been more than one death and there were no seat belts at that time yet.

(2)

My second escape from death was not too far from where the first escape happened. This second escape took place about ten miles east of Roblin, Manitoba or some forty miles west of Dauphin, Manitoba, some thirty miles west of where I escaped death the first time. Since those two escapes I have gone through that same area dozens of times. When I lived in Dauphin for nine years, there wasn't a week or so that I did not go through that corner turn-off to Ethelbert which is about ten miles west of Dauphin. I can't tell you what the exact year of the first escape happened, but I know it was during the summer time. This second escape occurred in the summer in July 1977.

This second escape happened when Mary and I were moving from Dauphin, Manitoba to Prince George British Columbia. We left Dauphin very early in the morning because we were looking to get to Edmonton before dusk. I had gone to the U-Haul dealer south of Dauphin and picked up a trailer. The dealer hooked everything up and we left for the house. Then we packed the trailer with our belongings and headed out of Dauphin towards the Saskatchewan border. Everything went well until we crossed the bridge over the CNR railway about ten miles east of Roblin, Manitoba. We started to go down an incline hill when trouble started. The car was picking up speed and as I stepped on the brakes, nothing helped. The trailer started to sway from side to side and from one side of the ditch to the other pushing the car in front from side to side and the brakes were not holding one single bit. Did I lose the brakes, brake failure?

As we are swaying with the trailer and the car, I shouted out to Mary to hold on, because we will be killed and if we make it to the bottom we will end up on the sides of the bridge or in the water below. Yes, I admit I was scared, because I knew death was eminent either in one ditch or the other or end up on top of the bridge on the bridge side wall or in the river below. God or the Guardian Angel was with us at that moment for as soon as we neared lower to the bridge and the river, the car started to straighten out with the trailer and we made it in one piece, Mary, me, the car and the trailer with our belongings. But I had the thought in my mind: "Why did the brakes not hold us down?" When we came to Roblin town and we had to stop, there was no problem. I knew that the brakes were working, but why did they not work when we were going down that hill?

I knew we were not out of the woods yet, because some eight miles west of Roblin could be a bigger disaster awaiting us. To get to the Saskatchewan border we have to go down, down, down a very steep and long hill and then climb up on the other side where the Saskatchewan border was on top of the hill on the other side of the lake. I had by now figured that before I attempt the drive down I will try something else. Before I start the drive down the long and steep hill, I will go a short few feet before the decent and put the car in a lower gear and see what will happen. If the trailer starts to fish tail, I will stop on the side of the road and will not go farther until someone will come and give me a hand explaining why the brakes do not work down the hill, but they work on straight level land. As we approached the big decent I put the car in low gear and slowly started to let the car move forward. Yes, the car is holding the trailer back and we crept down that long steep hill and unto the bridge. When we got unto the bridge I put the car in high gear and in no time we were on top of the hill and in Saskatchewan.

But what is going to happen when we get into British Columbia and it is filled with mountains, hills and curves? We are now on level road and pass through Yorkton and heading west on Highway #16. As we were passing Sheho and on the west side of the town a small decline in the road and I could feel the trailer was starting to sway again. I tried one other thing. I stepped on the gas and the trailer leveled off. I had been to Edmonton numerous times and knew there is a steep decline in the road at North Battleford and also east side of Edmonton. Having found out how to hold the car and trailer in position, I put the car in lower gear each time we went down any hill and had no problem. Now we can see the skyline of Edmonton and I knew I have a mechanic in Edmonton who will definitely want to have a look at the problem. That mechanic is non other than my kin brother John.

We arrived at John's place just before supper and we had supper with him and his son Gregory. During this time I tell John what had taken place just east of Roblin. John says there must be something wrong with the trailer. After supper we went out and John wants to check out the problem. He asks me to drive along side the curb and he will walk beside the trailer and see if he can find the problem. As I drove along John had asked me to step on the brakes from time to time. I guess he must have noticed something and told me to stop and turn the engine off. He went to his car and brought a wrench. On the trailer was a cylinder for brake fluid to apply brakes when one stepped on the brakes in the car. John opened the cylinder where the brake fluid was. He checked the cylinder and it was as dry as the Sahara Desert.

Our next stop was to the closest service station. I bought two cans of brake fluid and we drove back to where the car and trailer were. John filled the cylinder with fluid and asked me to drive slowly and apply the brakes. He saw the brakes were working. His next thing was to bleed the lines that went to the brakes on the trailer. Having done that he said that I will have no more problems. I was not sure of that, thinking of big mountains I still have before me.

Next morning Mary and I are continuing on our trip west. I was uneasy. After leaving Edmonton we came where there was one steep hill ahead of us. As we started the trip down I put on the brakes and the car stopped. Hey, it's working. Maybe the problem is fixed. Half way down the hill I tried again and sure enough the brakes are working. The remainder of the trip went well. When I returned the trailer to the U-Haul dealer in Prince George, I told him that we were nearly killed because the trailer had no brake fluid. That was my second escape from death which was staring me in my eyes some ten miles east of Roblin, Manitoba.

(3)

Now comes my third escape from death which could have been death to anyone who would have been near that place. This happened at Hyas, Sask. Mary had gone from Prince George to Winnipeg and was living there with her mother. In the meantime the church moved me from Prince George, British Columbia to Hyas, Saskatchewan in the fall of 1980. I lived in Hyas next to the church on a parcel of land that had the church and the manse on the same property.

When I arrived in the fall, there was no lawn cutting that year, but when spring came in 1981 I told the church executive I want to cut the lawn, so that I could have some exercise. This I did for the rest of my time I was there until 1988 when I moved out of Hyas. This third escape from death occurred on June 13-1984. Is the number thirteen lucky or unlucky? That day I found out it was unlucky to what took place but also lucky for I had beaten death again.

It was a clear, sunny, warm day. I cut the lawn each time with an old pair of shoes on my feet and bare hands on the handle of the lawnmower. I went into the garage to get the lawn mower, but someone whispered in my ear to put on rubber boots and gloves. I was going to do as I had done previously, but again the sound: "Put your boots and gloves on." Who is telling me to what to wear? It's not the first time I was going to cut that lawn, but I stopped for a moment and thought maybe I should do as someone is advising me, but then the thought: "Why?" Yes I pulled on the rubber boots and put gloves on and away I went to what I had come to do. At the same time I was thinking what the neighbors will think of me cutting the lawn wearing rubber boots on June 13th.

I finished the lawn around the church and the manse and then went outside the fence to do the lawn beside the curb-street and the fence. There were three sides to do this, because on the fourth side lived a neighbor. I did the west side of the curb side and then moved over to the south side. On the south side there are two hydro poles about eight or ten feet apart with guy wires into the ground supporting the poles from bending or falling over. Yes I had cut around those poles for the last three years. Today something different happened around those poles and guy wires. At other times I just went with the lawnmower and cut around the guy wires. Today I did the same thing, but it turned out it could have been a tragedy. I had cut around the poles and now came the guy wire. As the lawnmower touched the guy wire, a huge flash of flame flashed before me, the lawnmower jumped about eighteen inches into the air and out of my hands and killed the engine.

Yes, I am scared. What happened? Never had no problem here but today this? I stood in wonderment and started to study the situation over. The lawnmower had a one inch cut (melted steel) about quarter of an inch wide where it made contact with guy wire. My eyes started to follow the guy wire from the ground upward. As I gazed at the top, oh yes, how come the live wire between the two poles is touching the guy wire about twenty feet above me. I took another good look and rushed to the manse. Got out the phone directory, found the number and called Sask-Power at Norquay (about five miles east of Hyas) and told them what had happened. In that distance between Hyas and Norquay the Sask-Power people where by the church in about five minutes. When they arrived, I showed them what happened to the lawnmower and told them it looked like some wind must have moved the live power line so it touched the guy wire and the power was going into the ground through the guy wire. It took the two men just a few split minutes and they had the problem repaired. They told me there was anywhere from 5,000 to 25,000 volts of power going in that wire.

What would have happened if I had not worn rubber boots and gloves that day while cutting that lawn? I don't have to tell anyone what the result would have been. Tragedy for sure. But who told me to wear rubber boots and gloves that day? For the next few years that I lived there I put on rubber boots and gloves when I cut the lawn and each time I came to that guy wire I stopped first and looked up to see if it was safe to cut around it. This was the third time I escaped death in my life.

(4)

The next sequence where I escaped death happened again in Saskatchewan about a hundred miles west of Yorkton, Sask. Marusia and I had been married and we lived in Salmon Arm, British Columbia, than in Vernon and from Vernon we moved back to Saskatchewan to Yorkton. This happened in 1993 in the fall

Very good friends and "koomy" Godparents with me, the late Peter and Doris Chaykowski were living in Vernon. Marusia and I had received some bad news that Peter was not very well and he wanted to see both of us. Peter helped build the tool shed in Salmon Arm for us and also did the basement ceiling. They had gone to Ukraine in the summer of 1993. When Peter returned from Ukraine he fell ill and told us that someone must have put something in his food in Ukraine and he became ill from that.

Doris had called a few times to say that Peter wanted to see us before he dies. Marusia and I made a trip from Yorkton to Vernon, going through

USA and coming into British Columbia at Osoyoos, then up to Kelowna and Vernon. Yes Peter was ill and did not even get out of bed. It was cancer that was killing him. So Marusia and I visited him and some other friends in Vernon and Kelowna and then started our trek back home on the Trans-Canada Highway until we got to Calgary. In Calgary we took another Highway #9 heading to Saskatchewan.

We hit Saskatchewan, then at Rosetown, we took Highway #15 heading east towards home. All was going well, and we are about another two hours from home heading east to Yorkton. Near Semans, Saskatchewan we both nearly lost our lives. At the Semans corner we could see a car coming from the right (from Semans) towards the highway. Sure there is a stop sign and when you come to a highway you must stop - NOT? Well this car seemed to slow down somewhat so taking the chance the approaching car will stop before entering the highway we kept going. But things did not work out as they are supposed too. As we are just meters away from the crossroads, we notice that car was coming right at us and was not stopping. Had I put the brakes on we would have been hit broadside on the passenger side. To avoid a collision I turned towards the left side of the road and the car coming from the south missed our car probably by three feet behind us as we ended stopping on the wrong side of the road on the shoulder gravel part and partially in the ditch.

Now why did that car not stop? Was he/she blinded by the setting sun? Did he/she have two, too many (in the bar) and could not see us coming? There could have been a terrible crash and four lives could have been lost there. I know there were two people in the other car, what gender they were I could not say. What we should have done was to turn around on that spot and head north following that car and give them a few driving instructions to stop when entering a highway. But at a moment as that we both were shook up and just lucky enough nothing seriously happened. And then people wonder why accidents happen. But this was now the fourth escape from death. One more to come and that is the one most recent just over a year ago.

(5)

This last escape from death is absolutely unreal to me. As you read a few pages back you read about the start of the Osoyoos Kolomayka and it is the one that just about took my life. After having found out I will have to vacate the house in Osoyoos after it is sold, I started to look for something as you already read above in the " Osoyoos kolomayka." Because I did not know what funds I will receive from the sale of the house, I had to look for something so I would not be left without a penny for tomorrow and not even have a penny for bread. Yes Joyce and I had both put equal amounts of money into the purchase of the house, but when we were selling the house, the prices had gone way down, so I did not know how much I would receive so I started to look on the Internet for a modular home after I had canceled the plans for moving to Saskatchewan.

I looked in Kelowna, but there was nothing that I could have afforded so I took a few trips north to Lake Country and to Vernon. One day on the way back to Osoyoos after checking things out in Lake Country, I was going past the Kelowna International Airport when on the opposite side (west side) I noticed some beautiful modular homes. I might as well check and see what those people have. I turned off to the right from highway #97 towards the Okanagan College and on a circle drive (round-about) turned right again to the modular homes. The man said they could put me into a brand new modular home for $100,000.00 but I would need a lot where to place it. I asked about lots and he said there is a new modular home camp started at Creek Run, but before anyone can move a modular unto a lot they must first put up $20,000.00 because they need funds to build roads, water, sewer, etc.

Having heard that story, I walked out and started to drive back where I came from. I came back to the circle drive (round-about) and to get back unto the highway south, I drove around the circle and now headed a few meters towards the highway. I would turn right and be on the highway heading towards downtown Kelowna. When I got to the highway the light changed red and then I notice a sign beside the road saying: "No right turn."

Did you ever see such a thing where you can't turn right unto a highway? So I was stuck. The light is red and from the right side a large white tour bus is flying towards me. I had two choices, either let the bus smash right into me, or I go straight across the road and down into an embankment about thirty or more feet deep with big trees looking up from below. What happened next I do not know and remember. I don't know if the bus driver or the people saw anything or not, because I did not. The last thing I remember was a bus coming straight at me from the right. The next thing I remember was I was sitting in my blue Accent Hyundai car about three hundred yards to the north of where I was. To my right there was (and still is today) a fruit stand in the summer time. The car was facing towards the highway and I was sitting in the car watching the traffic flowing both ways. How I got some three hundred yards north from where I remember being the last time, I don't know. I didn't see anything and I didn't hear anything. Did the bus driver and people on the bus see anything, I don't know. I know the bus was gone and traffic was moving in both directions and I was sitting in the car, engine running and watching traffic fly by in both directions.

To this very day this is a mystery to me. Did God or a Guardian Angel picked me up with the car and settled me on the flat place by the fruit stand? I DON'T KNOW. This was my fifth escape from death, because it was either the big white tour bus hitting me broadside on the passenger side or I had to go upside down into the ravine into the big trees. This fifth escape from death is still a lingering suspense in my life. How did I and the car get from one place to the other? Each time I drive by to church in Kelowna and back, I think and wonder: How did I end up that the tour bus did not hit me and I did not end upside down in the ravine among the big trees down below? How did I get from one place to another and not knowing how it happened. **This is a mystery in my life till this very day.**